We dedicate this edition to very significant people in our lives:

To Betsy, Laura, and Linda, from Ralph
To Linda, Edward, Raquel, Naomi, and Nathaniel, from Bernie
To Emily, Paul, and Carol, from Bruce
To Sylvia, Eric, and Kay, from Richard

UNIVERSITY OF WINNIPEG, 515 Portage Ave., Winnipeg, MB. R3B 2E9 Canada

THE PSYCHOLOGY OF RELIGION

THE PSYCHOLOGY OF RELIGION

An Empirical Approach

Second Edition

RALPH W. HOOD, JR.
University of Tennessee at Chattanooga

BERNARD SPILKA
University of Denver

BRUCE HUNSBERGER
Wilfrid Laurier University

RICHARD GORSUCH
Fuller Theological Seminary

THE GUILFORD PRESS
New York   London

© 1996 The Guilford Press
Division of Guilford Publications, Inc.
72 Spring Street, New York, NY 10012

Printed in the United States of America

This book is printed on acid-free paper.

Last digit is print number: 9 8 7 6 5

Library of Congress Cataloging-in-Publication Data

The psychology of religion : an empirical approach / Ralph W. Hood,
    Jr. . . . [et al.].—2nd ed.
        p.   cm.
    Includes bibliographical references and index.
    ISBN 1-57230-116-3
    1. Psychology, Religious.   I. Hood, Ralph W.
BL53.P825   1996
200'.1'9—dc20
                                              96–22625
                                                 CIP

PREFACE

At the beginning of this century, those who were to become highly esteemed figures in the history of psychology and its sister disciplines focused much of their interest and attention upon religion. In academic psychology, such individuals as William James and G. Stanley Hall not only helped found the discipline of psychology; the psychological study of religion was also of interest to them. In psychoanalysis, a new discipline was created outside of academic psychology that nevertheless was to influence psychology immensely. One cannot read Freud or Jung for long without encountering extensive discussions of religion.

The second quarter of the 20th century saw a rapid decline in the study of religion among psychologists. Behaviorism was indifferent to the study of religion, while psychoanalysts relegated it to the province of psychopathology. The net effect was that research in this area remained on the periphery of scientific respectability. The mid-1950s saw a renaissance in the study of religion. Perhaps more secure as a science, psychology could once again look with some interest upon the serious investigation of religion. This time the study was less speculative, was not as concerned with grand theory, and focused on issues other than the origin of religion. In a word, an *empirical* psychology of religion emerged. This was a more limited view, to be sure, but it demanded that statements about religion be formulated as hypotheses capable of empirical verification or falsification.

In rapid succession, journals devoted to the empirical study of religion emerged in the middle of this century. Among these were the *Journal for the Scientific Study of Religion*, the *Journal of Religion and Health*, the *Review of Religious Research*, and the *Journal of Psychology and Theology*. More recently, additional journals and annuals have appeared, including the *International Journal for the Psychology of Religion*, the *Journal of Psychology of Religion*, and *Research in the Social Scientific Study of Religion*. In 1988 the *Annual Review of Psychology* included, for the first time, a summary of studies on the psychology of religion, affirming by its presence that a significant body of empirical research in this area is now available. This literature has continued to grow at a rapid rate. The domination of interpretative and conceptual discussions of religion in psychology is gradually yielding to empirical, data-based discussions that are pulling the psychology of religion into the mainstream of academic psychology. The occurrence of this second edition is itself an indication of the vigor of psychology of religion as we approach the beginning of another century.

Our aim remains the same as in the first edition: to present a comprehensive evaluation of the psychology of religion from an empirical perspective. However, we especially acknowledge the pervasive importance of *social* psychology within the more general psychology of religion. We are not concerned with purely conceptual or philosophical discussions of religion, or with grand theories that have little empirical support. Interesting as these approaches may be, they generate few if any empirical data. When they do, they are considered as are other hypotheses—as tentative claims to be judged by the facts. We have not imposed a single theoretical perspective across all the chapters. Instead, we have organized the findings in each chapter according to the theory or theories that best illuminate them. Although we are sensitive to the difficulties and limitations of a purely empirical approach, we have not abandoned the commitment to empiricism as the single most fruitful avenue to understanding the psychology of religion.

We have added an author to this edition, Bruce Hunsberger. Bruce takes up some of the slack resulting from Richard Gorsuch's schedule and commitments, which made him unable to be an active author here. However, Richard's considerable presence and influence remain represented in this edition. Much of his writing from the first edition has been updated and incorporated into the present text, so he remains very much an author and contributor.

The basic structure of the first edition remains. However, we have incorporated the data on the impact of family and schools into a more comprehensive chapter on religious socialization, and have added a chapter on religion and coping. The text itself is greatly expanded because of the richness and variety of empirical research conducted during the past decade, which itself is testimony to the vitality of the field. Our hope is not only that this text fairly represents the research and scholarly literature, but that it will encourage others to participate in the empirical study of one of the most truly human of life's adventures—religious faith.

Ralph W. Hood, Jr.
Bernard Spilka
Bruce Hunsberger
Richard Gorsuch

ACKNOWLEDGMENTS

Many people have contributed to the successful completion of this volume. It would be impossible to thank them all. However, we would like to single out individuals who have made significant contributions to the project at some point in its evolution.

Ralph Hood: I have benefited immensely from discussion with both Ron Morris and Paul J. Watson. Jean Tyrone was more than gracious in editing many chapters. Rich Metzger assured departmental support, for which I am grateful.

Bernard Spilka: Valuable information and significant direction on religion in adult life and religion and abnormal behavior was provided by Dr. Larry K. Graham, Dr. Joretta Marshall, and Dr. Paula D. Nesbitt of the Iliff School of Theology. Similar important and little-known material was offered by Dr. Peter Firmin of the University of Denver. Especially thoughtful and important ideas was the province of Dr. Harvey H. Potthoff, a man for whom the descriptive word "wisdom" was invented. Dr. Michael Kearl of the Sociology Department of Trinity University was an indispensable source of important and often obscure data of great relevance to this work. We are deeply appreciative of his kindness and contributions. Also, there are two stalwarts who know enough psychology to have kept me on the straight and narrow, and who can never be thanked enough: Daniel N. McIntosh (Danny) and Kevin Ladd. And finally my gratitude goes to Ellen Spilka, truly the long-suffering wife, who claims that during this effort, I had a secret affair with my computer. To all these the phrase "thank you" will never be enough.

Bruce Hunsberger: My friend, former mentor, and best critic, Bob Altemeyer, has, over the years, stimulated my plodding mind to think of religion in new ways (especially when we washed dishes together), and his encouragement has often led to research projects which otherwise would not have been carried out. My colleague Mike Pratt offered helpful comments on a couple of chapters, never having suspected that I would take him up on his offer to read them. My department chair, Keith Horton, kindly made departmental resources available for this project, sometimes knowingly. Others offered specific suggestions to improve the manuscript, including Professor Helmut Reich, and my graduate students Henry Danso and Bob Duck. Henry also deserves a medal for tracking down many references, as well as corrections to references. My undergraduate Psychology of Religion class tolerated the assignment of a draft of this book as the textbook for their course, and several of them offered helpful suggestions which improved a subsequent draft. Susan Alisat contributed to the preparation of drafts of the manuscript. Finally, my wife Emily, who has a policy of not asking about my research or writing, violated her own rule and actually read several chapters. Her comments helped make the book more readable.

We as coauthors also feel a great debt to each other. In spite of our diverse backgrounds, research interests, areas of expertise, and geographical locations, we came to rely heavily on each other for feedback, encouragement, and scholarly suggestions. We even learned to tolerate each other's idiosyncrasies and have not only remained on speaking terms, but have gained greater respect and appreciation for each other through our collaborative work on this difficult task.

The editorial team at The Guilford Press has been a pleasure to work with. They were knowledgeable, understanding, supportive, and they improved this book in countless ways. We would like to single out for special thanks Editor-in-Chief Seymour Weingarten and Senior Production Editor Anna Brackett for their editorial handling of the manuscript, and their patience with our various idiosyncrasies. We are also deeply indebted to Marie Sprayberry for her superb copy-editing of the book.

CONTENTS

ൟ

Chapter 1

THE PSYCHOLOGICAL NATURE
AND FUNCTIONS OF RELIGION

ะ๛

My religion is to do good.[1]

. . . dogma has been the fundamental principle of my religion.[2]

Things are coming to a pretty pass when religion is allowed to invade private life.[3]

Religion. n. A daughter of Hope and Fear, explaining to ignorance the nature of the Unknowable.[4]

I am an atheist still, thank God.[5]

WHY THE PSYCHOLOGY OF RELIGION?

The more important something is to people, the more they will personalize it, and find ways of distinguishing their views from those of others. The "definitions" and approaches to religion quoted above convey some of that flavor. Throughout history the importance of religion, both individually and culturally, has spawned innumerable interpretations of what religion is or should be. In different places and times, various faiths have dominated and then been replaced in paroxysms of war, rebellion, persecution, or simply revelation. Judaism in ancient and medieval Israel gave way to Catholicism, then Islam; it has now, of course, been reestablished in modern Israel. Roman religion was supplanted by Catholicism, which still reigns in modern Italy, but in some other countries Catholicism has been replaced by Protestantism. The latter still prevails in the North American milieu but over time has fractionated into a wide variety of forms, many of which have struggled with each other for converts and for social and political power. History tells us of holy wars, martyrdom, religious conflict, and bigotry, as well as ecumenism and a commitment to the highest human ideals. Still, we cannot confront the nature of faith without psychologically comprehending its many roles within the individual and the community. This is our purpose here—to look at religion from a psychological perspective in general and a social-psychological perspective in particular.

Few human concerns are more seriously regarded than religion. People surround themselves with spiritual reference, making it a context in which the sacred is invoked to convey the significance of every major life event. Birth is sanctified by christening, baptism, or circumcision. Marriages are solemnized by clergy, who readily interpret the roles of husband and wife in religious terms. Throughout life, religion mitigates death by associating it with gratifying images of an afterlife where only good prevails or justice demands that evil will be punished with pain and suffering. And, finally, some religious traditions assure the faithful of an ultimate resurrection at the end of time.

Why do people expend so much energy on religion? Simply because it is an ever-present and extremely important aspect of the historical, cultural, social, and psychological realities that humans confront in their daily lives. Our goal is to comprehend this complex world of personally significant values, beliefs, experiences, wishes, dreams, and actions. Individual expression in contemporary Western civilization, particularly in the North American milieu, is our primary focus. This approach emphasizes the empirical and scientific; we go where theory and data take us. Since most psychological research has been conducted within the Judeo-Christian framework, such material provides us with the overwhelming majority of our citations. Whenever information is available outside of this realm, we also pursue it. Our role is to search in mind, society, and culture for the nature of religious thinking and behavior; we want to know what religion is *psychologically*. We urge our readers to keep in mind that there is a big difference between religion per se and religious behavior, motivation, perception, and cognition. We study these human considerations, not religion as such.

Before we undertake this immense task, our proper role in this endeavor must be understood. A disclaimer is therefore in order. Let us recognize that psychologists have no calling to challenge religious institutions and their doctrines. God is not our domain; neither is the world vision of churches. We do not enter into debates of faith versus reason, of one theology versus another, or of religion with science. In addition, it is not our place to question revelation or scripture. Psychology as a social and behavioral science is our resource, and we expend our energies on this level of understanding. Beliefs, motivations, cognitions, and perceptions are psychological constructs that, when linked to religion, constitute the basis for a psychology of religion. As psychologists, we must always keep this emphasis and these considerations before us.

BASIC QUESTIONS AND DIRECTIONS

Some very basic issues confront psychologists of religion, and, for that matter, anyone who is seriously interested in religion. To begin, there is always the question "What is religion?" We certainly ought to be able to define the object of our concern and interest. However, this raises another question: "Can we offer a definition with which virtually all agree?" As we shall see, this is a very serious problem. Stated differently, we can suggest where one finds religion, and, in a practical sense, indicate what its major features are.

A second issue of special consideration to the social scientist concerns the vantage point from which religion is viewed. Anthropologists and sociologists examine religion as an aspect of culture. They want to know its institutional forms; that is, they want to know how churches, synagogues, and temples are formally and informally structured. This leads to an understanding of the place of religion in a social order—its historical, political, social, and economic functions, among other possibilities. Psychologists, especially social psychologists, try to focus on the individual in this matrix of sociocultural forces that are relevant to religion. They want to know what religion means to the individual, how it is expressed, what it does for people, and their thoughts and behavior in relation to its various forms. In the last analysis, however, a psychologist who does not look at personal faith in its societal context will be like a boxer fighting with only one hand. The institutional level and the individual level are inseparable, and the interaction between them means that both must be part of a thoroughgoing psychology of religion.

A third issue is the complexity of faith. It would be wonderful if things were as simple as we desire them to be, but that is not the way of the world. Whenever we look closely at something, it seems to grow in complexity, and personal faith is no exception. To many people, "religion" is one word, and therefore it must mean one thing—namely, what they think it is. It doesn't take rigorous research and observation to tell us that people express their religious inclinations in many different ways. We discuss some of these frameworks, and try to show the intricacies of religious belief, experience, and behavior. As Oscar Wilde put it, "The truth is rare, and never simple."[6]

A fourth concern deals with that most basic question, "Where does religion come from?" We would like to know the human sources of religious impulses and needs. Here we examine the roles of theorized "instincts"—genetic bases of faith, learning, and habit. On a higher plane, we need to show how religion defends and protects people, while also stimulating growth and self-realization.

Finally, we introduce in broad outline a point of view regarding how men, women, and children relate to their faith. People's personal religion is not an isolated thing; it concerns how they perceive and deal with themselves, others, and the world. The stress is on personal meaning, and on how it maintains and enhances people's sense of control and self-esteem.

We therefore feel it is necessary to unify as many of the research findings in the psychology of religion as we can by means of a theoretical framework. It may be that certain conceptualizations are most appropriate to specific aspects of the overall field. Other theories may be more broadly applicable. The principle that we wish to embrace is that thousands of isolated studies exist, and they need to be brought together in one or more consolidating frameworks. Our knowledge has to be meaningfully ordered, and theories do just that. They tell us what factors or variables may or may not be pertinent when certain problems and issues are examined. Psychologist Kurt Lewin is reported to have said that "there is nothing as practical as a good theory." Theories are the way we have of organizing our thoughts and ideas so that the data we collect make sense. In fact, even theologies can serve as psychological theories.[7] The theories we hold are "open"; they are always amenable to new information. To close our minds is the most impractical thing we can do. Our approach is therefore both theoretical and empirical, because neither aspect by itself is meaningful without the other.

Emphasizing a theoretically informed empirical approach does not mean that research and observations are made in a value-free vacuum. Humans are valuing beings, and if there is a specific human nature, it may be to act on values—to accept what is liked and reject what is disliked. People's interests complement their biases and prejudices, and religion is an area that people do not deal with dispassionately. Our problem as empirical scientists is to carry out research without letting our biases affect the outcome. The sociologist C. Wright Mills is reported to have affirmed this position by declaring, "I will make every effort to be objective, but I do not claim to be detached." As we will see, it is often not easy to remain "detached." Toward the end of this chapter, we offer more specific theoretical guidance.

We raise the foregoing issues in an effort to clarify how psychologists empirically study religion. The word "empirical" is crucial. It means (1) reliance on observation, and (2) the acquisition of knowledge that is objective. It is therefore based on the scientific method. We want information that is *public*; the findings of research should be understandable by all. A second requirement is that the data be *reproducible*: Each person can conduct his or her own research, and, ideally, can replicate results. More specifically, the same findings should result from studying the problem in the same way. This is the approach of science. It is a way of conveying an exciting and fascinating appreciation of the nature and place of religion in people's lives. This path is not always an easy one to follow, but it is the orientation with which we hope our readers will become acquainted in the following pages.

DEFINING RELIGION: IS IT POSSIBLE?

The famous theologian Paul Tillich harshly called upon all of us to clarify our muddled thinking about religion when he observed:

> There is hardly a word in the religious language, both theological and popular, which is subject to more misunderstandings, distortions, and questionable definitions than the word "faith." It belongs to those terms which need healing before they can be used for the healing of man. Today the term "faith" is more productive of disease than of health. It confuses, misleads, creates alternatively skepticism and fanaticism, intellectual resistance and emotional surrender, rejection of genuine religion and subjection to substitutes.[8]

Despite his unhappiness, Tillich could not find a substitute for "the reality to which the term 'faith'"[9] refers, and he devoted a volume to its exposition. We are confronted with a similar task, but our method and approach are different, and we hope that they will help to clarify Tillich's "reality."

Social scientists and religionists have teased out every abstraction, nuance, and implication in each word in any definition of religion that has ever been offered or is likely to be created. We therefore fully agree with the sociologist J. Milton Yinger that "any definition of religion is likely to be satisfactory only to its author."[10] Nevertheless, later, in a noteworthy book, Yinger struggled with the problem of definition in a very scholarly manner for some 23 pages.[11] It may have been a similar frustration that much earlier caused a noted psychologist of religion, George Coe, to state:

> I purposely refrain from giving a formal definition of religion . . . partly because definitions carry so little information as to facts; partly because the history of definitions of religion makes it almost certain that any fresh attempts at definition would necessarily complicate these introductory chapters.[12]

We do not feel that the situation has basically changed in the eight decades that have passed since Coe took his stand. We can, however, accept the guidance of another scholar who claimed that "religion, like poetry and most other living things, cannot be defined. But some characteristic marks may be given."[13] Let us therefore avoid the pitfalls of unproductive, far-ranging, grand-theoretical, general definitions of religion. Since we must still know what we are talking about, we utilize other definitions about which there can be little or no argument. These yield clear criteria, and are termed "operational definitions." They are discussed at length later.

Where Do We Find Religion?

Since we are not going to define religion theoretically, we might consider the "place" or "location" of religion. This should provide some focus in terms of where to look in order to increase our understanding of faith, both individually and collectively. The simple answer is to join all of those who claim that religion is to be found everywhere there are people; it is thus universal.[14] This seems to make sense, but if we can't arrive at a definition of what religion is, how do we know that it is universal? There is, moreover, some evidence that those who hold this "universalist" hypothesis enter the fray with ideas that are conditioned by Western culture. They then select the categories with which they are familiar, go out and look for these in other cultures, and somehow always manage to find what they are looking for.[15] Though they may be right, we do not know whether the religion they define as existing within another society is so defined by the members of that group. Maybe we need to have anthropologists from, say, various African or Asian cultures, and to listen to their interpretations. Religion might then take on quite a different character, but so far anthropology and the other social sciences, including psychology, are Western creations. Non-Western peoples may feel that they make little or no sense. We can well argue that, despite our scientific pretensions, we are often hardly objective and free of *our* values. In any event, believing that religion is universal is not much help, so we may have to accept a different perspective on its "location."

Staying, however, within our own bounds and intellectual limitations, we must recognize that we may find religion either "inside" a person or "out there" in a social order. But even this distinction may be too pat, too artificial, too simple an answer—because, as we have noted, person, culture, and society are inseparably related. There can be no individual independent of the environment, and even to conceive of an environment presupposes a person within it. The environment about which we are concerned is social, cultural, and historical. Just as people are products of their biological heritage, so they have internalized a wide variety of sociocultural influences. The language people use shapes their thoughts as much as they are molded by the past. To paraphrase one noted social scientist, the success and failure of individual men and women are problems of history, and this history includes some thousands of years of religious influence.[16]

Western culture gives us some leeway, and we are often rather arbitrary and expedient in what we choose to do. Just as we can view the person from many perspectives—biological, anthropological, sociological, and psychological—so we can claim that there are both "outside" and "inside" perspectives on religion.

The "Outside" Perspective

The "outside" or external point of view marks the approach of the sociologist or anthropologist. Religion is seen as an institution, a major element of culture that is defined in terms of some supraindividual group, category, or organization—a church, sect, or cult; the "faithful," the "believers," the "chosen." This collectivity has a history to justify its existence, and that history is associated with theological doctrines; the Bible or other sacred writings; and church dogma, liturgy, ritual, and whatever practices and beliefs the group considers spiritually meaningful.

From a psychological point of view, this is the context for individual religious expression. It is the foundation for one's religious beliefs, as well as the reference for acceptable or unacceptable thinking and behavior that every religious system advocates as the basis of living "the good life." Even though psychologists are not as a rule involved in the study of faith from this "outside" or external perspective, it is nevertheless indispensable to any understanding of religion.

The "Inside" Perspective

Now we enter the realm of the psychologist of religion. The essential point here is that psychologists of religion do not study religion per se; they study people in relation to their faith. This is what the humanist and religionist might term the domain of "inner experience" and "the perception of the infinite," respectively. Though more objective psychologists have not avoided the realm of religious experience, they stress religious beliefs, behaviors, attitudes, and knowledge. For example, the 19th-century philosopher/ethnologist Max Muller focused on the individuality of faith when he saw religion as "the *perception* of the infinite under such manifestations as are able to *influence* the moral character of man."[17] Walter Houston Clark, one of the giants of the contemporary psychology of religion, claimed that "religion can be *most characteristically* described as the *inner experience of the individual when he senses a Beyond*, especially as evidenced by the effect of this experience on his behavior when he actively attempts to harmonize his life with the Beyond."[18] William James, perhaps the single most influential psychologist of religion, noted that religion consists of the "belief that there is an unseen order and that our supreme good lies in harmoniously adjusting ourselves thereto."[19]

These definitions probably represent the dominant view of religion in Western culture. "Inner experience" or "perception" is anchored in something external and independent of us, and indeed transcendent—"the infinite," "a beyond," "the ultimate," or "the divine."[20] Here is the language of faith. It connotes a being, a deity, God, in whom resides universal, absolute truth; it is the object of adoration by people who earnestly believe and feel that their moral character and relationship to the world is constructively transformed in the religious process. It may also connote something more impersonal, and yet absolute and demanding of our ultimate concern. Our task is to understand what these ideas and words mean psychologically.

Finding Faith in Society and Culture

Social scientists are loath to use religious ideas in their work unless they are subtly masked, possibly even from themselves. Over 80 years ago, Edward Scribner Ames suggested that "religion is the consciousness of the highest *social* values."[21] "Social," of course, includes one's relationship with God. Even those who cross religion with psychology may embrace modern theological views, and replace the idea of God with something that moves humanity more to center stage. Wieman and Westcott-Wieman thus denoted religion as "a process of organizing the self around and toward the highest values."[22] The significant feature of this approach is its reference to a social and/or personal framework as the essence of religion itself. Subjective terms such as "self" or "highest values" are open to psychological definition and then become available for objective measurement.

Erich Fromm, one of the great movers of psychoanalytic thought into the realm of culture, demonstrated his social-scientific outlook when he described religion as "any system of thought and action *shared by the group* which gives the individual a frame of orientation and an object of devotion."[23] This view stresses an explicit social context and an "object of devotion" that is not in any way limited to a supernatural being. One can include here popular heroes or political, economic, or social ideologies that are in some ways analogous to traditional religions. We are probably all familiar with people who believe in some doctrine to such a degree that its effect on their lives is hardly different from what most people regard as religious. Yet analogies can mislead as well as clarify. Society is well populated with objects of devotion that elicit the fervor of the devout in every group from children to senior citizens. If our anchoring point is established religion, we will need more focused definitions than those that include every possible social referent.

The great theologians have always contended that no aspect of living, including the most commonplace of activities, can be divorced from a truly religious perspective. The poet Kahlil

Gibran said it well when he claimed that "your daily life is your temple and your religion."[24] Religion thus becomes life as lived in its prosaic, enlightened, and even seamy aspects. Even though our search for religion points in many directions, Yinger unites a number of these, offering a position with which it is hard to disagree:

> . . . where one finds awareness of and interest in the continuing recurrent problems of human existence—the human condition itself as contrasted with specific problems; where one finds rites and shared beliefs relevant to that awareness, which define the strategy of an ultimate victory; and where one has groups organized to heighten that awareness and to teach and maintain those rites and beliefs—there one has religion.[25]

Given some "outside" system, religion thus becomes the knowledge, beliefs, feelings, actions, and experiences of the individual as they are expressed in relation to that system. Studying this "inside" response to that "outside" framework is the task of the psychologist of religion.

Operational Definitions

We have seen something of the difficulties encountered in attempts to define religion. We have alluded earlier to the idea of "operational definitions" as a means of getting around these problems. The essential characteristics of such definitions need to be known in order to understand how psychologists and social scientists can study religion empirically. Simply put, they are necessary in order for scientific endeavors to have any validity or reliability. Operational definitions in the psychology of religion are always referenced to some tangible religious indicator. This may be as obvious as church attendance, answers to questions about the importance of religion in one's life, statements dealing with the details of religious beliefs, or descriptions of the nature of a religious experience. Whenever we identify some index or measure that we have used or intend to employ, we are providing an operational definition. It is a definition in terms of "operations"—the things we do, the methods and instruments we utilize.

For example, take the concept of "religiosity." If we are to treat it operationally, it must be identified by specific "operations." These may be a person's responses to a questionnaire that is designed to assess religious commitment—-the strength of one's beliefs in the doctrines of a church, as well as frequency of participation in church services and/or in other activities (e.g., Sunday school, Bible study, a prayer group, the "sisterhood" or men's club, evangelical or missionary behavior). The way people answer questions about such involvement can tell us much about their "religiosity." Very often we create questionnaires that ask about such beliefs, experiences, and actions. An early researcher, Ernest Chave, constructed over 50 inventories that evaluated, among other aspects of religion, people's views about God, Jesus, the Bible, the church, worship, and virtually every aspect of their knowledge of and personal attitudes toward traditional religion.[26]

Such operational definitions always let people know just what the researcher means when religious language is used. We can say, for example, "Religiosity was measured by the Attitude toward the Church Questionnaire." Another student of this topic may argue that a different measure is a better indicator of religiosity. All researchers must develop theories and justifications for the operational definitions they employ, and their arguments can help us progress by allowing different approaches to be tested and compared in order to determine which ones best support or counter theories about how religion functions in people.

Psychologists of religion have constructed literally hundreds of questions and question-naires to study different aspects of perceived religion. We must not view these efforts as ever fully describing or circumscribing religion or religiosity. Such simple indicators may point us in a meaningful direction; they can function as approximations to the religious life of the individual, but they cannot and do not treat it in its entirety. They are signs that point to those deeper, "behind the scenes" factors that often lie hidden in the personality or in social settings and relationships. Still, they are operationally definable, and everyone knows what was done. They can also show us the way to other empirical techniques that explore personal religion in greater depth.

BEING RELIGIOUS: ONE THING OR MANY?

Our passion to be efficient, to summarize the complex, to wrap it all up in "25 words or less," is often an enemy to real understanding. Words are symbols that place many things under one heading, and the term "religion" is an excellent example of this tendency. When psychologists first began research in this area, they simply constructed measures of religious-ness or religiosity. Sophisticated thinkers, however, soon put aside notions that people sim-ply vary along a single dimension with antireligious sentiments at one end and orthodox views at the other end. These proved unsatisfactory, and new ideas and indices began to appear in the research literature. We now read of "religious individualism," "religious institutional-ization," "ritualism," "idealism," "mysticism," "particularism," "ethicalism," "devotion-alism," "forgiveness," and a host of new religious labels. [27]

When we examine the many schemes that have been proposed, we see that some stress the purpose of faith, whereas others look to the possible personal and social origins of religion. Although some appear to mix psychology and religion, there are also those that take their cues exclusively from psychology and focus on motivation or cognition. How-ever, the real problem is twofold: the presence of a "hidden" value agenda that implies "good" and "bad" religion, and a lack of conceptual and theoretical clarity. There is also great overlap among the various proposals, with essentially the same idea being phrased in different words—testimony to the excellent vocabularies of some social scientists. On a surface level, we can say that most psychological researchers emphasize religious expres-sion in belief, experience, and behavior. There is, however, one point on which all agree: namely, that even though there is only one word for "religion," there may be a hundred possible ways of being "religious." John Wilson thus notes that "religion is clearly not a homogenous whole. Individuals who are religious in one respect might not be in another . . . religion is multidimensional."[28]

Theoretical versus Statistical Approaches

Given the many faces of religion, our concern with empirical evidence and with operational definitions leads to the question of where the many different forms or types of religion come from. Basically, there are two sources: theory and the objective analysis of data. The theoreti-cal approach relies on concepts and ideas, invariably derived from induction. This means that people have observed and thought about religion, and from their many observations, they sug-gest what its multifaceted essence is. The next step is to go out and attempt to demonstrate through research whether these ideas can be confirmed. In other words, do the findings support a theory that suggests certain kinds of religion? The theory must spawn hypotheses that can be assessed objectively. Their rejection might suggest modifications in the theory. Sometimes, even though we might like to reject the entire theory, we are rarely able to do so. Grand theories that cannot be totally tested (e.g., psychoanalytic theory) often yield "mini-" views that are amenable to research assessment.

The second, or statistical, approach starts with quantitative data. Most often, objective answers are provided by a sample of people to questions or statements about religion. We apply certain statistical techniques to these data, including correlation and factor analysis, as well as a wide variety of inferential statistics used to test empirical hypotheses (see the Appendix to this chapter). Complex analyses are carried out; a certain amount of subjectivity does enter the picture; and finally the result is a claim that there are so many "dimensions" of religiosity in some reasonably well-defined group, such as Roman Catholics or Methodists. Claims are, however, made that "religion in general" is being evaluated multidimensionally. Rather frequently, after the fact, researchers find out that the new system is not appropriate for non-Christians, or that it seems to work best with conservative Protestant groups and not with more liberal denominations (or vice versa). What we really need is a combination of theory and data analysis that can be continually tested and refined.

Some Multidimensional Frameworks

An excellent example of one effort to offer a comprehensive multidimensional system was advanced by Verbit.[29] He suggested that religion is composed of six components, each of which contains four dimensions. These are optimistically said to be best understood relative to Verbit's definition of religion as "man's relationship to whatever he conceives as meaningful ultimacy."[30] The proposed components are as follows:

1. *Ritual*: private and/or public ceremonial behavior.
2. *Doctrine*: affirmations about the relationship of the individual to the ultimate.
3. *Emotion*: the presence of feelings (awe, love, fear, etc.).
4. *Knowledge*: intellectual familiarity with sacred writings and principles.
5. *Ethics*: rules for the guidance of interpersonal behavior, connoting right and wrong, good and bad.
6. *Community*: involvement in a community of the faithful, psychologically, socially, and/or physically.

Each of these components is said to vary along the following four dimensions:

1. *Content*: the essential nature of the component (e.g., specific rituals, ideas, knowledge, principles, etc.).
2. *Frequency*: how often the content elements are encountered or are acted upon.
3. *Intensity*: degree of commitment.
4. *Centrality*: importance or salience.

This scheme might be a good theoretical guide for analyses of either institutional or personal religion, but it contains a number of potential problems. Obviously, there must be some overlap among both the components and the dimensions. For example, if we study the component of ritual, there is a high likelihood that the more frequently a ritual is carried out, the more likely it is to be central to the religion and to elicit considerable feeling. To state this problem differently, the dimensions sound good conceptually, but the relationships among frequency, intensity, and centrality may be so strong as to suggest that analyzing them independently would be redundant; they may all reduce to one dimension, which we could call something like "importance of religion." Another difficulty concerns the components. There is a good chance that each is in itself multidimensional, meaning that they possess a number of different facets relative to the way people perceive and act upon them. Finally, despite the construction of this potentially useful grand scheme (which is supposed to cover all religions), this framework does not appear to have ever been directly operationalized and evaluated in research.

The search for dimensions of religion often takes on the appearance of a game. Sometimes it is manifested as an exercise in complex statistics without any theoretical backing. In other cases there is good conceptual thinking, but no research support. This has become the psychology of religion's "gold rush," and there is reason to believe that some gold has been found. The valuable metal is evident in its stimulating effect on scholars, whose questions and arguments are leading to better definitions and improved theories along with theoretically guided research. Less and less of the time, however, are workers in the field succumbing to the lure of new "forms" of faith with appealing labels. Even an older, well-established scheme such as Allport's "intrinsic–extrinsic" distinction is being increasingly distrusted.[31] Despite challenges to the validity of these ideas, multidimensional constructions of religion are likely to continue and become more subtle and refined. Table 1.1 presents a sampling of some of the better-known of these frameworks.

We should not overlook the fact that there is overlap among the multidimensional schemes that different scholars have proposed. Some idea of this problem can be observed in Table 1.2.

Mention should be made of a shift in emphasis when forms of faith are conceptualized. For example, the distance between defining intrinsic and extrinsic religion and referring to people as "intrinsics" and "extrinsics" does not appear to be great. In reality, however, the criteria for placing individuals in one or the other of these categories are often quite debatable. This kind of terminology implies "pure types," and though these idealized images make for interesting discussion, in real life they are rare to the point of nonexistence. Still, both as scientists and as human beings, we like the appearance of unchallengeable certainty that classifications offer us. To be able to define everyone as a saint or a sinner would greatly simplify our lives. In our own eyes we might identify with the former; unhappily, others might see more of the latter in us. Such patternings of people are, however, quite commonly offered. Roof has recently looked at the religious propensities of the baby boom generation and come up with four types he terms the "loyalists," the "returnees," the "believers-but-not-belongers," and the "seekers."[32] When Benson and Williams studied religion in the U.S. Congress, they distinguished six kinds of religionists, which they called "legalistic," "self-concerned," "integrated," "people-concerned," "nontraditional," and "nominal."[33] All of these schemes point to the complexity of religious faith, as well as the uses to which it may be put. Let us be aware of the fact that there is invariably overlap among these categories, and that clear operational indicators of how their creators arrive at their designation are needed. Simple lines cannot be drawn from forms of faith to types of people. The usefulness of identifying types is a matter of debate in the contemporary psychology of religion.[34]

As already noted, some of these classifications are based on theory, whereas others are the product of sophisticated statistical analyses, particularly what is termed "factor analysis"

TABLE 1.1. Some Multidimensional Approaches to the Study of Individual Religion

Allen and Spilka (1967)

Committed religion	"Utilizes an abstract philosophical perspective: multiplex religious ideas are relatively clear in meaning and an open and flexible framework of commitment relates religion to daily activities" (p. 205).
Consensual religion	"Vague, non-differentiated, bifurcated, neutralized" (p. 205). A cognitively simplified and personally convenient faith.

Allport (1966)

Intrinsic religion	"Faith as a supreme value in its own right . . . oriented toward a unification of being that take seriously the commandment of brotherhood, strives to transcend all self-centered needs" (p. 455).
Extrinsic religion	"Religion that is strictly utilitarian; useful for the self in granting safety, social standing, solace, and endorsement of one's chosen way of life" (p. 455).

Batson and Ventis (1982)

Means religion	"Religion is a means to other self-serving ends" (p. 151).
End religion	"Religion is an ultimate end in itself" (p. 151).

Clark (1958)

Primary religious behavior	"An authentic inner experience of the divine combined with whatever efforts the individual may make to harmonize his life with the divine" (p. 23).
Secondary religious behavior	"A very routine and uninspired carrying out . . . an obligation" (p. 24).
Tertiary religious behavior	"A matter of religious routine or convention accepted on the authority of someone else" (p. 25).

Fromm (1950)

Authoritarian religion	"The main virtue of this type of religion is obedience, its cardinal sin is disobedience" (p. 35).
Humanistic religion	"This type of religion is centered around man and his strength . . . virtue is self-realization, not obedience" (p. 37).

Glock (1962)

Experiential dimension	"The religious person will . . . achieve direct knowledge of ultimate reality or will experience religious emotion" (p. S-99).
Ideological dimension	"The religious person will hold to certain beliefs" (p. S-99).
Ritualistic dimension	"Specifically religious practices [are] expected of religious adherents" (p. S-99).
Intellectual dimension	"The religious person will be informed and knowledgeable about the basic tenets of his faith and its sacred scriptures" (p. S-99).
Consequential dimension	"What people ought to do and the attitudes they ought to hold as a consequence of their religion" (p. S-99).

Hunt (1972)

Literal religion	Taking "at face value any religious statement without in any way questioning it" (p. 43).
Antiliteral religion	A simple rejection of literalist religious statements.
Mythological religion	A reinterpretation of religious statements to seek their deeper symbolic meanings.

(cont.)

TABLE 1.1 (*cont.*)

James (1902/1985)

Healthy-mindedness	An optimistic, happy, extroverted, social faith: "the tendency that looks on all things and sees that they are good" (p. 78).
Sick souls	A faith of pessimism, sorrow, suffering, and introverted reflection: "the way that takes all this experience of evil as something essential" (p. 36).

Lenski (1961)

Doctrinal orthodoxy	"Stresses intellectual assent [to] prescribed doctrines" (p. 23).
Devotionalism	"Emphasizes the importance of private, or personal communion with God" (p. 23).

McConahay and Hough (1973)

Guilt-oriented, extrapunitive	"Religious belief centered on the wrath of God as it is related to other people . . . emphasizes punishment for wrong-doers" (p. 55).
Guilt-oriented, intropunitive	"A sense of one's own unworthiness and badness . . . a manifest need for punishment and a conviction that it will inevitably come" (p. 56).
Love-oriented, self-centered	Belief "oriented toward the forgiveness of one's own sins" (p. 56).
Love-oriented, other centered	Belief that "emphasizes the common humanity of all persons as creatures of God, and God's love . . . related to the redemption of the whole world" (p. 56).
Culture-oriented, conventional	"Values which are more culturally than theologically oriented" (p. 56).

(see the Appendix to this chapter). Many of these schemes remain isolated and untested in the literature, but they are suggestive formulations that merit further study. Some stress the motives of religious people; others imply an emphasis on cognition and thinking; still other patterns refer to personality traits in relation to faith. Though these breakdowns are cited now for illustrative purposes, we expect to come back to them and show how they have been employed by workers in the psychology of religion.

Even though religion has been shown to be complex, we need to recognize one of those "behind the scenes" variables that is obviously of very great significance. This has been called "salience," or "the importance an individual attaches to being religious."[35] The connection between religious belief or experience and religious and nonreligious behavior may in part be a function of salience. In other words, the more important religion is to a person, the greater the likelihood that it will influence how that person responds in everyday life.

WHY ARE PEOPLE RELIGIOUS?

"Why are people religious?" is probably the most basic of all questions concerning faith. Some people find answers that cancel all doubt; others live in uncertainty and turmoil. To many, the presence of religion is all the proof they need that there is a deity. A man told one of us that the fact that he existed presupposed the existence of God—an argument that others might claim possesses a few fundamental weaknesses. Not a few claim that the existence of the Bible is all they require; in Islamic cultures, it may be the Koran. There is reason to believe that other peoples will respond similarly with reference to their own sacred writings. By

TABLE 1.2. A Comparison of Some Multidimensional Schemes for Studying Religion

Verbit (1970)	Glock (1962)	Fukuyama (1961)	Davidson (1975)[a]
Ritual	Ritualistic 　Ritual commitment 　Devotionalism	Cultic	Practice 　Public 　Private
Doctrine	Ideological 　Orthodoxy 　Particularism 　Ethicalism	Creedal	Belief 　Vertical 　Horizontal
Emotion	Experiential	Devotional	Experiential 　Desirability 　Frequency
Knowledge	Intellectual	Cognitive	Intellectual 　Religious knowledge 　Intellectual scrutiny
Ethics Community			
	Consequential		Consequential 　Personal 　Social

[a]In this system, the designations "public," "vertical," "desirability," "religious knowledge," and "personal" are regarded as conservative ends of the dimensions in question, while "private," "horizontal," "frequency," "intellectual scrutiny," and "social" constitute the liberal positions.

contrast, there are those whose personal religious orientation drives them on an unending search for truth and knowledge. They continually speculate on whether or not there is a God, and, if so, what God's nature is. When we phrase the question "Why religion?" it is to determine the psychological foundations for (1) religious behavior in general, wherever it exists and regardless of the form it takes; and (2) the development of and expression of faith by the individual. It is also obvious that these goals are closely related. Our immediate concern is with the first of these issues, and we again show that this is a field with few simple answers.

Biological Foundations for Religious Behavior

The Instinct Tradition

When psychology began to develop as a field worthy of study, there already existed in philosophy, science, and the popular mind a long tradition of speculation regarding the origins of human behavior. The Greeks provided a basis for both an empirical tradition that saw all mental content as the product of learning, and a parallel heritage that stressed a doctrine of innate ideas. Though the English empiricists Locke, Berkeley, and Hume later emphasized the former, the work of Darwin and his followers gave added impetus to the idea of inherent sources of motivation, cognition, and behavior. By the late 19th century, these biologically based notions dominated much of Western thinking about the essence of humanity. It was "nature over nurture," and the vehicle for accomplishing this hegemony was the concept of "instincts"—that is, inborn, native mental forces including motives, perceptions, and actions. Everywhere one turned, there were instincts to explain why people acted as they did.

People formed groups because of a gregarious instinct, war was a function of a pugnacious instinct, and all women possessed a maternal instinct. In a sense, each of these assumptions was explaining one unknown by postulating another unknown; however, they seemed to make sense because animals evidenced such instincts, and Darwinian thought demonstrated a continuity between humans and animals. Needless to say, it was not long before religion was explained on a similar basis. At the turn of the century, Le Bon proposed such an instinct, which he termed a "religious sentiment."[36] This was vaguely referred to as natural and unconscious. Soon after, in a similar manner, Trotter felt that religion was an expression of a more basic "herd instinct."[37]

The revival of the empirical tradition through behaviorism in the early 20th century generated strong attacks on instinctual explanations. The death blow to this tradition was probably administered by L. L. Bernard in 1924. His massive review of the literature turned up some 5,684 instincts, of which 83 were theorized to underlie religion.[38]

The difficulty of dealing with a specifically religious instinct prompted some psychologists to see faith as the product of a number of instincts and/or emotions. William McDougall,[39] one of the giants of early psychology, understood religion to be an outgrowth of what he called the instincts of curiosity, fear, and subjection. To these he added three religious emotions of admiration, awe, and reverence. One often needed a scorecard to distinguish the instincts from the emotions. Hardy postulated an instinct of approach (to be identified with the object of worship), which he erratically combined with an instinct of causation and an instinct of self-preservation to produce religion.[40] Bernard claimed that those who saw an instinctual basis for religion were naive with respect to heredity, and usually did not know that religion as they conceived it was not universal, as biology would have it.[41] Dresser put all of these attempts in perspective by observing:

> When a group of instincts is substituted for the alleged religious instinct as the origin of religious experience, the objection is that psychologists have not even been able to agree on the list of instincts and their corresponding emotions as attributed to life in general.[42]

Today, except in very well-defined situations involving animals, the term "instinct" is avoided in discussions of humans. Still, it lurks in the background in some conceptions even if the word remains unspoken. For example, Ostow and Scharfstein speak of "the need to believe," which they affirm "is almost as necessary to humans as eating . . . belief is essential to the efficient functioning of a human organism."[43] They claim that "religious and moral conceptions must have a primal source in the deep, often unconscious drives that lie behind our beliefs and practices."[44] Such vague, undefined inner sources for faith are not significantly different from instincts, and, though satisfactory to some people, are not acceptable to the scientific mind. Here is the appearance of knowledge, not its substance.

Sociobiology and Religion

A more sophisticated approach to this problem has been advanced by Edward O. Wilson, who created a stir in social science circles by proposing the concept of "sociobiology." This is "defined as the systematic study of the biological basis of all forms of social behavior, in all kinds of organisms, including man."[45] Asserting that "religious practices can be mapped onto the two dimensions of genetic advantage and evolutionary change,"[46] Wilson regards religious beliefs as "enabling mechanisms for survival."[47] Though he admits that "religion constitutes the greatest challenge to sociobiology,"[48] Wilson does not hesitate to offer a theory that views the roles religion plays in societal survival as important influences on gene selection and the shaping of the human gene pool. Hypothesizing ecclesiastical, ecological, and genetic forms of selection "over many lifetimes," Wilson claims "that religious practices that consistently enhance survival and procreation of the practitioners will propagate the physiological controls that favor acquisition of the practices. . . ."[49] Basically, this position declares that believers will survive, whereas nonconformists will be physically and/or socially excluded from society, thereby reducing the likelihood that they will be able to pass on their genes to succeeding generations.

An additional step is posited in this process. Religion is tied into the development and maintenance of moral and altruistic motivations; hence religion supports prosocial behavior that aids groups to survive, especially kinship groups. Indeed, many people feel that morality and ethics are primarily based on religion. Burhoe thus suggests that "religion transforms genetic selfishness into reciprocal altruism."[50]

Sociobiology is premised on innate genetic factors that affect social life. Most North American psychologists were and are nurtured by psychology courses that stress learning and experience, not biology; hence sociobiological explanations seem rather "far out" and uncongenial to the contemporary mind. The real test, however, is whether there are data that offer some insight into the extent of hereditary and environmental influences on religious beliefs and behaviors. Recently, such information has become available. Using five measures of religious beliefs, interests, and activities, a group from the famous investigation of thousands of twins at the University of Minnesota studied samples of identical and fraternal twins who were reared either together or apart. Obviously, identical twins possess the same genetic endowment whether they are brought up together or separately. In contrast, fraternal twins are no more closely genetically related than ordinary siblings, yet seem to encounter a similar environment if brought up together. Given these facts, it was possible to make an estimate of the degree to which genetics versus environment entered into the religious inclinations of those studied. The investigators concluded: "Our findings indicate that individual differences in religious attitudes, interests, and values arise from both genetic and environmental influences. More specifically, genetic factors account for approximately 50% of the observed variance on our measures."[51] In other words, religion, as measured in this study, was in equal parts a function of heredity and environment.

This is challenging work that needs further verification. In addition, we have to ask whether the genetics are influencing something intellectual or temperamental that religion taps. Sociobiology provides provocative hypotheses, including a possible scientific foundation for Jungian archetypes, as Wenegrat has argued.[52] Clearly, this approach is neither a complete nor a final answer; the findings of one research project can only be regarded as suggestive, and must be confirmed by more work that delves deeper into the issue. A door has been opened, but many have to pass through it in order to appreciate the view on the other side.

Religious Behavior: Between Biology and Psychology

There is a gradual shading from ideas that avow religion to be a pure creation of nature to a full environmental posture that simply looks on faith as learned in a social milieu. The old Scottish school of clergy/psychologists who wrote before William James's time held the former view, and felt that a full investigation of nature would reveal the active working hand of God behind behavior. The Darwinian revolution removed the deity from this sphere, and left psychology with a biological substrate to which behaviorism felt all human actions could eventually be referred. A century of writing and research on the physiological bases of behavior tells us that perception, learning, cognition, and motivation have biological roots; yet a considerable gap exists between the topics of social psychology, of which religion is one, and the neuromuscular correlates of the ideas and responses made in people's interactions with others. Having biological roots does not necessarily limit human potential, for much if not most of both the content and process of perception, motivation, and cognition is the result of learning and experience. Current theories of the origin of religion usually place us in this gray realm between psychology and biology.

It bears repetition that we must confine ourselves to the domain of nature and social life. Being objective may frequently conflict with personal beliefs; however, as psychologists we have no alternative but to stay with what we know, can theorize, and assess. This position forces us to raise questions that recognize that religious behavior may have roots in both nature and nurture.

An Example from Developmental Psychology: Cognitive Growth

Developmental approaches to religious behavior stress cognitive growth, and most often are based on the ideas of the great Swiss psychologist Jean Piaget. These are detailed in Chapter 2. Behind Piagetian discussions of "stages of growth" are somewhat muted notions of genetic and biological factors. Biological predispositions for a certain orderly pattern of development through physiological maturation are present. As one of the main interpreters of Piaget put it, "In Piaget's view, cognitive development must have its roots firmly planted in biological growth, and basic principles valid for the former are to be found only among those which are true of the latter."[53]

An excellent example of this kind of thinking, the biological basis of which remains implicit, is evident in David Elkind's fine article "The Origins of Religion in the Child."[54] Borrowing from Piaget, who is explicit about the innate sources of intelligence, Elkind selects four basic components of intelligence that are said to develop in the following sequence: "conservation," "search for representation," "search for relations," and "search for comprehension."

Conservation is a "life-long quest for permanence amidst a world of change."[55] "Permanence" tells us that something still exists even if it is not immediately present. For example, a mother may leave her child; however, when the concept of object permanence has developed, the child realizes that she continues to exist and will return. The greatest threat to permanence is death, and religion conserves life through images of an afterlife. The natural product of conservation is a deity that guarantees immortality.

By the age of 2 years, object permanence has been established, and its application to religion follows as a matter of course. Concurrently, language has started to develop and becomes the most important part of the thinking process. Thinking itself is fundamentally concerned with representing reality in symbolic form, and language is central in this search for representation, because it has the potential of embodying the most complex aspects of experience in single words. So it is that religion and God come to represent highly elaborate and intricate thoughts and images. These are associated with the resolution of what we would normally consider basic contradictions (e.g., making the sun stand still, virgin birth, immaculate conception, etc.). Symbolic representation develops into a powerful cognitive tool, which, it is claimed, intrinsically leads to a religious perspective.

Following the establishment of symbolization, a search for relations follows. Intellectual understanding entails awareness of how an individual is linked to others and to the world at large. A child gains personal meaning from knowing connections to family members, friends, school, neighborhood, and other objects and ideas of personal significance. With increasing age and exposure to new information from the media and schools, among other possibilities, the young person continually makes new inferences, associations, and relationships. Cognitive vistas expand from the family to the community, nation, world, and universe, and even further into the realm of ideas. The search for relations never ends, for people need to locate and understand who they are "in the scheme of things." Religion comes to satisfy this associational drive as it leads to ever broader horizons, even to those considered ultimate.

Finally, as childhood gives way to adolescence, the young person's intelligence increasingly utilizes abstractions, discriminations, and generalizations. As the person copes with the problems of personal existence, a sense of individuality gains strength. Reason and intellect struggle to integrate the person's ever-widening perspectives. This search for comprehension is well served by a faith that offers guidelines through its institutions, representatives, and theologies.

Elkind thus sees religion as a normal, natural outcome of mental development. The fundamentals of this process appear to be rooted in a biological substrate that manifests itself in physiological maturation with its various intellectual expressions. The contents of these expressions, however, are products of experience. People are not born into a spiritual vacuum; society, through parents, relatives, teachers, and clergy, among many others, offers religious solutions to problems. Most often, these solutions are accepted with minor variations.

Psychological Foundations for Religious Behavior

Obviously, the views described above contain many psychological elements, while leaving the door open to questions of biological origin. In contrast, many theoreticians explicitly state that they are not concerned with the origins of religion, yet their ideas are relevant to questions about the sources of religious activity.[56] Other thinkers embrace concepts that are strictly psychological, and they may even be quite open in suggesting that religion per se is exclusively a product of human psychology.[57] As a rule, these approaches fall into two large groupings which we might call the "defensive/protective tradition" and the "growth/realization tradition."

The Defensive/Protective Tradition

Facing Fear: The Need for Meaning and Control. The first framework we discuss here is fundamentally based on hedonism and need fulfillment. It has been part of a long-standing philosophical/psychological heritage that hearkens back to ancient Greece, and is one that still prevails as the dominant position in contemporary psychology. We might summarize it in the phrase "No one does something for nothing." This means that action only occurs when there is a need for it and something is to be gained by it. In biology, the concept of "homeostasis" is used; this suggests that when change occurs, invariably a deficiency, lack, or shortcoming exists and the body attempts to readjust in order to return to the desired state of balance. Psychologists have employed this notion to help them understand why people behave as they do. For example, if a person is hungry, he or she eats and satisfies this need. The body is satiated as far as various nutritive substances are concerned. Psychologically, the motivational tension that has caused the person to seek food is also alleviated.

In applications of these ideas to religion, the motivational base has been theorized as human weakness and inadequacy. When people can't make sense out of what is happening, and are unable to control a situation, fear often enters the picture; thus fear is said to be the source of religion. As Feuerbach claimed, "The explanation of religion by fear is eminently confirmed by the fact that most primitive peoples take the frightening aspects of nature as the principal if not exclusive objects of their religion."[58] Leuba cited the view of Lucretius that "Fear begets Gods," and Hume's contention "the first ideas of religion arose . . . from a concern with regard to the events of life and fears which actuate the human mind."[59] Gross summarizes this view succinctly by noting, "When misery is the greatest, God is the closest."[60] Finally, we must recognize that this association of fear with religion is well supported by research.[61]

How Does Fear Stimulate Religion? When people are truly afraid of something, they often confront circumstances that pose great uncertainty, ambiguity, and lack of meaning. Or, if the situation is clear, they lack a sense of control and mastery; they are powerless. It is not surprising that humans struggle to make the ambiguous clear, the doubtful certain, and the indeterminate sure. People search for ways to make sense out of life, to give them a feeling of control, to make the future predictable, and especially to insure a positive outcome. Religion offers such possibilities through scripture, theologies, prayer, liturgy, and ceremony. John Dewey captured the essence of this perspective thus:

> Man who lives in a world of hazards is compelled to seek for security. . . . One . . . attempt [is] to propitiate the powers which environ him and determine his destiny. It expressed itself in supplication, sacrifice, ceremonial rite and magical cult. In time these crude methods were largely displaced. The sacrifice of a contrite heart was esteemed more pleasing than that of bulls and oxen; the inner attitude of reverence and devotion more desirable than external ceremonies. If a man could not conquer destiny he could willingly ally himself with it; putting his will, even in sore affliction, on the side of the powers which dispense fortune, he could escape defeat and might triumph in the midst of destruction.[62]

Philosopher Josiah Royce referred to this "natural chaos" as a prime source of spiritual motivation, whereas noted psychologist of religion Paul Johnson sees faith as "the opposite of fear, anxiety, and uncertainty."[63] Once present, people's faith protects them from the storms of life that rage about them. Human frailty and vulnerability thus become the origins of a religion that offers hope.

A slight variation on this theme was provided by Dunlap, who claimed that "The only theory of religion which today seems to have value as a scientific working hypothesis is the theory that religion has its origins and its support in *dissatisfaction* with life, resulting from the failure of life to satisfy the primary desires of man."[64] Since this was written almost three-quarters of a century ago, it has been a somewhat productive "scientific working hypothesis," but by no means has it proven to be the *only* scientifically testable theory.

An alternative psychological version of human shortcoming focuses on the weakness of the child. According to Freud, the child confers upon the father a mantle of omnipotence. With age and experience, there is a growing awareness of paternal limitations; this awareness leads to the view that "God is the exalted father, and the longing for the father is the root of the need for religion."[65]

Catholic theologian Hans Küng perceives this as a defective religion. "Religious questions . . . become a form of self-deception and escapism . . . religion relies solely on wish-fulfillment and . . . is reduced to pure satisfaction of needs . . . a religion [of] infantile structures, a regression to childhood wishing."[66] Religion is again "a daughter of Hope and Fear."[67]

Modern life has introduced new sources of doubt and turmoil, which are said to sponsor religion. W. T. Stace notes:

> There has been growing up in men's minds, dominated as they are by science, a new imaginative picture of the world. The world, according to this new picture, is purposeless, senseless, meaningless. Nature is nothing but matter in motion. . . . If the scheme of things is purposeless and meaningless, then the life of man is purposeless and meaningless too.[68]

Stace then infers that "the essence of the [religious] spirit itself [is] belief in a meaningful and purposeful world."[69] Many scholars claim that the basic motivation of humans is to derive meaning from chaos, and this effort may be the taproot from which much religion springs.

Anxiety, Guilt, and Deprivation: Religion in the World. Looking for the origins of religion in the psychology of the individual confronts us with this issue: All of us are born into families that overwhelmingly represent the cultural mainstream of the society in which they and we exist. This means that the dominant religious framework will be communicated to children by parents, siblings, peers, and innumerable institutional expressions. These are typically accepted, and become integral aspects of the children's personalities.

One very significant aspect of personality concerns the motivational fact that when people are threatened physically or psychologically, anxiety is produced, and they attempt to cope with it. Freud recognized three forms of anxiety: "reality-based," "moral," and "neurotic."[70] Reality-based anxiety results from real, objective, independent sources of danger in the world, and these are likely to be powerful sources of religion. This is a faith that is established in the normal course of growing up in society. Moral anxiety concerns the distress that develops when one violates learned codes of proper behavior. Neurotic anxiety refers to extreme and inappropriate expressions of dread, tension, and worry that accompany behaving in ways that are considered normal by most people. Moral and neurotic forms of anxiety can be a function of one's religious background and current stance.

For many people, moral anxiety based on guilt and guilt feelings activates religious concerns. "Right" and "wrong" and "good" and "bad" are standards that are associated with religion from early childhood—particularly through such precepts as the Ten Commandments and the Golden Rule, which can be used by parents as means of child control. Sometimes such standards may have been acquired in a home where powerless parents form a "coalition with God" to enforce discipline.[71] Violation of moral codes becomes especially serious, as children are taught that this is an offense against the most powerful entity conceivable. Depending on family teaching and reinforcement, these ideas become foundations for moral and social life. In fact, the existence of morality is to many people impossible without established religion and belief in God.

"Straying from the fold" can arouse considerable guilt, which may only be resolved by a return to religion. Conversions, intense religious experiences, and other signs that imply a strengthening of faith have been reported in response to such motivations.[72] Religion can provide that additional spark of self-justification, that extra source of outside power to buttress inner doubt and weakness and to help control impulses (note the role of a "higher power" in Alcoholics Anonymous and similar groups). There is, however, another side to this coin, which bears on the development and expression of neurotic anxiety. Mowrer and others have pointed out the role of religion in enhancing feelings of guilt. Some people believe that God's punishment will follow those who are sinful, both in this life and in that to come. "Hellfire and damnation" have no limits.[73] Too often these views are part of a rigid, inflexible, unforgiving, and tyrannical belief system. Images of a threatening, unloving, and punitive deity may well be features of such a neurotically based faith. In Chapter 12, we provide more information relevant to this issue. Depending on the way religious beliefs operate—in terms of moral or neurotic guilt—the fundamental need is that "Religion must remain an outlet for people who say to themselves, 'I am not the kind of person I want to be.'"[74]

A General Deprivation Theory. Human shortcoming, weakness, and deficiency take many forms that a religious system may help to alleviate. The noted sociologist Charles Glock[75] studied the formation of religious groups and postulated five kinds of deprivation. Though the focus of his work was on group formation, the types of deprivation he emphasized affect individuals not only collectively, but, in the last analysis, individually. This is evident in Glock's definition of deprivation: "any and all of the ways that an individual or group may be, or feel disadvantaged in comparison either to other individuals or groups or to an internalized set of standards."[76] According to Glock, "economic," "social," "organismic," "ethical," and "psychic" forms of deprivation can stimulate religious activity.

Economic deprivation exists when people feel they lack enough money to meet survival needs and needs for other basic life satisfactions and enjoyments. Clearly, this has both objective and subjective aspects. One individual may have very little money, yet may not be unhappy with the degree to which his or her desires are met economically. Another may have much money, but may feel that he or she is in severe financial straits. Religion may tell the believer that money doesn't really count; it is the way life is lived spiritually and morally that is important. In contrast, historically, religion has sometimes been the rallying point for rebellion of the "have nots" against the "haves."

Social deprivation concerns the problem of how individual differences are socially regarded. For a wide variety of reasons, some people are much more highly esteemed and respected than others. Those who possess such qualities are the ones who are chosen for desirable positions; they accrue the social rewards of status, power, and prestige. Lacking the opportunities to acquire the admiration and recognition that others seem to achieve easily weighs heavily on some individuals. Walters and Bradley suggest that a lack of friends can stimulate religious activity.[77] Expressing these needs religiously can transform an outsider into an insider: A person can attain social approval and regard in religious circles through participation, piety, and commitment. In addition, such a person may come to believe that he or she has found favor in the eyes of God, and this takes precedence over all alternatives.

Organismic deprivation is related to individual variation in mental and physical health. People differ tremendously in these characteristics. Some are "hardy," whereas others seem to be ill much of the time. One person is physically strong, another weak; there are those who are handicapped visually, are hard of hearing, possess deformed limbs, have paralyses, or are neurotic or even psychotic. The list is almost endless, and the outcome is often a great deal of personal pain and psychological distress. People ask "Why me?" and for many the only satisfactory responses are through a religion that seems to provide both answers and solace. Perceiving oneself as Job also means that one has been chosen or is being tested by God. This conveys a special spiritual status on an individual. Religious mystical experiences may appear to change both the objective situation and the person's subjective outlook on it.[78]

In U.S. society, many people are dissatisfied with their own moral state and that of the social order. They feel ethically deprived; something is lacking—a constructive, meaningful, and honorable way of life. A competitive, "dog eat dog" philosophy is not for them. High rates of crime, abortion, and divorce trouble them. They decry a "lack of family values," political opportunism, or economic barbarism. Their silent revolution can ally them with traditional conservative religion. The Bible may become their moral guide to life; religion is the solution to their ethical dilemma.

Glock pointed out that ethical and psychic deprivation are somewhat similar. Whereas the former emphasizes moral concerns, the latter is more general in that the individual seeks meaning for life in general. Low self-esteem, lack of identity, the feeling that one doesn't belong—all these are aspects of psychic deprivation, and, from the individual's standpoint, religion may counter these very effectively. People may have accomplished much economically and socially, but they suffer from the feeling that "something is missing." A faith may be chosen to fill this void. Human weakness and deficiency, whether real or imagined, may take many forms that a religious framework can help resolve. It appears that wherever we observe conflict, frustration, distress, and inadequacy, there is a likelihood of faith entering the picture to rectify the situation. Anthropologist F. L. K. Hsu captures the central theme of this approach to religion thus:

> Man will always love and be in need of love. Man will always aspire to heights which he cannot reach; Man will always be fallible; Man will always die and be in distress; and Man will always have a seemingly ever-expanding universe before him even if he has conquered all earth. As long as man is subject to these and other circumstances, religion will have a place in human culture.[79]

The Growth/Realization Tradition

Religion as Overall Growth and Realization. Even though the motivational core of psychology is what we term "defensive/protective" in nature, a number of scholars have proposed a major alternative, which is positive rather than negative in its emphasis. Kurt Goldstein and Abraham Maslow utilized the concept of "self-actualization" to suggest that in all circumstances people attempt to utilize their capacities to their fullest, and to grow and improve at every opportunity, rather than simply to solve problems.[80] According to Maslow, self-actualization is most fully expressed in "peak experiences," those very special moments of emotional and intellectual enlightenment. He sees these as "the raw materials out of which not only religions can be built, but philosophies of any kind."[81] He further claims that "the peak experience may be the model of the religious revelation or the religious illumination or conversion."[82]

This approach counters the defensive view that "belief in God is a sign of man's alienation from himself, his projection onto God of that which is an unrealized possibility."[83] Movement from a deficiency outlook to one of growth may be inferred from Bertocci's notion of "religion as creative insecurity."[84] Johnson climbs the next step when he speaks of the "productive functions of faith," such as the integration of personality, personal betterment, the uniting of believers, and so on.[85] In like manner, Gardner claims that "all true religion is a path out of the quicksands of self-preoccupation and self-worship."[86]

Increasingly, the humanistic and phenomenological psychologies support the idea that people have the potential to create, grow, develop, progress, and become ever more competent and able. This theme of enlightenment, improvement, and uplift clearly finds more ready acceptance on a popular level than in mainstream psychology. Religionists are also prone to utilize such ideas; thus we read that "religion . . . is a process of organizing the self around and toward the highest values."[87] Ellwood calls it an "attitude toward the universe regarded as a social and ethical force."[88] Religion now becomes self-enhancement, growth, realization, actualization, the broadening of experiential horizons. This accords well with Tillich's perception that "faith as ultimate concern is an act of the total personality."[89]

Religion as Motivational and Cognitive Growth. Research utilizing a growth/realization perspective is rare in established professional psychology. Much humanistic writing has been devoted to these ideas, but what might be regarded as sincere efforts at conceptualizing the problem cannot be substituted for solid investigative study. Psychologists with an empirical/behavioral outlook often find this a difficult area in which to work. The main problem is one of operationalizing somewhat fuzzy concepts before research can be undertaken. Examination of this literature suggests an emphasis on motivation and cognition. Reference is primarily to the creation of meaning, and the assumption is usually made that this is the result of a basic, possibly innate drive. For example, Maddi claims "that the ultimate problem of motivational psychology is to understand how man searches for and finds meaning."[90] Nuttin suggests a fundamental composite need for self-preservation and self-development, which eventuates "in certain universal *religious tendencies* of mankind."[91] Though this may take many forms, Nuttin believes that there is "a need for contact with the whole order of reality, the only kind of contact which can give meaning to life."[92] This is also referred to as a "spiritual impulse," and its core is said to lie in a quest for meaning. Tageson refers to Nuttin as "describing . . . a basic thirst for an Absolute, a stable ground to serve as an anchor for our own ephemeral existence."[93]

Similar ideas about the importance of meaning to mental well-being have been widely espoused. Viktor Frankl's entire psychological system revolves around a "search for meaning" that is analogous to a universal striving for ultimate meaning in a "growth" sense.[94] The "search" is premised upon a "will to meaning" that is life's basic motivation.[95] Fabry states that "one gets the impression that Frankl uses the word 'meaning' where traditional writers speak of the 'will of God.'"[96] Religiously oriented psychologists have thus found Frankl's views productive for pastoral counseling and psychotherapy.[97]

Elkind's cognitive-developmental theory (described earlier) falls under this heading, as it literally sees meaning as part of a growth process. Since this approach is founded on assumed biological processes that are maturational, not motivational, it is exclusively cognitive in nature. This emphasis focuses on intelligence and its uses as intellectual horizons expand with age. It reaches its fullest expression in Einstein's concept of "cosmic religion . . . the strongest and noblest driving force behind scientific research."[98] One can argue that the goal is the same for religion: "We participate in an ultimate meaning of things."[99] O'Dea states this position impressively:

> . . . religion gives answers to questions that arise at the point of ultimacy, at those points in human experience that go beyond the everyday attitude toward life . . . because men are cognitively

capable of going to the "limit-situation," of proceeding through and transcending the conventional answers to the problem of meaning and of raising fundamental questions in terms of their human relevance.[100]

Religion as Habit

Completing our survey of psychological approaches to religion is the simple assumption that religion is nothing but a learned phenomenon. People are born into social orders in which religion already exists, and it is both formally and informally learned. This is the position of B. F. Skinner and those who advocate a more or less pure behaviorism.[101] It is basically the successor to William James's assertion that "Habit is . . . the enormous fly-wheel of society, its most precious conservative agent."[102] Though James thought of religion as much more than the product of simple learning, in a critical sense he might have had in mind the way most people seem to acquire and express their faith mechanically. Parents teach it to their children and these lessons are reinforced by society through the fact that births, marriages, deaths, and virtually every noteworthy personal and social event is solemnized by religious institutions, rituals, language, and concepts.

Robert Bellah states that U.S. society possesses a generalized religious atmosphere, a "civil religion" that is integral to public social and political life.[103] The U.S. milieu tells its inhabitants from early childhood that it is simply "un-American" not to believe in God, to deny this "object-less obsession with faith as faith."[104] Former president Franklin D. Roosevelt recognized this when he commented that no political figure would think of not including some "God stuff" in speeches.[105] Americans are supposed to believe without question and know enough not to think too deeply about these issues. This is a habitual religion, a mechanical religion, a convenient religion. It is a faith to which all are expected to give reverent assent, but one that will not otherwise interfere with people's personal lives. It is a religion of unthinking, automatic habit.

AN INTEGRATING FRAMEWORK FOR THE PSYCHOLOGY OF RELIGION

Even though scholars have offered thousands of discussions and research studies in the psychology of religion for over a century, to many critics our knowledge appears much more chaotic than scientific because of its seeming lack of structure. The scientific venture demands a conceptual organization of research under the direction of a theory. We have reviewed some broad formulations that attempt to coordinate all aspects of the psychology of religion. Unfortunately, the likelihood is that no one theory will ever completely suffice to explain this complex realm. Though many formulations may be necessary to comprehend religious expression, belief, motivation, cognition, development, and so forth, we hope to suggest some guidelines for psychological thinking about and investigation into religious behavior. The first step is to put this into its sociocultural context.

The Ever-Present and Always Influential Context

The word "context" implies something external, and we must recognize that religion has always been a powerful force in every known culture. On this level, the task of understanding is left to the historians, anthropologists, and sociologists. They tell us that religion is taught intentionally, actively, formally—and, just as influentially, passively, subtly, and informally. It infuses virtually every human setting and activity. Some people may reject "the faith of their fathers," but most accept it with variations that reflect individual experience in a climate of social change. Let us not, however, forget the study of twins from the University of Minnesota that implied the possibility of some genetic and biological potential. The psychology of personal faith may take us further than we expect.

Biology notwithstanding, there can be no question that parents and significant others are models for children during their formative years, and that these influences continue to be important regardless of how old the children become. They exemplify for each individual how religion functions. These lessons may have taught that faith is something that fills gaps, such as for personal problem solving (especially during crises). Or they may have taught that faith is a source of control for parents to keep children in line, and politicians to squelch dissent. This vengeful deity responds to sin and wrongdoing mercilessly.

In contrast, faith may have been represented as a positive force. Images of a loving and forgiving God support an open mind, the value of different kinds of people, and a world that is to be appreciated. Faith becomes a search for the truth and a life that can be cherished in its potential richness. In all probability, the religion that pervades people's lives has some elements that are positive and others that are negative. As researchers, we need to understand the psychology of both of these directions.

Forms of Personal Faith: Intrinsic, Extrinsic, and Quest Orientations

We subscribe to the idea that religion is complex and multidimensional. To date, however, though many different forms and types of religion have been proposed, and all have been criticized, certain of these have been involved in a great deal of research. Readers should keep in mind that these types may be weak when it comes to their being understood psychologically. They may also imply value judgments suggesting "good" and "bad" religion from the standpoint of religionists and even psychologists. Despite these basic problems, the scheme proposed by Allport and his students, which identifies "intrinsic" and "extrinsic" forms, has proven quite fruitful in stimulating research.[106] The partially parallel cognitive–personality conception introduced by Allen and Spilka—"committed" and "consensual" religious orientations—in part complements Allport's formulation, with apparently great overlap between the intrinsic and committed perspectives, but considerably less correspondence between the extrinsic and consensual forms.[107] This was first noted by Fleck and followed up by Kirkpatrick, who pointed out that the most widely used extrinsic scales were themselves multidimensional, being composed of two subforms that he designated "personal well-being" and "social well-being."[108] Short scales were developed to assess all of these tendencies. For our purposes, we often refer to "intrinsic/committed" and "extrinsic/consensual" forms of faith, but the terminology of "intrinsic" and "extrinsic" religious orientations is more firmly established, and is synonymously employed here.

Intrinsic and extrinsic orientations represent cognitive, motive, and behavioral patterns. Some would prefer to group these referents under the category of personality. Table 1.3 indicates a number of the characteristics of these forms. Extrinsic religion is described as "strictly utilitarian: useful for the self in granting safety, social standing, solace and endorsement for one's chosen way of life."[109] Intrinsic religion "regards faith as a supreme value in its own right. It is oriented toward a unification of being, takes seriously the commandment

TABLE 1.3. Characteristics of Intrinsic, Extrinsic, and Quest Orientations

Intrinsic religion	Extrinsic religion	Quest religion
Devout; strong personal commitment; universalistic; ethical; stress on love of neighbor	Religion of convenience; called on in crisis, when needed	Readiness to face existential questions; no reduction of complexity in life; resists traditional answers, but looks for "truth"
Unselfish, altruistic, humanitarian	Ethnocentric, exclusionistic, restricted to in-group, chauvinistic, provincial	Possibly "preintrinsic" religious conflict
Framework for everyday life; fills life with meaning	Expedient; not integrated into daily life	Self-criticism
Faith of primary importance; accepted without reservations; creed is fully followed	Faith and belief are superficial; beliefs selectively held	Religious doubt is positive
Faith of ultimate significance: a final good, supreme value, ultimate answer	Utilitarian: means to other ends, is in service of other personal and social needs	Openness to change
People seen as individuals	Views people in terms of social categories—sex, age, status	Concern with moral principles
High self-esteem	Low or confused self-esteem	Antiprejudice, humanitarian
Loving, forgiving God	Stern, punitive God	May reflect more general conflict and anxiety, but constructively
Open to intense religious experience; views death positively	Negative view of death; feelings of powerlessness, external control	
Feelings of power and competence		
Antiprejudice		

of brotherhood, and strives to transcend all self-centered needs. . . . A religious sentiment of this sort floods the whole life with motivation and meaning."[110]

Social psychologist C. D. Batson of the University of Kansas has also examined the intrinsic–extrinsic dimension. He claims that when it was first subjected to measurement, a very significant feature of Allport's original conception was overlooked—namely, "a critical open-ended approach to existential questions."[111] After a number of attempts to measure what Batson termed "quest" religion, he recently settled on a three-dimensional framework: (1) readiness to face existential questions without reducing their complexity; (2) self-criticism and perception of religious doubt as positive; and (3) openness to change. Though each of these realms is evaluated by four items, the most recent form of the Quest scale combines all 12 items into one instrument.[112] Now we await research that will tell us the extent to which this new measure contributes to our understanding of personal faith.

One criticism of intrinsic religion is that when measured, it is not distinguished from simple orthodoxy or religiosity. People for whom their faith is very significant are likely to agree with the intrinsic items. Quest religion might offer us a possible means of making this distinction. Our reading of Allport and Batson suggests that a true intrinsic orientation could combine a quest perspective with the other elements now found in measures of intrinsic faith. For example, those scoring high on intrinsic religion and high on quest may be "true" intrinsics—that is, if they also score low on extrinsic religion. Scoring high on intrinsic religion and low on quest may illustrate a simplistic religiosity or a narrow orthodoxy. This kind of thinking might also be used to identify "pure" questers or extrinsics. Initial work toward this end has been reported, but it used an old and questionable form of the Quest scale, plus less refined indices of intrinsic and extrinsic religion than are available today.[113] Obviously, more research is necessary to assess these possibilities.

It may be argued that much vagueness still plagues all of these religious forms. Falling back on the scales themselves as operational definitions does not resolve the conceptual difficulties that underlie these instruments. Unhappily, criticisms come much more easily to the tongue and pen than positive recommendations do. While we search for the latter, and try to understand intrinsic, extrinsic, and quest approaches to religion, we must still recognize that the first two types are still "the most empirically useful definitions of religion so far."[114] Still recognizing the problem of what intrinsic, extrinsic, and quest forms of faith really are, Pargament conducted a means–end analysis of these orientations; he concluded that all three are means to certain ends though as both means and ends they differ among themselves.[115]

In the first edition of this text, we noted that there were essentially no data on how intrinsic and extrinsic tendencies develop. The same is true for quest tendencies, and the situation has changed very little in the last decade.[116] Maybe one of our readers will look into this problem before too long.

We suspect that the overwhelming majority of people reveal differing degrees of intrinsic, extrinsic, and quest orientations toward religion. In some, one or another form may clearly dominate, but for most people the problem will be the extent to which they are inclined in one direction or another. The issue will still be denoting what these tendencies mean. It has also been shown that there are people who tend to be indiscriminately pro- or antireligious; however, what once seemed to be simple assents to or rejections of any religious proposition are now regarded as complex perspectives.[117]

ATTRIBUTIONAL APPROACHES
TO THE PSYCHOLOGY OF RELIGION

We have already commented that no single theory is likely to suffice for the entire realm of the psychology of religion. Those who study the development of religion may employ classical psychoanalytic views, object relations theory, a version of attachment theory, cognitive approaches, or perspectives derived from social psychology.[118] Many of these positions overlap to varying degrees, and whenever it is appropriate to do so, we utilize their ideas. However, most closely linked to social psychology are attributional approaches to religion; these constitute a theoretical perspective that has much to offer the psychological study of religion.

Nearly 40 years ago, the noted psychologist Fritz Heider offered a theory about interpersonal relations in which he asserted that people try to explain social situations in terms of both the characteristics of those who interact within these settings and the nature of the environment itself.[119] A process of organization, interpretation, and explanation takes place. Heider stated that "this ordering and classifying can be considered a process of attribution."[120] In other words, the process or processes of attribution are concerned with explanation—primarily causal explanation about people, things, and events. These are expressed in statements and ideas that assign certain roles and influences to various situational and dispositional factors. For instance, we might attribute a person's getting cancer to being exposed to the smoking of coworkers, to the person's own smoking, or to the view that "God works in mysterious ways." All of these are attributions. Examining such meanings and their ramifications, attributional approaches became the cornerstone of cognitive social psychology, and were soon extended to explain how people understand emotional states and much of what happens to themselves and to others.[121]

Motivational Bases of Attributions: Meaning, Control, and Self-Esteem Needs

The question of why people make attributions returns us to some basic motivational themes that underlie much religious thinking and behavior—namely, to needs for meaning, control, and self-esteem. Though other activating elements are important, depending on the topic and situation, we see these three as central concerns for the psychology of religion. These are further developed in Chapter 11 when we discuss religion in relation to coping and adjustment.

The three forms of personal faith discussed earlier—intrinsic/committed, extrinsic/consensual, and quest—can also be viewed as motivationally concerned with meaning, control, and esteem. Allport's idea of intrinsic faith as a sentiment flooding "the whole life with motivation and meaning," and as a search for truth, is explicitly directed toward the attainment of ultimate meaning.[122] Yalom terms this "cosmic" meaning as opposed to "terrestrial" meaning. The latter refers to the simple, everyday meanings necessary for ordinary living. Yalom suggests that one can have terrestrial meaning without cosmic meaning, but that the reverse cannot occur.[123] Quest is a similar effort to attain answers to basic questions. Insofar as both of these may represent a kind of informational control, the element of mastery enters the picture. Extrinsic faith with its stress on utility explicitly deals with control. Further analyses of these religious orientations easily yield connections with these motivations. Relative to religion per se, Clark's position will suffice: "religion more than any other human function satisfies the need for meaning in life."[124] In addition, there is much evidence that religious meaning is the prime component of faith that contributes to psychological well-being.[125] Fundamentally, the attributional process is an effort to acquire new knowledge; in other words, it appears to be a first step in making things meaningful.[126]

In addition to a "need to know," a "need for mastery and control" enters the picture. One of the central figures in attribution theory and research, Harold Kelley, has stated that "the theory describes processes that operate *as if* the individual were motivated to attain a *cognitive mastery* of the causal structure of his environment."[127] Especially when threatened with harm or pain, all higher organisms seek to predict and/or control the outcomes of the events that affect them.[128] This fact has been linked by attribution theorists and researchers with novelty, frustration or failure, lack of control, and restriction of personal freedom.[129] It may be that people gain a "sense" of control by making sense out of what is happening, and being able to predict what will occur, even if the result is undesirable.

Another motivational source of attributions that is buttressed by much research is self-esteem. Bulman and Wortman suggest that "people assign causality in order to maintain or enhance their self-esteem."[130] Self-esteem is also likely to be a consequence of the presence of meaning and a sense of control. The need for self-esteem, like the needs for meaning and mastery, has the ring of what we have called the "defensive/protective tradition."

Our theoretical position asserts that attributions are triggered when meanings are unclear, control is in doubt, and self-esteem is challenged. There is, as suggested, much evidence that these three factors are interrelated. For example, research on the concept of alienation—of which meaninglessness and powerlessness are major components—strongly affirms the correspondence between feelings of control and perceptions of the world and one's situation as being understood and making sense.[131] Likewise, self-esteem is a correlate of meaningfulness and control.[132]

Naturalistic and Religious Attributions

Given these three sources of motivations for attributions, the individual may attribute the causes of events to a wide variety of possible referents (the self, others, chance, God, etc.). These may be classified into two broad categories: "naturalistic" and "religious." The evidence is that most people in most circumstances initially employ naturalistic explanations and attributions.[133] Depending on a wide variety of situational and personal characteristics, there is a good likelihood of shifting to religious attributions when naturalistic ones may not satisfactorily meet the needs for meaning, control, and self-esteem.[134] The task is to identify and comprehend those influences that contribute to the making of religious attributions. For example, we already know that the attributions of intrinsically religious individuals differ from those who are extrinsically oriented.[135] In addition, Gorsuch and Smith have examined the bases of attributions to God.[136] Spilka and Schmidt, and Lupfer and his associates, have looked at a number of personal and situational possibilities that affect religious and secular attributions.[137] Hunsberger has focused on biases that enter this process.[138] Even though there is much potential in this theoretical framework, it has only been applied in a few areas.

Extending Attribution Theory

Theories usually become more useful when they are combined with other theoretical speculations, and Wikstrom has joined our attributional framework with Sunden's role theory of religion.[139] Though Sunden's theory is said to stress religious experience, it goes beyond this realm by pointing out that religion "psychologically speaking, seem[s] to provide models and roles for a certain kind of perceptual 'set.'"[140] A frame of reference is established in which the person's actions and cognitions are now structured by a religious role. We are told that "when the frame of reference is activated, stimuli which would otherwise be left unnoticed are not only observed but also combined and attributed to a living and acting 'other,' to God."[141] Furthermore, "as a condition and as a result of the feedback from the role-taking experience . . . [the self-perception] . . . can be seen as something that provides meaning and a feeling of identity, and strengthens self-esteem."[142] Control is also brought into the picture; this shows how role and attribution approaches seem to parallel each other. There is an unexplored potential here. For example, one might suggest that an intrinsic orientation goes with adopting the religious role reference, whereas an extrinsic perspective fails to do so. van der Lans also shows how this role theory aids in predicting various aspects of religious experience.[143] This could be coordinated with the work of Hood and his associates (see Chapter 6) and with the theory of Proudfoot and Shaver on attribution and religious experience.[144]

Clearly, there are both theoretical and research possibilities here. Our contention is that the attributional process, and that of role taking, are the products of interactions between external "situational factors" and internal "dispositional factors."[145] In other words, all thinking and behavior take place in an interpersonal, institutional, and sociocultural context of which situations are elements. We now identify some of the situational and dispositional influences that contribute to the making of religious attributions.

Situational Influences

For many years, social-psychological and attribution research has emphasized the role of situational and environmental factors in the determination of thinking and behavior.[146] This implies that most religious experiences, beliefs, and behaviors are subject to the vagaries of immediate circumstances. In other words, the information we obtain may be primarily a function of the settings in which people are studied and data collected. Without question, there is much evidence to support this approach. Schachter claims that the individual "will label his feelings in terms of his knowledge of the immediate situation."[147] Dienstbier has referred to this labeling as "emotion attribution theory," in order to explain how people define the causes of emotional states when ambiguity exists.[148] Proudfoot and Shaver use the same "basic idea" to denote the bases of religious experience.[149] The research does suggest that up to three-quarters of intense religious experiences occur when individuals are engaged in religious activities or in religious settings.[150] Still, we must be cautious, for some studies have not shown the influence of religious situations on religious attributions.[151] There is much reason to believe that personal factors must also be considered.[152] Since there is a need to understand attributions in general, rather than those that involve only emotion or ambiguity, Spilka and colleagues have called this approach "general attribution theory."[153]

We perceive situational influences as falling into two broad categories: "contextual factors"and "event character factors." The first category is concerned with the degree to which situations are religiously structured; the second stresses the nature of the event being explained.

Contextual Factors

Situations may be religiously structured by the locale in which activities or their evaluation take place (e.g., church or nonchurch surroundings; the presence of others who are known to be religious, such as clergy; or participation in religious activities, such as prayer or worship). The presence of such circumstances should elicit religious attributions, and, as noted above, this is obviously true when religious mystical or intense religious experiences occur. Certainly if other people are present and are religiously involved, their actions should aid in the selection of a religious interpretation. We might say that the "availability" of religious explanations is heightened by such factors. Work by Hood further demonstrates the importance of situational influences in the creation of nature and spiritual experiences.[154] Contextual elements apparently increase the chances that those affected will attribute what occurs to the intervention of God. The *salience* of religion seems to be the key factor here: The more salient, important, noticeable, or conspicuous religion is in a situation, the more probable it is that religious attributions will be offered. This suggests what has been called the "availability hypothesis" or "availability heuristic." Religious influences in situations increase the likelihood of making religious associations or arousing religious ideas.[155] One may argue that church settings in which religious attributions are not made may not be salient for religion. Research has shown that simply being present in a religious institution may not be enough.[156] As centers for community activity, churches and synagogues perform a wide variety of functions.

Event Character Factors

Religious attributions may be affected by the nature or character of the event being explained. A number of such influences are possible here: (1) the importance of what takes place;

(2) whether the event is positive or negative; (3) whether the event occurs to the attributing person or to someone else; and (4) the domain of the event (social, political, economic, medical, etc.). These factors have been shown to affect the intensity and frequency of making religious attributions, and we feel that they are influential to the extent that they enhance meaning, control, and self-esteem.

Lupfer and his associates speak of "meaning belief systems."[157] This concept stresses the adequacy of naturalistic versus religious explanations. As one set proves to be satisfactory, the alternative set should appear to be unsatisfactory, at least in terms of what the relative availability of explanations suggests. Another possibility that reintroduces questions of meaning and control concerns the degree of ambiguity and threat that events convey. For example, medical problems may be least understood and have the greatest potential for threat to life. As serious as economic disasters are, they seem to be comprehended more easily, because they leave the individual the possibility of starting over again. In other words, we hypothesize that situations involving high ambiguity and high threat may have the greatest likelihood of calling forth religious explanations. One problem is to determine the relative degrees of threat for the different domains.

Event Importance. Considering the awe with which the power of God is regarded, people may perceive a role for the deity only when events of the greatest significance are involved. A disaster takes place, and the insurance company defines it as an "act of God." A young person unexpectedly dies, and it is said to be an expression of "God's will." People who win millions of dollars in lotteries commonly see the "hand of God" in their success. The unanticipated is often explained by phrases such as "God works in mysterious ways." Despite the fact that science has provided detailed naturalistic interpretations of birth, death, the reasons for fortune and failure, defeat, and victory, for most people there still remains a sense of the miraculous about the rare and unique events that can greatly change their lives. From a personal perspective, science and common sense often do not answer satisfactorily such questions as "Why now?", "Why me?", "Why at this time?", or "Why here?" If someone is suffering from a severe illness or a terminal condition, attributions and pleas to God seem quite appropriate. Instances of remission when all appeared hopeless are frequently regarded as signs of God's mercy, compassion, favor, or forgiveness. Research confirms this view that God becomes part of the "big picture" for the significant things that happen.[158] Defining what is important has a very individual quality: Sports teams may pray for extra achievement in the "big" game, or gamblers may plead for divine intervention on a roll of the dice.[159] Attributions are therefore a function of event importance, but the subjectivity of importance cannot be overlooked.

Event Valence (Positivity/Negativity). If there is one tendency in making God attributions, it is that people rarely blame God for the bad things that happen to them. Attributions to God are overwhelmingly positive.[160] Bulman and Wortman studied the reasons given by young people who became paraplegics because of serious accidents. They saw a benevolent divine purpose in what happened to them. As one victim put it, "God's trying to put me in situations, help me learn about Him and myself and also how I can help other people."[161] In another study, a cancer patient told the researchers, "God does not cause cancer. . . . Illness and grief do not come from God. God does give me the strength to cope with any and all problems."[162] Rabbi Harold Kushner's well-known book *When Bad Things Happen to Good People* supports this idea that bad things should not be attributed to God.[163]

Even though positive attributions to God prevail, some people feel that they are being punished for their sins and thus may make negative attributions, but this is relatively rare. Clearly, the valence of events influences religious attributions, but we need to know more about why and under what circumstances positive or negative attributions are made to the deity.

Personal Relevance of Events. There is little doubt that when events occur to any of us, they acquire much greater personal importance than when they happen to others. We can be deeply moved when we hear about a friend's or relative's serious illness, but when we ourselves suffer from such a condition, the question "Why me?" is suddenly of the greatest significance, and attributions to God are commonly made. If something particularly good happens to someone else, such as the winning of a great deal of money, we might say, "That's luck for you," and feel happy for that person. The one benefited is more likely to claim that "God was looking out for me." The idea that personal relevance may elicit more religious attributions has gained support, but not consistently. It does seem to be involved in interactions with other variables, so additional research is called for to resolve these ambiguities.[164]

Event Domain. Certain domains appear "ready-made" for the application of secular understandings, while others seem more appropriate for invoking religious possibilities. We know that medical situations elicit more religious attributions than either social or economic circumstances; it may be that, historically and culturally, the latter realms have largely been associated with naturalistic explanations.[165] In addition, religious institutions have been quite averse to glorifying money and wealth. References in the Bible to "filthy lucre" and the difficulty the rich will encounter in attempting to enter heaven leave little doubt that economic and spiritual matters are not regarded as harmonious.

Without question, when people are in dire straits in any domain, it is not uncommon for them to seek divine help. The issue may, however, revolve about the clarity of meanings and the sense of control a person has in various situations. Religion may best fill the void when the person cannot understand why things are as they are, and control is lacking—in other words, when ambiguity is great and threat is high.

Situational Complexity and Event Significance. Reality tells us not only that any particular event includes all of the dimensions described above (importance, valence, personal relevance, and domain), but that event contexts are likely to vary greatly. It is also quite probable that event characteristics interact differently in different settings. It may be contended that each situation is a unique, one-time occurrence, and without question this is true. Still, there are commonalities across events and situations that need to be abstracted and categorized. Even within-situation dimensions still remain to be discovered. An empirical scientific approach must keep these considerations in mind when theories such as that proposed here are employed to direct research.

Though we somewhat arbitrarily distinguish situations and people, in life this really makes little sense. There are no situations or events that are meaningful without people to create such meanings. In the last analysis, person and situation are in transaction. It is a conceptual convenience to separate the two when in actuality they are inseparable. Many psychologists see their ultimate purpose as developing a psychology that treats the situation and the individual as a unit.[166] Though this is a goal to which we may aspire, we are nevertheless forced to consider the individual in the same way in which we look at the situation.

Dispositional Influences

The Individual in Context

In addition to the place of events and their contexts in attribution theory, it is obvious that human beings are an indispensable part of the attribution process; they make the attributions. The strong emphasis on individualism in North American society causes us to look at people as if they act independently of their surroundings. Just as events take place in contexts, persons always exist in their individual life spaces, and these vary with time and place. It may make a big difference if someone reacts in the morning before breakfast, or in the evening after supper. A religious experience that takes place in a church may have different repercussions from one that occurs when the individual is alone on a mountain top. Personal response is surprisingly situationally dependent.

Personal Factors

Individual characteristics may be termed "dispositional," and these fall into three overlapping categories: "background," "cognitive/linguistic," and, for lack of a better word, "personality." Since we are not in a position to denote constitutional and genetic influences or their effects, these three realms imply that people pattern their attributions regarding the causes and nature of events so that some explanations are much more congenial (meaning more "available" and/or "better-fitting") than other possibilities. This would hold true for people's selection of naturalistic as opposed to religious referents. Specifically, it would be true for their decisions as to whether positive or negative event outcomes are the results of their own actions or those of others; are due to fate, luck, or chance; or are attributable to the involvement of God. Research in this area is still needed, and slowly the challenge is being taken up.[167]

Background Factors. It is a psychological truism to state that people are products of their environment as far as most behavior is concerned. The overwhelming majority of individuals are exposed early in life to religious teachings at home and by peers and adults in schools, churches, and communities. These childhood lessons often persist throughout life, and are expressed by the use of religious concepts in a wide variety of circumstances. A common observation suggests that the stronger a person's spiritual background, the greater the chance that the person will report intense religious experiences and undergo conversion.[168] Frequency of church attendance, knowledge of a faith, importance of religious beliefs, and the persistence of religious ideas over many decades are correlates of early religious socialization.[169] In other words, the more conservatively religious or orthodox the home and family in which a person was reared, the greater the person's likelihood of using religious attributions later in life.

Cognitive/Linguistic Factors. Attributions depend on having available a language that both permits and supports thinking along certain lines. Bernstein has stated that "Language marks out what is relevant, affectively, cognitively, and socially, and experience is transformed by what is made relevant."[170] Such relevance is well demonstrated by studies showing that religious persons possess a religious language and use it to describe their experience. There is reason to believe that the presence of such a language designates an experience as religious instead of aesthetic or some other possibility.[171] Meaning to the experiencing individual appears in part to be a function of the language and vocabulary available to the person, and this clearly relates to the individual's background and interests. There is much in the idea that thought is a slave of language, and the thoughts that breed attributions are clearly influenced by the language the attributor is set to use.[172]

Personality/Attitudinal Factors. The broad heading of "personality/attitudinal factors" includes a wide variety of dispositional factors that almost seem to defy classification. The language of personality is both difficult and complex, and different thinkers often employ different concepts to cover the same psychological territory. Schaefer and Gorsuch propose a "multivariate belief-motivation theory of religiousness" in an effort to integrate the often scattered ideas and research notions that associate traits and attitudes with religion.[173] These scholars first recognize what they term a "superordinate domain" of religiousness, which consists of a number of subdomains.[174] Their intention is to define the components of these latter spheres. The three they select for study are religious motivation, religious beliefs, and religious problem-solving style. Depending on the variables chosen to represent these subdomains, there may be room for argument as to whether one is looking at a cognitive or a motivational factor. Unhappily, most workers in the field have not been as rigorous as Gorsuch and his students where variable definition is concerned. For example, many "personality" factors have been examined in relation to religiousness. Among these are self-esteem, locus of control, the concept of a just world, and form of personal faith. All four seem to possess a motivational quality, yet the last two strongly involve belief systems. The Schaefer–Gorsuch theory implies a need to distinguish motivational from belief components, or to identify a third, overlapping domain. Obviously, this work is in its infancy, but it suggests a potentially fruitful way of organizing a mass of somewhat disorganized, piecemeal findings into a coherent framework.

To illustrate the meanings of personality/attitudinal dispositions relative to the making of religious attributions, let us briefly look at what we know about self-esteem, locus of control, belief in a just world, and form of personal faith.

Self-Esteem. Research on self-conceptions has more than a 50-year history. For at least 30 years, many psychologists have focused on self-esteem—the regard people have for themselves.[175] The evidence suggests that this variable is quite basic to personality. One view is that attributions are often made to validate and enhance self-esteem; they perform a self-protective function.[176]

Needless to say, a fair number of researchers have examined self-esteem relative to religiosity. In general, high self-esteem relates to positive and loving images of God, and similarly to an intrinsic religious orientation.[177] There may be a need here for consistency, which counters distressing dissonance, suggesting that those who have negative self-views perceive God as unloving and punitive.[178] In other words, the person with such an opinion may be saying, "I am unlovable; hence God can't love me." Consistency further suggests that favorable God attributions ought to be associated with positive event outcomes as opposed to negative occurrences. This hypothesis has been supported.[179]

Self-esteem does not stand by itself. It is enmeshed in a complex of overlapping personality traits and religious concepts and measures, such as sin and guilt, as well as the nature of the religious tradition with which one is identified.[180] This work indicates that different patterns of self-esteem and God attributions may be a function of a person's religious heritage and its doctrines. If a prime role of attributions is to buttress self-esteem, we need to ask how religion performs such a function—especially with traditions such as fundamentalism, which may seem quite harsh on the individual's effort to express self-regard.

Locus of Control. Locus of control was initially conceptualized as a tendency to see events as either internally determined by the person or externally produced by factors beyond the control of the individual. This formulation has been extended and refined a number of times. External control was originally viewed as fate, luck, or chance until Levenson added control by powerful others and Kopplin brought in control by God.[181] Pargament and colleagues recognized the complexity of control relationships relative to the deity, and developed measures to assess what they termed a "deferring" mode (an active God and a passive person), a "collaborative" mode (both God and the person are active), and a "self-directive" mode (an active person and a passive God).[182] These notions illustrate different patterns of attribution for control to the self and to God. In the deferring mode, an individual may pray, and having done that may attribute all the power to God: "It's in the hands of God." Those with a collaborative style are basically saying that both they and God have control: "God helps those who help themselves." Utilizing these coping styles relates to further attributions to the nature of God. Though the associations are stronger with the collaborative than with the deferring mode, the tendency for persons who adopt such control perspectives is to attribute generally positive qualities to the deity, along with their recognition of God's power.[183]

Although belief in supernaturalism affiliates with external control, Shrauger and Silverman found that "people who are more involved in religious activities perceive themselves as having more control over what happens to them."[184] This sounds like intrinsic religion, or, at least, orthodoxy for this relationship is strongest among fundamentalists.[185] Studying highly religious people, Hunsberger and Watson found that attributions of control and responsibility are made to God when outcomes are positive, a well confirmed finding, but when the result is negative, the tendency is to attribute the blame to Satan ("The Devil made me do it").[186] Issues of control and to whom or what such are attributed have been extensively studied both within and outside of the psychology of religion. It is a concern that should be kept in mind throughout this book.

Belief in a Just World. The Western religious heritage holds dear the view of Robert Browning that "God's in his heaven—All's right with the world!"[187] Idealistic as it seems, this view suggests that people in general feel that even if things appear tragic and unfair, somewhere and somehow there is an element of justice in such occurrences. Apparently, as human beings, we are reluctant to accept the notion of chance happenings. There must be a reason for everything, and that reason must make sense even if, like Job, we are unable to fathom it. Individualistically oriented Western culture directs us to seek answers to all dilemmas, to search for meaning. A common tendency is to make what is termed "the fundamental attribution error"—the tendency to assign causality to the dispositional characteristics of specific beings—and for many people, the deity becomes a very significant attributional referent when concern is with ultimate justice.[188]

Psychologist Melvin Lerner and his students have conducted much research on this notion that what happens to us and others is premised on a justice principle—the notion that we live in a "just world." The implication is that good people will be rewarded (if not in this life, then in the next), and, of course, bad people will get their just deserts too. Trust that the world is just increases with belief in God, frequency of church attendance, and self-rated religiosity.[189] Studying health situations, Pargament and Hahn concluded that "attributions to God serve in helping people maintain a belief in a just world and to cope with the world."[190]

Form of Personal Faith. Earlier, we have discussed the three forms of faith that conceptually and operationally have dominated research in the psychology of religion. These are intrinsic (intrinsic/committed), extrinsic (extrinsic/consensual), and quest orientations toward personal religion. The research is quite conclusive that these inclinations represent very different ways of relating to one's faith and also of viewing and responding to the world.[191] They are therefore also associated with different patterns of attributions toward oneself, others, and religion. Unfortunately, we are in a much stronger position to discuss the intrinsic and extrinsic approaches than the quest approach, for even though the latter was formulated about two decades ago, the original form of the Quest scale proved to be unreliable and there was much argument concerning what it was measuring.[192] Batson and his students have recently produced a newer, better-defined, and more reliable instrument, and we await research with this measure that bears on issue of attributions. The earlier work should not be simply rejected, but it might be better to treat it as suggestive rather than definitive.

Intrinsic/committed religionists attribute primarily positive characteristics to their deity, seeing God as loving, benevolent, and forgiving; this is also a deity that is involved in human affairs, one upon whom people can rely and trust at all times.[193] In contrast, as extrinsic and consensual tendencies increase, so do attributions to God as wrathful, stern, and vindictive. Self-attributions parallel those to the deity, in that intrinsics look upon themselves as empowered whereas extrinsics impute relative powerlessness to themselves.[194] The former seem to consider themselves more strongly in collaborative control relationships with their God; the latter are more inclined to place themselves in a deferring, low-power association with God.[195]

Attributions of trust in the deity are further reinforced when attitudes toward death are studied. The intrinsic/committed person tends to show a low fear of death, viewing this ultimate threat in terms of courage and a final reward. Extrinsics see death as involving pain, loneliness, failure, and isolation.[196]

This overall pattern continues when attitudes toward others are examined. Empathic concern has been found to be a positive correlate of intrinsic faith, whereas an extrinsic orientation has been linked to prejudice, separation, and objectionable feelings toward others.[197] In like manner, extrinsics judge people in terms of their status, while intrinsics are concerned with them as individuals.[198] In other words, intrinsic attributions to others tend to be positive; extrinsic attributions tend to be negative.

Attributionally, we have (somewhat ideally) pictured opposites in their extreme forms. Extrinsic/consensual faith is tied to a perspective of oneself as relatively helpless. Extrinsics feel that the world is a dangerous place and that they must look out for "number one." God is sought mainly in crisis and times of trouble, but otherwise the deity is uninvolved in living—out of sight and out of mind. A reminder is, however, in order. Religious people are, as a rule, neither strictly intrinsic/committed nor strictly extrinsic/consensual; they invariably possess and express both orientations, and may do so equally or may lean more toward one approach than the other. We need to consider the nature of each situation where religion is relevant. It is nevertheless evident that intrinsics will see more circumstances as implying the meanings religion conveys than will extrinsics. In other words, we have been speaking of "pure" types when, in reality, trends are meant.

But what about those who seem to embrace a quest perspective? Despite some of the cautions noted earlier, Batson's work offers a number of possibilities that differentiate among intrinsic, extrinsic, and quest perspectives. Though controversial, these efforts raise many significant questions, and heighten our appreciation of the ways individuals approach issues of faith.

Batson and his coworkers cite a number of questionnaire studies that show empathy and altruism relating positively to intrinsic religion. These imply self-attributions of care and concern on the part of intrinsics. A similar pattern was not found for those scoring high on the Quest scale. Batson et al. argue that intrinsics want to look compassionate but may not really be so, while questers do not have this need.[199] The nonsignificant relationship found for the latter group suggests that they attribute social care and concern to themselves as often as not—a tendency that is unclear as to its motivation. Are questers more modest or intrinsics less immodest? Might questers be more situationally oriented or context-sensitive than intrinsics? Rather than simply desiring to appear compassionate, intrinsics may have internalized a more demanding cross-situational moral code than questers may have. In terms of the definition of intrinsic faith offered earlier, they may be living their religion, not just adapting it to situations. Intrinsics may, of course, show greater situational insensitivity than questers; their possibly higher levels of commitment to principle might appear thus. Obviously these are questions for research to resolve.

Even though Bolt and his coworkers did not include quest in their work on responsibility and nonspontaneous helping, their measure of the latter dealt with participation in specific altruistic activities. They found intrinsic inclinations related positively to such aiding behavior.[200] Does this imply lying on the part of the intrinsics so that they might "appear helpful"? This does seem farfetched. In other research that involved volunteering, neither the Intrinsic nor the Quest scale showed any relationship with such a propensity; this hardly supports the "appearance" hypothesis.[201] The complete lack of significant correlations across all variables for the Quest measure raises questions about the known unreliability of that early scale. Again, these are research questions.

Batson rightly states that the real test is whether one helps or doesn't in situations where altruistic behavior seems appropriate.[202] Once more, intrinsic faith is positively associated with helping others. Darley and Batson suggest that such helping is premised upon intrinsically oriented people's attributing the characteristics of concern and caring to themselves rather than to the needs of others for help (see Chapter 10).[203] Those who have been subjected to the sometimes insensitive proselytizing zeal of people with missionary intent can easily believe this.

In the case of helping, according to the Darley–Batson research, the preferred interpretation is that even though questers, like intrinsics, help, they do not attempt to do so if the potential recipient responds that such aid is not needed. The assumed quester's attribution is that the victim knows his or her own situation best; hence helper inaction does not appear to be a function of the aider's personal needs. One could, however, claim that intrinsics might feel that those requiring aid are more likely to deny such a need because in our society, people (especially males) are supposed to "stand on their own" and not be dependent. There may also be the feeling that someone clearly needing support might not be the best judge of the situation; hence extra effort to help could be appropriate. In a similar vein, the willingness of questers to trust the judgment of a person who appears to need help might not be due to believing a victim, but rather to relief on the potential helper's part that he or she will not be further inconvenienced. Though Batson and his students have conducted a number of studies to support their interpretation, this issue still remains unresolved.[204]

There can be little doubt that the concept of quest religion merits additional study, especially with the new measures that have been developed. Different attributional patterns are implied by the intrinsic, extrinsic, and quest forms of personal faith discussed here. All three present theoretical difficulties that can only be resolved by the research process, and there is obviously still much to do.

Using similar logic, Batson and colleagues have researched personal faith in relation to prejudice. Where low prejudice has been associated with an intrinsic orientation, this has also been viewed as motivated by a desire to appear unprejudiced. In contrast, evidence that the quest outlook is tied to tolerance is perceived as a genuine aversion to prejudice and discrimination, and hence also to negative stereotyping. To fully appreciate the nuances of this work, readers should examine the arguments presented by Batson, Schoenrade, and Ventis. They recognize, however, that to date definitive answers in this realm are also lacking.[205]

OVERVIEW

This chapter has been concerned with the basic problems and issues that the psychology of religion confronts. Unhappily, over a century's worth of thinking and research in this area has not resolved the most fundamental of questions—namely, those involved with the definition of religion. Indeed we have avoided direct confrontation with this matter. Our interest is focused on the psychological and especially the social-psychological relationship of people with their faith, however it is conceived. Given such a focus, religious thinking and behavior have been shown to be very complex, multidimensional phenomena. Though many schemes exist, we have selected for emphasis three forms that have been extensively involved in empirical research—namely, Allport's intrinsic and extrinsic orientations, and Batson's quest approach.

Our search for the motivational basis of religion has taken us to four broad traditions. The classical instinct heritage has been shown to be a dead end. Explaining one unknown in terms of other unknowns does not tell us anything about the psychological roots of religion. This tradition has opened a door to the field of sociobiology, which offers stimulating ideas but not data. Recent research on twins does suggest some biological possibilities; however, at this stage, until further work is done, this potential must be held in abeyance.

There is considerable information suggesting the fruitfulness of what we term the defensive/protective approach, which claims that religion grows from weakness, deficiency, and shortcoming. People are said to turn to religion to gain solace, security, and the illusion of safety and certainty. For others (maybe only a minority), religion appears to sponsor psychosocial growth and personal enrichment. Their faith is an attempt to gain an even deeper and broader perspective on life, a reaching out toward truth, perfection, and integration; it is a struggle to understand where they fit in the scheme of things.

There is no question that something much more prosaic and mundane is frequently involved in becoming "religious." Here we have simple, basic, unadorned social learning and habit. Religion is acquired in a cultural order that has maintained churches and their doctrines as central social, political, and moral forces throughout history. The result is that religion becomes an integral part of family life and child rearing. For most people it comes across as occasional churchgoing or dropping off the children for Sunday school, plus certain beliefs and ideas that not only are not questioned, but are simply not given much thought. Religion exists as an inviolable absolute that is just *there*.

Recognizing that there are serious conceptual and operational problems plaguing the psychology of religion, we have emphasized the importance of theory. Though many different theories are necessary at this stage of our development, we have offered an attributional perspective that is derived from social psychology. In many instances, this can be applied to various forms of faith that have been widely researched—namely, the intrinsic, extrinsic, and quest orientations. These represent complex motivational and cognitive patterns that appear fruitful for understanding the psychological roles of religion in life—how people deal with themselves, others, the world, and the religious system with which they are affiliated. We hope that we have provided a way of organizing thoughts about how a psychology of religion can help us to understand the complexities of human mental life within a religious context. This task perceives the individual's religious orientation to be a reflection of personal history, motivations, cognitions, and actions.

APPENDIX: STATISTICAL PROCEDURES AND CONSIDERATIONS

As we have stated, this book emphasizes the empirical psychological (especially the social-psychological) study of religion. Reference is made throughout the book to various statistical procedures, the chief ones of which are "correlation" and "factor analysis." To aid readers, we offer a brief explanation of these techniques.

Correlation

Correlation determines the strength of a relationship between two variables. The statistical calculations result in a number called a "correlation coefficient." This number can range from −1.00 through 0 to +1.00. If the coefficients are in the 0 to −1.00 range, the relationship between the variables is said to be "negative." This means that as the values of one of the variables increases, the other decreases. In other words, the scores of the two variables are related in the opposite directions. For example, we know that extrinsic religion correlates negatively with self-esteem, so a low score in extrinsic religion goes with a high score on self-esteem and vice versa.

If the computed correlation coefficient is in the 0 to +1.00 range, the association between the variables is said to be "positive." Now, as the values of one of the variables increases, so do the values of the other variable. Stated differently, the scores of the two measures increase and decrease together. To illustrate, we know that perceptions of a loving God correlate positively with an intrinsic religious orientation. The higher people score on a scale of intrinsic faith, the more they will usually profess belief in a loving deity.

The higher the correlation coefficient, meaning the closer it is to either −1.00 or +1.00, the stronger is the relationship between the two variables being studied. The importance of a coefficient is also a function of the size of the sample in which the relationship between the variables is calculated. For larger samples, smaller correlation coefficients will be "statistically significant." These can be looked up in a table, but all readers need to know now is that *when a correlation is said to be statistically significant, even if it is numerically low and close to 0, it indicates an association that has a very low probability of arising on the basis of chance alone.* When this probability is less than, say, 5% (or, as this is usually expressed, $p < .05$), we are inclined to infer that the association (relationship) between the variables is real; the variables are then assumed to be meaningfully related. In other words, if intrinsic faith and the likelihood of having a religious mystical experience are positively correlated (e.g., .40), and the sample is large enough for the researcher to claim that this is a statistically significant correlation coefficient, we are very likely to infer that the more a person is intrinsically religious, the greater the chance that the person has had or will have in the future a religious mystical experience.

Correlations are important, for they imply prediction. Using the appropriate formulas, the sophisticated researcher can use the correlation coefficient to predict the values of one variable when the scores on the other variable are available. Of course, the higher the correlation coefficient, the stronger the predictions that can be made.

Finally, we must state that if a correlation is not statistically significant, the two variables are considered to be "independent" of each other. No meaningful relationship is said to exist.

Factor Analysis

Factor analysis is a very complex statistical procedure that is often used to simplify correlational data. If we have a very large number of variables, it may be necessary to clarify the findings by using factor analysis. Consider first a simple situation with three variables. Variable A is correlated with variable B, which in turn is correlated with variable C. In turn, this last measure is also correlated with A. So we have three variables and, in this instance, three correlation coefficients. (Readers should not assume that the number of variables equals the number of correlations, even though it is true in this example.) The formula for the number of correlations is actually $n(n-1)/2$, where n is the number of variables. In this case, $n = 3$, and our formula results in $3(3-1)/2$ or $6/2 = 3$. Suppose, however, we have 50 variables. This would result in $50(49)/2 = 1,225$ intercorrelations, and making sense out of such a massive array or matrix of coefficients would be extremely difficult or indeed impossible without factor analysis.

Fortunately, today we have computers to do the complex calculations that will explain the large number of correlations by a much smaller number of "factors." It is possible that 5, 10, or 20 factors might result from the analysis of the 1,225 correlations among the 50 variables noted above. The findings would indeed become much clearer. This approach was used by a number of the researchers whose various dimensions of religion have been given in Table 1.1.

Other Considerations: Reliability and Validity

Since we use questionaires to a very great extent in our work, there must be some assurance that these really accomplish what we intend them to. Unfortunately, there are some very basic arguments about the possible discrepancy between "real life" and what the inventories tell us. Though we are unable to respond to this issue in detail, we do have reason to believe that our questionnaires usually get at the information we seek. This last inference deals with the concept of "validity": Does the test measure what it is supposed to measure? Probably the best way of determining this is by employing the test to confirm what theory says it should. There are also some other ways of approximating validity, and where possible these should be utilized.

Validity presupposes "reliability"—namely, consistency in the measure's assessment. This consistency may occur over time, or over the test items. Do they all measure the same thing? If a test is reliable, it may still not be valid, but not vice versa. Reliability has been termed "poor person's validity." If one cannot demonstrate reliability, the questionnaire must be invalid, so this is a good place to start. Reliability and validity can be evaluated by a variety of statistical procedures akin to correlation, so we may speak of reliability and validity coefficients. We would like the former to be above .75, but for research purposes sometimes we go as low as .60 and then try to find out how to raise reliability. For example, we may write more test items, or edit and improve those in use. There are no guidelines for the size of validity coefficients. We simply start by hoping to have these attain statistical significance, and the higher they are, the better.

When a questionnaire demonstrates at least reliability, we term it a "scale"; however, this label has other meanings in mathematics and the social sciences, so the interested reader should look to other sources and references for further information. Here we are concerned with the realm of "psychometrics," which treats issues of psychological measurement such as we have just mentioned.

We have just touched on a few statistical and psychometric concepts among many that are pertinent to work in our area. To be a psychologist, especially an empirical researcher, means that one must become familiar with a wide variety of other statistical concepts and procedures. It is our hope that in this volume, our presentations will not be too abstruse and difficult. Readers may want to make a list of psychometric and statistical terms that appear in these pages, and check them out in greater depth.

NOTES

1. Paine (1897, p. 497).
2. Cardinal Newman, quoted in Benham (1927, p. 238b).
3. Lord Melbourne, quoted in Cecil (1966, p. 181).
4. Bierce (1911/1967, p. 241).
5. Luis Buñuel, quoted in Rogers (1983, p. 175).
6. Wilde (1895/1965, Act I, p. 35).
7. Spilka (1970, 1976).
8. Tillich (1957, p. ix).
9. Tillich (1957, p. ix).
10. Yinger (1967, p. 18)
11. Yinger (1970).
12. Coe (1916, p. 13).
13. Dresser (1929, p. 441).
14. Nottingham (1954).
15. Cohn (1962).
16. Mills (1959, p. 3).
17. Muller (1889, p. 188). Emphasis added to stress Muller's use of individual terms.
18. Clark (1958, p. 22). Emphasis in original.
19. James (1902/1985, p. 29).
20. Williams (1962, p. 8); Clark (1958, p. 23).
21. Ames (1910, p. viii). Emphasis added.
22. Wieman and Westcott-Wieman (1935, p. 29).
23. Fromm (1950, p. 21). Emphasis added.
24. Gibran (1923, p. 88).
25. Yinger (1970, p. 33).
26. Chave (1939).
27. Brown (1962); Glock (1962); Maranell (1974).
28. J. Wilson (1978, p. 442).
29. Verbit (1970).
30. Verbit (1970, p. 24).
31. Kirkpatrick and Hood (1990).
32. Roof (1993).
33. Benson and Williams (1982).
34. Burris (1994).
35. Roof and Perkins (1975, p. 111).

36. Le Bon (1903).
37. Trotter (1919).
38. Bernard (1924).
39. McDougall (1909).
40. Hardy (1913).
41. Bernard (1924).
42. Dresser (1929, p. 185).
43. Ostow and Scharfstein (1954, p. 155).
44. Ostow and Scharfstein (1954, p. 37).
45. E. O. Wilson (1978, p. 16).
46. E. O. Wilson (1978, p. 172).
47. E. O. Wilson (1978, p. 3.)
48. E. O. Wilson (1978, p. 175).
49. E. O. Wilson (1978, p. 177).
50. Burhoe (1979, p. 157). For further discussions of this issue, see Austin (1980); Batson (1983); Campbell (1975).
51. Waller, Kojetin, Bouchard, Lykken, and Tellegen (1990, p. 140).
52. Wenegrat (1990).
53. Flavell (1963, p. 36).
54. Elkind (1970).
55. Elkind (1970, p. 37).
56. Oser and Gmunder (1984/1991, p. 4).
57. Skinner (1953). See especially Chap. 23, "Religion."
58. Feuerbach (1967, p. 26).
59. Leuba (1921, p. 81).
60. Gross, L. (1982, p. 242).
61. A vast literature supports this contention. See the following for an introduction: Acklin, Brown, and Mauger (1983); Johnson and Spilka (1991); Krause (1986); Krause and Van Tranh (1989); McIntosh, Silver, and Wortman (1989); O'Brien (1982); Yates, Chalmer, St. James, Follansbee, and McKegney (1981).
62. Dewey. (1929, p. 3).
63. Royce (1912, p. 44); Johnson (1959, p. 200).
64. Dunlap (1925, p. 99). Emphasis in original.
65. Freud (1927/1961, p. 22).
66. Küng (1979, p. 97).
67. Bierce (1911/1967, p. 241).
68. Stace (1960, p. 543).
69. Stace (1960, p. 547).
70. Hall and Lindsay (1978).
71. Nunn (1964).
72. Argyle and Beit-Hallahmi (1975); Clark (1929); Starbuck (1899).
73. Mowrer (1961); Fairchild (1971).
74. Herbert (1965, p. 506).
75. Glock (1964).
76. Glock (1964, p. 27).
77. Walters and Bradley (1971).
78. Spilka, Brown, and Cassidy (1993).
79. Hsu (1952, p. 133).
80. Goldstein (1939); Maslow (1954).
81. Maslow (1964, p. xii).
82. Maslow (1964, p. 26).
83. Browning (1975, p. 132).
84. Bertocci (1958).
85. Johnson (1959, pp. 201–202).
86. J. W. Gardner (1978, p. 33).
87. Wieman and Westcott-Wieman (1935, p. 29).
88. Ellwood (1922, p. 47).
89. Tillich (1957, p. 4).
90. Maddi (1970, p. 137).
91. Nuttin (1962, pp. 247–250).

92. Nuttin (1962, p. 249). Emphasis in original.
93. Tageson (1982, p. 186).
94. Frankl (1955, 1963).
95. Frankl (1969).
96. Fabry (1968).
97. Bulka (1979); Ungersma (1961).
98. Einstein (1931, p. 357).
99. Polanyi and Prosch (1975, p. 153).
100. O'Dea (1961, p. 30).
101. Skinner (1953).
102. James (1890/1950, Vol. 1, p. 121).
103. Bellah (1967); Bellah and Hammond (1980).
104. Marty (1959, p. 31).
105. Lerner (1957, p. 704).
106. Allport (1959); Allport and Ross (1967); Hunt and King (1971).
107. Allen and Spilka (1967).
108. Fleck (1981); Kirkpatrick (1989).
109. Allport (1966, p. 455).
110. Allport (1966, p. 455).
111. Batson, Schoenrade, and Ventis (1993, p. 166).
112. Batson and Schoenrade (1991a, 1991b).
113. McIntosh and Spilka (1990).
114. Gorsuch (1988, p. 210).
115. Pargament (1992).
116. Venable (1984).
117. Kirkpatrick and Hood (1990, pp. 449–450); Pargament et al. (1987).
118. Freud (1927/1961); Heimbrock (1991); Kirkpatrick (1992); McDargh (1983); Oser and Gmunder (1984/1991); Proudfoot and Shaver (1975); Spilka, Shaver, and Kirkpatrick (1985).
119. Heider (1958). Readers should keep in mind that the relationship of someone with his or her God might be conceptualized in interpersonal terms.
120. Heider (1958, p. 296).
121. Fiske and Taylor (1991); Hewstone (1983a).
122. Allport (1966, p. 455).
123. Yalom (1980).
124. Clark (1958, p. 419).
125. Chamberlain and Zika (1992).
126. Kruglanski, Hasmel, Maides, and Schwartz (1978); Valins and Nisbett (1971).
127. Kelley (1967, p. 193). Emphasis added.
128. Seligman (1975).
129. Berlyne (1960); Wong (1979); Wong and Weiner (1981); Wortman (1976).
130. Bulman and Wortman (1977, p. 351).
131. Dean (1961); Elmore (1962); Spilka (1976).
132. Becker (1973); Davids (1955); Oken (1973); Seeman (1959).
133. Lupfer, Brock, and DePaola (1992).
134. Hewstone (1983a); Spilka, Shaver, and Kirkpatrick (1985).
135. Watson, Morris, and Hood (1990a).
136. Gorsuch and Smith (1983).
137. Spilka and Schmidt (1983); Lupfer et al. (1992).
138. Hunsberger (1983c).
139. Wikstrom (1987).
140. Wikstrom (1987, p. 391).
141. Wikstrom (1987, p. 393).
142. Wikstrom (1987, p. 396).
143. van der Lans (1987).
144. Proudfoot and Shaver (1975).
145. Magnusson (1981, pp. 9–32).
146. Ross and Nisbett (1991).
147. Schachter (1964, p. 54).
148. Dienstbier (1979).

149. Proudfoot and Shaver (1975).
150. Spilka and Schmidt (1983).
151. Lupfer et al. (1992); Spilka and Schmidt (1983).
152. Epstein and O'Brien (1985).
153. Spilka, Shaver, and Kirkpatrick (1985).
154. Hood (1977b).
155. Fiske and Taylor (1991).
156. Spilka and Schmidt (1983).
157. Lupfer et al. (1992, p. 491).
158. Spilka and Schmidt (1983).
159. S. J. Hoffman (1992).
160. Bulman and Wortman (1977); Johnson and Spilka (1991); Lupfer et al. (1992).
161. Bulman and Wortman (1977, p. 358).
162. Johnson and Spilka (1991). Remarks by respondent no. 30 to question 33.
163. Kushner (1981).
164. Lupfer et al. (1992); Spilka and Schmidt (1983).
165. Spilka and Schmidt (1983).
166. Magnusson (1981); Rowe (1987).
167. Bains (1983); Lupfer et al. (1992); Schaefer and Gorsuch (1991).
168. Clark (1929); Coe (1900); Starbuck (1899).
169. McGuire (1992); Shand (1990); J. Wilson (1978).
170. Bernstein (1964), cited in Bourque and Back (1971, p. 3).
171. Bourque (1969); Bourque and Back (1971).
172. Carroll (1956).
173. Schaefer and Gorsuch (1991).
174. This use of the word "domain" does not refer to the same idea used earlier in our discussion of situational factors that affect the attributional research process.
175. Wylie (1979).
176. Hewstone, M. (1983b, p. 17).
177. Benson and Spilka (1973); Hood (1992c); Masters and Bergin (1992).
178. Benson and Spilka (1973).
179. Spilka and Schmidt (1983); Lupfer et al. (1992).
180. Hood (1992c).
181. Levenson (1973); Kopplin (1976).
182. Pargament et al. (1988).
183. Schaefer and Gorsuch (1991).
184. Shrauger and Silverman (1971, p. 15); see also Randall and Desrosiers (1980).
185. Furnham (1982); Silvestri (1979); Tipton, Harrison, and Mahoney (1980).
186. Hunsberger and Watson (1986).
187. Browning (1841a/1895, p. 133).
188. Fiske and Taylor (1991).
189. Rubin and Peplau (1973).
190. Pargament and Hahn (1986).
191. Batson et al. (1993); Wulff (1991).
192. Batson and Schoenrade (1991a).
193. Spilka and Mullin (1977).
194. Spilka and Mullin (1977); Spilka (1976).
195. Pargament et al. (1988).
196. Kahoe and Dunn (1975); Magni (1972); Minton and Spilka (1976); Spilka, Stout, Minton, and Sizemore (1977).
197. Bolt and Vermeulen (1986); Donahue (1985b); Watson, Morris, and Hood (1988).
198. Spilka and Mullin (1977).
199. Batson et al. (1993).
200. Bolt, Pyne, and Shoemaker (1984).
201. Bolt and Vermeulen (1986).
202. Batson et al. (1993).
203. Darley and Batson (1973).
204. Batson et al. (1993).
205. Batson et al. (1993).

Chapter 2

RELIGION IN CHILDHOOD

In infancy, of course, religion is lacking.[1]

He that spareth his rod hateth his son: but he that loveth him chasteneth him betimes.[2]

King Solomon must have been fond of animals, because he had many wives and one thousand porcupines.[3]

[When I was 10 or 11] I had a terrible fear of living forever. I couldn't grasp the concept of eternity; it really frightened me. I thought there would come a time when I would experience everything there is to experience and attain every piece of knowledge that could be attained and then I would be bored. But I'd be stuck living forever.[4]

IS RELIGION IN OUR GENES?

Does our DNA carry some genetic code for religiousness? Are we "naturally" religious, as Elkind has suggested?[5] As Chapter 1 has indicated, there is no shortage of "instincts" that have been theorized to underlie religion. Especially at the turn of the last century, when it became apparent that religion was almost universally present in societies around the world, there was speculation that it must somehow be a part of our biologically determined destiny.[6] Although the "theory of instincts" that was so popular early in the 20th century subsequently lost favor, especially in light of the growing dominance of behaviorism in North American psychology, the idea of a "religious instinct" did not go away. Many behavioral scientists would be skeptical of this notion, just as they would be suspicious of a claim that we humans are "naturally" inclined to like (or dislike) heavy metal music, or that we have a genetic destiny to be political or to be sports fans. Rather, social scientists would, on the basis of much evidence, point out that our love (or hate) of heavy metal music, and our inclinations toward politics and sports, come more from our socialization experience than from the DNA we have inherited from our parents. Albert Bandura's social learning theory,[7] which emphasizes the role of modeling and imitation of behavior, has been especially influential in this regard.

However, authors and theorists from the psychoanalyst Carl Jung[8] to developmental psychologist David Elkind[9] have concluded that at least some aspects of religiousness may be inherited. Jung believed that there exists an unconscious human need to hunt for and to find a deity. Elkind suggested that at least some aspects of religion "can be traced to certain cognitive need capacities that emerge in the course of mental growth."[10] These "nativist" speculations were given an injection of new life when some recent research seemed to lend empirical support to the notion that religion is innate. Thomas Bouchard and his colleagues followed more than 100 sets of twins who were separated in infancy and reared apart, as well as many more twins who were raised together.[11] They concluded that religiousness, like many other psychological characteristics, has strong heritability components, and family environment tends *not* to have a strong influence on children's religiosity. In our consideration of religious socialization in Chapter 3, we show that a considerable amount of research is inconsistent with this view.

Of course, this "heritability" research does not claim that one person is "born to be a Baptist" and another "born to be a Muslim." Rather, it is suggested (as by Jung) that there may be some genetically inherited predisposition to "believe" in a supreme power, or (as by Elkind) that we humans may have a need to use a kind of spiritual explanation for understanding ourselves, the world, and the universe.

The possibility that religiosity (or at least the capacity for religiousness) may somehow be passed genetically from one generation to another cannot be dismissed out of hand, but little empirical evidence beyond the twin research cited above exists to substantiate such claims. On the other hand, a mountain of evidence suggests that religion affects and is affected by our experiences as we grow up. "Religious development" has been an area of interest and study since the formative days of the psychology of religion,[12] and a number of major books and articles summarizing theory and research in this area have been published in the past half century, including works by Allport,[13] Hyde,[14] Oser and Scarlett,[15] Reich,[16] and Strommen.[17] The reader is referred to these scholars for more extensive treatment of the relevant research.

In this chapter we outline several major theoretical positions on religious development, describe relevant empirical work, and review research in several related areas. We begin with Gordon Allport's insightful reflections on child religious growth; we then turn to a brief consideration of Piaget's stages of cognitive development, since they have served as the basis for much subsequent theory and empirical work on cognitive religious development. This is followed by an exploration of the work of Elkind and Goldman, both of whom attempted to apply Piaget's concepts directly to religious growth. Subsequent developments in stage theories are then considered, including Kohlberg's theory of moral development, Fowler's conceptualization of faith development, and Oser's thinking on the development of religious judgment. After this a number of specific topics are discussed, including the development of God concepts, prayer, and religious experience, as well as other work. A new direction for theory and research comes from Kirkpatrick's adaptation of attachment theory to religious development. Finally, we reflect on the possibility of a unified theoretical approach to the study of religious growth, and turn to a critical assessment of previous efforts, especially with respect to "what's missing." Some potentially fruitful directions for future research are proposed.

In general, in this chapter we restrict our consideration of "religious development" to theory and investigations involving *children*—here taken to include persons up to their midteen years. This purposely avoids many studies of college students and adults, unless they have direct implications for childhood religious development. Some of this adolescent and adult material is discussed in the context of religious socialization processes in Chapter 3.

THEORIES OF RELIGIOUS DEVELOPMENT

Allport's Analysis

Gordon Allport, in *The Individual and His Religion*, described his ideas about how the child moves from essentially no religion to the point where faith becomes an integrated part of the personality.[18] Unlike those espousing the ideas of an "innate religion," Allport believed that religion is acquired, not inherited biologically, though he allowed that it does to some extent grow out of basic human needs. He suggested that, at least initially, babies are (psychologically) a bit like a ball of modeling clay—they can be shaped and molded into all sorts of interesting forms. Consequently, culture and environment shape religious orientation, just as they contribute to other aspects of the developing child. Thus, babies move from a state of no religion through the acquisition of social responses and habits (e.g., bowing their heads, clasping of hands—things as routine as brushing their teeth). Children do not understand why they are doing these things, but are taught to "go through the motions" of some religious rituals. Young children are also very egocentric, seeing the world as revolving around them; thus, prayer may be seen as a means of getting material things. Similarly, young children weave adult explanations and words into meaning that the *children* understand. For example, Allport told the story of a child who thought God must be the weathervane on top of the barn because the child heard that He is very high and bright, and the weathercock was the highest, brightest thing in the child's world. Furthermore, children's religious concepts tend to be anthropomorphic; for example, they tend to visualize God as a king, an old man, or a "superman."

According to Allport, children's egotism inevitably leads to disappointment and deprivations in the years preceding puberty (initiated by the death of pets, denial of material goods, etc.), and this in turn leads to revisions of their views of Providence. Essentially, Allport argued that children then pass from a "self-interested" type of religion to a "self-disinterested" religion. As time passes, older children begin to comprehend the abstract aspects of religiousness and no longer need to put everything in concrete terms; also, they begin to identify with an ingroup (i.e., their religious group). Ultimately, all of this leads, usually in adolescence, to the development of religion as an integral part of the personality. This has been described as moving from a faith which is really "second-hand fittings" (i.e., understanding and "believing" parental religious teachings) to a religion of "first-hand fittings" during adolescence (i.e., religion becomes part of an adolescent's own personality).[19]

This is an insightful analysis of children's religious development, but in fact it is rather nonspecific and unsystematic compared to other theories of development that posit specific stages. Moreover, there has been little research to assess Allport's suggestions. Allport did acknowledge that Piaget's conceptualization of cognitive development influenced his own description of religious growth, but Piaget's impact was apparently much stronger on some other theoretical work in the psychology of religious development, which in turn has stimulated many studies.

Stage Theories of Religious Development

There is little doubt that experiences relevant to faith development begin very early in children's lives, and it has been suggested that common "stages" in religious growth may exist. Allport has done this in a very general way, but we need to examine several important and more systematic theoretical positions in this regard. First, as Hyde has pointed out, "The study of religion in childhood and adolescence has been dominated for thirty years by investigations of the process by which religious thinking develops,"[20] and this has been largely attributable to the influence of Piaget.

Piaget's Cognitive Stages

Jean Piaget, the "giant" of developmental psychology, believed that the ways children think about their world change systematically as they proceed through childhood.[21] That is, Piaget argued that "cognitive development" proceeds through a series of stages as children grow older. Beginning in the 1920s, he studied the development of these stages—in part by sitting on street corners and playing marbles and other games with his own and other children, asking about the "rules" of each game, posing problems for the children to solve, and so on. He was just as interested in the "errors" the children made as he was in "correct" answers to his questions, and noted that there were striking similarities among the ways in which children of the same age reasoned about things. Piaget concluded that there are four major identifiable stages of cognitive development, which reflect the general reasoning abilities of children of different ages:

1. *Sensorimotor stage* (birth to about 2 years). During this stage, children seem to understand things through their sensory and motor ("sensorimotor") interactions with the world around them (e.g., by touching and looking at things, and putting them in their mouths). It is during this period that infants come to realize that objects continue to exist when not perceived ("object permanence"), and also that infants develop a fear of strangers ("stranger anxiety"); both of these cognitive changes appear at about 8 months or soon thereafter.

2. *Preoperational stage* (about 2 to 7 years). During this second stage, children live in a very egocentric world, being unable to see things from others' perspectives. Preoperational children become quite at home in representing things with language and numbers, but lack sophisticated logical reasoning capability, and are unable to grasp more than one relationship at a time. Also, children at this time are prone to errors, especially with respect to concepts of conservation. That is, they have difficulty grasping the idea that characteristics such as volume, mass, or length of objects remain the same in spite of changes in their outward appearance.

3. *Concrete operational stage* (about 7 to 12 years). During this stage, children become capable of understanding the concepts of conservation which gave them so much trouble at the previous level. They are also able to reason quite logically about concrete events, to understand analogies, and to perform mathematical transformation such as those involving reversibility (e.g., $4 + 3 = 7$; therefore $7 - 3 = 4$).

4. *Formal operational stage* (ages 12 and up). The last stage of cognitive development allows a move away from the concrete in thought processes. These older children are capable of complex abstract thinking involving the hypothetical—for example, generating potential solutions to a problem, and then creating a plan to systematically test different possibilities in order to arrive at a "correct" solution.

Although Piaget's proposals have not escaped criticism, one of his most important contributions in this stage conceptualization of cognitive development seems to have been his recognition that children are not simply miniature adults, and cannot think as adults do.

Rather, cognitive growth proceeds sequentially in order to allow growing children to assimilate and deal with their environment, and also to make alterations in thinking in order to accommodate new information. Each stage builds on the previous stages in order to further cognitive development. This would seem to have important implications for religious development; for example, it suggests that children are not cognitively capable of understanding the complex and abstract concepts involved in most religions of the adult world. Piaget did not write directly about the religious growth of children,[22] even though he wrote a book on moral development.[23] It was left to others to relate Piaget's theories of cognitive stages to religion.

Applications of Piaget's Stages to Religious Development

The Work of Elkind. In Chapter 1 we have described David Elkind's proposal that religion is a natural result of mental development, such that biological roots of intellectual growth interact with individuals' experiences. Specifically, Elkind suggested that four basic sequential components of intelligence (conservation, search for representation, search for relations, and search for comprehension) are critical in religious development which parallels the cognitive stages described by Piaget.[24] Three studies investigating Elkind's ideas about cognitive religious development are described in Research Box 2.1. Essentially, his research supported a Piagetian kind of progression as religious understanding emerges in children. A subsequent study by Long, Elkind, and Spilka revealed a similar cognitive sequence for children's ideas about prayer.[25]

Some authors have apparently seen in these findings implications for religious education; for example, it has been recommended that children not be taught basic concepts about God until they are capable of understanding them, at about age 6.[26] Abraham has also found that it may be possible to hasten the transition from concrete to abstract religious thinking by deliberately stimulating cognitive conflict in religious education instructional materials at the sixth-grade level.[27]

The Work of Goldman. Similarly, Ronald Goldman has attempted to apply Piaget's theory of cognitive development to religious thinking, claiming that "religious thinking is no different in mode and method from non-religious thinking."[28] Working in England, he asked 5- to 15-year-old children questions about drawings with religious connotations (e.g., a child kneeling at a bed, apparently praying), as well as questions about Bible stories (e.g., Moses at the burning bush). He then analyzed responses to the questions by looking for evidence of Piaget's different stages of development. He concluded, as did Elkind, that religious thinking does indeed proceed in a fashion similar to more general cognitive development.

A number of studies have confirmed these general "cognitive stage" conclusions, especially the implication that children are capable of more abstract religious thinking as they grow older (see, e.g., work by Degelman et al.,[29] Peatling,[30] and Tamminen[31]). There has also been some confirmatory cross-cultural work.[32] Some studies have examined specific predictions of the Piagetian approach for religious development. For example, Zachry concluded that his data, obtained from high school and college students, were "consistent with the prediction of Piagetian theory that abstract thought in a specific content area such as religion depends on an underlying formal logic."[33]

Evaluating Goldman's Findings. Some empirical work has not been entirely supportive of Goldman's conclusions—in particular, those regarding the development of religious thought. For example, Hoge and Petrillo studied 451 high school sophomores in different

⤜ ✿ ⤛

**Research Box 2.1. The Child's Concept of His or Her Religion
(Elkind, 1961, 1962, 1963)**

In three separate studies, Elkind posed a series of questions to Jewish, Catholic, and Protestant children, respectively, concerning their understanding of their religious identity and ideas. For example, in the 1961 study, Jewish children were asked questions such as these: "Are you Jewish?", "What makes you Jewish?", "Can a cat or a dog be Jewish? Why?", and "How do you become a Jew?" Elkind found considerable age-related cognitive similarity in children's responses to such questions across his three major religious groups. The development of religious ideas seemed to parallel Piaget's conceptualization of cognitive stages to some extent. For example, in the 5- to 7-year range (comparable to Piaget's late preoperational stage), children seemed to think that their denominational affiliation was absolute, having been ordained by God, and therefore it could not be changed. A few years later (ages 7–9, the age of Piaget's early concrete operational stage), religious ideas were indeed very "concrete." Religious affiliation was seen to be determined by the family into which one was born, and if a Catholic family had a pet cat, it was also thought to be a Catholic cat. At the next stage of religious development (ages 10–14, corresponding to Piaget's late concrete and early formal operational stages), children apparently began to understand some of the complexities of religious practices and rituals, and they could conceive of a person's changing his or her religion because they understood religion to come from within the person rather than being determined externally. Clearly, abstract and differentiated religious thinking was beginning to appear. In the end, Elkind concluded that children were not capable of an abstract "adult" understanding of religion before the age of 11 or 12 (i.e., the beginning of Piaget's formal operational period).

Protestant and Catholic churches,[34] and were led to conclude that Goldman had overestimated the importance of cognitive capacity and underestimated the role of religious training in the development of religious thought. This conclusion, however, was apparently based primarily on differences between public and private school Catholics. Hoge and Petrillo attributed such differences to religious education at the private school, but there might well have been self-selection factors at work. In this regard, Hoge and Petrillo acknowledged that there was bias in their sample, such that "the youth most alienated from the church refused [to participate] disproportionately often."[35]

Batson, Schoenrade, and Ventis reconsidered Hoge and Petrillo's results and concluded that their original conclusions were inappropriate. In fact, they suggest that Hoge and Petrillo's findings are "precisely what Goldman would have predicted."[36] The disagreement between these authors apparently hinges partly on a specific Goldman prediction concerning rejection of religious teachings. Goldman felt that faith rejection is initiated by a gap between the level of religious thinking (e.g., "concrete thinking" about religious content) and adolescents' overall capacity for higher, more abstract ("formal operational") religious thinking. In fact, Hoge and Petrillo did not measure this "gap" directly, but assumed that higher absolute scores on a measure of abstract religious thinking meant that a smaller "gap" existed. Furthermore, their findings were not consistent across different measures of religious rejection or across different participant groupings, and the majority of reported correlations did not achieve statistical significance. It is not surprising that there is some disagreement as to the interpretation of these findings.

Some authors, such as Godin[37] and Howkins,[38] have been quite critical of Goldman's general conclusions, especially the implications he drew for religious education. Apparently, Elkind's work has escaped the severe criticism applied to Goldman's, in part because Elkind avoided theological biases or assumptions,[39] whereas Goldman "assumed a particular theological point of view."[40] For example, Greer has suggested that the cognitive tests of Goldman and those of Peatling, who developed a measure of religious cognitive development, were biased in such a way that theologically conservative respondents would tend to endorse responses indicating concrete (rather than abstract) religious thinking.[41]

In the end, the efforts of Elkind, Goldman, and others have demonstrated the utility of a Piagetian framework for understanding the development of religious thinking. They have also set the stage for much subsequent research in related areas such as moral development, faith development, and the development of the God concept and prayer.

Kohlberg's Stages of Moral Development

Lawrence Kohlberg's theory of moral development[42] has served as a basis for the investigation of many issues related to morality. Building on Piaget's belief that the moral judgements of children derive from their cognitive development, Kohlberg attempted to identify cognitive stages that underlie the development of moral thinking. In a series of studies, Kohlberg asked people what they thought about different "moral dilemmas."

His most famous dilemma involved a woman near death from cancer who could potentially be saved by a new drug developed by a nearby druggist. The druggist, however, wanted 10 times what the drug cost him to make—more than the sick woman's husband, Heinz, could afford—and refused to sell it for less. Heinz subsequently considered breaking into the druggist's store to steal the drug for his wife. Respondents were asked to comment on the morality of Heinz's potential decision to steal the drug, and the reasoning behind their response. Based on such investigations, Kohlberg proposed that individuals pass through three levels of moral development, each with substages. As Sapp states, "each stage is distinguished by moral reasoning that is more complex, more comprehensive, more integrated, and more differentiated than the reasoning of the earlier stages."[43] Table 2.1 outlines the levels and stages of moral development proposed by Kohlberg.

Kohlberg's theory has been criticized,[44] and Bergling's extensive assessment of its validity suggests that the theory may have limited utility outside of Western industrialized countries.[45] But there is some support for Kohlberg's conclusions that children do progress through moral stages, especially from the preconventional level to the conventional level of morality, and Snarey's review of the literature suggests that this progression *is* reasonably similar in different cultures.[46]

One might expect that Kohlberg's conceptualization of moral development would be closely linked to religious growth, or that religious development would directly affect and possibly determine the emergence of morality. However, Kohlberg is very clear that moral and religious development are quite separate, and that the two should not be confused. For example, he has suggested that it is a fallacy to think that

> basic moral principles are dependent upon a particular religion, or any religion at all. We have found no important differences in development of moral thinking between Catholics, Protestants, Jews, Buddhists, Moslems, and atheists. Children's moral values in the religious area seem to go through the same stages as their general moral values, so that a stage-2 child is likely to say,

TABLE 2.1. Kohlberg's Stages of Moral Development

Preconventional level (develops during early childhood)

Stage 1. Punishment and obedience orientation
Is characterized by avoidance of punishment and unquestioning deference to power as values in themselves; morality is seen as based on self-interest; the goodness or badness of actions is determined by their physical consequences, regardless of any human meaning attached to these consequences.

Stage 2. Instrumental relativist orientation
Is defined by a focus on instrumental satisfaction of one's own needs as the determiner of "right"; reciprocity may be present, but is of the "you scratch my back and I'll scratch yours" variety.

Conventional level (develops during late childhood and early adolescence)

Generally involves a move toward gaining approval or avoiding disapproval as the basis for morality; law and social rules are seen as valuable in their own right.

Stage 3. Interpersonal concordance or "good boy/nice girl" orientation
Is driven by behavior that pleases or helps others and that receives their approval.

Stage 4. "Law and order" orientation
Focuses on the maintenance of the social order and the importance of authority and strict rules.

Postconventional level (may develop from late adolescence on)

Generally involves concern with morality as abstract principles; persons at this level are able to separate their own identification with groups from the principles and moral values associated with those groups.

Stage 5. Social contract/legalistic orientation
Involves a recognition of the relative nature of personal values, and the importance of having procedural rules to reach consensus; the individual can separate the legal world from individual differences of opinion.

Stage 6. Universal ethical principle orientation
Involves defining "right" in one's own conscience, consistent with one's own abstract ethical principles, but involving a sense of responsibility to others; there is a clear emphasis on universality, consistency, logic, and rationality; the highest stage of moral development discussed by Kohlberg.

"Be good to God and he'll be good to you." Both cultural values and religion are important factors in selectively elaborating certain themes in the moral life but they are not unique causes of the development of basic moral values.[47]

Other research by Gorsuch and McFarland,[48] and by Selig and Teller[49] confirms Kohlberg's conclusion in this regard; moreover, Nucci and Turiel found that older children and adolescents were able to distinguish between moral and religious issues, and viewed moral rules as unalterable by religious authorities.[50] However, this has not stopped many, many researchers from speculating about and investigating possible relationships between moral development and religiosity.[51] This has been facilitated by the development of a less subjective scoring system to evaluate stages of moral development. Rest's Defining Issues Test (DIT) asks people to respond to a series of 12 statements concerning each of six moral dilemmas.[52] The DIT was intended to be both simpler and more objective than Kohlberg's initial scoring of moral stages, and has stimulated numerous studies on moral development and religion, though apparently few with children. These investigations have reported some relationships between level of moral judgment and religious orientation, though typically not strong ones.[53] There have also been claims that fundamentalist denominations have lower DIT scores.[54] The validity of the DIT for conservative religious groups has been called into question, however, by Richards.[55]

Gilligan has criticized Kohlberg's theory and research for their failure to deal with unique aspects of women's moral development, especially the care and responsibility orientation of many women, as contrasted with the male justice orientation emphasized by Kohlberg.[56] This could conceivably have implications for religious development—for example, in terms of gender differences in images of God, if God is seen as a person's anchor for morality. Nelsen, Cheek, and Au found evidence suggesting that images of God diverge along gender lines, with women more likely to see God as supportive and men more likely to see God as instrumental.[57] In a forthcoming article, Reich considers more generally whether such considerations might suggest the need for a theory specifically for women's religious development. However, he concludes that there is no need to modify current theories of religious development, or to develop new ones, in this regard.[58]

In general, Kohlberg's stages of moral development can serve an important purpose in helping us to think about and conceptualize religious development. For example, Scarlett and Perriello have suggested that Kohlbergian conceptualization of moral development could help in understanding aspects of the development of prayer.[59] Furthermore, religion has much to say about morality, and understanding how moral development occurs is certainly relevant to the communication and understanding of moral issues at different ages. At the same time, we must take Kohlberg's warning to heart and not assume—as some researchers have—that moral and religious development are necessarily directly and causally related.

Fowler's Stages of Faith Development

James Fowler has suggested[60] that individual religious faith develops in a stage sequence similar to those described by Piaget for cognitive development and Kohlberg for moral development.[61] Faith is defined as "a dynamic and generic human experience . . . [which] includes, but is not limited to or identical with, religion."[62] That is, although Fowler's use of the term "faith" does have some overlap with institutionalized religion, the two are also independent to some extent. Faith is seen as a deep core of the individual, the "center of values," "images and realities of power," and "master stories," involving both conscious and unconscious motivations. That is, faith involves centers of values that vary from one individual to the next, but that are foci of primary life importance (such as religion, family, nation, power, money, and sexuality). Furthermore, people tend to align themselves with power in this dangerous world—possibly religious power, but also sources of secular power, such as nations and economic systems. "Faith is trust in and loyalty to images and realities of power."[63] Also, Fowler argues that faith involves stories or scripts that give meaning and direction to people's lives (e.g., what it means to be a good person or a part of a religious community).

Fowler and his colleagues have carried out extensive interviews with hundreds of people about these aspects of their faith, and have concluded that there are essentially seven stages in the "process of growth and transformation in faith,"[64] as described below:

1. *Primal faith* (*in utero* and during the first few months of life). This stage involves the beginnings of emotional trust. Subsequent faith development is based on this foundation.
2. *Intuitive/projective faith* (early childhood). In the second stage, imagination combines with perception and feelings to create long-lasting faith images. The child becomes aware of the sacred, of prohibitions, and of the existence of morality.
3. *Mythical/literal faith* (elementary school years). Next, the developing ability to think logically helps order the world, corresponding to the Piagetian stage of concrete operations.

The child can now discriminate between fantasy and the real world, and can appreciate others' perspectives. Religious beliefs and symbols are accepted quite literally.

4. *Synthetic/conventional faith* (early adolescence). During the fourth stage, there is a reliance on abstract ideas of formal operational thinking, which engenders a hunger for a more personal relationship with God. Reflections on past experiences and concerns about the future and personal relationships contribute to the development of mutual perspective taking, and to the shaping of a world view and its values.

5. *Individuative/reflective faith* (late adolescence or young adulthood). Here there is critical examination and reconstitution of values and beliefs, including a change from reliance on external authorities to authority within the self. This leads to consciously chosen commitments and to the emergence of an "executive ego."

6. *Conjunctive faith* (midlife or beyond). In the sixth stage, there is integration of opposites (e.g., the realization that each individual is both young and old, masculine and feminine, constructive and destructive), generating a "hunger for a deeper relationship to the reality that symbols mediate."[65] "Dialogical knowing" emerges, such that the individual is open to the multiple perspectives of a complex world. This enables the person to go beyond the faith boundaries developed in the individuative/reflective stage, and appreciate that "truth" is both multidimensional and organically interdependent.

7. *Universalizing faith* (unspecified age). The final stage involves a oneness with the power of being or God, as well as commitment to love and justice, and overcoming oppression and violence. People who have attained this stage of faith development "live as though a commonwealth of love and justice were already reality among us. They create zones of liberation for the rest of us, and we experience them as both liberating and as threatening. These people tend to confront others concerning their involvement in, and attachments to, dehumanizing structures which oppose 'the commonwealth of love and justice.'"[66]

Fowler concludes that it is extremely rare for people to reach the final stage, but examples of people who have attained it might include Mahatma Gandhi, Martin Luther King, Jr., and Mother Teresa. It is no coincidence that both Gandhi and King were assassinated. Fowler claims that people who reach the universalizing faith stage are in danger of premature death because of their confrontational involvement in solving serious problems in the world.

Fowler's analysis of stages of faith is rich in ideas, provides a framework for empirical work, and can potentially contribute to our understanding of what it means to be "religious." However, it has been pointed out that Fowler's conceptualization is abstruse and complex, and that it has generated relatively little rigorous empirical research.[67] Also, Fowler generally declined to analyze his own results statistically and ignored related work in the psychology of religion.[68] There have been attempts to simplify the measurement of Fowler's proposed stages. For example, Barnes and Doyles constructed a kind of "faith development" version of Rest's DIT[69] (which itself was intended to simplify measurement of Kohlberg's moral stages), though a strong, generally accepted "faith development scale" has yet to appear. In light of these problems, Fowler's conceptualization of faith stages has yet to live up to its potential as a useful and important explanatory construct in the psychology of religion.

Oser's Stages of Development of Religious Judgment

Fritz Oser has focused on a related aspect of religious development, which he calls "religious judgment."[70] Apart from the work of Elkind, Fowler, and others, Oser concludes, there have been few investigations directed at building up a theory about the development of an individual's constructions and reconstructions of the religious experiences and beliefs. For this reason, many of us in the field of religious development are attempting to formulate a new paradigm of religious development, using a structural concept of discontinuous, stagelike development and the classical semiclinical interview method as our primary research strategy.[71]

Oser suggests that people's developmental stages will underlie qualitatively different ways in which they relate their individual experiences to an "Ultimate Being (God)," and he concludes that his research indicates five stages in the development of religious judgment. Individuals move from a stage of believing that God intervenes unexpectedly in the world and that God's power guides human beings (Stage 1), through belief in a still external and all-powerful God who punishes or rewards depending on good or bad deeds ("Give so that you may receive") (Stage 2). Individuals in Stage 3 begin to think of God as somewhat detached from their world and as wielding less influence, with people generally responsible for their own lives, since they can now distinguish between transcendence (God's existence outside the created world) and immanence (God's presence and action from within). In Stage 4 people come to realize both the necessity and the limits of autonomy, recognizing that freedom and life stem from an Ultimate Being, who is often perceived to have a "divine plan" that gives meaning to life. Finally, in Stage 5 the Ultimate Being is realized through human action via care and love. There is "universal and unconditional religiosity."[72]

Overall, there is a growing need for autonomy as people advance through the five stages, as well as a "deepening appreciation for the unity or 'partnership' of opposites."[73] Certainly, various elements of this stage analysis of religious judgment parallel elements of the other stage theories considered above. For example, Oser's claim that people move from seeing God as all-powerful and guiding human behavior to a much more autonomous, self-defined view of the deity and world is similar to Kohlberg's move from unquestioning deference to power (at the preconventional level) to the recognition of the relative nature of personal values and an emphasis on universality (at the postconventional level). This in turn is similar to Fowler's conceptualization of early stages of faith development as a process of teasing apart the real from fantasy; of the middle stages as involving an increasing appreciation of other's perspectives, not just one's own; and of the later stages as characterized by the integration of opposites and the development of a universalizing faith.

Oser has pointed to limited empirical support for his stage conceptualization of the development of religious judgment,[74] and the results of Bucher's pilot study of people's understanding of parables were consistent with Oser's approach,[75] though there seem to have been no extensive studies that assess his proposals directly.

Stage Theories: Enough Is Enough?

How many different stage conceptualizations of religious development are needed, especially with respect to the cognitive aspects of religion? Given the overlap among current stage conceptualizations, it might be productive to attempt an integration and synthesis of Piaget's, Kohlberg's, Fowler's, Oser's, and others' stage theories of development, in order to delineate the common elements of these theories as they apply to the development of religious thought processes. Such an integration has been attempted by Helmut Reich; his work is discussed in a later section of this chapter. There has been a very strong emphasis in existing theories of religious development on *cognitive* components of such growth, and a tendency to ignore or underemphasize other aspects of religious socialization (see Chapter 3). Thus, there is a need for theoretical work outside of the traditional cognitive conceptualizations of religious development.

Is the stage approach to faith development the best way to conceptualize religious growth and change? Certainly, it has increased our understanding of the general processes involved in the emergence of adult religiousness. However, it is possible that the obsession with stages may detract from our ability to understand the complexity and uniqueness of individual religious development. That is, the tendency to assume that such growth involves cognitive commonalities across all members of specific age groups can to some extent "blind" us to the idiosyncratic nature of religion in childhood and adolescence.[76] Furthermore, the stage approach implies a certain amount of discontinuity in religious development, whereas it may actually be a reasonably continuous process.

RELATED EMPIRICAL RESEARCH

Much research has been carried out to evaluate different aspects of childhood religion and its development. This research sometimes incorporates elements of the stage theories of religious development described above, but specific issues are often studied empirically without direct reliance on one or more stage theories. We examine several of these empirical areas here, including the development of God concepts, prayer, and religious experience.

Concepts of God

Many studies of childhood religious development have focused specifically on children's images or concepts of God. Some of this research was based on psychodynamic theories about the development of an image of God. For example, Freud interpreted the God image as a father figure, a kind of projection of one's real father in the context of the resolution of the Oedipus complex.[77] Jung apparently agreed that there is some projection of one's earthly father into one's God image, but felt that "archetypes" (images/symbols found in many cultures) also play a role in concept of God.[78] Although such psychoanalytic theories of the origins and development of God image are difficult to test directly, they do suggest that there should be a firm link between how one sees one's real father and one's image of God.

Although research by Foster and Keating has confirmed that God images are typically male-dominated in Western culture,[79] Spilka, Addison, and Rosensohn found that empirical support for the prediction that God images should be related to one's own father has been mixed.[80] Vergote and Tamayo suggested that such images may bear more similarity to the mother than to the father,[81] and Roberts found that there is a correspondence between images of God and images of self.[82] There is also evidence that general qualitative aspects of relationships with parents may be related to positive (e.g., warm, loving) images of God.[83] At any rate, these psychodynamic approaches tend to focus on the underlying psychoanalytic explanation of the origin of God concepts, and the relevant psychodynamic research has been criticized for serious methodological and conceptual problems, as well as an inadequate theoretical basis.[84] Outside of this psychoanalytic emphasis, some approaches to God images have attempted to come to grips with the developmental aspects of God concepts, typically focusing on cognitive development. Some of these studies are clearly Piagetian in orientation, whereas others have a more general cognitive orientation.

For example, in the 1940s, Harms suggested that earlier investigations of children's images of God had erred by asking children to respond to fixed questions.[85] Instead, he asked more than 4,800 children (aged 3 to 18) both to talk about and to draw their representations of religion, especially God. Their responses led him to conclude that there were three stages in the development of God concepts:

1. *Fairy-tale stage* (3–6 years). Children see little difference between God and fairy-tale characters.
2. *Realistic stage* (6–11 years). As children's cognitive capacities begin to expand, they see God as more concrete, more human. They are more comfortable using religious symbols.
3. *Individualistic stage* (adolescence). Adolescents no longer rely exclusively on religious symbols. They take a more individualized approach to God, resulting in very different conceptualizations from person to person.

Another major study of the development of God concepts was undertaken by Deconchy in France in the 1960s,[86] though he did not include children under 7 years of age. He concluded that the development of God concepts occurred in three stages, revolving around themes of attributes, personalization, and interiorization, respectively; these are described in Research Box 2.2.

There have been variations on these themes, but different authors have come to conclusions that involve similar stage development of God concepts,[87] including some based on a Piagetian framework.[88] Others have simply noted the general change from fragmented, undifferentiated thinking through very simple, concrete God concepts to more abstract and complex images as children grow older.[89] However, attempts to further specify the parameters of such development, and the processes through which this development occurs, have not been particularly successful.[90] Recently, Janssen, de Hart, and Gerardts used open-ended questions about God in a study of Dutch secondary school students.[91] They concluded that

---

**Research Box 2.2. The Idea of God: Its Emergence
between 7 and 16 Years (Deconchy, 1965)**

In this investigation, Catholic children and adolescents were asked to free-associate when they heard words such as "God." An analysis of their responses led Deconchy to conclude that there were three major stages in the development of God concepts for these children. Those from about 7 or 8 to 11 years of age used predominantly "attributive" themes; that is, God was seen as a set of attributes, many anthropomorphic with overtones of animism. God concepts were relatively independent of other religious constructs, such as the historical events in the life of Jesus. The associations of children between 11 and 14 years of age emphasized "personalization" themes, such that God took on parental characteristics, and was seen in more sophisticated anthropomorphic terms (e.g., "just," "strong," "good"). Finally, by approximately the age of 14 a further shift began to take place, focusing on "interiorization" themes. That is, in middle adolescence anthropomorphic characteristics of God disappeared, and God concepts became more abstract and tended to reflect relationships with God (e.g., involving love, trust) emanating from within the individual, rather than simply involving descriptive characteristics.

percepts of God among their participants were complex and "can hardly be summarized."[92] Furthermore, although there was evidence of abstract thinking among their Dutch adolescents, there was no proof that it resulted from a developmental process. However, it is questionable whether a developmental process *could* have been demonstrated in a study of teenagers only.

Tamminen's extensive research with Finnish children and adolescents involved both structural questions about God and unstructured methods, such as sentence completion and "projective photographs."[93] His results were generally consistent with the stage approach outlined above. However, Tamminen noted that revealed images of God varied somewhat, depending on the measures used: "For example, God's effect on people, making them be good to each other, which was considered very important in the alternative answers chosen in the questionnaires, was not often mentioned in the fill-in sentences or essays."[94]

Ladd, McIntosh, and Spilka have recently obtained some empirical support for their proposal that God concepts develop similarly across various Christian denominations,[95] and these authors suggest that further research is necessary to understand how and why very different religious education experiences do not lead to divergent concepts of God by adolescence. Research by Vergote and Tamayo, however, has suggested that although there are certainly commonalities in God images across cultures, at least some cultural differences do emerge with respect to maternal and paternal symbolism.[96]

Harms's call for less constraining measures of ideas about God has not been ignored. In addition to his own attempt to allow subjects greater freedom in description of their God concepts, others have used quite a diversity of techniques: pictures or drawings;[97] word associations;[98] adjective ratings;[99] open-ended questions;[100] letters written to God;[101] semantic differentials;[102] Q-sorts;[103] standardized scales;[104] and sentence completions, essays, and "projective photographs."[105] Recently, there has been some concern with comparing the utility of different approaches to measuring images of God. For example, Hutsebaut and Verhoeven's study of university students compared open-ended and closed questions concerning God.[106] The authors concluded that the closed approach was slightly better.

However, it has been pointed out that despite the value of studies in this area, research has tended to be descriptive rather than carefully designed to test theories of cognitive development.[107] Furthermore, Hyde has suggested that research on children's ideas of God has been "occasional and sporadic, with no continuous theme and [it] has tended to remain so, following the varied interests of those undertaking it."[108] Additional research is needed, but it must address these problems.

Prayer

Evidence suggests that children's concepts of prayer develop in a manner consistent with Piaget's cognitive-developmental stages. For example, Long and colleagues interviewed 5- to 12-year-olds about prayer[109] (see Research Box 2.3). The authors concluded that there was a clear tendency for these children's concepts of prayer to evolve in three stages: They moved from habits and memorized passages, through concrete personal requests, to more abstract petitions. This change was interpreted as paralleling Piaget's conceptualization of cognitive development as moving from the preoperational and concrete to the abstract.

Other studies seem generally to be consistent with this,[110] from relatively direct replication research by Worten and Dellinger[111] to, for example, Brown's investigation of adolescents, which suggests that there is less emphasis on the material consequences of prayer

---

**Research Box 2.3. The Child's Conception of Prayer
(Long, Elkind, & Spilka, 1967)**

In a Piagetian context, these researchers interviewed 80 girls and 80 boys aged 5 to 12 about their concepts of prayer. They asked them various open-ended questions, such as "What is a prayer?" and "Where do prayers go?", as well as giving them sentence completion tasks (e.g., "I usually pray when . . ."). Three judges independently analyzed the children's responses according to a scoring manual that outlined levels of differentiation and degree of concretization–abstraction. The results suggested three stages of prayer concept development:

1. At the younger ages (5–7), children responded to the questions with learned formulas based on memorized prayers.

2. Children aged 7 to 9 identified prayer as a set of concrete activities, with time and place defined; the purpose was also concrete, typically centered on personal requests.

3. Between the ages of 9 and 12, prayer was more abstract, and tended toward shared conversation rather than specific requests. Prayer was more focused on abstract goals than on material objects.

Thus, across the 5- to 12-year age range prayer seemed to evolve from habits and memorized passages, through concrete personal requests, to more abstract petitions with humanitarian and altruistic sentiments. An emotional shift was also noted: Praying was emotionally neutral for the younger children, but by the older ages prayer had important emotional implications (e.g., expression of empathy and also identification with others and the deity). All of this is quite consistent with the Piagetian conceptualization of cognitive development, with the first two stages of prayer development paralleling the preoperational (preconceptual substage) and concrete operational stages. Long et al.'s third stage is best characterized as transitional, giving evidence of the abstract thought characteristic of Piaget's stage of formal operations, which he felt did not begin until approximately 12 years of age.

---

among older children.[112] Scarlett and Perriello asked seventh- and ninth-grade Catholic school students, as well as college undergraduates, to write prayers for six hypothetical vignettes (e.g., a woman's best friend is dying of cancer).[113] They found a shift from "using prayer to request changes in objective reality"[114] among the younger students, toward prayer as a way to deal with feelings and become closer to God among the older participants. This shift is apparently consistent with the second and third stages of prayer outlined by Long et al., though at slightly older ages for the Scarlett and Perriello sample.

Tamminen also found some divergence from Long et al.'s stages in his Finnish young people.[115] For example, personal conversation with God was important at younger ages (7–8) than Long et al. had found (9–12 years); moreover, petitionary prayer remained important up to age 20, whereas Long et al. reported decreasing importance of petitionary prayer as children grew older. More research is necessary to determine the reason for the differences across these studies. They could be attributable to culture, method, time period of the research, and so on.

Francis and Brown have carried out investigations of influences on prayer, rather than cognitive stages in development of prayer.[116] They found some denominational differences (e.g., Church of England schools exerted a small "negative" influence on attitudes toward prayer, compared to the lack of influence in Roman Catholic schools), as well as a shift in influence from parents (stronger among their 11-year-olds) to church (stronger among the 16-year-olds). They interpret their results as supporting a social learning or modeling interpretation of prayer, since prayer among children and adolescents seemed to result more from "explicit teaching or implicit example from their family and church community than as a spontaneous consequence of developmental dynamics or needs."[117] This research is highlighted in Research Box 3.2 (in Chapter 3), in the context of our discussion of religious socialization.

It is surprising that more research attention has not been focused on prayer as it relates to religious development. Although there are problems in operationalizing and studying prayer (especially spontaneous personal prayer), prayer is an important religious ritual that could potentially serve as a "window" into more general religious development, as well as the meaning of faith to religious persons. Further, there remain many questions about the nature and function of prayer in individual lives, and the nature of social and contextual factors in shaping prayer.[118] Brown's recent book *The Human Side of Prayer* initiates an exploration of some of these issues and provides an integrative review of the diverse research in this area, especially in his chapter devoted to the development and meaning of prayer.[119] He suggests, for example, that our understanding of prayer might be enhanced by drawing an analogy to the programming and "languages" of computers. In this context, prayer might be thought of as "an important 'source program' to express and help us understand what we know."[120] Such analogies can help us to think creatively about prayer and its development, and should help to stimulate additional empirical work.

Religious Experience

Kalevi Tamminen's studies of the religious experiences of Finnish children and adolescents,[121] highlighted in Research Box 2.4, deserve attention in this chapter for several reasons. First, almost 3,000 young people have been studied. Second, this research program has produced limited but important longitudinal data. Third, and possibly most important, these studies have moved a step beyond the more traditional cognitive stage approach by investigating the meaning and implications of religious *experiences* for children's lives, as well as aspects of religious cognitive development.

Tamminen's research program is not without problems. It is difficult to know what to make of written questionnaire responses from relatively young children; probably the younger children were not able to express themselves well in writing, and it is not clear that their self-reported "religious experiences" are consonant with what adults would call "religious experiences." Also, questionnaires were administered in school classrooms, suggesting that peer pressure, contextual influences, and other such factors may have influenced responses. For example, children may have been reluctant to reveal personal religious experiences to an unknown adult, especially while sitting among their classmates. As Scarlett has pointed out, "These are surveys carried out in impersonal settings not conducive to tapping into what God and religious experience *mean* to adolescents."[122] Furthermore, the children and adolescents were fairly homogeneous in terms of their religious background (Lutheran), and it is not clear to what extent Tamminen's findings may generalize to children from other religious backgrounds or no religious background at all.

**Research Box 2.4. Religious Experience in Childhood and
Adolescence: Finnish Research (Tamminen, 1994)**

The original study in Tamminen's series took place in 1974 and included 1,588 children
and adolescents (aged 7–20), mostly Lutheran, and fairly evenly divided between boys and
girls. Longitudinal data were then collected 2 years later on 277 of the original participants, and a final longitudinal wave of data was collected in 1980 on 60 of those who had
participated in the first and second stages. Two hundred and forty-two classmates of the
"third-wave 60" were also studied for comparison purposes. Finally, a study that was intended to some extent to replicate the 1974 investigation was carried out in 1986, involving
1,176 students. Most of the data were gathered by means of group questionnaires administered in classrooms, although the youngest students (first grade) were also interviewed.
Tamminen acknowledges that up to fifth grade, many students had difficulty expressing
themselves in writing, and this could have compromised his findings for the younger
children.

Religious experience was operationally defined by the question "Have you at times
felt that God is particularly close to you?" and its follow-up, "Would you like to tell me
about it, when and in what situations?" Interestingly, although 10–16% of the two youngest groups of students reported that they had *not* felt particularly close to God, this figure grew steadily to 53% of the 17- to 20-year-olds. That is, older children were significantly less likely to report any religious experiences involving closeness to God.

Closeness to God among the 7- to 11-year-old children was most likely to be linked
with "situations of loneliness, fear, and emergencies—such as escaping or avoiding danger—or when they were ill" (p. 81). Tamminen notes that these reports correspond to a
more general concreteness of thinking at these ages. Similar experiences were reported
by the 11- to 13-year-olds, though they also linked closeness to God with encounters with
death, loneliness, prayer, and contemplation. However, there was not much evidence of
more abstract thinking until later ages.

The 13- to 15-year-olds evidenced a variety of religious doubts (concerning, for
example, God's existence and trustworthiness, and the efficacy of prayer). Reports of decreased closeness to God were more common, and those reports that did appear were more
often linked with death and external dangers. Finally, the religious experiences of older
students (15- to 20-year-olds) tended to deal with personal identity issues and existential questions such as the meaning of life and death, and this material was more obviously
abstract in nature.

Overall, Tamminen concluded that the results of these far-reaching studies show "a
developmental line from concrete, separate, and external to more abstract, general, and
internalized. In addition, experiences in childhood were related almost exclusively to
everyday situations—as was the case also with evening prayer—whereas at the age of puberty and in adolescence, they were more frequently related to congregational situations
[i.e., church-related contexts]" (p. 82). In general, parallel findings appeared for other
questions dealing with God's guidance and direction in life.

Note. A more extensive treatment of Tamminen's research on religion in Finnish young people can be found
in his 1991 book *Religious Development in Childhood and Youth: An Empirical Study.*

In spite of these problems, this research program has made important contributions to our understanding of children's religious experiences. Tamminen's research has confirmed that there is a developmental sequence with respect to religious *experiences*, though his results are quite cognitive in nature. Although these investigations were not intended to test a Piaget-based cognitive-developmental theory of religious development, the results are certainly consistent with that approach (especially with respect to the shift from concrete to abstract thinking about religion as children move into adolescence). Also, the longitudinal trends in the data are consistent with cross-sectional findings. Furthermore, it has been pointed out that these studies "enlighten by countering the old view that God becomes important only after childhood."[123] Certainly there is a rich description of the nature and content of children's and adolescents' self-reported "close to God" experiences. Finally, this research should serve as a stimulus to other researchers to approach the topic of religious development from different perspectives, and not to be constrained by previous research carried out from within a Piagetian framework.

Other Work on Children's Religious Development

It is difficult to summarize the considerable literature on religious development in a chapter such as this one. To this point, we have attempted to outline several major theoretical and empirical directions of research, and the resulting knowledge that has accumulated from many studies. We have given little attention to other theories (e.g., psychodynamic) and to the many articles that do not offer novel theoretical advancement or lack an empirical base.[124] Furthermore, many empirical studies have not fallen neatly into the subheadings used in this chapter. Hyde has summarized much of this other work.[125] Here, we offer a sampling of recent research directions not discussed above.

Leslie Francis has summarized a considerable body of research on personality and mental aspects of religious development,[126] relying heavily on the work and orientation of Eysenck.[127] Francis's own studies suggest that among children, religiousness and introversion are positively related.[128]

Another line of research has focused on influences on religiousness and attitudes toward religion among young people (especially influence of parents, but also peers, schools, church, etc.). Some of this work has included samples of children or early adolescents,[129] but the majority of these studies have involved older adolescents and young adults, so a review of these efforts is left to the following chapter. Likewise, there has been some emphasis on the influence of religiously affiliated schools versus public institutions on values and other aspects of children's lives, but these have not shown much difference between the two types of schooling.[130] However, Francis has found variations between the influences of Catholic and Protestant schools in England.[131] The effects of schooling on religiousness are considered in more detail in Chapter 3.

Much other work has included religion as simply one of many variables of interest. For example, Archer's investigation of gender differences suggests that there is little difference between early to late adolescent males and females in the use of the identity process in religious development.[132] A study by de Vaus and McAllister concluded that gender variations in religiosity are not attributable to child-rearing roles of females,[133] and Albert and Porter found that liberal Christian and Jewish backgrounds are related to less rigid conceptions of gender roles in 4- to 6-year-old children.[134] Other research, such as that by Florian and Kravetz[135] and Stambrook and Parker,[136] has suggested a link between religion and concepts of death in childhood. Some efforts by Saigh have pointed to a link between religious symbols worn by examiners and performance on intelligence tests, such that performance may be better when young people are tested by same-religion examiners.[137]

There has been interest in the problems in getting children, especially at young ages, to understand and respond appropriately to questions about religion.[138] Similarly, tendencies have been noted by Francis for children's scores on attitudes toward religion to be positively related to lie scores on other scales,[139] and also for children to bias their responses in a proreligious direction when a priest, as opposed to a layman, is the test administrator.[140] Similar effects were not found by Hunsberger and Ennis in several studies of university students, however.[141] The best conclusion seems to be that caution must be exercised in studies of children involving measurement of religion, and appropriate checks should be included to assess possible biases or distortion of responses whenever possible.

This is not a complete summary of the religious development literature by any means.[142] However, we would argue that fresh conceptual approaches are needed to revitalize the study of children's religious development. The work stemming from attachment theory is one example of a promising new direction.

A DIFFERENT APPROACH: ATTACHMENT THEORY

Recently, Kirkpatrick[143] has extended Bowlby's[144] theory of parent–infant attachment to the realm of religion; in so doing, he has provided a very different approach for the study of links between early development and religion, and their implications for children's and adult's lives. As Kirkpatrick describes Bowlby's work, attachment theory "postulates a primary, biosocial behavioral system in the infant that was designed by evolution to maintain proximity of the infant to its primary caregiver, thereby protecting the infant from predation and other natural dangers."[145] Kirkpatrick has pointed out that this theoretical basis might help to explain individual differences in religiousness. For example, he has noted the extent to which the God of Christian traditions corresponds to the idea of a secure attachment figure. Similarly, religion more generally may serve as a comfort and a sense of security, especially during times of stress or other difficulties.

This has led Kirkpatrick and Shaver to suggest that attachment and religion might be linked in important ways.[146] For example, they posit a "compensation hypothesis," which predicts that people who have not had secure relationships with their parents (or other primary caregivers) may be inclined to compensate for this absence by believing in a "loving, personal, available God." On the other hand, consistent with Bowlby's theory, "one's working models of early attachment relationships might provide the basis for constructing images of God and other religious beliefs."[147] This latter approach has been labeled the "mental model hypothesis." In a study designed to test these ideas, they found that although there was some support for the compensation hypothesis, the relationship was not simple (see Research Box 2.5). The authors emphasize that their study represents "only an initial, exploratory step toward a systematic investigation of the role of attachment in the development of religious belief and involvement."[148] But it is a promising first step.

Kirkpatrick's subsequent writings on attachment and religion have provided a rich source of ideas for empirical investigation. For example, it has been suggested that attachment theory has relevance for understanding conceptualizations of God, religious behaviors such as prayer and glossolalia, and links between religious experience and romantic love.[149]

IS A UNIFIED APPROACH POSSIBLE?

Given the diversity of theoretical and empirical work cited in this chapter, one might wonder whether it is possible to integrate this material into a unified approach to the study of religious development. Recently, Helmut Reich has attempted to do just this.[150] He describes the problem succinctly:

Research Box 2.5. Attachment Theory and Religion
(Kirkpatrick & Shaver, 1990)

An examination of Bowlby's attachment theory suggested to Kirkpatrick and Shaver that it could potentially have links with religion. They speculated, on the one hand, that people from insecure attachment backgrounds may be inclined to compensate for this by adhering to a secure attachment type of religion (e.g., belief in a loving, personal, available God). This "compensation hypothesis" was contrasted with a "mental model hypothesis," which predicted that people's religiousness may be partially determined by early attachment relationships. That is, people may model their religious beliefs on the attachment relationships they have experienced early in their lives.

Data were collected from two surveys, one involving respondents to a questionnaire in a Sunday newspaper ($n = 670$), and the other including a subsample of 213 of these same people who agreed to participate in a further study. Various measures were used to tap aspects of religiousness, including the scale for assessing intrinsic–extrinsic religious orientation.[a] Child–parent attachment was measured in a standard way, which placed respondents into one of three categories (percentages in parenthesess are from Kirkpatrick and Shaver's study): secure (51%), avoidant (8%), and anxious/ambivalent (41%). Attachment did indeed serve as a predictor of religiousness, but in a somewhat complicated way. There was a tendency for those from avoidant (insecure) parent–child attachment relationships to report higher levels of adult religiousness, and also for persons with secure attachments to report lower levels of religiousness, but only for respondents whose mothers were relatively nonreligious.

The attachment classification apparently had a more direct relationship with reported sudden conversion experiences, with insecurely attached respondents much more likely to report conversions at some time in their lives (44%), compared to the other attachment groups (less than 10%). Home religiosity did not affect this relationship.

Of course, this study relied on adults' retrospective reports of earlier attachment and family religiousness, and memory and other biases may have affected their responses. The authors point out that their investigation is very much an exploratory study of attachment–religion relationships. However, their initial findings are provocative and tend to support the compensation hypothesis (but only for people from relatively nonreligious homes), and generally contradict the mental model hypothesis (i.e., that religiousness may be modeled after early attachment relationships). The reasons for this are not clear and call for further investigation.

---

[a]Allport and Ross (1967).

> Developmental psychology of religion is like a smorgasbord: For some authors conation is a major driving force, for others emotion, yet for others cognition, socialization, psychodynamics, and/or coping with critical or stressing life events, not forgetting attribution theory as a significant predictor.[151]

Reich has summarized many differing theoretical and empirical approaches to the study of religious development. In addition, he has attempted to distinguish between the degree of "hardness" and "softness" of stage theories. "Hard" stages

> describe organized systems of action (first-order problem solving), are qualitatively different from each other and follow an unchanging sequence with a clear developmental logic: A later stage denotes greater complexity and improved problem solving capacity. Each hard stage integrates the preceding stage and logically requires the elements of the prior stage.[152]

The stage models of Piaget, Kohlberg, Elkind, and Goldman would be considered "hard." "Soft" stages, on the other hand, "explicitly include elements of affective or reflective characteristics (metatheoretical reflection) that . . . do not follow a unique developmental logic."[153] Oser's and Fowler's theories would fall into this "soft" category. The "hard–soft" distinction could be helpful in understanding and categorizing theories of religious development, and also the circumstances under which one theory might be more appropriate than another. However, Fowler has criticized this approach,[154] suggesting that the use of hard and soft categories is obsolete; that Reich's formulation does not incorporate important work by Gilligan[155] on the ethics of responsibility and care; and that Reich fails to acknowledge important differences between Oser's and Fowler's stage theories.

Reich's articles do a considerable service by mapping common elements in different theories and empirical work, critically evaluating and integrating theories, and suggesting the need for clarification and some standardization in terminology and approaches. In reaction to Reich's proposed integration, Wulff has suggested that "in the long run . . . the psychology of religion and its practitioners will be best served if we not only recognize the limitations of these theories and their associated research techniques, but also strive to develop new ones more faithful to the traditions and life experience of the persons we seek to understand."[156] Reich's beginning could stimulate further integrative conceptualizations. However, a single major integrative theory of religious development remains an elusive goal.

WHAT'S MISSING?

As we have seen above, the area of religious development is rich in theoretical perspectives, many of which trace their roots back to Piaget's conceptualization of stages of cognitive development. Probably because of the mostly *cognitive* theme of the theoretical approaches, there has been a relatively narrow focus in empirical investigations of religious development. The resulting accumulation of knowledge typically confirms the development of patterns of religious thinking that parallel stages of more general cognitive development. However, this cognitive-developmental focus may have diverted attention from many other issues in childhood religious development.

A considerable body of relevant theoretical work stemming from a psychoanalytic perspective exists, but it has received little attention in this chapter. For example, the theories of Freud and Jung have been mentioned in the context of the development of concepts of

God. However, we have not discussed more general implications of psychoanalytic theory for religious development.[157] Nor have we mentioned the psychoanalyst Erik Erikson,[158] whose theory of psychosocial development could be interpreted as a model of religious development.[159] For example, Fowler made use of Erikson's theory in his conceptualization of faith development. Although these psychoanalytic theories can offer rich sources of ideas and insights into religious development, in general we have not given them more attention because (1) they have not generated much empirical research; (2) the relevant research that has been carried out has been compromised by the difficulties inherent in operationalizing and testing some psychoanalytic concepts; and (3) the conclusions of related studies are somewhat ambiguous and contradictory.

Meaning and Implications of Religion in Childhood

Aside from these psychoanalytic approaches, then, the general focus of theory and research on religious development in childhood has been on how religious *thinking* develops. Additional issues have tended to be ignored. For example, we know little about the meaning and implications of religion for children as they grow older, beyond the cognitive components. What impact (if any) does religion have on the day-to-day lives of children, including their physical and mental health, personal identity, and social relationships? How does childhood religion affect later religiosity, as well as nonreligious social attitudes? For example, does religious training affect a child's concept of death?[160] A broad survey of children and young adolescents (fifth through ninth graders) led Forliti and Benson to conclude that religion was related to increased prosocial action, and to a decreased incidence of sexual intercourse, drug use, and antisocial behavior; they also concluded that a restrictive religious orientation was linked to antisocial behavior, alcohol use, racism, and sexism.[161] These conclusions are not always consistent with those found with older adolescents and adults (see Chapters 3 and 10). Given the moderately strong associations among right-wing authoritarianism, religious fundamentalism, and prejudice observed by Altmeyer,[162] it would seem appropriate to investigate the childhood antecedents of such relationships, as well as the developmental dynamics that foster such connections.

Parenting and Religion

As Darling and Steinberg have pointed out, there is general agreement among developmental psychologists that parenting practices have important implications for child development.[163] In spite of the real possibility that parental religious orientation influences parenting style,[164] there has been little research relating parenting approaches, religion, and child development. A few early studies—for example, those by Bateman and Jensen[165] and by Nunn[166]—suggested the potential of such links. Subsequent theoretical and empirical work on "parenting styles" has provided new avenues for exploring the relationship between parenting and child religious development.

Baumrind has suggested that there exist four very different styles of parenting, based on parental responsiveness and demandingness: "authoritarian," "authoritative," "permissive," and "rejecting/neglecting."[167] Authoritarian parents are high on demandingness but low on responsiveness, preferring to impose rules on their children and to emphasize obedience. Authoritative parents tend to be both demanding and responsive, explaining why rules are necessary, and being open to their children's perspectives. Permissive parents make few demands, use little punishment, and are responsive to the point of submitting to their children's wishes. Rejecting/neglecting parents are neither demanding nor responsive, being generally disengaged from their children. Correlational and longitudinal research has suggested that the authoritative style of parenting may have benefits for children's development, whereas the authoritarian and rejecting/neglecting styles may have some negative implications.[168] Other research suggests that an emphasis on obedience has implications for behavior such as "cognitive accomplishment,"[169] as well as for personality development (e.g., right-wing authoritarianism).[170]

The authoritarian parenting style bears some similarity to Biblical injunctions to emphasize obedience among children and not to "spare the rod," and Zern has argued that, from a religious perspective, obedience is a preferred trait.[171] In fact, research by Ellison and Sherkat has found that conservative Protestants (and, to a lesser extent, Catholics) tend to endorse an authoritarian parenting orientation, valuing obedience in children.[172] Religion has also been linked with parental disciplinary practices,[173] including a preference, among those who subscribe to a literal belief in the Bible, for the use of corporal punishment at home[174] and at school.[175] Similarly, religiousness has been linked with emphasis on obedience to cultural norms generally.[176] One therefore wonders whether conservative religious groups, or religious fundamentalists more generally, might be inclined to use an authoritarian parenting style, with consequent implications for their children. A study by Neufeld has even noted similarities between child-rearing attitudes of religious fundamentalists and those of child-abusing parents,[177] though such a relationship must be regarded cautiously, pending additional research. Bottoms and colleagues have, in some detail, mapped possible links between religious beliefs and child abuse, broadly defined.[178]

Recently, Darling and Steinberg have suggested that parenting goals and values should be distinguished from parenting styles and parenting practices.[179] In light of the discussion above, it seems apparent that religious orientation is likely to have some impact on parenting goals and values. Certainly, some conservative Christian books on child rearing emphasize the importance of authoritarian-like goals for parents—for example, by explicitly advising parents that raising obedient children is an important goal.[180] Such goals in turn are likely to influence both general parenting style as delineated by Baumrind, and specific parenting practices such as the use of corporal punishment to teach obedience. The role of religion in this process might even help to explain variations in the prevalence of different parenting styles in American ethnic groups.[181] The role of religion in these aspects of parenting (and consequences for child development) has received little empirical attention to date.

Parenting techniques have been linked with religion in a somewhat different context. Nunn suggested that some parents invoke the image of a punishing God in an attempt to control their children's behavior.[182] He hypothesized that relatively ineffective, powerless parents may be inclined to use God in an attempt to gain some semblance of power, telling their children such things as "God will punish you if you misbehave." Nunn's data apparently supported this view of parents who form a "coalition with God," and also suggested that there were negative consequences of this "God will punish you" approach for the children, who were reportedly more inclined to blame themselves for problems and to feel that they should be obedient.

Nelsen and Kroliczak have pointed out that there has been a general decline in people's belief in a punishing God, and that this decline is at least partly attributable "to parents' being less likely to use coalitions with God. Hence, fewer children form this image."[183] Nelsen and Kroliczak examined data from over 3,000 children in Minnesota elementary schools in an attempt to replicate Nunn's findings.[184] They found a decreased tendency of parents to resort to the "God will punish you" approach (73% said that neither parent employed this approach, compared to Nunn's 33%). But the children whose parents tended to use the "coalition" also tended to view God as malevolent, to have higher self-blame scores, and to feel a greater need to be obedient. Essentially, Nelsen and Kroliczak replicated Nunn's finding some 20 years later.

These studies have implications for the development of God images, but they also suggest that parents' approach to discipline may be important for children's religiosity (e.g., how they view God), as well as for more general child development (e.g., tendencies toward self-blame and obedience). There may also be noteworthy ramifications for how parents deal with other child-rearing issues such as illness. For example, research has indicated that parents who believe more strongly in divine influence are more likely to seek spiritual guidance in coping with (hypothetical) child illnesses.[185] Finally, all of these findings are consistent with the suggestion that parenting goals, styles, and practices may have significant links with religious orientation. This represents an area ripe for further exploration.

Other New Directions

In the end, we must conclude that the area of religious development is top-heavy in theory, especially stage theories of religious cognitive development. There has been a considerable amount of overlap in research that "tests" these theories, but a lack of integrative work to make sense of it all. Furthermore, there has been little or no empirical research on many issues related to childhood religious development, and some studies of religious development have little to say about *children*, having focused on older adolescents or young adults.

We would encourage researchers to diversify their efforts in the area of child religious development. In particular, we would encourage them to consider the implications of more traditional developmental and social-psychological theories in the context of child religious development—for example, attribution theory,[186] attitude theories,[187] personality constructs,[188] attachment theory,[189] self-discrepancy theory,[190] schema theory,[191] and so on. We need to escape from the confines of the Piagetian approach to religious development. It is possible that extrinsic and intrinsic religious orientation,[192] and the religious quest orientation,[193] may appear in developmental sequence.[194] Furthermore, the implications of childhood religious development for the children themselves, as well as for other individuals and groups (e.g., peers, parents, social and athletic groups, schools), need to be investigated. These issues have generated considerable research with adolescent and adult populations, but not with children. There is a distinct paucity of longitudinal research on childhood religious development issues. Such research is critical if we are to escape the serious limitations of cross-sectional studies.[195] Gorsuch has noted a lack of strong experimental research in this area.[196] Finally, consideration needs to be given to the few studies that have investigated isolated child religious development topics (e.g., personality, gender differences, methodological issues), with an eye to integrating and making sense out of the diverse findings.

OVERVIEW

Clearly, Piaget's original description of stages of cognitive development has been important in guiding related theories and studies of religious growth, both explicitly and implicitly. There is evidence to suggest that children's conceptualizations of religious identity, morality, faith, images of God, and prayer all emerge in stages that parallel the Piagetian stages to some extent. In general, the progression involves a move from an inability to understand religious concepts at all early in life, through a very egocentric religion, to an understanding of religion limited to the concrete, and finally to a more abstract and complex religiousness.

Theoretical conceptualizations of religious growth generally (Elkind, Goldman), and of moral (Kohlberg) and faith (Fowler) development, have apparently been stimulated by Piaget's formulations. And much other work on religious development (e.g., images of God, concepts of prayer) has also used the Piagetian framework as the basis for empirical studies. The results of numerous investigations have confirmed the utility of Piaget's cognitive stages for understanding various aspects of religious growth. However, promising non-Piagetian theoretical conceptualizations have recently appeared in the psychology of religion. For example, Tamminen has directed attention to the religious experience of children, and Kirkpatrick has shown the potential of attachment theory for understanding aspects of religious growth.

In spite of attempts at integration of work on religious development, we are left with a kind of "smorgasbord" of differing directions, as Reich has noted.[197] This is not necessarily a bad thing, since this diversity has stimulated many different creative and useful empirical studies of religious development. Further integration of this work could eventually lead to a more comprehensive theory of religion in childhood. Beyond this integrative work, it has been suggested that future research in religious growth could take many potentially fruitful directions. The role of religion in parenting goals, styles, and practices, and the consequences for child development, are especially promising in this regard. Many other opportunities derive from important theoretical work in developmental and social psychology. In general, we expect that the research on the emergence of religion in childhood will move in a variety of promising new directions in the future.

NOTES

1. Allport (1950, p. 31).
2. Proverbs 13:24 (*The Holy Bible*, Authorized King James Version).
3. Child quoted by Goldman (1964, p. 1).
4. University student interviewed by one of us.
5. Elkind (1970).
6. See, e.g., Coe (1900).
7. Bandura (1977).
8. Jung (1933, 1938).
9. Elkind (1970).
10. Elkind (1970, p. 36).
11. Bouchard, Lykken, McGue, Segal, and Tellegen (1990).
12. See, e.g., Hickman (1926).
13. Allport (1950).
14. Hyde (1990).
15. Oser and Scarlett (1991).
16. Reich (1992).
17. Strommen (1971).
18. Allport (1950).
19. Allport (1950, p. 36).
20. Hyde (1990, p. 15).
21. Piaget (1932/1948, 1936/1952, 1937/1954).
22. Hyde (1990).
23. Piaget (1932/1948).
24. Elkind (1961, 1962, 1963, 1964, 1970, 1971).
25. Long, Elkind, and Spilka (1967).

26. Williams (1971).
27. Abraham (1981).
28. Goldman (1964, p. 5).
29. Degelman, Mullen, and Mullen (1984).
30. Peatling (1974, 1977); Peatling and Laabs (1975).
31. Tamminen (1976, 1991).
32. See Hyde (1990) for a review of these studies.
33. Zachry (1990, p. 405).
34. Hoge and Petrillo (1978b).
35. Hoge and Petrillo (1978b, pp. 142–143).
36. Batson, Schoenrade, and Ventis (1993, p. 62).
37. Godin (1968).
38. Howkins (1966).
39. Hyde (1990).
40. Hyde (1990, p. 35).
41. Greer (1983).
42. Kohlberg (1964, 1969, 1981, 1984).
43. Sapp (1986, p. 273).
44. Darley and Shultz (1990).
45. Bergling (1981).
46. Snarey (1985).
47. Kohlberg (1980, pp. 33–34).
48. Gorsuch and McFarland (1972).
49. Selig and Teller (1975).
50. Nucci and Turiel (1993).
51. Many papers could be cited in this regard, such as Bouhmama (1984); Clouse (1986); Eisenberg-Berg and Roth (1980); Ernsberger and Manaster (1981); Fernhout and Boyd (1985); Getz (1984); Hanson (1991); Kedem and Cohen (1987); Lee (1980); Mitchell (1988); and Wallwork (1980).
52. Rest (1979, 1983); Rest, Cooper, Coder, Masanz, and Anderson (1974).
53. Clouse (1991); Ernsberger and Manaster (1981); Holley (1991); Sapp (1986).
54. P. S. Richards (1991); Sapp (1986).
55. P. S. Richards (1991); Richards and Davison (1992).
56. Gilligan (1977, 1982).
57. Nelsen, Cheek, and Au (1985).
58. Reich (in press).
59. Scarlett and Perriello (1991).
60. Fowler (1981, 1991a, 1991b).
61. For an analysis of similarities between Fowler's and Kohlberg's theories, see Hanford (1991).
62. Fowler (1991a, p. 31).
63. Fowler (1991a, p. 32).
64. Fowler (1991a, p. 34).
65. Fowler (1991a, p. 41).
66. Fowler (1991a, p. 41).
67. Spilka, Hood, and Gorsuch (1985).
68. Hyde (1990).
69. Barnes and Doyles (1989).
70. Oser (1991); Oser and Gmunder (1984/1991); Oser and Reich (1990a, 1990b); Oser, Reich, and Bucher (1994).
71. Oser (1991, p. 6).
72. Oser (1991, p. 10).
73. Oser (1991, p. 13).
74. Oser (1991).
75. Bucher (1991).
76. See, e.g., Day (1994).
77. Freud (1913/1919, 1927/1961).
78. Jung (1948/ 1969).
79. Foster and Keating (1992).
80. Spilka, Addison, and Rosensohn (1975).
81. Vergote and Tamayo (1981).
82. Roberts (1989).

83. Godin and Hallez (1964); Potvin (1977).
84. Gorsuch (1988); Kirkpatrick (1986).
85. Harms (1944).
86. Deconchy (1965).
87. Ballard and Fleck (1975); Fowler (1981); Nye and Carlson (1984); Williams (1971).
88. Elkind (1970); Goldman (1964); Nye and Carlson (1984).
89. See, e.g., the review of European research on this topic by Tamminen, Vianello, Jaspard, and Ratcliff (1988).
90. Ladd, McIntosh, and Spilka (1994).
91. Janssen, de Hart, and Gerardts (1994).
92. Janssen et al. (1994, p. 116).
93. Tamminen (1991).
94. Tamminen (1991, p. 192).
95. Ladd, McIntosh, and Spilka (1994).
96. Vergote and Tamayo (1981).
97. Bassett et al. (1990); Graebner (1964).
98. Deconchy (1965).
99. Gorsuch (1968); Roberts (1989).
100. Janssen et al. (1994).
101. Ludwig, Weber, and Iben (1974).
102. Benson and Spilka (1973). The semantic differential technique requires that respondents rate a specific concept (e.g., "God") on a series of 7-point bipolar response scales (e.g., good to bad; cold to hot).
103. Benson and Spilka (1973); Nelson (1971); Spilka, Armatas, and Nussbaum (1964). In the Q-sort technique, individuals sort a set of cards containing statements into piles that range from "most characteristic" to "least characteristic" of an individual.
104. Gorsuch (1968).
105. Tamminen (1991).
106. Hutsebaut and Verhoeven (1995).
107. Spilka, Hood, and Gorsuch (1985, p. 70).
108. Hyde (1990, p. 64).
109. Long et al. (1967).
110. See, e.g., the review by Finney and Malony (1985c).
111. Worten and Dollinger (1986).
112. Brown (1966).
113. Scarlett and Perriello (1991).
114. Scarlett and Perriello (1991, p. 72).
115. Tamminen (1991).
116. Francis and Brown (1990, 1991).
117. Francis and Brown (1991, p. 120).
118. Francis and Brown (1991).
119. Brown (1994).
120. Brown (1994, p. 203).
121. Tamminen (1976, 1994); Tamminen et al. (1988).
122. Scarlett (1994, p. 88).
123. Scarlett (1994, p. 88).
124. There exist many published articles that attempt to draw practical implications from the theoretical and empirical work (e.g., implications for religious education or pastoral counseling).
125. Hyde (1990).
126. Francis (1994).
127. See, e.g., Eysenck (1981).
128. Francis, Pearson, and Kay (1982, 1983).
129. See, e.g., Francis and Gibson (1993).
130. See, e.g., McCartin and Freehill (1986).
131. Francis (1986).
132. Archer (1989).
133. de Vaus and McAllister (1987).
134. Albert and Porter (1986).
135. Florian and Kravetz (1985).
136. Stambrook and Parker (1987).
137. Saigh (1979); Saigh, O'Keefe, and Antoun (1984).

138. Tamminen (1994).
139. Francis, Pearson, and Kay (1988).
140. Francis (1979).
141. Hunsberger and Ennis (1982).
142. For a more thorough review, the reader is referred to Hyde (1990).
143. Kirkpatrick (1992); Kirkpatrick and Shaver (1990, 1992).
144. Bowlby (1969, 1973, 1980).
145. Kirkpatrick (1992, p. 4).
146. Kirkpatrick and Shaver (1990).
147. Kirkpatrick and Shaver (1990, p. 320).
148. Kirkpatrick and Shaver (1990, p. 331).
149. Kirkpatrick (1992); Kirkpatrick and Shaver (1992).
150. Reich (1993a, 1993b); see also Reich (1989, 1992, 1994).
151. Reich (1993b, p. 39).
152. Reich (1993a, p. 149).
153. Reich (1993a, p. 151).
154. Fowler (1993).
155. Gilligan (1977).
156. Wulff (1993).
157. See, e.g., Fitzgibbons (1987); Rizzuto (1991).
158. Erikson (1958, 1963, 1969).
159. Batson et al. (1993, p. 71).
160. Stambrook and Parker (1987); Florian and Kravetz (1985).
161. Forliti and Benson (1986).
162. Altemeyer (1988); Altemeyer and Hunsberger (1992).
163. Darling and Steinberg (1993).
164. Luft and Sorell (1987).
165. Bateman and Jensen (1958).
166. Nunn (1964).
167. Baumrind, D. (1967, 1991).
168. Buri, Louiselle, Misukanis, and Mueller (1988); Rohner (1994).
169. Holden and Edwards (1989).
170. Altemeyer (1988).
171. Zern (1987).
172. Ellison and Sherkat (1993).
173. Kelley, Power, and Wimbush (1992).
174. Wiehe (1990).
175. Grasmick, Morgan, and Kennedy (1992).
176. Zern (1984).
177. Neufeld (1979).
178. Bottoms, Shaver, Goodman, and Qin (1995).
179. Darling and Steinberg (1993).
180. Fugate (1980); Meier (1977).
181. Steinberg, Lamborn, Dornbusch, and Darling (1992).
182. Nunn (1964).
183. Nelsen and Kroliczak (1984, p. 269).
184. Nelsen and Kroliczak (1984).
185. De Vellis, De Vellis, and Spilsbury (1988).
186. Spilka, Hood, and Gorsuch (1985, p. 74).
187. Gorsuch and Wakeman (1991); Hill (1994); Hill and Bassett (1992).
188. Altemeyer (1988); Francis (1994).
189. Kirkpatrick (1992).
190. Higgins (1989).
191. McIntosh (1995).
192. Allport and Ross (1967).
193. Batson et al. (1993).
194. Batson et al. (1993).
195. Gorsuch (1988).
196. Gorsuch (1988).
197. Reich (1993b, p. 39).

Chapter 3

RELIGIOUS SOCIALIZATION AND THOUGHT IN ADOLESCENCE AND YOUNG ADULTHOOD

&

For approximately two-thirds of all children there is a reaction against parental and cultural teaching.[1]

Adolescence is a crisis of faith.[2]

I thought it was wrong to doubt the faith because—well, now I see that is kind of foolish, but back then it was really a serious concern of mine that I thought the teachers won't like this, my parents definitely won't like this. . . .[3]

One of the really frustrating things about Christianity . . . is how people claim to have such a deep faith in their religion, but I think it's absurd that you can just accept something you were born into without doubting it first.[4]

When I was a boy of fourteen my father was so stupid I could scarcely stand to have the old man around, but by the time I got to be twenty-one I was astonished at how much he had learned in the last seven years.[5]

RELIGIOUS SOCIALIZATION

Why do people believe what they do? Some people think that they have carefully considered different perspectives on issues and reached their own personal conclusions; that is why they hold certain religious beliefs. And they may feel that they would hold those beliefs regardless of their family upbringing, education, friends, cultural context, and so on. They feel that because they have reasoned things through, they have reached the best possible conclusions about religion, and because of the kind of people they are, they would have arrived at these same beliefs had they been raised in any family or culture. Others may feel that through divine revelation or historical precedent, they have special access to the "truth"—that God has singled them out to believe in the "one true religion."

The empirical evidence, of course, argues against such views. Study after study has shown the importance of the socialization process in determining people's present religious beliefs. In other words, you are what your environment has made you. If you had been born into a devout Muslim family, today you would be bowing toward Mecca. Or if you had been raised as a Pentecostal, you would sometimes speak in tongues. Or if your parents had been confirmed atheists, you would *not* believe in God today. (As Batson et al. put it, "If belief is a product of social influence, disbelief may also be."[6]) Or if you had grown up in a native culture you might believe in many gods.

In Chapter 1 we have discussed a variety of potential explanations for why people are religious. Similarly, various reasons have been proposed for people's underlying level of religious commitment, since the environment can influence individuals in many different ways. Five competing theoretical sources of religiousness have been suggested:[7]

1. *Deprivation* theory, often associated with the work of Glock and Stark,[8] suggests that religious commitment may somehow compensate for other deprivations in life.

2. *Status* theory suggests that religious commitment may in some ways be socially useful by increasing one's social status. For example, Goode found a positive correlation between church attendance and social status.[9]

3. *Localism* theory suggests that local communities may have well-defined and isolated community standards that encourage religious commitment. People living in more cosmopolitan contexts tend to be relatively free of such "local" expectations, and may therefore be less involved in religion.

4. In addition, it has been argued that *beliefs* are an important determining factor regarding religious involvement and commitment. That is, persons with strong religious beliefs are also likely to be strongly committed to their religion.

5. Finally, the *socialization* approach emphasizes the role of the culture in teaching children and adolescents religious beliefs and behaviors.

Other specific factors have also been suggested as determinants of religious commitment. For example, Ryan et al. have argued that guilt and fear determine religiousness;[10] Burris et al. have found that loneliness predicts religiousness;[11] and Erikson has linked religion to the "identity crisis," a major crisis that he argues occurs during adolescence.[12] These various explanations have been useful in helping to explain religious commitment. However, in this chapter we focus on the socialization explanation of religiousness— an approach that has marshaled a considerable body of empirical support, and that offers specific plausible explanations of religious influence, which have been studied in some detail.

"Socialization," as the term is used here, refers to the process by which a culture (usually through its primary agents, such as parents) encourages individuals to accept beliefs and behaviors that are normative and expected within that culture. As Long and Hadden put it, "The continuing thread in the socialization concept is the premise that society successfully shapes new members toward compliance with and adjustment to societal requirements."[13] Such socialization often involves a process of internalization, as noted by Ryan et al., "through which an individual transforms a formerly externally prescribed regulation or value into an internal one."[14] Johnstone has argued that people internalize the religion of their family or culture in essentially the same way that they learn their sex role, their language, or the lifestyle appropriate to their social class.[15] This is not to deny that people can become religious in other ways (e.g., see Chapter 8); rather, it is suggested that socialization (and internalization) serves as the usual basis for religiosity in adolescence and adulthood.

There is no single "socialization theory." As Slaughter-Defoe has pointed out, different theoretical traditions in the social sciences have influenced the study of socialization processes, including psychoanalytic, social learning, cognitive-developmental, and symbolic interactionist/role learning perspectives.[16] All of these have made contributions to our understanding of socialization, though we would argue that social learning theory has particular relevance for our consideration of the religious socialization process. As proposed by Bandura, social learning theory emphasizes the importance of observing and imitating others, as well as the role of reinforcement.[17] An important implication of this approach is that religiousness is typically strongly influenced by one's immediate environment, especially parents, through both modeling and reinforcement processes.

Many people find it difficult to accept the idea that, had they simply been born into a different cultural context, their religious beliefs would almost certainly be very different. And yet this is what the evidence regarding socialization suggests. There are exceptions to the rule, of course, and these require our attention. However, we first need to examine the childhood and adolescent religious socialization process; this then leads us to a discussion of adolescent and young adult thinking about religion, especially religious questions or doubts and their resolution. This in turn leads to a consideration of the processes involved in leaving the family religion (apostasy), which at first blush might seem to contradict socialization theory. But first, how and why does socialization exert such a strong influence on religiousness?

INFLUENCES ON RELIGIOUSNESS
IN CHILDHOOD AND ADOLESCENCE

Many external influences have the potential to affect people's religiousness: parents, peers, schools, religious institutions, books, the mass media, and so on. They can affect individuals directly through, for example, explicit religious teachings or family practices. They can also affect people indirectly in many ways—for example, by influencing school, marital, and career choices, or through cultural assumptions, subtle modeling, or lack of exposure to alternative positions. Persons may be conscious of some religious socialization influences, but quite unaware of others. Cornwall has noted that the religious socialization literature has traditionally focused on three "agents" of socialization: parents, peers, and church.[18] We examine each of these in turn, but consider church simply as one of a number of "other factors" that have been suggested to affect the religious socialization process. We also examine an additional factor that has been studied, education.

Our coverage of these potential influencing factors is largely restricted to the empirical work on religious socialization. There exists a rich body of literature in the psychodynamic and object relations traditions, especially with respect to the role of parents in the socialization process. The reader may wish to consult other sources for differing perspectives on these issues.[19]

The Influence of Parents

Parents constitute a good example of an influence that has both direct and indirect effects, and that may involve awareness or unawareness on the part of the children being socialized. Of the many different possible socialization influences, parents have typically been found to be the most important.

There is copious evidence that parents have considerable impact on the religiosity of their children, both when their offspring are younger and also when they are adolescents and young adults. We should not lose sight of the fact that socialization can be a two-way street, and children can also affect the attitudes and religiosity of parents, though there has not been a great deal of research on this issue.[20] But our focus here is on the many studies that have found parental religiousness and religious teachings to be major influences on their children's religiousness.

Some social scientists, such as Cornwall,[21] believe that parental influence occurs within the family as a "personal religious community" that may exist quite independently of institutionalized religion. This small community, of which the parents are an integral part, influences religiousness indirectly to some extent by affecting the "personal community relationship."[22] It is possible that this focus on personal religious communities may be most applicable in groups such as the Church of Jesus Christ of Latter-Day Saints (known to outsiders as the Mormons), which served as the empirical basis for Cornwall's conclusions about the religious socialization process. However, as Friedman[23] and Slaughter-Defoe[24] have pointed out, one's family of origin and the extended family are potentially very important in affecting one's socialization and functioning in a number of systems, including (but not limited to) religion. Although we recognize that parental influence may take place within the broader context of the family or a small community, we focus here specifically on parental influence.

To some extent, children lead sheltered lives; they may not be aware that there *are* other religions, or even people whose beliefs differ from their own. Parents often have a "captive audience" for their religious and other teachings, at least when their children are younger. Social learning theory would predict that children will be strongly influenced by these powerful and important parental models, as well as the reinforcement contingencies controlled by the parents.[25] Much evidence is consistent with this prediction, and social learning theory may be seen as the theoretical underpinning of the socialization process.

It is not a straightforward matter to tap "parental influence" in relevant studies of religious socialization. Some investigators simply focus on "keeping the faith"—the extent to which children identify with the family religion as they grow older. These investigators typically assume that keeping the family faith must result in large part from parental influence. Other researchers focus on parent–child attitudinal agreement regarding religious and other matters, assuming that greater agreement indicates more effective parental influence. Still others rely on direct self-reports of influence, asking children or adolescents about the extent to which parents influence their religiousness. Similarly, some investigators have asked older adolescents and adults to reflect back on their lives and consider to what extent parents (and other factors) influenced their religion.

All of these approaches have their problems. For example, identification with a religious group may mean different things for different denominations,[26] and may not always be a good indicator of parental influence. Parent–child attitudinal agreement does not necessarily mean that parental influence was strong, and people's self-reports and memories may be faulty. But, collectively, these different approaches offer insight into parental religious socialization influence.

Studies of "Keeping the Faith"

Hunsberger[27] studied several hundred university students from Roman Catholic, United Church[28] ("liberal Protestant"), and Mennonite ("conservative Protestant") families in Canada. These students were asked about the extent to which they accepted earlier religious teachings, as well as the strength of the emphasis placed on religion in their home. The correlation between these measures was +.44, indicating a self-reported moderate tendency for greater emphasis on religion in the childhood home to be linked with acceptance of religious teachings during the university years. However, a significant tendency remained for Mennonite students to be more accepting of religious teachings than United Church students (with Catholics being intermediate), even after differential emphasis on religious teachings in these groups was controlled for. This suggests that other factors unique to specific religious groups may also be important.

Elizabeth Weiss Ozorak has proposed a social-cognitive model of religious change in adolescence (see Research Box 3.1), which predicts that both social factors (such as parental

---

Research Box 3.1. Influences on Religious Beliefs and Commitment in Adolescence (Ozorak, 1989)

Elizabeth Ozorak noted that various explanations exist for adolescent change in religious beliefs and practices. For example, it has been proposed that influence from parents, peers, or others may be powerful factors; that "existential anxiety" may be an initiating factor; or (as we have seen in Chapter 2) that cognitive development can serve as the stimulus for such change. Ozorak sought to test a variety of possible effects within a "social-cognitive" model of religious change. She proposed that social influences, especially parents, are the most powerful factors affecting adolescent religiousness; that there is a gradual polarization of religious beliefs in the direction established relatively early in people's lives; and also that cognitive factors such as "existential questioning" are associated with decreased religious commitment.

After pilot-testing her materials on 9th- and 11th-graders, Ozorak studied 390 high school students and high school alumni from the Boston area. The subjects included 106 students in 9th grade, 150 students in 11th or 12th grade, and 134 alumni who had graduated 3 years earlier from two of the three high schools involved. Each participant completed a questionnaire including a wide variety of items and scales tapping religious affiliation, participation, beliefs, experiences, existential questioning, social "connectedness," family and peer influences, and religious change.

The data indicated that "middle adolescence is a period of [religious] readjustment for many individuals" (p. 455), with the average age of change being about 14.5 years. In general, social factors, especially parents, were powerful predictors of religiousness. For example, parents' religious affiliation and participation were positively related to children's religiousness. The influence of peers (discussed later in this chapter) was not so straightforward, though the data suggested that they too were related to adolescent religiosity. Cognitive factors also played a role in adolescent religiousness. More existential questioning and higher intellectual aptitude were associated with religious change, but only for the oldest age group (high school alumni). In addition, there was support for a "polarization" interpretation of the data, such that the most religious participants tended to report greater change in a proreligious direction and the least religious participants reported decreasing religiosity over time.

Ozorak thus concluded that "parents' affiliation and their faith in that affiliation act as cognitive anchors from which the child's beliefs evolve over time. Family cohesion seems to limit modification of religious practices but exerts less pressure on beliefs, which become increasingly individual with maturation" (p. 460). This study is important in that it reminds us of the powerful influence of *both* social and cognitive factors with respect to religious socialization. Furthermore, it emphasizes the critical role of parents in influencing their offspring's religiousness and religious change.

or peer influence) and cognitive variables (such as intellectual aptitude and existential questioning) will influence adolescent religiousness.[29] Her data support the social-cognitive model, especially with respect to the positive link between parental and adolescent religiousness, and she has concluded that parents are especially powerful influences in the religious socialization process. However, the influence of parents seemed more prominent for her high school subjects than for her college-aged respondents, suggesting that parental influence may decrease as adolescents make the transition to adulthood.

Other studies have also indicated that parental religiousness is a good predictor of adolescents' and even adult children's religiousness. For example, Benson et al. surveyed Catholic high school seniors and concluded that the three main factors predicting adolescent religiousness were perceptions of the importance of religion for the parents, positive family environment, and home religious activity.[30] Potvin and Sloane found, in a national probability sample of more than 1,000 U.S. adolescents, that parental religiosity was a significant predictor of adolescent religious practice.[31] Parker and Gaier noted that the religious participation of Jewish parents was a powerful predictor of the religious beliefs and practices of their adolescent children.[32] Hoge and Keeter reported that such influence might even extend into adulthood in a study of college teachers, who indicated that their parents' church attendance constituted the best predictor of their own religiousness.[33]

Similarly, studies by Hadaway,[34] Kluegel,[35] and others[36] have noted the very strong tendency for children raised within a specific familial religious denomination to continue to identify with that denomination through adolescence and young adulthood. In general, several different parental religion variables seem to be reasonable predictors of the extent to which adolescents and young adults maintain the family religion.

Parent–Child Agreement Studies

During the 1960s and 1970s there was interest in a possible "generation gap"—"a kind of organized rebellion against parents by their teenagers, one component of which supposedly involves considerable discrepancy between teenagers' attitudes and those of their parents."[37] Some researchers concluded that there was indeed a generation gap;[38] others contended that parent–adolescent attitudinal differences were relatively minor[39] or virtually nonexistent.[40] Bengtson and Troll have pointed out that parent–child attitudinal agreement may vary from one issue to another, and that religious attitudes in particular may involve more parent–child agreement than some other domains.[41]

A study of 143 Ontario university students, 127 of their mothers, and 109 of their fathers assessed agreement on religious as well as some nonreligious issues.[42] In general, there was moderate agreement on core religious beliefs, including scores on a scale of Christian Orthodoxy (correlations were .43 between students and their mothers and .48 between students and their fathers), and reports of frequency of church attendance (correlations were .58 and .57, respectively). Furthermore, there tended to be stronger parent–child agreement on religious matters than there was on some other issues (e.g., self-rated happiness, personal adjustment, political radicalism).

Other investigations of mother–father–adolescent triads have led to similar conclusions, though relationships are sometimes weak. Hoge, Petrillo, and Smith's study of triads from Catholic, Baptist, and Methodist homes showed weak to moderate correspondence between parents and their offspring on religious measures (higher for mothers than fathers), with creedal assent (i.e., endorsement of a specific creed) revealing stronger relationships.[43] These relationships remained significant when the effects of denomination, family income, and father's occupation were partialed out, though Hoge et al. emphasized that extrafamilial influences (e.g., denomination) were also important in religious socialization. Dudley and Dudley's mother–father–child triads from Seventh-Day Adventist homes revealed modest agreement across a series of religious and nonreligious values, with generally stronger relationships between offspring and mothers than between offspring and fathers.[44] Glass et al. carried out a study of three generations of family members, the youngest generation being between the ages of 16 and 26.[45] They concluded that there was substantial agreement on religious and political issues both for child–parent and for parent–grandparent dyads, suggesting that parental influence in these areas may persist into adulthood.

Hoge and Petrillo further reported that adolescent frequency of church attendance was correlated .60 with mothers' and .50 with fathers' attendance,[46] and Potvin, Hoge, and Nelsen found a correlation of .49 between the religious practice of Catholic parents and their adolescent offspring.[47]

Such findings of weak to moderately strong parent–adolescent agreement on religious issues do not "prove" that parents are important influences in their children's religious lives, of course. But such results are consistent with the data obtained through other approaches, which suggest that parents are indeed influential in this regard. Certainly, if parents play an important role in their children's religious development, one would expect to find at least modest correlations between measures of adolescent and parental religiousness. Interestingly, in Hunsberger's study,[48] parents were reasonably accurate estimators of the religious beliefs and practices of their college-aged children, *unless* those children had drifted away from the family religious teachings. When the children had become apostates (i.e., had abandoned the home religion), parents were significantly poorer predictors of their children's religious attitudes than when they had remained in the family religion. This might suggest that parents are relatively unaware of adolescent shifts away from the family religion when they occur, or, as argued by Bengtson and Troll,[49] that the parents tend to minimize differences between themselves and their adolescent children.

There also seems to be a tendency for adolescents to perceive that their parents are more conservative or traditional than the parents report themselves to be. Acock and Bengtson found that there was greater correspondence between adolescents' views and *perceived* parents' attitudes, compared to actual parents' views, in both religious and nonreligious realms.[50] Adolescents also perceived more attitudinal agreement between their parents than in fact existed. Thus, there seems to be a tendency for youths to perceive that their parents are more conservative and in more agreement than they really are, and these misperceptions may have some influence on the socialization process.

It is to be noted that the findings of these parent–adolescent agreement studies are generally consistent with recent conceptualizations of adolescence as a time of reasonably stable development and socialization, as well as considerable similarity in values and attitudes between parents and their adolescent offspring. This is in contrast to earlier conceptualizations of adolescence as a time of turmoil and rebellion, resulting in a sizeable "generation gap." This shift in our view of adolescence is reflected, for example, in Petersen's review of the adolescent development literature.[51]

Self-Reports of Religious Influence

In a pioneering study carried out in the 1940s, Allport and his colleagues found that about two-thirds of a Harvard and Radcliffe student sample reported having reacted against parental and cultural teaching.[52] However, these students indicated that the influences underlying their sense of need for religious sentiment included the following (with the percentage of respondents mentioning each particular influence shown in parentheses): parents (67%), other people (57%), fear (52%), church (40%), and gratitude (37%). Clearly, parents were perceived to play a central role in the development of religious sentiment.

More recent studies involving a wide variety of age groups in North America and elsewhere have confirmed that parents are perceived to be the most important influence on religiosity. Hunsberger and Brown asked 878 introductory psychology students at the University of New South Wales in Sydney, Australia to identify the three people who had the greatest influence on their religious beliefs.[53] Parents were clearly the "winners," being designated as the most important influence by 44% of all respondents (friends came next at 15%). In subsequent studies, Hunsberger asked several hundred students at a Canadian university,[54] and 85 older persons (aged 65 to 88 years), [55] to rate the extent of religious influence of 10 possible sources of influence in their lives. Both the students and the older persons ranked their mothers and fathers first and third, respectively. Church received the second highest ranking (see Table 3.1).

The difference in mean rating for adjacent categories is typically not large. However, one striking thing about Table 3.1 is the extent to which the students and seniors agreed in their rankings (rho = .67).[56] The seniors generally reported stronger absolute proreligious influence—a finding consistent with other cross-sectional studies by Benson[57] and Hunsberger,[58] and a panel study of Swedes by Hamberg,[59] showing a general increase in religiosity across the adult years. Substantial differences emerged only for friends (which students ranked as the fifth most important influence and seniors ninth) and reading (which students ranked eighth and seniors fourth). Given the huge age discrepancy and differing backgrounds of these two groups, it is impressive how similar their overall rankings of religious influences were. Furthermore, the rankings for the university students were quite similar to those given by Australian university students,[60] though the latter ranked only different *people* and therefore did not rate influences such as "church," "personal experiences," or "habit."

TABLE 3.1. Mean Rating of 10 Influences on Religious Development: University Students and Senior Citizens Compared

Source of influence	University students		Seniors	
	M rating	Rank	M rating	Rank
Mother	5.33	1	6.34	1
Church	4.99	2	6.28	2
Father	4.78	3	5.72	3
Personal experience	4.74	4	5.06	6
Friends	4.49	5	4.76	9
Habit	4.41	6	5.16	5
Relatives	4.39	7	4.98	7
Reading	4.35	8	5.28	4
School	4.32	9	4.78	8
Media	3.88	10	4.64	10

Note. Adapted from Hunsberger (1983b, 1985b). Copyright 1985 by the Gerontological Society of America. Adapted by permission. The student sample included 371 introductory psychology students. The senior sample included 85 people aged 65 to 88, typically from the same geographical area (southern Ontario) as the students. "M rating" is the average score derived from an item that asked participants to rate the extent to which each possible source had influenced their religious development, from −3 ("a strong negative influence") through 0 (neutral) to +3 ("a strong positive influence"), converted to a 1–7 scale. Thus, higher scores above 4 indicate stronger proreligious influence, on average.

Francis and Gibson explored parental influence on religious attitudes and practices of 3,414 secondary school students in Scotland (ages 11–12 and 15–16), with approximately equal numbers of males and females in each age category.[61] Primary dependent measures included self-report of frequency of church attendance, and scores on a 24-item Likert-type scale[62] measuring attitudes toward Christianity.[63] These authors concluded that parental influence was generally important across their participants with respect to church attendance, and there was a tendency for this influence to *increase* from the younger to the older age groups. Consistent with some of Hunsberger's[64] and Acock and Bengtson's[65] findings, they also concluded that mothers had more influence on children's religion than fathers overall, but there was some tendency toward stronger same-sex influence for both mothers and fathers. Also, parental influence was greater for overt religiosity (i.e., church attendance) than it was for more covert religiosity (i.e., attitudes toward Christianity).

In two separate studies of attitudinal predispositions to pray, described in Research Box 3.2, Francis and Brown concluded that parental influence was of primary importance with respect to church attendance for adolescents attending Roman Catholic, Anglican, and nondenominational schools in England.[66] Church attendance, in turn was positively related to attitudes toward prayer. Also, as in the Francis and Gibson study,[67] they found that mothers seemed to exert more influence than fathers, although parental influence was stronger when both parents attended church.

**Research Box 3.2. Social Influence on the Predisposition to Pray
(Francis & Brown, 1990, 1991)**

These two studies focused on predispositions to pray, as well as the practice of prayer, among two age levels of English adolescents. The first investigation involved almost 5,000 students aged 11, and the second about 700 students aged 16; in both studies, all students attended Roman Catholic, Church of England, or nondenominational state-maintained schools. As well as self-reports of their own and their parents' religious behavior, participants completed a six-item scale assessing attitudes toward prayer (e.g., "Saying my prayers helps me a lot").

Results confirmed that the parents were powerful factors with respect to children's church attendance at both age levels, though mothers consistently exerted more influence than fathers. However, there were indications that parental impact on children's prayer had decreased somewhat, and that church influences (e.g., attendance) had increased, for the 16-year-olds. Attendance at Roman Catholic or Church of England schools did not seem to affect adolescent *practice* of prayer, after other factors had been controlled for; however, there was a slightly negative impact of Church of England schools on *attitudes* toward prayer.

The authors concluded their 1991 paper by stating that their findings "support the importance of taking seriously social learning or modeling interpretations of prayer. Children and adolescents who pray seem more likely to do so as a consequence of explicit teaching or implicit example from their family and church community than as a spontaneous consequence of developmental dynamics or needs" (p. 120).

Mother versus Father Influence

Not all research findings confirm that mothers are more influential than fathers. Kieren and Munro, for example, concluded that fathers were more influential than mothers overall.[68] And the findings of some other studies have been equivocal in this regard.[69] But the weight of the evidence suggests that mothers are more influential than fathers. Mothers may well serve a primary nurturing role with respect to religious socialization, since in Western cultures women are, on average, more religious than men,[70] and women also tend to assume more child-rearing responsibilities.[71] They may, for example, assume primary responsibility for taking children to church and teaching them basic religious views. Because of this, it is not surprising that people typically perceive that their mothers exerted a stronger influence on their religiousness.

However, it is quite possible that fathers also play an important role, to the extent that their religious views are consistent or inconsistent with those of mothers and the church. Fathers may serve as role models for continued religiousness, or for rejection of religion after initial religious socialization. Thus, mothers and fathers may play somewhat different roles and have differential influence at different periods in their children's socialization. This could well contribute to seemingly contradictory conclusions in the literature concerning the relative importance of mothers and fathers inreligious socialization. Research is needed to assess this speculation.

Other Aspects of Parenting

A number of studies have suggested that the *quality* of one's relationships with parents can also affect religious socialization. For example, Wilson and Sherkat found, in a panel investigation spanning the years 1965 to 1982, that children who reported while in high school that they had a warm, close relationship with their parents were less likely to rebel against religious teachings.[72] Furthermore, the investigators' longitudinal data led them to conclude that "Lack of closeness and contact have created a religious gap between parents and children rather than religious differences creating a distant relationship."[73] In a similar vein, Herzbrun found evidence in a study of Jewish adolescents that fathers' communication and emotional support were related to father–adolescent religious consensus.[74] Hoge and his colleagues,[75] Dudley,[76] Nelsen,[77] and Thomas and Weigert[78] have come to similar conclusions regarding the importance of the emotional relationship between parents and adolescents.

Similarly, more general parental values and behavior may affect some aspects of the religious socialization process. Ellison and Sherkat found that parental valuation of obedience was associated with theological positions of Biblical literalism, belief that human nature is sinful, and punitive attitudes toward sinners.[79] Nelsen reported that parental disharmony (e.g., arguing and fighting) inhibited the transmission of religiosity across successive generations.[80] Moreover, as suggested in Chapter 2, adult parenting values, goals, and practices may have important implications for children's subsequent religious orientation.

Although it is clear that parents play an important role in the religious socialization process, the relationship is not always a simple one. The behavior, goals, attitudes, and values of the parents, as well as the quality of their relationship with their children, may facilitate or inhibit their children's religious socialization. Unfortunately, as D'Antonio and colleagues[81] and Cornwall and Thomas[82] have pointed out, there is a dearth of research on the subtle interplay between family life and religion.

Summary

All of the different approaches to studying parental influence in the religious socialization process converge on a single conclusion: Parents play an extremely important role in the developing religious attitudes and practices of their offspring. In fact, few researchers would quarrel with the conclusion that parents are *the* most important influence in this regard. Other reviewers of the related literature have come to similar conclusions.[83] However, Erickson[84] and Cornwall[85] have pointed out that parental influence can sometimes be more indirect than direct. For example, parents to some extent are "managers" who control which "other influences" their children are exposed to (e.g., through church attendance, selection of religious vs. secular schooling, etc.), and these in turn may have some influence on young people's religion. Furthermore, different aspects of the parental and parent–adolescent relationships can affect the strength of parental influence on young people's religion, and mother–father consistency and agreement also seem to enhance acceptance of the parental religious teachings.[86]

The Influence of Peers

Various authors have concluded that peer groups play an important role in influencing adolescents generally,[87] but relatively few studies have investigated peer influence on religiousness. Those that have done so, tend to report some, but relatively weak, peer group effects. Such studies almost always rely on self-reports of peer influence, and the direction of the influence (positive or negative) is not always specified.

David De Vaus[88] compared the impact of parents and peers in a study of 375 Australian youths aged 16 to 18. Consistent with previous research by Bengtson and Troll,[89] he concluded that parents were more influential for religious beliefs, and that peers tended to have more influence outside of the religious realm (e.g., with respect to self-concept); however, he found that peers also influenced religious practice to some extent, as noted by Hoge and Petrillo.[90] Erickson also found that peer influence was relatively unimportant in adolescent religiousness,[91] though he pointed out that peer influences might be hidden because of the way in which such influences and religious education were measured, since religious education "is also a social/friendship setting."[92]

Similarly, Hunsberger's studies involving self-ratings of religious influences showed that friends were well down the list of 10 potential influences for both university students (fifth) and seniors (ninth) (see Table 3.1).[93] Also, Ozorak concluded that peers do influence adolescent religiousness, though this relationship is rather complex and is overshadowed by more important parental influences.[94]

Of course, peer influence may be stronger in some areas than in others.[95] For example, Hoge and Petrillo found that peers may have little influence for core religion measures such as frequency of church attendance, but may be more important with respect to youth group participation and enjoyment of that participation.[96]

In an exception to the usual "self-report" studies in this area, Carey carried out a field experiment.[97] A total of 102 Catholic school students in seventh grade were randomly assigned to one of three groups: proreligion, antireligion, or no influence (control group).

Confederates (boys who were "leaders" in the same classes as the other participants) urged their classmates to comply or not to comply with a nun's talk on "Why a Catholic should go to daily Mass." Actual attendance at Mass was then monitored, and an effect did emerge for the position taken by the male confederates to influence their peers, but only for girls. Of course, the peer influence assessed in this study was very specific and short-term; we should be careful not to confuse such transitory impact with more general, long-term, and complex peer effects.

Finally, we should not assume that peer influence is relevant only to child and adolescent religion. Olson found that within five Baptist congregations, the number and quality of friendships were important predictors of adults' decisions to join or leave a denomination.[98] Unfortunately, there has been little investigation of possible peer influence on religiousness in adulthood, beyond friendship networks.

Does Education Make a Difference?

The Impact of College

The influence of education on religious socialization has been a somewhat controversial topic. Early studies generally concluded that education, especially college, tended to "liberalize" religious beliefs of students. For example, an extensive review of more than 40 studies led Feldman to conclude in 1969 that these studies

> generally show mean changes indicating that seniors, compared with freshmen, are somewhat less orthodox, fundamentalistic, or conventional in religious orientation, somewhat more sceptical about the existence and influence of a Supreme Being, somewhat more likely to conceive of God in impersonal terms, and somewhat less favorable toward the church as an institution. Although the trend across studies does exist, the mean changes are not always large, and in about a third of the cases showing decreasing favorability toward religion, differences are not statistically significant (considering only those studies that have given results of statistical tests of significance).[99]

These conclusions are consistent with those of Parker, whose 1971 review of the literature led to the conclusion that religious change may be considerable during the college years, especially in the first year.[100]

We must be cautious about "net" change, however, since it may mask substantial change in the opposite direction for *some* students.[101] In addition, if change occurs, it does not necessarily mean that education caused the change. Shifts away from orthodox religion may be part of a maturational or developmental change, or may result from the fact that some students are effectively away from parental control for the first time. Such shifts may also reflect peer influence or a tendency for less religious (or more questioning) students to attend (and not to drop out of) college, or at least to avoid campus religious involvement. Madsen and Vernon found a (not surprising) tendency for more religious students to be more likely to participate in campus religious activities; also, those students who participated in campus religious groups tended to increase in religious orthodoxy, but nonparticipants became less orthodox at college.[102] It is also possible that apparent effects of college are actually due to other factors. Hoge and Keeter found little effect of college on religion after they partialed out the effects of religious background.[103]

Furthermore, the findings of more recent studies have not always been consistent with Feldman's conclusion that there is a general shift away from traditional religion. For example, Hunsberger reported a cross-sectional study of more than 450 university students, and a separate longitudinal investigation of more than 200 students from their first to their third university years, including an interim assessment of about half of this longitudinal sample during their second year.[104] His data offered little support for the proposal that students generally become less religious over their years at university. The only consistent finding across both studies (cross-sectional and longitudinal) was that seniors reported attending church less frequently than did freshmen. Thus, there was limited support for a decrease in religious practices across the college years, but this change did not generalize to some other practices (e.g., frequency of prayer) or to a series of religious belief measures. Finally, the data indicated that measures of "average change" did not mask frequent or dramatic individual religious change in different directions.

Hunsberger speculated that college-related religious change may have been more characteristic of the 1960s, since other subsequent studies by Hastings and Hoge[105] and Pilkington et al.[106] also found little or no change. Moberg and Hoge, in fact, concluded that the decade 1961–1971 had seen considerable shifts toward liberalism in college students, but that the following decade (1971–1982) involved a slight change in the opposite direction (toward conservatism and traditional moral attitudes).[107] Finally, Hunsberger suggested that religious change may be more likely to happen in the high school years, and may be relatively complete by the time students reach college[108]—a suggestion supported by the research of Francis[109] and Sutherland.[110]

Parochial School Attendance

Some investigations have compared public with parochial schools regarding the religiousness of their students. These investigations have generated rather muddy findings, possibly because of methodological shortcomings, as noted by Benson et al.[111] and Hyde.[112] Although some researchers, such as Lenski[113] and Greeley,[114] have concluded that parochial school attenders are more strongly religious in some ways than their public school counterparts, the relevant research has sometimes failed to take background factors into account. Some investigators apparently assumed that differences between parochial and public school students were *caused* by the environments of the schools involved, and they ignored possible self-selection factors. Mueller found that when he held religious background constant, he could find no differences in religious orthodoxy and institutional involvement of college students.[115] He concluded that "high orthodoxy is a direct function of a strong religious background rather than specifically of parochial school attendance."[116]

Other research has supported this finding, including studies of fundamentalists by Erickson,[117] Jews by Parker and Gaier,[118] Lutherans by Johnstone,[119] Mennonites by Kraybill,[120] and Catholics and Church of England adherents by Francis and Brown.[121] The last authors argued that a positive relationship between Roman Catholic school attendance and positive attitudes toward prayer was really a result of "the influence of home and church rather than that of the school itself."[122] Furthermore, as indicated in Research Box 3.2, their investigation even detected a small *negative* influence of Church of England schools on attitudes toward prayer, after other factors were controlled for (gender, home, church, private practice of prayer)—a finding consistent with Francis's previous work with younger children.[123] However, these sorts of conclusions have been challenged by some authors, such as

Greeley and his colleagues,[124] and Himmelfarb has argued that church-related schools do indeed have a direct positive influence on the religiousness of their students.[125]

In the end, it is probable that there is variation across individual schools, different age groups (elementary, high school, and postsecondary students), and possibly different religious denominations. Self-selection factors may well be operating at parochial schools, and findings may differ across studies, depending on whether they focus on religious beliefs or practices.[126] Effects may be unique to specific studies, or may depend on combinations of factors. For example, Benson et al. found that Catholic high schools with a high proportion of students from low-income families tended to have a positive influence on religiousness *if* those schools stressed academics and religion, had high student morale, and also focused on the importance of religion and the development of "community of faith."[127] There may also be effects for some specific measures of religiousness, such as an increase in religious *knowledge*, as found by Johnstone.[128] As Benson et al. have pointed out, it is often very difficult to separate the influence of parochial schools from the effects of parents and the family generally.[129]

In light of the findings available, and the many qualifications these findings entail, we are led to this conclusion: The bulk of the evidence suggests that church-related school attendance has little direct influence on adolescent religiousness per se. The issue is not clear-cut, however, and the reader might wish to consult more comprehensive reviews of the relevant literature.[130]

Recently, Erickson reported that religious education was of "overwhelming influence" in adolescent religious socialization.[131] However, "religious education" was very broadly defined, including involvement in religious activities, knowledge gained from religious instruction, and perceptions of religious education programs. In fact, as defined by Erickson and some others, "religious education" apparently has little to do with formal (school) education or educational institutions, but is more a measure of church involvement and activity. In this sense, church-related involvement can clearly be an important contributor to the religious socialization process, as discussed below.

Other Influences

As noted in the preceding discussion of religious influences, parents, peers, and education are not the only potential sources of influence on religiousness. Some studies have suggested that the particular religious institution or denomination, as well as social class, sibling configuration, and many other factors (city size, the mass media, reading, etc.), can also have some effect on the religious socialization process.[132] Self-reported ratings of influence[133] and more indirect inferences[134] suggest that factors related to the institutional church (or religious education, broadly defined) are the most important. Francis and Brown have observed that church becomes a more important influence in middle adolescence, at roughly the time when young people are becoming less susceptible to parental influence with respect to religion.[135]

There seems to be some overlap in the consideration of church-related influences and more general educational influences in the literature. As noted above, the term "religious education" is sometimes used to describe this area where church and education boundaries blur. The *Review of Religious Research*, for example, devoted an entire issue to adolescent religious socialization in the context of religious education. It included articles by Hoge and his coresearchers examining the goals of religious educators and parents ("moral maturity" ranked highest in most denominations studied);[136] by Nelsen on the influence of religious denomination in affecting religious education goals;[137] and by Philibert and Hoge on the processes of religious education.[138]

In general, however, these other factors have received scant empirical attention. There is a need for further investigation of attitudes toward the church, the role of the clergy, the influence of church-related peers compared to non-church-related friends, and so on, as well as the subtle interplay among these and other religious socialization factors.

The Polarization Hypothesis

Earlier we have mentioned Ozorak's social-cognitive model of religious socialization processes, which allows for the possibility of a "polarization" effect in religious development. That is, Ozorak noted a tendency for more religious adolescents to report change in the direction of greater religiosity, whereas less religious adolescents reported a shift away from religion (see Research Box 3.1). Tamminen found a similar religious polarization tendency among Finnish adolescents.[139] This is consistent with Madsen and Vernon's observation that more religious college students joined campus religious groups and also increased in religious orthodoxy while at college, but that less religious students who did not join campus religious groups decreased in orthodoxy; in other words, the religious "distance" between these two groups increased at college.[140] Hunsberger found similar polarization tendencies among the most and least religious participants in his study of seniors.[141] Reflecting back over their lives and "graphing" their religiosity across the decades, these seniors indicated that they had gradually become more religious across their lives since childhood if they were highly religious at the time of the study. However, seniors who were relatively less religious indicated that they had become progressively *less* religious across their lives, compared to their more religious counterparts.

These studies are limited by the retrospective, cross-sectional, and self-report nature of the data, as well as by the possibility that we are learning more about people's perceptions of reality than we are about reality itself. However, the findings are consistent with the possibility that general trends toward greater or lesser religiosity may be established quite early in life, and that these trends may continue long after early developmental and socialization influences have had their immediate effects. More research is needed to evaluate the polarization hypothesis.

Gender Differences

Social influences (especially the influence of parents) in the religious socialization process can help to explain some important differences in adolescent and adult religiosity. For example, women have typically been found to be "more religious" than men.[142] They attend worship services more often, pray more often, express stronger agreement with traditional beliefs, are more interested in religion, and report that religion is more important in their lives. Batson et al. have proposed that this consistent sex difference is most likely attributable to social influence processes in sex role training, either through sex differences that have implications for religiousness (e.g., women are taught to be more submissive and nurturing—traits associated with greater religiosity), or through direct expectations that women should be more religious than men.[143] Similar "socialization" interpretations have come from others such as Nelsen and Potvin,[144] though these are not the only possible interpretations of gender differences in religion.[145]

It is likely that religious socialization processes have important implications for other areas of people's lives, such as (nonreligious) attitudes, careers and education. For example, an examination of national survey data from 19,000 U.S. women by Keysar and Kosmin led them to conclude that religious identification affects educational attainment more strongly than do other sociodemographic variables.[146] Women from more conservative, traditional, or fundamentalist backgrounds achieved less postsecondary education than did women from more liberal or modern religious backgrounds, on average. That is, "some gender inequality is indeed socially created by the influence of religion."[147] Thus, although this was a correlational study, it does raise the possibility that religious socialization can ultimately affect "nonreligious" aspects of one's life.

Summary and Implications

We must be cautious in drawing conclusions about religious socialization influences, since it is often difficult to isolate parental, church, educational, and other influences and their possible interactions. Also, relevant studies sometimes investigate very different samples. Some include a broad range of participants; others draw their samples from church or other religious sources; and still others focus on members of one specific religious group. Measures and data analysis techniques differ widely from one study to another, and the extent to which influence is positive or negative is not always assessed. However, given the large numbers of relevant studies and the convergence of some findings, we are able to offer some general conclusions.

Parents are potentially the most powerful influences on child and adolescent religion, though their impact becomes weaker as adolescents grow into adulthood, and some of their influence may be indirect. Mothers are often found to be more influential than fathers, though there is not complete agreement on this issue. Beyond parental impact, church is most often found to be a significant contributor to religious socialization, but there has been little investigation of specific components of this relationship. Education, parochial school environment, the mass media, and reading have *not* been found to affect religious socialization to any great degree. It has been suggested by Hyde, however, that when the parents and other potential influential agents (e.g., the church) reinforce the same religious perspective, the resulting combined religious socialization effects may be especially strong.[148]

Finally, it is important that we not lose sight of possible implications of religious socialization for other aspects of people's lives. We have seen that religious growth processes can have a potentially powerful impact on gender issues. No doubt the influence of religious socialization extends into many other aspects of people's lives as well, as discussed throughout this book.

HOW RELIGIOUS ARE ADOLESCENTS AND YOUNG ADULTS?

Findings have quite consistently confirmed that in general, adolescents and young adults are less religious than middle and older adults in North America and Europe.[149] Moreover, religiousness is typically found to decrease during the 10- to 18-year-old period,[150] at least for mainstream religious groups.[151] However, this should not be construed to mean that adolescents are not religious, or that religion has little impact on their lives.

In Allport et al.'s 1948 study of religion among college students,[152] they found that approximately 7 out of every 10 students sampled felt they needed religion in their own lives

(82% of the women and 68% of the men). Furthermore, only 6% of the men and 10% of the women reported a total absence of religious training. As might be expected, students trained in religion reported that they needed religion more often than others, leading Allport et al. to conclude that early training is likely to be the principal psychological influence upon an individual's later religious life. Overall, 15% of Allport et al.'s sample denied engaging in any religious practices or experiencing any religious states of mind during the preceding 6-month period.

Other early studies also point to the importance of religion in the lives of university students. In a 1962 study, Webster et al. observed that at entrance to college, about 90% of National Merit Scholarship winners felt a need to believe in a religion.[153] Havens noted in 1963 that about 12% of college students had a critical concern about, or even an acute crisis because of, their religious conflicts.[154] And Havighurst and Keating concluded in 1971 that "The data indicate most youth are honestly and at times somewhat desperately trying to 'make sense' of their religious beliefs."[155]

But have times changed? Some countries have apparently experienced considerable decreases in church attendance and religious belief in the last 50 years or so. For example, Bibby has estimated that about 6 in 10 Canadians were weekly church attenders in the 1940s.[156] However, this figure dropped steadily until the early 1990s, when the comparable figure was just over 2 in 10 people. A drop was noted for both adults and adolescents, though adolescents generally are less inclined toward regular church involvement than are their elders. Just 17% of 18- to 29-year-olds were weekly attenders in 1990, compared to 40% of those 50 and over. Also, the general "disengagement from religion" is apparent regardless of the measure of religion used (e.g., beliefs, practice, self-rated importance of religion).[157] Furthermore, the tendency toward decreased religious involvement has brought Canada more in line with other countries, such as Britain, France, Germany, the Netherlands, and the Scandinavian countries. Typically, in these European countries less than 10% of the population is involved in the churches,[158] and regular attendance is correspondingly low.[159] Francis has noted a progressive trend in the 1970s and 1980s for British adolescents to have less positive attitudes toward Christianity.[160] Also, professing "no religion" is more common in Australia than it is in the United States,[161] and religious involvement is much lower in Australia and Japan than in the United States.[162]

However, as Bibby has pointed out,[163] figures for the United States suggest that there has *not* been a general disengagement from religion, and religious involvement remains relatively high for both adults and adolescents. "As of the early 1990s, the U.S. has what many regard to be a world-leading weekly church attendance level of 40%, which has changed little in 60 years."[164] Although weekly church attendance among high school seniors declined modestly from about 41% in 1976 to just 31% in 1991,[165] almost 60% of these students said religion was "pretty" or "very" important to them in 1991—a finding almost identical to the 1976 percentage. Chaves and Cavendish[166] and Hadaway et al.[167] have argued that there is some evidence that self-reports of church attendance may be substantially inflated, at least in the United States. However, Campbell and Curtis have concluded that studies involving comparable data sources suggest that, relatively speaking, regular church attendance in the United States tends to be quite high, even when other factors are controlled for.[168] Overall, U.S. attendance rates have remained quite stable across recent decades, according to Chaves[169] and Firebaugh and Harley,[170] though the interpretation of this stability has been a source of some disagreement.[171]

Similarly, Harley and Firebaugh found that belief in an afterlife was high (about 80%) and stable from 1973 to 1991, according to General Social Survey data from the United States.[172] Benson and colleagues reported survey data for U.S. high school seniors, obtained by the Survey Research Center of the Institute for Social Research at the University of Michigan, concerning several indicators of religiousness—percentages of these adolescents who attended church weekly, who said that religion was very important to them, or who claimed no religious affiliation.[173] Figure 3.1 shows the trends for these variables across the 10-year period from 1976 to 1985. In general, the figure shows stability of religiousness across these 10 years, with a slight decrease in weekly church attendance.

Overall, it seems fair to conclude, as Cobb has, that "religious beliefs are an important aspect of adolescents' lives"[174] in the United States, and also, as Benson et al. have, that religion has a powerful impact on adolescents and their development.[175] It is not clear why the United States should be a "more religious" society than Canada, Australia, Japan, and highly developed European countries. However, it has been suggested by Bibby[176] and Finke and Stark[177] that cultural differences are important, particularly the role that religious groups have played in U.S. society over time. Bibby has also pointed to the successful tendency for U.S. religious groups to "service the spiritual needs of Americans."[178] Similar sentiments are expressed by Hadaway and Roof, who have concluded that in the United States, disaffiliation is not simply indicative of a shift in religiousness; rather, disaffiliation is also symbolic in an important way, representing "a deep shift in outlook and lifestyles."[179]

RELIGIOUS THINKING AND REASONING IN ADOLESCENCE AND YOUNG ADULTHOOD

Religious socialization processes clearly involve powerful influences during childhood and adolescence. In the past, these factors were characterized as affecting beliefs and practices, but little attention was devoted to the possibility that they might also alter *styles* of thinking about religion. In terms of Ozorak's social-cognitive model of religious development in adolescence,[180] previous research has emphasized social aspects. Here, we focus on cognitive change. It seems plausible that when individuals are being taught (directly and indirectly) about religion, they may be learning much more than simply what to believe and how to practice their faith. They may also be learning unique ways of thinking about religion.

As we have seen in Chapter 2, a developmental shift in thinking about religious (and other) issues occurs as young people move from childhood to adolescence. In Piagetian terms, this shift is from concrete to formal operations, which (especially for religious concepts) involves a move away from the literal toward more abstract thinking. It has also been suggested that this trend toward abstract religious thought may be linked with decreased religiousness, and possibly with a tendency to reject religion in adolescence. Possibly adolescents' emerging abstract thinking capability "complicates" their religious thought, and may even stimulate new styles of thinking in order to deal with "difficult-to-explain" religious concepts.

Reich's Complementarity Reasoning

Reich has pointed out that there are "many perceived contradictions and paradoxes that characterize religious life."[181] He suggests that "complementarity reasoning" may develop

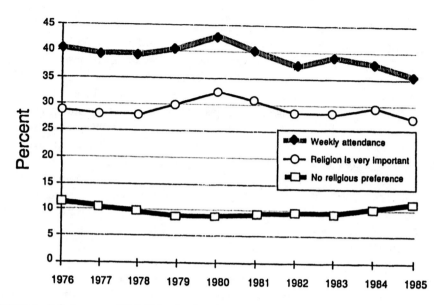

FIGURE 3.1. Religiousness of U.S. high school seniors, 1976–1985. From Benson, Donahue, and Erickson (1989, p. 156). Copyright 1989 by JAI Press, Inc. Reprinted by permission.

in order to deal with such religious contradictions. That is, people may develop "rational" explanations for specific perceived contradictions, which make the contradictions seem more apparent than real. Reich gives the example of a 20-year-old who attempts to explain the seeming conflict between creationist and evolutionary explanations of our origins and development as a species: "The possibility of evolution was contained in God's 'kick-off' at the origin . . . but God probably did not interfere with evolution itself . . . and perhaps so far not all of the initial potential has yet come to fruition."[182] Reich suggests that complementarity reasoning is crucial to religious development, though it "emerges in fully developed form relatively late in life, if at all."[183]

Reich proposes a kind of developmental analysis involving five different levels of complementarity reasoning. Essentially, these evolve from a very simplified (true–false) resolution of different explanations, through careful consideration of various competing explanations, to possible links between competing explanations and possibly even the use of an overarching theory or synopsis to assess complex relationships among the different factors. This analysis is similar to "integrative complexity" analyses of religious (and other) thinking (see below), and the complexity approach has the advantage of a well-established scoring system tapping different levels of thinking. Although we cannot at this time assess the developmental aspects of Reich's proposal, we can examine possible links between religious orientation and complexity of thinking processes. This has been done in several studies of university students.

Integrative Complexity of Thought

Defining and Scoring Complexity

Integrative complexity is defined by two cognitive stylistic variables. "Differentiation" involves the acknowledgment and tolerance of different perspectives or dimensions of an issue, and "integration" deals with the extent to which differentiated perspectives or dimensions are linked. A complexity scoring manual prepared by Baker-Brown et al. describes how integrative complexity is typically scored on a 1–7 scale.[184] Lower scores indicate the person's tendency not to reveal (1) or to reveal (3) differentiation; higher scores (4–7) indicate the extent to which people integrate these differentiated concepts into broader structures. As described in Research Box 3.3, a recent paper on the integrative complexity of religious doubts gives examples of responses receiving different scores.[185]

Are Religion and Complexity Related?

Batson and Raynor-Prince[186] found that a measure of religious orthodoxy was significantly negatively correlated (−.37) with the integrative complexity of sentence completions deal-

---

Research Box 3.3. Religious Fundamentalism and Complexity of Religious Doubts (Hunsberger, Alisat, Pancer, & Pratt, 1996)

This interview study of university students provides examples of the different integrative complexity anchor scores for content dealing with religious doubts. These young adults were asked a series of questions about their religious doubts, and their responses were then scored for complexity of thought.

When subjects were asked, "What would you say is the most serious doubt about religion or religious beliefs that you have had in the last few years?", the following response received a score of 1 (no differentiation), since it reveals just one dimension of religious doubt: "My only real doubt is why God could allow people to suffer so much in this world" (p. 207).

Full differentiation (a score of 3) is illustrated by the following response, which outlines two different dimensions of doubt: "I have doubted why God allowed me to become seriously ill a few years ago. What was His purpose? Also, I could never understand why there is war and famine in the world if there is a God" (p. 207).

An example of a response showing integration of differentiated doubts (score of 5) is as follows:

> Over the years I have had various "little doubts." For example, I was bothered by the hypocrisy of some "religious" people, and the Bible seemed to not be very relevant to a lot of things happening today. After a while I sort of sat down and put all of these little things together and realized that in combination they made me doubt organized religion in general (p. 207).

Scores of 7 are apparently quite rare in this type of research, and none was found in this study. Scores of 2, 4, and 6 represent transition points between the odd-numbered anchor scores.

Complexity scores were then examined to see whether they were correlated to other measures in this study. Results seemed to confirm that there was a weak but significant association between the extent of one's religious doubts and the integrative complexity of thinking about those doubts. This finding is consistent with previous conclusions that complexity–religion relationships are restricted to domains involving existential religious content.

ing with existential[187] religious issues (e.g., "When I consider my own death . . ."). That is, people with a more orthodox religious orientation tended to think more simply about existential religious issues, as indicated by the sentence completion task. Also, the quest religious orientation was significantly positively correlated (.43) with complexity scores for thinking about existential content. For both orthodoxy and quest, comparable correlations involving *non*religious sentence completions were not statistically significant.

In a series of investigations, Hunsberger and his colleagues have attempted to further specify the relationship between religious orientation and complexity of thinking about religious and nonreligious issues.[188] They moved away from sentence completion tasks, which they felt might be too constraining; they either had their participants write brief essays on issues, or interviewed people to allow them to give fuller expression to their ideas. Although at first glance there appears to be some inconsistency in the findings of the various related studies, Hunsberger, Pratt, and Pancer recently reviewed these different investigations and concluded that

> religiosity does not seem to have a general (negative) relationship with integrative complexity across various domains. Rather, such relationships are restricted to content dealing with existential issues. A reexamination of previous related research suggests that this observation can account for virtually all findings of complexity–religiousness relationships in the literature. Further, religious fundamentalism and orthodoxy measures are apparently equally predictive of integrative complexity.[189]

These authors also concluded that the unique relationship found between religious orientation and integrative complexity of thought about *existential* material adds substance to previous work by Batson et al.[190] and by Altemeyer and Hunsberger,[191] suggesting that dealing with (or avoiding) existential questions does indeed have important implications for religion. However, although we have apparently begun to fit together the jigsaw puzzle of how thought processes and religiousness might be linked, we are left to wonder about *why* the complexity–religion relationship is restricted to existential content. More research is needed to answer this "why" question.

Finally, although virtually all of the research cited above involved adolescent and young adult populations, there is no reason to conclude that the obtained relationships are characteristic of these groups only. If there is indeed a relationship between religious orientation or beliefs and the complexity of adolescent thought about existential issues, we might expect this relationship to hold for adult samples as well. To date, there have been few investigations of this possibility for people in middle or older adulthood. The findings of one study by Pratt et al.,[192] involving integrative complexity in middle and older adults, are consistent with our speculation here. In a rather different context, somewhat similar findings were obtained by van der Lans,[193] who concluded that adults who were inclined to a literal interpretation of religious material also "gave evidence of a low developed structure of religious judgment."[194]

Of course, the observed relationships between religiousness and complexity of thinking about existential religious issues are correlational, and one must be cautious in speculating about cause and effect. Thus, although our preferred interpretation is that the religious socialization process contributes to differential thought processes in dealing with existential content, other interpretations are possible. Research is needed to clarify this issue.

RELIGIOUS DOUBTS

Clearly, not all individuals are carbon copies of their parents when it comes to religion. If the socialization process is as efficient as outlined above, how do people who grow up in religious families come to change their religious beliefs, or to reject religion entirely? Here we consider the origins, characteristics, and effects of religious doubting. (In the next section, we consider the factors involved in abandoning one's religion entirely.)

Of course, people are not completely passive recipients of social influence when it comes to the religious socialization process. They think about religious issues, and may not be willing to accept all that they are taught. Almost everyone has questions related to religious teachings at some time. Questions may range from the relatively inconsequential (e.g., "Why does my minister insist that there be a long Bible reading to begin each worship service?") to the important (e.g., "Does God really exist?" "Should I abandon my religious faith?"). Many people apparently resolve their questions to their own satisfaction, and consequently their underlying religious beliefs are not substantially altered. Others, however, may not resolve their questions so easily, and their questions may grow into serious doubts and concerns about religious beliefs. The doubts may eventually lead them to abandon some or all of their beliefs. Let us examine this process in greater detail.

Questions and doubts about religion seem especially common in adolescence. Nipkow and Schweitzer analyzed 16- to 21-year-old German students' written reflections about God, and concluded that most of their respondents had "challenging questions" about God.[195] These primarily involved unfulfilled expectations of God, and whether or not the students continued to believe in God was determined by the extent to which their expectations were fulfilled. Similarly, Tamminen noted an increase in early adolescence in doubts about God's existence, and whether prayers were answered, among his Finnish students.[196] However, few psychological investigators ask about the religious questions and doubts of middle-aged and older adults, so we should not conclude that such doubts are less prevalent in adulthood than in adolescence until we have better comparative data.[197]

Doubt: "Good" or "Bad"?

The personal tension, distress, and conflict implied by religious doubt were noted by numerous early authors, including Pratt,[198] Allport,[199] and Clark.[200] Pratt further claimed that "The great cause for adolescent doubt is the inner discord aroused by some newly discovered fact which fails to harmonize with beliefs previously accepted and revered."[201]

Traditionally, religious doubt has been considered to be "bad," as pointed out by Clark:

> People differ in their estimate of the value of doubt. The official church attitude is that it is to be deplored as an obstacle to faith, at the worst a temptation of the Devil, at the best a sign of weakness.[202]

In this vein, Helfaer equated religious doubt with suffering and pain, and claimed that "religious doubt is in fact an example of the lack . . . of an integrated wholeness within the ego."[203]

In a recent investigation of students making the transition to university life, Hunsberger and his colleagues found that the extent to which students reported doubting religious teachings was related to several adjustment variables.[204] Doubting was positively related to measures of stress, depression, and daily hassles, and negatively related to self-esteem, relationship with parents, optimism, and adjustment to university life. These relationships were typically weak (ranging from .10 to .24) but statistically significant. A measure of Religious Fundamentalism was significantly related (positively) to just one of these measures, optimism. Thus, there seemed to be something unique about religious doubting, which was weakly but consistently associated with poorer adjustment in first-year university students.

However, Batson's conceptualization of the quest religious orientation as an open-ended, questioning approach to religion[205] has cast religious doubting in a somewhat more positive light. In fact, perception of doubt as positive is seen as one of three core characteristics of the quest orientation, the others being complexity and openness to change.[206] And Batson and his colleagues have shown that the quest orientation is linked with some characteristics that many people feel should be encouraged, such as greater openness, lower prejudice, a tendency to help others in need, and some aspects of mental health.[207]

Types of Doubt

Hunsberger et al. reported a series of three studies on religious doubt in which they investigated the kinds of doubts people have.[208] They suggested, first, that previous work had characterized doubt as involving unique events or situations:

> That is, the assumption seems to be that a person might have doubts about the existence of God because of certain educational influences, or that someone might doubt the validity of religious teachings because a respected religious person was revealed to have engaged in despicable behaviors. But it would be unlikely that an extensive series of doubts, having different sources, would be found in the same people very often.[209]

However, their research found evidence that argued against this assumption.

Initially, they attempted to categorize different kinds of doubting by building on Allport's[210] and Clark's[211] analyses of religious doubting, thus generating the following types of doubt:

1. *Reactive and negativistic doubt.* There is a general reaction against religion, with anything religious being viewed negatively.
2. *Violation of self-interest.* Self-centered expectations have not been fulfilled (e.g., unanswered prayer).
3. *Shortcomings of organized religion.* The person questions wars fought in God's name, commercialism, hypocrisy, dubious morality of some religious persons, or the like.
4. *God as a projection.* The person feels that God does not exist in reality and must be a "projection," since God's image changes across time and cultures.
5. *Religion as self-deception.* Religion is seen as fooling people—serving merely to ease their fears and anxieties, for example.
6. *Scientific doubt.* The person feels a need to verify statements before accepting them (a religion–science conflict).
7. *Ritual doubt.* The person questions the apparent ineffectiveness of some religious rites (e.g., failure of faith healing in curing someone may lead to doubts about God's ability to cure people).

These categories were not intended to be exhaustive, but rather represented a starting point for the investigation of religious doubting. Hunsberger et al.'s investigations of university students suggested that more orthodox religious persons reported lower absolute levels of religious doubting, and that doubting was associated with "apostasy, decreased church attendance, less agreement with religious teachings, and less family emphasis on religion."[212] That is, religious doubting seemed to be more characteristic of disengagement from religion—a finding replicated by Brinkerhoff and Mackie,[213] rather than being an integral part of ongoing faith as claimed by Allport[214] and Tillich.[215] Furthermore, varieties of doubting were moderately intercorrelated, leading Hunsberger et al. to conclude that doubting typically did not involve just one or more independent doubts. Rather, they suggested that doubts "tended to 'hang together' quite reliably in a general 'doubt syndrome.'"[216] Finally, there was a correlation between integrative complexity of thinking about religious doubts on the one hand, and the extent of religious doubting on the other, suggesting some relationship between ways of thinking about religious doubts and the content and extent of those doubts.

Correlates of Doubt

More recently, Hunsberger et al. interviewed 68 university students (33 high and 35 low religious fundamentalists who scored in the top and bottom quartiles of the Religious Fundamentalism Scale, respectively) about their own and others' perceived religious doubts.[217] Consistent with their previous investigation discussed above, they found reasonably strong negative correlations between religious doubting and measures of Religious Fundamentalism ($r = -.57$), Christian Orthodoxy ($r = -.61$), and Right-Wing Authoritarianism ($r = -.49$). Orthodox, fundamentalist, and authoritarian individuals apparently do not experience religious doubt (or at least do not admit it—see Research Box 3.4, below) to the same extent as their less orthodox, fundamentalist, or authoritarian counterparts.

Also, qualitative differences arose with respect to the nature of doubting, such that high fundamentalists did not typically doubt God or religion per se; rather, they focused their doubts on others' failure to live up to religious ideals, or relatively minor adjustments that they felt should be made within the church (e.g., improving the role of women in the church). Low fundamentalists, on the other hand, were more likely to question "the underpinnings of religion," such as the existence of God, the lack of proof for religious claims, or the unbelievability of the creationist account of human origins. Finally, again, there was some evidence that people who reported more religious doubts tended to think more complexly about such doubts, and about existential material more generally. The results of this study suggested that

> high and low fundamentalists may actually perceive and deal with their own (and others') religious experiences in different ways. Our findings seem consistent with the possibility that religious cognitive processing is "convergent" among high fundamentalists, tending to confirm and reinforce religious teachings. Any divergence (e.g., active questioning of God or religion) seems to be resolved by interpreting information as consistent with one's beliefs, or at least by accepting the religious "explanation" for the doubt or concern. Low fundamentalists, on the other hand seem to respond to divergent thinking (i.e., critical questioning and considering alternatives to their beliefs) by changing their religious beliefs. . . . Overall, a picture emerges of low fundamentalists and high doubters as being more complex, and critical, processors of information related to religion.[218]

Little empirical work has been done to extend these findings, though it is important that we further clarify the nature of doubt and factors affecting it. There does seem to be a link between religious doubting and apostasy or religious defection, though it is possible that this link is moderated by other factors, such as developmental level or cognitive stage.

Further, Wulff has argued that religious doubt "occurs most often as a temporary state, chiefly among adolescents and young adults in the 'irreligious twenties.'"[219] A study by Watson et al. did find a slight decline with age in scores on Batson's Quest measure ($r = -.19$),[220] suggesting a decreased tendency among older adults to doubt, insofar as the Quest scale taps doubting. However, we should be careful not to conclude that doubt is virtually nonexistent among older adults.[221]

As described in Research Box 3.4, Altemeyer has developed a "secret survey" technique[222] that assures anonymity, allows people to respond in very private circumstances chosen by themselves, and encourages respondents to be especially truthful about themselves in a way analogous to the "hidden observer" technique used by Hilgard[223] in studying hypnosis. Under these circumstances, Altemeyer found that about one-third of his participants who were high in right-wing authoritarianism admitted that they had *secret* doubts about God's existence, which they had *never* shared with anyone else. This suggests that many routine studies of doubting may not be tapping actual levels of doubt, but only what people are willing to admit to others.

We need direct investigations of the frequency, nature, and implications of religious doubting in middle and older adulthood, but we also need to be sensitive to the possible "secret" nature of some people's doubts. In at least some cases, doubt seems to be a precursor to abandoning one's religion. We now turn to an examination of this disengagement process, which is most likely to occur during late adolescence.

APOSTASY

The Work of Caplovitz and Sherrow

In the late 1970s, Caplovitz and Sherrow published what was until that time the broadest social-scientific investigation of "apostasy," or abandonment of one's religious faith.[224] These authors concluded that apostasy may be caused by one or more of the phenomena of secularization, alienation/rebellion, or commitment to the modern values of universalism/ achievement. Specifically, they proposed that four "germs" somehow infect young people, and that these germs predispose their "hosts" to become apostates. The germs were said to include poor parental relations, symptoms of maladjustment or neurosis, a radical or leftist political orientation, and commitment to intellectualism. Underlying all of these processes was the apparent assumption that apostasy represents "a purposeful rejection of previous identification and/or beliefs, and a conscious embracing of a new identification and/or beliefs."[225] In fact, Caplovitz and Sherrow concluded that apostasy represents rebellion against parents and other aspects of society, and that it results especially from "familial strain and dissociation from parents."[226] This thesis of apostasy's resulting from adolescent rebellion against parents has also been suggested by other researchers, such as Putney and Middleton[227] and Wuthnow and Glock.[228] Gordon Allport and his colleagues even used reaction to, or disagreement with, parental religious teachings as an operational definition of rebellion against parental authority.[229]

─────────────── ❧ ───────────────

Research Box 3.4. The Investigation of Religion: Right-Wing Authoritarianism (Altemeyer, 1988)

Altemeyer's book reports an imaginative and extensive program of research on right-wing authoritarianism (RWA). Our interest here is in some aspects of the research involving the investigation of religion, which is associated with authoritarianism. Altemeyer was intrigued by the fact that believing in an almighty God was a cornerstone of the belief system of high-RWA people. He suspected that doubts about God's existence probably arise for high RWAs as they do for others, but that possibly because of the strong anxiety these doubts arouse, high RWAs will not acknowledge them. But if doubts do exist in the mind of a "true believer," how can we possibly discover them when the person does not want to admit to them?

Altemeyer decided to attempt to probe these doubts by using a version of Hilgard's "hidden observer" research on hypnosis.[a] Hilgard had found that even people who endure pain without seemingly noticing it while under hypnosis will admit that they do feel pain when they are cued to allow a sort of "inner self" to discuss these experiences. This supposedly involves a part of the person that knows things that are not available to the person's consciousness.

So Altemeyer gave some students the following instructions in a survey study, after they had heard about Hilgard's research in their previous introductory psychology classes:

> You may recall the lecture on hypnosis dealing with Hilgard's research on the "Hidden Observer." Suppose there is a Hidden Observer in you, which knows your every thought and deed, but which only speaks when it is safe to do so, and when directly spoken to. This question is for your Hidden Observer: Does this person (that is, you) have doubts that (s)he was created by an Almighty God who will judge each person and take some into heaven for eternity while casting others into hell forever? (pp. 152–153)

Five alternatives followed, allowing respondents to answer with different versions of the type and extent of secret doubts they had experienced. About half of the high-RWA students in this study indicated that they had *no* doubts about God's existence. But, remarkably, about one-third of these people said that they did have *secret* doubts, which they had never shared with anyone else.

Of course, we cannot be sure that Altemeyer's participants were being truthful about their hidden religious doubts; however, this investigation raises important questions about the meaning of responses in typical survey research. It also suggests that creativity may be required to tap into very personal information about such topics as religious doubting.

───────────

[a]Hilgard (1973, 1986).

The Caplovitz and Sherrow work has been criticized on theoretical, methodological, and data-interpretational grounds.[230] Earlier findings—for example, those by Johnson[231] and Hunsberger[232]—had suggested that religious socialization tends to follow a "straight line," such that lower levels of religiousness are related to lower levels of emphasis on religion in the childhood home. That is, it seemed that apostasy may represent *consistency* with a lack of parental emphasis on religion, rather than rebellion against parents and society, as characterized by Caplovitz and Sherrow.

More Recent Research

Hunsberger carried out a series of three studies of university students to investigate this issue.[233] These are summarized in Research Box 3.5. These studies from different corners of the world were quite consistent in their finding that apostasy is most strongly related to weak emphasis on religion in the home. And although Hunsberger's work involved Canadian and Australian university students, his essential finding in this regard has been confirmed by other studies that have focused on specific groups, including work by Albrecht and his colleagues with Mormons[234] and Kotre's investigation of Roman Catholics,[235] as well as studies of more representative U.S. samples by Nelsen[236] and Wuthnow and Mellinger.[237]

Furthermore, in Hunsberger's studies, no support was found for two of Caplovitz and Sherrow's hypothesized predisposing "germs"—symptoms of maladjustment, and a radical or leftist political orientation. In a more recent study of more than 600 U.S. and Canadian college students, Brinkerhoff and Mackie found that apostates reported being less happy in their lives than did converts (people who grew up with no religious affiliation but now identified with a religious group), "religious stalwarts" (people who maintained the same denominational affiliation from childhood to young adulthood), and "denominational switchers" (people who had changed denominational affiliation since childhood).[238] However, apostates typically did not differ significantly from these other groups on measures of self-esteem or life satisfaction.[239] Although Brinkerhoff and Mackie conclude that apostates "are less satisfied in life, [are] less happy and have lower self-esteem,"[240] the statistical evidence supports this conclusion only for the general happiness item mentioned above. Brinkerhoff and Mackie did find that apostates had a more liberal world view, in the sense that they were "less traditional" than the "stalwarts."

Finally, although Hunsberger found weak evidence that poor parental relationships may be involved in apostasy, he suggested that one could interpret this finding as *either* a cause or a result of apostasy. However, Wilson and Sherkat have argued that their data suggest that poor relationships with parents are more likely to precede disengagement from religion.[241] Therefore, it would seem that such poor relationships contribute to disengagement rather than vice versa.

How to Raise an Apostate

It would seem that if parents want their children to abandon the family religion, they apparently can best encourage this by generally ignoring religion, or at least communicating (by teaching or by example) that religion is unimportant. This is just what a socialization explanation of religious development would predict: Homes that emphasize the importance of religion and model religious behavior will generally produce children who remain religious later in their lives, whereas homes that pay little attention to faith and model nonreligious behavior will generally produce children who pay no more attention to religion than their parents did. The related concept of "drift" has sometimes been used to describe the tendency for apostates to have been only marginally involved with a religious denomination before defection.[242]

This is not to deny the involvement of cognitive factors. Hunsberger and Brown's Australian study in particular suggested that people who say they have an intellectual approach to life, enjoy debating or arguing with others about religious issues, and the like are more likely to be apostates.[243] And this may well be associated with questioning and doubting reli-

Research Box 3.5. Three Studies of the Antecedents and Correlates of Apostasy (Hunsberger, 1980, 1983a; Hunsberger & Brown, 1984)

This series of three studies investigated the antecedents and correlates of apostasy. In the first investigation, Hunsberger screened about 600 introductory psychology students and found that his sample contained 51 "apostates" ("people who reported being raised in a religious denomination, but had changed their religious orientation to 'none'" [p. 160]) who could be paired with 51 "matched controls" (people who came from the same religious background, and who were the same sex, approximate age, and year in university, but who continued to identify with the family religion). As one would expect, apostates were significantly "less religious" on a series of measures, including frequency of church attendance and prayer, and belief in God. But the two groups did not differ on a number of other measures, such as self-reports of parental acceptance, personal happiness and adjustment, or grade point average—contrary to what Caplovitz and Sherrow would apparently have predicted. There was some tendency for apostates to report poorer relationships with their parents, consistent with Caplovitz and Sherrow's predictions. However, although emphasis placed on religion in the childhood home did significantly predict apostate versus matched control status, factors related to parental relationships and rebellion did *not* add to the explained variance in a factor analysis and subsequent multiple-regression analysis.

These findings were essentially replicated in the second study, which included 78 apostates and matched controls identified among introductory psychology students, and which involved additional variables that Caplovitz and Sherrow predicted would be related to apostasy. Again, it was concluded that the religious socialization process was the most important influence in determining apostate versus nonapostate status, since apostates reported considerably less emphasis on religion in the childhood home than did their matched controls. The findings from these two studies of apostasy were interpreted as being consistent with social learning theory, such that increased parental modeling and teaching of religion were associated with increased acceptance of the family religion. Factors that did *not* seem to predict apostasy included political orientation, intellectualism, academic orientation, adjustment and happiness in life, Minnesota Multiphasic Personality Inventory (MMPI) subscales, and general rebellion against parents. There was a weak tendency for poor relationships with parents to be associated with apostasy, but Hunsberger suggested that this might well be a result rather than a cause of apostasy.

The third study in this series involved a sample of more than 800 Australian university students. The apostasy rate (36%) was higher than in previous Canadian studies (10–20%). This investigation confirmed the tendency for apostates to be much less religious on various measures, and to report considerably less emphasis on religion in the childhood home. However, these students also reported themselves to have a more intellectual orientation in their lives, consistent with Caplovitz and Sherrow's prediction.

In the end, these studies from different corners of the world were quite consistent in their finding that apostasy seems most strongly related to weak emphasis on religion in the home. Also, Caplovitz and Sherrow's claim that symptoms of maladjustment and a radical or leftist political orientation are related to apostasy was not supported. Nor was there any indication that apostasy represents rebellion against parents and society. Weak support was found for two other "germs" suggested by Caplovitz and Sherrow (poor relationships with parents and an intellectual orientation), though these were clearly weaker predictors of apostasy than was reported emphasis on religion in the childhood home.

gious teachings, as discussed in the section on doubts. In this vein, Brinkerhoff and Mackie found that apostates reported more and earlier religious doubts in their lives than did nonapostates.[244]

Age of Apostasy

More broadly based survey studies suggest that disengagement from religion is most common among younger people, especially those in their late teens and early 20s. For example, Hoge et al. estimated that about two-thirds of all dropping out among Catholics occurred when people were between the ages of 16 and 25[245]—essentially the same peak "dropping-out" years reported for Mormons,[246] Presbyterians,[247] and more general religious groupings.[248]

Types of Apostasy

Some authors have attempted to typologize apostates, though the resulting groupings tend to focus on social and other characteristics of apostates (and some other disaffiliates) rather than the underlying apostasy process itself. For example, Hadaway used cluster analysis to derive five characteristic groups of apostates: (1) *successful swinging singles*—single young people who apparently were experiencing social and financial success; (2) *sidetracked singles*— single people who tended to be pessimistic and had not obtained the benefits of the "good life"; (3) *young settled liberals*—those who were dissatisfied with traditional values but who had a very positive outlook on life; (4) *young libertarians*—people who rejected religious labels more than religious beliefs; and (5) *irreligious traditionalists*—somewhat older conservative, married people who maintained some religious moral traditions in spite of their nonattendance and nonaffiliation.[249]

Others have offered different typologies,[250] but no generally accepted categorization has appeared. These studies do indicate that we should not assume that apostates constitute a homogeneous group. The social characteristics of apostates may vary considerably, and the underlying processes of disengagement are not uniform.

Problems in Definition and Measurement

Caution is necessary when one is comparing the results of different investigations of apostasy. As Bromley has noted,[251] the terminology used to describe disengagement from religion varies considerably from study to study, involving terms such as "dropping out," "exiting," "disidentification," "leave taking," "defecting," "apostasy," "disaffiliation," and "disengagement." Furthermore, operational definitions of these terms have varied from one study to the next. For example, some authors, such as Caplovitz and Sherrow[252] and Hunsberger,[253] have studied people who say they grew up with a religious identification or family religious background, but no longer identify with any religious group. Others, such as Hoge,[254] have focused on cessation of church attendance for a specified period of time. Hunsberger and Altemeyer incorporated elements of loss of faith as well as disidentification.[255]

Brinkerhoff and Mackie have pointed out that such differences could potentially lead to divergent findings;[256] it is important in relevant investigations to be clear about the criteria used to define apostasy operationally, and also to be sensitive to how this definition will affect the findings. Clearly, as Albrecht et al. have emphasized,[257] there are many reasons for cessation of church attendance that do not necessarily involve loss of personal faith. Wuthnow and Glock have even suggested that early studies may have underestimated rates of religious defection because of wording of survey items.[258] And as we have noted earlier in this chapter, there may be differences in religiousness across countries, and this could have implications for apostasy (e.g., apostasy probably has different meaning in the "religious" United States compared to "less religious" European countries).

Moreover, Roof's investigation of changing religious denominations indicated that "switching" is relatively common, especially in mainstream religious groups.[259] Switching usually occurs across relatively similar denominations (e.g., see Kelley's "exclusive–ecumenical" continuum, described in Chapter 9),[260] and it is often instigated by other life changes, such as marriage or moving to a new community.[261] In short, it should not be confused with abandonment of religious faith and identification.[262] Greeley has referred to the switching process as "religious musical chairs"[263]—a very different phenomenon from apostasy.

Clearly, we need greater precision and standardization of definition in research on apostasy, as well as careful consideration and integration of results of studies using different approaches and samples.

Is Apostasy Temporary?

As we have seen, polls and surveys typically show that adolescents and college students are "less religious" than are older persons. However, the disengagement from religion that is more common among adolescents and younger adults is often characterized as a temporary phenomenon. As noted in Chapter 9, some "dropping out" may simply represent youthful exploration of alternative ideas and religions (e.g., alternate philosophies or belief systems, sects, cults) for a relatively short period in young people's lives. Gordon Allport suggested that after youthful disaffection with traditional religious values, many people return to religion by the time they are in their 30s.[264] They may have children of their own and be concerned that their offspring should have some religious upbringing, or they may more generally have lost their rebellious tendencies and be settling down.

Similarly, Bibby has argued that disengagement from religion is typically temporary, and that many people who rejected religion in their teens eventually return to institutionalized religion, even if primarily to avail themselves of such "rites of passage" as marriage, funerals, and/or some religious instruction for their children.[265] Bibby relies on Canadian evidence showing that the percentage of people claiming "no religion" is consistently highest among younger adults (18–34). Furthermore, a cohort analysis by Bibby suggests that almost half of the 16% of people aged 18–34 who claimed to have "no religion" in 1975 were reabsorbed into the religious realm, since in 1990 just 9% of the 35- to 54-year-olds (i.e., apparently many of the same people in the 1975 statistics) claimed "no religion." But of course we do not know how many of the 9% were the same people who claimed "no religion" 15 years earlier; individuals could not be followed longitudinally, and we do not know, for example, how many people might also have become apostates in the interim. But this evidence certainly suggests (albeit indirectly) that some people do return to religion after claiming "no religion" when they were younger.

Not all research findings are consistent with this "return to religion" tendency. In a study of rural Pennsylvania young people, Willits and Crider asked them questions about religion when they were high school students in 1970, and again in 1981 when they were about 27 years old.[266] Data analyses were reported only for the 331 respondents who were married by 1981. The researchers concluded that these people were in fact *less* frequent church attenders at 27 than they had been in their middle teens. However, this study involved a relatively short-term follow-up, and it could be argued that the timing of the surveys (at ages 16 and 27, on average) might account for the unique findings. For example, a shift away from religion might well have occurred soon after the age of 16. Another follow-up when these people are in their 30s or 40s might be more informative.

An extensive longitudinal study of a U.S. national probability sample suggests that most religious "dropping out" probably occurs after age 16. Wilson and Sherkat followed the religious identification and other trends of more than 1,000 people from 1965, when they were seniors in high school, to 1973 and again to 1983.[267] In the third wave of their study, they managed to retain more than two-thirds of the original 1,562 participants. They focused their attention on those who reported a religious preference in 1965, but then reported no preference in 1973. For these "dropouts," they found few differences between those who retained their apostate status in 1983 and those who had returned to religion. The returnees did report closer relationships with their parents in high school than did the continuing apostates. Furthermore, there was a tendency for early marriage and forming a family to be related to returning to religion, though this relationship was found only for men. In general, women were less likely to become apostates than were men, but women apostates were also less likely to return to the fold than were men. Wilson and Sherkat speculated that men are more likely to be religiously affected by transitions to marriage and parenthood; they added, "Given the cultural understanding that the religious role is primarily allocated to women in the family, dropping out of the church is a stronger statement for women to make than for men, especially in a society where denominational affiliation of some kind is normative."[268]

Wilson and Sherkat's finding that marriage and parenthood are important factors in "returning to the fold" has been replicated elsewhere.[269] This is consistent with our conclusion that parental religious socialization effects tend to weaken, and that other factors become more important, as people move on through the life cycle and begin to live independent adult lives themselves. However, we should not be too quick to conclude that marriage and parenthood contribute to greater religiousness.

Ploch and Hastings methodically analyzed General Social Survey data from the United States from 1972 to 1991, and found a general trend toward increased religiousness with increasing age.[270] There was no indication in these correlational data that either marriage or childbearing was associated with an increase in church attendance. According to Ploch and Hastings, researchers who have concluded that family formation is positively related to church attendance may have confused a long-term trend toward an age-related increase in religiousness with short-term events such as marriage and childbearing. Recently, Stolzenberg and colleagues have continued this debate, finding that "family life cycle" attitudes and events (marriage, cohabitation, parenthood, divorce, etc.) *do* affect religion, though they may interact with age in complex ways. That is, their results "suggest that an aging hypothesis and the Family Life Cycle hypothesis are not incompatible."[271] This issue is a complicated one. However, we should be careful not to assume that church attendance and membership are ideal, accurate indicators of personal religiousness.

The studies described above do agree that some people apparently become lifelong apostates. Also, for example, the "no religion" category seems to be either holding fairly steady (at about 7% in the United States[272]) or increasing (in Canada[273]). Thus, in spite of the fact that some apostates do return to religion later in their lives,[274] apparently many people do remain "apostates for life."

Going against the Flow: "Amazing Apostates" and "Amazing Believers"

There is strong evidence that most people who become religious believers or apostates are behaving quite consistently with what socialization theory would predict. That is, most apostates come from homes where religion was only weakly emphasized and parental modeling of religion was not strong. And most religious believers come from homes where religion was relatively strongly emphasized and modeling was readily available. There are exceptions to the rule, although they are rare. For example, Bibby reported that just 2% of Canadian weekly church attenders in 1991 were going to church "seldom or never" as youngsters.[275] And Brinkerhoff and Mackie could find just 10 of 631 Canadian and U.S. college students (1.6%) who identified with a religious denomination after reporting that they grew up with no religion.[276]

This is consistent with research by Hunsberger and Altemeyer, who investigated "amazing believers" and "amazing apostates"—people who seem to contradict socialization predictions.[277] The researchers established strict criteria in an attempt to capture the exceptions to the socialization rule. "Amazing believers" scored in the top quarter of Fullerton and Hunsberger's 24-item Christian Orthodoxy scale,[278] but in the lower quarter of a 16-item Religious Emphasis scale, which tapped the extent to which religion had been emphasized in the childhood home; these findings suggested that they had come from relatively non-religious backgrounds but now held orthodox Christian beliefs. "Amazing apostates" scored in the bottom quarter of the orthodoxy scale and the top quarter of the emphasis scale, implying that they had come from highly religious backgrounds but no longer believed the basic tenets of their home religion.

Hunsberger and Altemeyer then interviewed all of the "amazing apostates" and "amazing believers" they could find at their respective universities, after screening several thousand students across two separate academic years. Since there were only a few amazing believers, they concentrated on the results of the interviews with 42 amazing apostates. The interviews confirmed that these 42 people had generally rejected family religious teachings, in spite of strong socialization pressures to accept religious beliefs. They were unique people whose "search for truth" had led them to question many things, especially religious teachings, often from an early age. Many of these people reported initial guilt and fear about dropping their religious beliefs, consistent with the findings of Etxebarria,[279] but in retrospect they believed that the benefits of leaving their religion far outweighed any costs involved. Also, they held very tolerant, nonauthoritarian attitudes toward others, in contrast to the more authoritarian views apparent among their highly religious counterparts.[280]

Why did these people reject religious teachings when the majority of their peers were accepting their religious backgrounds? The interviewees' own explanations typically revolved around their need to ask questions and get responses, and their unwillingness to accept "pat answers" that they felt did not really answer their questions. Most of these people had gone through some conflict over their beliefs, and had spent considerable time and effort weighing different arguments for and against religious beliefs. In the end, they decided that the religious arguments and evidence simply did not make sense to them, and they very deliberately chose a nonreligious path for their lives. Clearly, these apostates were "amazing," in that they seemed to reverse socialization influences through an intellectual search for truth in their own lives.

But as rare as these amazing apostates are, they are still more than twice as common as "amazing believers." And the few amazing believers studied by Hunsberger and Altemeyer rarely took the same carefully considered route to their newfound religiousness. Rather, they were more likely to have had some religious training early in their lives (in spite of a general lack of religiousness in the home), or to have "found religion" in an attempt to deal with crises in their lives. For example, some were attempting to escape from a dependence on drugs, alcohol, or sex; others were grappling with illness or tragedy (e.g., one woman had had four close relatives and friends die tragically in approximately a 12-month period).

This investigation of amazing apostates and believers must be regarded as preliminary in light of the small sample, but the initial findings are fairly clear and intriguing. A small percentage of the population does seem to "go against the flow" and reject religion in spite of strong childhood religious emphasis and training, and (fewer) others become strongly religious in spite of having nonreligious backgrounds. These exceptional cases do not necessarily fly in the face of socialization theory. Hunsberger and Altemeyer speculate that their amazing apostates may simply be acting on an important religious teaching from early in their lives: "Believe the truth." However, they have pursued the truth in a critical, questioning way that has led them away from their home religious teachings. Further research is needed to assess this interpretation. In the end, as rare as these amazing apostates are, such "exceptions to the rule" can potentially help our general understanding of the religious socialization process; thus, they deserve our attention.

OVERVIEW

In this chapter we have taken a socialization approach to the development of adolescent and young adult religiousness. There are certainly other ways of conceptualizing religious development as children move into adolescence; as we have seen, however, there is a considerable body of evidence that is consistent with a socialization perspective, especially one based on social learning theory. Much empirical work confirms that parents constitute the strongest influences on adolescent religiousness, though it would seem that their influence decreases as young people move into the postadolescent years. It is not entirely clear whether mothers or fathers exert the stronger influence, though the weight of the evidence suggests that mothers are more powerful. Certainly, both mothers and fathers have some influence, and interactive factors also play a role (e.g., warmth of the family environment, mother–father consistency in religiousness). Other religious socialization agents have been presumed to be active, such as the church, peer groups, and education. However, with the possible exception of specific effects of religious education (e.g., increases in religious knowledge) and the church, these other variables apparently exert relatively weak effects on adolescent religiosity.

Some studies have suggested that early tendencies for children or adolescents to increase or decrease in religiosity may continue into adulthood. This "polarization" tendency needs to be explored further.

Generational effects occur, such that adolescents and young adults are "less religious" than older adults. However, although religiosity has apparently decreased in many parts of the world, religion itself is hardly on the verge of disappearing. The United States is apparently an exception to the "decreasing religiousness" rule, since rates of regular church attendance have been relatively stable, with 30–40% of high school seniors attending weekly.

Some evidence suggests that the religious socialization process may affect the ways in which people think about some things, especially existential religious issues. Research using a measure of integrative complexity has shown that more orthodox and fundamentalist persons think less complexly about such issues. Possibly these stylistic thought differences are related to the ways in which people resolve conflicts, questions, and doubts concerning religious teachings. The evidence suggests that questions and doubts about religion are common during adolescence and early adulthood, and that those with more doubts tend to think in more complex terms about religious doubts and conflicts. There is some tendency for more fundamentalist persons to resolve their questions and doubts in ways that support their religious beliefs, whereas less fundamentalist persons are more likely to achieve resolutions that change their religious beliefs.

Finally, work on apostasy has suggested that leaving the family religion is generally consistent with socialization explanations of religious development. People who abandon the family faith tend to come from homes where religion was either ignored or only weakly emphasized. Thus, apostates often simply "drift" a bit further away from a religion that was not important to the family in the first place. Apostates tend to have poorer relationships with their parents, though it is not entirely clear whether this is a cause or an effect of the apostasy. Cognitive factors are probably involved in apostasy to some extent, with apostates more likely to question, doubt, and debate religious issues earlier in their lives than non-apostates. This critical approach to religion seems especially true of "amazing apostates"— people who become apostates in spite of considerable socialization pressure to accept religious teachings. Finally, some apostates apparently return to religion in adulthood, but others become "apostates for life." The explanation for this difference is unclear.

The research reviewed in this chapter constitutes a considerable body of knowledge concerning religious socialization processes. We continue to learn more about how young people become religious and sometimes leave a religious background. However, research has tended to focus on description rather than explanation. It *is* important to understand the integral role of parents (and the relative unimportance of some other factors) in the religious socialization process. It *is* valuable to gain insight into the thought processes and correlates of religious doubt and apostasy. And it *is* worthwhile to devise typologies of apostates. But it is also important that we generate testable explanations concerning *why* these processes occur as they do, and what the causative factors are with respect to religious development. We suspect that too much attention has been devoted to the social correlates of religious socialization and religious change, and that not enough attention has focused on factors within individuals (e.g., styles of thinking, and ways in which people approach and resolve information that challenges their beliefs). Correlational studies, which are the norm in this area, can help us to understand the processes involved, but they also make it difficult to extract cause-and-effect relationships. The issues discussed in this chapter have considerable potential for future research.

NOTES

1. Allport (1950, p. 36).
2. Campbell (1969, p. 852).
3. University student interviewed by one of us, 1994.
4. University student interviewed by one of us, 1994.
5. Quote attributed to Mark Twain.
6. Batson, Schoenrade, and Ventis (1993, p. 26).
7. Spilka, Hood, and Gorsuch (1985).

8. Glock and Stark (1966); Stark (1972).
9. Goode (1968).
10. Ryan, Rigby, and King (1993).
11. Burris, Batson, Altstaedten, and Stephens (1994).
12. Erikson (1958)
13. Long and Hadden (1983, p. 3).
14. Ryan et al. (1993, p. 586).
15. Johnstone (1988).
16. Slaughter-Defoe (1995).
17. Bandura (1977).
18. Cornwall (1988).
19. See, e.g., Rizzuto (1979).
20. Ambert (1992); Peters (1985).
21. Cornwall (1987, 1989); Cornwall and Thomas (1990).
22. Cornwall (1987, p. 44).
23. Friedman (1985).
24. Slaughter-Defoe (1995).
25. Bandura (1977). Social learning theory has been useful in explaining other aspects of adolescent development. See, e.g., DiBlasio and Benda (1990).
26. Spilka, Hood, and Gorsuch (1985).
27. Hunsberger (1976).
28. The United Church of Canada was formed in 1925 as a union of Methodist, Congregational, and Presbyterian churches.
29. Ozorak (1989).
30. Benson, Yeager, Wood, Guerra, and Manno (1986).
31. Potvin and Sloane (1985).
32. Parker and Gaier (1980).
33. Hoge and Keeter (1976).
34. Hadaway (1980).
35. Kluegel (1980).
36. See, e.g., Argyle and Beit-Hallahmi (1975); Benson, Donahue, and Erickson (1989); Spilka, Hood, and Gorsuch (1985).
37. Hunsberger (1985a, p. 314).
38. Friedenberg (1969); Thomas (1974).
39. Lerner and Spanier (1980).
40. Coopersmith, Regan, and Dick (1975); Nelsen, H. M. (1981b).
41. Bengtson and Troll (1978).
42. Hunsberger (1985a).
43. Hoge, Petrillo, and Smith (1982).
44. Dudley and Dudley (1986).
45. Glass, Bengtson, and Dunham (1986).
46. Hoge and Petrillo (1978a).
47. Potvin, Hoge, and Nelsen (1976).
48. Hunsberger (1985a).
49. Bengtson and Troll (1978).
50. Acock and Bengtson (1980).
51. Petersen (1988).
52. Allport, Gillespie, and Young (1948).
53. Hunsberger and Brown (1984).
54. Hunsberger (1983b).
55. Hunsberger (1985b).
56. Rho is a measure of association for rank-ordered data, similar to correlation.
57. Benson (1992a).
58. Hunsberger (1985a).
59. Hamberg (1991).
60. Hunsberger and Brown (1984).
61. Francis and Gibson (1993).
62. A Likert-type scale invites respondents to indicate the extent to which they agree or disagree with attitude statements. It might range, for example, from +3 ("strongly agree") to −3 ("strongly disagree").

63. Francis (1989a).
64. Hunsberger (1983b, 1985a).
65. Acock and Bengtson (1978, 1980); see also Dudley and Dudley (1986).
66. Francis and Brown (1990, 1991).
67. Francis and Gibson (1993).
68. Kieren and Munro (1987).
69. Benson, Williams, and Johnson (1987); Nelsen (1980); Hoge and Petrillo (1978a).
70. Batson et al. (1993).
71. Smith and Mackie (1995).
72. Wilson and Sherkat (1994).
73. Wilson and Sherkat (1994, p. 155).
74. Herzbrun (1993).
75. Hoge and Keeter (1976); Hoge and Petrillo (1978a); Hoge, Petrillo, and Smith (1982).
76. Dudley (1978).
77. Nelsen (1980).
78. Thomas and Weigert (1971).
79. Ellison and Sherkat (1993).
80. Nelsen (1981a).
81. D'Antonio, Newman, and Wright (1982).
82. Cornwall and Thomas (1990).
83. Batson et al. (1993); Benson et al. (1989); Brown (1987); Cornwall (1989); Havighurst and Keating (1971); Spilka, Hood, and Gorsuch (1985).
84. Erickson (1992).
85. Cornwall (1988); Cornwall and Thomas (1990).
86. Benson et al. (1989).
87. Allport (1950); Balk (1995); Cobb (1995); Newcomb (1962); Sprinthall and Collins (1995).
88. de Vaus, D. A. (1983).
89. Bengtson and Troll (1978).
90. Hoge and Petrillo (1978a).
91. Erickson (1992).
92. Erickson (1992, p. 151).
93. Hunsberger (1983b, 1985b).
94. Ozorak (1989).
95. Spilka, Hood, and Gorsuch (1985).
96. Hoge and Petrillo (1978a).
97. Carey (1971).
98. Olson (1989).
99. Feldman (1969, p. 23).
100. Parker (1971).
101. Feldman and Newcomb (1969).
102. Madsen and Vernon (1983).
103. Hoge and Keeter (1976).
104. Hunsberger (1978).
105. Hastings and Hoge (1976).
106. Pilkington, Poppleton, Gould, and McCourt (1976).
107. Moberg and Hoge (1986).
108. Hunsberger (1978).
109. Francis (1982).
110. Sutherland (1988).
111. Benson et al. (1989).
112. Hyde (1990).
113. Lenski (1961).
114. Greeley (1967).
115. Mueller (1967).
116. Mueller (1967, p. 51).
117. Erickson (1964).
118. Parker and Gaier (1980).
119. Johnstone (1966).
120. Kraybill (1977).

121. Francis and Brown (1991).
122. Francis and Brown (1991, p. 119).
123. Francis (1980, 1986).
124. Greeley and Gockel (1971); Greeley and Rossi (1966).
125. Himmelfarb (1979).
126. Hunsberger (1977).
127. Benson et al. (1986).
128. Johnstone (1966).
129. Benson et al. (1989).
130. See, e.g., Hyde (1990).
131. Erickson (1992, p. 151).
132. See, e.g., Benson et al. (1989).
133. Hunsberger (1983b, 1985b).
134. Francis and Brown (1991); Erickson (1992).
135. Francis and Brown (1991).
136. Hoge, Heffernan et al. (1982); Hoge and Thompson (1982).
137. Nelsen (1982).
138. Philibert and Hoge (1982).
139. Tamminen (1991).
140. Madsen and Vernon (1983).
141. Hunsberger (1985b).
142. Argyle and Beit-Hallahmi (1975); Batson et al. (1993); Benson et al. (1989); Nelsen and Potvin (1981).
143. Batson et al. (1993).
144. Nelsen and Potvin (1981).
145. Recently, Miller and Hoffman (1995) have suggested that gender differences in religiousness may be attributed to risk taking. Women tend to be "risk-averse," and it is argued that this is associated with religiousness, whereas men tend to be more inclined to take risks, and this is said to be associated with nonreligious behavior.
146. Keysar and Kosmin (1995).
147. Keysar and Kosmin (1995, p. 61).
148. Hyde (1990).
149. Dudley and Dudley (1986); Hamberg (1991).
150. Benson et al. (1989).
151. Potvin and Sloane (1985); Sloane and Potvin (1983).
152. Allport et al. (1948).
153. Webster, Freedman, and Heist (1962).
154. Havens (1963).
155. Havighurst and Keating (1971, p. 714).
156. Bibby (1987, 1993).
157. Bibby (1993).
158. Bibby (1993, p. 111).
159. Campbell and Curtis (1994).
160. Francis (1989b).
161. Hunsberger and Brown (1984).
162. Campbell and Curtis (1994).
163. Bibby (1993).
164. Bibby (1993, p. 112).
165. Youth Indicators (1993).
166. Chaves and Cavendish (1994).
167. Hadaway, Marler, and Chaves (1993).
168. Campbell and Curtis (1994).
169. Chaves (1989, 1991).
170. Firebaugh and Harley (1991).
171. See, e.g., Chaves (1989, 1990, 1991); Firebaugh and Harley (1991); Hout and Greeley (1990).
172. Harley and Firebaugh (1993).
173. Benson et al. (1989).
174. Cobb (1995, p. 523).
175. Benson et al. (1989).

176. Bibby (1993).
177. Finke and Stark (1992).
178. Bibby (1993, p. 113).
179. Hadaway and Roof (1988, p. 31).
180. Ozorak (1989).
181. Reich (1991, pp. 87–88); see also Reich (1989, 1992, 1994).
182. Reich (1991, p. 78).
183. Reich (1991, p. 82).
184. Baker-Brown et al. (1992).
185. Hunsberger, Alisat, Pancer, and Pratt (1996).
186. Batson and Raynor-Prince (1983).
187. The term "existential" is used as defined by Batson et al. (1993): as involving "questions that confront us because we are aware that we and others like us are alive and that we will die" (p. 8).
188. Hunsberger, Pratt, and Pancer (1994); Hunsberger, Alisat, et al. (1996); Hunsberger, Lea, Pancer, Pratt, and McKenzie (1992); Hunsberger, McKenzie, Pratt, and Pancer (1993); Pancer, Jackson, Hunsberger, Pratt, and Lea (1995); Pratt, Hunsberger, Pancer, and Roth (1992).
189. Hunsberger et al. (1994, p. 345).
190. Batson et al. (1993).
191. Altemeyer and Hunsberger (1992).
192. Pratt et al. (1992).
193. van der Lans (1991).
194. van der Lans (1991, p. 107).
195. Nipkow and Schweitzer (1991).
196. Tamminen (1991, 1994).
197. Bob Altemeyer (personal communication, October 31, 1995) has gathered some unpublished data that support our conjecture. He reports that, on a 20-item religious doubts scale, 163 parents of university students reported doubt levels ($M = 39.4$) almost identical to those of over 1,000 students ($M = 41.8$).
198. Pratt (1920).
199. Allport (1950).
200. Clark (1958).
201. Pratt (1920, p. 116).
202. Clark (1958, p. 138).
203. Helfaer (1972, p. 10).
204. Hunsberger, Pancer, Pratt, and Alisat (1996).
205. Batson and Schoenrade (1991a, 1991b); Batson et al. (1993).
206. Batson and Schoenrade (1991b, p. 431).
207. Batson et al. (1993).
208. Hunsberger et al. (1993).
209. Hunsberger et al. (1993, p. 28).
210. Allport (1950).
211. Clark (1958).
212. Hunsberger et al. (1993, p. 46).
213. Brinkerhoff and Mackie (1993).
214. Allport (1950).
215. Tillich (1957).
216. Hunsberger et al. (1993, p. 47).
217. Hunsberger, Alisat, et al. (1996).
218. Hunsberger, Alisat, et al. (1996).
219. Wulff (1991, p. 238).
220. Watson, Howard, Hood, and Morris (1988).
221. See note 197, above.
222. Altemeyer (1988).
223. Hilgard (1973, 1986).
224. Caplovitz and Sherrow (1977).
225. Hunsberger (1980, pp. 158–159).
226. Caplovitz and Sherrow (1977, p. 50).
227. Putney and Middleton (1961).

228. Wuthnow and Glock (1973).
229. Allport et al. (1948).
230. Hunsberger (1980).
231. Johnson (1973).
232. Hunsberger (1976).
233. Hunsberger (1980, 1983a); Hunsberger and Brown (1984).
234. Albrecht, Cornwall, and Cunningham (1988); Bahr and Albrecht (1989).
235. Kotre (1971).
236. Nelsen (1981c).
237. Wuthnow and Mellinger (1978).
238. Brinkerhoff and Mackie (1993).
239. The only pairwise comparison between apostates and each of the other three groupings that was statistically significant for either the life satisfaction or self-esteem measures indicated that apostates were lower in life satisfaction than were denominational switchers.
240. Brinkerhoff and Mackie (1993, p. 252).
241. Wilson and Sherkat (1994).
242. Bahr and Albrecht (1989).
243. Hunsberger and Brown (1984).
244. Brinkerhoff and Mackie (1993).
245. Hoge, McGuire, and Stratman (1981).
246. Albrecht et al. (1988).
247. Hoge, Johnson, and Luidens (1993).
248. Caplovitz and Sherrow (1977); Hadaway and Roof (1988); Albrecht and Cornwall (1989).
249. Hadaway (1989).
250. Bahr and Albrecht (1989); Brinkerhoff and Burke (1980); Condran and Tamney (1985); Hadaway and Roof (1988); Hoge et al. (1981); Perry, Davis, Doyle, and Dyble (1980); Roozen (1980).
251. Bromley (1988).
252. Caplovitz and Sherrow (1977).
253. Hunsberger (1980, 1983a).
254. Hoge (1988); Hoge et al. (1981).
255. Hunsberger and Altemeyer (1995).
256. Brinkerhoff and Mackie (1993).
257. Albrecht et al. (1988).
258. Wuthnow and Glock (1973).
259. Roof (1989).
260. Hadaway and Marler (1993).
261. Babchuk and Whitt (1990).
262. Albrecht and Cornwall (1989); Brinkerhoff and Mackie (1993); Sandomirsky and Wilson (1990).
263. Greeley (1981, p. 101).
264. Allport (1950).
265. Bibby (1993).
266. Willits and Crider (1989).
267. Wilson and Sherkat (1994).
268. Wilson and Sherkat (1994, p. 156).
269. Chaves (1991); Hoge et al. (1993).
270. Ploch and Hastings (1994).
271. Stolzenberg, Blair-Loy, and Waite (1995).
272. Hadaway and Roof (1988, p. 31).
273. Bibby (1993).
274. Hadaway (1989); Hoge (1988).
275. Bibby (1993, p. 31).
276. Brinkerhoff and Mackie (1993).
277. Hunsberger and Altemeyer (1995).
278. Fullerton and Hunsberger (1982).
279. Etxebarria (1992).
280. See Altemeyer and Hunsberger (1992).

Chapter 4

RELIGION IN ADULT LIFE

> People will do anything for religion, argue for it, fight for it, die for it, anything but live for it.[1]
>
> Religion can make good people better and bad people worse.[2]
>
> Like most Americans, my faith consists in believing in every religion, including my own, but without any ill-will toward anybody, no matter what he believes or disbelieves, just so his personality is good.[3]
>
> No creed is final. Such a creed as mine must grow and change as knowledge grows and changes.[4]
>
> What I want is, not to possess religion, but to have a religion that shall possess me.[5]
>
> Fax now available for messages to God. . . . The fax number is 011-972-2-612222. It is not toll-free.[6]

The history of psychology testifies to a great deal of selectivity in what has been studied over the last century. Whereas we can look back to G. Stanley Hall, James Mark Baldwin, Sigmund Freud, and Jean Piaget with their focus on child development, no dedicated researchers can be cited for their equivalent concern with adult life. Erik Erikson advanced a rather general theory that, interesting as it is, has provided little research direction. Simply put, there seem to be no giants in our psychological past who have stressed research and theory in adult development. For the most part, this realm has captured the attention of social scientists only within the past quarter century. The contemporary field of "lifespan developmental psychology" began with an emphasis on the elderly that still dominates this area of study, and research in it has yet to broaden significantly into the middle years of life. There has, however, been a movement toward more theory and research on postadolescent aging—and, with this trend, the appearance of scholars who will probably develop reputations as future psychological "giants" for this period of life.

The recognition of religion as a force in adult living has paralleled this general trend, with a dominating interest in faith during the closing years of life. Surprisingly little has been written on faith during the periods usually termed "early adulthood" and "middle adulthood." In less than rigorous formality, the former time is usually denoted as ranging from 17 or 20 years of age to about 45, with middle adulthood continuing to about 65 years of age.[7] The currently popular euphemism for those over 65 is "seniors," but they may just as accurately be described as the "elderly."

Our task in this chapter is to describe the role of religion in adult life. We need to know the nature and place of religious beliefs and activity, as well as their function in what Alfred Adler defined as the three great basic problems of life: "problems of behavior toward others; problems of occupation; and problems of love. The manner in which an individual behaves toward these three problems and their subdivisions—that is his answer to the problems of life."[8] Within Adler's system, the core motive is "a striving toward perfection, toward superiority, toward success," and the struggle to "overcome" is played out in these three problem areas of life.[9] In a similar vein, Erikson quotes Freud to the effect that a normal person should be able to do two things well—"*Lieben und Arbeiten*" (to love and to work).[10] Though adult life poses an almost unlimited number of concerns, most seem capable of being subsumed under the three problem areas described by Adler; hence we focus on the role of religion in these domains.

RELIGIOUS BELIEF AND BEHAVIOR AMONG ADULTS

Contemporary Beliefs and Behavior: Institutional Religion

The United States is generally regarded as one of the most religious nations in the world in terms of expressed beliefs and religious activities. This is illustrated by a study that showed belief in God to be higher in the United States than in 10 western European countries.[11] It is invariably assessed at 95–96%.[12] Table 4.1 presents recent data showing the rather considerable strength of institutionalized faith among Americans. Still, there have been noteworthy changes over the years. Though 55% of Americans claimed in 1994 that religion was very important in their lives, in 1952 this number was 75%.[13] Still, about 30% of those who did not attend church felt similarly in 1988.[14] Of even more graphic import is the observation that 28% of the population felt in 1994 that religion was increasing its influence in public life; in 1952, 69% believed similarly.[15] Of course, we do not know what the idea of "increasing its influence" is alluding to, and it could imply different issues and concerns.

Depending on the question asked, therefore, it is unclear whether faith's hold on the average American has really decreased. Some evidence suggests that this is true, but at other times it looks as if the religious members of the population have become even more committed as their less religious peers shift toward greater liberality. The overall national trend is admittedly toward a loosening of traditional religious bonds: The question in Table 4.1 about the relevance of religion to today's problems was answered positively by 59% in 1994, but by 82% of the population in 1952.[16] However, despite such a striking difference in the 42 years between these polls, there has only been a 5% reduction in church or synagogue membership.[17] Moreover, in the 8-year period from 1986 to 1994, the percentage of those describing themselves as "born-again" or "evangelical" increased from 33% to 39%.[18]

It is important not to make the generalization from reduced percentages to fewer people, for the U.S. population has increased by more than 100 million individuals in the last 40 years. For example, in spite of the 20% drop in those who felt that religion was personally very important to them, in 1952 112.5 million persons would have been included in this category, and in 1994 137.5 million people—an absolute increase of considerable size in the numbers. This shift is even more startling when we look at the 5% reduction in church or synagogue membership. In 1952, 73% meant approximately 109.5 million people; in 1994, 68% meant about 170 million Americans.

TABLE 4.1. Selected Religious Beliefs and Behaviors among Americans

1. How important is religion in your own life?[a]	
Very important	55%
Fairly important	30%
Not very important	14%
2. Is religion increasing its influence on American life?[a]	
Increasing	28%
Losing	67%
Not changing	2%
3. Are you a "born-again" or "evangelical" Christian?[a]	
Yes	39%
No	53%
4. Is religion currently relevant to answer all or most of today's problems?[a]	
Still provides answers	59%
Out of date	23%
5. Are you a church or synagogue member?[a]	
Yes	68%
6. Do you believe in a heaven?[b]	
Yes	77%
7. Do you believe in a hell?[b]	
Yes	58%
8. Do you ever pray to God?[c]	
Yes (overall)	88%
Men	85%
Women	91%
18–24 years	80%
65+ years	91%
White	87%
Nonwhite	90%
9. Do you engage in daily prayer?[d]	
Yes	64%

Note. Percentages in each category do not add up to 100, as some responses (e.g., "no opinion," "not sure," and some "no" responses) are not included.

[a]The data are from *The Gallup Poll Monthly* (1994, July, p. 37).

[b]The data are from Starr, Buckley, and Elan (1989).

[c]The data are from Poloma and Gallup (1991, pp. 2–3).

[d]The data are from Becker (1986, p. 5).

One could argue that even if a somewhat lower percentage of Americans see religion as the "real" answer to life's difficulties, there are now actually more people who feel this way. Furthermore, the average religionist may be more committed and involved than in past years (though, as noted, this is a debatable point that must await new research for its resolution). The 6% increase in those defining themselves as "born-again" or "evangelical" Christians between 1986 and 1994 may reflect a continuing trend in the growth of conservative churches at the expense of their more liberal and middle-of-the-road counterparts. In fact, it is not uncommon to find that evangelical and fundamentalist Protestant groups have increased their membership by threefold to fourfold in the last 25 years.[19]

The foregoing information may seem to be contradictory, as it first suggests a growing liberalism in religious ideas and attachments, and then a growing conservatism at the expense of moderation. In all probability, the main trend is toward more of a personal liberalism; however, within the general pattern, a sizeable group is also apparently becoming increasingly conservative. It is quite possible that people are moving more toward the possible extremes within Western religion while the center slowly loses its constituency. This is a hypothesis that merits close scrutiny.

The issue of institutional loyalty deserves a brief comment, for many Americans literally sample different faiths. Whereas up to 40% of Protestants shift their religious affiliation at least once, 13% of Jews and 15% of Catholics exhibit similar movement.[20] This does not appear to be a function of theological conservatism or liberality, but rather of one's attachments to family and ethnic group. Age is a big factor in switching, with younger people moving away from formal affiliation, while older Protestants are likely to associate with more liberal denominations and groups. Roof and McKinney claim that "the big 'winner' in the switching game is the growing secular community."[21]

Religion and the "Baby Boomer" Generation

In the two decades after World War II, an estimated 76 million "baby boomers" were born in the United States. In recent years, they have been the objects of much investigation regarding virtually all aspects of their lives. With respect to faith, the noted sociologist of religion Wade Clark Roof has called them "a generation of seekers."[22] The propensity of some of this group to pursue spirituality outside of the religious mainstream is discussed below, but their main direction is of a much more mundane nature, which may say much for the future of religion in the United States for some time to come.

In his major study of the religion of the "baby boomers," in which he employed a sample of 1,599 people in four states spanning the nation, Roof has distinguished three groups: "loyalists," "returnees," and "dropouts." Loyalists, as the word implies, stayed with traditional religion; the returnees often deviated considerably in their personalized experiments with faith before coming back to the mainstream. The dropouts were those who simply moved away from standard religious institutions or were never affiliated to begin with. Table 4.2 offers some insight into the journeys of those who were reared as Catholics and as mainline and conservative Protestants.

Apparently both conservative Protestants and Catholics were more successful in keeping their members than were mainline Protestants. This may again be an indication of the power of conservative religious bodies, noted earlier. More of the mainline Protestants also became nonreligious than did members of the other groups. Still, before their possible return, over 60% of all the young adults with religious backgrounds had dropped out of their faith.[23] When they did come back, 13% moved toward fundamentalism and 21% were denoted as conservative (technically "evangelical moderates").[24]

We see some possible contradictions when we look at attitudes toward churchgoing and actual weekly attendance among Roof's subjects. With respect to the latter, as we move from liberal to conservative, the attendance percentages for men ranged from 31% to 51%; for women, they ranged from 30% to 80%.[25] When subjects were asked, however, whether a person "can be a good Christian and not attend church," the percentages varied from 66% (conservative) to 94% (not conservative). Churchgoing has thus become an issue of personal determination and choice, which Roof describes as the "new voluntarism."[26]

There is no doubt that exposure to the 1960s "revolution against the establishment" had a rather pervasive effect. Among those little affected by this time, 56% dropped out; in cases

TABLE 4.2. The Diverse Religious Paths Taken by Baby
Boomers Reared as Catholics, Mainline Protestants, and
Conservative Protestants

Religious path taken	%
Reared as Catholics	
Loyalists (identify selves as Catholics)	33
Currently active as Catholics	50
Shifted to other faiths*a*	12
Currently religiously active	8
Initial dropouts	67
Returnees	25
Final dropouts	42
Inactive Catholics	31
Reared as mainline Protestants	
Loyalists (identify selves as mainline Protestants)	31
Currently active as mainline Protestants	39
Shifted to other faiths*a*	24
Currently religiously active	5
Initial dropouts	69
Returnees	24
Final religious dropouts	45
Inactive mainline Protestants	26
Reared as conservative Protestants	
Loyalists (identify selves as conservative Protestants)	39
Currently active as conservative Protestants	55
Shifted to other faiths*a*	13
Currently religiously active	9
Initial dropouts	61
Returnees	25
Final dropouts	36
Inactive conservative Protestants	25

Note. Adapted from Roof (1993, pp. 176–179). Copyright 1993 by HarperCollins
Publishers. Adapted by permission.

*a*For Catholics, this includes shifts to conservative and mainline Protestant groups
along with a variety of undefined faiths; for mainline Protestants, this includes
shifts to conservative Protestant groups; for conservative Protestants, this includes shifts to mainline bodies.

where such influence was high, 84% left the institutional fold.[27] Still, in terms of belief in a
deity, the baby boomers essentially matched the overall population, with 94–95% of the total
group affirming this stance.[28] An interesting and subtle shift may be inferred from the finding that, as Roof puts it, "these intense seekers prefer to think of themselves as 'spiritual' rather
than as 'religious.'"[29]

The Search for Spirituality

"Spirituality" is a very popular word, but its meaning is extremely obscure. Efforts to clarify
the concept point vaguely toward a holistic relational perspective, which, appealing as it is,
has not proven useful for empirical research.[30] One wonders whether this ambiguity is not a

major source of its attractiveness, countering Western society's valuation of what is often viewed as a dehumanized scientific and technological exactitude. In any event, without specifying what it really is, one poll reports that 58% of Americans seek "spiritual growth."[31]

Though the idea of spirituality has been a core conception of mainline religion for millenia, it has been revitalized in modern life through a wide variety of sects, cults, personally constructed faiths, and what has been loosely termed "New Age religion." There is no core set of beliefs that characterizes this poorly defined collection of ideas and groups. It is composed of a melange of cliques and individuals that sometimes stress nature and environment, the power of mind and crystals, and extraordinary mental and physical possibilities— even to the point of "out-of-body frequent flier programs."[32]

Though one may question certain New Age enthusiasts' grip on reality, the movement speaks to a search for meanings that stand outside of, and are emotionally and intellectually at variance with, accepted mainstream religion, science, and life as normally lived and experienced. Whereas in the 1960s similar ideas appealed strongly to adolescents and young adults, contemporary supporters are said to be middle-aged. They may, in part, be that earlier generation grown older. Though direct evidence to this effect has not been forthcoming, there are data that show the continuing influence of exposure to the ideas of the 1960s. For example, when such a potential effect was low, only 33% of the boomers in Roof's sample considered themselves "spiritual"; when the impact of that decade was high, 81% of the sample regarded themselves as "spiritual."[33] Similar trends were found in a number of related areas. Exposure to the 1960s reduced theistic beliefs but enhanced mystical and individualistic ones.[34]

One view is that the baby boomers are now confronting the meaning of aging and its long-range eventuality without mitigating beliefs that place their lives in a larger, if not universal, perspective.[35] Another general feature of this development is the use of a "religious" and "spiritual" language, which may reflect an attempt to conceptualize these ideas and bodies as inspirational variants of well-established historical faith traditions. In part, these new forms may reflect the common complaint among churchgoers that formal religious institutions are overly involved with "organizational as opposed to theological or spiritual issues."[36]

The outcome of these largely adult struggles for an institutional religious revitalization and a personal "rebirth" has been the development of an estimated 400 new spiritual/religious associations in the late 1980s alone—a trend that seems to be continuing.[37] Estimates of the number of New Agers in the United States range from 6% to 15% of the population.[38]

Futurists forecast that, in the short term, the main religious developments will take place on the fringes of the Judeo-Christian tradition, with the evangelical/fundamentalist heritage holding down one end of the continuum and New Age faiths growing at the other extreme. Though the first population far exceeds the second, both movements seem quite adept at using modern business methods and the mass media to get their messages across to potential consumers.[39]

The Significance of Religion for Adults

Theorized basic psychological needs for religious belief and activity are explicated at length in Chapter 11, where we suggest that faith satisfies personal requirements for meaning, control, and self-esteem. These may be especially true for the baby boomer generation, as one discussion of the this generation claims that the "search for meaning is a powerful motivation [for this group] to return to the pews."[40] For many young marrieds, this quest may become critical when children come along; for middle-aged people, this may happen when they confront the obvious fact that life will not go on forever. In either case, a struggle ensues to locate oneself in the scheme of things, and this elicits an effort to establish that one's existence matters and is not just a product of biology, chance, and fate. Obviously, religious doctrines are well suited to cope with such a necessity.

If we view the religious search in terms of motivations to attend church, a number of possibilities exist. Relative to participation in a fundamentalist congregation, Monaghan has suggested three basic motivations: authority seeking, comfort seeking, and social involvement.[41] Those in the first group want an authority upon whom they can be dependent, and to whom they can submit themselves for guidance. For these people, "the minister provides meaning for church members where none existed before."[42] Is it possible that the baby boomers described above are searching for authorities who offer ultimate meanings? There could, of course, be overlap with Monaghan's second type, in that comfort seekers are also looking for answers (particularly regarding death and its aftermath). Certainly such concerns and interests increase as people get older. By contrast, Monaghan's third type really consists of persons for whom the church becomes their life, but more relationally and interpersonally than ideologically. This may be a rather small group.

In a study of 11,122 people from 561 congregations, Benson and Eklin speak of "horizontal," "vertical," and "integrated" faith.[43] The first two forms, introduced earlier by Davidson, refer respectively to an orientation toward other people and an orientation toward God and the supernatural.[44] When both orientations are strong, one's faith is said to be integrated. Benson and Eklin note that the overall tendency for adults is for a vertical perspective to be dominant, but that both types generally increase with age, with an integrated faith prevailing for those over 70.

One popular image must be dispelled: Simplistic categorization implies that religious people must be more alike than different in their religious beliefs. Even when individul churches and denominations are considered, the view persists that homogeneity within these groups is the rule. Research, however, suggests quite the opposite, showing that considerable heterogeneity exists in both vertical and horizontal beliefs among religionists within specific congregational settings.[45] Davidson points out that such variation can be quite constructive in fostering breadth in religious outlooks; it can also "insure that the organization will remain meaningful for both the otherworldly and the this-worldly oriented members."[46] Though heterogeneity can sponsor conflict, it may spur the development of church programs with wide appeal, as well as the appearance of new and creative theological outlooks.

Age is apparently a factor in the homogeneity–heterogeneity issue. One national sample of 4,444 Lutherans showed a reduction of heterogeneity from young adulthood, where it was greatest, to a steady increase in belief homogeneity to age 65.[47] A landmark study by Shand of a group of Amherst College graduates over a 40-year period revealed a surprising overall stability in their views, despite the fact that there were marked reductions in beliefs in hell, heaven, and resurrection.[48] If there is an underlying theme behind all of this research, it is that people not only vary meaningfully among themselves in religious beliefs, but do not manifest rigidity over the lifespan; they may change their views as a result of personal experience.

In the last analysis, the psychological significance of religious belief and involvement is to be found in what may be viewed as the common, rather taken-for-granted trials, tasks, and needs of everyday existence. This brings us back to Adler's three great problems of life—work, interpersonal relations, and love and marriage. On a more basic level, we must simply ask whether religious faith relates to personal satisfaction. The answer is generally that it does. In fact, much research and writing reveal that the way people feel about themselves often underlies their performance and success in other domains.[49]

The role of religion in these relationships seems quite clear. A number of national and international surveys are consistent in the finding not only that religious faith is personally important (something we have already noted), but that faith is positively affiliated with perceptions of self-satisfaction and happiness. Those with the greatest religious involvement report the greatest degree of happiness.[50] Part of this association is undoubtedly a function of the role of faith in aiding people to cope with both adversity and the ordinary difficulties of living; this role is described in detail in Chapter 11. Such people have thus surmounted the first hurdle in adult living—living successfully with themselves. The next step is to meet the economic responsibilities of mature adulthood, and this now brings us to the realm of work.

RELIGION IN WORK, PROFESSIONS, AND OCCUPATIONS

From Biblical prescriptions to modern-day endorsements, the call to work and labor has been endowed with religious sanction and public approbation. Whether it be the Biblical "the people had a mind to work"[51] or the rule that "if any would not work, neither should he eat,"[52] precept and practice are clear: Work is endowed with a sacred quality and purpose that is ennobling. Though always central to the Judeo-Christian tradition, the valuation of labor reached new heights with the advent of Protestantism and the Calvinistic quest for grace. This has been well stated, if not sociologically codified, in Max Weber's *The Protestant Ethic* and *The Spirit of Capitalism*.[53]

Achievement Motivation and the "Protestant Ethic"

Calvinism's emphasis on achieving grace and salvation defined the path to such glory through predestination and the exercise of one's earthly calling. Worldly duties were thus endowed with an overriding moral quality. As one author has noted, "work, as all good Calvinists knew, justified one's existence to God."[54] This was rapidly translated into a celebration of success and achievement, hence labor and piety were idealistically regarded as a unity. Capitalism and the motivation to acquire and achieve were now legitimized. Though such imagery has faded in contemporary society, the goal of work as an avenue to wealth and personal satisfaction continues as a central, even if muted, part of our modern cultural mythology.

Almost from the time it was first proposed, this "Protestant ethic" came under attack. Despite efforts to demonstrate its influence as a pervasive and continuing force primarily among Protestants, the data supporting this view have been extremely weak.[55] This is not to say that such elements are not present, but that comparisons of Protestants with Catholics and Jews often fail to show any consistent differences in adherence to these ideas. As Roberts claims, "the rational pursuit of wealth (spirit of capitalism) is so thoroughly secularized in the Western world that it has become independent of any one religious tradition."[56]

In untangling the web of factors that contribute to the struggle for riches, particularly what has been termed "achievement motivation," one encounters a maze of sociological and psychological factors. Male Jews, for example, are overrepresented in the professions and among managers and proprietors, and underrepresented in blue-collar occupations. Along with Presbyterians and Episcopalians, they fall at the high end of occupational income, and also join these groups at the top echelons of occupational prestige ratings.[57] Catholics are much lower in this last dimension, implying their greater presence in more modest occupations. Greeley has observed, however, that Catholics and Protestants share similar economic aspirations.[58] In early work on achievement motivation per se, the levels reported for Jews and Protestants were higher than for Catholics. This was attributed to greater independence training for the first two groups—an emphasis likely to reflect class and cultural factors.[59]

Jewish–Christian Differences

Variation among religious groups in the U.S. milieu appears to be slowly but surely disappearing; however, with respect to economic factors, some indications of Jewish–Christian differences still exist. A long history of anti-Semitism plus a corresponding pattern of self-segregation contributed to the development of a Jewish subculture that, among other elements, valued knowledge and education and reinforced family pressures toward achievement motivation.[60] The outcome has been a disproportionately high number of Jews coming to the forefront of U.S. society. For example, a study of the 1974–1975 edition of *Who's Who in America* revealed that Jews had a rate of inclusion two and a half times higher than expected for the overall population.[61] Recent work by Davidson and his associates with the 1992–1993 edition of *Who's Who* suggests that this incidence has increased for Jews to over four times the rate that would be expected from their numbers in the United States.[62] Study after study further reveals the presence of Jews among the U.S. intellectual elite at rates from 4 to 10 or more times their percentage in the population, the latter being less than 3%.[63] This has been most evident for some time among U.S. Nobel laureates, of whom 30–40% are Jewish.[64] A strong attraction of Jews toward science has also been observed among applicants for the Westinghouse Science Talent Search.[65]

Rising to the Top: Religion, Work, and Money

An interesting variation on the observations above comes from the imagery that in part translates the Protestant ethic into the notion of a Protestant elite in our nation. This has been termed "the Protestant establishment."[66] Here the idea is that those who represent the Protestant ethic should and actually do rise to the top of society—socially, politically, and economically. U.S. history testifies to the place of Protestants in the foremost positions in all three domains: in "the 400" or "the upper crust"; among our highest government officials; and in that noteworthy group pejoratively termed by Lundberg "the rich and the super-rich."[67] Davidson and colleagues testify to the persistence of a Protestant elite; however, diversity has been increasing at a rapid rate, with Catholics and Jews making sizeable inroads in the last half century into the circles of economic power and their political, cultural, and social correlates.[68]

Integrating Religion and Work

In a very significant recent work, Robert Wuthnow points out that we really know very little about how Americans integrate their rather strong religious beliefs with their correspondingly clear and zealous economic motivations and behaviors.[69] Using over 2,000 respondents and almost 200 in-depth interviews, this impressive survey reveals that even though religion's role in U.S. economic life is greatly muted, it nevertheless exerts some subtle, "behind the scenes" influence. Calvinistic/Puritan ideas are still present, counseling morality in business dealings. Likewise, appeals to thrift and economic advantage probably find a responsive ear, as they continue to be featured in advertisements by banks, investment firms, stockbrokers, insurance agencies, and other financial "movers and shakers."

When asked directly about the role of religion in choosing a job, about 22% of Wuthnow's sample suggested that their faith might have had some role in their decision.[70] Comparing churchgoers and the total labor force on a wide variety of characteristics, Wuthnow found that essentially nothing seemed to distinguish these two groups. With regard to sense of personal worth, churchgoers placed considerably more weight on their relation to God than was found in the overall labor force. Though the inference was tenuous, slight differences showed churchgoers favoring familial, social, moral, and community values over personal pleasure and gain.[71] These tendencies are in line with research showing intrinsic/ committed leanings to be positively associated with social, altruistic, and religious values. As Wuthnow has theorized, those who subscribe to a utilitarian, extrinsic/consensual faith orientation are more concerned with status, materialism, achievement, income, and security.[72] Wuthnow further confirms that the classical Calvinistic view that hard labor is pleasing to God still prevails in the work force (53% of his sample endorsed this view), and moreover relates to church attendance (68% of Wuthnow's weekly churchgoers affirmed this view).[73]

One notable characteristic of contemporary U.S. society has been the growing number of females in the work force. When the 20th century began, fewer than 20% of all women and fewer than 5% of married women were working. Currently, both of these numbers are in the vicinity of 60%, and both will undoubtedly continue to grow.[74]

The relationship between work and religiosity has proven to be complex, for whether adult females work or not, they continue to be burdened by the demands of home and motherhood. Some research therefore suggests a negative association between working and religious activities. Other work suggests the replacement of religious values by those of the workplace, and/or the substitution of new social ties from one's occupation for those previously developed in church.[75] Despite such possibilities, large-scale survey research has not shown any reduction in church attendance on the part of Christian working women.

Examining these issues for a traditionally conservative group—namely, Mormons— Chadwick and Garrett obtained survey data on over 1,100 women. There was little doubt that employment had a negative impact on church activity, both subjectively in terms of belief and objectively in relation to behavior. Despite these tendencies, it appeared that most of the women sampled tried hard to maintain their religious commitment and church involvement.[76]

Given the foregoing, one might reasonably ask about the relationship between religiosity and job satisfaction. There is much literature showing that women who work are happier than those who do not hold jobs.[77] Validating earlier research, Wuthnow found that religiosity was generally positively correlated with job satisfaction. He suggests that religious beliefs and activities may serve to reduce job stress (see Chapter 11).[78] The data accumulated to date suggest that one's faith makes work more meaningful by helping to integrate it positively into one's life.

Religion and Ethics in the Workplace

Continuing his examination of the potential influence of religion in work settings, Wuthnow examined the possible role of ethics and found a number of differences that were linked with faith commitments. When it came to defining what work ethics entail, weekly churchgoers were more likely than the work force in general to stress honesty and fairness. There was also a tendency to see such concerns in a more absolutist than relativistic manner.[79] With regard to making major work decisions, moral absolutism was again present, along with a theistically premised moralism and altruism. These inclinations countered an individualistic utilitarianism. In other words, Wuthnow's churchgoers felt that personal desires and benefits must give way to religious and humanitarian considerations.[80] Moral concerns were seen as taking precedence over individual ones; thus those who subscribed to moral and theistic absolutist perspectives were likely to adhere to ethical rules and regulations in the workplace.[81] These positions were held more strongly by persons who were affiliated with religious fellowship groups, again revealing the "behind the scenes" role of religious involvements.

Religion, Money, and Materialism

It may be one of those subtle yet understandable holdovers from classic Christianity and the Protestant ethic, but religious individuals seem more concerned than their less involved peers about the relationship of money and materialism to spiritual issues.[82] Differences between these groups are often small to nonexistent; however, committed religionists associate hard work with using money and wealth as avenues to charity and helping others. Wuthnow points out that religious people justify wealth by associating it with generosity and hard work.[83] This view is realized in church giving, where the main predictors are a strong religious commitment, theological conservatism, and church activity.[84] In other words, intrinsic religiosity is a significant element in making religious donations, though it is by no means the only reason. This perspective combines two orientations—strong personal religious involvement, and social awareness and sensitivity.[85] It is seen clearly in Research Box 4.1, which briefly overviews the important work of Davidson and Pyle.

We should note that spirituality and materialism have been traditionally conceptualized as being in opposition. Idealistically, this may appear true; however, once again, Wuthnow points out that the relationship is not simple. Even though churches and churchgoers support materialism, there is still a small, underlying, but consistent tendency for

---

Research Box 4.1. Passing the Plate in Affluent Churches
(Davidson & Pyle, 1994)

Studying financial giving in a number of affluent churches in northeastern Kansas, these researchers attempted to test two theoretical views: "social exchange" and "symbolic interactionism." The former stresses donations as a function of benefits to be gained in relation to costs; the latter pertains to religious self-concepts and beliefs. Three independent variables were defined: "benefit orientation," "intrinsic religiosity," and "belief orientation." The dependent variable was the amount given to the church.

The biggest direct contributors to giving were income and participation. Since the details of this work are quite complex, we may summarize the findings thus: Neither benefits and costs per se nor beliefs by themselves were primary independent predictors of giving. Participation and intrinsic religiosity, representing a linking of social exchange and symbolic interactionism, came into play. Future research must therefore consider relationships between these frameworks and church giving.

religious commitment to counter materialistic emphases.[86] That image of "filthy lucre" still lurks in the religious background.

Religion as a Profession

No discussion of the relationship of religion to work would be complete without some examination of those who seek fulfillment by uniting their work lives with their faith. Much writing and research has been carried out on seminary students and clergy; yet drawing conclusions about factors that direct a person toward church-related professions is risky.[87]

Dittes examined this area 25 years ago and raised many questions, and it does not appear to have changed appreciably since then.[88] As he demonstrated, serious methodological problems plague this area; theory is lacking; and the research can best be termed "conceptually scattered." Almost every kind of psychological instrument has been applied at one time or another to clergy or aspirants to the profession.[89] In Chapter 12, we give this literature some attention as regards questions about abnormality and deviance as motivators for becoming a religious professional. Here we look at other issues, more to give readers a sense of the thinking in this area than to solve any of the many fundamental questions that have been raised.

Why Become a Religious Professional?

Dittes suggested a "little adult" theory as directing individuals toward becoming clergy.[90] Basically psychoanalytic in nature, this theory posits a continuation of childhood and adolescent roles, in which approval and dependency needs gain expression when a person becomes a religious professional. Unfortunately, there is a dearth of solid research supporting this view.

Approximately 40 years ago, the Ministry Studies Board of the National Council of Churches produced the Theological School Inventory (TSI), which was primarily intended to assess constructive personal reasons for becoming a cleric.[91] This instrument suggested two motivational–behavioral patterns for entering the ministry: "special leading" and "natural leading." The former stresses the role of God in making one's choice to enter the ministry; one essentially perceives oneself to be "chosen" by God for such a profession. In contrast, natural leading focuses on finding an identity, and this is felt to be best realized by meeting the religious, spiritual, and psychosocial needs of both oneself and others. The emotional–transcendental link is converted into a rational decision-making process.[92]

However, in an interesting study of college students who were directing themselves toward the ministry, Embree explored a variety of religious variables and found the distinction between natural leading and special leading to be a weak contributor to motivation to enter the ministry.[93] This work is representative of the kinds of conflicting results that pose a dilemma for workers in this area.

The hopes, needs, and desires of those seeking to become religious professionals require a much more open-minded approach to motivations than the dichotomy between natural and special leading is capable of including. Studies of occupational satisfaction among ministers and priests indicate a very broad and clearly multidimensional pattern of views and concerns.[94] The age of the professional cannot be omitted from these efforts, as a very large number of those seeking to become clergy are now choosing this avenue as a second vocational path in their lives.[95] Much has been done to bring these issues under consideration, but the involved nature of the problem, the variation among the samples selected for study, and the lack of cross-validation all make it extremely difficult to arrive at definitive conclusions.

&

Research Box 4.2. Differentiation of Clergy Subgroups on the Basis of Vocational Interests (Webb & Hultgren, 1973)

This study attempted to determine whether vocational interests might distinguish among 10 different clergy occupations (i.e., parish ministers, directors of Christian education, scholars, missionaries, counselors, musicians, social workers, campus ministers, administrators, and evangelists). Comparisons were made on seven dimensions: music versus scholarship; teaching versus counseling; scholarship versus administration; personal relationship versus impersonality; involvement versus noninvolvement in social concerns; and emotionalized versus institutionalized religion. To this end, 3,617 male clergy in these positions were given the Inventory of Religious Activities and Interests plus a biographical questionnaire. The groups were then compared by means of various procedures. Of 45 possible two-group comparisons (e.g., parish ministers vs. counselors), differences were found for 22 of the pairings. In terms of vocational interests, 51% of all participants were classified correctly in their specialty. This is a very significant number, suggesting the validity of the measure. The findings indicate that clergy aspirants have a broad range of interests and possible motivations for the ministry; results also suggest early use of a vocational interest inventory to aid clerical aspirants in choosing a religious career.

Even superficial observation of a few researches directed at revealing the complexity of the clerical domain makes the difficulties evident. The massive study by Schuller, Strommen, and Brekke of 47 Protestant denominations implies that variation among these bodies may well render any simplistic search for overriding motivational or personality commonalities among clerics conceptually invalid.[96] It is also abundantly clear that the atmosphere of churches is changing, in response to rather sweeping changes in U.S. culture over the last half century. Hadden and Quinley noted a rising tide of clerical social activism during the 1960s and 1970s; they pointed to a widening gulf between clergy and laity during this period.[97] This trend may perhaps have begun to reverse itself in the 1980s.[98] Similar conflicts and diversity have been found and extensively discussed with regard to Catholic priests.[99] Such tendencies may well influence one's choice of a religious profession.

The issue of complexity also comes to the fore when one examines how the single word "clergy" masks a host of occupational specialties and a surprising variety of vocational interests on the part of clerics. Studying over 3,600 male clergy, Webb and Hultgren showed that at least 10 roles and seven dimensions could be employed to understand and classify clerical subgroups.[100] This study is described in detail in Research Box 4.2.

Gender and the Religious Professional

That the domain of the religious professional has been a male preserve for millenia goes without saying. There have been some variations on this theme. The Catholic church has provided for sisterhoods of nuns; of course, nuns have always been secondary in power and prestige to priests, and all higher church offices were and still are limited to men. There is evidence that this gender pattern may have been different in early Christianity.[101] Traditional male–female power relationships have prevailed in Judaism and Protestantism as well; however, some of these are yielding to pressure, and others are increasingly being challenged. The modern movement for the religious professionalization of women appears to have begun, though in muted and rather controlled fashion, in the late 19th century.[102] This is merely one expression of a much broader and more basic set of issues that cannot be handled here, and the interested reader should seek out this literature which is rapidly growing in breadth and understanding.[103] The literature also describes a surprising level of cultural insensitivity and callousness.[104] It may not be amiss to speculate that we are witnessing the change from a caste to a class system, as opportunities slowly increase for women to compete with men for church positions that were formerly restricted to males.

The impressive studies of Paula Nesbitt on Episcopalian and Unitarian/Universalist clergy illustrate clearly some of the current differential treatment afforded males and females.[105] Nesbitt shows how multiple ordination tracks serve to keep female clergy in lower occupational levels and to reduce their opportunities for advancement. At the same time, in the Episcopal Church, one observes an "increasing concentration of [women] in lower-level positions regardless of ordination track."[106] With respect to the Unitarian/Universalist ministry, "persistent inequality, particularly at denominational leadership levels, suggests that ordination holds different value for women and men in accessing opportunities for their ministerial careers."[107] An even more heinous and extreme expression of gender inequality among clergy is found in data indicating that the majority of female clergy have been sexually harassed or abused by their male colleagues.[108]

Whether antifeminists like it or not, female clergy are here to stay. Their increasing numbers illustrate, as Nesbitt has put it, the "feminization" of the clergy.[109] This growing trend for women to become clerics is not restricted to the more liberal faiths, but may be found among very conservative religious bodies such as Pentecostal sects.[110] In these groups, a woman must work especially hard to affirm her role in the home as a wife and mother, deny her sexuality, and recognize herself as inferior to males. This delicate balance is essential for even tentative acceptance of her clerical role.[111]

Nesbitt sees "dim prospects in the near future for women to develop parity with men," and adds that

> the prognosis points to continued movement toward occupational feminization, including occupational sex segregation and the accompanying struggle among women priests and ministers for full-time positions leading to the levels of responsibility held by men, in their cohort, with comparable educational background. There does not seem to be much evidence that women and men will be competing for the same set of occupational opportunities. Thus, structurally, the best and brightest of the young male clerics still may have the greatest occupational life chances.[112]

Not all research is quantitative and "hard-nosed." Much good information can be obtained by skilled interviewers using relatively small samples. These idiographic approaches are often excellent sources of theory and hypotheses that can be further assessed by more objective and quantitative methods. The work of Martha Long Ice is a fine example of such an effort.[113] This is described in Research Box 4.3.

Summary

There is not a great deal of research on religion relative to Adler's first great task of life, work. A few recent studies, such as that of Wuthnow, demonstrate the complexity of such ties. The importance of work in personal satisfaction cannot be underestimated.[114] Faith can, however, serve as a substitute for the loss of work. One study of 62 societies revealed that the elderly appear to compensate for their decreasing economic role by increasing their religious involve-

⠶

Research Box 4.3. Clergywomen and Their Worldviews (Ice, 1987)

Work on female clergy is truly in its infancy. This in-depth study of 17 clergywomen demonstrates the breadth of this domain and the rich variety of outlooks that exist among such women. In a sense, they are pioneers charting a new and difficult path for the many others who are rapidly following in their footsteps.

The women studied by Ice represented 12 denominations and spanned a broad range of ages, from the 20s to the mid-70s. Fifteen of the women were actively serving in congregations. Only one, a Catholic, was not officially ordained. There were 15 Protestants, a Catholic, and a Jew in the sample. Ice attempted to get as full an autobiographical perspective as possible, and to this added concerns with gender orientation, views of authority, religious institutional administration, moral leadership, the issue of theological truth, and other related matters.

Though the subjects felt quite comfortable with themselves as women, a flexible androgynous orientation seemed to prevail. Their situation called on a variety of characteristics that are sometimes stereotypically male and sometimes female; no gender limitations were evident. This does not mean that these women were not aware of gender differences in power, or that such could be ignored. Their preference was for egalitarian ideals and democratic relationships, and the women displayed a positive, confident perspective in attempting to realize such human goals. Evidences of struggle for personal growth were indeed present, marking many of these women as "transcenders"—those who grow above the difficulties and restrictions they have faced in life.

A holistic outlook stressing people, not things and mechanics, tied together the faith and lives of these women. This could be characterized as a fundamentally intrinsic religious orientation. A stress on moral modeling was also evident. In like manner, the women demonstrated what might be termed an integrative theologizing, which was linked with their moral and administrative leadership.

Of special significance is the fact that as a social scientist, Ice perceived her observations as contributing to a theoretical approach and hypotheses that could be assessed in future work.

ment. The evidence further suggests that institutionalized religion and personal faith commitments probably influence work and career. Koltko sees "an indirect influence on vocational development through an influence on values."[115] He cites research to the effect of "a *general* religious influence on precursors to vocational choice [and] . . . a *specific* influence based on denomination."[116] This is a realm that still poses problems of interest to both religion and psychology, and therefore merits much more research than has yet been afforded it.

RELIGION IN SOCIAL RELATIONSHIPS

The second great task of life noted by Adler concerns how people deal with their interpersonal perspectives, relationships, and social outlook. Apparently, as people enter adulthood, the number of close personal relationships decreases.[117] Levinson and his associates suggest that becoming an adult involves a concern with the "balance between the needs of the self and the needs of society."[118] Religion may help resolve these choices. Initially, such satisfaction is evident in simply being identified with a formal religious system. More specifically, involvement in a church aids integration into the community, and, as we will see in Chapter 12, such activities perform important cultural socialization roles. The result is that regular churchgoers appear to be better off psychologically than their nonattending peers.[119]

Most of the research on interpersonal relations has dealt with the issues of prejudice, discrimination, and altruism. These are significant concerns throughout life; however, in the present volume, we treat them as primarily falling under morality broadly conceived. They are therefore discussed in Chapter 10. Some overlapping ideas and research leading to the more detailed treatment of these areas are introduced here.

Religious and scriptural themes such as the Golden Rule clearly convey the concern of basic institutional religion with the idea of how people evaluate and behave toward others. Unhappily, such constructive notions are placed under great strain in daily life in individualistically oriented U.S. society. The mass media shower the public with horror stories of crime in endemic proportions, as well as of people taking advantage of the sick, elderly, and infirm (both legally and illegally). Inhumanity often appears to reign undiminished; it frequently seems that one can easily speak of the "skim milk of human kindness." On the other side of this coin, however, one reads about the billions of dollars people give to charities and those ever-present good Samaritans who risk life and limb to help persons in dire straits. The picture is not simple, and religion does play a role in its expression.

For millenia, religious institutions and their representatives have played noteworthy social roles; people have commonly been levied for monetary contributions or voluntarily made such contributions to aid those requiring support. In corresponding fashion, churches and synagogues have often engaged in activities to aid those needing help. In 1992, for example, U.S. religious sources made charitable bequests in excess of $56 billion.[120]

At the same time, estimates of giving to religious bodies range from about $40 billion annually to over $50 billion.[121] Study after study has also shown that such giving relates positively to religious commitment and involvement.[122] As one might expect, there is, as Wuthnow states, a "culture of giving" that separates responsible giving from materialistic motivation.[123] Regular churchgoers are consistently more willing to give money and volunteer to assist others than the population in general has been found to be. One large-scale study of over 11,000 churchgoers found that approximately 85% of members saw their church as placing some to very strong emphasis on "involving members in helping people in [their] town or city."[124] The numbers were even higher when the recipients of such aid were the "poor and hungry."[125] Benson points up the primary importance of a "caring church" and Christian education in fostering a mature faith among Protestants, a major component of which is "social justice and social welfare behavior."[126] Using a measure based on Alfred Adler's idea about social interest, Edwards and Wessels, like Benson, have described such concern as central to religious maturity.[127] The social message of Western religion is obviously quite strong, and it appears to be widely accepted.

The idea of a socially sensitive mature faith has recently become a part of seminary education through the concept of "globalization."[128] The idea is to sensitize theological students and potential clergy to cultural diversity and the modern multicultural social environment. Efforts to join such training and issues to personal faith outlooks, orientations, and religious activities such as prayer are in their infancy; yet they already demonstrate a variety of ties, such as links with prayer directed toward self-growth, constructive worldly concerns, and positive God images.[129]

Research on religion and specific interpersonal outlooks outside of the realms of prejudice and altruism is not prolific and manifests some contradictions. Kirkpatrick observed a negative association between humanitarianism and religious conservatism, but this relationship has been shown to be more complex than was first believed.[130] When faith is defined in terms of intrinsic/committed and extrinsic/consensual forms plus other expressions among adults 22 to 56 years old, social interest, empathy, and interpersonal understanding decrease as extrinsic/consensual tendencies increase.[131] By contrast, the intrinsic orientation is positively related to social interest.

In one noteworthy study, dealing with somewhat variant notions about trust and faith in people, no associations were shown with either church attendance or intrinsic perspectives.[132] These apparently conflicting findings gain some support from other work with questionnaires, which revealed weak correlations at best between faith in people and intrinsic religion.[133] This last effort also utilized a variable termed "interpersonal distance"—namely, how closely an individual will allow others to approach before becoming uncomfortable. We look more closely at this work in Research Box 4.4, as it reveals other subtle considerations that merit additional investigation.

Considering the contemporary emphasis in mainstream social psychology on interpersonal perception, influence, attraction, and so forth, it is surprising that so little research has attempted to examine these variables in relation to religious belief, experience, and behavior. Here is an area that seems "wide open" with regard to research potential.

RELIGION IN LOVE AND MARRIAGE

Adler's third great task of life—that of establishing deep and lasting love relationships—has been of great concern to institutional faith and individual religionists for thousands of years.

Research Box 4.4. Personal Religion and Psychosocial Schemas: Interpersonal Distance (Spilka & Mullin, 1977)

A broad sample of 437 persons ranging from high school students to older adults was administered an instrument designed to assess "interpersonal distance." It permitted one to indicate how closely they would allow others to approach them physically from front, rear, and sides. Several different everyday interpersonal situations were pictured, in which the reference person's sex, age, and social status were varied. The distances indicated were correlated with measures of intrinsic and extrinsic, and committed and consensual, faith orientations.

It was observed that consensually and extrinsically oriented persons tended to keep others at greater distances than those who were intrinsically and committedly oriented. Extrinsically and consensually oriented persons also varied their distances in relation to the age, sex, and status of the reference person; this was not true for their intrinsic/committed peers. The implication is that extrinsic/consensual tendencies relate to viewing people in terms of social categories. This may be regarded as a utilitarian evaluation of others in terms of their personal acceptability, and opposes the more individualistic perspective of an intrinsic/committed faith.

It has also been an area illustrating much personal and social conflict that, if anything, is more evident today than in past times. A good deal of this dissension and friction centers around questions of sexual expression.

Sexual Behavior: The Religious View

Religion and sexual behavior have had a long and troubled relationship. We might call it both close and conflicted, suggesting (as some of the writing on issues in marriage contends) that this is an instance of "neurotic interaction in marriage."[134] We might, of course, paraphrase another noteworthy book title and call religion and sex "intimate enemies," for they have often been poor bedfellows.[135]

Historically, the Christian perspective on sex fits into a broader context. In part, it reflects an earlier Greek view that placed pleasures of the mind above those of the body. This was sometimes equated with the notion that the body is corrupting, whereas the exercise of mind through reason is the way toward enlightenment.[136] Early Christian ascetics added the idea that the body interferes with the attainment of a mystical union with the divine. In certain quarters, this translated into an association of body with sexuality and the denial of reason; hence the body and sexuality developed an affiliation with evil (both potential and actual), in large part because evil was seen as countering reason. Another step in this process was to identify sexual activity with women and associate the two with evil, as in Tertullian's reference to woman as "the Devil's gateway."[137] One could also selectively treat scripture emphasizing the prescription to "be fruitful and multiply," implying a positive and constructive purpose to sex. By contrast, stress might be placed on the role of Eve in the fall of humanity, and hence the guilt of all females by association. Finally, elements of Manicheism[138] filtered into Christianity, and may have influenced Augustine and other early church fathers; the result was that sensuality, sexual relations, and women were all relegated to a lower and more sinful realm.[139]

Religion and Sex in Marriage

Adler described a mutually satisfying marital relationship as the essence of his third great task of life; Freud similarly extolled such a state, viewing it as a sign of maturity and further as the framework in which procreation should occur.[140] This has fundamentally been the Judeo-Christian position for over two millenia. Though concern with love and respect has always been present, the notion of intercourse only for the purpose of producing children has increasingly given way to a more liberal treatment of sexual activity for both affectional and pleasurable purposes.[141]

Sexual Activity in Marriage

The early research on religion and sexual activity supported a popular view that religion tended to suppress sexual activity. In the Kinsey reports of almost 50 years ago, this held for males but not for females.[142] No adequate explanation for this contradiction was ever provided. The issue may now be moot, however, as more recent research suggests that religiosity has no inhibiting effect on sexual behavior, and there are even data indicating that religiosity either is positively correlated with frequency of sexual relations or is independent of it.[143]

Those who perceive faith as a sexual inhibitor may also be the ones holding the view that religious women are not as likely to experience orgasm and sexual satisfaction as their less religious counterparts. Both inferences appear to be false. In one study, the "very religious" and those who were "not religious" were essentially equal in designating sex as "deliciously sensuous." There was some suggestion that Protestants agreed with this assessment slightly less than Catholics and Jews or those who claimed no religious affiliation.[144] Another large-scale research effort implies a positive relationship between general happiness and sexual satisfaction. In this work, both measures increased with religiosity.[145]

An interesting study by Matthews focused on sexuality among conservative Christians, whose churches advocate a leading and controlling role for men in marriage, and hence a submissive stance for women.[146] Extensive interviews of 55 women and 21 men revealed considerable variance from church doctrine. Fewer than half of both the men and women viewed sexual activity as necessarily restricted to the marital state. More in line with what liberal critics might believe was the finding that fewer than one-third of the respondents felt sex was primarily to be enjoyed. Under one-quarter saw sex as a gift of God. Still, there was an awareness of males' responsibility to be sensitive to females' sexual needs. In reciprocation, the wives often regarded sex as a "privilege," "pleasure," or "gift" to be realized within a loving relationship.

With respect to their actual experiences, 57% of the men and 49% of the women described their sexual lives within marriage in extremely positive terms; another 29% of both the husbands and wives considered their sexual lives as fair to good. Only one male and 13% of the women viewed their marital sexual relations as poor. Generally, the wives felt that their husbands were sensitive to their needs. To some degree this may be due to the fact that the churches have increasingly moved away from the view of sex as a male privilege and a female duty, and toward concerns with love, responsibility, and sensitivity on the part of both partners. That husbands should learn about and meet their wives' needs before their own is part of this modern teaching. Interestingly, about one-third of both the husbands and wives were in conflict regarding traditional views about male leadership and female submission.

Sexual Behavior and Marital Satisfaction

The relationship between marital satisfaction and sexual behavior has always been muddled. In the broader context of marital concerns (money, children, security, love, commitment, etc.), sex has often taken a secondary role. The view has been advanced that religiosity may act as a buffer between sexual gratification and marital happiness, especially among women.[147] This does not appear to be true. *The Redbook Report on Female Sexuality* claims that very religious women report greater satisfaction with marital sex than do less religious or nonreligious women.[148] The report also states that religious women are more satisfied with their frequency of sexual intercourse, and claim to be more orgasmic, than their less devout peers. Moreover, they seem to have better communication with their spouses and rather strong beliefs that they are in good to very good marriages.

Some social scientists seem reluctant to accept such positive testimony of religious women. Suggestions have been made that they probably "don't know what they are missing," or are responding to researchers in a socially desirable way.[149] No evidence to support such interpretations has been forthcoming. Tavris and Sadd theorize that these women may have lower sexual expectations and are less willing to believe widely purveyed popular fantasies about ecstatic sexual gratification.[150] Again, no data to back such an interpretation have been produced. These problematic efforts to cast religion in repressive or suppressive roles relative to sexual expression have not gained support from research. The great majority of Americans are obviously religious, and there is little reason to believe that personal religiosity has any adverse effects on sexual activity in marriage.

Religion and Marriage: The Broader Context

Many factors clearly take precedence over sexual activity in the long-term marital relationship. Commitment in marriage is a very complex phenomenon, reflecting a wide variety of personal and social perspectives, social pressures, relationship investments, and moral outlooks, plus a host of other structural and individual concerns and expectations.[151] It behooves us, therefore, to ask whether faith is related to marital happiness and commitment in general. Before doing so, we must recognize that religious institutions constitute an important arena for social interaction of the sort that can lead to marriage. People who meet in churches or synagogues are quite likely to possess similar backgrounds (socioeconomically and ethnically similar in particular), and therefore to share views regarding many aspects of life. Such similarity is a well-known correlate of a happy marriage. Many sources of potential conflict are thus absent or minimized at the start of a relationship.

Religion, Marital Happiness, and Commitment

In this realm, it was not long ago that the verdict was clear: Religion, marital satisfaction, and marital stability went together. A portion of the literature still claims that the more religiously involved people are and the stronger their religious beliefs, the lower their divorce rate, the less extramarital sex they engage in, the fewer disagreements they have, and the more they are satisfied with both themselves and their mates.[152] Chances are that where these conditions exist, such people live within a moral system that considers marriage a lifetime commitment requiring the dedication and hard work of both parties for its success. Stanley has recently shown that various indicators of marital commitment, satisfaction, and quality are positively associated with an intrinsic faith orientation, but not with an extrinsic outlook.[153] Similarly, Hunt and King observed that the greater spousal agreement is on religious matters and the more there is joint participation in church activities, the more pleased both spouses are with their union. In contrast with the work of Stanley, they also found that extrinsic faith was linked with marital happiness.[154] It may well be that religion is used in a constructive, utilitarian manner to create a successful marriage. As we will see below, however, religious involvement and conservatism are no longer easily taken as guarantees for a happy home and a stable marriage.

In the modern world, many wives are employed outside the home, and such external involvement is correlated with greater marital and personal satisfaction on the part of women. This is true in spite of the fact that they usually continue being the primary homemakers. The latter role combined with holding down a job greatly stresses many, if not most, women.[155]

Though little work has been done on the role of religion relative to female employment, the traditional view, especially among religious conservatives, is that "woman's place is in the home." Today, this view conflicts with some new realities: (1) Two incomes are much better than one when it comes to maintaining a home and realizing the "good" life; and (2) many women do not want to be confined to the home, and find great fulfillment in holding down a job. Research on the marital satisfaction of the husbands of working wives over the past three decades has produced all possible findings, from depression through no effects to increased happiness.[156] Such apparent confusion is understandable, as many confounding factors may enter the picture: degree of religiosity, educational level, the presence of children, age of children, and, of course, the relative conservatism of the religious group with which one is associated. These considerations hold for both husbands and wives.

Johnson and his coworkers studied this problem among Mormons, a very conservative group.[157] Controlling for many of the potential influences described above, and using multiple indicators of marital contentment, the researchers found that part-time employment of the wives resulted in the lowest degree of satisfaction for both spouses. The men were most pleased when their wives were employed full-time, but the latter's marital gratification fell beneath that of full-time homemakers, though it was still above that of women who were employed part-time. Neither degree of religiosity, nor the status level of a woman's employment, adversely affected happiness. Though the age of children had a negative effect, this was largely a problem with part-time employment, implying again the negative effects of the latter. The very high value Mormons place on family roles may have overridden the additional stresses for the wives of taking on both the expected home tasks plus those of a job. We also do not know the extent to which the Mormon husbands took over some homemaker functions. It is possible—even among conservative religious bodies—that the desire for two incomes, and the social pressures caused by increased awareness of changes in women's roles, are slowly forcing husbands of working wives to take on duties usually associated with women in the home.

The situation of working women within a conservative religious body raises the conventional argument about woman's "place." Classic Christianity holds that the man should be leader and head of the household. One survey of evangelicals, both males and females, indicated that approximately 90% of this group affirm the Biblical injunction of male domination in the family; about 40% would deny women any positions of power in the church.[158] The woman is clearly defined as subject to male control. The more orthodox a religious body is, the more such a doctrinal view appears to be verbalized and accepted—on a theoretical level.

Carolyn Pevey's study of a fundamentalist Southern Baptist church shows that tenet or theory is one thing and practice is another.[159] Pevey concludes that wifely submission is sometimes forced, but that religiously conservative women apparently learn how to meet their own needs, not infrequently subverting masculine claims to authority when necessary. Husband–wife relationships in the main, however, seem to be mutually supportive and cooperative rather than combative within an authoritarian framework.

Religion and Spousal Abuse

Recent years have witnessed a growing awareness of and sensitivity to the issues of child and spousal abuse. It is commonly averred that fundamentalists who rigidly maintain an authoritarian patriarchal role in the home are likely to show high rates of abuse. This has been shown with regard to children, but not where more general familial violence is concerned. Male control backed by scripture is not as simple as it may seem. There is a strong suggestion that work on the abusive family often confounds religion with education and socioeconomic status.[160]

Using data from a national survey in Canada, Brinkerhoff and his colleagues confirmed one U.S. study showing that very high rates for spousal abuse occurred among those who were least religious. Still, conservative Christian women reported even higher abuse rates. This was not confirmed by the men's data, but a self-serving desirability bias could be present. The men admitting abuse tended to be religiously unaffiliated, but when they were attached to a church they attended one to three times a month. The researchers interpreted this rate as representing an extrinsic religious orientation. The women reporting most abuse were those, religiously conservative in outlook or not, who never attended church.[161] This is clearly a troubled area and is desperately in need of solid research.

Religion and Family: How Many Children?

When we think of a family, it consists of more than the two marital partners. It includes children. As noted earlier, the Judeo-Christian tradition emphasizes the scriptural prescription to "be fruitful and multiply." Judaism, Catholicism, and Protestantism all repeatedly stress the role of the family as an institution for bearing and rearing children. As Western religion has been liberalized, the issue of having children has moved from absolute expectations to considerations of personal choice. In the background, however, the parental role is regarded as an integral part of adult self-realization and maturity.

Antipathy toward birth control has always been a central theme in Catholic teachings, and one that is periodically reinforced by papal pronouncements. It is probably one factor in Catholic families' being larger than Protestant and Jewish families, but socioeconomic factors may also be influential.

For some time, changes in birth control attitudes and practices have been occurring among Catholics. In 1968, Pope Paul VI reaffirmed Catholicism's strong stand against artificial birth control; by 1970 in the United States, however, 70% of Catholic women were violating this principle, and only 14% of a sample of over 1,000 Catholic women had ever used the church-approved rhythm method.[162] By 1985, 83% of Catholics in their childbearing years (18–39) supported personal choice in this area.[163] In fact, immediately after the 1968 encyclical, 76% of Catholics approved dissemination of birth control information.[164]

Even diocesan priests have demonstrated opposition to the church in these matters. This is also a function of the age of a priest, with younger priests taking a more liberal stand. Prior to the 1968 encyclical, only 11% of priests in the 26–35 age range considered artificial contraception immoral and forbidden by the church. Among priests over 55, 68% agreed with the official stand. Following the 1968 restatement of the traditional Catholic position, the percentages for these two groups of priests became 7% and 59%, respectively.[165] Apparently, the encyclical decreased the numbers of priests opposing birth control, but not markedly. General national trends in the last two decades suggest that in all likelihood, more priests now favor artificial contraception than previously.

Historically, Catholicism has resisted family planning, but by the mid-1970s over 80% of Catholics, 88% of Protestants, and 98% of Jews championed efforts to make birth control information available to married persons.[166] Considering the high likelihood that these percentages have increased further, we do not believe it is amiss to suggest that for all practical purposes, the birth control issue has become academic. The evidence indicates that family size at present is overwhelmingly a function of personal preference, socioeconomic status, and the educational level of parents. Among Western religionists, the influence of faith is minimal.

Religion and Divorce

Clearly, religion often plays a positive role in love and marriage. Along with the sour note introduced by the problem of spousal abuse, however, another off-key tone must be sounded: In U.S. society, almost one in two marriages ends in divorce. By 1990, the number of one-parent families in the United States exceeded those with two parents in the home.[167] Faith can act and often does act as a restraining force against divorce, but even this function is not simple. Table 4.3 presents recent data on divorce rates for the major religious groups.

The table indicates that though divorce among the religiously affiliated occurs less often than in the general population, the formerly low incidence of family dissolution among Jews has been dramatically reversed. The classic image of Jewish family solidarity appears to have succumbed to the contemporary readiness to make marriage a transitory state. The strong stand of the Catholic Church against divorce, however, seems to be holding in a relative sense, as evidenced by Catholics' having the lowest divorce rate of the groups listed in Table 4.3. Still, most U.S. Catholics have disagreed with the church's stand on divorce for over 25 years.[168] There is no doubt that divorce is increasingly seen as a major way of resolving marital problems. Kosmin and Lachman point out that though the ideal of a good marriage still remains important, it may currently be taking a back seat to the desire for personal happiness. In 1985, over 80% of women chose family dissolution over staying with husbands "because of the children."[169]

The relationship of religious conservatism to marital stability and divorce is not to be taken at face value. Many traditional religious groups evidence a surprisingly high incidence of family breakup. The 1990–1991 General Social Survey of the National Opinion Research Center revealed the highest divorce rates to be among fundamentalists, but this decreased within the range of sampling error to become equivalent with the rate for moderate Protestants by 1994, as shown in Table 4.3.[170] Readers should keep in mind that the question asked here concerns "ever having been divorced." This pertains to a previous divorce, and is not necessarily relevant to one's current marital status.

Many religious bodies are strongly influenced by class and ethnic factors, and marital stability may be more dependent on these influences than on faith per se. Since those who get divorces tend to be in the early years of their marriages, they are also usually young. Moreover, there is a fair likelihood that they will be religiously unaffiliated; this implies that

TABLE 4.3. Responses to the Question "Have You Ever Been Divorced in the Past?" by Religious Group

Religious group	Percentage answering "Yes"
Protestant	
Fundamentalist	33.2
Moderate	34.7
Liberal	30.5
Catholic	26.6
Jewish	47.1
No religion	44.8
Total	32.8

Note. The data are 1994 General Social Survey data from the National Opinion Research Center (Davis & Smith, 1994), and were selectively tabulated by Michael Kearl of Trinity University, San Antonio, Texas.

they are unlikely to use religious institutional channels to meet potential mates, and that their chances of matching up with others of similar religious background are thus lower. They may also be less conforming to the cultural mainstream, and, as noted in Chapter 12, the incidence of psychosocial disturbance among those not associated with churches is higher than among churchgoers. All these factors do not bode well for marital stability.

Intermarriage

The Definition and Nature of Intermarriage

Problems of Definition. At first glance, it seems that all we need to determine intermarriage is to learn the religious preferences of spouses. If these vary, *voilà!* We have intermarriage, or, as it is more technically labeled, "religiously exogamous marriage." Once more, as we have frequently seen, few things are as simple as they first appear. What about varying degrees of religious commitment? A devout Methodist may have much in common with a devout Presbyterian; however, two mates from the same denomination may differ substantially in belief and commitment. Religious institutions can vary much in theology, but few parishioners know the fine distinctions made by theologians. Frequently a person affiliates with a church for a combination of social and spiritual reasons, rather than solely for the latter. Moreover, considering the variety and great number of Protestant groups in the United States, we may well ask when a denominationally mixed couple qualifies for definition as an intermarriage. There is certainly no distance along a scale of liberalism–conservatism that has ever been accepted as an indication of difference connoting intermarriage.

Then there is the issue of conversion. One of the four of us knows of two spouses from quite different religious backgrounds who found common cause through conversion to a Pentecostal sect. In terms of their past, this is an intermarriage; relative to their current state, no such definition is appropriate. How many conversions take place simply to please the more committed spouse?[171] The result is often a formalized shift in apparent identification when in actuality religious self-definition is superficial and nominal. There is also the matter of considering a convert as totally a member of the new faith group, or anchoring one's judgment in that person's original preconversion identification. The significance of this last concern is evident in McCutcheon's assertion that approximately half of U.S. intermarriages result in conversion, and that analyses of intermarriage "based solely on contemporary religious identification underestimate intermarriage rates by half."[172]

These are only a few of the problems of definition that can arise when the issue of intermarriage is posed. Most are overlooked by researchers; hence many of the data resources in this area are suspect.[173] Questions such as these have caused scholars to emphasize the most evident religious differences that historically and culturally can be denoted. In U.S. society, Herberg's image of "the triple melting pot" of Catholicism, Protestantism, and Judaism offers the clearest framework for the study of intermarriage.[174]

Historical and Contemporary Factors. Among the various theories of intermarriage that have been offered, the one obtaining most support concerns the proximity and availability of potential mates. If one's religious group is small compared to others in a certain environment (e.g., Jews in a predominantly Christian setting, or Catholics in overwhelmingly Protestant surroundings), the likelihood of interaction with the majority group increases, and with it the probability of emotional attachments that often eventuate in marriage. The data support this position.[175]

In other words, the demographic framework may be the prime factor leading to intermarriage. A second consideration, probably not unrelated to the first, reflects changing attitudes toward religious exogamy. Polls taken 50 to 60 years ago indicated that most Christians were negative toward intermarriages with Jews, but by the mid-1980s opposition had decreased to 10%; among non-Jews below the age of 30 (the time at which most people are marrying), only 4% disapproved of such unions.[176] This represents a broader shift toward increasing intermarriage across the entire religious spectrum. About 22% of Americans live in religiously mixed homes, and most religious groups evidence a slow erosion of homogamous marriages.[177] There are still some exceptions among recent immigrants from Asia and the Middle East. Among U.S. Christians, however, exogamy increases with having attended college. This is probably a result of both the liberalization normally associated with higher education and the likelihood of greater exposure to potential spouses who differ in religion.[178]

The intermarriage situation represents very clearly the borderline between sociology and psychology. Specific studies translating demographics into personal attitudes and behavior are rarely undertaken on the level of individuals. Comparative research on outlooks and conflicts within both homogamous and exogamous households would be very useful adjuncts to our understanding of intermarriage problems. Some insight into these issues may be gained by looking more closely at intermarriages of (1) Jews and non-Jews, and (2) members of different Christian faiths (primarily Catholics and Protestants).

Jewish Intermarriage

In the 20th century, radical changes have occurred in the rates for Jewish intermarriage. Unfortunately, even though controversy surrounds the gathering of these data, the trends are clear even if the absolute numbers vary.[179] Some instability in the findings is also attributable to variations in sample size. The best estimates suggest that prior to 1965 about 10% of marriages involving Jews were exogamous, but that after 1985 this number increased to 57%.[180] If we look back to the first 40 years of this century, the rate was only 2–3%, as shown in Table 4.4.

Biblical proscriptions against intermarriage have been buttressed by Jewish fears that the survival of Judaism is seriously threatened. There are predictions that if the current rate of increase in exogamous marriages continues, there will be a slow decline, possibly as great as 10% in the number of Jews in the United States early in the 21st century.[181] As might be expected, orthodoxy correlates negatively with intermarriage. For marriages contracted since 1985, exogamy occurred in 24% of unions involving Orthodox Jews, 52% of those involving Conservative Jews, and 66% of those involving Reform Jews.[182] This pattern, of course, reflects the amount of Jewish education and exposure to a Jewish environment and community.[183] The greater such investment, the less probable is intermarriage. Another pertinent factor is that "Jews who married out were four to five times more likely to describe themselves as 'unconventional' or 'rebellious.'"[184] An interesting psychological consideration is that these exogamously marrying Jews reported high levels of conflict with their parents.[185] We may wonder to what degree such estrangement preceded or followed intermarriage, and how it was expressed.

The intermarriage tendency in terms of gender has been for Jewish men to marry outside of their faith, but intermarriage has recently increased geometrically among Jewish women. By the mid-1980s, it was estimated that 45% of the latter were marrying exogamously.[186] Silberman predicts that this situation is likely to change, and he points to Canadian statistics revealing a shift back to homogamous Jewish marriages by Jewish men.[187]

TABLE 4.4. Jewish Intermarriage and Conversion to Judaism by Time of Marriage

Time period	Homogamous marriages	Exogamous marriages	Conversions to Judaism
Pre-1965	89%	9%	2%
1965–1974	69%	25%	6%
1975–1984	49%	44%	7%
1985–	43%	52%	5%

Note. The data are from the Council of Jewish Federations, and appeared in Steinfels (1992).

When conversion to Judaism occurs within a marital context, it is more likely to be the non-Jewish woman who changes her faith. This is largely motivated by the desire to achieve marital harmony and consensus.[188] In such homes, the convert is usually quite committed to her new faith. There is rather strong devotion to traditional Jewish practices, and the almost unbelievable estimate is that up to 99% of the children in these families are raised as Jews.[189]

This, however, does not describe the general situation for exogamous marriages involving Jews. For some time, secularization has been the growing choice for Jews. Jewish cultural identification has replaced formal religious involvement. The result is that 38% of the children from such homes receive no religious training; 40% are religiously brought up as non-Jews; and only 25% are reared as religious Jews.[190]

The response of the Jewish community to intermarriage has been mixed, ranging from outright hostility through indifference to fear. As a rule, converts to Judaism are easily accepted into Jewish circles, but the issue becomes one of retaining Jews who marry non-Jews, and therefore keeping the family unit identified with things Jewish. The sociologist Egon Mayer reported in 1992 that nationally some 561 programs existed in 373 Jewish institutions in order to keep these exogamous unions within Judaism.[191] One estimate suggests that about half of those who participate in these efforts commit themselves to Judaism, as opposed to 14% for spouses who are not involved in such programs.[192]

Intermarriage among Christians

As indicated earlier, we barely touch on marriages across the 200-plus Protestant groups, because any barriers that once existed appear to have largely disappeared. In other words, the number of Protestants intermarrying across denominational lines continues to increase, and intragroup resistance to such unions is rare.

Circumstances are different when it comes to Catholic–Protestant marriages. Just as more and more Jews are marrying non-Jews, more and more Catholics are marrying Protestants. This is not to say that disapproval of such religiously mixed marriages does not exist, even among Protestants. One study revealed opposition to these marriages ranging from 31% to 94%, depending on denomination. Overall, 43% of Protestants and 65% of Catholics have been found to disapprove of cross-faith unions.[193] Apparently, such opinions become quite secondary when potential spouses from different faiths reach the point of contemplating a future life together. Table 4.5 offers some recent data on interfaith marriages in general.

Because of the disparity in numbers for the various religious groups, the relative effect of exogamous marriages on Protestants is less than on Catholics, and (as noted) much less than the effect on Jews. Stated differently, Catholics are likely to lose a higher proportion of their coreligionists than Protestants, and Jews are likely to lose the most. Table 4.6 looks more

TABLE 4.5. The Pattern of Interfaith Marriages

| Marriages with | Marriages by | | |
	Protestants ($n = 976$)	Catholics ($n = 443$)	Jews ($n = 36$)
Protestants	85.4%	31.2%	19.3%
Catholics	14.5%	67.9%	16.0%
Jews	0.7%	1.2%	63.9%

Note. The data are 1994 General Social Survey data from Davis and Smith (1994), and were recomputed by Michael Kearl of Trinity University, San Antonio, Texas. The column percentages may not add up exactly to 100 because of rounding errors.

closely at the Christians by defining Protestants along a liberal–conservative dimension. Once more we see the expected pattern of intrafaith marriages dominating over interfaith possibilities, even within the three Protestant subgroups. As suggested, in all probability this is explainable by the high likelihood of interaction with members of the opposite sex of similar mind and orientation. Still, there is exposure to others who vary from one's own religious outlook, and this has its effects. Nevertheless, the trend remains for Protestants to choose Protestants and Catholics to marry Catholics. Why fundamentalist Protestants are more apt to wed Catholics or liberal Protestants than moderate Protestants is not clear, but it could be a chance finding because of the relatively small samples in these cells. Even though one's faith may be an influence in mate selection, we must recognize that the choice of a spouse in U.S. society depends a great deal on individual emotional attachments. It is therefore quite unlikely that evangelical fervor and missionary inclinations are factors in these preferences.

Obviously, religious conservatism is involved in marital selections among the Protestants, as the percentage of ingroup choices increases from liberal to fundamentalist groups. Maintaining the integrity of the ingroup apparently grows with religious conservatism. One study of Catholic university students revealed that even though they were more willing to marry outside of their religion than Protestant students, they were less ready to change their

TABLE 4.6. The Pattern of Christian Interfaith Marriages among Protestants (by Degree of Conservatism) and Catholics

| Marriages with | Marriages by | | | |
| | Protestants | | | |
	Fundamentalists ($n = 509$)	Moderates ($n = 256$)	Liberals ($n = 305$)	Catholics ($n = 441$)
Protestants				
Fundamentalists	73.9%	11.3%	17.4%	11.6%
Moderates	5.7%	62.9%	7.9%	9.5%
Liberals	10.4%	9.4%	59.3%	10.6%
Catholics	10.0%	16.4%	15.4%	68.2%

Note. The data are 1994 General Social Survey data from Davis and Smith (1994), and were recomputed by Michael Kearl of Trinity University, San Antonio, Texas. The column percentages may not add up exactly to 100 because of rounding errors.

faith.[194] Chances are that similar reluctance increases with religious conservatism and commitment within Protestantism. The fact that interfaith marriages are steadily increasing must mean, even despite this sort of reluctance, that a slow erosion of religious solidarity is continuing. It may also be argued that the rate of such change is probably increasing.

The Happiness and Stability of Interfaith Marriages

Interfaith marriages may be increasing, but we also know that divorce rates in general have more than doubled in the last 30 years.[195] Cross-religion marriages make a substantial contribution to these statistics. When both spouses share the same religious heritage, the divorce rate tends to be low; when faith backgrounds vary, the incidence of divorce is high. In Catholic–Protestant marriages where children are present, the divorce rate is three to four times greater than in unmixed marriages; the highest incidence occurs in those unions where the wife is Protestant.[196] One factor causing this split seems to be the prenuptial agreement required by the Catholic church in mixed marriages. After children appear and their religious education becomes a concern, conflict over their religious identification and schooling often ensues, whether there was earlier consensus or not.

A more general overview of the marital stability issue is presented in Table 4.7. Without question, the fragility of interfaith marriages is clear: Christian–Jewish marriages are most unstable, with ecumenical Protestant–Catholic and exclusivist Protestant–Catholic unions following closely. Institutional opposition, together with personal commitment to one's faith, seems to constitute a seedbed for conflict and divorce. Given the statistics shown in Table 4.7, it will come as no surprise that national data from 1974 to 1994 assessing the happiness of intra- and interfaith marriages reveal consistently higher satisfaction for both spouses in intrafaith unions.[197]

To reduce such disharmony, the serious conversion of one of the spouses to the other's faith has been suggested.[198] For example, according to one major study that covered a 15-year period, 44% of the Christian spouses in Jewish–Christian marriages converted because of concern for the religious rearing of children.[199] In addition, under such circumstances, it was common for the converts to perceive Judaism in positive terms. These conversion patterns are interesting in that 58% converted before the marriage, and 18% before the birth of their first child. There still appeared to be some basis for conflict, as some of the converts to Judaism continued to engage in Christian practices, such as decorating a Christmas tree (10%) or exchanging Christmas presents in the home (25%). Five percent attended a Christmas service; at Easter, this dropped to 3%. As a rule, however, the converts showed a high degree of participation in Jewish practices, such as involvement in a seder (96%), attendance at Yom Kippur services (93%), and attendance at Rosh Hashanah services (91%). Ninety-nine percent of these mixed couples belonged to a synagogue. In cases where marital discord occurred, religious factors did not seem to be a significant source of such difficulties. By contrast with these findings, Ellman reported divorce rates in marriages where there was no conversion to be five to six times higher than in marriages where both spouses identified themselves as Jews.[200] Since Jews who intermarry frequently identify little with Judaism, high divorce rates suggest that religion may still possess some latent potential for dissolution of these unions.[201]

Troublesome differences in religious background and commitment between spouses may include different expectations about marriage, sex roles, economic and social relationships, and the place and treatment of children.[202] When these are combined with changing

TABLE 4.7. Dissolution of Marriages in the United States within 5 Years by Marital Religious Composition, 1987–1988

Marriage type	5-year probability of dissolution
Intrafaith marriages	
Ecumenical Protestant (same NSFH code)[a]	.20
Exclusivist Protestant (same NSFH code)[a]	.19
Catholic	.20
Jewish	.27
Interfaith marriages	
Ecumenical Protestant (different NSFH code)[a]	.24
Exclusivist Protestant (different NSFH code)[a]	.31
Ecumenical Protestant–exclusivist Protestant	.29
Ecumenical Protestant–Catholic	.38
Exclusivist Protestant–Catholic	.38
Christian–Jewish	.42

Note. Adapted from Lehrer and Chiswick (1993). Copyright 1993 by the Population Association of America. Adapted by permission.

[a]The "NSFH codes" are based on the 1986–1987 National Survey of Families and Households (NSFH), which used a sample of 9,643 males and females that was analyzed into more than 60 religious groups. Imposed on this is Kelley's (1972) "exclusivist–ecumenical" gradient, which is largely a conservative–liberal continuum, but more accurately a distribution ranging from groups that are relatively closed (exclusivist) and oppose interfaith marriage to those that are open and accepting (ecumenical).

gender roles in the mainstream society, as well as other contributors to marital instability (e.g., personal immaturity, parental pressures, contemporary socioeconomic stresses, and an increasing readiness to break up a marriage over conflicts that should be resolvable), the burden may be too much for an interfaith marriage to withstand. Unhappily, the trend toward settling such problems by divorce is still increasing. More research is needed to determine the kinds of strains religious differences place on interfaith marriages. According to the data presented here, these unions are more fragile. We need to know how faith in the home may exacerbate or help settle marital difficulties. Though talk about religious and family values often prevails in a platitudinous way, the actual psychosocial mechanisms involving religion that either enhance conflict or aid in its resolution have yet to be specified.

Religion and Homosexuality

If sex and heterosexual relationships are themselves not sensitive enough topics for public discussion, homosexuality is an even more touchy issue. It frequently arouses extreme emotions, which too often serve as substitutes for information and understanding. Religion is often found at the center of these concerns, with conservative and orthodox religionists condemning homosexuality, while their liberal counterparts call for tolerance, compassion, and knowledge. Apparently, religiosity leads to a generalized personal ethical conservatism, which in turn spawns homophobia or homonegativism.[203] Such attitudes appear primarily to be value-expressive, rather than ego-defensive, utilitarian, or simply cognitive; in other words, they represent identification with the classical conservative Christian outlook.[204] A fundamentalist orientation and church attendance have been found to be positively correlated with homophobia and fear of AIDS.[205] In contrast, Fulton and Gorsuch report that intrinsically religious persons are relatively accepting of homosexuals.[206] The implication is that to the extent that intrinsic faith represents religious maturity, the often-found negative relationship of this perspective with open-mindedness and lack of prejudice is now extended to the understanding of homosexuality. This is obviously a subject that will excite much debate for years to come, and already involves theologians and every facet of institutional faith. It is a topic that has come "out of the closet" and must be acknowledged as a fact of life.

There is no question that gays and lesbians do not appear to differ from their heterosexual counterparts in terms of religious or spiritual inclinations. At the same time, we are speaking about a group that always has been and continues to be the object of prejudice and discrimination because of sexual orientation. A natural concomitant of such a state of affairs is personal conflict, which is often severe and involves self-deprecation and low self-esteem. Such conflict may be exacerbated among those with strong religious commitments.[207] For the religiously oriented homosexual, it can also bring to the fore pastoral counseling concerns with sexual identity issues.[208]

Though writing about religion and homosexuality has been increasing at a rapid pace over the past decade, this literature has largely focused on conceptual, political, social, pastoral, and clinical issues. These are beyond the scope of this book. Empirical research in this realm is sorely lacking—a deficiency that we hope will be shortly remedied. Serious efforts to obtain information are, of course, hampered by fears of disclosure; yet a few efforts have been undertaken. Those willing to take part in research may be highly selected and therefore not representative of homosexuals, either in general or in the specific group being studied. Representative of these pioneering works is a book edited by James Wolf, *Gay Priests*.[209] This volume is a compilation of hard data plus much humanistic commentary; it is a noteworthy beginning. A parallel work by Curb and Manahan on lesbian nuns is basically a subjective, compassionate document not intended for social-scientific scrutiny.[210] Still, a perspicacious behavioral scholar may gain some hypothetical insights from its personal approach. A relatively rare and interesting initial study in this area is presented in Research Box 4.5.

Summary

We have surveyed Adler's third great problem of adult life—namely, love and marriage—in its interactions with religion. Though psychologists have studied this domain extensively in regard to personality, interpersonal relations, and emotion, work involving the influence of personal faith is relatively sparse. It is also evident that this is an area that our sociological colleagues have examined in depth. They have provided much material for psychological investigation, and solid efforts such as that by Stanley[211] mark a significant beginning.

RELIGION IN OTHER AREAS OF ADULT LIFE: POLITICS AS AN EXAMPLE

The tasks of adulthood and maturity go beyond making a living, interpersonal behavior, and love and marriage. People relate themselves to the larger community through a variety of social, political, and economic avenues. Many of these issues are examined in other chapters, such as those dealing with morality (Chapter 10) and the social psychology of religious organizations (Chapter 9). Again, we encounter topics that have traditionally been studied by so-

---
&a.

Research Box 4.5. Pastoral Counselors' Attitudes toward Gay and Lesbian Clients (Hochstein, 1986)

In view of the generally negative attitude within Christianity toward homosexuality, Hochstein studied the degree to which such sentiments might affect the pastoral counseling of homosexual clients. A sample of 190 members of the American Association of Pastoral Counselors responded to a mailed summary and questionnaire about an interview with a client with a grief reaction or depressive symptoms. Four gender and sexual preference scenarios were distributed; two were of males and two of females. For each gender, a heterosexual and a homosexual client was pictured. Each counselor was asked to rate the hypothetical client and "any healthy adult" on the 38 items of a sex role stereotype questionnaire. Additional questions regarding diagnoses, treatment, demographic data, and attitudes toward homosexuals were also collected.

No differences were found between psychological health ratings for the hypothetical heterosexual and homosexual clients. Male clients were perceived as less healthy than their female peers, with the former also rated as possessing fewer male-valued stereotypic traits than the females. All clients were rated as less competent and healthy than the "healthy adult" referent.

Thirty percent of the counselors scored in the homophobic range on the measure of attitudes toward homosexuals; 70% were nonhomophobic. The more theologically conservative a counselor was, the more homophobia was present. In nine instances there was rejection of, or only conditional acceptance of, the homosexual for counseling. Still, homophobia did not appear to affect responses to the hypothetical client, though sexism did influence the counselors.

---

ciologists and anthropologists. However, we touch here briefly on a few adult psychological concerns relative to politics. These are important and controversial matters in today's world.

There was a time not so long ago when the relationship between faith and politics in the United States seemed simple: Catholics and Jews voted Democratic; Protestants were Republicans. The former supported liberal causes; the latter were conservative. The shadows of that time are still found in the loyalty these groups bring to such issues as affirmative action, health, welfare, the military, and "big government." The political waters have become roiled, however, and new concerns and factions call for religious perspectives on the likes of abortion, women's rights, gay rights, pornography, family values, prayer in the schools, and other controversial issues. Some observers also claim that the traditional separation of church and state is under attack. Though religion was always an element on the sociopolitical scene, it is currently employed with a motivational intensity rarely seen in past times. On one level, it has infused U.S. cultural life through what has been termed "civil religion."

Civil Religion

Utilizing Rousseau's term "civil religion," Bellah has recognized the pervasive influence of religion in U.S. public and political life.[212] Greeley has observed that despite the legal separation of church and state in U.S. society, "there is an official religion, if not an official church in the American republic. This religion has its solemn ceremonials, such as the inauguration, its feast days, such as Thanksgiving, Memorial Day, the Fourth of July, and Christmas."[213] Bellah indicates that civil religion, without conflicting with the churches, has been fueled by a selective borrowing of religious ideas. These have performed as "powerful symbols of national solidarity and . . . mobilize deep levels of personal motivation for the attainment of national goals."[214] Benson adds that "Civil religion provides a kind of divine stamp of approval of the social order as it now exists."[215] Connections are thus established to virtually all social institutions, and a central coordinating theme becomes the classic religion–morality association.[216] This has a strong emotional appeal that strengthens the role of religion in public life.

In recent decades, civil religion has been employed as an avenue to abrogate the principle of church–state separation. Regardless of the issue, a number of conservative Christians have tried to identify their Biblically based faith with U.S. history, political actions, values, and destiny. Usually dubbed the "religious right" or the "Christian right," this group includes some who seek to transform the superficiality of civil religion into the "real thing" to such a degree that the United States becomes a "Christian nation." This movement has powerful friends, and is heard in high government circles on many contentious issues.[217] And for good reason: By the mid-1980s, it was estimated that this group included some 35 million adult Americans.[218] An illustrative recent effort to influence Congress was provided by the Christian Coalition, an organization with 1.5 million members. In the presence of leading members of Congress, including presidential candidates, the leader of the coalition offered a conservative 10-point legislative agenda that was termed a "Contract with the American Family."[219]

Psychologically as well as socioculturally, this infusion of faith into the public domain often functions to control thinking and stifle debate. There is a "stop thinking" quality to pronouncements that associate the deity and faith with freedom, flag, and family. Such statements convey a moral aura that is not to be questioned. They appear to validate the affiliation of religion with politics, so that this association seems natural and appropriate. A recent example of this method is the "Contract with the American Family," which includes "individual religious expression in schools and a ban on abortion."[220] Additional issues with which members of the Christian right are concerned are "school prayer, pornography, gay rights, the Equal Rights Amendment, busing, school textbooks, and tuition tax credits."[221]

Individual Ramifications of the Religion–Politics Connection

Faith performs a number of personal political functions for the individual. It may support personal views and behaviors that motivate people to enter into public discussion and action. Religion can also justify inaction and withdrawal from the political arena. Specifically, faith can act as a source or sanction for political loyalty or conflict, or can offer opportunities to avoid dissension.[222]

Religion as a Source or Sanction for Political Loyalty

Politicians often seek to legitimate their programs and ideas by identifying them with sacred sources. According to Franklin D. Roosevelt, it was essential that all political speeches include what he (possibly too candidly) referred to as "God stuff."[223] For many people, the presence of such language endows the content of the speech and the speaker with the aura of doing "God's work." In keeping with the recent alliance between the Republican party and evangelical Protestantism, Roosevelt's advice was apparently adopted by Ronald Reagan when he referred to God 10 times in one speech and 24 times in another.[224] When it came to offering more substantive support for the legislative program of the Christian right, Reagan was much more circumspect and cautious in his pronouncements, avoiding some of the controversial topics altogether and selectively using few words to support other points.[225]

The mass media are reticent about calling such uses of religion to the attention of the electorate, because doing so might have adverse effects on sponsors and their audience.[226] This becomes critical when phrases such as "moral majority," "Christian virtues," "family values," "freedom foundation," and the like are bandied about rather easily and uncritically. In the "stop thinking" tradition described above, no one wants to be viewed as against morality, Christianity, virtue, family, and freedom. Whereas these notions were once associated with "the Great Society," social welfare, and other indirect derivatives from the social gospel movement, political power (or at least the appearance of such power) has shifted to the opposite end of the religious spectrum.

Another way of looking at this politics–religion relationship is to note that, in a sense, these are control systems. They are concerned, not by any means in a negative sense, with directing and focusing thought and behavior. Religion is thus used to select and reinforce political ideas. The result is enhanced loyalty both to churches and to certain political ideologies.[227] Historically, this has often pitted liberal religionists against their conservative counterparts; hence we see different concepts of human nature and different readings and interpretations of scripture, plus the variations that may exist in theology under the broad rubric of Christianity. The use of these arguments also serves to keep the more crass considerations of social and economic stratification and power out of the picture. The skillful manipulation of religious–political ideas in sermons, church publications, and radio and television programs has its effects both at the ballot box, and in establishing faith as a source and a sanction for political loyalty.

Religion as a Sanction for Political Conflict

Where factions exist, as they invariably do when either religion or politics enters the picture, loyalties imply conflict. Not only in wartime do we hear that "God is on our side"; in peacetime, "doing God's work" becomes a muted expression of the same sentiments, depending on how such "work" is defined by a particular person's theological stance. Those who do not feel similarly are "unbelievers," often meaning that loyalty to one doctrine implies conflict with another. For example, even the use of the label "Christian" is no guarantee of similarity in outlook in any major area, least of all religious belief.

When a religious body supports a political issue, it must oppose variant positions. Truth, good, and evil are not concepts open to negotiation, and political ideas that gain sacred backing come to share religion's absolutist fate. The "enemy" is likely to include members of other faiths, and to do battle becomes a religious obligation. God, scripture, cross, and star are invoked, along with other symbols designed to call the faithful to the colors. Morality and immorality are introduced into the fray, and righteous impulse and emotion are called to support the fight of newly broadened perceptions of good versus evil. This "primitive moralism" blurs relevant differences.[228] Issue complexity is denied, and simplistic dichotomies prevail. If opportunity and group identifications allow, extremists may create an ethnocentric gauntlet, and ingroup–outgroup distinctions are treated with an alienating rhetoric. Abortion and sexism are unlikely to be distinguished; prayer in the schools may take on an anti-Semitic tint; and brotherhood can be restricted to an exclusive within-group bond. "True believing" knows few bounds, especially when religion is an organizing force. Conspiracy fantasies ask who is behind pornography, evolutionary theory, secular humanism, women's rights, opposition to "voluntary" prayer in the schools, and so forth. The approved answers often excite bigotry. Purity of purpose is distorted into a group purity advocating a separatism that ruptures the social fabric. Religion thus becomes a source and sanction for many kinds of conflicts, not the least of which are political.

Religion as a Sanctuary from Political Conflict

There have always been religionists who feel that faith can be tainted by the immorality that pervades the world. These individuals feel that God and the spiritual good are above politics and public affairs, and true religion does not deal with such things; people's concern should therefore be with the transcendental and the world to come.[229] A recent version of this theme may be found in a book that is subtitled *How American Law and Politics Trivialize Religious Devotion*.[230] Quite a case can be made for such an assertion, and the desire to counter it feeds the motivation to keep faith out of politics.

This is a perspective that has a strong following in the United States. One study of 1,580 California clergy revealed that over one-third had never given a sermon on a political topic.[231] The more traditional the cleric, the less likely it was that mundane, worldly matters would be presented. Because of a sampling bias, the authors of this work felt that they underestimated the aversion of ministers toward politics.

Conflict between being in and being out of the world varies greatly within conservative religious groups. Some, like the Amish, work hard to maintain their separation from all aspects of the broader community.[232] Fundamentalists frequently oppose "things of the world" and explicitly take stances to combat modernism as defined by the religious right.[233] Political involvement may, however, be taken as creating a value system that competes with religion, implying that politics must be resisted unless it is subsumed under the categories of faith. Its influence can then be limited and made acceptable. The last two decades have witnessed such conflict, with radical politics being replaced internationally by radical religious regimes that rather enthusiastically exercise governmental power. In all probability, the effort to move religion away from the world will become increasingly restricted to ever-smaller local situations and circumstances.[234]

Religion as a Reconciler of Political Conflict

Paradoxically, just as religion exacerbates conflict, it is also concerned with its reduction. Church pronouncements against dissension and strife, whether in the form of the Golden Rule or ever-increasing efforts at ecumenism, are widespread in our society. The involvement of Jimmy Carter in various peace efforts in Bosnia and Haiti, and in work for the organization Habitat for Humanity, represents attempts at reconciliation that have religious roots. In a similar mode, many Protestant denominations have joined with Catholics to found the Council of Evangelical Churches of Nicaragua to aid the people of that nation in overcoming natural and human-made disasters.[235]

The World Council of Churches sponsors a program on Justice and Peace for the Integrity of Creation, which also stresses the basic unity of peoples. Recently, a Parliament of World Religions meeting was held in Chicago and attended by over 8,000 representatives of a wide sampling of world faiths. The outcome was a Declaration of a Global Ethic, which was designed to "promulgate a set of 'irrevocable, unconditioned ethical norms' for the entire human community."[236] For many years, the Catholic Worker movement founded by Dorothy Day has taken stands on a wide variety of economic and political issues. Its supporters assert that their aim is "to live in accordance with the justice and charity of Jesus Christ," [237] and this has spurred many social and political actions. Environmental concerns have also been expressed through such developments as an ongoing ecumenical Institute for Ecology, Justice and Faith. This institute sponsors seminars and workshops, such as one on "Aspects and Models of the Green Theological Community," designed to sensitize people to environmental threats.[238]

The foregoing are illustrative of religiously sponsored actions that have been taken against all forms of prejudice and discrimination, sexism, racism, poverty, war, nuclear arms, animal rights, environmental pollution, and a host of other humanistic concerns. The churches are obviously not united on these issues. Indeed, religionists of the same persuasion frequently take opposing positions, and are able to use scripture and theology to justify their conflicting stances.

Religion and politics are necessarily interwoven in a complex tapestry of attitudes, feelings, and behaviors in which each of these realms finds expression in the other. People look to their faith to authenticate their political outlooks, and in turn see religious principles in their political stands. Over a century and a half ago, Alexis de Tocqueville asserted that "There is in each religion a political doctrine which by affinity is joined to it."[239] In other words, whatever religious posture adults take, it has political implications.

Religion and Politics: The Research Scene

The factors that cause people to take specific political positions are a complex compound of sociological and psychological components. Surprisingly little research has exhaustively tried to identify such influences. One truly creative and impressive project that attempted to unravel such forces was conducted by Benson and Williams.[240] This is summarized in Research Box 4.6.

Benson and Williams's research demonstrates how psychologists of religion can conduct creative studies of ties between faith and politics. Clearly, many other factors may affect voting behavior and political attitudes; these also need to be researched. This is a realm that begs for exacting research, particularly in the present era of political controversy.

OVERVIEW

Adult life is much more complex than can be illustrated here. We have selectively organized the conceptual and research data according to Adler's theorized major concerns of adulthood—achievement and work, interpersonal relations, and love and marriage. To illustrate another possibility, we have briefly touched upon the political domain. Some topics have not been presented here because related material is offered in the chapters on religion, coping, and adjustment (Chapter 11) and religion and mental disorder (Chapter 12), especially concerning women and the elderly. Still, much more can be said about these latter two groups, particularly the effects of the women's movement of recent decades. Some additional attention is given to the elderly in the next chapter, but it is necessarily limited by the focus on the main psychological issue of death and dying.

Research Box 4.6. Religion on Capitol Hill: Myths and Realities (Benson & Williams, 1982)

The purpose of this study was "to chronicle the religious beliefs and values held by members of the United States Congress, and to track how they connect with the legislative decisions of the Congress" (p. 2). Eighty senators and representatives from an initial random sample of 112 were interviewed. On a wide variety of pertinent demographic variables, this group closely matched the characteristics of those not interviewed. Seven categories of beliefs were assessed: (1) "the nature of religious reality," (2) "religious reality's relationship to the world," (3) "means of apprehending religious reality," (4) "salvation and paths to salvation," (5) "about the last things," (6) "people and society," and (7) "values and ethical principles" (p. 24).

Eighty-six percent of the participants affirmed a belief in God, and tended to describe images of a transcendent, loving deity. Religion was viewed as addressing the lack of meaning and purpose in life. The path to salvation was seen as one of doing good works, practicing one's faith, and living a virtuous life.

Ninety percent of the respondents were formally members of churches and synagogues, and 74% attended services once a month or more. The same percentage reported praying at least once a week, and 37% also read scripture weekly. Ninety-seven percent considered religion to be moderately to very important in their lives. The authors concluded that Congress well reflects the dominant religious beliefs and behaviors present among the U.S. public: "It is not true, as some contend, that the members of Congress are less religious than the people they serve" (p. 82).

After extensive and sophisticated statistical analyses of the data, Benson and Williams distinguished six types of religionists in the Congress:

1. *Legalistic religionists* (15%). These believers placed "very high value on rules, boundaries, limits, guidelines, direction, and purpose" (p. 126). They also stressed self-discipline and self-restraint.

2. *Self-concerned religionists* (29%). This religious type was "visible, articulate, enthusiastically shared, regularly practiced, apparently genuine—and almost entirely concerned with the relationship between the believer and God. . . . [There was] little impetus toward concern for fellow creatures" (p. 128).

3. *Integrated religionists* (14%). "These people's beliefs work[ed] to liberate, to free them to speak and act. . . . God not humankind [was] their audience" (p. 129). They were likely to vote in terms of religious principle.

4. *People-concerned religionists* (10%). These individuals emphasized the connection between faith and action, and possessed well-examined religious concepts and God images.

5. *Nontraditional religionists* (9%). These intellectually perceptive members of Congress held abstract God concepts plus many individualized religious ideas. They also shared a secular-humanist orientation.

6. *Nominal religionists* (22%). This group rejected most traditional religious ideas and had rather superficial church attachments. Holding a rather vague, unanalyzed religion, they were more concerned with it as a source for solace, unlikely to affect daily life and thought.

Ninety-nine percent of the sample felt there were connections between religious outlook and voting behavior; 24% saw a strong association. Political conservatives held images

(*cont.*)

of God as omnipotent, strict, guiding, protective of social institutions, and playing an active role in life. They believed that an afterlife is assured, and that the path to salvation is personal and accomplished by doing good. Liberals stressed justice, love, and the social nature of salvation.

Studying eight political issues on which the Congress had voted, Benson and Williams found noteworthy associations between the various religionist types and voting records. These data are summarized in the table below. Most conservative votes were cast by the legalistic and self-concerned religionists, whereas the majority of liberal votes were cast by people-concerned and nontraditional religionists.

Voting behavior	Percentage of votes cast, by religionist type					
	Legalistic	Self-concerned	Integrated	People-concerned	Non-traditional	Nominal
Pro-						
Civil liberties	32	30	60	80	81	51
Foreign aid	21	26	63	97	88	55
Hunger relief	30	29	78	90	83	60
Abortion funding	23	28	71	87	86	44
Anti-						
Government spending	47	45	25	23	22	34
Pro-						
Strong military	84	78	44	19	26	58
Private ownership	50	54	29	19	18	37
Free enterprise	65	61	35	23	20	42

Note. Adapted from Benson and Williams (1982, p. 161). Copyright 1982 by the Search Institute. Adapted by permission.

Even though some fine work has been done in the areas covered in this chapter, it should be abundantly evident that there seem to be almost no limits on what remains to be done. So often, religion appears to function as a subtle, "behind the scenes" factor. This in itself may be one major reason why so little effort has been put into studying faith relative to interpersonal relations, apart from prejudice.

Similarly, though much has been reported on religion in connection with love and marriage, the steadily increasing fragility of marital unions and the high rates of nonsolemnized liaisons may indicate that religion is becoming increasingly irrelevant in this sphere. However, the importance of faith varies with the age of people, socioeconomic status, and the presence of children. More sensitive research looking at such influences is called for.

Sociocultural recognition of a long-suppressed aspect of sexual reality—namely, homosexuality—calls for rigorous research in this area. The great sensitivity this subject calls for an insightful attention to objectivity that few other topics currently require. Much that has been written on homosexuality by knowledgeable scholars needs to be examined for its theoretical potential. To say that pertinent research involving religion is in its infancy is to suggest that it is further advanced than it actually is; we might more accurately state that research on faith and homosexuality is in an embryonic phase.

Obviously, a great deal still needs to be done with regard to work. Though many early research investigations were directed at understanding religion as a profession, this subject too has changed in the past few decades, especially in relation to gender. Rigorous studies of this factor have begun, and a significant door has been opened to a fundamentally conflicted area.

Unfortunately, research on religion in adult life has barely been informed by our knowledge of the complexity of different forms of personal faith. The role of religion in the 40-plus years of adulthood pleads for much more research and a clearer understanding.

NOTES

1. C. C. Colton, quoted (with slight modifications) in Edwards (1955, p. 535).
2. Source unknown.
3. Saroyan (1937, p. 130).
4. Sir Arthur Keith, quoted in Edwards (1955, p. 539).
5. Charles Kingsley, quoted in Edwards (1955, p. 540).
6. *The Denver Post* (1993, January 21, p. 17A).
7. Levinson, Darrow, Klein, Levinson, and McKee (1978).
8. Adler (1935, p. 6).
9. Adler (1935, p. 6).
10. Erikson (1968, p. 136).
11. Rosten (1975, p. 339).
12. Becker (1986, pp. 4–5).
13. *The Gallup Poll Monthly* (1994, July, p. 37).
14. *Denver Post* (1988, June 17, p. 3A).
15. *The Gallup Poll Monthly* (1994, July, p. 38).
16. *The Gallup Poll Monthly* (1994, July, p. 41).
17. *The Gallup Poll Monthly* (1994, July, 39).
18. *The Gallup Poll Monthly* (1994, July, p. 41).
19. Bedell (1994); Jacquet (1983); Naisbitt and Aburdene (1990, pp. 277–279).
20. Roof and McKinney (1987).
21. Roof and McKinney (1987, p. 170).
22. Roof (1993).
23. Roof (1993, p. 55).
24. Roof (1993, p. 99).
25. Roof (1993, p. 222).
26. Roof (1993, p. 110).
27. Roof (1993, p. 57).
28. Roof (1993, p. 72).
29. Roof (1993, p. 79).
30. Spilka (1993).
31. Kantrowitz et al. (1994, p. 54).
32. Myers (1992, p. 180).
33. Roof (1993, p. 123).
34. Roof (1993, p. 125).
35. Kantrowitz et al. (1994).
36. Naisbitt and Aburdene (1990, p. 275).
37. Kantrowitz et al. (1994); Naisbitt and Aburdene (1990, p. 276); Woodward et al. (1990).
38. Naisbitt and Aburdene (1990, pp. 280–281).
39. Naisbitt and Aburdene (1990, pp. 290–294).
40. Woodward et al. (1990, p. 51).
41. Monaghan (1967).
42. Monaghan (1967, p. 239).
43. Benson and Eklin (1990).

44. Davidson (1975).
45. Davidson (1972).
46. Davidson (1972, pp. 202–203).
47. Johnson, Brekke, Strommen, and Underwager (1974).
48. Shand (1990).
49. Wylie (1979).
50. Myers (1992, p. 183).
51. Nehemiah 4:6 (*The Holy Bible*, Authorized King James Version).
52. II Thessalonians 3:10 (*The Holy Bible*, Authorized King James Version).
53. Weber (1904/1930).
54. Mazlish (1975, p. 63).
55. Lenski (1961); Warren (1970).
56. Roberts (1984, p. 278).
57. Roberts (1984, p. 284); Spilka, Hood, and Gorsuch (1985 p. 99); Wilson (1978, p. 291).
58. Greeley (1963).
59. McClelland, Atkinson, Clark, and Lowell (1953, 1955); McClelland, Rindlisbacher, and DeCharms (1955).
60. Greenberg (1960); Katz (1961); Maller (1960).
61. Silberman (1985, p. 143).
62. Davidson, Pyle, and Reyes (1995).
63. Silberman (1985, pp. 144–146).
64. Levitan (1960); Silberman (1985, p. 145).
65. Datta (1967).
66. Baltzell (1966); Wyllie (1966).
67. Lundberg (1968).
68. Davidson (1995).
69. Wuthnow (1994).
70. Wuthnow (1994, pp. 48–49).
71. Wuthnow (1994, p. 58).
72. Spilka (1977).
73. Wuthnow (1994, p. 61).
74. Chadwick and Garrett (1995).
75. Chadwick and Garrett (1995, p. 279).
76. Chadwick and Garrett (1995, pp. 288–291).
77. Bridges and Spilka (1992).
78. Wuthnow (1994, pp. 66–67).
79. Wuthnow (1994, p. 85).
80. Wuthnow (1994, p. 101).
81. Wuthnow (1994, p. 105).
82. Wuthnow (1994, p. 123).
83. Wuthnow (1994, p. 133).
84. Donahue (1994); Hoge and Yang (1994).
85. Davidson and Pyle (1994).
86. Wuthnow (1994, pp. 174–187).
87. Fichter (1961); Greeley (1972a); Kennedy and Heckler (1972); Schuller, Strommen, and Brekke (1980).
88. Dittes (1971b).
89. Dittes (1971b, pp. 426–427); Menges and Dittes (1965).
90. Dittes (1971b).
91. Kling (1958, 1959); Kling, Pierson, and Dittes (1964).
92. Kling (1959, pp. 14–16).
93. Embree (1968).
94. Hartley (1973).
95. Donovan and De Jong (1986); Kobasa (1986).
96. Schuller et al. (1980).
97. Hadden (1969); Quinley (1974).
98. Hadden and Swain (1981); Hill and Owen (1982).
99. Fichter (1965, 1968).
100. Webb and Hultgren (1973).

101. Fiorenza (1979).
102. Brereton and Klein (1979).
103. Lehman (1985, 1994).
104. Plaskow and Romero (1974); Ruether (1974).
105. Nesbitt (1993a, 1993b, 1994).
106. Nesbitt (1993a, p. 27).
107. Nesbitt (1994, p. 16).
108. Fortune and Poling (1994).
109. Nesbitt (1990).
110. Lawless (1988).
111. Lawless (1988, p. 164).
112. Nesbitt (1990, p. 274).
113. Ice (1987).
114. Campbell (1981).
115. Koltko (1993, p. 2).
116. Koltko (1993, p. 2). Emphasis in original.
117. Levinson et al. (1978).
118. Levinson et al. (1978, p. 242).
119. Myers (1992).
120. U.S. Bureau of the Census (1994, p. 389).
121. U.S. Bureau of the Census (1994, p. 389); Wuthnow (1994, p. 227).
122. Hoge (1994); Hoge and Yang (1994).
123. Wuthnow (1994, pp. 229–238).
124. Benson and Eklin (1990, item 1).
125. Benson and Eklin (1990, item 7).
126. Benson (1988).
127. Edwards and Wessels (1980).
128. Arinze (1986); Browning (1986); Schuller (1986).
129. Beck, Spilka, and Mason (1991).
130. Kirkpatrick (1949).
131. Edwards and Wessels (1980).
132. Pargament, Steele, and Tyler (1979).
133. Spilka and Mullin (1977).
134. Eisenstein (1956).
135. Bach and Wyden (1969).
136. Bottomley (1979).
137. O'Faolain and Martinez (1973).
138. Manicheism, a religion founded in the 3rd century A.D., stressed (among other issues) the conflict between good and evil. Marriage and sexual involvement were regarded most negatively and were forbidden.
139. Mathews and Smith (1923); Ruether (1972, 1974).
140. Adler (1931, 1935); Jones (1955a, 1955b).
141. Douglass (1974); Janus and Janus (1993); Tavris and Sadd (1977).
142. Kinsey, Pomeroy, and Martin (1948); Kinsey, Pomeroy, Martin, and Gebhard (1953).
143. Janus and Janus (1993); Tavris and Sadd (1977).
144. Janus and Janus (1993, pp. 255–256).
145. Tavris and Sadd (1977, p. 141).
146. Matthews (1994).
147. Wallin and Clark (1964).
148. Tavris and Sadd (1977).
149. Tavris and Sadd (1977).
150. Tavris and Sadd (1977).
151. Stanley and Markman (1992).
152. Hunt and King (1978); Stanley (1986).
153. Stanley (1986, p. 126).
154. Hunt and King (1978).
155. Bridges and Spilka (1992).
156. Johnson, Eberly, Duke, and Sartain (1988).

157. Johnson et al. (1988).
158. Kosmin and Lachman (1993).
159. Pevey (1994).
160. Brinkerhoff, Grandini, and Lupri (1992).
161. Brinkerhoff et al. (1992, p. 22).
162. Reynolds and Tanner (1995, p. 72).
163. McGuire (1992, p. 65); Rosten (1975, p. 368).
164. Rosten (1975, p. 367).
165. Greeley (1972a, pp. 105–107).
166. Rosten (1975, p. 368).
167. Kosmin and Lachman (1993, p. 224).
168. J. Wilson (1978).
169. Kosmin and Lachman (1993, p. 225).
170. 1991 and 1994 General Social Survey data from Davis and Smith (1994).
171. Gordon (1967).
172. McCutcheon (1988, p. 213).
173. Yinger (1968a, 1968b).
174. Herberg (1960, p.46).
175. McCutcheon (1988).
176. Silberman (1985, p. 287).
177. Kosmin and Lachman (1993, p. 244).
178. McCutcheon (1988, p. 221).
179. Silberman (1985). There is an old saying that if you have two Jews, you have three opinions and four organizations. This seems especially true when it comes to computing Jewish intermarriage rates. This debate is well explicated by Silberman, who thoughtfully justifies his choices in this complex realm. Needless to say, there is much disagreement with his position, and we have to employ data from a number of sources, not all of which agree with one another.
180. Kosmin and Lachman (1993, p. 246). These data differ slightly from those offered by Steinfels, which are presented in Table 4.4.
181. Steinfels (1992).
182. Kosmin and Lachman (1993, p. 248).
183. Goldstein and Goldscheider (1968).
184. Silberman (1985, p. 301).
185. Silberman (1985, p. 300).
186. Silberman (1985, p. 296).
187. Silberman (1985, p. 297).
188. Kosmin and Lachman (1993, p. 247).
189. Kosmin and Lachman (1993, p. 247); Silberman (1985, p. 304).
190. Kosmin and Lachman (1993, p. 248).
191. Mayer, cited in Steinfels (1992, p. 40).
192. Steinfels (1992, p. 40).
193. Stark and Bainbridge (1985).
194. Rosten (1975, p. 560).
195. M. S. Hoffman (1992, p. 942).
196. Rosten (1975, p. 561).
197. 1974–1994 General Social Survey data from Davis and Smith (1994), selected and arranged by Michael Kearl of Trinity University, San Antonio, Texas.
198. Rosten (1975, p. 561).
199. Forster and Tabachnik (1993).
200. Ellman (1971).
201. Goldstein and Goldscheider (1968).
202. Rosten (1975).
203. VanderStoep and Green (1988).
204. Chalfant, Beckley, and Palmer (1981).
205. Fulton and Gorsuch (1990); Kunkel and Temple (1992).
206. Fulton and Gorsuch (1990, p. 12).
207. Curb and Manahan (1985).
208. Marshall (1994a, 1994b).

209. Wolf (1989).
210. Curb and Manahan (1985).
211. Stanley (1986).
212. Bellah (1967).
213. Greeley (1972b, pp. 156–157).
214. Bellah (1970, p. 181).
215. Benson (1981, p. 50).
216. Hughey (1983).
217. Carter (1993); Colombo (1984); Hill and Owen (1982).
218. Quebedeaux (1989, p. 128).
219. Berke (1995, p. 2A).
220. Edsall (1995, p. 2A).
221. Moen (1990, p. 200).
222. Geyer (1963).
223. Lerner (1957, p. 704).
224. Cannon (1984, p. 21A).
225. Moen (1990).
226. Wills (1990).
227. Kelly (1983).
228. Lane (1969).
229. Lipset (1964).
230. Carter (1993).
231. Stark, Foster, Glock, and Quinley (1970).
232. Hostetler (1968).
233. Lawrence (1989).
234. Lawrence (1989).
235. Council of Evangelical Churches of Nicaragua (n.d.).
236. Skidmore (1993, p. 15).
237. *The Catholic Worker* (1991, p. 5).
238. Institute for Ecology, Justice and Faith (1995).
239. Quoted in Lipset (1964, p. 120).
240. Benson and Williams (1982).

Chapter 5

RELIGION AND DEATH

❧

Our son, thou art finished with the sufferings and fatigues of this life. It hath pleased our Lord to take thee hence, for thou hast not eternal life in this world; our existence is as a ray of the sun . . . we shall all follow thee for it is our destiny, and the abode is broad enough to receive the whole world.[1]

To every thing there is a season, and a time to every purpose under the heaven: A time to be born and a time to die. . . .[2]

For God's sake, let us sit upon the ground
And tell sad stories of the death of kings.[3]

[F]aith alone represents the victory over the prison of this world and its lethal power.[4]

It is impossible to experience one's death objectively and still carry a tune.[5]

A bit of wry humor states that we are all born terminally ill, and that none of us will get out of this world alive. In a more serious vein, these ideas are central in Western religion, as not getting out of our current existence alive is considered a prerequisite to the continuation of life in another realm. This constitutes the essence of immortality as a fundamental principle of most spiritual systems—so much so that philosophers and critics often claim that death invented religion.[6] The theologian Paul Tillich has championed such an inference by averring that "the anxiety of fate and death is the most basic, most universal, and inescapable."[7] Following this one step further, the noted anthropologist Malinowski claimed that "Death, which of all human events is the most upsetting and disorganizing to man's calculations, is perhaps the main source of religious belief."[8] In one study of clergy, only 2% felt that concern about death was not a factor in religious activity.[9]

Throughout this volume, we have stressed the role of religion in offering people meaning. The need to have acceptable answers is at no time greater than when the mystery of death is confronted. It is, of course, a mystery because most people cannot deal with the possibility of a simple, final termination when life ends. Understandably, no one does well when faced with the likelihood of ultimate extinction; it is not just that people want to live on indefinitely, but that they desire conviction and certainty that this will occur. Religion offers the assurance that this will eventually take place. The famous philosopher Unamuno has thus asserted that the theme of "immortality originates and preserves religions."[10]

Institutionalized faith, as we have seen, plays many roles in life, but the issue of death lies at its core. Kearl gets to the heart of the matter when he points out that "religion has historically monopolized death meaning systems and ritual," and further that it helps "create and maintain death anxieties and transcendence hopes as mechanisms of social control."[11] Here social control easily translates into personal control, another major function of religion (see Chapter 11). Expectations of judgment in an afterlife can prompt socially conforming behavior and give people the feeling that they are in charge of their final destiny. In individualistic, achievement-oriented U.S. society, this means, as the historian Arnold Toynbee observed, that death is "un-American, an affront to every citizen's inalienable right to life, liberty, and the pursuit of happiness."[12] Religion therefore stands as the only major bulwark against the threat of death—culturally, socially, and psychologically.

RELIGION, DEATH, AND IMMORTALITY

Belief in an Afterlife

When death is present in thought or reality, probably the most personally significant meaning that faith conveys is its claim of continued existence in an afterlife. Indeed, few if any formulations can be as consoling and gratifying as this. Estimates of belief in an afterlife range upwards of 65% with some U.S. national data indicating a rate as high as 86%.[13] The best current estimates, however, suggest that just under 80% of Americans hold afterlife beliefs.[14] When heaven alone is specified, recent survey data indicate that 63% of Americans "definitely" believe in its existence, and another 22% feel that it probably exists. In regard to hell, these numbers drop to 50% and 21% respectively.[15]

If the nature of life after death is specified, the dominant view is that this new realm will contrast with the present one by being a place of bliss. A Gallup poll of believers in a life after death found that 93% felt their postlife state would be positive. Terms such as "better," "good life," "peaceful," "no sickness or pain," "happy," "joyful," "no sorrow," and the like were generally employed as descriptive.[16] From 82% to 98% of those surveyed in other studies felt that their afterlife existence would be pleasant and enjoyable.[17] One poll reported that even though 97% believed in the existence of a heaven, only 83% expected to go there.[18] Some people are apparently not sure that their behavior will be acceptable when they get to the "pearly gates."

There is, of course, the alternative potential of an unpleasant eventuality if one goes to hell. Despite the fact that 86% in one of the studies cited above believed in hell, there was little desire to place anyone there, including extremely heinous historical figures—and, of course, least of all oneself.[19] Even though 46% of Protestants and 71% of Catholics claim that what one does in this life will determine one's fate in the hereafter, there seems to be considerable reluctance to change one's ways to avoid hell.[20] A certain vagueness attends afterlife beliefs, as continuation is more likely to apply to the spirit than to the body. Still, for many believers, the afterlife is succeeded by actual resurrection of the body. Contemporary Christianity prefers to conceptualize this as a "spiritual" body rather than a physical one.[21] Those desiring further details are often referred to faith and "trust in the Lord." Under such circumstances, imagery in this area rapidly takes on an individual quality. Nevertheless, the promise that one will not go into oblivion is present and is widely believed.

Some Cautions and Qualifications

Lifton points out that there are a number of ways of transcending death. He offers five forms under the rubric of "symbolic immortality."[22] "Biological immortality" lets a person live on through offspring, but this extends to a broader biosocial framework in which the person continues through contributions to larger social units—groups such as organizations, institutions, nations, and eventually the species. Above, we have been discussing what Lifton terms "theological immortality" or "religious immortality." "Creative immortality" is attained through works and achievements, whereas "nature immortality" deals with being part of nature and continuing in this mode. Lastly, there is a state of "experiential transcendence" or a mystical kind of immortality.

A few research efforts have related these modes of immortality to personal faith. Gochman and Fantasia found the religious form to be strongest among devout persons, as might be expected, whereas the remaining types appeared to be independent of religion. Religious immortality was also associated with short- and long-term life planning, implying a flexible yet long-range time perspective—a tendency also noted by Hooper and Spilka.[23]

Utilizing a cognitive theoretical framework, Hood and Morris constructed a more rigorous quantitative assessment of Lifton's modes, relating these to forms of personal faith and death perspectives.[24] They found that the religious mode countered fear of death and the loss of experience and control in death—tendencies not found with the other modes. An intrinsic religious orientation was found to be associated with all of the death transcendence modes, but was strongest with the religious perspective; by contrast, the religious mode was independent of extrinsic faith. These findings suggest that a deep religious commitment may act as a buffer against negative emotions, and yet may have additional ramifications relative to a wide range of death outlooks.

Many factors influence belief in an afterlife. As one might hypothesize, church members affirm these views more strongly than people in general.[25] When the major religious groups were compared over an 18-year period (1973–1991), Protestants were slightly above Catholics in contending that there is a hereafter, and both of these groups were considerably higher than Jews. Interestingly, among the Christians, there was no tendency for this belief to change over the almost two decades studied; Jews, however, showed a slow, regular increase of about 10% averring such ideas during this period.[26] The 1991 national data presented in Table 5.1 illustrate well the kind of religious patterning in afterlife beliefs held by Americans.

TABLE 5.1. Percentages of Americans Affirming the Existence of Heaven and Hell by Religious Group

Religious group	Agreement percentages	
	Heaven	Hell
Protestant		
Fundamentalist	97.1	88.8
Moderate	87.8	75.5
Liberal	83.6	74.4
Catholic	87.6	69.9
Jewish[a]	29.6	10.0

Note. The data are 1991 General Social Survey data from Davis and Smith (1994), and were retabulated by Michael Kearl of Trinity University, San Antonio, Texas.

[a]Small sample size makes this estimate tentative.

We might theorize that older individuals would profess such outlooks more than their younger contemporaries, but national data fail to show such a trend; hence no overall national effects of age appear to be present.[27] However, a different pattern emerges from a study of over 11,000 church members by Benson and Eklin, with the youngest respondents (20–29 years) and the oldest (over 70 years) revealing the lowest incidence of afterlife belief. From age 30 to age 69, there was little variation in the holding of these perspectives, with approximately two-thirds of churchgoers claiming absolute faith in the existence of an afterlife. Another 12.5% believed that such views are "mostly true."[28] The great distance young people may feel they are from death may make afterlife beliefs appear unrealistic. Elderly persons (even religious ones), who are confronted with the high probability of dying within a short time may come to feel that afterlife beliefs are nothing but illusions.

Differences in beliefs about the existence of an afterlife are found between the sexes, and such beliefs also appear to be affected by education and class level, among other influences. Table 5.2 offers a picture of these variations from a 1991 nationwide survey. Among the most striking features of the data in this table are the very high percentages of belief in heaven and hell in the U.S. population. In addition, the belief in heaven is stronger than that in hell, as we have already noted; this has a self-serving and self-protective quality about it. The higher percentages of assent for women than for men probably reflect the well-known inclination of the former to be more religious than the latter. In all likelihood, the dropoff in agreement

TABLE 5.2. Percentages Affirming Belief in Heaven and Hell by Gender, Age, and Socioeconomic Class

	Agreement percentages[a]	
	Heaven	Hell
Gender		
Male	79.5	65.9
Female	89.6	74.2
Age		
18–29	87.7	70.7
30–39	82.6	67.6
40–49	84.8	73.2
50–59	89.6	71.4
60–69	78.5	70.9
70+	91.3	74.0
Education		
0–11 years	92.9	73.9
High school graduate	92.1	78.8
Some college	80.3	69.6
4+ years college	74.7	58.6
Class level		
Lower	87.6	78.9
Working	88.9	75.9
Middle	83.4	67.3
Upper	64.3	44.8

Note. The data are from 1991 General Social Survey data from Davis and Smith (1994), and were retabulated by Michael Kearl of Trinity University, San Antonio, Texas.

[a]These percentages include "definite" and "probable" beliefs.

at the upper ends of the educational and socioeconomic dimensions is a function of the often-observed positive correlation among these demographic factors.

The Threat of Death and Its Effects on Afterlife Belief

A fairly popular view is that belief in an afterlife correlates positively with anxiety about death. Support for this hypothesis has been elusive, with research showing all possible relationships from negative through independent to positive.[29] Utilizing a fairly rigorous approach to this problem, Osarchuk and Tatz conducted an experiment and found evidence that concern about death can increase belief in an afterlife.[30] This study is summarized in Research Box 5.1.

Generalizing from Belief in an Afterlife

Throughout this volume, we have demonstrated that religious beliefs, attitudes, and values have relevance well beyond the sphere of faith. Subtly yet pervasively, religion manifests itself

---

Research Box 5.1. Effect of Induced Fear of Death on Belief in an Afterlife (Osarchuk & Tatz, 1973)

To test their hypothesis that making one's fear of death more salient would increase belief in an afterlife, these researchers constructed two equivalent and reliable 10-item scales of belief in an afterlife (forms A and B). Half of the people in each group received form A initially; the other half received form B first. Within each of these groups, 10 members were assigned to a death threat subgroup; 10 were assigned to a shock threat subgroup; and 10 were designated as controls. Six subgroups were thus formed—three with high belief in an afterlife, and three with low belief. To the death threat subgroups, a taped communication was played giving an exaggerated estimate of the probability of an early death for individuals 18 to 22, due to accident or disease related to food contamination. The tape contained a background of dirge-like music. A series of 42 death-related slides was coordinated with the communication, including scenes of auto wrecks, realistically feigned murder and suicide victims, and corpses in a funeral home setting.

   The members of the shock threat subgroups were informed that they would receive a series of painful electric shocks, to which, of course, they never were subjected. The control groups engaged in ordinary play for the same amount of time that the other groups underwent the death or shock threats. All subjects were then given the alternate form of the belief-in-afterlife scales that they had not filled out earlier. The results were partially as predicted. Those with low belief in an afterlife, regardless of what group they were in, revealed no changes in their beliefs. In contrast, only those initially holding strong after-life beliefs who were exposed to the death threat manifested a meaningful increase in these views. It appears that heightening the concern with death can influence belief in an afterlife. It would have been interesting to see whether other religious views (such as belief in God) were also similarly affected, but this was not done here. The question is one of focus, for, as Dr. Johnson put it, "when a man knows he is to be hanged in a fortnight, it concentrates his mind wonderfully."[a]

---

[a]Quoted in Boswell (1791/n.d., p. 725).

in a wide variety of developmental, personality, and social concerns and expressions. In particular, this is very true of belief in an afterlife. Using survey data, Richardson and Weatherby examined the ties between these views and a variety of structural and secular concerns.[31] They confirmed the already stated influences of religious affiliation and church involvement. They further showed that even though education countered an afterlife stance, the latter appeared to increase with occupational prestige, and also demonstrated greater relevance to white than to black churches. The authors have interpreted some of their findings to suggest that belief in an afterlife performs social control functions—specifically, maintaining morality and controlling sexual behavior. For example, with regard to the latter, the prospect of an afterlife may well be associated with concerns about premarital sex, divorce laws, and abortion. Here again is the classical implication that behavior in this world is linked to existence in an afterlife, which, of course, should have relevance to whether people perceive this eventuality in terms of their going to heaven or hell. We have already seen how this expectation is often held with reservations and qualifications.

Inferring the Existence of an Afterlife

People invariably seek information to buttress their convictions, sometimes making interpretations that go beyond the data in order to reassure themselves that they are right. How often do we hear of conflict between facts and figures, and opinions where the former are disbelieved because of people's ego involvement in the latter? An excellent illustration of such a tendency may be seen in making inferences to an afterlife from near-death experiences (NDEs).

Near-Death Experiences

The 1970s greatly popularized the concept of NDEs. Rather easily, many people transformed the idea of "near death" into "after death." The belief was that those undergoing these episodes had really died, encountered an aspect of the afterlife, and then returned to describe what happened to them. Little does more to legitimate extraordinary occurrences than to have such events backed by experts. The volume *Life after Life* by psychiatrist Raymond Moody performed such a function,[32] and, in the process, Moody became quite celebrated. Criticality, logic, and alternative explanations were acceptable only in certain quarters.

The noted pollster George Gallup, Jr., points out that NDEs (which he terms "verge-of-death experiences") have much in common with mystical and religious experiences, in that all may be triggered by extreme threats to life. He even suggests seven different situations that can elicit these episodes.[33] Readers should keep in mind, as we indicate elsewhere in this volume, that at least a third of the U.S. population reports having had mystical encounters, and that among religious persons the percentage is far higher. Gallup, however, notes that 15% of Americans claim they have had NDEs. The possible identification of religious encounters with NDEs suggests that those who report the former may be inclined to have the latter, and this appears to be true. Gallup has found that 23% of those who claim religious experiences also state that they have had NDEs—a percentage 8 points higher than that of the general populace.[34] Another possible variation on this theme is apparent in a consistently found correlation between NDEs and belief in other extraordinary phenomena, such as UFOs, reincarnation, and the likelihood that the living can contact the dead.[35]

Turning to a group that is likely to question NDEs—namely, scientists—Gallup reported that 10% admitted to personal involvement in an NDE. Though 32% believed in an afterlife, only 3% felt they had had a supernatural encounter. The overall tendency of scientists was to separate NDEs from the idea of an afterlife, and many attempted theoretical explanations of these phenomena in terms of physiological changes related to brain chemistry and function under oxygen deprivation, anesthetic effects, or the operation of endorphins. It is also significant to note that many religionists are also reluctant to claim that NDEs represent proof of an afterlife.[36]

Further doubt is cast on the supernatural origins of NDEs by the fact that these seem to have changed over time, and are affected by place.[37] In addition to much individuality entering the picture, cultural influences are obviously present. To some critics, the common absence of religious content in NDEs raises questions. The claim has also been made that NDEs often profoundly affect the lives of those who undergo these encounters. Suggestions of increased social concern and compassion, less materialism, improved self-esteem, and greater internal control have been reported.[38]

We need further confirmation of such radical transformations that cover extended periods of time; such have yet to be offered. The initial enthusiasm that greeted NDEs in the 1970s and 1980s now needs to be tempered with solid research. Interpretation of these experiences varies widely, from their explication as "spiritual experiences" to discussions in terms of consciousness and brain function.[39] As psychologists, we assume that the latter may prove to be of greater utility to a scientific perspective than the former.

Contact with the Dead

Another basis for inferring the existence of an afterlife comes from the widespread reporting of contacts with those who have died. MacDonald terms this "idionecrophany," an interesting term that is surely more a tribute to vocabulary construction than to any real need for such language.[40] Data on the prevalence of such interactions vary greatly, from about 40% of Americans who have lost one or more loved ones in the past year to over 90%, depending on ethnic group, religiosity, and age.[41] It is difficult to know whether the sense of actual contact is distinguishable from almost obsessive thinking about the one who has died.

A study of widows revealed that 64% still thought a great deal about their deceased husbands a year after the husbands' deaths.[42] In this work, almost every subject reported that she frequently experienced a sense of the presence of the departed one. The descriptions often fell into an intermediate category between thinking about the dead spouse and a sense of actual contact.

A recent Gallup poll indicated that 24% of the population believe that contact with the dead is possible; Kalish and Reynolds, however, found that over 40% of those they interviewed claimed some degree of contact with a deceased individual.[43] When a person is affected by a death, the combination of desire, need, hope, and other factors may create the conditions necessary for the person to experience some alteration of consciousness that leaves the impression of contact with the dead.

Religion may enter this picture, but, in general, its effects do not appear to be major. This is seen in Table 5.3, which presents national survey data. These data indicate that even though most people do not feel they have had contact with the dead, there is a slight tendency for more perceptions of contact as one's religious perspective becomes more conser-

TABLE 5.3. Responses to the Question "How Often Have You Felt as Though You Were Really in Touch with Someone Who Died?"

Religious group	Percentages reporting contact with the deceased			
	Never	1–2 times	Several times	Often
Protestant				
Fundamentalist	59	24	12	5
Moderate	62	23	10	5
Liberal	65	22	9	4
Catholic	57	26	12	5
Jewish	66	23	8	3

Note. The data are 1991 General Social Survey data from Davis and Smith (1994), and were retabulated by Michael Kearl of Trinity University, San Antonio, Texas.

vative. Another study that utilized General Social Survey information claimed an interaction between race and images of God relative to contact with the dead. Blacks who believed in God as a judge, and whites who conceptualized the deity as the incarnation of love, tended to be high in reporting contacts with deceased persons.[44] This researcher theorizes that when a relative dies, people may hold on to comforting God images, offering the possibility that these respective God percepts for blacks and whites perform such a function.

In the last analysis, people appear to seize on virtually anything in order to maintain a belief in immortality. The final possibility, which may have mental health ramifications, is simply to believe that someone has not died. In a rapidly transitory manner, probably most people toy with such an idea immediately after a death. The problem comes when someone refuses to give up such an outlook. In a less serious mood, we may ask what should be done with all of those who claim that Elvis Presley, Hitler, or other notables still walk the earth in disguise. We doubt that the claimants' faith can be implicated in such notions.

RELIGION, DEATH ANXIETY, AND DEATH PERSPECTIVES

The widespread prevalence of beliefs in immortality and an afterlife may be ascribed to both historical tradition and contemporary influences. For millenia, Western culture has been molded by a religious heritage that affirms ideas such as resurrection and life after death in the strongest terms. In one form or another, these views seem to be worldwide.[45] For those who adhere strongly to frameworks that advance these claims, such beliefs offer much gratification and must alleviate a rather basic source of anxiety. This last concern has been central to much work on the association of religion and death, for it deals with the immediate issue of how people conceptualize and confront death.

Death is always present. The mass media reveal it in daily reports that detail accidents, crimes, natural disasters, and war, and more specifically in ever-present semipersonalized obituaries. People usually appear inured to death and dying, as in most cases it is impersonal and distant. The front page is easily put aside; the young ignore funeral and death notices, but their elders increasingly attend to this information, not so infrequently seeing the names of those with whom they have been in contact. And finally, all encounter death in its personal form—for children, commonly in the loss of pets and the demise of grandparents.

Explanations are nearly always sought in afterlife notions, which receive reinforcement from one's elders and, of course, religious figures.

What we are suggesting here is that people know from childhood onward that death is inevitable, and they don't like this; it is to be feared, and therefore elicits a pervasive level of death concern and anxiety. Many psychologists have attempted to comprehend this phenomenon, and have found it to be rather consistently correlated with religious beliefs and behavior.

Religion and Anxiety about Death and Dying

The principal death-related variable that has been studied in relation to faith has been variously termed "fear of death," "death anxiety," or "death concern." These terms have all been rubricized under the general heading of "thanatophobia"—a word that is rarely employed and, once mentioned, can be put aside.

Research Problems

Certain problems have attended this research. First, the domains of religion and death fear have been confounded by measures from both areas containing similar items (e.g., belief in an afterlife). Second, a number of scholars have commented on such deficiencies as poor experimental designs, weak measurement indices, inadequate controls, inappropriate statistical analyses, and the use of questionable samples.[46] With respect to the last of these, most workers have examined college students, but others have studied the elderly, psychiatric patients, student nurses, medical students, the terminally ill, seminarians, and regular church-going community members. Finally, we have noted in Chapter 1 how measurement in the field of religion has gone from simple unidimensional scales to much more refined and complex multidimensional instruments. A parallel development has occurred in efforts to assess death anxiety. Unitary approaches once dominated the field; now measures are usually multiform in nature. It appears as if every possible combination of these approaches has been employed.

Despite all of these problems, it has been claimed that "one of the major functions of religious beliefs [is] to reduce a person's fear of death."[47] On the basis of the information we have—and there has been a great deal of research on this issue—we may reasonably ask whether faith does lessen concern about death. Initially, we encounter inconsistency. One survey of 36 studies revealed that 24 of these did find negative relationships between death fear on the one hand, and faith and afterlife beliefs on the other. Seven found independence between these domains, while three showed an unexpected positive association. Two other studies that were more complex (e.g., assessing different levels of death fear, such as conscious and unconscious expressions) demonstrated two of the three possible relationships.[48] Examining 16 studies conducted in the 1980s, Gartner and colleagues noted that six evidenced a negative relationship, three a positive association, and five no affiliation between religion and death concern; there were also two studies with curvilinear patterns.[49] These inconsistencies may be a function of the shortcomings noted above, plus other factors such as cultural influences.[50] Again, we feel the necessity of appreciating the complexity of the religion and death realms; unfortunately, some workers in this area seem to overlook this complexity.

These discrepant findings cannot be further debated here. However, our overview of this literature suggests that the better-defined research, particularly in terms of samples and instruments, argues in favor of religious commitment's reducing the fear of death. We are not foreclosing other options, but feel that the best case can be made for this alternative, theoretically and operationally. Some support for this position is now offered.

The Issue of Multidimensionality

Considering the issue of religious complexity, Batson, Schoenrade, and Ventis have done yeoman service by surveying studies utilizing measures of intrinsic and extrinsic faith relative to death fear.[51] In this work, religion is multiform in character, while the death realm remains unidimensional. The findings are quite clear: An extrinsic religious orientation is usually associated with death fear, concern, and anxiety, whereas an intrinsic outlook counters such negative outlooks.[52]

The next step in this research has been to develop dimensionalized measures of fear of death. A number of schemes have resulted in anywhere from five to eight forms. Minton and Spilka suggest five components: (1) lack of death fear; (2) sensitivity to death; (3) fear of the dying process; (4) awareness of the nature of death; and (5) loss of experience and control.[53] Focusing on Christianity, Clark and Carter have implied that different features of death anxiety may distinguish among persons varying in religious commitment—specifically, in intrinsic versus extrinsic perspectives.[54]

Additional efforts to dimensionalize the fear of death have been advanced by Hoelter and Epley, Leming, and Nelson and Nelson; though there seems to be a fair amount of conceptual and operational overlap among these instruments, they have proven useful in research.[55] Not only are such aspects of death anxiety differentially related to religion, but curvilinear associations have also been demonstrated.[56] For example, Leming observed relationships between fear of death and overall religiosity, religious belief, experience, and ritual. He suggested "that religiosity may serve the dual function of afflicting the comforted and comforting the afflicted."[57]

A different approach to the issue of the complexity of death anxiety has been introduced by Feifel, who has pointed out that there are both conscious and unconscious considerations to be evaluated when the death realm is examined. In other words, one's fear may be either conscious or unconscious, or both. Initially, Feifel was unable to find differences between religious believers and unbelievers with respect to these levels of death fear among persons who were either physically healthy or terminally ill.[58] When this work was expanded to three degrees of awareness, the deepest level (most unconscious) failed to relate to religion, but a midlevel fantasy approach did contribute markedly to associations with religious indices.[59] Employing different measures, Rosenheim and Muchnik found religiosity to be a factor at the unconscious level of analysis, but it was less significant than the personality trait complex of repression–sensitization.[60]

Death Anxiety and Death Perspectives

An additional development in this area recognizes that there are various perspectives on death, which may or may not overlap with the various dimensions of death fear. This approach was initiated and refined by Hooper and Spilka.[61] Research Box 5.2 describes a later development of this work.

èa

Research Box 5.2. Death and Personal Faith: A Psychometric Investigation
(Spilka, Stout, Minton, & Sizemore, 1977)

Early research on attitudes and feelings toward death focused on the very evident fact that the main emotion people expressed toward death specifically or in general was fear. It soon became evident that different facets of the death and dying process were being emphasized, and also that a simple positive–negative continuum had to give way to more complex cognitions regarding this ever-present and inevitable phenomenon. Hooper originally conceptualized 10 different ways of looking at death: (1) as a natural end, (2) as pain, (3) as loneliness, (4) as an unknown, (5) as forsaking dependents, (6) as failure, (7) as punishment, (8) as an afterlife of reward, (9) with courage, and (10) with indifference.[a] A number of scales were designed to assess these outlooks, but encountered various psychometric problems. In the work discussed here, Spilka and colleagues undertook a rigorous analysis of statements that might assess the 10 perspectives. It was found that the following eight reliable scales could be constructed:

Death as Pain and Loneliness	Death is viewed as painful, and associated with loss of mastery, consciousness, and isolation.
Death as Afterlife of Reward	Death leads to reward, personal justification, and a benevolent eternity.
Indifference toward Death	Death is of no consequence, a trivial occurrence in the scheme of things.
Death as Unknown	The end of life is an unfathomable, an ambiguous mystery.
Death as Forsaking Dependents	Death involves guilt over leaving one's dependents.
Death as Courage	Death is a final test of one's highest values, strength of character, and courage.
Death as Failure	Death is personal failure and defeat— the ultimate in frustration and helplessness.
Death as Natural End	Death is the natural conclusion to life, with nothing beyond it.

A number of studies related these death perspectives to two overlapping dichotomous religious orientations: intrinsic versus extrinsic faith, and committed versus consensual religious forms. The table below shows the differential pattern of correlations between the death perspectives and religious forms in the Spilka et al. study and a later confirmatory one by Cerny and Carter.[b] In further work, Clark and Carter obtained similar findings.[c]

---

[a]Hooper (1962).
[b]Cerny and Carter (1977).
[c]Clark and Carter (1978).

(*cont.*)

❧

Research Box 5.2 (*cont.*)

	Personal religion							
	Committed		Consensual		Intrinsic		Extrinsic	
Death perspectives	Spilka	Cerny	Spilka	Cerny	Spilka	Cerny	Spilka	Cerny
Loneliness and pain	−.08	−.19**	.13	.18**	−.26**	.21**	.36**	.41**
Afterlife of reward	.35**	.77**	.20*	.51**	.37**	.72**	−.07	.05
Indifference	−.09	−.38**	.18*	−.14*	−.25**	−.38**	.39**	.14*
Unknown	−.24**	−.41**	.12	−.23**	−.18*	−.47**	.21**	.14*
Forsaking dependents	−.11	−.07	.14	.12	−.13	−.13*	.31**	.31**
Courage	.20*	.45**	.14	.35**	.12	.41**	−.01	.10
Failure	−.18*	−.15*	.17*	.25**	−.23**	−.17**	.49**	.41**
Natural end	.04	.11	.19*	−.03	−.13	.04	.29**	.04

*$p < .05$. **$p < .01$.

It is noteworthy that this table shows only two instances of disagreement in the direction of a relationship where both correlations were statistically significant. Full agreement in both direction and significance occurred in 15 of the 32 coefficients. In addition, of the nine correlations that attained significance in only one of the studies, seven occurred in the Cerny and Carter research. The generally higher coefficients and the greater significance in this research are probably functions of Cerny and Carter's larger sample and their use of less stringent criteria to denote religiosity. These factors permit greater meaningful variance, and hence more significance.

The pattern of correlations was as expected. Intrinsic and committed religious orientations were positively related to favorable outlooks on death (e.g., death as an afterlife of reward, death with courage). Negative associations were obtained with undesirable death perspectives, with one exception (intrinsic faith with death as pain and loneliness). The latter may simply be an artifact (i.e., a chance occurrence). Again, we observe that religious commitment endows the individual with strength and reason not to fear death.

RELIGION, DEATH, AND THE ELDERLY

Death Concern among the Elderly

Death is too far from the young and too near the elderly, both in fact and perception—but not always, as one might expect. Persons over the age of 65 do account for more than 80% of the deaths in our nation; therefore, as people age the reality of death grows, and this invariably becomes a coping issue.[62] Erikson and his associates claim that "those nearing the end of the life cycle . . . [struggle] to balance consequent despair with the sense of overall integrity that is essential to carrying on."[63] Still, in one study of people over the age of 65, only 4% were troubled over their relative temporal proximity to their own deaths.[64]

It may be that more frequent thoughts of death and dying are replaced by "more optimistic life-affirming involvement."[65] In a personal contact, a centenarian responded to a question about whether she thought about death with the response, "Of course, but I'm too busy to die."[66] She was indeed, and survived for another 3 years. Hers is not an isolated perspective. The notion of not wanting to die because of "unfinished business" may be quite prevalent.[67] This view counters the most popular social-scientific perspective on aging—namely, disengagement theory, which suggests that people are supposed to lead themselves toward death when they are old by slowly and surely withdrawing from their connections with the world.[68]

The question of what constitutes withdrawal is controversial. A common type of involvement for older people is with their church, and to regard this as "disengagement" may be more pejorative than accurate. The constructive aspect of this behavior is most evident. Elderly people who are religious generally reveal low levels of anxiety and concern about dying. Though a minority of studies show no relationship between these variables, no studies have found a positive association.[69]

Faith apparently buttresses older people against the idea of impending death; it may accomplish this protective and beneficial function not only by providing the assurance of an afterlife, but also by currently affirming the elderly's worth and dignity. As people age, their social and occupational roles are usually reduced (e.g., through disengagement), and religious involvement may be substituted for other lost positions. Church activities offer a number of social possibilities by sponsoring the acquisition of new contacts and opportunities to demonstrate that a person is still effective and has value. Blazer and Palmore thus noted that "religious activities . . . were correlated with happiness, feelings of usefulness, and personal adjustment" among those over 70 years of age.[70] The emotion-controlling and directive functions of ritual should also be considered here. Not a few of the elderly regard these as reassuring.[71]

Here is a time, as Erikson puts it, of dealing with the issue of basic meaning; as Chapter 11 indicates, this is one of the most fundamental of religious purposes. Facing death implies the attainment of integrity and what Erikson calls "wisdom." The task is to gain a sense of place in the universe—a religious function if ever there was one. The final chapter of life is thus a period of taking stock, coming to terms with the past, and looking into a future in which the individual is not included. This raises the surprisingly complex matter of transcendence, which has already been alluded to, and was treated in a sophisticated manner in one study of the elderly (see Research Box 5.3).

Religion, the Elderly, and Longevity

Even though in the 19th century Galton rejected the idea that piety and longevity may be positively correlated, people have been reluctant to accept such a judgment. In research that has dealt with this issue either directly or indirectly, the results have not been either clear or consistent. Richardson's study of over 1,300 octogenarians found religion to be unrelated to 1-year survival rates.[72] More recent work by Koenig has confirmed this finding.[73] Idler and Kasl also found that neither public or private religiousness predicted mortality; yet for both Christians and Jews, there were significantly fewer deaths in the 30 days prior to a major religious holiday than for the same period afterwards.[74]

Other research on the institutionalized elderly who were chronically ill claimed that those who died within the year were less religious. This picture is muddied by the fact that they also had poorer prognoses and were more cognitively impaired.[75] In a similar vein, there is work reporting that religion is positively correlated with longevity, but only among the elderly who are in poor health.[76] Evidently this is an area that merits more rigorous study, along with theory that offers reasons why faith and mortality should be related, especially among the elderly.

ᨀ

Research Box 5.3. Toward a Theory of Death Transcendence
(Hood & Morris, 1983)

With sensitivity to the necessity of theoretically guided research, Hood and Morris described what they termed "transcendent" and "reflexive" facets of the self. The former is conceptually associated with immortality, in which the person "survives" this world. The reflexive self or selves, which exist in this world in a real sense, can also survive after bodily death. Cognitive issues come to the fore in thinking about transcendent–reflexive relations and the various forms of the latter. Robert Lifton's modes of "biological," "creative," and "nature" transcendence, which have been cited earlier, fall into the reflexive category.

Applying these ideas, Hood and Morris developed reliable measures of the Lifton modes from interviews with 39 persons averaging 65 years of age. Independent judges agreed 94% of the time on classifying the responses to the modes. In terms of their presence or absence, 27 people were identified with nature transcendence, 30 with biological (now viewed as biosocial) transcendence, 31 with religious transcendence, and 33 with the creative mode. These people were then administered scales of death anxiety, death perspectives, and intrinsic and extrinsic religious orientations. Patterns of meaningful relationships were obtained, suggesting the usefulness of both the Lifton modes and Hood and Morris's transcendent–reflexive distinction with elderly persons.

RELIGION AND EUTHANASIA

Among the more troubling and controversial topics in the United States today is the question of euthanasia. This is an issue that is often conceptually oversimplified and biased by such terminology as "mercy killing," "assisted suicide," "right to die," and "death with dignity." A distinction must, however, be made between passive and active euthanasia. The former usually implies the withholding of heroic measures to sustain life when death is imminent and the quality of life is very poor. In contrast, active euthanasia suggests the intentional, active termination of life under the same conditions, especially when great pain and suffering are present. Frequently, this is practiced when a patient makes impassioned pleas to die.

General and Medical Support for Euthanasia

Though euthanasia is illegal in most jurisdictions, the overwhelming majority of medical professionals favor passive euthanasia. Surveys reveal that anywhere from two-thirds to over 90% of health practitioners approve such approaches, while 17% of physicians and 36% of nurses have positive attitudes toward active euthanasia.[77] It should not come as a surprise that in 1993, a Gallup poll reported that 43% of Americans approved the "assisted suicide" actions taken by Dr. Jack Kevorkian. A slightly greater number (47%) disapproved.[78] The Gallup organization has taken a sophisticated view of this problem, revealing how attitudes are dependent on a number of factors. Table 5.4 illustrates some of these considerations.

Religious Perspectives on Euthanasia

As might be expected, the general attitudes toward euthanasia described in Table 5.4 are mirrored in the views of members of the major religions in the United States. Though scripture and theology are usually interpreted as opposing euthanasia, there is much deviation from such a position. If euthanasia is approved by a physician, 61% of Protestants, 62% of Catholics, and 78% of Jews agree with such a stance.[79] The strength of one's religious position does affect these findings, as the comparable data for "strong" Protestants, Catholics, and Jews are 49%, 51%, and 67%, respectively.[80] It is abundantly evident that euthanasia under certain circumstances is supported widely, regardless of religious affiliation. There are also data indicating that such approval is a positive function of belief in an afterlife.[81]

A conceptual variation on euthanasia is physician-assisted suicide (PAS). This takes one of two forms: (1) The physician may offer the individual the means (pills, injections, or equipment) to induce death; or (2) the doctor may accede to the patient's wish to die by actively causing the person's death.[82] Dr. Kevorkian has generally utilized the first procedure. Though PAS is against the law in the Netherlands, the law is not enforced, and it is estimated that up to 10,000 persons there utilize PAS annually. Despite the fact that these procedures are also illegal in the United States, there is much tacit approval of their use, and in a number of states

TABLE 5.4. Attitudes of Americans toward Euthanasia

1. Do you think a person has the moral right to end his or her life under these circumstances?[a]

	Yes	No
When the person is suffering incurable disease	58%	36%
When the person is suffering great pain with no chance of improvement	66%	29%
When an otherwise healthy person wants to end his or her life	16%	80%

2. A terminally ill person wants treatment withheld so that he or she may die. The patient has the right to stop treatment[a]:

	Yes	No
If the doctor agrees	75%	22%
If the person is in great pain	78%	18%
If the family agrees	76%	22%
Under any circumstances	59%	4%
Under no circumstances	11%	87%

3. If you yourself were on life support systems and there was no hope of recovering, you would prefer to[a]:

	Yes
Remain on life support	9%
Have treatment withheld	84%

4. Do you think a doctor should be allowed by law to assist a person to end his or her life?[b]

	Yes	No
When the person is suffering from incurable disease	52%	42%
When the person is suffering great pain	64%	31%
When the person is a burden on the family	22%	71%
No reason	8%	88%

[a]The data are from Gallup (1992, p. 4).

[b]The data are from *The Gallup Poll Monthly* (1992, December, p. 34).

efforts to pass laws permitting PAS are in progress. However, in states where the electorate has voted on such proposals, they have been narrowly defeated.[83]

Opposition to PAS has come more from formal religious organizations than from their members. Scriptural arguments are usually employed in resisting PAS. Still, the more liberal Christian and Jewish groups seem to be moving slowly toward support for PAS. The United Church of Christ already backs it.[84]

Indications that it is probably just a matter of time before more religious bodies justify euthanasia come from the increasingly favorable positions taken by members of the clergy. In one investigation, Carey and Posavec found that 96% of the clerics they surveyed advocated passive euthanasia, and 21% espoused its active form.[85] Backing for passive euthanasia varies with the reasons advanced for such action. Another study found that support was offered, depending on the justification, by anywhere from 34% to 73% of Protestant clergy; for Catholic priests, there was little difference, with the comparable figures ranging from 30% to 69%. In regard to active euthanasia, the percentages were significantly lower: For the Protestant clergy they varied from 13% to 25%, and only 1–3% of the priests countenanced such action.[86]

Even though this last investigation failed to designate the Protestant denominations sampled, some data reveal that approval of euthanasia increases with the liberality of a cleric's theological position and group. Conservative clergy balance their opposition with strong beliefs in a rewarding afterlife.[87]

Despite the fact that a study by Gillespie did not bear directly on the question of euthanasia, he demonstrated clerical differences on a variety of death perspectives across religious groups.[88] This research implies that pastoral outlooks on euthanasia may be dependent on factors other than denominational conservatism and afterlife beliefs. It opens a significant door to further study.

RELIGION AND BEREAVEMENT

That life entails death goes without saying. In fact, it has been said that once people are born, the only predictable thing about them is that they will die. Living also means encountering the demise of loved ones, for there must inevitably come that time when a beloved person "goeth to his long home, and the mourners go about the streets."[89] When someone dies, the likelihood is high that family and friends will turn to religion for solace and understanding. Faith is often a basic part of the process of coping, and death is a common problem that is often confronted and dealt with in religious terms.

Grief is a surprisingly complex process. The literature offers discussions about stages of grief, models of grief, ritual in grief, religion as a resource in bereavement, the grief of parents and grandparents for deceased children and grandchildren, the grief of spouses for deceased mates, and so on and on. In all of these areas the role of faith is significant. For example, Flatt suggests some 10 grief stages, which range from "initial shock" to what he terms "growth." In most of these stages, God is given a role—whether it be a questioning of how the deity could let someone die or how the divine actively brings about a death, to a place for "God's grace" in recovery from the depression resulting from grief. Another possibility is that the recovery from grief may move the person along to new stages and tests, such that the deity is seen to care as the person is reintegrated into "God's world." This means that the bereaved gains new strength to realize "God's purpose" in his or her remaining life.[90] Here we observe how significant attributions to God may be when death is confronted.

Though the majority of research on religion and bereavement points to the beneficial role faith often plays in such distressing circumstances, it should be noted that not all work in this area supports such inferences and observations.[91] This is indeed an involved realm, which needs more sensitivity to theory and the possibility of confounding factors.

Sanders undertook a rather interesting study, in which she compared grief reactions to the death of a spouse, child, and parent.[92] Though the most intense responses occurred when a child died, church attendance was positively related to more optimism, less anger, and a better appetite. When church attendance and family interaction were treated together, the findings even more graphically favored the religion–family combination. This may imply the significance of religion not only in terms of meaning, but in regard to a broader beneficial basis for social support from one's kin.

Religious Schemas and Bereavement over Child Loss

A creative and useful theoretical treatment of bereavement has been advanced by McIntosh and his colleagues.[93] McIntosh has also extended this approach to religion in general and its role in life.[94] Noting that "a schema is a cognitive mental structure or representation containing organized prior knowledge about a particular domain, including a specification of the relations among its attributes," McIntosh further notes that "people have different schemas for many domains."[95] Schemas influence what is perceived, speed up cognitive processing of information, and offer meaning in difficult situations by filling in gaps in knowledge. In sum, they orient people to the world and the problems with which they must cope. As such, they influence behavior and can help people adapt to trying and problematic circumstances. With respect to death and bereavement, one salient aspect of a religious schema may be belief in an afterlife. Apparently such belief is "associated with greater recovery from bereavement regardless of the cause of death."[96]

For many reasons (largely experiential and cultural), most people possess religious schemas, and these are often called into play when ambiguity and threat become troublesome. In their significant work on how parents coped with the death of an infant from sudden infant death syndrome (SIDS), McIntosh and his colleagues demonstrated how parents' faith, through the use of religious schemas, indirectly facilitated their adjustment—both cognitively and behaviorally. The schemas both made the death meaningful and also supported parents' efforts to come to terms with their loss. Behaviorally, via religious participation, social support and meaning were elicited. Cognitively, religious importance contributed to meaning, and also to cognitive processing. Both avenues aided in the reduction of distress.[97]

McIntosh et al.'s work explains similar findings in other studies that have dealt with parental and grandparental bereavement.[98] Studying the influence of church attendance, Bohannon was able to show that it was inversely related to anger, guilt, loss of control, obsessive thoughts about the child's death, somatic complaints, and death anxiety on the part of the grieving mothers. Similar effects were found for anger, guilt, and death anxiety on the part of the fathers.[99] The research on the grandparents of SIDS children revealed that religious beliefs were strengthened in 46% of the sample, and 90% felt that their faith aided them in coping with the SIDS death.[100]

Further work by Gilbert with bereaved parents stressed the perceived role of God in this situation. She found that in cases where religion was a resource, the views were that (1) God did not do bad things, (2) God was in control and could be relied on to make the wisest decision, (3) God had good reasons for the child's death, (4) God inflicted this tragedy upon the parents because they had the strength to deal with it, (5) God wanted them to appreciate life more, and (6) God wanted them to change their lives for the better. Interestingly, those who claimed that religion was not initially helpful gained a more positive perspective over time. Lastly, those who claimed that religion was irrelevant seemed to possess an extrinsic orientation.[101] The implication is that for faith to be of significance in this kind of tragedy, it must have an intrinsic quality, not a superficial, utilitarian one. A further good example of theoretically guided work in this area that is also methodologically sophisticated is presented in Research Box 5.4.

Conjugal Bereavement

The classic work of Glick, Weiss, and Parkes stresses the benign effects of faith on bereavement when a spouse dies.[102] To the extent that the widows surveyed in this research were devout, they were described as turning "to the formal doctrine of their religions for explanation."[103] Again we see the significance of meaning and understanding in alleviating negative feelings. In parallel work, social and religious support appeared to operate independently, both working to counter depression and subjective stress.[104] Study after study confirms these findings: Personal adjustment is positively related to religious commitment and activity, and,

---

Research Box 5.4. The Stress-Buffering Role of Spiritual Support (Maton, 1989)

Positing two major avenues for religion to mitigate the effects of stress, Maton has defined these as the "cognitive mediation" and "emotional support" pathways. The former implies a positive reframing of negative life events, whereas the latter concerns perceptions of God as valuing and caring for the distressed individual. Treating these as independent, Maton assessed the contributions of each within two samples: (1) bereaved parents who had lost a child, and (2) college students. In the first sample, 33 parents who had been bereaved within the preceding 2 years constituted a high-stress group, and 48 whose child had died more than 2 years previously made up a low-stress group. Measures of spiritual, social, and friendship support and of depression were completed by the respondents.

Spiritual support was correlated negatively with depression and positively with self-esteem for the high-stress group, but not for the low-stress sample. A similar pattern was noted for support provided for the high-stress group, but not the low-stress group. A prospective study with college students ruled out the likelihood that spiritual help followed rather than contributed to well-being. Maton concluded that "spiritual support may influence well-being through directly enhancing self-esteem and reducing negative affect ('emotional support' pathway) or through enhancing positive and adaptive appraisals of the meaning of a traumatic event ('cognitive mediation' pathway)" (p. 320). Various forms of spiritual support were theorized, and other research possibilities were suggested to explore this domain further.

as might be expected, religious involvement is likely to increase following the death of a spouse.[105]

The Significance of Ritual

Among the diverse aspects of faith that play a constructive role in grief is ritual. Variously said to create a sense of safety and impart new constructive meanings, it may also be self-alienating. In other words, ritual distances a person from emotions and permits him or her to return to the world—a process that obsessive self-concern hinders.[106] Reeves and Boersma thus maintain that "rituals can provide a sense of positive personal power for an individual who is feeling out of control and clarify and provide meaning to an issue so that it is easier to work on."[107]

On another level, rituals introduce structure, elicit social support, and not infrequently serve as a distraction from the grief itself. Formal ceremonies allow the bereaved to work through the pain of loss. A death is a disruption in the survivors' lives, and religious ideology and ritual can function to restore stability to the bereaved.[108]

Illustrative of this principle is the Jewish practice of *shiva*, a 7-day, repetitive set of mourning rites that evokes community support in the form of a group. Group members often bring food to the griever's home, and they participate in a well established set of ceremonies. *Shiva* has been compared to group therapy.[109] Gerson describes in detail the formalized mourning process in Judaism, and notes how it is designed to thwart the development of pathological grief by specifying degrees of return to normal social interaction.[110] For these reasons, the symbolic power of religious rituals has recently become part of the psychotherapeutic armamentarium of pastoral counselors.[111]

RELIGION AND SUICIDE

Even though death itself is often terribly distressing, the way a person dies cannot be overlooked. When people are terminally ill and in great pain, death may be regarded as a blessing; when people (especially those who are young) kill themselves, it is frequently devastating to family and friends.[112] When religion is brought into the picture, the general tendency is for suicide to become even less acceptable.[113]

Institutionalized religion has rather uniformly treated suicide in the most negative terms. The Judeo-Christian tradition has taught that suicide is immoral and therefore sinful.[114] Those who commit suicide may not be allowed to be buried with the other faithful in religiously sponsored cemeteries, or may be consigned to certain sections that indicate severe condemnation and rejection. Because of the disgrace and stigma attached to suicide both historically and contemporaneously, medical, religious, and civil authorities are often reluctant to identify a death as a suicide. The more modern religious perspective is to consider these individuals as mentally disturbed—a diagnosis that removes the burden of sin, and mitigates the opprobrium that members of the surviving family may otherwise incur from the religious community. There is reason, however, to believe that the influence of religion on attitudes toward suicide has decreased considerably in the contemporary world, especially in the United States.[115]

That institutionalized faith can affect the incidence of suicide has been well documented for over a century.[116] Cross-national studies suggest a weakening of the impact of religion, such that the inverse relationship between faith and suicide may no longer hold for men; it continues to exist among women.[117] Attitudinally, the classic finding that religious commitment and conservatism oppose suicide nevertheless persists.[118] Furthermore, church attendance remains negatively correlated with suicide rates.[119]

The elderly are at much greater risk of suicide than are young people. A summary of data from 1960 to 1986 shows a steady growth of suicide rates with increasing age. For those 15 to 24 years of age, the suicide rate is 13.1 per 100,000 people; for those aged 65–74, the rate is 19.7; and it reaches 25.2 in the 75–84 age range.[120] Men are much more likely than women to take their own lives, with rates as high as 61 per 100,000.[121] We may hypothesize that men are less able than women to cope with a loss of independence and self-determination. As Kearl notes, "for some elderly individuals, suicide is preferable to loneliness, chronic illness, and dependency."[122] This may be especially true for physically ill older men, the group with the highest suicide rate in the United States. Again, however, among the elderly, religion plays its traditional role in countering self-destruction. Koenig suggests that faith suppresses suicidal thinking in this group.[123] One possible explanation might emanate from a generation effect—namely, that religious elderly persons often identify with their faith's opposition to suicide, as well as with the promise of a happy afterlife.[124] A related finding is that the recovery from bereavement of those who lose a loved one via suicide is enhanced by high belief in an afterlife.[125] Direct research relating suicide to belief in an afterlife would indeed make a contribution to this literature.

The need for a sophisticated theoretical approach to the association of religion with suicide has been addressed by Stack and Wasserman.[126] Though they treat suicide ideology rather than suicide per se, their thinking suggests a more direct assessment of the latter. These authors note three possibilities: (1) Religion fosters general social integration, which opposes suicide; (2) specific religious views such as belief in an afterlife may counter self-destructive impulses; and (3) religious organizations foster networking and social support, which should thwart suicidal inclinations. Using sophisticated statistical techniques on national data, these authors found evidence supporting all three views. On the basis of church attendance data, however, they concluded that the social connections faith can create and reinforce may constitute the main element hindering suicide.

A SPECIAL CASE: RELIGION, DEATH ANXIETY, AND AIDS

The association of the invariably fatal disease AIDS with homosexuality and drug usage has resulted in a troubled role for religion. Some of the ramifications of homosexuality have been treated in Chapter 4; however, when AIDS enters the picture, homophobia becomes even harsher. For example, certain religious extremists claim that AIDS is God's punishment for homosexual behavior.

Research on religion in relation to AIDS is slowly revealing what we might theorize—namely, that faith can be of benefit to those confronting the eventuality of death via this disease. Unhappily, the overall pattern of negativism toward homosexuality and AIDS displayed by the churches, especially conservative ones, has been reciprocated by the gay and bisexual community. High levels of antireligious hostility have been manifested by the latter groups.[127]

In one comparison of groups of gay men with and without AIDS, the former showed higher levels of death anxiety than those without AIDS, and this was positively associated with more formal church activity.[128] Interestingly, the AIDS group evidenced less belief in an afterlife than their non-AIDS peers. We may hypothesize either the presence of denial on the part of those with AIDS or a tendency to consider afterlife beliefs a luxury that they could not intellectually accept as strongly as the non-AIDS group did. Could this be a function of their facing death, in all probability, rather shortly?

Research on religion and AIDS has been beset by a number of design shortcomings, such as the use of unidimensional measures of death concern and religion, as well as the employment of single-item indices (which have a high likelihood of being unreliable). These problems may account for some inconsistency in the findings of the few studies available.[129] In an effort to correct for these potential deficiencies, Bivens and his coworkers undertook a much more refined investigation; this is described in Research Box 5.5. Bivens et al.'s study charts a path to even more complex and insightful work regarding how religion may be employed as a resource to reduce fear of death by individuals suffering from a chronic disease known to be fatal.

DEATH AND THE CLERGY

Like the rest of us, piety notwithstanding, the clergy also die. However, one thing that does separate this profession from virtually all others is that ministers, priests, and rabbis are almost always called upon to use their pastoral skills on behalf of those who are in the process of

---

ᢒᢒ

Research Box 5.5. Death Concern and Religious Beliefs among Gays and Bisexuals (Bivens, Neimeyer, Kirchberg, & Moore, 1994–1995)

Bivens and colleagues studied a sample of 167 gay or bisexual men, of whom 24 were HIV-positive (HIV+) and 19 had full-blown AIDS. These 43 were collectively termed the "HIV+" group. The remaining subjects were HIV-negative (HIV–). Sixty-nine of these subjects were defined as an "AIDS-involved" group, as they helped AIDS patients in a variety of settings. The remaining participants were denoted "AIDS-uninvolved." All subjects were administered a multidimensional fear-of-death scale that yielded eight measures of death concern. An index of personally perceived threat from the potential of one's own premature death was also used. This instrument yielded three factors plus a total score. Intrinsic and extrinsic religious orientations were assessed by the Allport–Ross scales. Also included were a scale of Christian orthodoxy and a more general inventory of religious beliefs and practices.

The HIV+ group displayed greater fear than the other two groups with respect to the likelihood of a premature death. No difference was found between the AIDS-uninvolved and AIDS-involved groups on this measure. The AIDS-involved group, however, (1) manifested less global threat and less threat regarding meaningfulness and survival concerns, and (2) were significantly more religious, than the AIDS-uninvolved participants. A consistent pattern of negative correlations was observed between the measures of religiosity and fear of the unknown. Intrinsic faith, belief in God, and church attendance were also associated with less global threat, lower threats to meaningfulness, lower survival concerns, and less negative emotional appraisals.

dying. Furthermore, once death has occurred, the clergy conduct the final rituals that consign the souls of the deceased to their ultimate divine destiny. Concurrently, they turn their attention to grieving family members and friends, attempting to bring solace to the bereaved. In sum, one of the prime clerical tasks is to situate death in ultimate perspective. The goal of pastoral interpretations and actions is often to engender hope in the face of death.

In work with the dying and their survivors, members of the clergy have three aims: (1) to make the death meaningful to all concerned in terms of the perspective of a religious or spiritual system; (2) to transform the distress of the death and dying process into a vista of personal strength, self-identity, and a natural closing to a life well lived—an existence in which one has contributed to a better future and a richer heritage; and (3) to attempt to convince all that death is not an end, but a new beginning, a doorway to immortality, a personal permanence, a new kind of life.[130] We have already shown how these efforts may take a number of forms.

Training the Clergy to Deal with Death

The last 30 years have witnessed a new sensitivity to death and dying that has profoundly affected seminary education. Programs to develop pastoral skills in this area have proliferated, along with a plethora of books and articles detailing the complexities of the tasks pastors must confront.[131]

That the clergy themselves feel deficient in this area was illustrated by one study of priests, ministers, and rabbis, which revealed that only 15% of practicing clerics felt their education had prepared them adequately to deal with death and dying. Forty percent considered themselves poorly trained to do death work.[132] However, the increased emphasis on death education for prospective clergy during the last 30 years has imparted a heightened sense of competence in dealing with terminal patients. Some 64% of clerics-to-be in the study just mentioned felt that they were moderately to well educated in this area.[133] In contrast, older clergy had to learn about death and dying via direct experience in the pastorate. Today, these important skills are acquired both in seminary and through internships prior to ordination. Opportunities are currently provided for neophyte clerics to model themselves selectively after mentors who have been engaged with the dying and their families for long periods of time.

With relatively little variation, those to whom the clergy provide their services tend to be quite pleased with the pastoral efforts of hospital chaplains and home pastors.[134] An interesting exception occurs with breast cancer patients: Both male and female clerics usually avoid discussing some of the central concerns of these women about their identity as female and the surgical mutilation of their bodies.[135] Obviously, there is still a need for additional pastoral training to deal with such sensitive personal issues.

Clerical Feelings about Death and Dying

Even though most clergy appear to buffer themselves against death and dying with strong beliefs in a life after death, the more theologically liberal they are, the more they see death as a natural end to life or simply as a mystery.[136] None of these perspectives implies that the clergy are not afraid of death. The evidence is that, like everybody else, they too manifest anxiety about death and dying.[137]

Clerical Involvement and Effectiveness in Death-Related Situations

Spilka has participated in a number of workshops designed to aid clergy and other death workers in their interaction with the dying and their families. The growing hospice movement has also undertaken such training. Unfortunately, the proliferation of these efforts has not been accompanied by research to evaluate the effectiveness of these programs. Still, in two studies of over 400 clergy, about 60% claimed that they dealt often or very often with terminal patients and their families; only 1% are not at all engaged in this kind of work.[138]

But what do home pastors (i.e., people's regular clerics making home visits) and hospital chaplains do when they interact with the dying and their kin? Over 90% of clerics claim that they make two or more calls to the home of the bereaved in the year following a death.[139] Table 5.5 gives us some idea of the variety of actions that may take place in these encounters.

Table 5.5 suggests some interesting differences between home pastors and hospital clergy, some of which may be attributable to the longer personal history of contact between the recipients and their regular clerics. In most instances, especially with cancer patients, hospital chaplains were not as pastorally involved with the patients as home pastors were. This was less true when the clerics were dealing with the families of children with cancer. Still, for both groups, there was considerable reluctance to discuss the future. There may be a number of critical interactive subtleties in this process that call for additional research. Certainly, we still need to know the characteristics and behavior of successful pastors—that is, successful from the recipients' viewpoint.

Theology, Personal Faith, and Clergy Effectiveness

Spilka and colleagues found that among clergy dealing with death and dying, two-thirds claimed that the theology of their church was "very helpful," while only 2–3% felt it was of little or no use. Surprisingly, these numbers held whether the clerics were affiliated with a conservative or a liberal religious body. An interesting variation on this theme suggests that clerics' own personal faith is of greater importance than their church's theology, as 83%

TABLE 5.5. Activities of Home Clergy and Hospital Chaplains Working with Cancer Patients and the Families of Children with Cancer

Activity	Cancer patients		Families of children with cancer	
	Home clergy	Hospital chaplains	Home clergy	Hospital chaplains
Offering to pray for	43%	47%	42%	44%
Offering to pray with	42%	35%	51%	44%
Actually praying with	46%	22%	56%	48%
Reading religious material	17%	14%	20%	20%
Counseling	21%	16%	20%	24%
Talking irrelevancies	21%	18%	34%	36%
Seeming to understand	44%	28%	44%	44%
Talking church matters	15%	6%	7%	12%
Talking about family	47%	12%	46%	40%
Discussing the future	15%	8%	15%	12%
Other	9%	22%	17%	8%

Note. The data are from Spilka and Spangler (1979). Percentages add up to more than 100, because clergy engaged in more than one activity per contact.

regarded the former as providing them with the most support in their death work.[140] Apparently, as important as formal theology is, the crucial issue may be the degree to which a cleric identifies with that position.

There is little doubt that working with terminality is a very trying experience for clerics. Almost 70% of the clergy studied by Spilka et al. were less than "very satisfied" with their exertions, and 11–14% were quite unhappy with themselves. Some 43% of pastors described themselves in this work with qualifying adjectives such as "frustrated," "inadequate," "apprehensive," and the like.[141] In addition, Parkes observed that clergy "are often embarrassed and ineffectual when face-to-face with those who have been or are about to be bereaved."[142] At least, with the families of the dying, theological conservatism implies more personal satisfaction; this may be a concomitant of afterlife beliefs that are more strongly held and more clearly defined by orthodox as opposed to liberal institutions.

Some research suggests that clergy from the liberal end of the theological spectrum are sometimes more concerned with their own psychological state than with that of a patient and family when they are doing death work.[143] In these circumstances, the more conservative clergy emphasize religious, scriptural, and spiritual referents and convey these to those to whom they minister. It is not amiss to note that terminal patients and their kin seem to want these kinds of support, rather than what might be taken as strictly psychological pastoral actions. As important as the latter are in these situations, the appeal is clearly to God, not to psychotherapy.[144]

That the bereaved consider the clergy helpful at this troubled time is abundantly evident. Carey studied the satisfaction of widows and widowers with physicians, nurses, chaplains, social workers, and family members. Although family members were viewed as most helpful, the hospital chaplains came in a close second.[145]

Like virtually everyone who confronts death, the clergy probably never become immune to the feelings that death and dying engender. They have entered a profession in which they must continually confront these hard realities. Undoubtedly, pastoral effectiveness in death work is a function of experiences that force clerics to face their own mortality while expressing the empathy and humanity these situations call for. Fortunately, most pastors develop the skills, compassion, and understanding to handle these trials. Additional consideration of these difficulties from the consumer's viewpoint is offered in Research Box 5.6.

DEATH IN THE RELIGIOUS–SOCIAL CONTEXT

We have commented on the role of religious ritual in relation to death, and have indirectly alluded to the fact that ceremonial practices are invariably associated with certain religious groups or peoples (e.g., the Jewish custom of *shiva*). When cultural settings and religious rites are coordinated, their combined power is often quite compelling to those associated with various traditions. Death has always been circumscribed by rites that are usually quite meaningful to believers. The Mormons and the Amish offer excellent illustrations of the power of religious regulations and traditions concerning death.

The Mormon Case: Religion, Health, and Death

It is no accident that the lowest death rates in the contiguous 48 United States are found in Utah.[146] These numbers hold for deaths from cancer, cardiovascular problems, and a varira

---

Research Box 5.6. Spiritual Support in Life-Threatening Illness
(Spilka, Spangler, & Nelson, 1983)

In the last analysis, the effectiveness of clerics must be determined by those to whom the clergy demonstrate their skills. This effectiveness was assessed in a study of 101 cancer patients and 45 parents of children with cancer. All subjects were questioned about their interactions with home pastors and hospital chaplains. The participants were generally quite religious. All respondents were administered a 45-item questionnaire, of which 6 items were open-ended, permitting a free response.

Twenty-nine percent of the patients were visited at home by their pastors, and 66% received hospital visits. With regard to the families of the children with cancer, 42% had home visits and 56% hospital visits. About 55% of both the patients and parents saw hospital chaplains. From 78% to 87% of the patients and parents were satisfied with the home and hospital visits. (Table 5.5, earlier in this section, has indicated what went on during these contacts.) The subjects expressed most satisfaction with situations where home clergy actually prayed with the patients and the family members. Engaging in religious reading was also positively regarded. In the hospital, the families regarded discussions of the future by the chaplain quite favorably. Finally, the willingness of a cleric simply to be present and to devote time to this troubling situation was considered most desirable.

As is so frequently true, subjects were often clearer about the undesirable characteristics of clerics than about those they approved of. Most that was displeasing was broadly attributed to poor communication and lack of understanding on a pastor's part. Specifically, conveying the impression of visiting out of a sense of duty alone, and/or failing to appreciate or to be sensitive to the pain of the circumstances, was upsetting to these people. Extremely distressing were efforts (fortunately rare) to effect "deathbed conversions." For example, one cleric harangued a patient to "change his pagan ways." Much more common were indications of the pastors' own discomfort—looking at their watches, acting "nervous," verbalizing clichés, standing at a distance from patients, being painfully silent and unresponsive, and finally being in a rush to leave.

Pastoral identity was also a problem. A fair number of patients reported difficulty in discovering who was and was not a chaplain. This resulted from the wearing of informal sports clothes, the absence of a badge defining a person as a chaplain (or the use of a badge too small to read at any distance), and/or a person's failing to state that he or she was a chaplain.

The many things pastors do and may represent can bring comfort, solace, and happiness to those greatly in need of such aid. In most instances, this is what takes place. Still, clergy sometimes convey a lack of feeling and compassion without intending to do so. There is clearly a need for "on-the-job" training in these critical situations.

---

ety of other diseases.[147] Utah is, of course, the "Mormon state"—that is, the state having the highest population of members of the Church of Jesus Christ of Latter-Day Saints in the nation. The evidence is that being Mormon and being healthy go together, and the mechanism for this relationship is that the church strongly promotes doctrines regarding health and food practices that contribute to good health and low mortality.[148]

Throughout its history, Mormon theology has associated evil with illness, and therefore maintains a high valuation of the way the body is treated.[149] Specification of the latter stresses abstinence from alcohol, caffeine-containing beverages, and tobacco. Nutritional counsel emphasizes "wholesome" foods, among other healthful directions.[150] Those who have traveled in Utah and/or associated with devout Mormons rapidly become aware of the seriousness with which they take prescribed food practices. In regard to deaths from conditions not known to be affected by violation of eating proscriptions (e.g., accidents), the data suggest that Utah is representative of the rest of the country.[151]

The Mormons are an excellent example of how a strong and pervasive religious system that is well integrated with the sociocultural context can influence nutrition and health.

The Amish: Religion and Family Support

Like the Mormons, the Amish have been able to blend their social setting with their religious ideology. To do so, they have been quite successful in preserving their religious and cultural unity by creating relatively isolated communities. Under such conditions, daily life is often inseparable from one's spiritual existence.

The Amish illustrate well what occurs when a distinctive faith group maintains its unity through separation from others with variant beliefs and practices. This is also found among Orthodox Jews, Mormons, and members of various sects and cults. A situation is created in which people rely primarily on their kin and close neighbors, and death is first a familial–religious obligation that is rapidly and willingly embraced by the community.[152] A semiformal organization develops to provide mutual support and to perform various ceremonial functions, such as preparing the deceased for burial. In this way, the Amish view of "death as a spiritual victory over temporal life" is reinforced.[153] Other families who have also lost members visit and help the bereaved to work through the grieving process. Death is not denied, but openly accepted as a necessary and essential fact of life, every aspect of which is encompassed by theological doctrine and meaning.

Under such circumstances, we may reasonably hypothesize that death, rather than diminishing the community and family, strengthens social and familial ties and enhances religious commitment. In addition, this kind of religious–social support may be very effective in resolving the grief process, so that the likelihood of developing undesirable psychological aftereffects may be low.

Summary

The foregoing examples of how the Mormons and Amish deal with death can be easily extended to innumerable groups that have been studied.[154] For example, Scheffel's research on the Old Believers of Alberta describes the burial process, and specifies in great detail every aspect of body preparation, clothes, symbols, artifacts, body position, and activities that must take place at various times following the burial.[155] The important thing is that the role of ceremony is made very clear, and ritual can be viewed in its structuring and emotion-controlling function. Considerations of meaning and control are ever present, and we can easily see how well religion performs these functions (see Chapter 11 for further details of this process). Death is thus an individual concern and a cultural matter—both of which are important to the psychology of religion, which recognizes that the person must always be understood in context.

OVERVIEW

With respect to religion, the psychology of death has not resolved the problem of theory. Stating that this is an area that "may require a theoretical model that is more descriptive than valuative," Florian and Kravetz suggest attributional considerations.[156] Sociological thinkers may have an advantage over psychologists, as they can refer individual responsivity to socio-cultural referents and to social constructions of ideas and attitudes about death. Leming thus utilizes Homan's notion that religion both creates and resolves death-related anxiety.[157] Coping theory has recently put in an appearance, and looks as if it may be quite productive, for death is unquestionably a problem people must confront many times in their lives.[158]

We have seen a common development in research in this area—namely, from the use of simplistic and unitary notions of death fear and religiousness to multidimensional conceptualizations in both domains. Even though more sophisticated instrumentation is now available, it does not seem to be employed as much as it might in current research, possibly because many researchers are much more knowledgeable in the coping realm than they are about advances in the psychology of religion. We now see these trends in work on religiosity in relation to coping with AIDS, bereavement, and euthanasia. Convenience samples in which testing must be kept to a minimum may be impeding the use of more sophisticated measurement of religious perspectives.

Our position is that the deaths of others and the prospect of one's own death pose for each individual the very basic coping questions we have often emphasized in this volume—namely, the issues of meaning, control, and self-esteem. Death arouses these concerns in their ultimate form, and it is here that faith may, for most people, manifest its greatest adaptive contributions.

The contemporary world has united death more strongly with moral and religious considerations than ever before. Vacuous platitudes such as "God works in mysterious ways" and "The good die young" are highly likely to elicit rapid and vehement rejection in a time of AIDS, high suicide rates for adolescents and the elderly, and calls for active euthanasia *à la* Dr. Jack Kevorkian. Simple, easy, dichotomous yes–no answers must give way to deeper, more thoughtful considerations, in which institutionalized religion will invariably play a significant and central role. Death in the modern world has become increasingly complicated, and challenges faith and the role of the clergy more and more on both the individual and the societal levels.

NOTES

1. Aztec funerary ritual, quoted in De Sahagun (1974, p. 26).
2. Ecclesiastes 3:1–2 (*The Holy Bible*, Authorized King James Version).
3. King Richard in Shakespeare's *Richard II*, quoted in Ulanov (1959, p. 5).
4. German pastor quoted in Shneidman (1982, p. 185).
5. Woody Allen, quoted in Peter (1977, p. 134).
6. Becker (1973); Weisman (1972).
7. Tillich (1952, p. 40).
8. Malinowski (1965, p. 71).
9. Spilka, Spangler, Rea, and Nelson (1981).
10. Unamuno (1954, p. 41).
11. Kearl (1989, p. 172).
12. Quoted in Woodward (1970, p. 81).

13. Gallup and Proctor (1982, p. 183); Gallup (1992, p. 5); Kearl (1989, p. 184); Stark and Bainbridge (1985, p. 82).
14. Harley and Firebaugh (1993).
15. 1991 General Social Survey data from Davis and Smith (1994), organized and provided by Michael Kearl of Trinity University, San Antonio, Texas.
16. Gallup and Proctor (1982, p. 184).
17. Dixon and Kinlaw (1982–1983); Litke (1983).
18. Litke (1983).
19. Litke (1983); Marty, Rosenberg, and Greeley (1968).
20. Litke (1983); Stark and Bainbridge (1985, p. 53).
21. Badham (1976).
22. Lifton (1973).
23. Gochman and Fantasia (1979); Hooper and Spilka (1970).
24. Hood and Morris (1983).
25. Harley and Firebaugh (1993).
26. Harley and Firebaugh (1993).
27. Harley and Firebaugh (1993).
28. Benson and Eklin (1990).
29. Berman (1974).
30. Osarchuk and Tatz (1973).
31. Richardson and Weatherby (1983).
32. Moody (1976).
33. Gallup and Proctor (1982).
34. Gallup and Proctor (1982, p. 205).
35. Gallup and Proctor (1982, p. 142).
36. Gibbs (1988).
37. Zaleski (1987).
38. Ring (1984).
39. Shaver (1986).
40. MacDonald (1992).
41. M. Kearl (1995), personal communication on 1984, 1988, and 1989 General Social Survey data from Davis and Smith (1994).
42. Glick, Weiss, and Parkes (1974, p. 143).
43. Kalish and Reynolds (1976); Gallup and Proctor (1982).
44. MacDonald (1992, p. 221).
45. Reynolds and Waugh (1977).
46. Lester (1967, 1972); Martin and Wrightsman (1964).
47. Groth-Marnat (1992, p. 277).
48. Spilka, Hood, and Gorsuch (1985, p. 131).
49. Gartner, Larson, and Allen (1991).
50. Pressman, Lyons, Larson, and Gartner. (1992).
51. Batson, Schoenrade, and Ventis (1993).
52. Batson et al. (1993, pp. 264–265, 273–275).
53. Minton and Spilka (1976).
54. Clark and Carter (1978).
55. Hoelter and Epley (1979); Leming (1979); Nelson and Nelson (1975).
56. Florian and Mikulincer (1992–1993); Hoelter and Epley (1979); Nelson and Cantrell (1980).
57. Leming (1980, p. 347).
58. Feifel (1974).
59. Feifel and Tong Nagy (1981).
60. Rosenheim and Muchnik (1984–1985).
61. Hooper and Spilka (1970).
62. Kearl (1989, p. 124).
63. Erikson, Erikson, and Kivinick (1986, p. 56).
64. Munnichs (1980, p. 6).
65. Munnichs (1980, p. 63).
66. Answer given by Dr. Ruth Underhill to a student in a 1977 course on the psychology of death and dying, which was taught by Dr. Bernard Spilka at the University of Denver. Dr. Underhill was then almost 100 years old, and was still both mentally and physically very active.

67. Tobin, Fullmer, and Smith (1994).
68. Kearl (1989, p. 125).
69. Koenig (1994a, p. 252).
70. Blazer and Palmore (1976, p. 85).
71. Erikson et al. (1986, pp. 69–70).
72. A. H. Richardson (1973).
73. Koenig (1995).
74. Idler and Kasl (1992).
75. Reynolds and Nelson (1981).
76. Zuckerman, Kasl, and Ostfeld (1984).
77. Carey and Posavec (1978–1979); Hoggatt and Spilka (1978); Rea, Greenspoon, and Spilka (1975).
78. *The Gallup Poll Monthly* (1993, December, p. 47).
79. Kearl (1989, p. 191).
80. Kearl (1989, p. 191).
81. Klopfer and Price (1979).
82. Koenig (1994a, p. 478).
83. Koenig (1994a, p. 480).
84. Koenig (1994a, pp. 489–491).
85. Carey and Posavec (1978–1979).
86. Nagi, Pugh, and Lazerine (1977–1978).
87. Spilka, Spangler, and Rea (1981).
88. Gillespie (1983).
89. Ecclesiastes 12:5 (*The Holy Bible*, Authorized King James Version).
90. Flatt (1987).
91. Sanders (1979–1980).
92. Sanders (1979–1980).
93. McIntosh, Silver, and Wortman (1993).
94. McIntosh (1995).
95. McIntosh (1995, p. 2).
96. Smith, Range, and Ulmer (1991–1992).
97. McIntosh et al. (1993).
98. Bohannon (1991); De Frain, Jakub, and Mendoza (1991–1992).
99. Bohannon (1991).
100. De Frain et al. (1991–1992).
101. Gilbert (1992).
102. Glick et al. (1974); see also Parkes (1972).
103. Glick et al. (1974, p. 133).
104. Levy, Martinkowski, and Derby (1994).
105. Bahr and Harvey (1980); Haun (1977); Loveland (1968).
106. Reeves and Boersma (1989–1990).
107. Reeves and Boersma (1989–1990, p. 289).
108. Honigmann (1959).
109. Kidorf (1966).
110. Gerson (1977).
111. Flatt (1987).
112. Deluty (1988–1989); Lo Presto, Sherman, and Dicarlo (1994–1995).
113. Domino and Miller (1992); Hoelter (1979); Lo Presto et al. (1994–1995).
114. Kastenbaum (1981).
115. Wasserman and Stack (1993).
116. Dublin (1963); Kastenbaum and Aisenberg (1972).
117. Stack (1983).
118. Lo Presto et al. (1994–1995).
119. Martin (1984).
120. U.S. Bureau of the Census (1992, p. 80).
121. Koenig (1994a, p. 464).
122. Kearl (1989, p. 145).
123. Koenig (1994b).
124. Nelson (1977).
125. Smith et al. (1991–1992).

126. Stack and Wasserman (1992).
127. Clark, Brown, and Hochstein (1989).
128. Franks, Templer, Cappelletty, and Kauffman (1990–1991).
129. Bivens, Neimeyer, Kirchberg, and Moore (1994–1995).
130. Cook and Oltjenbruns (1989, pp. 18–19).
131. Bendiksen, Hewitt, and Vinge (1979); Clemens (1976); Jernigan (1976); Kalish and Dunn (1976); Malony (1978); O'Brien (1979); Wood (1976).
132. Spilka, Spangler, and Rea (1981).
133. Spilka, Spangler, and Rea (1981).
134. Brabant, Forsyth, and McFarlain (1995); Johnson and Spilka (1991); Spilka, Spangler, and Nelson (1983).
135. Johnson and Spilka (1991).
136. Spilka, Spangler, and Rea (1981); Spilka, Spangler, Rea, and Nelson (1981).
137. Kierniesky and Groelinger (1977); Yudell (1978).
138. Spilka, Spangler, and Rea (1981).
139. Spilka, Spangler, Rea, and Nelson (1981).
140. Spilka, Spanger, and Rea (1981).
141. Spilka, Spangler, and Rea (1981).
142. Parkes (1972, p. 169).
143. Spilka and Spangler (1979).
144. Spilka and Spangler (1979).
145. Carey (1979–1980).
146. U.S. Bureau of the Census (1992, p. 75).
147. U.S. Bureau of the Census (1992, p. 81).
148. Vernon and Waddell (1974).
149. Hansen (1981).
150. Vernon and Waddell (1974, p. 201).
151. Vernon and Waddell (1974).
152. Bryer (1979).
153. Bryer (1979, p. 259).
154. Reynolds and Waugh (1977).
155. Scheffel (1991).
156. Florian and Kravetz (1983, p. 602).
157. Leming (1980).
158. Maton (1989); Park and Cohen (1993); Park, Cohen, and Herb (1990).

Chapter 6

RELIGIOUS EXPERIENCE

> The very beginning, the intrinsic core, the essence, the universal nucleus of every known high religion . . . has been the private, lonely, personal illumination, revelation, or ecstasy of some acutely sensitive prophet or seer.[1]

> Belief, ritual, and spiritual experience: these are the cornerstone of religion, and the greatest of them is the last.[2]

> Drug experiences took this small town, straight girl to the fact that there were other realities.[3]

> I have had many spiritual experiences but rarely talk about them because people regard you as "slightly peculiar" or you "give them the shivers"; or they devalue the experience by diminishing it and trying to find plausible explanations.[4]

> If humans were no longer taught any religions, they would, I think, spontaneously create new ones from the content of ecstatic experiences, combined with bits and pieces transmitted by language and folklore.[5]

The study of religious experience can be perplexing, partly because so much time and effort can be wasted on defining precisely what is meant by "experience." At a common-sense level, everyone is aware that experience is something other than mere action or behavior. Yet it would be queer indeed to think of experience without any action involved—for even to do nothing is to do something. Similarly, experience is not simply thought or belief, even though people are often thinking when they have an experience. Finally, many people try to equate experience with emotions or feelings; yet feelings and emotions are only part of what is sometimes meant by experience, and they cannot be equated with the experience. "Experience" refers to a total way of reacting or being and cannot be reduced to its parts, even if such parts could be identified. To experience is to identify some totalizing aspect of life—an event or episode that is "experienced." Perhaps we can say of experience what St. Augustine is reputed to have said of time: We know what it is until we are asked to *say* what it is.

What then of *religious* experience? Surprisingly, it may be easier to identify specifically religious experience than to identify experience in general. It would appear that "experience" identifies something particular. "Religious experience" distinctively separates from the vast domain of experience that which is religious. Thus, as psychologists, we are free to identify religious experience as any experience that is identified within faith traditions as religious. This tautology need not disturb us. Religious traditions define the distinctively religious for the faithful. What is religious within one tradition may not be so within another. With the possible exception of mystical and numinous experiences (discussed in Chapter 7), it is probably not fruitful to define religious experiences by their inherent characteristics. Whether an experience is religious or not depends upon the experiencer's interpretation of it. Interpretations provide meanings not inherently obvious to those outside the tradition that provides the context for identifying any particular episode as a religiously meaningful experience. Almost any experience humans can have can be interpreted as an experience of God.[6]

CONCEPTUAL CONSIDERATIONS
IN DEFINING RELIGIOUS EXPERIENCE

William James's classic work *The Varieties of Religious Experience* has continued to influence psychologists since it was first delivered in Edinburgh, Scotland, as the Gifford lectures at the turn of the last century.[7] Although we can speculate as to the varying reasons for the persistence of this work (continually in print since first published in 1902), the simple fact remains that James set the tone for contemporary empirical work in the psychology of religious experience.

James's Formula for Religious Experience

James's definition of "religious experience," for purposes of the Gifford lectures, clearly revealed his sympathy for the extreme forms of religious experience. James defined "religion" as "*the feelings, acts, and experiences of individual men, in their solitude, so far as they apprehend themselves to stand in relation to whatever they may consider the divine.*"[8] The presence of something divine within all religious traditions can be debated. Buddhism is often cited as an example of a faith tradition without a god.[9] However, we need not equate belief in something divine with belief in God or in supernatural beings. James's clarification of what he meant by the "divine" makes the case for the near-universal application of this concept. As he saw it, the divine is "such a primal reality as the individual feels compelled to respond to solemnly and gravely, and neither by a curse nor a jest."[10] James's divinity is close to what we have termed a "foundational reality" in Chapter 7—that which each tradition finds most basic and foundational to its existence.

Thus, influenced by James's notion of divinity, religious experience—ultimately, the experience of the solitary individual—is placed at the forefront of the psychology of religion. Culling from a wide variety of written and personal testimonies, James's Gifford lectures minimized belief and behavior, focusing instead upon experience. Yet in his justly famous lectures, James was parsimonious in his conclusion regarding the value of religious experiences in general. As he perceived it, the infinite variety of religious experiences can be subsumed under a simple formula: discontent and its resolution. Placed in the context of individual lives, responses to the divine are resolutions. Studies derived from documents similar to those solicited and used by James support this sweeping generalization. However, as we shall see, the issue may be confounded by the methodology of focusing upon personal declarations of religious experience. As noted in Chapter 11, the resolution of discontent is an appealing formula that can mask the often complex relationships between religion and coping.

Varieties of Religious Experience from the Alister Hardy Centre

Perhaps most congruent with the Jamesian tradition of the use of personal documents to understand religious experience has been the work associated with the Alister Hardy Centre at Westminster College, Oxford, England.[11] The work of this research center continues to be funded largely by the Templeton Prize money for research in religion awarded to Alister Hardy, who achieved scientific accolades as a renowned zoologist. Yet his lifelong interest in religious experience led him, upon retirement from his career in zoology in 1969, to form a research unit devoted to the collection and classification of religious experiences. The basic procedure has been and continues to be to solicit voluntary reports of religious experiences— typically through requests in newspapers, as well as newsletters distributed to various groups, mostly in the United Kingdom. Requests are not simply for the more extreme and intense types of experiences favored by James, but for the more temperate variety of religious experiences as well.[12] Often, individuals simply submit unsolicited experiences. In *The Spiritual Nature of Man*, Hardy published an extensive classification of the major defining characteristics of these experiences from an initial pool of 3,000 experiences.[13] A summary of his major classification categories is presented in Table 6.1.

Although Hardy's classification scheme is admittedly provisional, it demonstrates that even a preliminary effort to classify what people regard as religious experiences can quickly become cumbersome. As Leech has argued, there is hardly any experience that could fail to qualify as religious or spiritual under some framework.[14] In this sense, it would be a vain attempt to try to define elements that all religious experiences have in common. It is better to think of religious experiences in light of Wittgenstein's notion of "family resemblance."[15] We can identify the family resemblance among experiences we classify as religious, but not by finding a single element they all must share. The factors that make an experience religious are clearly not the discrete, isolated components that can be identified in any experience.

Hardy's significant effort to classify religious experiences would not have appealed to James, who preferred to let the experiences speak for themselves, unfettered by what he would probably have seen as the tyranny of classification schemes. However, Hardy's conclusions, reached ostensibly independently of James's, are interesting because they are precisely what James concluded much earlier. Both James and Hardy have affirmed the evidential value of religious experiences, at least as hypotheses suggesting the existence of a transcendent reality variously experienced. As for the psychological consequences, the power of prayer is acknowledged; early childhood experiences are considered significant; and feelings of safety, security, love, and contentment are regarded as concomitants of religious experience. Few religious experiences are negative. By the very understanding of religion, at least in the West, experiences attributed to God must be ultimately positive.[16]

Other studies of voluntarily submitted reports of religious experience are not inconsistent with either James's or Hardy's claims.[17] However, much of this research favors a methodology that is probably biased toward the simple conclusion that religious experiences are resolutions of discontent. This research most likely solicits reports of religious experiences congruent with a simple, if not naive, view of religion. Such reports are often evaluated by persons committed to a positive assessment of religious experience. Few negative experiences are reported; almost none that are inconsequential, or failed to produce positive results, are volunteered. In this sense, asking persons to report religious or spiritual experiences may be tapping general cultural views (especially in a culture heavily influenced by the Judeo-

TABLE 6.1. Classification and Percentages of Various Elements Found in the Solicited Reports of 3,000 Religious Experiences

1. Sensory or quasi-sensory experience: Visual

a.	Visions	18.1
b.	Illumination	4.5
c.	A particular light	8.8
d.	Feeling of unity with surroundings and/or other people	5.9
e.	Out-of-the-body experiences	6.0
f.	Déjà vu	0.5
g.	Transformations of surroundings	2.4

2. Sensory or quasi-sensory experience: Auditory

a.	Voices, calming	7.4
b.	Voices, guiding	7.0
c.	Glossolalia (speaking in tongues)	3.1
d.	Music and other sounds	2.3

3. Sensory or quasi-sensory experience: Touch

a.	Healing	1.5
b.	Comforting	2.9
c.	Feeling of warmth, etc.	5.4
d.	Being hit, shocked, etc.	1.8
e.	Guiding	0.5

4. Sensory or quasi-sensory experience: Smell — 0.1

5. Extrasensory perception

a.	Telepathy	3.4
b.	Precognition	6.9
c.	Clairvoyance	1.5
d.	Contact with the dead	8.0
e.	Apparitions	3.4

6. Behavioral changes: Enhanced or "superhuman" power

a.	Comforting, guiding	2.7
b.	Healing	3.4
c.	Exorcism	0.3
d.	Heroism	0.6

7. Cognitive or affective elements

a.	State of security, protection, peace	25.3
b.	Sense of joy, happiness, well-being	21.2
c.	Sense of new strength in oneself	6.5
d.	Sense of guidance, vocation, inspiration	15.8
e.	Awe, reverence, wonder	6.6
f.	Sense of certainty, clarity, enlightenment	19.5
g.	Exaltation, excitement, ecstasy	4.7
h.	Sense of being at a loss for words	2.5
i.	Sense of harmony, order, unity	6.7
j.	Sense of timelessness	3.8
k.	Feeling of love, affection (in oneself)	5.7
l.	Yearning, desire, nostalgia	1.4
m.	Sense of forgiveness, restoration, renewal	4.0
n.	Sense of integration, wholeness, fulfillment	1.3
o.	Hope, optimism	1.5
p.	Sense of release from fear of death	3.6
q.	Fear, horror	4.2
r.	Remorse, sense of guilt	2.4
s.	Sense of indifference, detachment	1.1

(cont.)

TABLE 6.1 *(cont.)*

7. Cognitive or affective elements

t. Sense of purpose behind events	11.4
u. Sense of prayer answered in events	13.8
v. Sense of presence (not human)	20.2

8. Development of experience

Intrapersonal

a. Steady disposition; little development noted	0.01
b. Gradual growth of sense of awareness	9.1
c. Sudden change to a new sense of awareness	17.5
d. Particular experiences, no growth noted	14.6

Interpersonal

a. Identification with ideal human figure	0.06
b. Development of personal encounter	11.3
c. Participation in church, institutional, or corporate life	3.0
d. Development through contact with literature/arts	11.8
e. Isolation or rejection of others	2.7

9. Dynamic patterns in experience

Positive or constructive

a. Initiative felt beyond self; grace	12.4
b. Initiative felt with self but answered from beyond	32.3
c. Individuation (Jung) or self-actualization (Maslow)	0.05
d. Differentiation of initiative and response illusory (merging of self into the all; unitive experience)	2.2

Negative or destructive

a. Sense of external evil force as having initiative	4.0

10. Dream experiences

10. Dream experiences	8.8

11. Antecedents or "triggers" of experience

a. Natural beauty	1.3
b. Sacred places	2.6
c. Religious worship	11.8
d. Prayer, meditation	13.6
e. Music	5.7
f. Visual arts	2.5
g. Literature, drama, film	8.2
h. Creative work	2.1
I. Physical activity	1.0
j. Relaxation	1.7
k. Sexual relation	0.04
l. Happiness	0.07
m. Depression, despair	18.4
n. Illness	8.0
o. Childbirth	0.09
p. Anticipation of death	1.5
q. Death of others	2.8
r. Crises in personal relations	3.7
s. Silence, solitude	1.5
t. Psychedelic drugs	0.07
u. Anesthetic drugs	1.1

12. Consequences of experience

a. Sense of purpose or new meaning to life	18.5
b. Changes in religious belief	3.9
c. Changes in attitudes toward others	7.7

Note. Adapted from Hardy (1979, pp. 25–29). Copyright 1979 by the Clarendon Press. Adapted by permission of Oxford University Press and the Religious Research Center.

Christian tradition) that religious experiences are "good" and can resolve problems. For instance, Lupfer and his colleagues have demonstrated that attributions are likely to be made to God only for events with positive outcomes.[18] Although their research applies primarily to conservative Christians, other research suggests the general tendency among all believers to attribute to God only experiences with positive outcomes.[19]

If we look at more sophisticated studies of religious experience, conducted with more methodological rigor, we may have a firmer data base with which to judge James's simple formula. The fact that Hardy interprets his data to support James does not provide a sufficiently firm basis on which to make such sweeping assertions. To organize religious experience under some framework that can guide our understanding of the literature is essential. It is probably premature, in a text such as this, to endorse a single theoretical perspective. Hood has identified 13 theoretical orientations, each of which organizes the empirical literature in a clearly identifiable if not unique manner.[20] In addition, which empirical literature is deemed relevant is largely determined by which theory one adopts. The more distant the theories are from one another in terms of basic assumptions and orientations, the less likely they are to appeal to congruent research literatures. Table 6.2 presents a listing of major theoretical orientations in the study of religious experience, and the most typical methodologies favored by each.

Given our commitment to empirical psychology, largely defined by orientations that are measurement-based, our theoretical affinities can be readily surmised from an inspection of Table 6.2. Even phenomenological and depth psychologies have influenced the empirical literature on religious experience. Thus, we do not exclude any theoretical orientation, but rather seek to illuminate religious experience from a variety of perspectives. Our test of any perspective is simply whether it generates measurable empirical research. There is no perspective listed in Table 6.2 that has not generated some interest among empirical researchers. Yet it is equally true that no theory has sufficient empirical support to be presented as *the* theory of religious experience. Indeed, in light of a postmodern perspective on the social sciences, perhaps seeking a single best orientation is chimerical.[21] Still, we must organize the richness and vastness of religious experience in some fashion. We have chosen James's formula as a guide, and broadened its reference to include contemporary discussions of limits and their transcendence as the most general framework within which to discuss religious experience. Later we borrow from role theory, particularly as developed by Sundén, to add the specific influence of religious traditions and texts to the understanding of experience that is interpreted as meaningfully religious.

Limits and Transcendence: The James–Boisen Formula

Again, before looking at particular studies of religious experience, we suggest the wisdom of James's simple formula for religious experience. Although James is most often noted for his insistence on the richness and diversity of religious experience, he also suggested that a resolution to a previously experienced uneasiness is the thread from which all religious experience is woven. James is not alone in this.

Boisen noted that what distinguishes religious experience from otherwise intense pathological experience is that religious experience brings a resolution of what would otherwise be a devastating defeat.[22] For Boisen, as for James, it is not the nature of the experience but its results that define it as religious. Religious experiences, like some pathological experiences, are accompanied by a great personal disharmony. But there is a difference: the outcome. A

TABLE 6.2. Theoretical Orientations in the Study of Religious Experience

Theoretical orientation	Most common research methods
Depth psychologies	
Freudian theory	Clinical case study; Oedipal interpretations
Jungian theory	Clinical and literary case studies; interpretation
Object relations theory	Clinical case study; pre-Oedipal interpretations
Major psychological orientations	
Developmental theory	Experimental; correlational studies; measurement
Affective theory	Experimental; correlational studies; measurement
Behavioral theory	Experimental studies (often with small sample size).
Cognitive theory	Experimental; measurement
Specific psychological perspectives	
Attachment theory	Experimental; correlational studies; measurement
Attribution theory	Experimental; correlational studies; measurement
Role theory	Correlational; participant observation; measurement
Specialty concerns	
Feminist theory	Correlational; interpretive
Phenomenological theory	Descriptive; introspective reports
Transpersonal theory	Interpretive; correlational; experimental

Note. Adapted from Hood (1995a). Copyright 1995 by Religious Education Press. Adapted by permission.

religious experience marks the successful resolution of an inner conflict defined in transcendental terms. A limit has been reached and meaningfully transcended.

This James–Boisen formula meshes nicely with both theological and psychological perspectives in which the concepts of limits and transcendence are related.[23] In the simplest sense, a total involvement and an awareness of limits produce the discontent and disharmony (James's uneasiness or discontent) that create the possibility of transcendence. It is the very confrontation with limits, however conceived, that can produce either despair and the tragedy of defeat (when such limits are oppressively interminable) or produce joy and the ecstasy of transcendence (when such limits are overcome). This is the sense in which Bowker has emphasized that the psychological origin of the sense of God must be rooted not in the particulars of experience, but rather in terms of content that meaningfully points to limits to be surpassed.[24] In this sense, God is always "beyond," and the psychology of religious experiencing is the experience of this "beyondness" through the mode of transcendence of previously experienced limits.

We have rather a basic perspective within which to organize the empirical literature on religious experience. It can be traced back to James's notion of discontent and resolution, but only if we keep in mind the fact that both discontent and resolution are *interpretations* rooted in James's definition of religion. In a fundamental sense, religious experience is the meaningful transcendence of limits of the resolution of discontent, rooted in a sense of the divine. Not surprisingly, then, religious experience is almost infinite in its varieties. It is the *understanding in a religious vocabulary* of the process of discontent and its resolution that makes an experience religious.

If there is a typicality to religious experience, it comes from the uniformity of interpretation found within particular traditions; traditions define what relevant religious experiences are. The experience of being religious varies across traditions. Perhaps most compatible with this perspective is the work of the Swedish psychologist Hjalmar Sundén.[25] His theory of religious experience is truly social-psychological in nature. Most important for our present purposes is Sundén's emphasis upon religious traditions. Particularly in the form of sacred texts, traditions provide the templates or models that make religious experience possible. The interpretation or perception of events—often in terms taken from or suggested by stories from sacred texts—makes experience religious. What others are blind to, the devout see. Without knowledge of a religious tradition and its sacred texts, religious experiences are not possible. For example, many would not associate the handling of serpents with religion. However, in some southern Appalachian churches in the United States, serpent handling is a religious experience perceived to be in obedience to God's will as one of the five signs specified in Mark 16:17–18. These "sign-following" churches obey what they perceive to be God's will. The signs include speaking in tongues, casting out of demons, laying of hands upon the sick, handling serpents, and the drinking of poisonous substances. Kimbrough has extensively documented the history of sign-following churches in eastern Kentucky,[26] and Hood and Kimbrough have argued for the relevance of Sundén's role theory to understanding this tradition.[27]

Serpent Handling as a Religious Experience

In 18th-century North America, "rattlesnake gazing," or staring at snakes in the wild, was a common practice. Settlers, strongly informed by Biblical narratives, found in rattlesnake gazing a significance that attributed supernatural powers to this "agent of Satan." As one historian of popular religiosity notes, "[A] people familiar with the biblical story of the serpent's tempting of Eve might well be predisposed to assume that the rattlesnake and other serpentine creatures did indeed possess supernatural power."[28] However, rattlesnake gazing was never practiced as a religious ritual or acknowledged by any formal religious denominations.

At the turn of this century, Holiness sects in Appalachia emphasized numerous Biblical texts (e.g., Mark 16:17–18; Luke 10:19) by which the handling of serpents gained a religious significance. In its early history, the Church of God championed serpent handling as one of the "five signs."[29] In obedience to their interpretation of scripture, believers handle serpents or (with reference to Luke 10:19) walk upon them. Serpent handling was initiated by George Hensley, who made it religious by actually modeling the handling of serpents in churches. Later abandoned by the Church of God (whose members continue to practice some of the signs, such as speaking in tongues), the practice persists in Holiness sects throughout Appalachia. In Sundén's role theory, both text and the modeling of text in actual practice permit believers to handle serpents as a religious act. In addition, in terms of our notion of limits and transcendence, the actual handling of serpents in services permits a transcendence of the real possibility of death that lies at the rational basis of the fear of handling rattlesnakes and other vipers.[30] Whether serpent handlers are bitten or not, whether they live or die, they believe that they live and act in obedience to God's word. Despite clinical prejudices to the contrary, there is no empirical evidence that serpent handlers exhibit more independently assessed objective indices of psychopathology than do more mainstream religious controls.[31]

The example of serpent handling illustrates one criticism of the study of religious experience in North American psychology—a criticism leveled against James and to some extent inherent in the appeal to "experience." In general, it would appear that the demand to describe "experience" is a plea to identify something unique, intense, or exceptional in one's life. "What did you experience?" is one of those questions that focus on the extremes, much as the expletive "What an experience!" is likely to identify something exceptional in one's life. In one of the early critiques of James's *The Varieties of Religious Experience*, Crooks bemoaned James's fascination with the extreme and unusual in religious experience at the expense of the more common experiences characteristic of religion.[32] In a similar vein, Starbuck urged other psychologists of religion to avoid a focus upon the extremes in religious experience.[33] The echoes of such criticism are heard today, but fall largely upon deaf ears. For many social scientists, ordinary piety and the commonplace elements of religious experience are apparently as James saw them—the duller religious habits. What fascinated James most were the more passionate expressions of the extremes of religious experience. Little has changed in this regard since James published *The Varieties*. The empirical literature has a Jamesian focus, if not in method, then in terms of the topics that have elicited interest and study. Thus, although we cover a broad terrain in our survey of the contemporary literature—from recent discoveries in the physiology of the brain to psychedelic drugs; from altered states of consciousness to speaking in tongues; from visionary reports of the Virgin Mary to the immersion of subjects in isolation tanks—it is a decidedly uneven terrain. However extreme, this range in the proper context reflects the richness of experience that is religious.

THE BODY IN RELIGIOUS EXPERIENCE

In her presidential address to the Society for the Scientific Study of Religion, Meredith McGuire posed this interesting question: "What if people—the subjects of our research and theorizing—had material bodies?"[34] McGuire answered her own rhetorical question by noting three broad themes in which the social sciences might better appreciate what she aptly termed the "mindful body": in the experience of self and others; in the production and reflection of social meanings; and in the body's significance as the subject and object of power relations.[35] Although McGuire's concern is more sociological than psychological, her appeal to reconsider the body is useful for psychologists who tend to reduce the body to the study of physiological processes. This is a particularly pernicious tendency in the psychology of religion.

Perhaps one of the most shortsighted views of religious experience is to assume that such experiences are merely emotional. The "merely" here has a negative connotation; it suggests that since what is perceived as religiously meaningful is physiological in origin, it can be discounted. James identified such disclaiming views as "medical materialism." Medical materialism dismisses Saint Paul by calling his vision on the road to Damascus a discharging lesion of the occipital cortex, since Paul was an epileptic. It snuffs out Saint Teresa of Avila as a hysteric, Saint Francis of Assisi as a hereditary degenerate. George Fox's discontent with the shams of his age, and his pining for spiritual veracity, it treats as a disordered colon.[36]

The point, of course, is not that physiological processes may not be involved in religious experience, but that some think that the identification of the physiological processes involved in a religious experience "reduces it away." Yet no experience is identical to the processes involved in its occurrence. This is not to say that physiological processes, such as arousal, may not be involved in some aspects of religious experiencing. What is crucial is that such arousal be appropriately identified as part of a broader context that is identified as religious because of other than merely physiological processes. The consideration becomes not simply arousal, but arousal contextualized and interpreted.

Physiological Arousal and Religious Experience

It has long been noted that when persons describe their experiences, there are often large physiological components to their descriptions. It appears that as embodied selves, human beings must have feelings to claim to have experienced something. Yet in a critical survey of current psychological theories of feeling, Hill flatly states that "there are no general overarching theories of affect guiding research on religious experience."[37] However, in the conceptual literature on religious experience, there is a broad-based theory that has generated considerable discussion. It is essentially a social-constructionist theory, which argues that there are no natural emotions; instead, emotions are constructed, interpreted, and recognized on the basis of cognitive interpretations of physiological arousal. Much of this theory is based upon Schachter's psychological research on his two-factor theory of emotion.[38]

Within the conceptual literature on religious experience, Proudfoot has focused upon Schachter's two-factor theory of emotion as providing a conceptual critique in support of constructionist theories of religious experience.[39] Schachter's theory essentially argues that the identification of an emotional experience requires both physiological arousal and a cognitive framework within which to identify the meaning of the arousal. Neither alone is sufficient to determine an emotional experience. In other words, persons tend to know how they feel or what they experience in terms of two quite different processes: (1) what the arousal circumstances were (external, perceptual, or cognitive factors), and (2) what internal physiological processes the persons are aware of. Hence, the labeling of physiological arousal is not just the result of physiological arousal per se, but also of the specific circumstances in which the physiological arousal occurs. In this view, otherwise unanticipated physiological arousal may be labeled as "fear," "awe," or "anger," depending upon the circumstances in which it occurs. Proudfoot relies upon Schachter's theory to defend the thesis that experience cannot be religious until and unless it is identified and interpreted to be religious.[40] Thus, consistent with Sundén's role theory as discussed above, a person cannot have a religious experience without religious training and instruction to provide a context for interpretation.

In a now classic study, Schachter and Singer gave injections to persons participating in an experiment they were told was for testing the effects of a vitamin compound on vision.[41] In fact, half the participants received an injection of epinephrine (adrenaline), which reliably produces increased respiration and heart rate, slight muscle tremors, and an "edgy" feeling. The other participants received a placebo (saline solution), which produces no physiological feelings. Hence, the experimenters could be fairly assured that only the experimental group would experience physiological arousal. The participants in the experimental group were further divided into three groups: One group was told truthfully what physiological effects to anticipate; one group was misinformed and told to anticipate numbness, itching, and perhaps a headache; and one group was given no information. Contextual cues were then provided for all persons in the experiment. The cues were provided by "stooges" of the experimenter, who were in the room with the real subjects, presumably as participants in the experiment. The stooges acted either euphoric or angry.

Results of the experiment were generally as predicted and support a cognition-plus-arousal theory of emotional experience. Persons who experienced no physiological arousal (the placebo [saline solution] group), or who were given correct information as to expectations, did not use environmental cues to label their emotions. On the other hand, those with incorrect information or no information tended to interpret their emotions to be congruent with the cues—as euphoric when the stooges acted euphoric, and as angry when the stooges acted angry. Both observation (through one-way mirrors) and self-report measures were used in this study. In both experimental groups, physiological arousal was generally properly identified (e.g., change in heart rate). The placebo group reported no physiological changes. Hence, Schachter and Singer argued that, given a situation of unanticipated physiological arousal, external cues (in this case, the stooges' feigned emotional behavior) influence the labeling of what emotion is occurring—angry, happy, or sad, depending upon the context for unanticipated physiological arousal. Specific emotions are thus socially constructed.

Since its inception, Schachter's two-factor theory has generated much debate. Despite major methodological criticisms of the Schachter and Singer study,[42] its importance for a theory of religious experience is that physiological processes per se cannot account for emotional experiences; cognitions must also occur, at least in ambiguous circumstances.

It is important to note that Schachter's theory gives a place to both cognition and physiological arousal. Recently, theorists have begun to champion more extreme views that minimize the role of physiology in emotions. For example, the almost purely cognitive view of Lazarus argues that emotions are organized psychophysiological reactions.[43] The organization requires cognitive appraisal. Thus, without cognitive appraisal, emotions are impossible; they are merely unspecified physiological activation.

The pertinence of cognition–arousal theories such as Schachter's, and cognitive appraisal theories such as Lazarus's, is that the articulation of the experience gains religious relevance from the tradition within which experience gains its validity. The more a person knows about a tradition, the more the person can experience what it is the tradition defines as religious. Sundén's role theory meshes nicely with the cognitive aspect of these theories, insofar as familiarity with religious texts and traditions is the rich source from which come appraisals deeming a situation religiously relevant. Traditions provide the relevant cognitions.

In our own view of limits and transcendence, cognition–arousal and cognitive appraisal theories suggest that physiological arousal may be a factor in initiating feelings that become meaningfully religious only if other appropriate conditions are met. The relevant question is this: Under what conditions will physiological arousal be interpreted religiously? Modern research suggests what James long ago insisted: When a person interprets an experience as religious, the immediate content and context of religious consciousness are important factors to examine. However, much of the research literature of religious practices has been more interested in aspects of arousal than in the context in which arousal is interpreted. For example, both prayer and meditation have been studied in terms of the state of the brain's arousal during these practices.

Brain Waves and Meditation

The activities of prayer and meditation have in common an effort to withdraw from normal waking consciousness and a concern with attention to another reality, often considered to be transcendent. Of course, we must be careful with language here: To the devout, prayer and meditation are affirmed to be meaningful confrontations with a "deeper" or "higher" reality, or perhaps, as in the case of Zen, simply a full appreciation of reality as it is. For instance, Preston has shown how converts to Zen are socialized into an interpretation of reality based upon nonconceptual meditative techniques, which demand attentiveness to reality presumably as it is, in and of itself.[44]

Naranjo and Ornstein distinguish between "ideational" and "nonideational" meditation.[45] The former encourages and utilizes imagery common within a tradition; the latter seeks an imageless state and avoids attention to unwanted imagery that may occur during meditation. Much imageless meditation is widely recognized as a spiritual practice—a fact that has contributed to psychophysiological studies of the practice. Rather than assess either verbal reports or behavior, investigators have focused upon physiological measures, particularly of brain activity. This has proven an especially useful technique for studying a person who is otherwise apparently "just sitting."

Seeking a precise physiology of either prayer or meditation may be one of those chimeric tasks that serve to satisfy those whom James referred to as the "medical materialists"—those who will accept the reality of things spiritual only if they can identify bodily correlates.[46]

It is well established that there is at least a gross relationship between brain wave patterns and modes of consciousness. Table 6.3 reveals that within particular brain wave frequencies, typical states of consciousness can be identified. However, it is also obvious that despite physiological correlates of consciousness, the mere fact that a person is "in" a certain brain state as measured by frequencies does not tell us much about what is being experienced. Reading a book, playing baseball, and watching a great movie would all probably register as "beta" states; yet this is to equate them only in a trivial sense with all activities a person engages in when awake and attending to something external. Not surprisingly, prayer and meditation states can be either alpha or beta states. Imageless states are more likely to be alpha; image states may be alpha or beta, depending upon the degree of focused awareness on specific imagery. However, even these conclusions are qualified generalizations.

Specific studies of meditative traditions have focused upon the brain wave correlates of those learning to meditate and those adept at meditation. Kasamatsu and Hirai have identified four stages that occur as one progresses in *zazen* (Zen meditation): (1) alpha waves in spite of eyes being open; (2) an increase in the amplitude of alpha waves; (3) a decrease in alpha wave frequency; and (4) the appearance of rhythmic theta waves in some adept meditators.[47] Furthermore, dividing 23 Zen disciples into three groups according to years of training revealed a difference in typical brain wave patterns during meditation for these groups. These results are presented in Table 6.4. As the table indicates, Kasamatsu and Hirai found that Zen disciples appeared to progress through stages (defined by brain wave patterns) as they became more adept at *zazen*. Those practicing *zazen* for over 20 years had increased alpha amplitude (assumed to measure intensity), but some also developed rhythmic theta waves.

In an important aspect of their study, Kasamatsu and Hirai linked these advanced stages to the Zen master's evaluation of the mental state achieved by the 23 disciples. Importantly, the Zen master made his evaluation of the quality of the mental state (low, medium, or high) without knowledge of the brain wave data. These results, presented in Table 6.5, provide some added support for the finding that particular brain wave patterns were reliably associated with

TABLE 6.3. Modes of Consciousness Associated with Identifiable Brain Wave Frequencies

Brain wave frequency	Mode of consciousness
Beta (above 13 cps[a])	Active thought; focused attention with eyes open. Oriented toward "external world."
Alpha (8 to 12 cps[a])	Relaxed yet aware. Eyes closed. Oriented toward "internal world."
Theta (4 to 7 cps[a])	Drowsiness. Fluid, dream-like (hypnagogic) images.
Delta (less than 4 cps[a])	Deep sleep. Conscious but unaware.

Note. See Johnston (1974).

[a]Cycles per second.

TABLE 6.4. Number of Disciples Experiencing Different Brain Wave Patterns, by Years Spent in *Zazen* Training

Brain wave changes	Years of training		
	< 5 years (*n* = 13)	5–20 years (*n* = 4)	>20 years (*n* = 6)
Alpha with eyes open	8	1	0
Increased alpha amplitude	2	1	0
Decrease in alpha frequency	3	2	3
Rhythmical theta waves	0	0	3

Note. Adapted from Kasamatsu and Hirai (1969, p. 494). Copyright 1969 by the Folia Publishing Society. Adapted by permission.

advancement in *zazen*. The Zen master's independent ratings of those most adept at *zazen* were clearly associated with brain wave patterns assumed to be indicative of the higher stages of *zazen*. It is also noteworthy that these objective, qualitative electrophysiological correlates of a meditative stage have supported the claims within the Zen tradition that advancement in *zazen* can be identified appropriately by Zen masters. This supports earlier research by Maupin, who found that those most adept at *zazen* had higher tolerances for anomalistic experiences and were able to take advantage of what, in psychoanalytic terms, were regressive experiences.[48] Maupin noted that if meditation is considered to foster such regression, then each stage of meditation, successfully mastered, permits further adaptive regression.

Associated with efforts to meditate or pray is the difficulty of attending to one's prayerful or meditative activity without being disrupted by external stimuli. Research with yogis suggests that those with well-marked alpha activity in their normal resting states show a greater aptitude and enthusiasm for practicing *samadhi* (yoga meditation).[49] In laboratory studies, external cues can be introduced while persons meditate, and the effects of these on their alpha activity can be examined. In terms of brain wave patterns, external stimuli force attention so that alpha states are disrupted or blocked (alpha blocking), and beta waves are noted. Meditators must then attempt to return to their inward states, characterized by alpha waves. It has been postulated that those adept at meditation are less likely to exhibit alpha blocking when external stimuli are introduced. Several investigators have confirmed this prediction, both with Zen meditators[50] and with those who practice yoga.[51] Research Box 6.1 reports a classic study of brain wave patterns of yogis in meditation and during the experience of pain, which is consistent with the research on *zazen* discussed above.

TABLE 6.5. Quality of Meditative State and Wave Patterns for 23 Zen Disciples

Brain wave changes	Zen master's rating of quality of meditation		
	Low (*n* = 7)	Medium (*n* = 12)	High (*n* = 4)
Alpha with eyes open	5	4	0
Increased alpha amplitude	2	1	0
Decrease in alpha frequency	0	7	1
Rhythmical theta waves	0	0	3

Note. Adapted from Kasamatsu and Hirai (1969, p. 494). Copyright 1969 by the Folia Publishing Society. Adapted by permission.

Research Box 6.1. Electroencephalographic Studies on Yogis
(Anand, Chhina, & Singh, 1961)

Disciples of Raj yoga practice a form of meditation called *samadhi*. Those adept at *samadhi* claim to experience an imageless state identified as *mahanand* (ecstasy), in which they are unaware of internal or external stimuli. They also claim to be able to reach a state that surpasses the experience of pain. When not in *samadhi*, yogis claim to be attentive to the world. Anand, Chhina, and Singh studied six yogi volunteers, four of whom were studied before and during *samadhi*, and two of whom were studied before and during the introduction of a normally painful stimulus (immersion of a hand in 4°C water for 45–55 minutes). The primary measures were brain waves as identified by scalp electroencephalographic recordings.

All four of the yogis who were studied before and during *samadhi* exhibited high-amplitude alpha. Two of these yogis were introduced to external stimuli during *samadhi* but showed no evidence of alpha blocking to strong light, a loud banging noise, a tuning fork, or being touched with a hot glass tube. When not in *samadhi*, these same yogis showed alpha blocking. The two yogis whose hands were immersed in 4°C water continued to exhibit alpha, apparently not responding to a painful stimulus.

Brain wave correlates of meditative states present a fairly consistent gross pattern. However, they can be misleading, and may be interpreted to carry more weight than they should in terms of documenting religious experiences. Experience is no more "real" because we can identify its physiological correlates than it is the case that identical physiological correlates of meditative states mean that the experiences are necessarily the "same." For instance, numerous differences exist between *samadhi* and *zazen*, not to mention varieties of prayer. These difference are not necessarily reflected in brain wave patterns (though they may be). For a person to be in alpha may not tell us whether the person is practicing *zazen*, *samadhi*, or Christian contemplative prayer. The experience of mediation and prayer is more than its physiology.

Sundén believed his role theory to be particularly useful in addressing the question "How are religious experiences at all psychologically possible?"[52] Jan van der Lans utilized Sundén's theory in a study of students selected to participate in a 4-week training course in Zen meditation.[53] They were told simply to concentrate on their breathing for the first 14 sessions. Then they were told to concentrate without a focus upon any object—a method called *shikantaza* in Zen. Participants were divided into those with ($n = 14$) and those without ($n = 21$) a religious frame of reference, based upon intake interviews. Instructions varied for each group: The religious group was told to anticipate experiences common to meditation within religious traditions, and the control group was told to anticipate experiences common to meditation used for therapeutic purposes.

Dependent measures included writing down every unusual experience after each daily session, and filling out a questionnaire on the last day of training that asked subjects specifically whether they had had a religious experience during meditation. The daily experiences were content-analyzed according to a list of 54 experiences categorized into five types: bodily sensations; fantasies, illusions, and imagery (hallucinations); changes in self-image; new insights; and negative feelings. Responses per category were too low for any meaningful statistical analyses. However, the number of persons reporting a religious experience during their Zen meditation varied as a function of the presence or absence of a premeditative religious frame. Half of the religious participants reported a religious experience during meditation, whereas none of the control group (those without a premeditative religious frame) did. In addition, all participants were asked a control question at the end of the study: Had their meditations made them feel more vital and energetic? Groups did not differ in their responses to this question.

The conclusion we may draw from this research is that the actual practice of meditation elicits a specifically religious experience only for those with a religious frame of reference. If we assume equivalent meditative states in both groups (e.g., achievement of an alpha state), the meaningfulness of such a state is dependent upon the interpretive frame one brings to the experience. Of course, a paradox is that within Zen, interpretive frames are minimized; hence this research employed a technique more compatible with prayer within the Christian tradition. (Particular prayer experiences are often sought and interpreted as religiously meaningful within the Christian spiritual tradition.)[54] Still, it is clear that experience, meaningfully interpreted, is dependent upon what framework for interpretation can be brought to, or derived from, the experience. Sundén's role theory simply argues that familiarity with a religious tradition is the basis from which religious experiences gain meaning—and without which *religious* experiences are not possible. Religious experience is less likely to be derived from an experience than to be an interpretive frame brought to an experience.

Deikman empirically investigated contemplative meditation.[55] In this type of meditation, the emphasis is on focused concentration upon a single object, rather than no object (as in Zen). What is important about Deikman's work is that contemplative meditation is often associated with the mystical tradition, in which the goal is a state of unity, devoid of content or imagery. This is introvertive mysticism as discussed in Chapter 7. However, it is also known that various experiences are likely to occur during such concentration, including diverse imagery. Much of this imagery is readily understandable in the psychology of perception as afterimages, stabilized retinal images, and hypnagogic imagery. If not interpreted as meaningful, such imagery is largely irrelevant; it is left as minimal experience without meaning. However, if such experiences are specifically interpreted to be distractions and not part of one's meditative goal, they have no inherent religious meaning and are only clues that one has yet to reach the desired imageless state. Furthermore, to focus upon such imagery will distract one from achievement of the imageless, introvertive mystical state as discussed in Chapter 7.

Deikman's study is rare in that it reports the results of a prolonged series of meditative sessions derived primarily from two subjects. They simply sat in comfortable chairs and for 30 minutes focused their attention upon a blue vase. Contemplative meditation requires that one simply contemplate the meditative object, without attention to thoughts or peripheral sensations. In Deikman's study no religious object was used as a meditative focus, and hence, in term of Sundén's theory, religious frames of reference were unlikely to be elicited. Deikman's study was thus phenomenological (i.e., an effort to provide a clear description of whatever appeared to the subjects' consciousness). Wulff notes that phenomenological studies try to reclaim for psychology the preeminence of experience.[56] Deikman's study is one of the few in this tradition. He carefully described and documented the subjects' reports of light, motion, and a sense of force present during contemplation—phenomena that were neither expected by the subjects nor easily interpreted as merely subjective. Deikman thus left open the possibility that contemplative meditation, like classic mystical and religious experiences, creates an openness to experience that permits other aspects of reality to be revealed.

Other descriptive studies of meditation by Goleman[57] and by Naranjo and Ornstein[58] reveal a rich variety of experiences, many of which also cannot simply be dismissed as subjective states. The fact that during contemplative meditation subjects experience an unexpected sense of force relates to survey reports of the commonality of this experience, discussed in Chapter 7. It may be that phenomenological studies are the most appropriate method by which to descriptively explore experiences that are apparently quite common and can be facilitated by such simple techniques as meditation. As Wulff has stated, "Indeed, systematically appropriated and developed by even a handful of investigators, phenomenological psychology could revolutionize the field."[59]

Altered States of Consciousness

At the other extreme from phenomenological and introspective descriptions of consciousness are studies that focus upon neurophysiological states. Part of their appeal is the obvious scientific legitimacy of "hard" data—the pure descriptive facts of identifiable physiological processes. Three areas have gained some considerable influence among those interested in the psychology of religion.

The catchall phrase "altered states of consciousness" emerged in the 1960s, signifying what has become a loosely knit area in which the focus is upon the empirical study of experiences previously assumed to be pathological or anomalous.[60] Included are such phenomena as hypnosis, dreaming, meditation, drug experiences, and a number of other "fringe" topics, such as parapsychology and near-death experiences. Much of this literature is more popular than academic. The serious academic study of such experiences, many of which fit Zusne and Jones's phrase "anomalistic psychology,"[61] has assumed that such experiences have no objective validity. However, among sympathetic researchers there has been a shift in attitude: The experiences themselves are positively valued and assumed to have ontological validity. In other words, previous efforts to provide reductive explanations of such experiences are now overshadowed by descriptive efforts to explore the meaning and validity of such experiences, including their objectivity. Much of this is incorporated into modern "transpersonal psychology"—an area yet to be clearly defined or to have general academic and research support among mainstream psychologists.[62] However, it is apparent that investigators are beginning to study empirically a wide variety of experiences that are immensely relevant to religion. Much of this research promises to enliven the psychology of religion by including within the discipline phenomena that religious traditions take seriously.

Tart has been extremely influential in linking transpersonal psychology and altered states of consciousness.[63] Basically, an altered state of consciousness is characterized by an introspective awareness of a different mode of experiencing the world. Loosely speaking, for example, everyone experiences dreaming as an altered state of consciousness relative to the normal waking state. Each altered state of consciousness has a typical pattern of functioning, recognized as such by the person. Hence, things that might seem strange or bizarre are not really so when recognized as normal for that particular state of consciousness. Furthermore, persons move in and out of various states of consciousness. In Zinberg's terms, there are alternate states of consciousness, not simply one normal and appropriate state of consciousness.[64] Generally, the more open to experience one is, the more states of consciousness one can experience. More controversial is Tart's claim that knowledge is state-specific—in other words, that it is derived from, and appropriate to, a particular state of consciousness and may not be applicable to other states.[65] Thus, many religions are seen as state-specific sciences, with knowledge claims valid only within the parameters of the experiences and interpretations provided by these traditions. This parallels the concept of "ideological surround," discussed in Chapter 9. In a sense, new religious movements represent the sociological counterpart to the psychology of alternate states of consciousness.

Although much of transpersonal psychology and the claim to state-specific knowledge is controversial, the concept of altered states of consciousness is often supported by a physiological base. Most typically, this consists of identifying alterations in neurophysiology assumed to be associated with altered states of consciousness. None of these models has achieved any degree of consensus, and all are at best speculations, in neurophysiological terms, of processes assumed to underlie various altered states of consciousness. Perhaps most often cited is Fischer's cartography of mental states, linked to a continuum of arousal.[66] This continuum ranges from tranquility to ecstasy; between these extremes of hypoarousal and hyperarousal is found a so-called normal, everyday consciousness. Although the neurophysiology of consciousness is beyond the scope of our concerns, the important point is that neurophysiological correlates (verified or not) have given altered states of consciousness a respectability within mainstream science, especially insofar as consciousness is studied as a brain process. This respectability comes at the same time that others are affirming the much more controversial claim that the objects revealed in such altered states of consciousness cannot be dismissed as merely subjective phenomena.

The Split-Brain Hypothesis

Closely related to research on altered states of consciousness is the discovery of the perplexing duality of the human brain. It has long been noted that the cortex of the human brain is apparently doubled, with the two cerebral hemispheres connected by a structure known as the corpus callosum.[67] Of interest to psychologists of religion is the claim that this structure underlies a dual mode of human consciousness—a mode of direct relevance to religious experience.[68]

The lateral specialization of the cortex is particularly relevant to issues involving language and the ability to describe experience, which are largely left-hemispheric functions. The right hemisphere is more involved with tactile and visual memories, but, lacking high linguistic capabilities, cannot allow description of tactile and visual experiences. This has led Ornstein to argue that people have two distinct minds: the left (or the logical, analytical, and linguistic) mind, and the right (or the creative, intuitive, and ineffable) mind.[69] In this view, many religious experiences, including those difficult to express or verbalize, are attributable to right-hemispheric activity. On the other hand, the ability to articulate experience clearly and in logical terms is a left-hemispheric capacity. Thus, an individual's mode of experiencing the world is assumed to be a function of the individual's dominant hemisphere. Although extreme claims to lateralization are inaccurate,[70] dichotomies apparently exist in both language and human experience. For example, laypeople and scientists alike often contrast religion with science, rationality with intuition, and verbal with nonverbal expression. The list of dichotomies seems endless, causing Gardner to bemoan the emergence of "dichotomania" among contemporary scientists.[71] Many scholars have leaped to the inference that religious experience is essentially a right-hemispheric phenomenon, whereas the articulation of that experience is essentially a left-hemispheric phenomenon. Few theories are as provocative in this sense as Jaynes's bicameral theory of religious consciousness.

Jaynes's Bicameral Theory

In a provocative theory that postulates a neurophysiological basis for religion, Jaynes links modes of human consciousness with forms of culture that emerged through evolution.[72] He speculates that reflexive consciousness (including the sense of a personal "I") is a recent evolutionary phenomenon, rooted in the earlier failure of bicameral consciousness—a God-centered consciousness that increasingly became dysfunctional and was unfavored by natural selection.

Jaynes argues that early humans were bicameral, in that their left and right hemispheres functioned independently. The effect of this lack of interconnection between the hemispheres was that persons acted unconsciously, simply doing what they were commanded to do by unseen "gods." Such orders came from "inside" a person's head via the right hemisphere, as a complex of visions/voices from gods who could not "speak" but could command and be understood.[73] As such, obedience to an inarticulate will of the gods was assured by those whose consciousness was dominated by the right hemisphere. Jaynes speculates that even today a residual function of the right hemisphere may be an organizational one, "that of sorting out the experiences of a civilization and fitting them together into a pattern that could 'tell' the individual what to do."[74] Of course, the left hemisphere remains neither passive nor silent. Rather, it confronts and attempts to articulate the meaning of the experiences it receives from the right hemisphere. Here then are the well-known dichotomies of religion: its ineffable, experiential base (rooted in the right hemisphere), and its rational attempt to articulate the meaning of experience (rooted in the left hemisphere). Often it appears that one has little direct relevance to the other. However, in Jaynes's bicameral model these differences are but reflections of the hemispheric difference between persons and gods. Often overlooked in discussions of Jaynes's theory is that the more fully one tries to articulate the meaning of one's experience, the more the left hemisphere becomes involved and probably inhibits the recounting of the actual experience. Thus, religious experience often requires an "abandonment" or "letting go," which can be facilitated by left-hemispheric acceptance of a safe set or setting within which right-hemispheric actions can be facilitated. In this sense, Sundén's role theory remains relevant: Familiarity with texts and traditions facilitates experience through right-hemispheric activity (often assumed to be a religious trance state), and sanctions it interpretively through left-hemispheric activity.

Jaynes further speculates that when the stable world order broke down, bicameral consciousness became less effective and was no longer favored by natural selection. A more rational, reflectively directed consciousness emerged, typical of modern consciousness and associated with the inevitable silence (if not death) of the gods. The powerful visions/voices and ineffable experience of the gods survive as isolated religious experiences, probably elicited by stress, or as aspects of the traumatic experiences of the mentally ill. Jaynes proposes a general bicameral paradigm that incorporates the logical structure of his theory and yet remains relevant to modern inductions of experience based upon the neurological structures (as yet unspecified) assumed to operate in the bicameral mind. This paradigm is presented in Table 6.6.

The merit of Jaynes's admittedly speculative theory is that it represents a creative effort to relate religious experience to the neurophysiology and anatomical structure of the human

TABLE 6.6. Jaynes's General Bicameral Paradigm

1. *Collective cognitive imperative:* A culturally agreed-on expectancy or prescription that defines the particular form of a phenomenon and the roles to be acted out within that form. This is essentially a belief system.
2. *Induction:* A formally ritualized procedure whose function is the narrowing of consciousness. The major technique used is similar to contemplative meditation, but, instead of attention's being focused on a single object, it is focused on a small range of preoccupations.
3. *Trance:* An altered state of consciousness characterized by a restriction of consciousness or its loss. The sense of "I" is diminished or lost. In this state one adopts a role accepted by or encouraged by the group.
4. *Archaic authorization:* The individual (god or person) to whom the trance is related. This authority is accepted by the group and within its belief system is attributed the power to produce the trance state.

Note. Adapted from Jaynes (1976, p. 324). Copyright 1976 by Houghton-Mifflin Co. Adapted by permission.

brain. In addition, his theory requires cultural considerations—for instance, historical patterns of social control that are maintained by left-hemispheric ideological justifications of the imperatives issued by the voices/visions of the right-hemispheric gods or God. Yet this leaves pitifully little comfort for the modern religiously devout, whose religious experiences seem to lose their ontological validity in the curious neuroanatomy of the gods. Indeed, the appeal to evolutionary theory leaves the validity of the gods to a previous history and the content of their experience to those contemporaries who now are woefully inadequate to the modern world. If there is a residue of right-hemispheric experience supported by contemporary religious institutions, it lies in "glossolalia," or speaking in tongues—a phenomenon as old as the bicameral mind and as recent as Pentecostal and Holiness churches that support and sanctify this phenomenon.

Glossolalia (Speaking in Tongues)

Glossolalia is a universal religious phenomenon.[75] Jaynes asserts that it is always a group phenomenon and that it fits well into the general bicameral paradigm, including the strong cognitive imperative of religious belief in a cohesive group, the induction procedures of prayer and ritual resulting in the narrowing of consciousness (trance), associated with the archaic authorization of the divine spirit in a charismatic leader.[76] Whereas Jaynes asserts the musical and poetic nature of glossolalia,[77] Samarin finds it to be merely a meaningless, phonologically structured human sound.[78] Lafal, Monahan, and Richman dispute the claim that glossolalia is meaningless.[79] Hutch claims that glossolalia aims to amalgamate the sounds of laughing and crying—signs of both the joy and pain of life.[80] Early psychologists attributed glossolalia to mental illness, but modern researchers have made a strong conceptual case for distinguishing glossolalia from what are only superficial clinical parallels.[81] Empirically, glossolalia is normative within many religious traditions, including some Pentecostal denominations in the contemporary United States. Thus, it is not surprising that empirical studies comparing glossolalic with nonglossolalic controls have consistently failed to find any reliable psychological differences, including indices of psychopathology between the two groups.[82] However, it is also true that, as Lovekin and Malony found in their study of participants in a Catholic charismatic program of spiritual renewal,[83] glossolalia per se may not be particularly useful in fostering personality integration.

The real focus of research has been on whether or not glossolalia occurs only in a trance or altered state of consciousness. The anthropologist Goodman has documented the cross-cultural similarity of glossolalic utterances.[84] She attributes this similarity to the fact that glossolalia results from an induced trance. The trance state itself, for neurophysiological reasons, accounts for the cross-cultural similarity of glossolalia.[85] Her model of the induction of a trance state is very similar to Jaynes's general bicameral paradigm.[86] She argues for induction techniques generated by religious rituals in believers; the resulting trance state produces an altered perceptual state in which previous limits are transcended. One participant in her research stated the case for limits and transcendence succinctly: "At first you feel that you have come to a barrier, and you are afraid. All of a sudden you are beyond it and everything is different."[87] This altered perceptual state is identified by Goodman as the "sojourn." It is followed by dissolution and by the joy and euphoria of having had this sacred experience.

Samarin has challenged Goodman's cross-cultural data on the basis that all her samples were from similar Pentecostal settings, even though the data were collected within different cultures.[88] Samarin also points out that vocal patterns identified in typical Appalachian mountain preachings are similar to those found in glossolalia. This is the case, even though such preaching is not done in a trance state; hence, there is no reason to infer that glossolalia can only be elicited in trance states. This view is also supported by Hine.[89]

Obviously, the debate on whether or not trance states are necessary for religious experiences such as glossolalia or serpent handling is conceptually clouded. It would require a clear operational definition of glossolalia at one level and a clear operational definition of trance at another level to test whether the two covary, much less to see whether glossolalia can only be elicited in a trance state. Although such research has yet to be done, the debate has been useful as another instance of religious experience's gaining a foothold in mainstream social science by raising issues of possible physiological correlates. It is assumed that since such physiological processes can be identified in hard scientific terms, the experiences they facilitate have at least some validity. Of course, once again, to religiously committed individuals, such faint praise is less than sufficient. Experience attributed to the gods or to God must have more reality than the physiological conditions that facilitate them. A participant observation study of glossolalia, conducted over many years in Scandinavian countries, is presented in Research Box 6.2; it suggests that trance is unlikely to be necessary for glossolalia to occur.

The issue of whether or not trance states are required for glossolalia is paralleled in participant observation studies of serpent handlers. Williamson has emphasized that serpent handlers have historically been associated with denominations such as the Church of God, which once sanctioned *both* serpent handling and glossolalia.[90] Hood and Kimbrough note that some handlers believe that faith alone is sufficient for handling serpents, whereas others argue that only when "anointed" should one handle serpents.[91] Anointing is the case that most closely parallels the claim to trance. That believers can handle serpents either through faith or through anointing supports the claim that trance is not necessary for serpent handling. However, in one unique study, a serpent handler in an anointed state agreed to be videotaped and to have his electroencephalogram taken. Research Box 6.3 presents the results of this study.

RELIGIOUS IMAGERY: THE RETURN OF THE OSTRACIZED

It has been more than a quarter of a century since a distinguished psychologist prophesied the "return of the ostracized" to psychology.[92] The ostracized that Holt spoke of was imag-

~

Research Box 6.2. Sundén's Role Theory and Glossolalia (Holm, 1987)

Holm is among the foremost researchers who have focused upon the social and contextual factors that facilitate glossolalia. He collected recordings of hundreds of Pentecostal meetings in Scandinavian countries over several years; thus, he studied the speaking of tongues within religious contexts where it was normative. He found that there were few linguistic impediments to producing glossolalia, and therefore that a trance state was not necessary for one to speak in tongues. However, he also noted that a trance state could remove social inhibitions and hence facilitate glossolalia in some Pentecostalists.

Relying heavily upon Sundén's role theory, Holm conducted in-depth interviews with 65 Pentecostalists. Tongue speaking is modeled both by relevant Biblical texts regarding the Pentecost story, and by those who speak in tongues during services. Individuals must wait for this experience to occur as a true "baptism of the Holy Spirit" and not attempt to produce the experience themselves. Holm notes that approximately two-thirds of his sample first spoke in tongues at some kind of religious meeting. An initiate, surrounded by others speaking in tongues and having glossolalia also modeled in Biblical texts, thus receives the "gift of tongues." The emotional excitement that accompanies this experience is a function of a true "baptism of the Holy Spirit" and a religious sense of its presence. Subsequent doubts as to whether or not the glossolalia was self-produced are allayed by church members and authorities, who assure the initiate of its validity. Repeated glossolalic experiences confirm and solidify them as routine. It is important to note that in Holm's sample, 12 persons never spoke in tongues. Personality factors such as inhibitions (and perhaps neurophysiological factors as well) may help to explain why, even with appropriate readiness and textual and actual modeling, the experience is not available to all.[a]

---

[a]See also Holm (1991, especially pp. 142–145) and Hood (1991).

---

ery, and its return has fostered the development of the psychology of religion in two ways. First, as Bergin has emphasized, it has helped shift the emphasis of psychology from the study of behavior to psychology as the study of inner experience.[93] Second, it has fostered interest in religious experience, given the unquestioned centrality of imagery within the world's great faith traditions.[94] Imagery as a central fact of much human experience often gains unique relevance when interpreted religiously. The spontaneous presence or cultivated facilitation of imagery is central to many religious traditions. However, before we discuss religious imagery, we must briefly consider the issue of hallucinations.

Hallucinations

Recent studies have questioned the existence of hallucinations as a unique phenomenon. Fischer has identified a perception–hallucination continuum.[95] Whether or not an image is considered hallucinatory depends upon cultural and social factors, not simply neurophysiology. Recent research focuses upon cultural and social processes that facilitate the report of imagery, whether or not it is defined as hallucinatory.[96] Religions have long been noted

---

Research Box 6.3. Electroencephalogram Taken from Liston Pack (Woodruff, 1993)

In Holiness sects, as in many Pentecostal groups, anointment by the Holy Ghost is believed to occur when the spirit of God possesses an individual. Anna Prince, a member of a serpent-handling Holiness sect, partly defined anointing as follows: "It's a spiritual trancelike strand of power linking humans to God; it's a burst of energy that's refreshing, always brand new; it brings on good emotions. One is elated, full of joy."[a] The famous serpent handler Pastor Liston Pack stated, "The anointing is hard, real hard to explain; and 'cause if I was to tell you that you had to feel just like me, I might tell you wrong, you see, but if you didn't know me, you would think I was havin' a stroke or somethin' tremendous was takin' place."[b]

At Thomas Burton's request, Liston Pack agreed to be videotaped and to have electroencephalographic (EEG) recordings taken while he was in an anointed state. Michael Woodruff did the recordings and interpreted them. His four major conclusions were as follows: (1) Liston Pack's EEG showed no abnormal clinical signs; it was not a self-induced epileptic seizure, nor was it brought on by some idiopathic state. (2) Liston Pack had a great deal of control over his mental state, given his ability to prepare for anointment in a laboratory setting among skeptical scientists. (3) There was a sudden conversion from alpha to beta when anointment began, with beta predominant throughout the experience. The EEG was that of an aroused individual, but was accompanied by observations of an individual having a religious experience. It was *not* similar to that of a Zen monk in contemplation. (4) Overall, the EEG patterns of Liston Pack were more similar to patterns found in hypnosis than in meditation. However, Woodruff cautions that self-hypnosis is only a hypothesis worthy of further study and ought not to be confused with self-delusion.

---

[a]Burton (1993, p. 140).
[b]Burton (1993, p. 140).

---

for their interest in fostering such activities as prayer and meditation, which either are aimed at or indirectly facilitate the elicitation of religious imagery.[97] Similarly, apparently spontaneously experienced imagery can take on great significance when it is sanctioned as meaningful within religious traditions. For instance, Roman Catholicism makes a distinction between a "vision" and an "apparition" that parallels psychological distinctions between "imagery" and "hallucinations." Volken notes that apparitions are perceived as "exterior" and are a special case of visions within Catholicism.[98] A purely secular person would be tempted to call an apparition an hallucination. However, social scientists have gained some insight into factors influencing the report and sanction of images of Mary within the Catholic tradition, whether these are considered apparitions or hallucinations.

Images of Mary within the Catholic Tradition

Several investigators have focused attention upon reports of images of the Virgin Mary associated with the Catholic faith tradition. We use the term "image" in a neutral sense, to cover the possibility that such occurrences are either hallucinations (nonveridical perceptions) or apparitions (veridical perceptions accepted within the Catholic tradition). In either case, social-psychological factors clearly determine the frequency of the report of such experiences, their acceptance as authentic by the Catholic Church, and the differential appeal of the cult of the Virgin Mary. Much of the current research has been stimulated by the work of Carroll.[99]

Catholics have long accepted the veneration of Mary as part of their faith tradition. Included in this is the recognition by Catholicism of apparitions of the Virgin Mary that have appeared throughout history. Modern apparitions have ranged from the Miraculous Medal of the Immaculate Conception in France in 1830 to the visions at Medjugorje in the former Yugoslavia in 1981.[100] Sociological studies have focused upon the factors that influence the Catholic Church to accept only *some* reported apparitions of Mary as legitimate. For instance, Warner provides critical historical documentation in support of her claim that the sanctioning of apparitions of the Virgin Mary has often been linked with official support for sexual suppression.[101] Perry and Echeverría argue that apparitions have been used both to facilitate social control on the part of the Catholic Church and to boost national prestige.[102] Their latter claim is congruent with Carroll's claim that even when countries have similar frequencies of reports of Marian apparitions, such as Spain and Italy, social and political factors have led to differential legitimation of the apparitions by central church authorities.[103]

More relevant to the empirical psychology of religion is the fact that Carroll's theoretical orientation is primarily classical Freudian theory, in which it is assumed that repressed sexual desires account largely for hallucinations and fantasies. Thus, Carroll treats apparitions of the Virgin Mary as hallucinations, differentially legitimated by central church authorities. His empirical efforts focus upon predicting characteristics of Marian apparitions from history in terms of classical Freudian theory. His thesis can be readily summarized in three major claims.

First, the Catholic doctrine of the Virgin Mary incorporates three beliefs: Mary was conceived without sin; her hymen was never ruptured (*in partu* virginity); and Mary remained a lifelong virgin. Thus, Mary is unique in religious mythology in that she is a perpetual virgin, totally devoid of sexuality. In Freudian theoretical terms, Mary symbolizes sexual denial.

Second, Carroll provides demographic and historical data to document that the Marian cult is strongest in countries where the machismo complex is most common. The machismo complex essentially entails fierce sexual domination of women by males, and is often strongly culturally supported.

Third, Carroll provides anthropological and ethnographic data to show that in areas where the Marian cult and the machismo complex are strongest, males come from father-ineffective families. In Freudian terms, father-ineffective families assure strong and delayed attachment to the mother on the part of her male children. Using Freudian Oedipal theory, Carroll argues that males strongly attached to their mothers have intense erotic repressions that can effectively be expressed in attraction to the cult of the Virgin Mary. The idealized Virgin represents the denial of sexual attraction to one's mother; the machismo complex displaces eroticism onto other women, who are treated primarily as sex objects; guilt is assuaged by attraction to the passion of Christ, in which the male identifies with the need for punishment. Thus, sexual sublimation accounts for the appeal of the cult of the Virgin Mary.

Carroll's provocative thesis is rare in the psychology of religion, as it incorporates historical, anthropological, ethnographic, and social-historical facts into a single, coherent theoretical framework. It has also led to several empirical studies. For instance, Carroll[104] utilized Walsh's[105] massive identification of Marian apparitions associated with the Catholic Church, including those officially recognized by the church as well as those not legitimated. All apparitions from 1100 to 1896 for which three empirical criteria could be documented resulted in a sample of 50.[106] The three empirical criteria were as follows: (1) The seer was in a waking state; (2) the seer both heard and saw Mary; and (3) the image of Mary was not provided by an identifiable physical stimulus. Assuming sexual sublimation to foster susceptibility to Marian hallucinations (apparitions), Carroll predicted that the seers would be unmarried (and hence most likely celibate). Table 6.7 presents the results of Carroll's study for 45 of the 50 separate apparitions for which the celibacy status of the seers could be assumed. Inspection of this table shows that 94% of the seers could be assumed to be celibate; this supports the sublimation thesis. Of course, we cannot be assured that every nonmarried seer was celibate, but the available data do suggest that married and assuredly noncelibate seers were unlikely to report apparitions for the years studied (1100 to 1896).

What of women seers? Freudian theory suggests that sexual sublimation applies to females as well as males. In the female case, identification with Mary permits expression of repressed sexuality, since a daughter obtains the father by identifying with her mother. Granted the controversial nature of Freudian Oedipal theory,[107] Carroll's use of this theory does lead to specific, empirically testable predictions. In this case, Carroll predicted that the gender of the seer would be related to whether or not apparitions of Mary contained additional male figures (such as Jesus or adult male saints).[108] He based this prediction upon the fact that in Oedipal theory, males desire exclusive possession of the mother and do not want father figures present. Since females identify with the mother in order to obtain access to the father, they should want father figures present. Classifying the same 50 apparitions noted above, this time for gender of the seer, permitted Carroll to cross-tabulate this with whether or not male figures were present in the reported Marian apparitions. These results are presented in Table 6.8 for the 47 of 50 seers for whom the gender and adulthood of male figures appearing with Mary could be clearly identified. Inspection of the table indicates that most apparitions studied did not have adult males in them. However, a gender effect was clearly identified for males, with males unlikely to report a male present in their Marian apparitions. For females, the likelihood of a male's being present was as great as that of a male's not being present. Most importantly for Carroll's thesis, females were much more likely to

TABLE 6.7. Assumed Celibacy Status of Seers at Time of Their First Apparition of the Virgin Mary

Status	n	%
Assumed celibate		
Cleric	18	40
Unmarried		
Child	8	18
Adolescent	9	20
Adult	8	18
Assumed not celibate		
Married	2	4

Note. Adapted from Carroll (1983, p. 210). Copyright 1983 by the Society for the Scientific Study of Religion. Adapted by permission.

TABLE 6.8. Relationship between Sex of Seer and Likelihood of One or
More Adult Males in a Marian Apparition

| | Did male/males appear in Marian apparition? | | | |
| | Yes | | No | |
Sex of seer	*n*	%	*n*	%
Male	2	7	25	93
Female	10	50	10	50

Note. Adapted from Carroll (1983, p. 220). Copyright 1986 by the Society for the Scientific Study of Religion. Adapted by permission.

report apparitions with males present than were males, whose Marian apparitions seldom included other adult male figures.[109]

If we assume Marian apparitions to be hallucinations (non-sensory-based imagery), then Carroll's theory argues that psychological factors predispose individuals to experience hallucinations that may be compatible with religious traditions legitimating such imagery in the form of apparitions. Thus, religious tradition and psychological dispositions interact to allow powerful experiences for some, which, when formally sanctioned by the authorities of the tradition, become powerful vicarious experiences for others within that tradition as well. They can believe through faith what the original seers have experienced firsthand. A test of Carroll's thesis using a sample of Protestant males and the preference for images of Mary and Christ is presented in Research Box 6.4.

Studies of hallucinations or apparitions of the Virgin Mary have important conceptual relevance for the empirical study of religion. What is crucial is the fact that the meaningful status of imagery varies with the context within which it is interpreted, as does the nature of the ontological status the image is given.[110]

The Facilitation of Religious Imagery

Studies of imagery associated with the Virgin Mary are specific to one religious tradition—Roman Catholicism. However, religious imagery plays a role in many religious traditions and is of immense relevance to any empirical psychology of religion. Much of the more clinical and conceptual literature in the psychology of religion—for instance, that associated with Jungian, object relations, and transpersonal theory[111]—explores images in depth. However, Jungians use images as either dependent or independent variables in empirical research. The experimental study of imagery has been of interest in the long tradition of studies of "sensory deprivation" or isolation. As we shall see, restricting external perception enhances the probability of imagery. Not surprisingly, psychologists have sought ways to enhance both solitude and isolation to facilitate the occurrence of imagery.

Although imagery has long been of central concern to religious traditions, has been granted important ontological status, and has often been cited for its evidential value in supporting the claims of various faith traditions, psychologists have only recently begun to focus upon the study of imagery. Few contemporary psychologists would dispute Pylyshyn's claim that "Imagery is a pervasive form of human experience and is clearly of utmost importance to humans."[112] Indeed, as both Shephard[113] and Lilly[114] have noted, situations of isolation, solitude, and focused concentration often elicit unanticipated and undesired imagery that

---

Research Box 6.4. Non-Catholic Male Attraction to the Cult of the Virgin Mary (Hood, Morris, & Watson, 1991)

Carroll's thesis that sexual sublimation is involved in the male attraction to the cult of the Virgin Mary in Roman Catholicism was tested by Hood et al. in a sample of non-Catholic, Christian males. First, an independent sample of raters was used to identify (1) crucifixes ranked according to the degree of Christ's suffering they represented, and (2) artistic rendering of the Virgin Mary ranked and rated for (a) eroticism and (b) nurturing quality. Four crucifixes reliably varying in the degree of suffering expressed (and one plain cross, as a control) were used as stimuli. Five pictures of the Virgin Mary, reliably varying in erotic and nurturing quality (with one identified as equally nurturing *and* erotic, as a control) were also used. These stimuli were then rated for personal preference by 71 non-Catholic males, all of whom either agreed or strongly agreed on a 5-point Likert scale that "My whole approach to life is based upon my religion." These males also completed a measure developed by Parker to assess self-recalled maternal bonding.[a] This was used as a measure of strong attachment (ambivalently erotic and nurturing) to one's mother.

Participants were taken one at a time into a room in which the crucifixes and cross were mounted on one wall and the pictures of the Virgin Mary were mounted on another wall. The subjects were first seated in front of the wall on which the crucifixes and cross were randomly numbered and hung, and were asked to take a moment to contemplate them. They then answered the question "Which cross or crucifix best expresses what Christ means to you?", followed by "Which cross or crucifix next best expresses what Christ means to you?" This was continued until one remained and participants were asked, "Why did you not choose this cross/crucifix?" Next, a similar procedure was followed as participants were seated in front of the wall with the five pictures of the Virgin Mary.

Consistent with the theory of the role of sexual sublimation in reports of Marian hallucination or apparitions, Hood et al. predicted that males strongly but ambivalently attached to their mothers would have a preference for (1) a suffering Christ and (2) the ambivalently erotic/nurturing Virgin Mary representation. Results supported these predictions. The more males recalled ambivalent and strong attachments to their mothers as measured by the bonding scales, the more likely they were to prefer a suffering Christ figure and the ambivalent Virgin Mary figure. In terms of Freudian theory, the ambivalent attraction to one's mother also involves the unconscious sense of guilt and the identification with a Christ who suffers painfully. Freudian theory is often controversial and susceptible to varying interpretations. It is best viewed as one means of interpreting any set of data—even those proposed as a test of Freudian theory, as in this study of Carroll's speculative theory.

---

[a]See Parker (1983); Parker, Tupling, and Brown (1979).

---

can disrupt ongoing activities. Examples of such situations include focusing upon a radar-scope, attending to concerns during space travel, and surviving during prolonged periods of isolation. Thus, it is not surprising that early experimental studies of isolation, using isolation tanks, often documented imagery that was disruptive and disturbing to research participants.[115] The very phrase "sensory deprivation" emphasizes the negative. However, within many religious traditions, withdrawing from "worldly" perceptions and "turning within" have long had a valuable and privileged status. For instance, some forms of both prayer and meditation involve withdrawal from external sensory attention that may produce imagery that is religiously meaningful. LaBarre has gone so far as to claim:

> Every religion in historic fact, began in one man's "revelation"—his dream or fugue or ecstatic trance. Indeed, the crisis cult is *characteristically* dereistic, autistic, and dreamlike precisely *because* it had its origins in the dream, trance, "spirit" possession, epileptic "seizure," REM sleep, sensory deprivation, or other visionary state of the shaman–originator. All religions are necessarily "revealed" in this sense, inasmuch as they are certainly not revealed consensually in secular experience.[116]

Although LaBarre's position may be extreme, it does emphasize the obvious relevance of imagery to religious traditions. It is thus curious that sensory isolation research neither has focused upon the elicitation of imagery with religious samples nor has concerned itself with the specific elicitation of religious imagery among samples, whether religious or not.

The exclusion of external sources of stimulation in isolation studies led early investigators to coin the term "sensory deprivation."[117] Many assumed that the images present in such studies must be hallucinations. However, early isolation ("deprivation") studies produced exaggerated results that are now readily identifiable largely as artifacts of the experimental setting. In particular, the use of isolation tanks provided the means to control external sources of stimulation. A typical isolation tank is an enclosed, soundproofed, and lightproofed container filled with magnesium salt solutions, heated to external body temperature (34.1° C), and adjusted for specific gravity so that a person simply floats partly submerged. The uniqueness of the isolation tank situation, combined with excessive experimental forewarnings and precautions, elicited panic and bizarre reactions in some early research participants. However, as studies progressed, it was discovered that if participants were knowledgeable (i.e., were initiated into the experiences likely to be facilitated by the isolation tank), negative reactions became exceedingly uncommon. Instead, participants explored the variety of experiences common to altered-states research in an almost universally positive fashion.[118] Most important for our interests is the imagery elicited in isolation tank experiences—imagery seldom appropriately identified as merely hallucinatory.[119]

Imagery is readily elicited in isolation tanks if participants are relaxed and unfearful, and are given specific instructions to attend to internal states, contents, and processes. Unstructured phenomena such as focused or diffuse white light, as well as various geometric forms and colors, are common and rapidly explained by the psychology of perception. For instance, spontaneous neural firing in the retina, a common phenomenon, is attended to in isolation studies and hence becomes a part of conscious awareness. Some of these phenomena are common in meditation and prayer, as discussed above.

More detailed instructions and time in the isolation tank can lead to more meaningful images—some similar to hypnagogic forms, and others similar to meaningful figures not unlike those found in dreams. Both the report and content of the imagery are heavily influenced by set and setting.[120] As in psychedelic research, hallucinations are rare in isolation tanks. Persons do not see things they mistakenly expect to exist in time and space, as they would objects of everyday perception. However, with appropriate set and setting, participants do experience imagery that has ontological significance. These figures are not simply dismissed as "subjective." In this sense, isolation tanks can facilitate genuine religious experiences. Research Box 6.5 reports one experiment in which set and setting were used to facilitate religious experiences under isolation tank conditions.

ひ

Research Box 6.5. Sensory Isolation and the Differential Elicitation of Religious Imagery (Hood & Morris, 1981b)

Hood and Morris utilized an isolation tank to provide a setting in which the elicitation of imagery could be facilitated. The isolation tank was 7.5 feet long, 4 feet high, and 4 feet wide. The tank contained a hydrated magnesium sulfate solution with a density of 1.30 grams/cc, a depth of 10 inches, and a temperature of 34.1°C (approximate external body temperature). Participants were totally enclosed in the tank, which was also soundproofed and lightproofed. The tank itself was in a small soundproofed room. Participants were nude in the tank and floated there for 1 hour.

A person can expect a variety of imagery phenomena under isolation conditions, including geometric forms, light, and images of meaningful figures. As part of the appropriate ethical concerns in doing such research, participants were forewarned to anticipate such experiences. However, the participants were also instructed to try to control their images.

In a double-blind procedure, half the participants were instructed to try to imagine religious figures, situations, and settings, while the other half were instructed to try to imagine cartoon figures, situations, and settings. Thus, the researchers attempted to encourage specific imagery among religious types, for whom such imagery should be relevant. Furthermore, it was predicted that intrinsic persons would report more religious imagery, based upon the assumption that their participation in religion would be more devoutly experientially based than that of extrinsics. Twenty intrinsic and twenty extrinsic participants had been selected for their extreme scores on either the Intrinsic or Extrinsic Religious Orientation Scale.[a] The results of this study are presented in the table below.

		Religious type			
		Intrinsic		Extrinsic	
Reported imagery	Set condition	Mean	SD	Mean	SD
Religious figures	Cartoon	2.10	0.86	1.10	0.32
	Religious	3.10	0.74	1.90	0.74
Cartoon figures	Cartoon	2.30	0.95	2.50	1.27
	Religious	1.30	0.68	1.50	0.71
Meaningful figures	Cartoon	2.30	0.95	2.30	1.06
	Religious	2.00	1.16	2.50	0.97
Geometric forms	Cartoon	2.40	1.08	1.60	0.70
	Religious	2.00	1.05	2.30	0.82
Light	Cartoon	2.30	1.16	2.10	0.88
	Religious	2.10	0.74	2.90	0.57

Note. From Hood and Morris (1981b, p. 267). Copyright 1981 by the Society to the Scientific Study of Religion. Reprinted by permission.

Inspection of this table reveals that there was no overall tendency for either religious group to report more imagery when the images were those well documented to occur under isolation conditions (e.g., geometric forms, meaningful figures, light). However,

---

[a]The intrinsic participant group had an intrinsic mean of 38.9 (SD = 4.01) and an extrinsic mean of 26.4 (SD = 5.12). The extrinsic participant group had an extrinsic mean of 35.4 (SD = 3.93) and an intrinsic mean of 20.9 (SD = 4.22). The Allport and Ross (1967) scale was used.

(cont.)

---

under the set conditions intrinsic persons reported more cued religious imagery than extrinsics, whereas the groups did not differ on cartoon imagery.[b] Thus, the report of more religious imagery under cued conditions was not a function of the intrinsics' greater tendency to report imagery. Indeed, the intrinsics even reported more religious imagery under the cartoon cue than extrinsics reported under the religious cue. That these results were not simply functions of demand characteristics—with intrinsics more sensitive to reporting more religious imagery when cued—was supported by a control study in which intrinsics did not report more religiously relevant imagery than extrinsics when asked to give religious responses to Rorschach cards.

---

[b]Results were tested by both multivariate and univariate statistical tests. See pp. 267–268 of the Hood and Morris paper for details.

Other researchers have begun to explore other ways to experimentally induce imagery and other facets of religious experience. Masters and Houston, noted for their pioneering work on the varieties of psychedelic experience, have developed a mechanical device to induce altered states of consciousness.[121] It is essentially a vertical canvas stretcher hooked to a suspended platform. Blindfolded subjects are strapped into the device, which responds to the slightest movement and is claimed to induce a trance state rapidly in most participants. With proper set and setting, individuals report imagery and similar experiences. Once again, the relevant point is that when investigators take a serious interest in the elicitation of experiences, participants, especially when selected for their interest and sensitivities, may report significant religious experiences.

In a similar vein, Goodman claims to have discovered 30 specific body postures that can reliably elicit altered states of consciousness.[122] These postures are derived from ancient cave drawings as well as from anthropological research. Unique in Goodman's research is her claim that these specific postures elicit states of consciousness in which perceptions of an expanded reality are accessible. Although her thesis is controversial, it is clearly empirically testable. Again, the issue is that sympathetic researchers are taking seriously not simply the induction of altered states of consciousness, but the ontological reality of what is revealed in the experience. In this sense, the psychology of religion is forced to confront spiritual claims as it explores the reports of individuals whose experience may have evidential force.

Prayer and Religious Imagery

One of the earliest topics in psychology, and one that continues to occupy the interests of psychologists of religion, is the efficacy of prayer. However, psychologists have only recently become interested in empirical (much less experimental) studies of prayer, which Heiler argued to be central to religion.[123] Since there are few firm data on which to base a theory of prayer, it is not surprising that Janssen, de Hart, and den Draak note that "no convincing psychological theory [of prayer] exists."[124] Part of the problem is that instead of focusing upon the content and phenomenology of prayer, researchers have focused upon its correlates. Galton, one of the earliest measurement psychologists, argued persuasively on the basis of statistical analysis that prayer had no demonstrable objective benefits.[125] However, he argued just as persuasively for the beneficial effects of prayer on subjective well-being. The shift to a focus upon subjective well-being in prayer research has been helpful for the study of religious experience in two senses. First, subjective well-being involves experience—that is, how a person feels or reacts to situations as a function of prayer. Second, few religionists or scientists would find a test derived from a subject's own wishes to be very meaningful; thus there is a shift away from studying the mere efficacy of prayer in objective terms. Scientists find such studies deficient because people obviously cannot wish the world to conform to their desires in any efficacious sense, and few researchers would bother to think further empirical tests of such hypotheses worthwhile. The religionists find such theorizing inadequate because the movement toward mature faith in virtually every tradition is likely to be seen as a shift from requesting that a person's own will be done to asking that a divine will be done. In the latter case, apparently unanswered prayers (outcomes not corresponding to those requested) can be successfully interpreted as meaningful in terms of a more mature reflection upon the nature of faith, as Godin has emphasized.[126]

Poloma and her colleagues have made significant contributions to the contemporary empirical study of prayer.[127] Not only have they reliably measured several types of prayer (colloquial, meditative, petitionary, and ritualistic), but they have focused upon the more psychologically meaningful measures of (1) experiences during prayer and (2) subjective consequences of prayer. Thus, much of Poloma et al.'s work on prayer is in the quality-of-life tradition that meaningfully assesses the subjective aspects of human experience.[128]

"Quality of life" is a multidimensional construct that includes existential well-being, happiness, life satisfaction, religious satisfaction, and negative affect (reverse-scored). Prayer is also multidimensional, with various types of prayer differentially relating to an experienced quality of life. For instance, meditative prayer is most closely related to religious satisfaction and existential well-being. On the other hand, only colloquial prayer predicts the absence of negative affect, whereas ritual prayer alone predicts negative affect.[129] Thus, not simply the frequency of prayer, but also the nature and type of prayer, determine experiential consequences.

Another contribution of Poloma and her colleagues is to focus upon the measurement of actual experiences during prayer. Poloma's prayer index is presented in Table 6.9. This index has consistently been correlated with quality of life, regardless of the objective status of those who pray. Thus, as others have noted, in the specific case of variables used in religion, assessing objective outcomes may be less relevant than assessing subjective ones.[130] Specifically, in research on prayer, Brown has noted that the belief in the objective efficacy of even petitionary prayer lessens with age and spiritual maturity.[131]

The turn from attempting to document the physical consequences of prayer makes work such as Loehr's[132] (on the efficacy of prayer on plant growth) less worthy of critical methodological commentary than irrelevant. It is simply the wrong kind of issue to address. If the focus is upon the change in intentionality, consciousness, or affect of those who pray, then the focus of research on prayer is rightly on its subjective quality.

In this regard, both Poloma and her colleagues, and Hood and his, have derived remarkably similar factors in their multidimensional approach to the measurement of prayer. Table 6.10 presents their similar factor structures, remarkable for their independent derivation—one by a team of sociologists, the other by a team of psychologists. Furthermore, the high reliability of all scales suggests the robust nature of the multidimensional criteria of prayer that Poloma's and Hood's groups have both identified.

Both Poloma's and Hood's groups have noted that "contemplative" (Hood's term) or "meditative" (Poloma's term) praying—a nonpetitionary attempt merely to become aware of God—leads to unique experiences. For instance, Poloma and Pendleton note that with the exception of life satisfaction, each of their quality-of-life measures relates to only one type of

TABLE 6.9. Poloma's Index of Prayer Experience

1. How often during the past year have you felt divinely inspired or "led by God" to perform something specific as a result of prayer?
2. How often have you received what you believed to be a deeper insight into a spiritual or Biblical truth?
3. How often have you received what you regarded as a definitive answer to a specific prayer request?
4. How often have you felt a strong sense of God during prayer?
5. How often have you experienced a deep sense of peace and well-being during prayer?

Answer options: _____ once or twice, _____ monthly, _____ weekly, _____ daily.

Note. Adapted from Poloma and Pendleton (1989, p. 53). Copyright 1989 by the Religious Research Association. Adapted by permission.

prayer.[133] Consistent with our focus on subjective experience, meditative prayer relates most closely to an existential quality of life. Similarly, Hood and his colleagues found in one study that contemplative (Poloma's meditative) prayer related most strongly to measures of mystical awareness (a feeling of unity), religiously interpreted for intrinsics who prayed.[134] On the other hand, extrinsics who prayed had disruptions of both religious and nonreligious imagery during contemplative prayer—suggesting the inability to quiet the mind and eliminate such images. Furthermore, they did not experience a sense of unity, as intrinsics did. Thus, it may be that different interpretations of experience reflect actual differences during an experience, as well as differences in the types of prayer in which intrinsics and extrinsics engage.

TABLE 6.10. Poloma's and Hood's Prayer Factors Compared

Poloma's four factors[a]	Hood's four factors[b]
Meditative (alpha = .81)	**Contemplative (alpha = .82)**
How often do you spend time just feeling or being in the presence of God?	When you pray or meditate, how often do you seek to be one God or ultimate reality?
How often do you spend time worshipping or adoring God?	When you pray or meditate, how often do you seek a perfect harmony?
Ritualistic (alpha = .59)	**Liturgical (alpha = .81)**
How often do you read from a book of prayers?	When you pray or meditate, how often do you recite sacred phrases or words?
How often do you recite prayers that you have memorized?	When you pray or meditate, how often do you read from sacred texts?
Petitionary (alpha = .78)	**Petitionary (alpha = .90)**
How often do you ask God for material things you might need?	When you pray or meditate, how often do you seek blessings for others?
How often do you ask God for material things your friends or relatives may need?	When you pray or mediate, how often do you seek forgiveness for yourself?
Colloquial (alpha = .85)	**Material (alpha = .65)**
How often do you ask God to provide guidance in making decisions?	When you pray or meditate, how often do you seek material things for yourself?
How often do you talk with God in your own words?	When you pray or meditate, how often do you seek material things for others?

[a]Adapted from Poloma and Pendleton (1989, p. 48). Copyright 1989 by the Religious Research Association. Adapted by permission.
[b]Adapted from Hood, Morris, and Harvey (1993). Adapted by permission of the authors.

Although more research is clearly needed, it is readily apparent that the shift away from the study of the efficacy of petitionary prayer is a step in the right direction. Brown has recently argued that if the definition of prayer is restricted to the narrow view of merely "asking for things," then prayer is perhaps more characteristic of unbelievers.[135] Measurement-based research has clearly established the multidimensionality of prayer, and future research will undoubtedly contribute to a deeper understanding of the subjective experience of prayer. In this sense, theories such as Sundén's role theory will become more relevant, as knowledge of traditions and texts is required to illuminate the meaningfulness of prayer within the communities of those who pray. Research Box 6.6 reports one of the few empirical studies of the needs stated for prayer, the content of prayer, and its effects.

PSYCHEDELIC DRUGS AND RELIGIOUS EXPERIENCE

It has long been recognized that many religions have employed various naturally occurring and synthetic substances in their rituals. However, until the discovery of psychedelic drugs, it was rather arrogantly assumed that concern with the facilitation of experience by drugs was the domain of anthropology and sister disciplines concerned with less "advanced" religions. In a new and controversial discipline by the cumbersome name of "archeopsychopharmacology," researchers combine ancient texts and artifacts with contemporary cross-cultural studies of the use of naturally occurring psychedelic substances to speculate on the origins of religions. For example, Allegro contends that the origin of the Judeo-Christian tradition may have been heavily influenced by altered states facilitated by the use of naturally occurring psychedelic substances, such as the mushroom *Amanita muscaria* or fly agaric.[136] So influenced, too, Wasson argues, was the sacred *Soma* of the ancient Indian text *Rig Vedat.*[137] To complete the picture, Kramrisch, Otto, Ruck, and Wasson argue that all religion originated from the use of psychedelic mushrooms.[138] Finally, Wasson, Hofmann, and Ruck argue that an ergot similar to LSD was integral to the Eleusinian mystery cults of ancient Greece, and from there influenced Western philosophy.[139] Although the widely speculative theories of archeopsychopharmacology cannot be empirically confirmed, they have raised a crucial question at the center of the social-scientific study of religion and the more general study of psychedelic drugs: Can psychedelic drugs facilitate or produce religious experiences?

The literature on the psychology of psychedelic drugs is immense, easily running to several thousand studies. Much of the U.S. research has been halted by legislation against these drugs, so that Rätsch has concluded, "Since the beginning of the 1970s, there has been little new research into psychedelic substances."[140] Although Rätsch's claim must be qualified, given the significant current research by anthropologists and ethnobotanists on psychedelic plants and drugs in European countries (where laws are more flexible), the measurement-based empirical study of psychedelic drugs has clearly been drastically curtailed by U.S. drug laws.[141] However, there nevertheless remains an extensive body of research on psychedelic drugs. Critical reviews are readily available, including the general overall review by Aarson and Osmond,[142] Dobkin de Rios's cross-cultural survey,[143] Barber's methodological review,[144] a review by Masters and Houston of research on varieties of psychedelic experience,[145] and Lukoff et al.'s review of studies on religious and transpersonal states facilitated by psychedelic drugs.[146]

Curiously, very few studies have been conducted using religious variables for directly assessing the religious importance of psychedelic drugs, despite a vast and often contentious

---

Research Box 6.6. A Content Analysis of the Praying Practices of Dutch Youth (Janssen, de Hart, & den Draak, 1990)

In 1985, a sample of 192 Dutch high school students was asked to respond to three open-ended questions regarding prayer: (1) "What is praying to you?", (2) "At what moments do you feel the need to pray?", and (3) "How do you pray?" Using a computer technique to analyze the content of the responses to these three questions, Janssen and colleagues were able to summarize prayer structure according to the following sentence: "Because of some reason, I address myself to someone in a particular way, at a particular place, at a particular time, to achieve something." They diagrammed this sentence as follows:

1. Need	2. Action	7. Effect
(conditional adjunct)	(predicate)	(direct object)
	3. Direction (indirect object)	
	4. Time (adverbial adjunct 1)	
	5. Place (adverbial adjunct 2)	
	6. Method (adverbial adjunct 3)	

The percentages of content references to each structural category for the four most frequent citations within that category were as follows[a]:

1. *Need (83%):* personal problems (60%); sickness (23%); happiness (20%); death (16%).
2. *Action (83%):* talk/monologue (38%); talk/dialogue (36%); ask/wish (33%); meditate (22%).
3. *Direction (60%):* God/Lord (80%); Spirit/power (13%); Someone (11%); Mary/Jesus (2%).
4. *Time (20%):* evening/night (90%); at day (8%); dinner (8%); anytime (5%).
5. *Place (34%):* bed (86%); home (11%); church (11%); outside (9%).
6. *Method (55%):* alone (55%); prayer, formal (17%); low voice (19%); aloud (4%).
7. *Effect (37%):* help/support (38%); favor (34%); remission (13%); rest (10%).

---

[a]Percentages for the seven structural aspects are based upon *n* = 192. Percentages for content within each structure are based upon number of participants who reported that structural aspect. See the Janssen et al. paper, p. 102, Table 1.

---

conceptual literature on drugs and religion. Although Wasson's and his colleagues' archeo-psychopharmacological speculations may be extreme, their basic assumption has been common within both psychological and religious studies. It has long been noted that there is an obvious similarity between various religious experiences and drug-induced experiences. At the end of the 19th century, this similarity was used by Leuba to argue that religious experience in advanced traditions must be invalidated because it is similar to drug-induced states in less advanced traditions.[147] The essentials of Leuba's argument have been recently advanced by Zaehner, who argues that because an experience is drug-induced, it cannot be genuinely religious.[148] These largely conceptually based debates do little to advance a scientific under-standing of the possible religious importance of psychedelic drugs. We can no more invali-date an experience because its physiology is known than we can invalidate physiology be-cause its biochemistry has been identified. As Weil has emphasized, the similarity of psychedelic substances found within plants, animals, and the human brain suggests that any simple distinction between natural and artificially induced states is arbitrary.[149]

Our concern is with the religious significance of psychedelic drugs. In particular, we focus upon the question of whether or not psychedelic drugs can either induce or be used to facili-tate a religious experience. We include under the heading of "psychedelic" such drugs as LSD, mescaline, and psilocybin, since users in both scientific studies and on the street report simi-lar psychological experiences from these drugs.[150] However, as Brown cautions, drugs that produce similar psychological effects need not have identical biochemical properties.[151]

The term "psychedelic" has a controversial history.[152] Debates over the common name for the class of drugs we are discussing have produced a range from "hallucinogenic" to "psy-chotomimetic" to "psychedelic." Ironically, "hallucinogenics," a common term for psyche-delics, is the most inadequate term. Hallucination is one of the *least* common responses to psychedelic drugs.[153] Although these drugs do produce various visual effects and imagery, whether users' eyes are open or closed, they do not produce false perceptions mistaken as real (hallucinations). "Psychotomimetic" is a term favored by early researchers who thought that this class of drugs produced psychoses or psychotic-like states. Given the cultural evalu-ation of psychoses, the negative connotations of "psychotomimetic" are obvious; however, it is well established that the ability of psychedelics to elicit sudden psychoses in otherwise normal persons is highly exaggerated.[154] Ironically, "psychedelic" was the term preferred by those who favored the "mind-manifesting" aspect of these drugs. It is the most common term today, despite its association with the illicit street drug culture and its positive connotations among participants of the 1960s deviant drug culture.[155]

For well-established physiological reasons, psychedelic drugs can be expected to pro-duce reliable alterations in visual phenomena, which, to an informed and stable participant, are likely to be interesting objects of conscious exploration.[156] Meaningful images that occur under the influence of these drugs, with the user's eyes closed, are not typically attributed to an object expected to exist in the world (in the sense that if the user were to open his or her eyes, the object would be physically real). Likewise, when the user's eyes are open, alterations in the perception of objects are noted as perceptual alterations of existing objects, not as changes in the actual physical objects or in the perception of objects that in fact are not real. However, the user's ability to interpret perceptions in terms of a meaningful frame can trans-form his or her perception of the world. In Sundén's theory, a religious frame of reference should enhance the power of psychedelics to facilitate religious experiences. With a condu-cive religious set and setting, psychedelic drugs can facilitate religious experiences, insofar as a person under the influence of these drugs may, for the first time, see the world in terms appropriate to a particular system of meaning. In this sense, the "other-worldly" property of psychedelic drugs is well established and provides their obvious link to religion. Religious beliefs often assert realities and possibilities of experience that are quite foreign to everyday secular experience. In addition, as noted in Chapter 9, religions often encourage such expe-riences in believers (or, at a minimum, urge believers to respect these experiences in others).

Masters and Houston found that under the influence of psychedelic drugs, religious imagery was quite common, even when many participants did not identify themselves as having a "religious" drug experience.[157] For instance, religious architecture was one of the most common images reported, but Masters and Houston claimed that this was more a sense of aesthetic appreciation than a genuine religious interest.[158] Still, the commonality of religious imagery in their sample of 206 subjects is impressive. These data are presented in Table 6.11.

The frequent report of religious imagery is likely to be a function of set and setting, long known to be major determinants of the content of imagery elicited by psychedelic drugs.[159] In light of Sundén's role theory, we would expect that if users possess the appropriate familiarity with religious frames, many drug-facilitated experiences will be felt as religious. It would be naive to claim that such religious experiences are merely drug-specific effects. Rather, the power of psychedelic drugs to facilitate religious experience lies in the extent to which states of consciousness, altered by drugs, are seen as relevant in religious terms. Within U.S. culture, the ironic fact is that mainstream religion sends mixed signals relative to religious experience—often encouraging and validating experiences when these are interpreted as originating in God, but discouraging and invalidating experiences known to be drug-facilitated. The fact that many participants in psychedelic drug studies experience religious imagery and use religious language to describe otherwise secular imagery (for instance, cosmological events) is difficult to assess. Masters and Houston noted that the use of sacramental or religious metaphors was a common practice among their research participants, even though genuine religious experiences may have been rare.[160] Here, the problem is how to judge the genuineness of any experience; obviously verbal reports of religious imagery and religious language are necessary, but not sufficient, criteria for establishing the validity of religious experience.

Grof has argued that the therapeutic use of psychedelic drugs often provides a set and setting that encourage the report of religious and transpersonal experiences.[161] Many of these

TABLE 6.11. Spontaneous Religious Imagery Elicited during
Psychedelic Experiences

Imagery	%
Overall religious imagery of some kind ($n = 206$)	96
Specific religious imagery	
Architecture such as temples, churches	91
Sculpture, paintings, stained-glass windows	43
Symbols such as cross, yin and yang, star of David	34
Mandalas	26
Persons such as Christ, Buddha, and saints	58
Devils and demons	49
Angels	7
Abstract imagery interpreted religiously	
Numinous visions, such as pillars of light, God in the whirlwind	60
Cosmological imagery such as heavenly bodies, galaxies	14
Religious rituals	
Christian, Jewish, and Muslim rites	8
Oriental rites	10
Ancient rites (such as Greek, Egyptian, Mesopotamian)	67
Primitive rites	31

Note. Adapted from Masters and Houston (1966, p. 265). Copyright 1966 by Robert Masters and Jean Houston Masters. Adapted by permission.

are interpreted in terms of Jungian theory, which is particularly favorable to describing religious imagery. Thus, one would expect religious imagery in LSD psychotherapy sessions to be common and to increase if the set and setting are made even more explicitly religious—for instance, by having religious symbols in the therapeutic room. Leary compared the reported LSD experiences of some clients of two different therapists—one who used an explicitly religious context for therapy, and one who did not.[162] These data are presented in Table 6.12. Inspection of the table indicates that whether an experience was interpreted as religious or not was clearly affected by the religious context of the therapy; in addition, therapy within a religious context produced a greater percentage of persons reporting it as the greatest personal experience. Although these results are confounded by other possible differences between the therapists, if we ignore these differences it appears that having a religious context clearly facilitates a religious experience. Research Box 6.7 presents a study in which autobiographical accounts of various experiences, including hallucinogenic drug experiences, were shown to differ reliably in the way they were described.

Although the hostility of mainstream religion to the psychedelic movement is well documented, the irony is that psychedelic drugs have relevance to the range of experiences typically called "religious." It is a mistake not to acknowledge the possibility that drug-facilitated states of consciousness may have ontological validity. Indeed, to identify them as religious is to contextualize and to validate them. However, the mere elicitation of a single experience, however "religious," probably lacks sustaining, life-transforming power if it is not contextualized within some tradition. Roszak has argued that the focus upon specific behaviors or experiences elicited as "religious" can be distorting:

> The temptation, then, is to believe that the behavior which has thus been objectively verified is what religious experience is *really* all about, and—further—that it can be appropriated as an end in itself, plucked like a rare flower from the soil that feeds it. The result is a narrow emphasis on special effects and sensations: "peak experiences," "highs," "flashes" and such. Yet even if one wishes to regard ecstasy as the "peak" of religious experience, that summit does not float in midair. It rests upon tradition and a way of life; one ascends such heights and appreciates their grandeur by a process of initiation that demands learning, commitment, devotion, service, sacrifice. To approach it in any hasty way is like "scaling" Mount Everest by being landed on its top from a helicopter.[163]

TABLE 6.12. LSD Therapy Experience as a Function of Religious Set and Setting

	Percentage of clients saying yes	
	Therapist A, using no religious context ($n = 74$)	Therapist B, using religious context ($n = 96$)
Felt LSD was greatest personal experience	49	85
Felt LSD was a religious experience	32	83
Felt a greater awareness of God, higher power, or ultimate reality	40	90

Note. Adapted from Leary (1964, p. 327).

Research Box 6.7. The Language of Altered States
(Oxman, Rosenberg, Schnurr, Tucker, & Gala, 1988)

Oxman and his colleagues collected 94 autobiographical accounts of personal experiences that fulfilled four criteria: (1) The account was from a published source; (2) the passage was written after an acute episode or important experience; (3) the account was written in English; and (4) the passage was of sufficient length for textual analysis (at least several hundred words). The texts were divided into four categories: 19 schizophrenic experiences; 26 drug-induced hallucinogenic experiences; 21 mystical/ecstatic experiences; and 26 autobiographical controls, identified as personally important experiences. The texts were coded into 83 thematic categories by means of standardized computer programs.[a] The four groups were significantly different in word frequencies in 49 of the 83 lexical categories. More stringent statistical analysis (to minimize Type I errors) yielded differences on 13 variables. Multidimensional scaling of a two-dimensional solution of the correlation matrix for these 13 variables was used to identify the key-word categories that significantly differentiated one group from the other three. Schizophrenic experiences were characterized by an abnormal illness experience associated with a negative self-evaluation. The major word categories for these experiences were "medical" and "deviation." Drug-induced hallucinogenic experiences were characterized by positive, aesthetically experienced visual and auditory phenomena. "Sense" was the major word category differentiating this group. Mystical/ecstatic experiences were characterized by life-altering encounters with God, associated with a sense of power and certitude. The major word categories differentiating these experiences were "ideal value" and "religious." "Economic" was the word category that primarily differentiated autobiographical episodes. When discriminant functional analysis was employed, 84% of the experiences could be correctly identified by their word frequencies. The authors assumed that the actual experiences were different, given that different words were used to describe them.

---

[a]These were the General Inquirer Computer Content Analysis Program and the Harvard-111 Psychosociological Dictionary. See Stone, Dunphy, Smith, and Ogilvie (1966).

Stevens has documented the history of the psychedelic movement and its failure to have psychedelic drugs accepted for sacramental use within a religious frame.[164] In this sense, the psychedelic movement must be judged in terms of cultic and sectarian movements discussed in Chapter 9. However, exceptions include some Native American religions, whose long history of sacramental use of peyote demonstrates that psychedelic substances can be incorporated into sacred frameworks and used to facilitate experiences in which the meaning is truly religious.[165]

The cultural bias against psychedelic drugs not only has affected serious study of these drugs, but has also made it difficult to take a balanced view of the range of their effects.[166] Furthermore, several reviewers have argued that typical double-blind studies are particularly inappropriate ways to investigate psychedelic drugs, especially since subjects who are assigned to the control conditions are likely to be immediately aware of that fact.[167] Many researchers have supported the view that ingestion of psychedelic substances on the part of researchers is a valid (and, some claim, necessary) method of study. Such self-involvement has plagued the history of the psychedelic movement in the United States and promises to fuel future controversies in which research on psychedelic drugs and religion takes on many of the characteristics of religious movements, as discussed in Chapter 9.

OVERVIEW

Religious experience is as varied as the interpretations individuals can bring to their lives. It is less relevant to seek the common elements of religious experiences than to find higher-order abstractions for identifying a class of varied phenomena. The James–Boisen formula that religious experience is a successful resolution of discontent is basic to most faith traditions. However, few studies have placed religious experience within a context to determine its functionality over time. The particulars of discontents and resolutions are provided by Sundén's role theory, which not only allows tradition, text, and practice to model appropriate perceptions and interpretations to facilitate religious experiences within a faith tradition, but also permits the longitudinal studies needed for true tests of the James–Boisen formula.

Common religious practices, such as prayer and meditation, have been studied in terms of the physiological correlates and subjective contents of these experiences. Speculations as to the neurophysiology of dramatic religious experiences, such as glossolalia and hallucinations, demand additional empirical investigation. Dynamic theories illuminating the processes involved in determining the content of hallucinations have been tested and promise to foster both controversy and additional research.

Imagery has returned as a focus of study, with new psychological orientations offering interpretations sympathetic to various faith traditions concerned with the reality of images. Psychedelic drugs remain of interest, despite legal impediments in the United States to research involving them. The fact that religious imagery can be facilitated by psychedelic drugs, in the appropriate set and setting, assures the continued relevance for the psychology of religion of techniques used to alter states of consciousness.

NOTES

1. Maslow (1964, p. 19).
2. Lewis (1971, p. 11).
3. Quoted in Volinn (1985, p. 151).
4. Quoted in Maxwell and Tschudin (1990, p. 167, subject #4465).
5. Goodman (1988).
6. Leech (1985).
7. James (1902/1985).
8. James (1902/1985, p. 34). Emphasis in original.
9. Hong (1995).
10. James (1902/1985, p. 39).
11. Formerly the Religious Experience Research Unit of Manchester College, Oxford.
12. Chapter 7 of this text discusses one specific question used by Hardy and the extent to which it elicits reports of mystical or numinous experiences.
13. Hardy (1979, pp. 25–29).
14. Leech (1985).
15. Wittgenstein (1953).
16. Spilka and McIntosh (1995).
17. See Ahern (1990); Hardy (1966); Hay (1987); Laski (1961); Maxwell and Tschudin (1990); Robinson (1983).

18. Lupfer, Brock, and DePaola (1992); Lupfer, DePaola, Brock, and Clement (1994).
19. Spilka and McIntosh (1995).
20. Hood (1995a).
21. Rosenau (1992); Roth (1987).
22. Boisen (1936, 1960).
23. See Corssan (1975); Johnson (1974).
24. Bowker (1973).
25. Sundén's work is largely untranslated into English. However, authoritative summaries and use of his theory are readily available. See Holm (1995); Holm and Belzen (1995).
26. Kimbrough (1995).
27. Hood and Kimbrough (1995).
28. Lippy (1994, p. 79).
29. Williamson (1995).
30. Hood and Kimbrough (1995).
31. Tellegen, Gerrard, and Butcher (1969).
32. Crooks (1913).
33. Starbuck (1904).
34. McGuire (1990, 284).
35. McGuire (1990, p. 285).
36. James (1902/1985, p. 20).
37. Hill (1995, p. 355).
38. Schachter (1964, 1971).
39. Proudfoot (1985).
40. Proudfoot (1985, pp. 98–102).
41. Schachter and Singer (1962).
42. See Kemper (1978); Marlasch (1979); Plutchik and Ax (1967).
43. Lazarus (1990).
44. Preston (1988).
45. Naranjo and Ornstein (1971, p. 7).
46. James (1902/1985).
47. Kasamatsu and Hirai (1969).
48. Maupin (1965).
49. Anand, Chhina, and Singh (1961).
50. Kasamatsu and Hirai (1969, p. 495).
51. Bagchi and Wenger (1957).
52. Wikstrom (1987, p. 390).
53. See van der Lans (1985, 1987).
54. Holmes (1980).
55. Deikman (1966).
56. Wulff (1995).
57. See Goleman (1977, 1988).
58. Naranjo and Ornstein (1971).
59. Wulff (1995, p. 197).
60. Reed (1974).
61. Zusne and Jones (1989).
62. Greenwood (1995).
63. See Tart (1969, 1975b).
64. Zinberg (1977).
65. Tart (1975a).
66. Fischer (1971, 1978).
67. See Segalowitz (1983); Springer and Deutsch (1981).
68. Ornstein (1986).
69. Ornstein (1986).
70. Kolb and Whishaw (1990, p. 3).
71. H. Gardner (1978).
72. Jaynes (1976).
73. Jaynes (1976, pp. 100–125).
74. Jaynes (1976, p. 118).
75. May (1956).

76. Jaynes (1976, p. 360).
77. Jaynes (1976, pp. 361–378).
78. Samarin (1972).
79. Lafal, Monahan, and Richman (1974).
80. Hutch (1980).
81. See Kelsey (1964); Kildahl (1972).
82. See Goodman (1972); Hine (1969); Malony and Lovekin (1985); J. T. Richardson (1973).
83. Lovekin and Malony (1977).
84. Goodman (1969).
85. Goodman (1972).
86. Goodman (1988, pp. 37–39).
87. Quoted in Goodman (1988, p. 37).
88. Samarin (1972).
89. Hine (1969).
90. Williamson (1995).
91. Hood and Kimbrough (1995).
92. Holt (1964).
93. Bergin (1964).
94. LaBarre (1972b).
95. Fischer (1969).
96. Al-Issa (1977).
97. See Clark (1983); Larsen (1976); Pelletier and Garfield (1976).
98. Volken (1961, p. 10).
99. Carroll (1986).
100. Perry and Echeverría (1988).
101. Warner (1976).
102. Perry and Echeverría (1988).
103. Carroll (1983, especially pp. 217–219).
104. Carroll (1983; 1986, Chap. 6).
105. Walsh (1906).
106. See Carroll (1986, pp. 225–226) for a listing of these apparitions.
107. Shafranske (1995).
108. Carroll (1986, p. 145).
109. Carroll (1986, p. 145): $p = .005$ using Fisher's exact test (one-tailed), phi = .35. Strictly speaking, this test was not appropriate, as the cases were probably not independent; later apparitions were probably influenced by earlier ones. Carroll acknowledges this problem (p. 145).
110. See Bettelheim (1976); Klinger (1971); Singer (1966); Watkins (1976).
111. See Beit-Hallahmi (1995); Greenwood (1995); Halligan (1995).
112. Pylyshyn (1973, p. 2).
113. Shephard (1978).
114. Lilly (1977).
115. See Lilly (1977); Zubeck (1969).
116. LaBarre (1972a, p. 265). Emphases in original.
117. Zubeck (1969).
118. See Lilly (1956, 1977); Lilly and Lilly (1976); Suedfeld (1975).
119. Suedfeld and Vernon (1964).
120. See Jackson and Kelly (1962); Rossi, Sturrock, and Solomon (1963).
121. Masters and Houston (1973).
122. Goodman (1990).
123. Heiler (1932).
124. Janssen, de Hart, and den Draak (1990, p. 99).
125. Galton (1869).
126. See Godin (1968, 1985).
127. See Poloma and Gallup (1991); Poloma and Pendleton (1989).
128. Poloma and Pendleton (1991b).
129. Poloma and Pendleton (1989, pp. 50–51).
130. See Hood (1983).
131. See Brown (1966, 1968).
132. Loehr (1959).

133. Poloma and Pendleton (1989, p. 43).
134. Hood, Morris, and Watson (1989). A difficult methodological confound is that measures of contemplative or meditative prayer overlap conceptually with assessments of unity. Thus positive correlations between such measures are partly "built in" conceptually.
135. Brown (1994, pp. 45–46).
136. Allegro (1971).
137. Wasson (1969).
138. Kramrisch, Otto, Ruck, and Wasson (1986).
139. Wasson, Hofmann, and Ruck (1978).
140. Rätsch (1990, p. 2).
141. Lukoff, Zanger, and Lu (1990).
142. Aarson and Osmond (1970).
143. Dobkin de Rios (1984).
144. Barber (1970).
145. Masters and Houston (1966).
146. Lukoff et al. (1990).
147. Leuba (1896).
148. Zaehner (1972).
149. Weil (1986).
150. See Aarson and Osmond (1970); Wells and Triplett (1992).
151. Brown (1972).
152. Stevens (1987).
153. Barber (1970).
154. Barr, Langs, Holt, Goldberger, and Klein (1972).
155. Stevens (1987).
156. Durr (1970).
157. Masters and Houston (1966, p. 265).
158. Masters and Houston (1966, pp. 265–266).
159. Barr et al. (1972); Barber (1970).
160. Masters and Houston (1966, p. 260).
161. Grof (1980).
162. Leary (1964).
163. Roszack (1975, p. 50). Emphasis in original.
164. Stevens (1987).
165. See Bergman (1971); LaBarre (1969).
166. Walsh (1982).
167. See Bakalar and Grinspoon (1989); Yensen (1990).

Chapter 7

MYSTICISM

> "Since we cannot change reality, let us change the eyes which see reality," says one of my favorite Byzantine mystics.[1]

> Confirmation of the genuineness of mystical experience is to be found in the high degree of unanimity observable in the attempts to describe its nature.[2]

> This problem of the secularized interpretation of amorphous mystical experiences has been raised repeatedly since the Enlightenment.[3]

> Out of my experience . . . one fixed conclusion dogmatically emerges . . . there is a continuum of cosmic consciousness, against which our individuality builds but accidental fences, and into which our several minds plunge as into a mother-sea or reservoir.[4]

> Nowhere are religions closer than in mysticism, where experience takes over from formal statement and communal organization.[5]

The focus upon mysticism in this chapter highlights the central role that mystical experience has occupied in conceptual discussions of religion in the 20th century. The claims of mystics dominate contemporary discussions concerned with the evidential value of religious experience. "Evidential force" and "evidential value" are the phrases most often linked to debates as to whether or not religious experiences such as mysticism provide sufficient grounds for asserting the truth of various religious beliefs.[6] For some, mysticism is simply a delusional belief that a person has united with God or has experienced ultimate reality. For others, mysticism is an experience that provides sufficient warrant for belief in God or ultimate reality. As Katz notes, those who assert the evidential force of mystical experience provide an ecumenical umbrella under which diverse religious claims can be sheltered as but different expressions of one fundamental truth.[7] This avoids the embarrassing particulars of religious experiences that, like the particulars of religious belief expressed in dogmatic terms, tend to separate one faith from another.[8] Although as social scientists we need not address theological or philosophical debates directly, our methods and analyses will inevitably have philosophical and religious implications. As Jones has noted, though science and religion are not identical, neither can they be categorically separated or viewed as mutually exclusive orientations.[9] Our confrontation with the conceptual issues debated by both philosophers and theologians will give us a framework to organize and guide our review of the empirical research.

CONCEPTUAL ISSUES IN THE STUDY OF MYSTICISM

The theological and philosophical literature on mysticism is extensive.[10] Our concern as social scientists is restricted to the aspects of these literatures that have direct relevance for empirical research. Of immediate concern is the clarification of the nature of mystical experience, as well as of its relationships to other forms of religious experience.

Thorner,[11] following the work of the philosopher Kaufman,[12] contrasts mystical and prophetic experiences. He first notes that persons having any religious experience believe three things: (1) Their experience is different from everyday, normal experience; (2) the experience is more important than everyday experiences; and (3) the perceptual referents are not simply to be found in the discrete aspects of the empirical world.[13] These claims are consistent with our analysis of the wide variety of religious experiences discussed in Chapter 6. However, the third point raises serious problems. How are social scientists to respond to a claim that refuses to locate the perceptual referents of experience within discrete aspects of the empirical world? Within the conceptual literature on religion, scholars have focused upon numinous and mystical experiences as the most likely candidates for revealing a transcendent dimension to human experience. Social scientists have concurred, noting that the numinous and the mystical are empirically the most common claims of those who assert that they have experienced a transcendent reality, however conceived. Social scientists differ widely in their own claims to have identified the true perceptual referents in such experiences. However, most also share the belief that the true perceptual referents need not include reference to God or an ultimate reality, and hence attempt to explain the transcendent in purely scientific terms.

Thorner notes that the claim of the mystic is that the perceptual referent in religious experience is a unity within the world. This unity is not linked to any one perceptual object; instead, all objects are unified into a perception of totality or oneness. However, the mystical experience of a unity within the world as emphasized by Thorner is but one form of mysticism. Following Stace,[14] we refer to this as "extrovertive mysticism." We contrast extrovertive mysticism with another form, "introvertive mysticism." This is an experience of unity devoid of perceptual objects. It is literally an experience of "no-thing-ness." Perceptual objects disappear, and a pure consciousness devoid of content is reported. Forman has referred to this as "pure conscious experience."[15] What is important for now is that only extrovertive mysticism has as its perceptual referent a unity that transcends individual, discrete objects of perception. There are discrete objects of perception, but they are all seen unified in their particularity as nevertheless one. The unity in extrovertive mysticism is with the totality of objects of perception; the unity in introvertive mysticism is with a pure consciousness devoid of objects of perception. Stace has suggested that the extrovertive form is a less developed mysticism, perhaps preparatory to introvertive mysticism.[16] Forman argues that extrovertive mysticism is a higher form of mysticism, for which introvertive mysticism is only preparatory.[17] Hood has argued that extrovertive mysticism is likely to follow upon introvertive mystical experience, but does not claim it to be a "higher" experience.[18] The conceptual arguments as to whether they are two separate mysticisms has important consequences for empirical research. As we shall see, if introvertive and extrovertive mysticism can be measured, the relationship between the two can be studied as an empirical issue. Yet whether the experience of unity is introvertive or extrovertive, it is this experience that, by scholarly consensus, uniquely characterizes mysticism.[19]

Many scholars have contrasted prophetic or numinous experience with mystical experience. A numinous experience is an awareness of a "holy other" beyond nature, with which or whom one is felt to be in communion. More typically, this experience is identified with the classic work of Otto, whose phenomenological analysis illuminates the human response to the transcendent.[20] For Otto, the essential fact of religious experience includes a non-rational component that is psychologically characterized by a numinous consciousness. The term "numinous" is based upon the Latin word *numen,* denoting a power implicit in a sacred object. It is the object that elicits a response from the subject. Thus religion, as Hick has also argued,[21] is a response to the transcendent. Social scientists can study this response, noting that from the believer's perspective it is a response to a transcendent object experienced as real. Numinous experiences identify a personal transcendent object, often referred to as God or Allah or Yahweh. Obviously, religious traditions assert the reality of this object, refusing to identify it merely with empirical realities described by the scientist. Hood refers to the transcendent object as the "foundational reality" of a faith tradition.[22]

The numinous consciousness is both compelled to seek out and explore this transcendent object (*mysterium fascinans*), and to be repelled in the face of the majesty and awfulness of this object, in whose presence one's own "creatureness" is accentuated (*mysterium tremendum*). Efforts to rationally confront the feelings of *tremendum* are articulated in personal conceptualizations of a holy other such as God or Allah or Yahweh. The *fascinans* is explicated in rational concepts such as grace, in which the inadequacy of personal analogies to conceptualize the holy other is revealed. The *fascinans* thus has a mystical element, insofar as the personal analogue revealed in the *tremendum* is found to be inadequate and an impersonal language is sought to describe it. Not surprisingly, Stace's categories of "introvertive mysticism" and "extrovertive mysticism" are derived from Otto's "mysticism of introspection" and "unifying vision," respectively.[23] Thus, although it is possible to separate the numinous and the mystical as two poles of religious experience, they are ultimately united. Mystical experiences of unity (variously expressed) can be numinous as well, eliciting the *mysterium fascinans* when the object is experienced in impersonal terms and the *mysterium tremendum* when the object is experienced in personal terms. Hick has articulated this duality as the *personae* and *impersonae* of "the Real."[24] Hood has emphasized that William James accepted both impersonal (the absolute) and personal (God) interpretations as compatible with the facts of mystical experience.[25] Hood has also emphasized the numinous and the mystical as two interrelated ways of experiencing foundational reality. [26] As we shall see, empirical studies use measurements that tend to emphasize experiences of either a sense of presence (favoring numinous experiences) or a sense of unity (favoring mystical experiences).

The focus upon the numinous and the mystical as two poles of religion is important, in that it links the empirical studies of mysticism to current theological and philosophical considerations of mysticism. Much as modern physics employs both wave and particle conceptualizations of light, Hick argues that what he simply refers to as "the Real" can be either personal or impersonal.[27] Similarly, Smart has argued that although the numinous and the mystical must be carefully conceptually distinguished, they are incorporated into a single unifying doctrine in some religions traditions.[28] Elsewhere, Smart has noted that "nature mysticism," the extrovertive experience of unity in nature, is in fact a numinous experience.[29] This parallels Stace's view that extrovertive mystical experiences incorporate an awareness of an inner subjectivity to all that is perceived.[30] Likewise, Stace has emphasized that the category of "the holy" applies to both introvertive and extrovertive mystical experiences, and most probably accounts for their religious quality.[31] Thus, for conceptual purposes we can separate the numinous and the mystical according to whether the personal or impersonal aspects of foundational reality are emphasized. Mysticism tends toward the impersonal; the

numinous tends toward the personal. As we shall soon note, measurement studies can identify both numinous and mystical experiences on the basis of whether one experiences a sense
of presence (numinous experience) or a sense of unity (mystical experience).

For purposes of this chapter, we refer to mystical experiences either as "mystical experiences proper" when experiences of unity are emphasized, or as "numinous experiences"
when a sense of a holy other's presence is emphasized. That both components are properly
mystical has been briefly noted above and extensively argued by Hood.[32] Their importance
is that from a social-psychological perspective, they are part of what religions defend as the
experience of the sacred. Hood has argued that the human response to the transcendent is
most effectively analyzed in light of the possibility that the response is at least potentially a
response to that which is real.[33] Empirically, reports of transcendent experiences include the
belief in the reality of transcendent objects. It may also be true that the belief in their reality
is necessary for the experience to occur. Thus, although social scientists cannot confirm any
transcendent realities, they can construct theories compatible with claims of the existence
of such realities. Hodges has argued that the scientific taboo against the supernatural can be
broken as long as hypotheses about the supernatural can be shown to have empirical consequences.[34] In Garrett's phrase, the "troublesome transcendent" must be confronted by social
scientists as much as by theologians and philosophers.[35]

There is no reason why scientists cannot include specific hypotheses derived from views
about the nature of transcendent reality in empirical studies of religious experience, as long
as specific empirical predictions can be made. The source of the predictions may reference
even the unobservable and the intangible. All that is required is that there be identifiable
empirical consequences. As Jones has stated the case, "Invoking Occam's Razor to disallow
reference to factors other than sensory observable ones is question begging in favor of one
metaphysics building up an ontology with material objects as basic."[36] Jones echoes the classic
claim of William James[37] that mystics base their experience upon the same sort of processes
that all empiricists do—direct experience. Although James would restrict the authoritative
value of mystical experience to the person who had the experience, foundational realities are
the shared basis of faith; this suggests that many share such experiences or that some are
united in the belief that such experiences are real, even if they personally have not had them.
Thus, as Swinburne argues, mystical experience is also authoritative for others:

> . . . if it seems to me I have a glimpse of Nirvana, or a vision of God, that is good grounds for me
> to suppose that I do. And, more generally, the occurrence of religious experience is prima facie
> reason for all to believe in that of which the experience was purportedly an experience.[38]

What makes numinous and mystical experiences so important to study is that they are
the strongest claims that people can experience foundational realities. Social scientists are
often too quick to boast that their own limited empirical data undermine ontological claims.
Whether we use Hick's term "the Real" or Hood's phrase "foundational reality," the point
is that religious traditions cannot be adequately understood without the assumption that transcendent objects of experience are believed to be real by those who experience them. It is also
possible that not only are they believed to be real, but also that they are in fact real. Presup-
posing a totally reductionistic interpretation of the objects of religious experience is less persuasive than was once thought. Bowker, after critically reviewing social-scientific theories of
the sense of God, has noted that it is an empirical option to conclude that at least part of the
sense of God may come from God.[39] In our terms, religious views of the nature of the Real

suggest ways in which it can be expressed in human experience. This can work in two directions, both deductively and inductively. Deductively, we can note that if the Real is conceived to be a particular way, then certain experiences of the Real can be expected to follow. Thus we anticipate that expectations play a significant role in religious experience, often confirming the foundational realities of one's faith tradition. Inductively, we can infer that if particular experiences occur, then the possibility that the Real exists is a reasonable inference—a position forcefully argued by Berger.[40] Thus we can anticipate that experiences, some of which are unanticipated, may lead some to seek religions for their illumination. O'Brien has gone so far as to include in his criteria for a mystical experience that it must be unexpected.[41] Religious traditions adopt both options in confronting mystical and numinous experiences.

Not surprisingly, then, these experiences have long been the focus of empirical research and provocative theorizing among both sociologists and psychologists. We first explore classic efforts to confront these experiences. These classic views are of more than historical interest, as they set forth the various conceptual issues that continue to plague the contemporary empirical study of mysticism. Our focus upon classic views is not exhaustive; we focus upon representatives of three major social-scientific views regarding mystical experience. These are as follows:

1. *Mysticism as erroneous attribution.* Mystics attribute to transcendence objects and processes that can in fact be explained in social-scientific terms. These processes have been variously identified as physiological, psychological, or sociological. The misattribution is to assume that something more is involved in such experiences. Most commonly the "more" is believed to be something transcendent, including, in cases of personal mysticism, God, Allah, or Yahweh.

2. *Mysticism as heightened awareness.* Mysticism is an awareness of ultimate reality that occurs with heightened or altered awareness. This awareness may be cultivated or may occur spontaneously. The awareness may be variously interpreted, or the interpretations may reflect different reality claims. Although social-scientific processes can be identified that permit the experience of transcendence to occur, they need not deny genuine ontological status to the object of transcendence. In simple terms, both the mystical experience and its object are real in the terms of which they are experienced.

3. *Mysticism as evolved consciousness.* Mysticism is the most evolved form of consciousness. It is variously interpreted to be potentially common to all humans or to currently characterize only some humans (a few advanced or "evolved" persons). Typically, this form of consciousness is interpreted in purely natural scientific terms. The transcendent is merely the naturally evolved form of consciousness.

REPRESENTATIVE CLASSIC VIEWS OF MYSTICISM

Mysticism as Erroneous Attribution

Preus has emphasized that the classic social-scientific theorists of religion, with only a few exceptions, had little doubt that they could provide genuine explanations of religion.[42] Such explanations purported to replace religious attributions with purely secular claims to processes involved in mystical experience as illuminated by science. Furthermore, it was commonly assumed that once the social sciences illuminated the true nature of religious experience, then religious claims based upon such experiences would lose much of their persuasive force.

The early psychologists of religion could not help confronting mysticism in light of this assumption. The mystical claim to have experienced God could not be uncritically accepted by psychologists. Much of the scientific validity of psychology was seen to rest upon its ability to provide scientific explanations for spiritual and religious claims. Thus, despite the fact that in the popular mind psychology was seen as a spiritual discipline, most psychologists saw the public interest in spiritual matters as a way to help develop the science of psychology, if psychology could explain the spiritual in natural scientific terms.[43] In *The Psychology of Religious Mysticism*, Leuba provided one of the earliest physiological theories of mysticism.[44] Considerably less sympathetic to religion than James, Leuba insisted that mystical experience can be explained in physiological terms. He also insisted that no transcendental object is necessary for mystical or numinous experience, and that only physiological processes and a natural-scientific framework can illuminate these experiences. He was one of the first psychologists to argue forcefully that mystical experience provides no evidential force for religious beliefs. Mystics do not encounter God in their experience, Leuba claimed; instead, mystics use their beliefs to interpret their experience, ultimately erroneously. His now-classic study of mysticism was echoed in the general French tradition of the emerging discipline of psychiatry, in which mental states—including many religious ones interpreted by those who experienced them—were understood in terms of their origins in physiological and psychological processes often deemed pathological. Charcot, who was part of this French tradition, heavily influenced Freud, whose attitude toward religion was complex but ultimately unsympathetic.

In *The Future of an Illusion*, Freud argued that religious *beliefs* are illusory—the products of wishes rather than responses to the reality of the world.[45] Later, he responded to a criticism of the Nobel laureate Romain Rolland that he had focused only upon religious beliefs and had underestimated the value of religious *experience*. Rolland found the essence of religion in what he termed the "oceanic feeling," a state of unity with the world (mysticism); Rolland claimed validity for this feeling, independent of Freud's devastating challenge to religious beliefs. Freud's response, in *Civilization and Its Discontents*, was that this feeling is not originally religious but only later becomes attached to religious beliefs.[46] The actual "oceanic feeling" is but a recollection of an infantile state, perhaps of unity with the mother. Mysticism is thus a regression to an earlier infantile state. Thus, mystical experience does not provide evidence for unity with the world or even of God; it is simply a feeling attached to religious beliefs that God exists and can be experienced. The religious beliefs themselves are not simply illusional but delusional as well. Religion is thus a double error: an erroneous belief in the existence of a God, and the erroneous interpretation of regressive experiences as evidence of union with God. Thus, Freud was one of the first theorists to argue that there is no essential relationship between mystical experience and religious beliefs.[47]

Leuba and Freud represent examples of genuine explanations of mysticism, if one assumes that the experience is capable of being reductively explained by either physiological processes (Leuba) or psychological processes (Freud). Basic to both views is that persons who believe they have confronted or merged with transcendent objects are wrong. Similar arguments have been made by sociologists. For instance, Durkheim argued for mystical experience as the apprehension of the dependence of individuals upon a transcendent object; however, that object is society, not a divine being or reality.[48] The genuine experience of being part of a larger unity is correct, but a misattribution applies this to God instead of its real origin, society. Thus, any theory that claims to explain experiences of union with the Real by processes identified at the physiological, psychological, or social level must claim to explain mysticism by misattribution. A corollary is that when individuals realize the true source of their experience of union, the religious quality (in terms of transcendent claims) will disappear.

These classic theories set the tone for modern studies of mysticism. Inherent in their views is that mystical experiences offer no ontological proof for religious belief, and assuredly no proof that one has experienced union with God. Although they may be acted upon as authoritative by those who have them, insofar as they are misattributions, the individual who so acts risks being defined as delusional or pathological. The authoritative basis of the experience for the individual who has it may be susceptible to destructive analyses by experts, in which the experience itself is demonstrated to be attributable to processes more appropriately identified by social scientists, whether they are physiologists, psychologists, or sociologists.

Mysticism as Heightened Awareness

Although most early social scientists reveled in the apparent power of psychology to explain religion in general and mystical experiences in particular, William James best represented the paradoxical position of the emerging science of psychology. Hood has traced the efforts of James to avoid religious concepts, such as the soul, in developing psychology as a natural science.[49] In *The Principles of Psychology*, James saw no need for the concept of a soul or for any transcendent dimension to human consciousness; however, in *The Varieties of Religious Experience*, James noted that the facts of mystical experience require a wider dimension to human consciousness.[50] He favored Myers's notion of a subconscious,[51] in which, James argued, a wider self may emerge. Furthermore, he argued that this natural process may be one in which the human self merges with God. Thus, although the empirical facts cannot prove the existence of a God, mystical experience provides the basic experiential fact from which God as a genuine "overbelief" to explain the process is a viable hypothesis. Mystical experiences thus have reasonable evidential force, in James's view.

James's views created much controversy among early psychologists, who were anxious to separate psychology from religious views associated with the science in the popular mind. But, as Hood has shown, James's insistence that mystical experiences are valid forms of human experience—incapable of being reductionistically explained by either physiological or psychological processes—provided a counter to the emerging natural-scientific and psychoanalytic psychologies, which denied the possibility that religious experiences may have a truly transcendent dimension.[52] James's view was simply that in numinous and mystical experiences one may encounter God, regardless of the processes identified by the scientists as operating during the experience. In the terms used previously, science cannot rule out that a mystical or numinous experience is an experience of the Real or of a foundational reality that may be necessary for the experience to occur. At a minimum, the *belief* in the reality must be there. As James stated in his notes for his lectures on mysticism in *The Varieties*, "Remember, the whole point lies in really *believing* that through a certain point or part in you you coalesce and are identical with the Eternal."[53]

Mysticism as Evolved Consciousness

Evolutionary theory has been a continuing influence on psychology since its inception. Mysticism has been proposed by some as a form of consciousness that is evolving, much as consciousness has evolved from the nonreflective consciousness that characterizes animals to the reflective consciousness that characterizes people. Not only are persons aware, but they are also aware that they are aware. They can reflect upon their awareness. Bucke is most closely identified with the theory that following upon reflexive awareness in the evolution of consciousness is a cosmic consciousness or mystical state of awareness of unity with the world.[54] He documented the increased presence of individuals over time whom he saw as examples of persons expressing this cosmic consciousness. Basic to his theory is the notion that cosmic consciousness is evolving in the human species and becoming more frequent (although by citing as exemplars of mystics such persons as Buddha and Christ, Bucke made the absolute frequency of mystical experience quite rare in any population). Nevertheless, as opposed to theorists who described mysticism as pathological or as a union with a religiously defined transcendent object, Bucke saw cosmic consciousness as the natural, advanced form of consciousness toward which the human species is moving. As consciousness evolves, it evolves into a mystical consciousness. The philosopher Bergson gave the major impetus to evolutionary theories of mysticism by identifying mystical experience with the direct awareness of the evolutionary process itself (*élan vital*), which he saw as the basis of all life. Kolakowski has argued that sociological studies of mysticism both support and are compatible with Bergson's linking of mystical experience and his *élan vital*.[55]

Alister Hardy proposed a similar theory of evolution, in which a cosmic consciousness is gradually emerging within the human species as a whole and is providing a thoroughly naturalistic basis for mystical experiences that were previously interpreted in religious terms.[56] Unlike Bucke, Hardy assumed that mystical states are common. Late in his life, after his retirement from a career in zoology, Hardy began soliciting reports of religious experiences and initiated efforts to provide a classification system of them. We have discussed his empirical work in Chapter 6, and discuss it further in the section on survey research below.

Jung, who was perhaps the most mystical of the dynamic theorists, offered a different twist to evolutionary theories of mysticism.[57] Indeed, many have claimed that Jung's entire psychology is inherently mystical. For our purposes, it is sufficient to note that in terms of evolution, Jung's theory assumes that archetypes are evolutionarily based tendencies to experience the world in particular ways. When imagined, experience is archetypal and has a numinous sense.[58] The archetypes are collectively shared as profound religious symbols, inherent in the human psyche. Thus, followers of Jung expect numinous experiences to occur in everyone, whether or not these are expressed in religious language. In Catholicism the symbols are objectively protected and identified; in Protestantism the symbols are allowed to emerge outside of institutional controls.[59] Yet, even when these experiences occur in dreams outside of religious interpretations, as normal processes inherent in the human psyche, only the absence of their report is problematic. Jung had these words carved in the arch to his home: *Vocatus atque non vocatus deus aderit.* The phrase has been variously translated, but a good English rendering is "Whether called or not, God will be present."

From our brief consideration of the conceptual issues involved in the study of mysticism, as well as the three classic theories of mysticism, four key issues can be identified that have significant empirical consequences:

1. How is mysticism to be operationalized and measured? Clearly, the way in which mysticism is measured brings with it the conceptual consequences that have been well dis-

cussed in the scholarly literature. It is unlikely that any empirical measure can avoid serious conceptual criticism, given the controversies that dominate this literature.

2. What empirical relationships exist between mystical experience and its interpretation? How does language affect experience? The conceptual literature ranges from the claim that mystical experiences are identical despite different interpretations (the unity thesis) to the claim that differences in descriptions of experience constitute different experiences (the plurality thesis).

3. What kind of persons report mystical experiences? Do such experiences occur across the developmental spectrum? Are they characteristic of the healthy or of the sick? Do they occur only among the religiously committed?

4. What triggers such experiences? Can they be facilitated, or do they occur only spontaneously? Is an experience affected by how it is produced? For instance, are experiences reported under drugs possibly the same as those reported during prayer?

These four issues are central to the conceptual literature on mysticism and have generated extensive discussion. Much of this discussion is quite philosophically and theologically sophisticated. However, our task in the remainder of this chapter is to focus on the empirical literature. As we shall see, many of the issues raised in the conceptual literature are paralleled in the empirical literature. By interrelating these two, we hope to contribute to what McGinn has termed the "unrealized conversation" between social-scientific investigators and those involved in the history and theory of mystical traditions.[60]

THE EMPIRICAL STUDY OF MYSTICISM

Central to any empirical study of mysticism is measurement based upon operationalized terms. There are almost as many definitions of "mysticism" as there are theorists. At the end of the 19th century, Inge evaluated at least 26 definitions of it and concluded that no word in the English language had been employed more loosely.[61] Not surprisingly, much of the current conceptual literature on mysticism debates various definitions and classifications of mysticism—often, obviously, on the basis of prior theological or religious commitments. For instance, Zaehner has argued for a clear distinction between "theistic mysticism" and other forms of mysticism, primarily on theological grounds.[62] Likewise, in an often-cited example, the renowned Jewish scholar Buber referred to his own experience of an "undivided unity," which he had thought to be union with God but later felt to be an inappropriate interpretation.[63] In a similar vein, James refused to give serious consideration to the considerably refined classification systems of mystical states associated with the Catholic mystical tradition, believing them to be primarily driven by theological considerations unrelated to actual experience.[64] Finally, the Protestant theologian Ritschl claimed that neo-Platonism had so influenced the history of mysticism that it had become the theoretical norm for mystical experience, and that the universal being viewed as God by mystics is a "cheat."[65]

From this sampling of views, it is clear that any definition of mysticism is likely to encounter conceptual criticism. However, at the empirical level it is clear that the distinction between experience and its interpretation and/or evaluation carries some weight. Thus, even in the case of Buber cited above, an experience of unity can be identified, regardless of how it is interpreted. The measurement of mysticism is possible once some operational indicator is identified. There is considerable agreement that an experience of unity is central to mystical experience. Indeed, debates on mysticism often center on precisely how this unity is to be interpreted. Accordingly, measurements of mysticism identifying an experience of unity that is variously interpreted are quite congruent with the conceptual literature. As we note later in this chapter, Hood has developed just such a measure.[66]

Whereas unity is agreed to characterize mysticism proper, we have noted above that numinous experiences focus more upon a fascinating and awe-inspiring sense of presence. Again, theological traditions determine how this presence is identified. In social-psychological terms, expectations determine interpretations of experiences (and, as we shall see, perhaps the nature of the experience itself). The measurement of a sense of presence is another indicator of mystical states, one that has been operationalized in a measure derived from the work of William James—the Religious Experience Episodes Measure (REEM).[67] We also discuss this measure later in this chapter. However, more sociologically oriented social psychologists utilize survey data; this necessitates limited numbers of questions, which can be answered via phone surveys or interviews. Thus, on the sociological side, both numinous and mystical experiences have been measured by a limited number of questions that have been repeatedly used across a variety of survey studies. These too must be noted. Finally, several investigators have simply asked respondents to reply to a single item they believe to tap mystical experiences.

In summary, there are three major ways in which mysticism has been operationalized and measured in empirical research:

1. Open-ended responses to specific questions intuitively assumed to tap mystical or numinous experiences. These responses may then be variously coded or categorized.

2. Questions devised for use in survey research. Of necessity, these questions are brief, limited in number, and worded in language easily understandable for use in random surveys of the general population.

3. Specific scales to measure mysticism, including (a) a numinous sense of presence, and (b) a mystical experience of unity.

As we shall see, how mysticism is operationalized and measured is related to the kinds of data provided to answer the various key issues in mysticism noted above. Accordingly, we discuss empirical studies in terms of the predominant operational and measurement strategies employed.

Studies Using Open-Ended Responses to Assess Mystical Experiences

Laski's Research

One of the more curious mainstream references in the empirical study of mysticism is Laski's research on ecstasy[68]—curious because of its severe methodological inadequacies. Laski, a novelist untrained in the social sciences, became interested in whether or not the experience of ecstasy she had written about in a novel was experienced in modern life. Initially using a convenience sample of friends and acquaintances sampled over a period of 3 years, Laski essentially asked persons to respond in an interview to the primary question: "Do you know a sensation of transcendent ecstasy?"[69] If she was asked to explain what was meant by "transcendent ecstasy," Laski told her respondents to "Take it to mean what you think it means."[70] It took only 63 persons to produce 60 affirmative responses, perhaps because of the highly educated and literary nature of Laski's friends (20 of the 63 identified themselves as writers). Laski's own belief was that transcendent ecstasy is most likely to be related to a family of terms that includes "mysticism," "oceanic feeling," and "cosmic consciousness."[71] However, an attempt to replicate her interview results with a sample distributed through mailboxes to 100 homes in a working-class area of London resulted in only 11 returns, with only 1 of these responses answering affirmatively the reworded question: "Have you ever had a feeling of unearthly ecstasy?"[72] We need only note here that different methods with different samples radically alter the nature of data one may collect!

Thus Laski's text primarily analyzed responses obtained from her original 60 interviews and from comparisons to 27 literary and 24 religious excerpts from published texts (selected for their intuitive demonstration of ecstatic experiences similar to those reported by the interview group). Her work consisted of an extensive discussion of various means of classifying and identifying the nature of these experiences, primarily in terms of the language used to describe them. Laski's own limited data-analyzing skills were balanced by her perceptive analysis of language. The citations of the primary texts and interviews make it easy for the reader to judge the value of Laski's own analyses. Her conclusions raise several issues that have been the focus of additional more rigorous studies, to be discussed below.

Among Laski's conclusions is that transcendent ecstasy is a subset of mystical experience, defined and demarcated by the language used to describe it. It can be of three subtypes: experience of knowledge, of union, or of purification and renewal. It is transient, and is triggered or elicited by a wide variety of circumstances and contexts. Generally, it is pleasurable and has beneficial consequences; however, it need not have unique religious value or provide evidential force for the validity of religious beliefs. Laski herself preferred to interpret transcendent ecstasy as a purely human capacity to experience joy in one's own creativity; she believed that in both the past and the present, those who believe they have experienced God are indeed mistaken.[73]

Social scientists continue to cite Laski's work less for its methodological rigor than for its powerful description and analysis of instances of mystical experience. The assumption of many that mysticism is a rare phenomenon, characteristic of only a few, is belied by Laski's work. Her examples ring true to many persons' experiences, as we shall see. Furthermore, her interview procedures and willingness to use the participants' own terms and language to analyze experiences have parallels in modern phenomenological research.[74]

Pafford's Research

One of Laski's contributions was to identify mystical experiences among adolescents. In her interview sample, there were two girls aged 14 and 16, and one boy aged 10. This unwittingly opened the door to a series of studies identifying mystical experiences among children and youths. Especially among those influenced by literary works, the poet Wordsworth has given an implicit model of mystical experience relevant to children and adolescents. Laski used two excerpts from Wordsworth's poetry in the literary texts she analyzed.[75] In his autobiography, *Surprised by Joy*, C. S. Lewis extensively analyzed three boyhood experiences central to his religious development, noting that such descriptions had also been furnished by such poets as Wordsworth and could be "suffocatingly subjective."[76] However, they gained ontological validity as they pointed to something "outer" and "other."[77] The work described by Pafford in his book *Inglorious Wordsworths* was partly based upon questionnaire responses from both grammar and university students.[78] Implicit in all these is a model purporting that children have an intense longing for transcendent experiences, which often are realized. Much of adult life is assumed to involve a longing for such experiences once again. Such a model can be contrasted with psychoanalytic and object relations theories, which assume mystical experiences to be regressive in a pathological sense. "Inglorious Wordsworths" have transcendent experiences that are valuable and healthy, and are capable of being recovered once again in adulthood.

As part of a questionnaire study, Pafford had both university and grammar school students respond to a literary description of an experience typical of Wordsworth's poetry—an experience that was specified as occurring in childhood, and one that was conscious of something more than a mere child's delight in nature.[79] Participants were to describe in writing any experience of their own that they felt was in any way similar to the description provided. Pafford analyzed responses from 400 participants, half each from the university and grammar school samples; there were equal numbers of males and females in each sample.[80] He found that 40% of the grammar school boys and 61% of the grammar school girls had had such experiences. In the university sample, the percentages were 56% for the men and 65% for the women.[81]

Although Pafford's samples can be classified and analyzed in as many intuitive ways as Laski's, he did at least attempt some crude quantitative and statistical analyses. One quantitative effort was to have respondents check off, on a list of 15 words, those that applied to their experience. These results are presented in Table 7.1. It is interesting to note that whereas Pafford claimed, partly from his own transcendental experiences, that such experiences are part of the essence of what he termed "real" religion,[82] his own respondents checked the two words most closely related to religion ("holy" and "sacred") quite infrequently. It is unlikely that the most frequently checked word ("awesome") was interpreted by the respondents in a religious sense.

Pafford found that transcendental experiences were most typical in the middle teens, under conditions of solitude. The experiences were positive, and most respondents wished

TABLE 7.1. Endorsement of Words Characterizing Transcendental Experiences

Word	Frequency of endorsement	Percentage of subjects endorsing
Awesome	119	54
Serene	87	39
Lonely	81	37
Frightening	77	35
Mysterious	65	29
Exciting	64	29
Ecstatic	47	21
Melancholy	45	20
Sacred	39	18
Sad	33	15
Holy	28	13
Sensual	21	10
Irritating	7	3
Erotic	5	2

Note. Number of respondents = 222. Adapted from Pafford (1973, p. 262). Copyright 1973 by Hodder and Stoughton. Adapted by permission.

to have such experiences again. However, they were less frequent in adulthood. One of the most common outcomes of the experience was some effort at creativity, although Pafford (influenced by Laski) specifically asked about creative acts following the experience, perhaps setting an expectation among respondents to list such activities.

Other Research on Children and Adolescents

Both Laski and Pafford found most mystical-type experiences to be uncommon in childhood—Laski because she sampled so few children, and Pafford because his samples reported most such experiences in middle adolescence, even though the literary example he used stated 8 years of age as the beginning of such experiences. Since in Pafford's British sample sixth-form grammar students would have tended to be 18 and university students 19 or above, his respondents may simply have reported their most recent experience; thus reports of possible experiences in childhood may have been minimized. Some have argued that the frequency of religious experience reported in adolescence reflects a North American Protestant bias, linked to the early focus on conversion experiences discussed in Chapter 8.

One such critic, Klingberg, sought to focus upon the study of religious experience in children, sampling only the age ranges from 9 to 13.[83] Klingberg's study was done in Sweden in the mid-1940s, but was not published in English until 1959. Two sets of data were collected, intended to be "mutually supplementary"; one of these consisted of adults' religious memories from childhood.[84] Our concern is with the compositions collected from 630 children (273 boys and 357 girls) in Sweden from 1944 to 1945. Most were 10 to 12 years of age. All children responded in writing to the statement "Once when I thought about God. . . ." Of the 630 compositions received, 566 contained accounts of personal religious experiences (244 from boys and 322 from girls).[85] Assessing the experiences for depth indicated "phenomena which call to mind the experiences of the mystic."[86] These primarily included apparitions of objects of religious faith, such as Jesus, God, and angels; more importantly for our interests, however, they also included a felt sense of an invisible presence. Although Klingberg recognized the facilitating role of a religious culture, school, and home in encouraging such reports among children, he claimed that the value of the study is that it shows that mystical experiences *can* take place during childhood.[87] Klingberg further argued that maturational mechanisms cannot eliminate mystical experiences in children, and suggested their universality.[88] Fahs has persuasively argued for the awakening of mystical awareness in children by avoiding a narrow religious indoctrination that might preclude a sense of wonder, curiosity, and awe.[89]

David and Sally Elkind studied the compositions of 149 ninth-grade U.S. students who were asked to respond to the questions "When do you feel closest to God?" and "Have you ever had a particular experience of feeling especially close to God?"[90] The former question was assumed to tap recurrent religious experiences, and the latter acute religious experiences.[91] The researchers concluded that the majority of respondents regarded personal religious experiences as a significant part of their lives, even though many resisted formal religious activities and participation. Across all respondents, 92% wrote compositions indicating recurrent experiences, and 76% wrote compositions indicating acute experiences.[92] Again, asking people in friendly or institutional contexts to write or talk about religious and mystical experiences readily yields responses from most participants.

Hood's Research

Open-ended responses to specific questions such as the ones we have been discussing can yield massive material, difficult to summarize. Statistical rigor and classification often yield to a rich descriptive presentation. However, such studies can be used to test empirical hypotheses as well. Hood selected two extreme groups from a sample of 123 college students who responded to Allport's Religious Orientation Scale. [93] The 25 highest-scoring intrinsic (mean = 41.8, SD = 2.9) and highest-scoring extrinsic (mean = 49.2, SD = 3.7) subjects were invited to participate in interviews regarding their "most significant personal experience." The 41 participants (20 intrinsic and 21 extrinsic) described a wide variety of experiences, few of which were explicitly identified as religious. However, coding experiences for their mystical quality on five criteria revealed that, as predicted, the most significant personal experiences of intrinsic subjects were reliably coded as mystical more frequently than were those of extrinsic subjects (see Table 7.2). This finding held not only for the total, global assess-

TABLE 7.2. Most Significant Personal Experiences Coded for Mystical Criteria in Intrinsic and Extrinsic Persons

Mystical criteria	Intrinsic (n = 20)	Extrinsic (n = 21)	Chi-square	Contingency coefficient[a]
		Total		
Mystical	15	3		
Nonmystical	5	18	13.0***	.49
		Loss of self		
Yes	14	3		
No	6	18	10.9***	.46
		Noetic		
Yes	17	3		
No	3	13	7.6**	.39
		Ineffable		
Yes	19	4		
No	1	17	21.0**	.58
		Positive		
Yes	19	12		
No	1	9	6.0*	.36
		Sacred		
Yes	18	6		
No	2	15	13.8***	.56

Note. Adapted from Hood (1973b, p. 446). Copyright 1973 by the Society for the Scientific Study of Religion. Adapted by permission.

[a]Upper limit of contingency coefficient = .71.

*p < .02. **p < .01. ***p < .001.

ment of mysticism, but for each of the five individual criteria used to identify mysticism. Despite the wide diversity of actual experiences (from childbirth to drug experiences), these could be coded as mystical more often for the intrinsic subjects than for the extrinsic subjects. It is important to note that few participants spontaneously described any experience as mystical; coders using theory-derived criteria categorized experiences as mystical or not. The role of language in defining experience from both first-person and third-person perspectives is complex and has become a focus of intense conceptual debate.[94] At the purely empirical level, Hood's study indicates that experiences can be judged to be mystical by trained raters using theory-based criteria, even if the respondents do not spontaneously define their experiences as either "religious" or "mystical."

In a methodologically similar study, Hood selected a sample of 54 persons equated for degree of religious commitment.[95] However, they were divided into three groups based upon the *nature* of their religious commitment: primarily personally religiously committed ($n = 25$), primarily institutionally religiously committed ($n = 14$), and an equally personally and institutionally committed group ($n = 15$). Once again, interviewing these persons regarding their most significant personal experiences and rating their responses for Stace's specific criteria of mysticism revealed that all the groups differed significantly. The personally religiously committed group had the most mystical experiences, and the primarily institutionally committed had the fewest. Again, few participants spontaneously defined their experiences as mystical; rather, they were coded as mystical by raters trained to use a particular theory-based rating system.

Research by Thomas and Cooper and by the Alister Hardy Centre

However, if individuals respond affirmatively to an item measuring mysticism, does it mean that their experience was mystical as judged by others? Thomas and Cooper suggest that it may not be so.[96] In two studies, these researchers had persons from colleges, religious groups, and civic organizations respond to one of the items most frequently used in survey research (to be discussed later) to assess mystical experience. The item was "Have you ever had the feeling of being close to a powerful spiritual force that seemed to lift you out of yourself?"[97] Research Box 7.1 describes these two studies in greater detail.

The findings of Thomas and Cooper are supported by classifications of the religious experiences solicited from and sent in to the Alister Hardy Research Centre, as described in Chapter 6. Much as samples of plankton were collected and classified by Alister Hardy during his career as a zoologist, numerous samplings from over 5,000 reports of religious experience at the Alister Hardy Centre have been collected and variously classified. The most extensive classification is based upon the initial 3,000 cases Hardy collected.[98] Variations occurred in the wording of the appeal for reports of such experiences, depending on the source of publication. In some cases, brief descriptions from literature illustrating the type of experience of interest were given.[99] Most common was this one in a pamphlet widely circulated in the United Kingdom:

> All those who feel they have been conscious of, and perhaps influenced by, some Power, whether called God or not, which may either appear to be beyond their individual selves or partly, or even entirely, within their being, are asked to write a simple account of their feelings and their effects.[100]

Not surprisingly, Hardy and his colleagues found that the reports of the materials submitted defied easy classification: "So many of them were a mixture of widely different

---

Research Box 7.1. Measurement and Incidence of Mystical Experiences (Thomas & Cooper, 1978 [Study 1], 1980 [Study 2])

In Thomas and Cooper's first study, only young adults aged 17 to 29 were used (44 males, 258 females). In the second study, 305 persons representing three different age groups— 17 to 29 years ($n = 120$), 30 to 59 years ($n = 110$), and 60 years and older ($n = 75$)—responded to the same survey question. In each study, those who answered "yes" went on to describe their experience in open-ended fashion, and raters coded the responses to place them in one of the categories described below. The percentage who answered "yes" was identical in both studies and is typical for survey research (34%). However, when the open-ended descriptions were analyzed for frequency and type of experience reported, all experiences were reliably placed into one of four response categories derived from a portion of the initial sample.

The frequencies and types of experiences reported, based upon open-ended descriptions to "yes" responses to the question "Have you ever had the feeling of being close to a powerful spiritual force that seemed to lift you out of yourself?", were as follows. (Note that these percentages are based on n's of 302 for Study 1 and 304 for Study 2; coder agreement was 94% overall for both studies.)

Type 0: No experience (*Study 1, 66%; Study 2, 66%*). Respondents answered "no" to question.

Type I: Uncodable (*Study 1, 8%; Study 2, 10%*). Respondents answered "yes," but responses were irrelevant or could not be reliably coded.

Type 1: Mystical (*Study 1, 2%; Study 2, 1%*). Responses included expressions of such things as awesome emotions; a sense of the ineffable; or a feeling of oneness with God, nature, or the universe.

Type 3: Psychic (*Study 1, 12%; Study 2, 8%*). Responses included expressions of extraordinary or supernatural phenomena, including extrasensory perception, telepathy, out-of-body experiences, or contact with spiritual beings.

Type 4: Faith and consolation (*Study 1, 2%; Study 2, 16%*). Responses included religious or spiritual phenomena, but without indications of either extraordinary or supernatural elements.

Despite minor variations in frequencies of experience categories between these two studies (perhaps because of the larger age range in Study 2), there is remarkable agreement not only in the identical percentage of affirmative responses in both studies, but also in the fact that the *least* frequent content category for the open-ended responses was mystical.

The importance of these two studies is that if affirmative responses to a single-item survey question are accepted at face value, many diverse experiences may be clustered together. In terms of our specific concern with mystical experiences, no more than 2% of the 34% who responded to the survey question presumed to be a measure of mysticism actually described mystical experiences in open-ended descriptions. The criteria for mysticism compatible with those typically cited in the conceptual literature—such as an ineffable sense of union with God (personal) or the universe (impersonal)—were not evident. Thus, survey items to assess mysticism may do so poorly according to more rigorous criteria, and may overestimate the actual incidence of reported mystical experience in samples.

items."[101] Hardy's own elaborate classification system, composed of 12 major categories (most with numerous subclassifications), yielded a total of 92 classifications (see Chapter 6, Table 6.1). Some of these refer to the development and consequences of the experience and do not describe the experience proper. Each experience was rated for the presence or absence of any classification category. Most relevant to our concerns in this chapter are those experiences that were coded in terms of mystical or numinous criteria, and few were thus coded. The most specific mystical category, "Feeling of unity with surroundings and/or other people,"[102] characterized only 168 of the initial 3,000 experiences, or 5.6%. The most numinous classification, "Sense of presence (not human),"[103] characterized 369 of these 3,000 reports, or 12.3%. Thus, despite the fact that Hardy felt his appeal would yield reports of evidential value, akin to spiritual reports in the Bible and of the mystics,[104] only a small minority of the experiences were either mystical or numinous when coded for relevant criteria by independent raters.

However, a cautionary note must be sounded in regard to materials from the Alister Hardy Research Centre. Access to these materials by various scholars has led to numerous classification systems, few of which have been rigorously established by methodological or statistical means. Hence, widely varying reports of the content of these materials persist. For instance, Hay has identified six major types of religious experiences in the Hardy archives,[105] one of which is "an awareness of the presence of God,"[106] and the other "experiencing in an extraordinary way that all things are 'One.'"[107] Although these correspond to numinous and mystical experiences, respectively, why Hay's results differ dramatically from Hardy's own analysis as described above is unclear. Current efforts to place the Hardy material on computer files that will be readily available to scholars may solve radical discrepancies in classification of these reports.[108]

Hay's Research

Hay and Morisy conducted a random sample of 266 residents of Nottingham, England.[109] They asked their respondents a version of the Hardy appeal: "Have you ever been aware or influenced by a presence or power, whether you call it God or not, which is different from your everyday self?"[110] Of the 172 who consented to be interviewed, 72% (124) answered "yes." Eliminating 17 of these (who appeared to have misunderstood the question or who could not describe the experience) left 107 persons who were able to describe the experience in detail (or the most important experience, if they had had more than one). Using the respondents' own language, the researchers classified the experiences into one of seven categories as follows: presence of or help from God (28%), assistance via prayer (9%), intervention by presence not identified as God (13%), presence or help from deceased (22%), premonitions (10%), meaningful patterning of events (10%), or miscellaneous (8%).[111] Athough these categories were purely provisional, once again it is evident that persons who were responding to a particular question were in fact reporting many different types of experiences. This was true even though the specific wording of the Hardy question used in this study was field-tested and assumed to draw out both the mystical and numinous qualities of religious experience.[112] Yet no mystical experiences could be coded (except perhaps if included under "miscellaneous"), and only 28% were explicitly numinous in terms of a sense of presence identified with the holy (God).

In a similar study, Hay surveyed 100 randomly selected students in a postgraduate teacher certificate course at Nottingham University, England.[113] Hay found a high (65%) affirmative response rate to whether an individual could ever remember being "aware of or influenced by a presence or a power, whether you call it God or not, which is different from your everyday self."[114] Despite the fact that the question was worded to cover mystical or numinous experiences—by focusing upon whether the experiences could be classified as personal ("presence") or impersonal ("power")—it yielded only 32 of 109 (29.4%) experiences described that were clearly either mystical or numinous.[115] These were 10 (9.2%) experiences of unity (mystical experiences) and 22 (20.2%) experiences of an awareness of God (numinous experiences).

Further Research by Hood

Open-ended questionnaire studies have been also used to identify "triggers," or the conditions that facilitate the report of mystical experience. The more deeply a person is committed to a particular religious ideology and view of mysticism, the more the person's religious beliefs should be used both to interpret the experience and to identify relevant triggers for the experience. Among those researchers influenced by Maslow's humanistic psychology, persons seen as self-actualized are hypothesized to have "peak experiences"—a concept loosely related to, but perhaps broader than, mystical experience, as we have discussed in Chapter 6. Humanistic and transpersonal psychologists have carefully tried to develop spiritual rather than religious measures avoiding religious language, especially language associated with particular faith traditions, such as Christianity.[116]

A widely used scale to measure self-actualization, the Personal Orientation Inventory (POI),[117] was found by Hood to relate significantly to Factor I but not Factor II of the Mysticism Scale (the M Scale, discussed later in this chapter) in a sample of 87 psychology students.[118] This is consistent with the idea that measures of self-actualization should relate to nonreligiously interpreted mystical experiences, insofar as such experiences overlap with peak experiences. However, in a sample of 400 students, the 50 persons scoring lowest and the 50 persons scoring highest on the POI who also scored high on the M Scale created two groups reporting equally intense mystical experiences but differing on a measure of self-actualization.[119] Hood predicted that, given the antireligious bias of the POI, triggers cited for the elicitation of mystical experience among those scoring highest on the POI should be less traditional. On the other hand, given that the lowest scorers on the POI should be more traditional, the triggers of their mystical experiences should be from the more traditional sources. Independent raters' categorizations of open-ended questionnaire responses to the conditions that facilitated each respondent's mystical experience supported this hypothesis. Six categories of triggers were reliably identified. When the miscellaneous category was ignored as not meaningful, only introspection was a commonly shared trigger for both low and high scorers on the POI. Low-POI persons had their experiences more frequently triggered by the traditional triggers of religion and nature. High-POI persons had their experiences most frequently triggered by the nontraditional triggers of sex and drugs. Thus, persons differing on a measure of self-actualization differed not so much in the report of mystical experiences as in the triggers that facilitated the experiences. Obviously, nontraditional triggers as such can be used by some to doubt the legitimacy of an experience.

Personal and cultural factors that affect what might be appropriate triggers for mystical experiences have been studied. Survey research has long established that many different triggers can elicit mystical experiences. Although some triggers are consistently reported— prayer; church attendance; significant life events, such as births and deaths; and experiences associated with music, sex, and drugs—one seeks in vain for a common characteristic shared

ᨠ

Research Box 7.2. Social Legitimacy, Dogmatism, and the Evaluation of Intense Experiences (Hood, 1980)

Hood was interested in how the evaluation of intense experiences would vary as a function of the identification of triggers among open- and closed-minded persons. From published sources, he selected one true report each of an aesthetic, a mystical, and a religious experience, independently operationalized for equal intensity. These unlabeled experiences were then presented in a booklet along with Rokeach's Dogmatism scale, claimed to be a measure of "open-mindedness." Three versions of the booklet were constructed, so that the experiences described could be described as a result of drugs, prayer, or unspecified factors. The experiences were rated on an evaluative semantic differential scale, with higher scores indicating a more positive evaluation. This part of the study clearly showed that the more normative the experience, the more positively it was viewed, so that religious experiences were evaluated more positively overall. Aesthetic and mystical experiences were evaluated less positively overall than religious ones, but did not differ from each other in valence of evaluation. In addition, as predicted, the more normative the trigger, the more positively it affected the evaluation of the experience. Experiences triggered by prayer were more positively evaluated than those with unspecified triggers. Drug triggers lowered the evaluation of all experiences. These effects were most pronounced for the high-dogmatism persons. The actual mean evaluations for each experience coded by trigger for high- and low-dogmatism groups were as follows. (This table is based upon 93 low- and 93 high-dogmatism subjects; 31 subjects in each group rated the three experiences as triggered by drugs, 31 as triggered by prayer, and 31 as triggered by unspecified factors [none].)

Subjects		Aesthetic experience triggered by			Religious experience triggered by			Mystical experience triggered by		
		Drugs	Prayer	None	Drugs	Prayer	None	Drugs	Prayer	None
High-dogmatism	Mean	53.16	62.65	59.94	55.97	66.68	60.03	47.87	59.87	54.00
	SD	9.4	4.1	8.3	9.6	8.9	9.3	12.3	9.5	10.7
Low-dogmatism	Mean	51.988	61.32	57.86	54.50	62.10	59.61	48.02	57.45	53.65
	SD	9.9	7.3	9.0	8.7	8.1	8.6	11.4	9.7	10.7

Note. From Hood (1980). Copyright 1977 by the Religious Research Association. Adapted by permission.

by such diverse triggers. Empirically, it is more useful to focus upon what triggers function to elicit mystical experience in different persons. Research Box 7.2 presents the results of a study in which the evaluation of experience was shown to be a function (1) of the normative legitimacy of the trigger, (2) of the experience, and (3) of the alleged open-mindedness of respondents.

Sex and eroticism are often cited as triggers of mystical experience. Noting the vast conceptual literature relating mysticism and eroticism, Hood and Hall hypothesized that individuals would use similar gender-based descriptions to describe both mystical and erotic experiences.[120] Results indicated only partial support for this hypothesis. Open-ended descriptions of mystical and erotic experiences by both males and females were coded for the use of active, agentive language or receptive language. As predicted, females used receptive terms to describe both their erotic and mystical experiences. However, whereas males used agentive language to describe their sexual experiences, they did not describe their mystical experiences in agentive terms. Rating subjects' expressions of mystical and erotic experiences in words independently established to be either agentive or receptive also showed that females described both erotic and mystical experiences in receptive terms, but that males described only their sexual experiences in agentive terms. The researchers have suggested that the compatibility of erotic and mystical experiences for females is aided by the masculine imagery common in the Christian tradition, which facilitates a congruent expression of eroticism and mysticism for females but inhibits it for males.

Summary

Overall, we can conclude that open-ended responses to specific questions presumed to elicit reports of either mystical or numinous experiences reveal little of scientific value beyond the facts that individuals from children through seniors readily report such experiences. The richness of their reports varies with their linguistic capacities. Such reports cannot be taken as uncritical evidential values for the realities they describe, and they may be highly influenced by the personal concerns of those making the reports. Finally, depending on investigators' own classification interests, such reports can be almost interminably classified and cross-referenced. This means that first-person descriptions of experience are unlikely to correspond closely to third-person classifications of these same experiences. Perhaps the very richness of these descriptions means that they are best approached through techniques of literary criticism. However, this research tradition does remind us that responses to such questions, even if reliably quantified, mask a rich subjective variation of immense importance to those whose experiences are studied.

Survey Research

Emerging simultaneously with and influenced by open-ended reports of mystical and numinous experiences are survey studies. As noted earlier, such studies use a few specific questions, often answered simply "yes" or "no." What survey studies lose in terms of the range and depth of description of experiences, they gain in terms of identifying the frequency and reporting of such experiences in the general population. Their results are also easily quantified and allow correlations with a wide variety of demographic and other variables to provide a distinctive empirical base that complements merely conceptual discussions of these experiences. We focus here on the body of survey research that has asked questions intended by the researchers to be direct measures of mystical and numinous experiences. Fortunately, several surveys have used identical questions over several years and even within different cultures, so some comparisons over time and cultures can also be made, at least at the descriptive level.

One caution must be noted before we begin. Intercorrelations among different items to measure mystical experiences across different surveys are not available. Although we can anticipate positive correlations, it is not clear that this will always be the case, nor can we be certain of the magnitude of such correlations. Hence, each item must be judged in itself as an operational measure of the experience in question. Four major questions have dominated the majority of surveys covering a span of a quarter of a century. Accordingly, we summarize these data in terms of the survey questions used; each of these is identified by the name most closely associated with the formulation of the initial question. Therefore, we have the Stark, Bourque, Greeley, and Hardy questions.

The Stark Question

As part of an early multidimensional model of religion, Glock and Stark proposed five dimensions to religion, one of which is the experiential dimension.[121] This dimension includes religious emotions as well as claims to direct experiential awareness of ultimate reality. The survey question used in their initial sampling of churches in the greater San Francisco area in 1963 was this: "Have you ever as an adult had the feeling that you were somehow in the presence of God?"[122] With a sample size just under 3,000 respondents (2,871), 72% answered "yes."[123] Although we might expect the various dimensions of the Glock and Stark model of religion (ritual, belief, consequences, experience, belief) to intercorrelate simply because they are all religious items, the model attempts to assess experience independently; hence the question refers to a *feeling* of God's presence, which is presumed to tap religious experience rather than belief. Not surprisingly, the majority of religiously committed, institutionally involved persons answered "yes." Only 20% of all Protestants sampled ($n = 2,326$) and 25% of all Catholics sampled ($n = 545$) answered "no."[124]

Vernon isolated a small sample of 85 persons who indicated "none" when asked about religious commitment.[125] In this same sample of "religious nones," 25% nevertheless answered the Stark question affirmatively. Thus, even among those with no institutional religious commitment, a significant minority of adults reported experiencing a sense of God's presence.

More recently, Tamminen used the five religious dimensions of Glock and Stark to organize his longitudinal study of religious development in Scandinavian youths.[126] Modifying the Stark question slightly by omitting the phrase "as an adult," he asked, "Have you at times felt that God is particularly close to you?"[127] Percentages of responses by grade level for the 1974 sampling are presented in Table 7.3.

The steady decline in the percentage of students reporting experiences of nearness to God by grade level (and hence age) is obvious. This decline is further evident in Table 7.4, which presents responses to the same question in 1986 from this longitudinal study. Tamminen's study is thus the only major longitudinal study to document the steady

TABLE 7.3. Scandinavian Students' Reports of Experiencing Nearness to God (1974)

Response	Percentage responding by grade level					
	I	III	V	VII	IX	XI
Yes	84	—	—	—	—	—
Very often	—	42	17	10	10	8
A few times	—	30	40	33	31	27
Maybe once	—	18	12	15	14	13
No	16	10	31	43	44	53

Note. $n = 1,336$. Level I answered only "yes" or "no." Adapted from Tamminen (1991, p. 42). Copyright 1991 by Soumalainen Tiedeaktemia. Adapted by permission.

TABLE 7.4. Scandinavian Students' Reports of Experiencing Nearness to God (1986)

Response	Percentage responding by grade level						
	III	IV	V	VI	VII	VIII	IX
Very often	19	19	13	10	5	1	4
A few times	31	33	44	29	20	13	15
Maybe once	18	20	19	27	24	18	22
No	32	28	24	34	52	68	59

Note. n = 971. Adapted from Tamminen (1991, p. 43). Copyright 1991 by Soumalainen Tiedeaktemia. Adapted by permission.

decline in the report of religious experience from childhood through adolescence. It suggests that such experiences (or their report) are quite common in childhood, and therefore supports the claims of Pafford and others discussed above.

The Bourque Question

In a series of surveys, Bourque and her colleagues utilized the following question to assess religious experience: "Would you say that you have ever had a 'religious or mystical experience'—that is, a moment of sudden religious awakening or insight?"[128] They also cited results from three Associated Press surveys using this question. These surveys were conducted in 1962, 1966, and 1967 in the United States. Over time the percentage of persons answering "yes" increased from 21% in 1962 (*n* = 3,232) to 32% in 1966 (*n* = 3,518) to 41% in 1967 (*n* = 3,168).[129] In 1966 Bourque administered this question, along with the Stark question above and another question, to a sample of 3,168 and found that 32% answered "yes."[130] Gallup used this item in a national survey in the United States in 1976 and found that 31% answered affirmatively in a sample of 1,500.[131] More recently, Yamane and Polzer[132] reported the results of two Gallup surveys in 1990—one in June[133] and one in September,[134] each using a sample of 1,236—and found a stable affirmative response frequency of 53%.

Thus, over a period exceeding a quarter of a century, representative samples of persons in the United States have reported having a religious or mystical experience, defined as a moment of sudden religious awakening or insight. The range of affirmative responses is large (from 21% to 53%), but lower than the typical affirmative response to the Stark question, which asks active, institutionally affiliated religious persons whether they have ever have a sense of God's presence.

The Greeley Question

Another question widely used in survey research and accepted as an operational measure of reported mystical question is associated with the work of Greeley.[135] The question most typically used is "Have you ever felt as though you were close to a powerful spiritual force that seemed to lift you out of yourself?"[136] It has been administered as part of the annual General Social Surveys of the National Opinion Research Center. The General Social Surveys are independent cross-sectional probability samples of persons in the continental United States living in noninstitutional homes who are 18 years of age and English-speaking.[137] It was found that overall, in a General Social Survey sample of 1,468, 35% of the respondents answered "yes" to this question.[138]

Hay and Morisy administered the same question to a sample of 1,865 in Great Britain and found that 30% answered in the affirmative.[139] In the studies by Thomas and Cooper discussed above, the 34% affirmative responses included few responses that were truly mystical when independently coded for criteria of mysticism.[140] On the other hand, Greeley found that a very high percentage (29%) of those who positively answered his question agreed with "a sense of unity and my own part in it" as a descriptor of their experience.[141] Thus, most of the 34% answering "yes" to the Greeley question also appeared to accept a mystical description of unity as applying to the experience. It may be that methodologically checking descriptors of experience increases the positive rate of mystical experiences over spontaneous descriptions of the experiences in open-ended interviews.

McClenon, in a survey of 339, found the lowest affirmative response rate to the Greeley question (20%).[142] Most recently, Yamane and Polzer have analyzed all affirmative responses from the General Social Surveys of the National Research Opinion Center to the Greeley question in the years 1983, 1984, 1988, and 1989.[143] A total of 5,420 individuals were included in their review. Using an ordinal scale where respondents who answered affirmatively could select from three options—"once or twice," "several times," or "often"—yielded a 4-point range from 0 (negative response) to 3 (often). Using this 4-point range across all individuals who responded to the Greeley question yielded a mean score of 0.79 ($SD = 0.89$). Converting these to a percentage of "yes" as a nominal category, regardless of frequency, yielded 2,183 affirmative responses or an overall affirmative response rate of 40% of the total sample who reported ever having had the experience. Independent assessment of affirmative responses for the year suggested a slight but steady decline. The figures were 39% for 1983–1984 combined ($n = 3,072$), 31% for 1988 ($n = 1,481$), and 31% for 1989 ($n = 936$).[144]

Bourque and Back created an index of religious experience composed of three questions—the Stark and Bourque questions already noted, plus a third: "Have you ever had a feeling of being saved in Christ?"[145] In a sample of 3,168, 990 (31.2%) responded affirmatively to all three questions,[146] 794 (25%) to any two, and 566 (17.8%) to at least one.[147]

The Hardy Question

As noted above, Alister Hardy's interest in religious experience focused methodologically on soliciting open-ended responses from persons to both literary examples and descriptions of religious experiences. The most common description used by Hardy (quoted earlier) has been slightly modified by Hay and Morisy and used in several survey studies.

The precise wording of the Hay and Morisy question was "Have you ever been aware of or influenced by a presence or power, whether you call it God or not, which is different from your everyday self?"[148] Their survey was conducted in Great Britain. Respondents were chosen from a two-stage stratified sample: names randomly drawn from the electoral register, supplemented with names drawn at random of nonelectors from the households of the selected electors. In their sample of 1,865, 36% answered the question affirmatively. In the more restricted sample of 172 residents of an industrial area in England described earlier, Hay and Morisy found the high affirmative response rate of 72%.[149] The high rates were probably a function of face-to-face interviews, which have been shown to increase the number of affirmative responses to survey questions dealing with religious experience.[150] However, Hay also found a 65% affirmative response rate to his version of the Hardy question in a random sample of postgraduate students at Nottingham University, England.[151] He extensively interviewed respondents regarding their experiences, but the actual affirmation of the experience occurred before the interview. It may be that anticipating a discussion of reports of religious experience increases the rate of report. Hay has also cited a study by Lewis in which a high affirmative response rate to the Hardy question was obtained in a British sample of 108 nurses from two different hospitals in Leeds.[152] Again, face-to-face interviews may have been a factor increasing response rates.

In a Gallup sample of 985 British citizens, Hay and Heald found a rate more typical of other general surveys using the Hardy question: 48% of their sample responded affirmatively to the question.[153] This closely matches the 44% rate found in previously unpublished data based upon an Australian sample of 1,228 by Morgan Research (the Australian affiliate of the Gallup Poll organization) and cited by Hay.[154] A survey in the United States of 3,000 produced a 31% affirmative response rate, closely matching the 35% response rate produced in a sample of 3,062 from the Princeton Research Center a few years earlier.[155] Hay has also cited two unpublished Gallup polls commissioned by the Alister Hardy Research Centre in 1985, indicating a 33% affirmative response to the Hardy question in a sample of 1,030 in Britain, and a 10% higher rate (43%) for a similar sample of 1,525 in the United States.[156] Finally, Back and Bourque reported three different Gallup surveys done in the United States, with affirmative response rates to the Hardy question of 21% in 1962 ($n = 3,232$), 32% in 1966 ($n = 3,518$), and 41% in 1967 ($n = 3,168$).[157]

Thus, surveys from 1962 through 1987 in the United States, Britain, and Australia suggest a fairly wide range (21–72%) of affirmative responses to the Hardy question. However, when higher rates obtained from anticipated in-depth interviews are ignored, the affirmative response rates average in the 35–40% range for the Hardy question—paralleling fairly closely the rates for the Greeley and Bourque questions, and for the Stark question when the respondents are not restricted to church or synagogue members. Thus, it appears overall that 35% of persons sampled affirm some intense spiritual experience, felt by the researchers to measure mystical and/or numinous experience. At a minimum, then, the reports of such experiences have been clearly and conclusively established by survey studies to be statistically quite common among normal samples. What are we to make of these reports?

Most survey studies have included additional questions and demographic characteristics that can be correlated with the reports of religious experience. No simple pattern has emerged from the studies mentioned above, and unfortunately each study must be considered in terms of its sampling and the statistical models used. The range of data analysis is large, from naive to state-of-the-art sophistication. The major consistent findings are easily summarized: Women report more such experiences than men; the experiences tend to be age-related, increasing with age; they are characteristic of the educated and affluent; and they are more likely to be associated with indices of psychological health and well-being than with those of pathology or social dysfunction. Thus, Scharfstein's "everyday mysticism"[158] is supported by survey research in affirming the commonalty of mysticism among both institutionally and noninstitutionally committed religious persons within the United States, the United Kingdom, and Australia.

Several studies have focused upon communication patterns of persons who have such experiences, noting that these persons do *not* discuss their experiences with others. Even Tamminen noted this among his young Scandinavian sample; the failure to communicate such experiences starts in childhood.[159] This may well account for the persistence of the belief that such experiences are uncommon. The irony is that at least one-third of the population claims to have such experiences, but that few people talk about them publicly. This hidden dimension of religious experience is well documented and can be clarified by other studies, to be discussed below. However, before we begin to discuss these studies, a cautionary note is needed—one that confronts the issue of the language and experience central to much of the conceptual and empirical literature on mysticism.

A Cautionary Note: Mysticism and the Paranormal

Since its inception, North American psychology has been linked in the popular mind with psychic phenomena. As Coon has documented, many founding North American psychologists fought hard to separate the emerging science of psychology from "spiritualism" and "psychic," to which it was connected in the popular mind.[160] Few psychologists, then or now, believe in the reality of parapsychological phenomena. Hood has identified religion and parapsychology as perhaps the most controversial research area in the psychology of religion.[161]

Yet within research on mysticism, several empirical facts emerge that are problematic. Some of the key theoreticians and empirical researchers have explicitly linked mysticism to parapsychology, with varying degrees of sympathy to both. These include such major figures as Greeley,[162] Hardy,[163] and Hood.[164] Second, in classifications of open-ended responses to single-item questions to measure mysticism, one of the most common code categories is "paranormal." Thus, many persons who affirm what the researchers assume to be a mystical or numinous item are in fact reporting paranormal experiences, such as telepathy, clairvoyance, or contact with the dead. Third, survey studies of mysticism commonly include items to assess paranormal experiences. For instance, paranormal experiences were included in the 1984, 1988, and 1989 General Social Survey data.[165] In virtually every survey, paranormal and mystical experiences are positively correlated: Persons who report paranormal experiences often report mystical experiences as well, and vice versa. Seldom is only one type of experience reported. Further support for this claim is that factor analysis of survey items that include mysticism and paranormal experience indicates that extrasensory perception, clairvoyance, contact with the dead, and mysticism form a single factor, meaning that these are empirically measuring one thing in the popular mind. If we exclude *déjà vu* experiences, which are also included in survey studies but neither conceptually nor empirically linked to paranormal experiences,[166] the range of affirmative responses is as high as or higher than the range of affirmative responses to religious items. As an example, Table 7.5 compares the distribution of affirmative responses to three items assessing paranormal experiences with the distribution of such responses to the Greeley question about mysticism.

Clearly, Table 7.5 reveals that reports of parapsychological experiences are at least as common as those of mystical experiences. This fact, combined with the strong intercorrelation among parapsychological and religious items that in a general sample yield a single factor, suggests that what is being tapped in these surveys is some assertion of experiencing a reality different from that postulated by mainstream science. However, the nature of that reality, is open to serious question. We have seen that open-ended responses to survey questions yield a wide range of experiences. It is likely that some respondents simply want to affirm experiences that offer evidential support not only for alternative beliefs, but for their own self-importance as well. Furthermore, it is likely that to tease out separate reports of such experiences as mystical and numinous experiences would require studies of sophisticated populations for whom such distinctions could be made, in terms of both conceptualizations

TABLE 7.5. Comparison of Affirmative Responses to Four Questions about Mystical or Paranormal Experiences in Three General Social Surveys

Year	Extrasensory perception	Clairvoyance	Contact with the dead	Mysticism
1984	$n = 1,439$	$n = 1,434$	$n = 1,445$	$n = 1,442$
	67%	30%	42%	41%
1988	$n = 1,456$	$n = 1,440$	$n = 1,459$	$n = 1,451$
	64%	28%	40%	32%
1989	$n = 922$	$n = 983$	$n = 991$	$n = 988$
	58%	23%	35%	30%

Note. The four questions asked were as follows:

> *Mysticism:* Have you ever felt as though you were close to a powerful spiritual force that seemed to lift you out of yourself?
>
> *Extrasensory perception:* Have you ever felt as though you were in touch with someone when they were far away from you?
>
> *Clairvoyance:* Have you ever seen events that were happening at a great distance as they were happening?
>
> *Contact with the dead:* Have you ever felt as though you were in touch with someone who had died?

Adapted from Fox (1992, p. 422). Copyright 1992 by the Association for the Sociology of Religion. Adapted by permission.

and actual experience. However, it would seem that sampling from religiously committed persons would best allow distinctions between the religious and parapsychological experiences often associated with religion but perhaps best independently identified. For instance, the conceptual literature on mysticism clearly separates paranormal experiences from mystical ones. Moreover, many religious traditions carefully dissociate themselves from what they would term "occult" practices.

Some empirical evidence for this view is that when samples are carefully selected for their religious identification, paranormal experiences are infrequently cited, if at all, as instances of religious experiences. For instance, Margolis and Elifson carefully solicited a sample of persons who were willing to affirm that they had had a religious experience that researchers accepted as indicating some personal relationship to an ultimate reality.[167] Forty-five respondents were then carefully interviewed about their experiences; to avoid interviewer bias, a structured format was employed. The 69 experiences described were content-analyzed, yielding 20 themes. These were then factor-analyzed, yielding four factors, the major one of which was a mystical factor "very similar to the classical mystical experience described by Stace and others."[168] Two of the other three factors (a life change experience factor and a visionary factor) were clearly religious experiences. One factor, vertigo experience, was a loss of control experienced negatively, often triggered by drugs or music. No paranormal experiences were reported. Thus, it is likely that survey questions worded to avoid religious language probably elicit a variety of experiences, including paranormal ones, that otherwise would not be identified as religious by the respondents.

However, in a survey study in the San Francisco Bay area, Wuthnow found not only that the majority of all respondents claimed to have experienced paranormal phenomena, but also that those who affirmed that they had ever been "in close contact with the sacred or holy" were the most likely to report paranormal experiences.[169] The conceptual literature on mysticism is replete with discussions of traditions warning against confounding paranormal and mystical experiences, even though they are often related.[170] It is unlikely that general populations make such distinctions, because they usually lack either the experiential base or the conceptual sophistication to make such distinctions. As Yamane and Polzer have argued, religiously committed persons may be quite adept at distinguishing religious experiences from other types of intense or anomalous experiences.[171] Of course, some outside mainstream traditions may define paranormal experiences as "religious," or more likely by the more general term "spiritual." It is likely that the use of the term "God" or not in survey items produces different results, in that persons committed to a mainstream religion are most likely to respond to religious language and to make distinctions among various experiences on the basis of religious knowledge.

Clearly, avoiding religious language in survey questions encourages the reporting of a wider range of experiences. Teasing out reports of experiences from a whole host of complex factors affecting their reporting requires more complex techniques than the methodology of survey research permits. Some of these issues have been explored in more measurement-based studies, many of which are correlational. However, there are also more laboratory-based and quasi-experimental studies. These permit even more precise identification of determinants of the reports of mystical experience.

Measurement Studies

Academic psychology of religion is heavily committed to what Gorsuch has called the "measurement paradigm."[172] One goal of measurement is to create reliable scales from clearly operationalized concepts. Many have thought that religious experiences, particularly the numinous and mystical varieties, cannot be reliably measured. However, two approaches to their measurement have been reasonably successful and have been used in several studies.

The Religious Experience Episodes Measure: The Influence of James

One approach to the measurement of mystical and numinous experiences has been to operationalize and quantify what might be called the "literary exemplar approach" of many of the more open-ended studies discussed above. Laski, Pafford, and Hardy gave particular examples of experiences and asked respondents whether they had ever had an experience like the one described. Hood essentially systematized this procedure in constructing the Religious Experience Episodes Measure (REEM).[173] He selected 15 experiences from James's *The Varieties of Religious Experience*, presented them in booklet form, and had respondents rate on a 5-point scale the degree to which they had ever had an experience like each of these. Hood's approach standardized the experiences presented to research subjects and allowed a quantification of the report of religious experience by summing the degree of similarity of one's own experiences to those described in the REEM. Rosegrant modified the REEM by rephrasing "the elegant 19th century English" and reducing the number of items from 15 to 10.[174] Examples of REEM items as modified by Rosegrant are presented in Table 7.6.

Both Hood's initial version[175] and Rosegrant's modified version[176] of the REEM have high internal consistencies, suggesting that the experiences described cluster together. Unpolished factor analysis of the REEM also yields a single factor. Overall, the mixture of more numinous and mystical items, along with explicit or implicit religious language, suggests that the REEM is best used with religiously committed samples.[177] It also reflects elements of religious experience perhaps most common in North American Protestant experience—a common criticism leveled against James's classic text, from which items for the REEM were originally selected. Holm found it difficult to make a meaningful translation of the REEM into

TABLE 7.6. Items from the Modified REEM

To what extent have you ever had an experience like this?

God is more real to me than any thought or person. I feel his presence, and I feel it more as I live in closer harmony with his laws. I feel him in the sunshine, or rain, and my feelings are best described as awe mixed with delirious restfulness.

Or like this?

I would suddenly feel the mood coming when I was at church, or with people reading, but only when my muscles were relaxed. It would irresistibly take over my mind and will, last what seemed like forever, and disappear in a way that resembled waking from anesthesia. One reason I think that I dislike this kind of trance was that I could not describe it to myself; even now I can't find the right words. It involved the disappearance of space, time, feeling, and the things I call my self. As ordinary consciousness disappeared, the sense of underlying essential consciousness grew stronger. At last nothing remained but a pure, abstract self.

Or like this?

Once, a few weeks after I came to the woods, I thought perhaps it was necessary to be near other people for a happy and healthy life. To be alone was somewhat unpleasant. But during a gentle rain, while I had these thoughts, I was suddenly aware of such good society in nature, in the pattern of drops and every sight and sound around my house, that the fancy advantages of being near people seemed insignificant, and I haven't thought about them since. Every little pine needle expanded with sympathy and befriended me. I was so definitely aware of something akin to me that I thought no place could ever be strange.

Note. From Rosegrant (1976) as adapted from Hood (1970). Copyright 1976 by the Society for the Scientific Study of Religion. Reprinted by permission.

Swedish, and had to create a version of the REEM appropriate to Swedish culture by selecting Nordic tales.[178]

Hood initially created the REEM to test the hypothesis that intrinsically religious persons would score higher on the REEM than extrinsically religious persons.[179] In a sample of college students this hypothesis was supported, with intrinsic persons scoring significantly higher on the REEM than extrinsic persons. These findings are compatible with the survey research noted above, in which religiously committed persons often are identified to have high rates of reported mystical experiences. It further suggests, however, that among the religiously committed, intrinsic persons have higher scores (and hence perhaps report more experiences) than extrinsic persons. Using Allport's Intrinsic–Extrinsic scales to create a fourfold typology, based upon median splits on the Intrinsic and Extrinsic scales, indicated that "indiscriminately pro" (high extrinsic/high intrinsic, or IP) persons could not be distinguished from intrinsic persons on the basis of their REEM scores. Likewise, "indiscriminately anti" (low extrinsic/low intrinsic, or IA) persons could not be distinguished from extrinsic persons on the basis of their REEM scores. Survey researchers have often worried about "false positives" and "false negatives" in their surveys. How do we know that persons who report experiences are telling the truth? Some may not have the experiences they report (false positives). On the other hand, how do we know that persons denying these experiences are telling the truth? Some may refuse to admit experiences they have had (false negatives).

In this study Hood linked the methodological problem of distinguishing between intrinsics and IPs, and between extrinsics and IAs, with the possibility that the IPs are often false positives and the IAs false negatives in regard to the report of mystical experience. The basis for this hypothesis is that Allport believed the indiscriminate types to be motivated by conflicting stances with respect to religion: The IAs may be denying religious impulses they may in fact feel, whereas the IPs may be feigning religious impulses they may not actually experience. It is this sort of dynamic and conflictual process that Allport felt made the indiscriminate categories potentially of significant research interest and of "central significance" for his theory.[180]

In a second study, Hood replicated the relationship between Allport's fourfold typology and his own REEM scores.[181] This time, using Rosegrant's modification of the REEM and categorizing persons according to their religious type produced similar high REEM scores for intrinsic and IP persons, and similar low scores for extrinsic and IA persons, as indicated in Table 7.7.

In order to directly test the possibility that the indiscriminate categories might represent false positives (in the case of IPs) and false negatives (in the case of IAs), Hood had interviewers in a double-blind condition conduct a bogus interview that included nearly 40 personal and religious questions. These served as baseline data and served to mask the key final question, which was prefaced by the comment that many of the preceding questions were designed to tap into whether or not respondents had ever had a mystical experience. Persons were then asked whether they had in fact ever had such an experience. The answer to this key question, whether "yes" or "no," was then analyzed with a "Stress Analyzer," a device that measures stress by means of detecting small voice tremors. Each subject's stress level was measured by comparing the affirmation or denial of a mystical experience to the baseline levels of stress in response to the bogus inventory. The numbers of persons affirming and denying mystical experiences, and the numbers showing stress when responding, are reported in Table 7.8 according to religious type.

As predicted, the proportions of persons affirming mystical experiences were similar for intrinsics and IPs, as were the proportions denying mystical experiences for extrinsics and IAs. However, intrinsic persons as a group expressed little stress, whereas IPs showed much more stress, when affirming mystical experiences. The case was less clear for extrinsics. Still, more than half the IA persons exhibited stress, and while many did so when reporting mystical experiences, it may be that indiscriminates as a group (whether pro or anti) indicated stress when talking about their religion (or the lack of it) because of their conflictual stance. In any case, the large number of IP persons affirming mystical experiences with great stress is consistent with the possibility that such persons are "false positives," attempting to appear religious by reporting experiences they believe they should experience but perhaps have not.

However, it is also possible that, as Rosegrant found, stress is often associated with the report of mystical experience; this was indicated by a .29 ($p < .05$) correlation between REEM scores and a measure of stress in a nature setting with 51 students.[182] Although Rosegrant did not measure religious orientation in his study, it may be that the *lack* of correlation be-

TABLE 7.7. REEM Scores According to Religious Type

Religious type	Score
Intrinsic ($n = 31$)	Mean = 48.81, $SD = 12.21$
IP ($n = 46$)	Mean = 50.89, $SD = 14.79$
Extrinsic ($n = 39$)	Mean = 39.51, $SD = 17.07$
IA ($n = 31$)	Mean = 39.13, $SD = 18.80$

Note. $F (1, 143) = 5.69$, $p < .05$; post hoc comparisons grouped according to significant differences *between* clustered categories, at least $p < .05$. Categories *within* parentheses did not differ: (IP, I); (IA, E). Adapted from Hood (1978b, p. 426). Copyright 1978 by the Society for the Scientific Study of Religion. Adapted by permission.

TABLE 7.8. Numbers of Subjects Affirming and Denying Mystical Experience, and Showing Associated Stress, by Religious Type

Religious type	Mystical experience		Stress level	
	Affirming	Denying	High	Low
Intrinsic ($n = 31$)	28	3	3	28
IP ($n = 46$)	40	6	31	15
Extrinsic ($n = 39$)	3	36	8	31
IA ($n = 31$)	12	19	18	13

Note. There was an error in the original article: The numbers for mystical experience for extrinsics were reversed. All differences were significant at least at $p < .05$ for all groups except IAs for both mystical experience and stress. Adapted from Hood (1978b, p. 427). Copyright 1978 by the Society for the Scientific Study of Religion. Adapted by permission.

tween mysticism and a measure of meaningfulness used in his study indicates that mystical experiences are felt as stressful only when subjects are asked for a meaningful religious framework for interpretation. Consistent with this claim is that mystical experience as measured by the REEM is higher not only among intrinsically oriented persons, but also among religious denominations with strong norms for eliciting and interpreting mystical experiences.[183]

Rosegrant's finding that mystical experiences as measured by the REEM were associated with stress experiences in a solitary nature setting[184] may be misleading. Hood has argued that stress per se is unlikely to elicit mystical experience; rather, an incongruity between anticipatory set stress and actual setting stress is likely to facilitate the report of mystical experience. In a study to test this hypothesis specifically in a nature setting, Hood administered Rosegrant's modification of the REEM to 93 males who, as part of the requirements for graduation from a private high school, participated in a week-long outdoors program.[185] One portion of this program entailed having students "solo." Each student was taken alone by Hood into a wilderness area; was issued minimal equipment (a tarp, water, and a mixture of nuts and candy for food); and was then left to spend the night in solitude. Various students were taken out over a five-night period, regardless of weather conditions. As some indication of the power of this experience, 29 of the 93 participants "broke solo," meaning that they returned to base camp before dawn. Before each outing, anticipatory stress was measured by having the students fill out a measure of subjective stress. In addition, setting stress was fortuitously varied by the fact that some students soloed on nights when there were strong rain and thunderstorms. Table 7.9 presents the means on the REEM for participants in this

TABLE 7.9. Mean REEM Scores for Participants under High- and Low-Stress Nature Solo Conditions, According to Anticipatory Stress Levels

Anticipatory stress	Setting stress	
	High	Low
High	32.44 ($SD = 12.75$) ($n = 16$)	52.83 ($SD = 14.72$) ($n = 12$)
Low	51.43 ($SD = 9.37$) ($n = 21$)	42.07 ($SD = 4.95$) ($n = 15$)

Note. Adapted from Hood (1978a, p. 283). Copyright 1978 by the Society for the Scientific Study of Religion. Adapted by permission.

exercise, according to anticipatory stress levels and setting stress conditions. Appropriate statistical tests indicated not only that set–setting incongruity elicited higher REEM scores, but also that it made no difference whether the incongruity was between high anticipatory stress and low setting stress or between low anticipatory stress and high setting stress. Either incongruity would work.

Subcultural differences in the emphasis upon and support of intense religious experiences should also be reflected in REEM scores. Hood and Hall had anthropologists select five "culturally fair" REEM items with which to compare four samples.[186] All subjects were Roman Catholics and were matched for education, gender, age, and social class. The four groups were Native Americans, acculturated Mexican-Americans (spoke English 100% of the time), Mexican-Americans (spoke Spanish at least 25% of the time), and Caucasians. As hypothesized, the two groups whose subcultures encourage intense experiences (Native Americans, Mexican-Americans) had higher REEM scores than either the Caucasians or the acculturated Mexican-Americans. The matching on relevant variables suggests that differences in the REEM scores reflect genuine subcultural differences in either the experiences themselves or the reporting of such experiences.

Several investigators have postulated that mystical and other intense religious experiences are related to and perhaps often elicited by hypnotic trance states. For instance, Gibbons and Jarnette suggest that at least some religious experiences may be trance states induced by stimuli located outside awareness.[187] Anthropologists have long argued for the similarity between hypnotic and religious ecstatic states.[188] Hood[189] found a correlation between the original form of the REEM and the Harvard Group Scale of Hypnotic Susceptibility[190] of .36 ($p < .01$) in a sample of 81 fundamentalist Protestants willing to be hypnotized. This is consistent with the finding that fundamentalist Protestants who report significant conversion experiences are also hypnotically suggestible.[191] Perhaps the loss of sense of self reported in mystical experience parallels the loss of self in hypnotic states. However, we must be careful *not* to equate mysticism and hypnosis on the basis of similar processes that may operate in both.

It is also worth hypothesizing that the many different triggers or facilitating conditions for mystical experiences noted in survey research and other studies may have in common the fact that an individual fascinated by any given trigger acquires a momentary loss of sense of self, being "absorbed" or "fascinated" by his or her object of perception. Tellegen and Atkinson have proposed "absorption," or openness to absorbing and self-altering states, to be a trait related to hypnosis.[192] The only empirical study using their measure of absorption and a measure of mysticism is a study by Mathes relating mysticism, absorption, and romantic love. Unfortunately, he did not report the correlation between mysticism and absorption.[193] However, in Mathes's study, Rubin's measure of romantic love[194] was correlated with mysticism for both males and females. This is consistent with being fascinated or "absorbed" by the object of interest in both experiences. It is also consistent with the fact that both love and sexuality are frequently cited as triggers of mysticism in open-ended questionnaire and survey studies.

The relationship between mysticism and hypnosis has been negatively interpreted, particularly by psychodynamically oriented investigators. Both hypnotic susceptibility and religious experiences, especially mystical ones, are interpreted either as regressions to early states of ego development or as signs of adult weak ego development.[195] Hood has noted that claims to a relationship between weak ego development and religious experience are derived from primarily a priori theoretical commitments of dynamic theorists that not only are conceptually unwarranted but also lack empirical support.[196] In the only direct empirical test of a relationship between weak ego development and intense religious experience, both the conceptual and empirical inadequacies of this hypothesized relationship were demonstrated.[197]

In this study, Hood administered the most psychometrically sophisticated measure of ego strength (Barron's Ego Strength scale[198]) to a sample of 82 college students who also took the initial 15-item version of the REEM. Overall, there was a significant negative correlation ($r = -.31$) between the REEM and Barron's total scale, appearing to support the claim that intense religious experience is related to weak ego. However, part of the problem is conceptual, in that Barron's scale contains several religiously worded items; these religiously worded items are scored so that agreement indicates weak ego.[199] This suggests a conceptual bias against religious experience, so that one can simply assume that many religious beliefs reflect poor ego development and then use them as a measure of weak ego strength. Hood separated Barron's scale into two parts: the religiously worded items and the residual, nonreligiously worded items. Correlating these with the REEM yielded markedly different results, as shown in Table 7.10.

Inspection of Table 7.10 is instructive in two senses. First, negative correlations, supposedly indicating weak ego among persons reporting mystical experiences, were found with religiously worded items scored to indicate weak ego strength! This link reveals the conceptual basis of these items, and confounds many supposedly empirical findings. Removing the religious items removed any significant relationship between weak ego and religious experience. Furthermore, using a nondynamically oriented measure developed for use in survey research (Stark's Index of Psychic Inadequacy) revealed that among a sample of 114 college students, those with higher adequacy in psychological functioning as measured by this index had significantly higher REEM scores than those with lower adequacy as measured by this index.[200]

Thus, not only is there little conceptual or empirical support for the claim that weak ego strength must characterize persons who have intense religious experiences; such persons may also be more psychologically adequate than those who do not report such experiences. This latter claim is consistent with the normality of the report of mystical and numinous experiences noted in survey studies and with those theorists who are more sympathetic to religion. For instance, Maslow's popular theory of self-actualization postulates that more actualized persons are most likely to have and to report "peak experiences," Maslow's term for mystical and other related experiences.[201] Although his theory has generated little rigorous empirical research to support this claim, it serves as a useful conceptual counter to dynamic theories that postulate a relationship between regression and religious experience, for which there is also little rigorous empirical support.

TABLE 7.10. Correlations between the REEM and Barron's Total Ego Strength Scale, Religiously Worded Items, and Residual Items

	Religiously worded items	Nonreligiously worded items	REEM
Total ego strength scale	.47*	.93*	−.31*
Religiously worded items	—	−.46*	−.55*
Nonreligiously worded items	—	—	−.16

Note. Adapted from Hood (1974, p. 66). Copyright 1974 by the Society for the Scientific Study of Religion. Adapted by permission.

*$p < .01$.

The Mysticism Scale (M Scale): The Influence of Stace

James was the source for the range of experiences, both numinous and mystical, selected for the REEM. One criticism of the REEM is that although it does contain both numinous and mystical experiences according to the criteria discussed earlier, it is not particularly theory-driven. However, this is not the case with the Mysticism Scale (M Scale). It was developed by Hood[202] as a specific operationalization of Stace's[203] phenomenological work, in which he identified both introvertive and extrovertive mysticism and their common core. It is currently the most widely used empirical measure of mysticism.[204]

Prior to the development of the M Scale, Stace's criteria of mysticism had influenced assessments in psychedelic research seeking to document the ontological validity of experiences elicited under drugs. Stace's criteria were developed under the assumption of causal indifference. Examples used by Stace were accepted as mystical, whether elicited under drug conditions or not.[205] Research Box 7.3 presents a summary of, and recent follow-up data from, what is perhaps the most famous study in the psychology of religion—Pahnke's Good Friday experiment.

Pahnke's original study and Doblin's long-term follow-up are important in demonstrating the effect of set and setting on drug-facilitated mystical experiences, using Stace's explicit criteria. The general discussion of drugs and religious experience in Chapter 6 obviously applies to this experiment. Yet, in terms of this chapter, Pahnke was the first investigator to attempt explicitly to operationalize Stace's criteria of mysticism. His original questionnaire has been variously modified through the years, with many additional nonmystical items added. However, basic items relating to Stace's core criteria of mystical experience have remained virtually unchanged.[206] The most recent expanded versions of Pahnke's questionnaire include items relevant to peak experiences, which we have discussed in Chapter 6. It is clear that the concept of "peak experience" has been broadened to include a wide variety of experiences, only some of which are mystical in Stace's sense of the term. The M Scale is explicitly designed to measure Stace's criteria of mysticism, distinct from a wide range of other experiences, including peak experiences.

Given that the M Scale is based upon Stace's demarcation of the phenomenological properties of mysticism, it is also of necessity driven by some of Stace's theoretical concerns. Most central is the fact that Stace has become the central figure in the debate between what we call the "common-core theorists" and the "diversity theorists." Common-core theorists assume that people can differentiate experience from interpretation, such that different interpretations may be applied to otherwise identical experiences. This theory is often characterized by its opponents as if it claims that there is an absolute, unmediated experience. In fact, Stace[207] and other common-core theorists simply distinguish between degrees of interpretation, arguing that at some level different descriptions can mask quite similar (if not identical) experiences.

Diversity theorists—led by Katz, who edited an entire volume in response to Stace's work[208]—argue that no unmediated experience is possible, and that in the extreme, language is not simply used to interpret experience but in fact constitutes experience. Proudfoot is among the contemporary theorists (heavily influenced by psychology) who argue for the role of language in the constitution of, not simply the interpretation of, experience.[209] Although we cannot engage this rich conceptual literature here, let us note that three fundamental assumptions implicit in Stace's work should be emphasized. First, the mystical experience is itself a universal experience that is essentially identical in phenomenological terms, despite

 За

Research Box 7.3. Drugs and Mysticism: Pahnke's "Good Friday" Experiment (Pahnke, 1966; Doblin, 1991)

In the psychology of religion's most famous and controversial study, Pahnke, as part of his doctoral dissertation, administered the drug psilocybin or a placebo in a double-blind study of 20 volunteers, all graduate students at Andover–Newton Theological Seminary. The subjects met to hear a broadcast of a Good Friday service after they had been given either psilocybin (experimental group) or nicotinic acid (placebo group). Participants met in groups of four, each consisting of two experimental subjects and two controls matched for compatibility. Each group had two leaders assigned, one of whom had been given psilocybin. Immediately after the service and then 6 months later, participants were administered a questionnaire, part of which consisted of Stace's specific common-core criteria of mysticism.

Nearly a quarter of a century later, from November 1986 to October 1989, Doblin contacted the original participants in the experiment. By either phone or personal contact, he was able to interview nine of the control participants and seven of the experimental participants from the original study. In addition, he was able to administer Pahnke's questionnaire to them. Thus, we have the responses on Stace's criteria of mysticism immediately after the service, then 6 months later, and finally nearly 25 years later. Assigning each score as the percentage of the possible maximum for that criteria, according to Pahnke's original procedure, yields the following results.

| | Original Pahnke study | | | | Doblin follow-up study (nearly 25 years later) | |
| | Immediate | | 6 months later | | | |
Stace category	Exptls. (*n* = 10)	Controls (*n* = 10)	Exptls. (*n* = 10)	Controls (*n* = 10)	Exptls. (*n* = 7)	Controls (*n* = 9)
1. Unity:						
a. Internal	70%	8%	60%	5%	77%	5%
b. External	38%	2%	39%	1%	51%	6%
2. Transcendence of space/time	84%	6%	78%	7%	73%	9%
3. Positive affect	57%	23%	54%	23%	56%	21%
4. Sacredness	53%	28%	58%	25%	68%	29%
5. Noetic quality	63%	18%	71%	18%	82%	24%
6. Paradoxicality	61%	13%	34%	3%	48%ʻ	4%
7. Ineffability	66%	18%	77%	15%	71%	3%
8. Transience	79%	8%	76%	9%	75%	9%

Note. Our table has been constructed to allow direct comparison between Doblin's percentages and Pahnke's. Terms have been altered to correspond more closely to M Scale terminology where relevant. Some of Pahnke's criteria were not Stace's (e.g., transience), and some of Stace's criteria were not employed by Pahnke (e.g., inner subjectivity). Exptls., experimental participants.

wide variations in ideological interpretation of the experience (the common-core assumption). Second, the core categories of mystical experience are not all definitionally essential to any particular mystical experience, since there are always borderline cases, based upon fulfillment of only some of the criteria. Third, the introvertive and extrovertive forms of mysticism are most conceptually distinct: The former is an experience of unity devoid of content (pure consciousness), and the latter is an experience of unity in diversity, one with content. The psychometric properties of the M Scale should reflect these assumptions, and insofar as they do are adequate operationalizations of Stace's criteria. Of course, they also reflect in measurement terms what diversity theorists criticize conceptually in Stace's work. The issue for now is what light empirical research can shed on mysticism and its interpretation.

Psychometric Properties. The M Scale consists of 32 items (16 positively worded and 16 negatively worded items), covering all but one of the original common-core criteria of mysticism proposed by Stace.[210] Hood's original work indicated that the M Scale contains two factors.[211] For our purposes, it is important to note that Factor I consists of items assessing an experience of unity (introvertive or extrovertive), while Factor II consists of items referring both to religious and knowledge claims. This is compatible with Stace's claim that a common experience (mystical experience of unity) may be variously interpreted. A factor analysis of the M Scale by Caird supports the original two-factor solution to the M Scale.[212] Reinert and Stifler also support a two-factor solution, but suggest the possibility that religious items and knowledge items emerge as separate factors.[213] This splits the interpretative factor into religious and other modes of interpretation, which would not be inconsistent with Stace's theory. This would allow for an even greater range of interpretation of experience—a claim to knowledge that can be either religiously or nonreligiously based. However, the factor-analytic studies cited above are far from definitive; notably, they suffer from inadequate subject-to-items ratios. Overall, however, they are consistent in demonstrating two stable factors—one an experience factor associated with minimal interpretation, the other an interpretative factor that is probably heavily religiously influenced.

More recently, Hood and his colleagues have proposed a three-factor solution to the M Scale, based upon more adequate sample size.[214] This three-factor solution fits Stace's phenomenology of mysticism quite nicely, in that both introvertive and extrovertive mysticism emerge as separate factors, along with an interpretative factor. This version of the M Scale is presented in Table 7.11. Because the three-factor solution to the M Scale is clearly the most adequate overall measure of mysticism in terms of Stace's theory, and because it permits the separate measurement of each type of mysticism as well as an interpretative factor, it is preferred for future research. However, the research to date has used the two-factor solution initially reported by Hood, in which introvertive and extrovertive mysticism are not independently measured, forming as they do part of the minimal phenomenological Factor I. Thus, the majority of studies of mysticism to date using two-factor solutions do not separately identify differential predictions for introvertive and extrovertive mysticism, but rather merge these two as a single factor expressing experiences of unity.

Relation to Other Measures of Mystical Experience. The initial publication of the M Scale related it to several other measures. The M Scale might be anticipated to correlate with the REEM, since the latter contains a mixture of items relating to numinous and mystical experiences. However, given the overall religious language explicit or implicit in the REEM, it was anticipated that the interpretative factor would correlate more strongly with the REEM

TABLE 7.11. Three-Factor Structure of the Mysticism Scale (M Scale)

Factor I: Extrovertive Mysticism (12 items; alpha = .76)

6. I have never had an experience in which I felt myself to be absorbed as one with all things.
8. I have never had an experience in which I felt as if all things were alive.
10. I have never had an experience in which all things seemed to be aware.
12. I have had an experience in which I realized the oneness of myself with all things.
15. I have never had an experience in which time and space were nonexistent.
19. I have had an experience in which I felt everything in the world to be part of the same whole.
24. I have never had an experience in which my own self seemed to merge into something greater.
27. I have never had an experience in which time, space, and distance were meaningless.
28. I have never had an experience in which I became aware of a unity to all things.
29. I have had an experience in which all things seemed to be conscious.
30. I have never had an experience in which all things seemed to be unified into a single whole.
31. I have had an experience in which I felt nothing is ever really dead.

Factor II: Religious Interpretation (12 items; alpha = .76)

5. I have experienced profound joy
7. I have never experienced a perfectly peaceful state.
9. I have never had an experience which seemed holy to me.
13. I have had an experience in which a new view of reality was revealed to me.
14. I have never experienced anything to be divine.
16. I have never experienced anything that I could call ultimate reality.
17. I have had an experience in which ultimate reality was revealed to me.
18. I have had experience in which I felt that all was perfection at the time.
20. I have had an experience which I knew to be sacred.
22. I have had an experience which left me with a feeling of awe.
25. I have never had an experience which left me with a feeling of wonder.
26. I have never had an experience in which deeper aspects of reality were revealed to me.

Factor III: Introvertive Mysticism (8 items; alpha = .69)

1. I have had an experience which was both timeless and spaceless.
2. I have never had an experience which was incapable of being expressed in words.
3. I have had an experience in which something greater than myself seemed to absorb me.
4. I have had an experience in which everything seemed to disappear from my mind until I was conscious only of a void.
11. I have had an experience in which I had no sense of time or space.
21. I have never had an experience which I was unable to express adequately through language.
23. I have had an experience that is impossible to communicate.
32. I have had an experience that cannot be expressed in words.

Note. Negatively worded items are reverse-scored. Items are numbered to correspond to the original two-factor solution reported in Hood (1975) and to allow easy comparison to Caird (1988) and Reinert and Stifler (1993). From Hood, Morris, and Watson (1993, p. 1177). Copyright 1993 by *Psychological Reports*. Reprinted by permission.

than would the phenomenological factor. This was the case in a sample of 52 students enrolled at a Protestant religious college in the South: Factor I correlated .34 with the REEM, whereas Factor II correlated .56 with the REEM. It was also found in another sample of 83 college students that Factor I correlated (−.75) more strongly with a measure of ego permissiveness than did Factor II (−.43).[215] Insofar as Taft's ego permissiveness measure[216] is related to openness to a wide range of anomalous experiences, including ecstatic emotions, intrinsic arousal, and peak experiences, it is not surprising that Factor I correlated more strongly with this measure than Factor II. The differential correlation of Factors I and II in the two studies is congruent with Stace's theory that experience can be separated from interpretation in varying degrees. Factor I correlates more strongly with measures of experience minimally interpreted, and Factor II with measures of experience more extensively interpreted in religious language.

In Hood's original report, the M Scale factors correlated with a measure of intrinsic religion in roughly the same magnitude in a sample of 65 fundamentalist college students enrolled in a religious college in the South (I = .68, II = .58), supporting research as noted above between the REEM and intrinsic religion.[217] Furthermore, if in light of the assumption that intrinsic persons are likely to be frequent church attendees, Hood's finding that both frequent attendees and nonattendees had similar high scores on Factor I of the M Scale, but that only frequent church attendees had high Factor II scores,[218] makes sense in terms of Stace's distinction between experience and interpretation. Both frequent attendees and nonattendees reported mystical experiences in terms of their minimal phenomenological properties of an experience of union, but frequent church attendees were likely to interpret these experiences in religious terms. Nonattendees did not use traditional religious language to describe their experiences.

Holm prepared a Swedish translation of the M Scale and administered it to a sample of 122 Swedish informants.[219] Unlike the REEM, the M Scale could be meaningfully translated into Swedish and could be studied similarly to the way it was investigated in North America. Holm not only confirmed a two-factor solution closely paralleling Hood's initial mysticism and interpretation factors, but also found that in correlating the M Scale with ratings of a person's most significant personal experiences, Factor I correlated best with experiences reported by individuals without a Christian profile, whereas Factor II best related to more traditional Christian experiences. The revised Swedish version of the REEM, using Nordic accounts of intense experiences appropriate to a Finnish–Swedish culture, also showed patterns similar to those found in Hood's research with the REEM in the United States. In Holm's words:

> We also discovered one factor which could be called a general mysticism factor and another where the experience was interpreted on a religious/Christian basis. The "religious interpretation factor" had strong correspondences with religious quality in the interviews and with the background variables of prayer frequency, bible study, church attendance and attitude towards Christianity. This factor thus covered experiences with an expressly Christian profile. It showed high correlations with the intrinsic scale, with the expressively Christian narratives on the REEM and with the religious quality on the interviews. Thus, overall, in a Finnish–Swedish culture the M Scale and REEM functioned very closely to how they function in American culture.[220]

Interestingly, Holm also noted that the distinction between a general mysticism factor (or impersonal mysticism) and a religious factor (or personal mysticism) has parallels with early research on mysticism in Sweden by Soderblom, who identified these as "infinity mysticism" and "personality mysticism," respectively.[221] This also parallels our earlier discussion of the distinction between impersonal and personal aspects of mystical experience, as noted by several investigators.

Relation to Measures of Other Personality Factors. Although the relationship between the religious factor of the M Scale and the more explicitly religiously worded REEM items is reasonable, the question of more general personality factors related to mysticism is of interest. M Scale scores have been correlated with standardized personality measures in two studies. In one, Hood found that most scales of the Minnesota Multiphasic Personality Inventory (MMPI), a widely used measure to assess pathology, failed to correlate with the M Scale.[222] Furthermore, differential patterns of significant correlations between Factors I and II were compatible with a nonpathological interpretation of mysticism. For instance, Factor II (But not factor I) correlated significantly with the Lie (L) scale of the MMPI. This scale presumably measures the tendency to lie or present oneself in a favorable social light. However, insofar as Factor II represents a traditional religious stance, Hood suggested that high L scores for Factor II may represent the fact that the traditionally religious are less likely to engage in deviant social behaviors as measured by the L scale.[223] Factor I did significantly correlate with two scales on the MMPI concerned with bodily processes (Hypochondria) and intense experiential states (Hysteria), which, in nonpathological terms, are likely to be compatible with mystical experience.[224]

Possible relationships between mysticism and absorption or hypnosis, discussed above in connection with the REEM as a measure of religious experience, are consistent with the work of Spanos and Moretti.[225] They directly correlated the M Scale with the Tellegen and Atkinson Absorption scale and with three measures of hypnosis: the Carleton University Responsiveness to Suggestion Scale, which yields both an objective and a subjective score (CURSS-O and CURSS-S);[226] the Field Hypnotic Depth scale;[227] and the widely used Stanford Hypnotic Suggestibility Scale, Form C (SHSS:C).[228] Overall, the M Scale correlated .53 with the Absorption scale, .37 with the Hypnotic Depth scale, .40 with the SHSS:C, and .36 with both the CURSS:O and CURSS:S in an all-female sample of university students. When mysticism was used as the criterion variable, regression analyses using the four hypnosis measures, absorption, and two other variables (neuroticism and psychosomatic symptoms) indicated that Absorption was the single best predictor, accounting for 29% of the variance, with Hypnotic Depth second best, adding an additional 5%. None of the other hypnotic scales, or the neuroticism or psychosomatic symptom scales, added predictive power.[229] Spanos and Moritti concluded that while mystical experience can occur among the distraught and troubled, it is as frequent among the psychologically untroubled. However, mysticism per se is unrelated to psychopathology.

Using a measure of positive functioning, designed to measure "common-sense" personality characteristics of the healthy person,[230] further supports the normality of those who report mystical experiences. Hood and his colleagues[231] administered the Jackson Personality Inventory (JPI)[232] to a sample of 118 college students. Factor I scores on the M Scale correlated significantly with 6 of the 15 JPI scales, suggesting a pattern of consistency with a general openness to experience, including tolerance, breadth of interest, innovation, and willingness to take risks. Not insignificantly, Factor I was also associated with a tendency to be critical of tradition and related negatively to value orthodoxy, whereas Factor II revealed the reverse pattern (i.e., value orthodoxy and a tendency to accept tradition). Factor II also correlated negatively with risk taking.[233] Thus, consistent with much of the research noted above with the REEM and the M Scale, persons who report mystical experiences can be represented as open to experiences outside those accepted within various religious traditions. Again, one interpretation of this type of data is that conventionally religious persons have mystical experiences interpreted within their traditions and hence meaningful as confirming religious experiences, whereas less traditionally religious persons have mystical experiences they are unwilling to interpret within traditional frameworks and hence do not see them as confirming or verifying beliefs within an established tradition.

Two studies not directly employing the M Scale are relevant to this issue. Hood and Morris took virtually all items used in the empirical assessment of mysticism and factor-analyzed them into scales, all with adequate reliability.[234] These were then administered to a sample of respondents who rated the items for their applicability to defining mysticism as they understood it, and then rated them for whether or not they ever had experienced that item. Respondents did not differ on knowledge about mysticism, whether or not they personally identified themselves as having had a mystical experience. However, persons who denied having had such an experience did not mark items they knew to define mysticism as experiences they themselves had had, whereas those affirming mystical experience did. Thus, persons equally knowledgeable about mystical experiences differ on whether or not they mark an item as a function of having a mystical experience. This suggests that persons can know what mysticism is and yet not experience it.

In an additional analysis of these data by Morris and Hood, all those who indicated no religious identity ("nones," $n = 40$) were compared to a randomly selected sample ($n = 40$) of those who identified themselves as Baptists.[235] Persons were asked to indicate whether they had ever had a mystical experience. Using two factors developed to identify unity and religious interpretation (paralleling Stace's distinctions and those found in the M Scale), Morris and Hood found that both "nones" and Baptists who reported mystical experiences used religious language to describe them, although Baptists scored higher on the use of religious language. Consistent with the larger study, the results suggest that individuals can distinguish between knowledge about mysticism and whether or not they have had a mystical experience. However, if they have had one, religious language is used to describe it—even by the "nones." These results are consistent with survey research discussed above, in which Vernon found that religious "nones" nevertheless reported religious experiences. It may be that for many, the language of religion is the only language available to express these profound experiences.

In light of the research described above, it is worth noting that Troeltsch's church–sect theory, extensively discussed in Chapter 9, was initially a church–sect–mysticism theory in which he postulated two mysticisms.[236] One was simply the affirmation within religious traditions of a spiritual accessibility to the holy as defined by tradition. The other was a radical individualistic form of mysticism assuming no traditional support or mediation, since an individual experiencing this form has direct access to the transcendent. Garrett has tried to reintroduce these two mysticisms into contemporary discussions of church–sect theory, but with little success.[237] This is unfortunate, since Troeltsch's two mysticisms nicely fit the empirical data on the reporting of mystical experience, based upon Stace's distinction between experience and its interpretation.

Mystical experiences within traditions are both interpreted and partly structured by an awareness of an experience meaningfully described within the beliefs of a tradition. They are the direct validation of what we have referred to above as "foundation realities." The term "direct" does not mean absolutely unmediated; rather, it means that the tradition structures and provides a language framework within which experiences can be fully existentially encountered. As Katz[238] and the diversity theorists have rightly insisted, Jews have Jewish mystical experiences and Buddhists have mystical experiences common to Buddhism. Indeed, most mystics have historically struggled to maintain themselves within established traditions—that is, to use the language and concepts of a given tradition to clarify and confirm their experiences.[239] However, others experience mysticism outside established traditions and hence fail to find the language of established traditions meaningful. Such experiences are no less mystical and probably most correspond to what Factor I of the M Scale measures: the minimal phenomenological properties of a sense of union. For these mystics, the experience does not confirm an established tradition, except insofar as direct access to the transcendent outside of tradition has itself become a mysticism of radical individuality.[240] Such persons are unlikely to use the established language of a tradition to describe their experience, and may be seeking alternative frameworks to understand their experience or may merely be satisfied with a nonlinguistic recognition of the experience. This is consistent with Rosegrant's finding that mystical experiences may be reported but may not be perceived as meaningful.[241] It also reflects that the claim to ineffability can be a tactic to refuse to describe experiences, such that they become confirming of the reality claims of any established tradition. Obviously, the demand that experiences be described entails the use of language. Thus, not surprisingly, those who have focused upon having persons describe their "ineffable" experiences have found language to be a major factor affecting experience (or, better, experience as described). However, minimalist language, referring to such things as "unity," can produce agreement among persons; this may suggest a common element to experience even if that unity is variously described.

The report of mystical experience is firmly established as a normal phenomenon among healthy individuals, who, if lacking a religious commitment, are unlikely to use traditional religious language to describe the experience, or are likely to use it reluctantly as the only available language to express their experience. That mystical experience is a normal phenomenon reported among healthy individuals does not mean that others cannot also report these experiences. In the only empirical study administering the M Scale to both healthy and normal populations, Stifler and his colleagues administered the M Scale along with other measures to three relevant samples ($n = 30$ each): psychiatric inpatients meeting formal diagnostic criteria for psychotic disorders; senior members of various contemplative/mystical groups; and hospital staff members (as normal controls).[242] Using total M Scale scores, Stifler et al. found that psychotics (mean = 141.9, $SD = 10.4$) and contemplatives (mean = 142.8, $SD = 3.7$) could not be distinguished from each other, but that both differed from hospital staff controls (mean = 124.9, $SD = 3.9$).[243] Thus, both psychotics and contemplatives reported mystical experiences more often than normal controls. Although these data are correlational, it is reasonable to assume that mysticism neither causes nor is produced by psychoses. Rather, psychotics, like contemplatives, can have or can report such experiences.

Consistent with this research is the work on temporal lobe epilepsy, commonly assumed to be associated with reports of mystical and other religious experiences. For instance, Persinger has argued that what he terms the "God experience" is an artifact of changes in temporal lobe activity.[244] However, in a study of 46 outpatients in the Maudsley Epilepsy Clinic, Sensky found that patients with temporal lobe epilepsy did not have a higher rate of mystical experiences (or general religious experiences), compared to a control population.[245] By contrast, a study by Persinger and Makarec found positive correlations between scores of their measure of complex epileptic signs and the report of paranormal and mystical experiences in a sample of 414 university students.[246] Although neither of these studies used the M Scale to measure mystical experience, findings overall suggest that even if mystical experience is commonly associated with temporal lobe activity, it is no more common in actual temporal lobe epileptic patients than in control populations with normal temporal lobe activity. Hence, there is no firm empirical basis from which to assume neurophysiological deficiencies in those reporting mystical experiences.

Relation to More Abstract Concepts. Rather than focusing upon particular concrete triggers, Hood has argued that more abstract conceptualization may permit a more empirically adequate investigation of the conditions and circumstances that trigger mystical experience.[247] In particular, theological and philosophical interest in the concept of limits is useful.[248] At the conceptual level, the idea of limits entails transcendence; in fact, awareness of limits makes the experience of transcendence possible. Perhaps the sudden contrast that occurs when a limit is suddenly transcended yields a contrast effect similar to a figure–ground reversal, in which what was previously unnoticed is thrown into stark relief. Hood has noted that such sudden contrasts are common in nature settings, particularly those in which stress is involved. Nature as a common trigger of mystical experiences is well documented in survey studies; often such experiences are associated with stress, which is itself sometimes cited as a trigger of mystical experience. In one study described earlier, the set–setting incongruity hypothesis was supported when the REEM was used as a measure. It has also been supported in research using the M Scale.

Hood took advantage of a week-long outdoors program at a private all-male high school.[249] During this program, graduating seniors engaged in a variety of outdoor activities varying in degree of stress. Three particularly stressful activities were examined: rock climbing/rappelling (for the first time, for many students); whitewater rafting (down a river rated as difficult); and the experience (described earlier in this chapter) of staying alone in the woods one night with minimal equipment. A nonstressful activity (canoeing a calm river) was selected as a control. Just prior to participating in each activity, participants were administered a measure of subjective anticipatory stress for that activity. Immediately after each activity, the participants took the M Scale to assess mystical experience. The comparisons between set and setting stress for each high-stress activity supported the hypothesis that the interaction between these two types of stress elicits reports of mystical experience. It is important to note that anticipatory stress varied across situations, such that whether or not a particular person anticipated a given situation as stressful was not simply a function of its independently assessed situation stress. Also, in stressful situations, those anticipating low stress scored higher on mysticism than those anticipating high stress. Thus, set and setting stress incongruity elicit reports of mystical experience—not simply stress per se, either anticipatory or situational. Additional support for this hypothesis was found by using the canoe activity as a control; no student anticipated this activity to be stressful. Given the congruity between low anticipated stress and low setting stress, low M Scale scores resulted, as predicted. However, in high-stress activities anticipated as high in stress, M Scale scores were also predicted and obtained. Only the incongruity between setting and anticipatory stress produced high M Scale scores. Furthermore, with only one exception, these results held for both Factor I and Factor II scores; this suggests not only that the minimal phenomenological properties of mysticism are elicited, but also that they are seen as religiously relevant in the broad sense of this term. This replicates the findings discussed above with solo experiences in a nature setting when the REEM was used as a measure. Thus, it would appear that anticipatory and setting stress incongruities can elicit both mystical experiences of unity (M Scale) and more numinous religious experiences (REEM) in nature.

The fact that both nature and prayer settings reliably elicit reports of mystical experience in traditionally religious persons has led some to suggest that prayer should be correlated with the report of mystical experience, particularly if the prayer is contemplative in nature. Hood and his colleagues, using a modified form of the M Scale, documented such a correlation in two separate studies.[250] They found that among persons who prayed or meditated regularly, intrinsically religious persons had higher mysticism scores than extrinsics, in terms of both the minimal phenomenological properties of mysticism and its religious interpretation. This finding is consistent with survey research by Poloma and Gallup, in which meditative prayer was related to experiences of closeness to God.[251] Thus, several studies suggest that meditative prayer, as opposed to petitionary or other forms of prayer, relates to both mystical (unity) and numinous (nearness) experiences of God. Finney and Malony have developed a theoretical model in which contemplative prayer should be a useful adjunct in psychotherapy when spiritual development is a treatment goal, and therapeutic progress should be associated with greater mystical awareness.[252] However, they failed to find empirical support for their theory when mysticism as measured by the M Scale did not increase during successful therapy aimed at spiritual development, even though time spent in contemplative prayer did increase.[253]

Mystical experiences are common in nature and in meditative prayer—two conditions that are often solitary. Hence, it may be that factors that meaningfully enhance solitude facilitate the report of mystical experience. Experimentally, it is possible to enhance solitude through the use of an isolation tank. If a religious set is given in an isolation tank, will the combination of set and enhanced isolation facilitate the report of mystical experience? Research Box 7.4 reports a study in which Hood and his colleagues explored this question.[254]

Summary. Overall, studies employing the M Scale have been successful in correlating the scale with predicted variables of theoretical significance. The M Scale has also proven useful in quasi-experimental studies eliciting mystical experience. Most studies to date have used a two-factor solution to the M Scale, in which introvertive and extrovertive mysticism are collapsed into a single experiential factor. Separating introvertive and extrovertive into separate scales, as recommended earlier, should permit theory development based upon the differential predictions that should follow from these two experiences of unity.

OVERVIEW

Clearly, mystical experience remains a central concern for those who would link the conceptual and empirical literatures on religious experience. The mystical and the numinous remain contenders for the unique in religion. They also provide an experiential basis that may require serious attention to the ontological claims of those who have such experiences. McClenon has argued that the uniformity of the report of a wide range of anomalous experiences suggests that cultural determination of these interpretations may account for less variance than many suppose.[255] Although social scientists may not offer "proofs" for claims of mystical experience, neither can they—without hubris—deny the possibility that religion contains truths. Indeed, such truths may be as necessary for the experience as the more restricted claim that the *belief* in such truths is necessary. Few persons have such experiences without believing in their possibility in advance or becoming converted to their truth after the fact.

Research on mystical experiences is best approached in terms of what each methodology can contribute. The descriptive material of open-ended and qualitative studies enhances the narrowness and precision of survey research. Yet the two methods have revealed similar triggers and consequences of these experiences, and both methods have confirmed the normality of their occurrence. Survey research provides suggestive correlations and patterns for laboratory and quasi-experimental studies, which in turn have shown that mystical experience can be facilitated and follows patterns compatible with results from open-ended and

---

❧

Research Box 7.4. The Differential Elicitation of Mystical Experience in an Isolation Tank (Hood, Morris, & Watson, 1990)

Solitude is often cited as one trigger of religious and mystical experiences. Hood and his colleagues placed individuals in a sensory isolation tank to maximize solitude. The tank was approximately 7.5 feet in diameter and 4 feet high. It contained a hydrated magnesium sulfate solution with a density of 1.30 grams/cc, a constant temperature of 34.1°C, and a depth of 10 inches. The tank was totally enclosed, lightproof, and soundproof. It was equipped with an intercom system so that a participant could communicate with an experimenter in another room.

Each participant in the study was placed in the isolation tank after being told about the typical images likely to occur under these conditions. In addition, participants were given a specific religious set (in boldface) or a nonreligious control set (in italics) as follows:

> I am now going to invite you to keep silent for a period of 10 minutes. First you will try to attain silence, as total silence as possible of heart and mind. Having attained it, you will expose yourself to whatever [**religious revelation**/*insight*] it brings.[a]

Participants had previously completed the Allport Religious Orientation scale and could be classified as intrinsic, extrinsic, and "indiscriminately pro" (IP) individuals. A modified version of the M Scale was used that allowed a simple "yes" or "no " response to each item, so that participants could respond over the intercom while still in the isolation tank. Results were as predicted: Under the religious set, both intrinsic and IP participants reported more religious interpretation of their experiences (higher Factor II scores) than extrinsics. However, the IP participants reported less minimal phenomenological properties of mysticism (lower Factor I scores) than either the intrinsics or the extrinsics. This suggests that the IP participants wished to "appear" religious by affirming religious experiences they did not actually have. Extrinsics had these experiences, as indicated by their Factor I scores, but did not describe them in religious language. Intrinsics both had the experiences and described them in religious language.

Further support for these views was evident in the control conditions. When participants were not presented with a religious set, none of the groups differed in the minimal phenomenological properties of mysticism (Factor I). However, intrinsics still interpreted their experiences in religious terms (Factor II), whereas neither extrinsic nor IP persons described their experiences in religious language in the control condition. Thus, the isolation tank elicited similar experiences in subjects of all religious types. The difference in Factor II under set conditions for the types suggests that the intrinsics consistently interpreted their tank experiences as religious; extrinsics consistently interpreted their tank experiences as less religious; and IP persons only interpreted their tank experiences as religious when given an explicit religious set.

---

[a]These instructions were adapated from those used by de Mello (1984) in his study of prayer.

survey research. All these are then given various alternative interpretations by the theological, philosophical, and historical literature.

If there is any picture to be suggested at this point, it is to be sketched in broad lines; yet even this picture is helpful. Mysticism is a normal phenomenon, reported by healthy and functioning persons struggling to find a meaningful framework within which to live out their experience as foundational—as at least what is real for them, if not in some sense as the ultimate "Real." Mysticism, real or Real, has proven itself susceptible to empirical investigation. Clearly, much remains to be done. Future progress will surely be interdisciplinary. Even if McGinn is correct in his fear that an empirical reading of mystical texts from a psychological perspective has only an "ambiguous contribution" to make, he is correct in noting that psychological investigators and those involved in studying the history and theory of mysticism must cooperate in what to date is an "unrealized conversation."[256]

NOTES

1. Kazantzakis(1961, p. 45).
2. Blofeld(1970, p. 24).
3. Scholem (1969, p. 16).
4. W. James, quoted in McDermott (1967, pp. 798–799).
5. Smith (1978, p. ix).
6. Clark (1984); Davis (1989); Swinburne (1981).
7. Katz (1977).
8. Schuon (1975).
9. Jones (1994).
10. An excellent summary of this literature is provided in McGinn (1991).
11. Thorner (1966).
12. Kaufman (1958).
13. Thorner (1966, p. 82).
14. Stace (1960).
15. Forman (1990).
16. Stace (1960, p. 131).
17. Forman (1990, p. 8).
18. Hood (1989).
19. Hood (1985).
20. Otto (1917/1958).
21. Hick (1989).
22. Hood (1995b).
23. Stace (1960); Otto (1932, especially pp. 47–72).
24. Hick (1989, pp. 252–296).
25. Hood (1995c).
26. Hood (1995a).
27. Hick (1989, p. 162).
28. Smart (1964, pp. 121–122). Smart cites the religion of the Upanishads as one example.
29. Smart (1978).
30. Stace (1960, pp. 11–12).
31. Stace (1960, pp. 11–12).
32. Hood (1995b).
33. Hood (1995b).
34. Hodges (1974).
35. Garrett (1974).
36. Jones (1986, p. 225).
37. See Hood (1992a, 1995c).
38. Swinburne (1981, p. 190).
39. Bowker (1973).

40. Berger(1979).
41. O'Brien (1965).
42. Preus (1987).
43. See Coon (1992); Hood (1994).
44. Leuba (1925).
45. Freud (1927/1961).
46. Freud (1930/1961).
47. See Hood (1976a, 1992b); Shafranske (1995).
48. Durkheim (1915).
49. See Hood (1992a, 1995c).
50. James (1890/1950, 1902/1985).
51. Myers (1903/1961).
52. Hood (1995c).
53. Quoted in Perry (1935, Vol. 2, p. 331). Emphasis in original.
54. Bucke (1901/1961).
55. Kolakowski (1985).
56. See Hardy (1965, 1966).
57. Jung (1938).
58. Jung (1954/1968).
59. Jung (1938).
60. McGinn (1991, p. 343).
61. Inge (1899, p. 3). The definitions are reviewed in an appendix to the text (pp. 335– 348).
62. Zaehner (1957).
63. Buber (1965, p. 24).
64. James (1902/1958).
65. Quoted in McGinn (1991, pp. 267–268).
66. Hood (1975).
67. Hood (1970).
68. Laski (1961).
69. Laski (1961, p. 9).
70. Laski (1961).
71. Laski (1961, p. 5, footnote 1).
72. Laski (1961, pp. 526–533).
73. Laski (1961, pp. 369–374).
74. Wulff (1995).
75. Laski (1961, p. 399, texts 1a, 1b).
76. Lewis (1956, p. viii).
77. Lewis (1956, p. 238).
78. Pafford (1973).
79. Pafford (1973, p. 251). The actual text was from W. H. Hudson's autobiography. See Hudson (1939).
80. Pafford obtained 475 questionnaires, but primarily analyzed only 400. He took the first 100 by gen-
    der in both the university and grammar school samples for the 400. His analyses were generally based
    upon the 264 respondents of the 400 who reported experiences similar to the one described. In a few
    instances some persons described more than one experience, and these were used in some analyses
    not discussed here.
81. Pafford (1973, p. 91).
82. Pafford (1973, p. 19).
83. Klingberg (1959).
84. Klingberg (1959, p. 212).
85. An unspecified number of compositions contained more than one experience.
86. Klingberg (1959, p. 213).
87. Klingberg (1959, p. 212).
88. Klingberg (1959, p. 215).
89. Fahs (1950).
90. Elkind and Elkind (1970).
91. Elkind and Elkind (1970, p. 104). Students were also asked to respond to the question "Why does God
    permit war, murder, disease?", but few did, and this item is ignored in our discussion.
92. Elkind and Elkind (1970, p. 104).

93. Hood (1973b).
94. See Katz (1992); Proudfoot (1985); Scharfstein (1993).
95. Hood (1973b).
96. See Thomas and Cooper (1978, 1980).
97. Thomas and Cooper (1978, p. 434).
98. Hardy (1979).
99. Hardy (1979, p. 18) cites an example from Beatrice Webb, reported in an address given by Mary Stokes of the World Congress of Faiths.
100. Hardy (1979, p. 20).
101. Hardy (1979, p. 23).
102. Hardy (1979, p. 26). See Table 6.1 of the present book, item 1d.
103. Hardy (1979, p. 27). See Table 6.1 of the present book, item 7v.
104. Hardy (1979, pp. 19–20).
105. Hay (1994, especially pp. 20–23).
106. Hay (1994, p. 21).
107. Hay (1994, p. 22).
108. The materials may be completed by the time this book goes to press. Interested scholars can contact L. B. Brown, Director, Alister Hardy Research Centre, Westminster College, Oxford, England OX2 9AT.
109. Hay and Morisy (1985).
110. Hay and Morisy (1985, p. 214).
111. Hay and Morisy (1985, p. 217).
112. Hay and Morisy (1985, p. 214).
113. Hay (1979).
114. Hay (1979, p. 165).
115. It is typical of this research tradition that more than one experience may be described by a respondent and included in analyses. Hay (1979, p. 167) reports a total of 109 experiences from the 65 affirmative responses to the question.
116. Mathes, Zevon, Roter, and Joerger (1982).
117. Shostrom (1964).
118. Hood (1977a).
119. The groups did not differ on Factor I or Factor II; the use of extreme scores and the fact that Factors I and II correlate probably account for this. See Hood (1977a, p. 270, footnote 3).
120. Hood and Hall (1980).
121. Glock and Stark (1965).
122. Glock and Stark (1965, p. 157).
123. Glock and Stark (1965, p. 157).
124. Glock and Stark (1965, p. 157).
125. Vernon (1968).
126. Tamminen (1991).
127. Tamminen (1991, p. 42).
128. Back and Bourque (1970).
129. Back and Bourque (1970).
130. Bourque (1969).
131. Gallup (1978).
132. Yamane and Polzer (1994, p. 4).
133. Gallup and Newport (1990).
134. Gallup and Casteli (1990).
135. See Greeley (1974, 1975).
136. Greeley (1975, p. 58).
137. Davis and Smith (1994).
138. Greeley (1974).
139. Hay and Morisy (1978).
140. Thomas and Cooper (1978, 1980).
141. Greeley (1975, p. 65).
142. McClenon (1984).
143. Yamane and Polzer (1994, p. 25).
144. The total *n* for these years varies slightly (5,489) from the 5,420 in the Yamane and Polzer text, prob-

ably depending upon how missing responses to some questions resulted in inclusion or exclusion of subjects. Rounding of percentages also produced slight variations between the years, considered both independently and cumulatively.

145. Bourque and Back (1971, p. 8).
146. Thirty-one percent is often reported as indicating the total affirmative response to the Bourque question. However, since an index of three items was used, the data reported by Bourque and Back (1971, p. 10) cannot isolate the effect of one particular item from the effects of the other two.
147. Bourque and Back (1971, p. 10).
148. Hay and Morisy (1985, p. 214).
149. Hay and Morisy (1985).
150. See Back and Bourque (1970).
151. Hay (1979).
152. Hay (1994, p. 8).
153. Hay and Heald (1987).
154. Hay (1994, p. 7).
155. Princeton Research Center (1978).
156. Hay (1994, p. 7).
157. Back and Bourque (1970).
158. Scharfstein (1973, pp. 63–70).
159. Tamminen (1991, p. 62).
160. Coon (1992).
161. Hood (1994).
162. Greeley (1975).
163. Hardy (1965, 1966).
164. Hood (1989).
165. Fox (1992).
166. *Déjà vu* emerges as a single factor in Fox's analysis of survey items included in the 1984, 1988, and 1989 General Social Surveys. See Fox (1992, pp. 423–424).
167. Margolis and Elifson (1979, p. 62).
168. Margolis and Elifson (1979, p. 64).
169. Wuthnow (1978, p. 72).
170. Zollschan, Schumaker, and Walsh (1995).
171. Yamane and Polzer (1994).
172. Gorsuch (1984).
173. Hood (1970).
174. Rosegrant (1976, p. 306).
175. Hood (1970, p. 287) reported a Kuder–Richardson internal consistency of .84.
176. Rosegrant (1976, p. 306) reported a Cronbach's alpha internal consistency of .73.
177. It is not clear what the effects may be of explicit instructions that the religious language of the REEM is not essential and that one ought to focus upon the underlying description, not the language used. See Rosegrant (1976, p. 306). This is especially pertinent in light of recent conceptual debates on the relationship between religious language and experience, as well as the empirical studies described later in this chapter.
178. Holm (1982).
179. Hood (1970).
180. Allport and Ross (1967, p. 442).
181. Hood (1978b).
182. Rosegrant (1976, p. 307).
183. Hood (1972).
184. Rosegrant (1976).
185. Hood (1978a).
186. Hood and Hall (1977).
187. Gibbons and Jarnette (1972).
188. Lewis (1971).
189. Hood (1973a).
190. Shor and Orne (1962).
191. Gibbons and Jarnette (1972).
192. Tellegen and Atkinson (1974).

193. Mathes (1982).
194. Rubin (1970).
195. See Allison (1961); Owens (1972); Prince and Savage (1972).
196. Hood (1985).
197. Hood (1974).
198. Barron (1953).
199. The one exception is the item referring to church attendance.
200. Hood (1974, p. 68). The means on the REEM for the two groups were 40.7 (*SD* = 12.9) and 33.0 (*SD* = 2.9), respectively. A *t* test of difference between means was significant, t (112) = 3.10, $p < .01$.
201. Maslow (1964).
202. Hood (1975).
203. Stace (1960).
204. Lukoff and Lu (1988).
205. Stace (1960, pp. 29–31).
206. Doblin (1991, p. 8).
207. Stace (1960, pp. 31–38).
208. Katz (1977).
209. Proudfoot (1985).
210. Hood (1975) excluded paradoxicality as a criterion of mysticism. Also, Stace (1960, pp. 270–276) seemed to waiver on how essential a property it is for mysticism.
211. Hood (1975, pp. 30–34).
212. Caird (1988).
213. Reinert and Stifler (1993).
214. Hood, Morris, and Watson (1993).
215. Hood (1975, pp. 35–36).
216. Taft (1970).
217. Hood (1975).
218. Hood (1976b).
219. Holm (1982).
220. Holm (1982, p. 273).
221. Soderblom (1963), cited in Holm (1982, pp. 275–276).
222. Hood (1975, pp. 37–39).
223. Hood (1975, pp. 38–39).
224. Hood (1975, pp. 38–39).
225. Spanos and Moretti (1988).
226. Spanos, Radtke, Hodgins, Stam, and Bertrand (1983).
227. Field (1965).
228. Weitzenhoffer and Hilgard (1962).
229. Spanos and Moretti (1988, p. 110).
230. Jackson (1978).
231. Hood, Hall, Watson, and Biderman (1979).
232. Jackson (1976).
233. Hood et al. (1979, pp. 805–806). We ignore Hood et al.'s discussion of gender differences (see p. 805) in favor of a general description of these data.
234. Hood and Morris (1981a).
235. Morris and Hood (1980).
236. Troeltsch (1931).
237. Garrett (1975).
238. Katz (1977).
239. Katz (1983).
240. Troeltsch (1931).
241. Rosegrant (1976).
242. Stifler, Greer, Sneck, and Dovenmuehle (1993).
243. The variance for psychotics on the M Scale was much greater than that for either normals or contemplatives. This was also true for other measures used in the study. See Stifler et al. (1993, p. 369).
244. Persinger (1987).
245. Sensky (1983).

246. Persinger and Makarec (1987).
247. Hood (1977b).
248. Grossman (1975).
249. Hood (1977b).
250. See Hood, Morris, and Watson (1987, 1989).
251. Poloma and Gallup (1991).
252. Finney and Malony (1985b).
253. Finney and Malony (1985a).
254. Hood, Morris, and Watson (1990).
255. McClenon (1990).
256. McGinn (1991, p. 343).

Chapter 8

CONVERSION

There are two lives, the natural and the spiritual, and we must lose the one before we can participate in the other.[1]

He was down and out, the Catholics took him in and before he knew it, he had faith. So it was gratitude that decided the issue most likely.[2]

But the Muslim believes that the propositional tenets of his faith are self-evident if they are properly presented and understood, and the focus of his proselytization is the proclamation of these tenets rather than the experiences of human beings.[3]

All conversions (even Saul's on the road to Damascus) are mediated through people, institutions, communities, and groups.[4]

And Priests in black gowns were walking their rounds,
And binding with briars my joys & desires.[5]

In the early months of 1881, G. Stanley Hall delivered a series of public lectures at Harvard University. His topic was religious conversion, and much of the material he covered was later incorporated into his classic two-volume study of adolescence.[6] The young science of psychology was courageous enough to tackle some of the most profound and meaningful religious phenomena of the times. Because the emerging psychology was linked in the popular mind with religious and parapsychological phenomena,[7] some of the first North American psychologists divided along lines claiming to debunk or support such phenomena.[8] Hall eventually went on to write a two-volume treatise with the title *Jesus, the Christ, in Light of Psychology*.[9] The title is relevant in revealing the Christian bias of the young science of psychology: When they said "religion," most psychologists meant "Christianity."

At the turn of the century, religious revivals were common in North America, especially in evangelical Protestantism.[10] Evangelicals focused upon the "born-again" experience. In his Gifford lectures, William James distinguished between those "once-born," who are cultivated within and gradually socialized to accept their faith, and those "twice-born," with a more melancholy temperament, who are literally compelled through crises to accept or realize their faith within an instant.[11] Not surprisingly, North American psychologists were fascinated by this predominantly Protestant phenomenon, and conversion became the earliest major focus of the psychology of religion.

Sociologists were also concerned with conversion. In 1908, George Jackson chose conversion as his topic when he gave the Cole lectures at Vanderbilt University.[12] James devoted two of his Gifford Lectures in Edinburgh to the specific topic of conversion.[13] He relied heavily upon the research of his contemporaries, especially Edwin Starbuck and James H. Leuba. Both had been students of Hall's at Clark University. Leuba published the first psychological journal article on conversion; this was rapidly followed by Starbuck's article on conversion, and by his book-length treatment of the topic.[14] Not surprisingly, Leuba's and Starbuck's research methods paralleled Hall's, including the use of questionnaires and personal documents. Despite James's aversion to questionnaire studies, he utilized material supplied by Starbuck from his questionnaire studies of religious converts. Another early investigator, Coe, added quasi-experimental techniques to the investigation of religious converts.[15]

Whereas early investigators tended to focus upon dramatic cases of sudden conversion, others argued against the selection of such extreme cases as the basis for developing a general model of conversion. For instance, J. B. Pratt, a student of James at Harvard, emphasized the study of gradual converts, whose experiences were less dramatic, required intellectual seeking, and were hypothesized to be more genuinely characteristic of conversion both within Christianity and within other religious traditions.[16] As we shall soon see, from the beginning of the study of conversion, the fundamental issues that continue to characterize the contemporary study of the subject were identified and debated. Yet as the psychology of religion waned in North America, conversion was ignored by psychologists. By the late 1950s, W. H. Clark bemoaned the fact that psychology had all but abandoned the study of conversion:

> For students of religion and religious psychology there is no subject that has held more fascination than the phenomenon called conversion. Yet of recent years a kind of shamefacedness becomes apparent among those scholars who mention it . . . among the more conventional psychologists of the present day, who infrequently concern themselves with the study of religion and practically never with the subject of conversion. It is quite obvious that the latter is regarded as a kind of psychological slum to be avoided by any respectable scholar.[17]

It is primarily social psychologists who produce the majority of the empirical measurement-based research in the psychology of religion. Social psychology is divided into sociological social psychology and psychological social psychology.[18] Although contemporary research on conversion is rapidly increasing in volume, the clear tendency is for sociological social psychology to dominate the field. Much of this can be attributed to the sociological interest in new religious movements, discussed in Chapter 9. For instance, a major bibliography on new religious movements by Beckford and Richardson has at least 145 references pertinent to conversion, only 5% of which appeared prior to 1973.[19] An earlier bibliography on specifically conversion literature prepared by Rambo listed 252 references, only 38% of which were published prior to 1973.[20] Conversion has reemerged as a major focus of concern for the contemporary social psychology of religion, but with a distinctive sociological rather than psychological emphasis.

Quite naturally, we can focus upon two major approaches to conversion, roughly identified with what we term the "classic" and the "contemporary" periods in the social-psychological study of conversion. The classic approach, influenced primarily by psychological social psychology, has been dominated by a concern with North American Protestantism. Many different techniques and methods characterize this research, but the focus is primarily upon intraindividual psychological processes. The contemporary approach is influenced primarily by sociological social-psychological studies of conversion. The research is focused upon new religious movements, or varieties of communal Christian groups; it is less likely to be strongly measurement-based than psychologically oriented social psychology, and the focus is upon interpsychological rather than intrapsychological processes. These major distinctions are not exclusive and overlap in significant ways, but as we shall see, they provide differing (and to some extent even contradictory) views of conversion. The extent to which the differences between the classic and contemporary approaches are confounded by claims about the nature of conversion processes is an open question.

THE CLASSIC RESEARCH PARADIGM: PSYCHOLOGICAL DOMINANCE

What we have chosen to call the classic research approach to conversion is not merely of historical interest. The early psychologists utilized a number of methods to study conversion. They also accepted as raw data for analysis various types of material; these included personal documents such as private letters and confessions, as well as autobiographical and biographical materials. Questionnaires, interviews, and public confessions were also employed. Although contemporary psychology tends to minimize the use of many of these sources, especially personal documents, their value can be immense.[21] They cannot be used to identify the causal processes in conversion, but they are essential and valid as rich descriptions of the process of conversion as a human experience.

Classic Conceptualizations of Conversion

Snow and Machalek have appropriately noted that any effort to understand the causes of conversion presupposes the ability to identify converts.[22] However, they also note that few investigators have bothered to give clear conceptualizations of conversion.[23] Most psychologists define conversion as a transformation of self; these definitions emphasize intrapersonal processes. Furthermore, early psychologists such as Cutten and Pratt emphasized that such definitions rely heavily upon a Protestant understanding of Saul's (Paul's) conversion on the road to Damascus as typical of all conversion.[24]

The use of Paul's conversion as prototypical so dominates the classic paradigm of conversion research that Richardson refers to the "Pauline experience" as the exemplar for conversion research in an article contrasting the classic paradigm with an emerging contemporary paradigm.[25] Ironically, contemporary views echo Pratt, who argued that the fascination of psychologists with Paul's conversion as a model for all crisis-precipitated sudden conversion accounted for its overrepresentation in textbooks on the psychology of religion. In Pratt's own words, "I venture to estimate that at least nine out of every ten 'conversion cases' reported in recent questionnaires would have no violent or depressing experience to report had not the individual in question been brought up in a church or community which taught them to look for it if not to cultivate it."[26] As was the case with psychology at the turn of the century, much of the contemporary psychology of religion is really a study of Christianity, particularly Protestantism.[27] Gorsuch has appropriately sounded a note of caution about extending the psychology of Christianity to other religions.[28] Social psychologists have, however, not been properly hesitant in generalizing not only from Paul's conversion to all conversion within Christianity, but to conversion experiences in other religions as well.

The regarding of conversion as a radical transformation of self is probably itself heavily influenced by the conversion of Paul. Most psychologically oriented investigators view conversion as a radical transformation of self, and even sociologically oriented investigators tend to define conversion in terms that imply a radical change in self, even if conversion is empirically assessed by other indicators. For instance, in an often-cited definition, Travisano refers to conversion as "a radical reorganization of identity, meaning, life."[29] Heirich refers to conversion as the process of changing one's sense of "root reality," or of one's sense of "ultimate grounding."[30] After a critical analysis of treatments of conversion as radical personal change, Snow and Machalek define conversion in terms of a shift in the universe of discourse that carries with it a corresponding shift in consciousness.[31] However, as Coe long ago noted, if self-transformation is used to define conversion, "Conversion is by no means co-extensive with religion."[32] Indeed, most psychologists are likely to focus upon changing the self outside religious contexts.[33] What then makes conversion, contextualized as a radical transformation of self, distinctively religious?

It does little good to identify conversion in distinctively religious terms by imputing causal power to a deity to distinguish religious from nonreligious conversions. For instance, Rambo admits his own predilection to accept as genuine only conversions defined as transformation of the persons by the power of God,[34] but he recognizes that this is not a useful definition for empirical psychology. However, differential attributions of the self-transforming power of God are capable of being empirically investigated. The use of religious attributions or a religious universe of discourse is what makes conversion religious conversion.[35] After conversion, religious attributions defining and identifying the new self become master attributions, replacing the secular or peripheral religious attributions that existed prior to conversion.[36] In this sense, early clarifications of conversion mesh nicely with contemporary considerations. Coe spoke of "self realization within a social medium" as defining conversion.[37] James noted, "To say a man is 'converted' means . . . that religious ideas, peripheral in his consciousness, now take a central place, and that religious aims form the habitual center of his energy."[38]

Most empirical studies of conversion implicitly, if not explicitly, utilize criteria that correspond to Coe's analysis of conversion. First, conversion is a profound change in the self. Second, the change is not simply a matter of maturation, but is typically identified with a process (sudden or gradual) by which the transformed self is achieved. Third, this change in the self is radical in its consequences—indicated by such things as a new centering of concern, interest, and action. Fourth, this new sense of self is perceived as "higher" or as an emancipation from a previous dilemma or predicament. Thus, conversion is self-realization or self-transformation, in that a person adopts or finds a new self. Moreover, the process occurs within a social medium or context; specifically, religious conversion entails a religious framework within which the transformed self is described, acts, and is recognized by others. The fact that conversion may result in new habitual modes of action links any purely *intrapsychological* processes of conversion to the *interpsychological* processes that maintain them. Over 70 years ago, Strickland argued against James's distinction between once- and twice-born believers on the grounds that anyone who consciously adopts a religious view, whether gradually or suddenly, is twice-born: "And if action from new ideals and changed habits of life do *not* follow, there has been no conversion."[39]

Contemporary Distinctions Refining the Classic View

Numerous investigators have recognized that self-transformation within a religious context is a useful definition of conversion, capable of a variety of operational indicators.[40] However, the study of conversion requires additional conceptual refinements so that variations in phenomena closely related to conversion in this ideal sense can be identified. Among these refinements are apostasy, deconversion, intensification, switching, and cycling. We define these terms as follows:

"Apostasy" refers to the abandonment of one's religious commitment in favor of the adoption of a nonreligious framework.

"Deconversion" refers to the process by which a previous convert leaves. Deconversion does not necessarily imply apostasy.

"Intensification" refers to a revitalized commitment to the religion in which one was raised or of which one has been only a nominal member. It is distinguished from conversion proper, as one does not adopt a faith commitment *de novo* or change one's religion. Many religious traditions have routinized procedures whereby intensification experiences are to be anticipated by the faithful. For instance, for many evangelicals, there is a moment when one is "born again."

"Switching" refers to a change of religious membership without radical change in one's self. Typically, changing from one denomination to another closely related denomination entails no radical self-transformation and hence is merely switching. We discuss denominational switching in Chapter 9.

"Cycling" refers to patterns of religious participation that vary across the lifespan. Participation is episodic; many people drop out of religious participation, only to return at various points in their lives. We also discuss religious cycling in Chapter 9.

It is important to clarify what is meant by conversion and closely related phenomena, so that measures used in empirical research can be appropriately selected, constructed, and evaluated.[41] It is unreasonable to expect a single model of conversion to account for what we have termed conversion, apostasy, deconversion, intensification, switching, and cycling.

Age and Conversion

Investigators have persistently studied the relationship between age and conversion. Although conversion can conceivably occur at any age, it is reasonable to hypothesize that it is most likely to occur in adolescence. Adolescence is a time in which individuals challenge and test normative systems, eventually selecting and identifying with those within which they forge their identity or sense of self.[42] It is also a time when secondary socialization provides a variety of options in a world that is largely recognized to be socially constructed.[43] Religions exist as one type of meaning system within which individuals can orient themselves and can understand, interpret, and direct their lives. Adolescence is a likely time in which the very existence of a variety of religions testifies to the necessity of choice, even if only to affirm one's already existing religious faith.[44] As Starbuck noted, "Theology takes the adolescent tendencies and builds upon them; it seems that the essential thing in adolescent growth is to bring the person out of childhood into the new life of mature and personal insight."[45]

In a review of five major studies of conversion that had a total sample size in excess of 15,000 persons, Johnson found the average age of conversion to be 15.2 years, with the range from 12.7 to 15.6 years.[46] Roberts found adolescence to be the most common time of conversion in Britain; the typical age at conversion was 15.[47] Gillespie found 16 to be the common age of conversion in samples he reviewed.[48] These data correspond to critical summaries of the literature fixing adolescence as the customary time for conversion.[49] Thus, in general the empirical literature on age of conversion is consistent and has been for nearly 40 years, although it is admittedly based upon a severely biased sampling range that seldom extends beyond youth.[50]

There is a fairly narrow age range for conversion, centering around middle to late adolescence. If sex differences are considered, females convert 1 to 2 years earlier than males. However, this is true only for conversion in Western countries—primarily in the United States and Canada, and to a lesser extent the United Kingdom and some parts of Europe. Furthermore, in most cases studied, the phenomena reported as "conversion" are mixed with intensification experiences, in which adolescents come to consciously adopt the faith within which they were raised or switch to a similar faith commitment. Few investigations linking age to conversion have adequately empirically assessed the possibility of radical self-transformation by means of sophisticated psychometric procedures. Most rely upon either verbal reports of conversion or reported church participation. Furthermore, age-related conversion phenomena cannot be generalized to non–Western contexts. Finally, anticipating a bit, we might note here that conversion to new religious movements also appears to be age-related. Most often, conversion is likely to occur in late adolescence and young adulthood. Unfortunately, few investigators have directly assessed age and participation in new religious movements, other than to report mean ages for their samples. As a rule these are college students, who are readily available to be sampled but are perhaps not truly representative of the age of conversion to new religious movements in general.

Age and Apostasy

The secularization thesis discussed in Chapter 9 is relevant to contemporary studies of conversion, in that apostasy has increasingly become a topic of social scientific interest. Secularization provides the context within which the complete rejection of religion is possible and perhaps increasingly frequent. However, it remains true that most North Americans are religious, insofar as they at least affirm some religious identification. However, when asked in surveys for their religious identification, a minority mark "none."[51] Hadaway notes that from 1972 to 1988, 93% of U.S. residents identified themselves as either some variety of Protestant, Catholic, or Jew, according to National Opinion Research Center surveys.[52] However, 7% identified themselves as having no religion.[53] Brinkerhoff and Burke note that religious disidentification is an extreme form of apostasy only when persons both sever ties with religious institutions and disavow religious self-identification.[54] However, the most common operational indicator of apostasy is refusing to indicate a religious identity in questionnaire or phone survey studies. These are religious "nones." Often it is simply assumed that these "nones" were raised within a religion and hence are apostates. Furthermore, Hadaway and Roof note that U.S. apostates have dropped a religious identity within a culture in which religion remains a dominant value.[55] They report that the rate of apostasy increased by 2% from 1972 to 1987, remaining fairly constant (ranging between 7.2% and 7.8%) for the most recent years surveyed.[56]

Studies using this operational indicator have found that like conversion, apostasy is age-related. Apostates tend to be late adolescents or very young adults.[57] Thus, both apostasy and conversion are primarily phenomena of adolescence or young adulthood. However, one must not lose sight of the fact that the ages of conversion and apostasy reported are often confounded by limiting sampling to adolescents and young adults, typically in high school or college. It does not mean that these phenomena do not occur across the lifespan, from early adolescence through old age. In Chapter 9, apostasy and cycling are explored across a broader spectrum of the lifespan.

Efforts to Explain Conversion

The process of conversion or apostasy can be gradual or sudden. It is the speed of these processes that has led to the most intense theoretically guided discussions purporting to provide explanations of both reactions.

Sudden Conversion

Early investigators did not fail to classify conversion types into simple dichotomies. The most obvious was derived from a continuum of duration. Some persons convert quickly, appearing suddenly to adopt a faith perspective previously unknown (conversion) or to make a faith that was previously of peripheral concern a central concern (intensification). Others seem to mature and blossom gradually within a faith perspective that in some sense has always been theirs. We have already noted the dispute surrounding James's "once-born" and "twice-born" types. James acknowledged the possibility of gradual conversion, but focused upon sudden conversion, probably precipitated by crises.[58]

In his fascination with sudden conversion, James was not alone. Starbuck stressed "conversions of self-surrender" and "voluntary conversions."[59] The former were thought to be elicited by a sense of sin, suddenly overcome; the latter by a gradual pursuit of a religious ideal. Ames favored restricting the term "conversion" to sudden instances of religious change associated with intense emotionality.[60] Coe noted at least six kinds of conversion, but favored limiting the term to intense, sudden religious change.[61] Johnson later echoed these views succinctly when he stated, "A genuine religious conversion is the outcome of a crisis."[62]

So influential were the early psychologists in viewing conversion as a sudden, intense experience of religious self-transformation that Richardson describes their implicit conceptualization as the "old conversion paradigm."[63] Its major characteristics can be summarized from Richardson's article as follows:

1. Conversion occurs suddenly.
2. It is more emotional than rational.
3. External forces act on a passive agent.
4. There is a dramatic transformation of self.
5. Behavior change follows from belief change.
6. Conversion occurs once and is permanent.
7. It typically occurs in adolescence.
8. The prototype is Paul's conversion.[64]

Richardson emphasizes that what we have called the classic model implies a passive subject transformed by forces that may be variously identified. However, whether these forces are described as "God" or as "the unconscious" makes little difference. The convert is not seen as an active agent; instead, emotion dominates the irrational transformation of self.

Richardson's model has similarities to Strickland's summary of the success of sudden conversions common among evangelical and fundamentalist Protestant groups in North America, including those occurring during revivalist meetings. Strickland also emphasized the institutionalization of Paul's conversion as the valued form of entering the Christian faith, with a stress upon sin and guilt as eliciting conditions joyously relieved in the emotionality of a sudden conversion.[65]

Not surprisingly, several studies have related emotional states to sudden conversions. For instance, in a classic study by Clark (discussed more fully in Research Box 8.1), 2,174 cases of adolescent conversions were classified as either sudden or gradual.[66] Approximately one-third were sudden, either emotion- or crisis-precipitated, and linked with a stern theology. Starbuck studied adolescent conversions and found that two-thirds were at least partially triggered by a deep sense of sin or guilt.[67] However, he found that in later adolescence, conversion was likely to be more gradual. Pratt went so far as to claim that prior to their conversions, the twice-born wallow in extreme feelings of unworthiness, self-doubt, and depreciation that are released or overcome via conversion, as in the James–Starbuck thesis.[68] This position thesis recognizes conversion as a functional solution to the burdens of guilt and sin, which are found to be unbearable prior to conversion. In light of the James–Starbuck thesis, we must be careful not to interpret negative emotions such as guilt, sin, and shame as necessarily psychologically unhealthy.

Research Box 8.1. The Psychology of Religious Awakening (Clark, 1929)

In this classic study, E. T. Clark classified 2,174 conversions as to whether they were sudden or gradual. Sudden conversions (32.9%) were subdivided into two types: (1) "definite crisis awakening," in which a personal crisis is suddenly followed by a religious transformation (6.7%, majority males); and (2) "emotional stimulus awakening," in which gradual religious growth is interrupted by an emotional event that is suddenly followed by religious transformation (27.2%, equal proportions of males and females). Gradual conversions were described as "gradual awakening," a steady, progressive, slow growth resulting in gradual religious transformation (66.1%, slightly more females). A stern theology was associated with sudden conversions, equally distributed between crises and emotional awakenings; this was as would have been predicted from the James–Starbuck thesis. Almost all gradual conversions were associated with compassionate theologies that emphasized love and forgiveness.

Clark suggested that sudden conversions were associated with fear and anxiety. In addition, 41% of these conversions occurred during revivals, which were likely to be highly emotional settings. The dominant emotional states reported were joyful reactions, assumed by Clark to result from the alleviation of the negative feelings existing prior to conversion, which were elicited by stern theologies emphasizing sin and guilt. This study suggests that negative emotional states can precipitate experiences within a religious setting, and that the conversion then provides positive relief of these negative feelings.

Watson and his colleagues have provided a series of studies relevant to the James–Starbuck thesis. Watson argues that negative emotions such as shame and guilt can function positively when interpreted within an ideological surrounding that provides a context for both their meaningfulness and their resolution.[69] Clearly, one person's personal religious reaction may be another's madness. Just as many refuse to experience the necessity of salvation from sin insisted upon by some fundamentalist groups, so may others perceive fundamentalists to be encased in a rigid, outmoded religious framework. Nevertheless, the functionality of sin, shame, and guilt within fundamentalism is hard to dispute.[70] As Hood has documented, the empirical issues involved in studying fundamentalist religious groups are clouded by differences, often value-based, between investigators and those investigated.[71]

That sudden conversion is often correlated with emotionality seems well established. However, correlations do little to provide meaningful support for the causal claims that emotional feelings trigger conversions, or that guilt and sin are resolved by such conversions. Nevertheless, essentially correlational studies can be suggestive. A classic study by Coe compared 17 persons who anticipated striking conversions that actually occurred with 12 persons anticipating conversions that did not occur.[72] Emotional factors were dominant in the first group; cognitive factors were dominant in the second group. In addition, the actual converts were more suggestible than the others. Although Coe's research suggests that emotional factors may be causally involved in sudden conversions, no true experimental studies or longitudinal studies documenting this claim exist. However, recent research in cognitive psychology suggests a reason to link emotionality and sudden, dramatic conversions. McCallister has noted that emotional situations such as dramatic conversions may restrict the encoding of knowledge about experience, leading dramatic converts to utilize narrative formats to reconstruct their experience.[73]

Still, in many studies it may be that emotionality and sudden conversions are merely correlated phenomena. For instance, Spellman, Baskett, and Byrne divided persons in a small Protestant town into sudden or gradual converts and compared them to nonconverts.[74] They found that sudden converts scored higher on an objective measure of anxiety than did gradual converts or the nonconverted. Yet this difference was found *after* conversion; there was no evidence that greater emotionality differentiated the groups prior to their conversion, as postulated by the James–Starbuck thesis. Furthermore, as Poston has noted, emotional and crisis-triggered conversions are uncommon in many non-Christian religions—they do not, for instance, characterize conversion to Islam.[75] Woodberry notes that traditional Islamic thought does not even have a term for conversion.[76] Finally, the special case of sudden conversion along with claims to mind control and "brainwashing" is discussed in Chapter 9. It is a recent and special case of emotion-induced sudden conversion associated with analyses of new religious movements, primarily sects and cults.

Gradual Conversion

Like sudden religious conversions, gradual conversions result in a transformation of self within a religious context. Yet gradual conversions occur almost imperceptibly; they are usually distinguished empirically by not being identified with a single event. Some investigators have argued that gradual conversions need not result in radical shifts in personality, self, or even religious beliefs.[77] These researchers have essentially redefined conversion or accepted as empirical criteria such actions as merely joining a new religious group. Scobie even argues for "unconscious conversion," referring to persons who cannot recall *not* having been religious.[78] Clearly, characteristics associated with joining a new religious group often do not precisely parallel those defining conversion in the classic sense. Neither do continual faith commitments without an intensification experience. We must note in each case the empirical criteria used to assess conversion, and must keep these in mind when comparing individual empirical studies.

Over 70 years ago, as noted earlier, Strickland contrasted gradual and sudden conversions.[79] In gradual conversions, the emphasis is upon a conscious striving toward a goal. The convert is not likely to experience a single decisive point at which conversion is either initiated or completed; there is also an absence of emotional crises and of feelings of guilt and sin. The process is cognitive rather than emotional.

THE CONTEMPORARY RESEARCH PARADIGM: SOCIOLOGICAL DOMINANCE

Strickland's distinction between gradual and sudden conversion laid the foundation for the emergence of what we describe as the contemporary paradigm of conversion. The focus upon an active agent, seeking self-transformation, has become the target of extensive research among more sociologically oriented investigators. No single theory dominates the research literature, but most theories share enough common assumptions to enable us to contrast them with the classic psychological paradigm.

Five characteristics of the contemporary paradigm are notable. First, the research is done primarily by sociologists or sociologically oriented social psychologists, rather than by psychologists or psychologically oriented social psychologists. Second, the research examines new religious movements—many of non-Western origin or influence, or, if Christian, often fundamentalist groups of a sectarian nature. Third, the research is often participatory in nature, with single groups studied over a period of time. Investigators are less likely to take a single set of measurements on a group, as typical of classic conversion studies by psychologists. Both structured and unstructured interviews with religious converts are common. Fourth, almost by definition, the research highlights gradual rather than sudden conversion. Finally, the process of deconversion is investigated, in which individuals who have converted and then leave new religious movements are studied.

Major Differences between the Classic and Contemporary Paradigms

Richardson has been the most articulate theorist arguing that the old standard, based upon the "Pauline experience," is being abandoned in favor of an emerging paradigm.[80] Some have debated the claim that there is a new emerging model; they argue instead that perhaps the nature of conversion itself has changed over time.[81] It is difficult to compare the classic and contemporary paradigms empirically, given differences in the research methods used and the nature of religious groups studied.

What undoubtedly characterizes the contemporary approach is the use of typologies, often based upon assumed contrasts widely acknowledged in the classic model. In the classic approach, as noted earlier, sudden change was contrasted with gradual transformation. Associated with this distinction were other contrasts:

Sudden conversion	Gradual conversion
Middle to late adolescence	Late adolescence to early adulthood
Emotional, suggestive	Intellectual, rational
Stern theology	Compassionate theology
Passive role for convert	Active role for convert
Release from sin and guilt	Search for meaning and purpose[82]

Despite this acknowledged series of contrasts, empirical research in the classic paradigm was concentrated upon the more dramatic case of sudden religious conversion. Perhaps it was this narrowed focus in the empirical literature that allowed the contemporary paradigm to emerge. In addition, the emergence of new religious movements and their obvious appeal to converts altered that typical pattern of research, almost by definition. Thus, intensification experiences within traditions accentuating intrapsychological processes gave way to interpersonal processes involved in converting to new religious movements.

The characteristics of the emerging approach to conversion research as suggested by Richardson can be summarized as follows:

1. Conversion occurs gradually.
2. It is rational rather than emotional.
3. The convert is an active, seeking agent.
4. There is self-realization within a humanistic tradition.
5. Belief change follows from behavior change.
6. Conversion is not permanent; it may occur several times.
7. It typically occurs in early adulthood.
8. No one experience is prototypical.[83]

It is apparent that, ironically, Richardson's claim to an emerging standard meshes quite closely with earlier psychological research on gradual conversion. Perhaps appropriate is the fact that the Lofland and Stark model, seen by Richardson as transitional between the old and new paradigms, is still useful insofar as it permits identification of both predisposing psychological factors (typically studied in sudden conversions) and situational and contextual factors (usually studied in gradual conversions).[84] This model is based upon Lofland's provocative research in what was then only a minor new religion.[85] He was one of the earliest investigators to study the Unification Church (popularly known as the "Moonies") at a time when it was a minor cult and had not yet achieved prominence on the world scene. As discussed in Chapter 9, research on the Unification Church, like research on many religious cults, is often dichotomized into psychological and sociological studies of conversion. In the former, sudden conversion is associated with denigrating metaphors such as "brainwashing" and "mind control." Yet more sociologically oriented studies of the gradual and voluntary process of conversion to the Unification Church are consistent with empirical findings concerning a variety of new religious movements, and are not compatible with demeaning images of conversion as pathological.[86]

Long and Hadden have argued for a "dual-reality" approach, in which conversion may involve either sudden, emotional responses (associated with intrapsychological processes and the "brainwashing" metaphor) or more gradual responses (associated with interpsychological processes).[87] However, we need not consider conversion in an either–or manner, based upon dichotomies such as sudden–gradual or passive–active. The distinction primarily reflects differing psychological and sociological interests. Investigators would best profit from studying actual processes of conversion in particular cases, and the degree to which the characteristics typically assumed to operate in what we have termed the classical and contemporary paradigms can be empirically identified. We may assume, as Rambo does,[88] that there are no fundamental differences among the processes of conversion to various religions; however, we must be careful to identify the factors that actually do operate before we can take such an assumption as proven.

Conversion Motifs

The emphasis upon gradual processes has suggested a variety of empirical phenomena operating in conversion, which is viewed as a process occurring over time. Several investigators have attempted more diversified classifications of types of conversion, identifying various possible "conversion careers."[89] It is undoubtedly true that personal accounts of conversions often reflect biases elicited by investigators who rely upon interviews and observation after the fact to assess the factors operating in conversion, as Beckford has noted.[90] Classifications that rely upon psychological dispositions and intrapsychological processes ought not to be simply opposed to those that involve social contexts and interpsychological considerations. The union of both is needed.

One classification system admirably linking the classic and contemporary models, the psychological and the sociological is that of Lofland and Skonovd.[91] These scholars have coined the phrase "conversion motif" to take account of the "phenomenological validity" of "holistic subjective conversion experiences."[92] They have postulated six conversion motifs, and five major dimensions that apply to each motif; these are presented in Table 8.1.

The Lofland and Skonovd typology allows for variation in conversion without forcing arbitrary dichotomies. It permits distinctions among basic objective phenomena, identified along the five dimensions; it also respects the subjective account of conversion by the convert. Thus, their six conversion motifs provide "phenomenological validity" to objective factors (dimensions) postulated to be operative in conversion.[93] Their motifs are capable of operationalization and empirical study. They also cut across psychological and sociological concerns. For instance, the mystical motif fits the Pauline prototype of conversion, empha-

TABLE 8.1. The Lofland and Skonovd Conversion Motifs

	Intellectual	Mystical	Experimental	Affectional	Revivalistic	Coercive
Degree of social pressure	None or low	None or low	Low	Medium	High	High
Temporal duration	Medium	Short	Long	Long	Short	Short
Level of affective arousal	Medium	High	Low	Medium	High	Low
Affective content	Insight	Awe or love	Curiosity	Affection	Love and fear	Fear and love
Belief–behavior sequence of change	Belief first	Belief first	Behavior first	Behavior first	Behavior first	Behavior first

Note. Adapted from Lofland and Skonovd (1981, p. 374). Copyright 1981 by the Society for the Scientific Study of Religion. Adapted by permission.

sizing intrapsychic factors. The experimental motif focuses upon the processes by which "seekers" creatively transform themselves, often by interacting with others who model proper converted behavior.[94]

Embedded in the typology of conversion motifs is the assumption that there are three levels of reality to consider. The first is what Lofland and Skonovd call "raw reality," or the actual truth of conversion, which is only imperfectly available to the social scientist.[95] The second level is the convert's experience and interpretation. The third is the analytic interpretation provided by the social scientist. The change in conversion motifs over time may reflect a change in any one or all of the levels of reality. Obvious examples are the clearly historical contingency of coercive motifs, discussed in detail in Chapter 9, and the revivalist motif, now less common among nonevangelical forms of Protestantism.

The processes of conversion within each motif need to be empirically researched. Once again, psychological and sociological social psychologists actually parallel each other in their analyses. For instance, whereas sociological social psychologists tend to focus on accounts, a parallel literature exists among psychological social psychologists in terms of attributions.[96] To a large extent, various conversion motifs exist because of the linguistic frameworks within which conversion is understood. These include biographical reconstructions, the adaptation of master attribution schemes, and a variety of rhetorical indications that a person has indeed been converted.[97]

Active Conversion

Much of the sociological literature on the process of conversion emphasizes how people behave in such a way that they essentially "convert themselves." Whereas classic conversion research focused upon what happened to a passive convert, the contemporary research identifies what converts actively do to produce their conversions. For instance, Balch has emphasized how individuals must learn to act like converts by performing the particular role-prescribed behaviors expected of one who has been converted. Thus, behavior change occurs before the individual internalizes beliefs and perceptions characteristic of the convert.[98] Perhaps actual perceptual changes require a deconditioning of habitual patterns of perception, aptly captured by Deikman's notion of "deautomatization."[99] However, it is only after the individual participates in activities associated with the new religious group that such alteration in perceptions can occur. Thus, behavior change precedes belief change. Several investigators have documented this via participation research with new religious groups: Wilson has demonstrated such a process with converts to a yoga ashram,[100] and Preston has studied the same tendency among converts becoming Zen practitioners.[101]

In terms of empirical assessment, it is important to note that the use of either behavior change or belief change as an indicator of conversion will determine at what point conversion occurs (if at all). The two types of change need not occur at the same time. In addition, the temporal duration of conversion may be different for belief change and behavior change, even within a single conversion process. An individual may gradually be socialized into a new religious group and may suddenly experience a deautomatization, resulting in new perceptions congruent with the group's world view. Deautomatization occurs when habitual modes of perception are replaced with new ones. This is apparently particularly true of some Eastern traditions that emphasize practice over belief, such as Zen and yoga.[102] In this sense, a person may not be able to actively pursue deautomatization as a goal; it is a product of successful socialization into religious groups, and becomes possible once proper techniques and practices are mastered.[103] Much of the research literature has reintroduced classic cognitive dissonance theory to provide theoretical justification for a behavior–belief change sequence. Dissonance theory is a counterintuitive theory, in that it proposes behavior change's occurring prior to belief change. Festinger long ago proposed empirical conditions under which behavior change can be expected to precede, and to produce, belief change.[104]

CONVERSION PROCESSES

As emphasized above, contemporary research has been guided by a focus upon gradual conversion to new religious movements. In addition to typologies, numerous investigators have presented models of the process of conversion. Some are formal in scope and propositional in nature.[105] However, the majority are qualitative models inductively arrived at and used to organize the empirical literature;[106] it is not clear that such models can be easily submitted to empirical tests.[107] Most models share a recognition that conversion is a complex process in which a variety of factors must be considered. In general terms we can identify these factors under four headings: context; precipitating events; supporting activities; and finally participation/commitment.

Context

Conversion always takes place within a context. The term "context" is broad and vague enough to incorporate the historical, social, cultural, and interpersonal situations that make conversion possible. For instance, Wallace notes that historical figures such as Jesus, Mohammed, and Buddha have become the foci of revitalization movements.[108] Within varieties of North American Protestantism, we have already seen how Paul's conversion has served as a prototype for a model of transformation that permits the expected "born-again" experience associated with conversion or intensification experiences. Yet the cautionary note that this is only one model of transformation is now well substantiated by empirical research. Indeed, Research Box 8.2 describes an example of research on conversion within Islam, in which emotional, Pauline-type experiences are neither encouraged by the religion nor typically reported by converts. Clearly, the context of Islamic culture does not facilitate such experience.

Included among the contextual factors facilitating religious conversion are purely social and cultural phenomena that alter the probability of conversion. For instance, Bulliet has argued from a historical perspective that conversion to new religions follows the typical S-curve established to characterize diffusion of innovation in cultures.[109] Psychologists will readily recognize the S-curve as a normal (bell) curve. What is important for studies of conversion is Bulliet's classification of those who converted at various points in history along the curve. Using the history of Islam as his example, he described the first 16% who converted as the "innovators" (2.5%) and "early adopters" (13.5%). Then came the 34% constituting the "early majority," followed by the next 34%, the "late majority." Finally, the remaining 16% who converted were the "laggards."[110] Figure 8.1 illustrates Bulliet's classification curve.

**Research Box 8.2. An Empirical Study of Conversion to Islam
(Poston, 1992)**

Poston attempted to obtain questionnaire responses from 20 Muslim organizations. Only 8 of these 20 organizations responded at all, and from these 8, only 12 completed questionnaires were obtained. Poston notes that this is typical of Muslims (at least in North America), who are suspicious of research into their beliefs and practices. This is in contrast to Christians and members of many new religious movements in North America, who readily cooperate in completing inventories about their conversion experiences.

Reverting to reports of conversion experience in Islamic publications, Poston was able to obtain 72 testimonies of conversion, 69% of which were from males. Classifying these testimonies, Poston found that most converts (57%) had been raised as Christians. Only 3 of the 72 converts reported an emotional, Pauline-type conversion in which supernatural factors were perceived to account for the conversion. All but one of the converts were seekers who sought out a variety of religious options before becoming converted to Islam, with 21% stating the reasonableness of the faith as the motive for conversion, and 19% the universal brotherhood of all as the reason.

Bulliet's theory has been operationalized and tested for the historical dominance of Islam in various cultures, but this model is capable of empirical testing within other temporal contexts as well. What is important is the fact that the social-psychological processes of conversion may vary, depending upon the time a person converts to a religion and its dominance at that time in the culture. It may be that the kinds of persons and the processes by which they convert to new religious movements vary as such movements gain ascendancy within the culture.

Precipitating Events

The effort to dichotomize theories of conversion often focuses upon whether or not precipitating events can be identified, and, if so, within what time frame they operate. We have seen how proponents of sudden conversions often cite crises or emotional events as the turning point; yet, as Rambo has noted, crises can vary in length, scope, and duration.[111] Advocates of gradual conversion emphasize interpersonal processes and the active seeking of meaning and purpose over a longer time interval as key factors in conversion.[112]

The use of the conversion motifs discussed earlier allows for variations compatible with the existing empirical literature. There are many pathways to conversion, varying in length, scope, and nature.[113] For instance, crisis-precipitated conversions, including the affectional and coercive types, vary widely among themselves in terms of duration, intensity, and scope.[114] Furthermore, the crisis may be intrapsychic or interpsychic; the former often refers to some form of personal stress, the latter to some variety of social strain.[115] Likewise, actively seeking meaning and purpose (as in the experimental and intellectual motifs) varies in the range and nature of the meaning sought, as well as in the motivation for seeking such meaning.[116] It may be, as Gerlach and Hine have shown, that some converts gradually employ new systems of rhetoric that allow them to see themselves and the

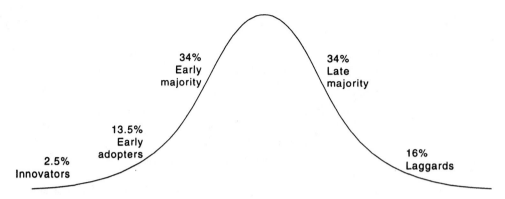

FIGURE 8.1. A bell curve model of conversion types, based upon time of conversion relative to percentage of population converted. The data are from Bulliet (1979, pp. 31–32).

world transformed.[117] Similarly, in a study that employed a comparison group to look at differences among Catholic Pentecostals, Heirich found that converts were most likely to be persons introduced to a group by a friend or spiritual advisor who facilitated the gradual use of new religious attributions in the process of conversion; nonconverts were not introduced to the group by a friend or spiritual advisor, and failed to acquire the appropriate language (attributions or rhetoric) of conversion.[118] Thus, mundane factors can precipitate conversion. Straus has documented how converts to Scientology managed to seek and find beliefs, and to enter groups that allowed them to convert themselves by "creative bumbling."[119]

Thus, no one process of conversion applies to all conversion motifs. Generalizations concerning the conversion process are highly suspect if proffered as other than hypotheses for empirical investigation.[120] Furthermore, it is not clear how the nature of the religious group to which one converted interacts with whatever general conversion processes have been empirically proposed. For instance, Seggar and Kunz found that a widely cited process model of religious conversion accounted for only 1 of the 77 cases of conversion to Mormonism in their study.[121]

Ullman is the only investigator to have made empirical comparisons of conversion processes across different religious groups.[122] She studied people who were converts to either Orthodox Judaism, Roman Catholicism, Hare Krishna, or the Baha'i faith. Emotional factors rather than cognitive factors differentiated converts to all four religious groups from nonconverts. This was not a direct test of the relative contribution of cognitive and emotional factors in conversion, given that all converts were selected on the basis of criteria that included actual changes in religious identity but excluded such changes when they were made for interpersonal reasons (e.g., marrying a spouse in the new faith). We have already noted the role of interpersonal factors in some conversion motifs, especially those unlikely to be elicited by crises or emotional factors. In addition, all four of Ullman's groups cultivated intense, emotional experiences, perhaps biasing the sample toward an affectional conversion motif. Still, Ullman's study is one of the few empirical studies that have used appropriate measurement procedures to compare converts to a variety of religious groups with matched controls. Some highlights of this research are presented in Research Box 8.3.

Research Box 8.3. Cognitive and Emotional Antecedents of Religious Conversion (Ullman, 1982; see also Ullman, 1989)

Ullman studied 40 white, middle-class individuls raised as Jews and Christians, who had converted from 1 to 10 months prior to the study. Half the converts were male and half female. They were compared on the basis of both objective measures and in-depth interviews to one another and to 30 controls (unconverted subjects). All converts actually changed religious denomination. The four converted groups consisted of 10 subjects each, who were now Orthodox Jews, Roman Catholics, Hare Krishnas, and Baha'i adherents. The major differences between the four converted groups and the nonconverted group were on emotional, not cognitive, indices. Among the significant differences between all converts and the control group were more indications of both childhood and adolescent stress, as well as a greater frequency of prior drug use and psychiatric problems, among the converted subjects. Converts recalled childhoods that were less happy and filled with more anguish than those of nonconverts. The emotions recalled for adolescence followed similar childhood patterns, with the addition of significant anger and fear in adolescence for the converts but not the nonconverts. Converts also differed from the unconverted in having less love and admiration for their fathers, and more indifference and anger toward them. Differences among the converted groups were less relevant than the consistency across all groups, suggesting that similar processes operated regardless of the faith to which a subject converted.

Supporting Activities

The classification of conversion motifs is helpful in directing research into factors in the conversion process that have long been ignored. Among these are interpersonal relationships between the potential convert and what Rambo refers to as "the advocate."[123]

Often the advocate is a friend who initiates and sustains the potential convert in the group. Sometimes simple factors such as marriage convert one partner. Much of the literature has documented the importance of social networks in facilitating conversion, especially among noncommunal religions. Snow and Machalek found that the vast majority (from 59% to 82%) of Pentecostals, evangelicals, and Nichiren Shoshu Buddhists that they studied were recruited through social networks.[124]

Much of the research has focused upon how social networks may facilitate gradual emotional conversions by the mere fact of intensive interaction's increasing the likelihood of affective bonding between group members.[125] Jacobs has reintroduced the analogy between conversion and falling in love into the contemporary literature on conversion to groups with charismatic leaders.[126] William James used the same analogy, as did Pratt, who went so far as to state that "In many cases getting converted means falling in love with Jesus."[127] Several investigators have noted that new religious movements provide alternative pathways to intimacy and love.[128]

More psychologically oriented social psychologists have also focused on affective bonding, operationalized more rigorously in terms of attachment theory (discussed in Chapter 2). Kirkpatrick and Shaver found that individuals of one attachment type in particular, the avoidant, reported higher rates of sudden conversions in adolescence or adulthood, regardless of the religiosity of their parents.[129] Once again, the literature of sociological and psychological social psychology have accentuated similar concerns, although the writings are unfortunately not often cross-referenced.

Social networks may also function to facilitate more cognitively motivated conversions, by providing interpersonal support for world views associated with what are in effect cognitive reformulations of converts' sense of themselves and others. Religious converts not only use more religious attributions, but employ those associated with their new group. For instance, Beckford has demonstrated the process by which Jehovah's Witnesses converts gradually come to assess the world in light of a master attribution scheme consistent with Jehovah's Witnesses' theology.[130] One rhetorical indicator that conversion is occurring is the utilization of such a master attribution scheme, which both defines and produces conversion. Interacting within a given social network supports the scheme and serves to differentiate the newly emerging convert. It is the new religious attribution scheme that permits a biographical reconstruction of the transformed self. Often such reconstructions are solidified by participation in appropriate rituals confirming one's conversion.[131]

The more sociologically oriented research on rhetorical indicators of conversion meshes nicely with psychologically oriented measurement research on cognitive change among converts. For instance, Paloutzian demonstrated an increase in scores on a measure of purpose in life for converts, as compared to unconverted controls or controls who were unsure they were converted.[132]

Participation/Commitment

It is not likely that conversion as a process can be identified in temporal terms as having been completed once and for all. After conversion, commitment and participation may be expected to vary. It is not uncommon for converts to new religious movements to follow conversion careers, joining and leaving a variety of religious groups over time.[133] Bird and Remier note that only a small percentage of converts to new religious movements remain members of one movement.[134] Furthermore, participation in religious groups is not necessarily higher among the converted than among those born and socialized into the religious groups.[135]

DECONVERSION AND RELATED PHENOMENA

The concept of conversion careers emphasizes that for some people, a variety of conversion experiences can be expected. This is especially true for converts to new religious movements, the majority of whom can be expected to leave within a few years. "Deconversion" is the term most typically used to identify this process. Compared to the massive research literature on conversion, little literature on deconversion exists, and the few existing studies are of recent origin. Wright could document only three investigations of deconversion published prior to 1980.[136]

Not surprisingly, the literature on deconversion parallels that for conversion. With the exception of the special case of "brainwashing" discussed in Chapter 9, most studies of deconversion have been done by sociologists using participant observation or descriptive research strategies. Measurement is often in terms of interviews, either structured or open-ended, with former members. Most deconversion studies have utilized defectors from new religious movements, paralleling the tremendous literature on new religious movements and conversion discussed above. Unlike the literature on apostasy, the deconversion literature focuses upon the processes involved in leaving religious groups, not simply correlates and predictors of leaving.

Deconversion within New Religious Movements

Skonovd studied fundamentalist Christian groups, as well as former members of Scientology, the Unification Church, the People's Temple, and a variety of Eastern groups.[137] He identified a process of deconversion consisting of a precipitating crisis, followed by review and reflection, disaffection, withdrawal, and a transition to cognitive reorganization. His model, however, does not distinguish between voluntary and involuntary leaving—an issue of concern, given the current debate on deprogramming as discussed in Chapter 9.

Wright studied matched samples of those remaining and those voluntarily defecting from the Unification Church, Hare Krishna, and a fundamentalist Christian group.[138] He focused upon precipitating factors that initiated the process of deconversion. Among these were breakdown of insulation from the outside world, development of unregulated interpersonal relationships, perceived lack of success in achieving social change, and disillusionment. Wright's research parallels conversion research, in that both emotional and cognitive factors can trigger the process of deconversion, and the process itself can be sudden or gradual. Furthermore, he identified the mode of departure, based upon the length of time a person was committed to the group. Most of those who were members for 1 year or less (92%) left by quiet, covert means. Those who were members for more than a year left by either overt means or direct confrontation, often emotional and dramatic in nature ("declarative" means).

Downton has documented the gradual process of deconversion from the Divine Light Mission (the sect associated with Guru Maharaj Ji).[139] Intellectual and social disillusionments predominated. The breaking of ties within the group occurred only as new bonds were established outside the group. Another study found that converts to the Unification Church who had not completely severed nonsanctioned emotional attachments within the group were likely to deconvert even when they believed in the doctrine of the group.[140]

Jacobs studied 40 religious devotees, most of whom were involved in either charismatic Christian, Hindu-based, or Buddhist groups.[141] All groups had charismatic leaders, were patriarchal in orientation, and had structured hierarchies with rigid disciplines of behavior and devotion. The 21 male and 19 female participants were predominantly middle-class, white, and well educated. Among the 40 deconverters, both social distress and disillusionment with a charismatic leader were major reasons cited for discontent leading to deconversion, as noted in Table 8.2. Jacobs notes that the total process of deconversion for these individuals required severing ties with both the group and the charismatic leader. This process included a period of initial separation, often accompanied by an experience of isolation and loneliness. It was followed by a period of emotional strain and readjustment, culminating in the reestablishment of identity outside the group.[142]

Descriptive studies of deconversion, like those on conversion, run the risk of confounding the natural history of groups with the causal processes assumed to operate in them.[143] Furthermore, investigators tend to avoid measurement in favor of utilizing subjective accounts, placed within descriptive systems proposed by the investigators as explanatory. Few tests of these models have been undertaken. Longitudinal research is virtually absent. Finally,

TABLE 8.2. Sources of Disillusionment among 40 Deconverters

Source	%
Disillusionment with a charismatic leader and his actions	
Physical abuse	31
Psychological abuse	60
Emotional rejection	45
Spiritual betrayal	33
Social disillusionment	
Social life	75
Spiritual life	50
Status/position	35
Prescribed sex roles	45

Note. Adapted from Jacobs (1989, pp. 43, 92). Copyright 1989 by Indiana University Press. Adapted by permission.

no studies have compared subjects who have deconverted from several religious groups to see whether the same process of deconversion occurs each time.

Disengagement within Mainstream Religious Groups

Although most of the research on deconversion has examined new religious movements that are sectarian or cult-like in nature, most religious participation in the United States is within denominational religious groups. Such established bodies have long been noted to have transitional memberships. As a general pattern, participation in religious groups waxes and wanes. Probably 80% of denominational members withdraw at some point in their life, only to return at some later point.[144] Thus, only a minority of persons socialized into religious groups in North America ever truly reject religious identity or participation. As we have noted, the percentage of apostates in North America has remained fairly constant at around 7%. This means that well over 90% of the U.S. population belonging to a religious group engages in some form of religious participation, whether this takes place at a church, mosque, or synagogue. However, the frequency of this participation fluctuates. For instance, Albrecht, Cornwell, and Cunningham mailed questionnaires to a stratified random sample of 32 active and 45 inactive families in each of 27 different Mormon wards (similar to congregations).[145] Seventy-four percent of the active and 44% of the inactive families responded; phone follow-ups to the inactive families raised their participation rate to 64%. Two measures of disengagement were used: (1) behavioral (a period of at least 1 month or more of no church attendance), and (2) belief (a period of at least 1 year when the Mormon church was not an important part of a family's life). Summarizing the results for every 100 families revealed that 74 became disengaged, in terms of either behavior (55) or belief (19). Only 4 families remained engaged nonbelievers; only 22 remained engaged believers. Of the 55 families that were disengaged nonbelievers, 31 returned to church participation.[146] These data are consistent with studies of disengagement and reengagement among Catholics.[147] They are also consistent with the studies of denominational switching and the cycling of religious participation discussed in Chapter 9. However, in light of the historical context within which new religious movements have emerged, it appears that many persons disengaged from mainstream religion have explored new religious movements as one form of reengagement.

Baby Boomers and Disengagement/Reengagement

Several investigators have been concerned with what has been called the "baby boom" generation. Although not precisely defined, this generation includes those raised in the 1960s in North America during a period of intense social upheaval.[148] Associated with this turmoil was the emergence of new religious movements, competing with and often congruent with a variety of countercultural movements.[149] Participants in these movements were largely youths reared in a mainstream religious tradition. For instance, Roof notes that two-thirds of all baby boomers reared in popular religious traditions dropped out or disengaged from mainstream religious participation in their late adolescence or early adulthood.[150] The average ages of disengagement for different birth cohorts are presented in Table 8.3.

Roof used a commercial firm to conduct focused group interviews with subjects from randomly digit-dialed samples. Households in four states (California, Massachusetts, North Carolina, and Ohio) were sampled. A 60% participation rate was obtained from an initial sample of 2,620 households. Baby boomers were defined as those born between 1946 and 1962 ($n = 1,599$; 61% of sample). The sample was further divided into older boomers (1946–1954; $n = 802$) and younger boomers (1955–1962; $n = 797$). Follow-up interviews were conducted with older boomers, and eventually 64 in-depth, face-to-face discussions and 14 group dialogues were conducted with these participants.[151]

As discussed in Chapter 3, disengagement tends to follow a pattern that includes religious socialization and participation, followed by youthful rebellion and departure, and subsequently by later return. Thus, high rates of leaving among baby boomers would not be surprising, nor would the return of most of these to normal religious participation. Indeed, Roof found that a return to mainstream religion occurred as expected for many of those who were disengaged. Furthermore, categorizing participants by the extent to which they were part of the mainstream culture (in terms of having settled into a community, married, and had children) indicated that the more normalized a subject's current lifestyle was in terms of the dominant culture, the more likely the subject was to have returned to mainstream religious involvement, as noted in Table 8.4.

The fact that those who disengage from religion tend to return as they participate more fully in the dominant culture is readily understandable in terms of life cycle theories of socialization. Youth may be a time for exploration and rebellion, both of which may play a part in searching for identity.[152] However, it is also the case that theories of social change suggest the relevance of youthful participation in radical social movements aimed at altering society.[153] Whereas religious denominations tend to be at ease with the dominant culture, religious sects and cults are at tension with at least some aspects of this culture, as discussed in Chapter 9. New religious movements are likely to appeal to individuals not committed to the dominant culture. Montgomery has argued that the spread of new reli-

TABLE 8.3. Average Age of Religious Disengagement by Birth Cohort

Birth cohort	Average age at disengagement
1926–1935	29.4 years
1936–1945	25.1 years
1946–1954 (older baby boomers)	21.1 years
1955–1962 (younger baby boomers)	18.2 years

Note. Adapted from Roof (1993, pp. 154–155). Copyright 1993 by HarperCollins Publishers. Adapted by permission.

TABLE 8.4. Baby Boomers' Reengagement in
Mainstream Religion

Normative criteria	% reengaged
Single, no children, not settled	14 ($n = 51$)
Married, no children, not settled	16 ($n = 50$)
Married, children, not settled	52 ($n = 71$)
Married, children, settled	54 ($n = 124$)

Note. Adapted from Roof (1993, p. 165). Copyright 1993 by HarperCollins
Publishers. Adapted by permission.

gions is facilitated when the new religions either are a threat to society or come from a source
other than the society; they provide sources of identity and resistance for those alienated from
the dominant culture.[154] Although Montgomery's theory applies to the emergence of new
religions within a historical context and focuses upon macrosocial relations. It also applies
to the emergence of new religions within a subculture opposed by the dominant culture—a
phenomenon characteristic of the 1960s in North America. The subculture is likely to accept
new religious movements that promulgate behaviors and beliefs at odds with the dominant
culture, as cults and sects do.

One empirical prediction that is congruent with these macrosocial assumptions is that
exposure to countercultural values should make a person more susceptible to new religious
movements and to disengagement from mainstream religion. Roof's research provides data
relevant to this claim. Using an index of exposure to the 1960s counterculture, Roof found
that the preference for sticking to a mainstream cultural expressions of faith varied as a function of such exposure, as did willingness to explore other teachings and religions. These results
are summarized in Table 8.5.

The high rate of former drug use among those converted to new religious movements
is well documented. In some new religious movements, the rate of former drug use is reported
to be almost 100%. For instance, Volinn used in-depth interviews and extensive participatory observation to study 52 members of an ashram in New England.[155] Of these, 47 admitted to smoking marijuana, and 46 had used it 50 times or more. Likewise, all but 8 admitted
to using LSD, but only 6 had used this more than 50 times, and 14 had used it only "once or
twice."[156] Other investigators have documented former drug use among converts to new

TABLE 8.5. Responses to the Question "Is It Good to
Explore the Many Differing Religious Teachings, or Should
One Stick to a Particular Faith?" as a Function of Exposure
to the 1960s

Exposure to 1960s index[a]	Explore many teachings	Stick to faith
0	49%	39%
1	60%	32%
2	63%	23%
3	80%	14%

Note. Adapted from Roof (1993, p. 124). Copyright 1993 by HarperCollins
Publishers. Adapted by permission.

[a]Exposure to 1960s index: "Did you ever: 1. Attend a rock concert? [67% yes];
2. Smoke marijuana? [50% yes]; 3. Take part in any demonstrations,
marches, or rallies? [20% yes]." For each positive response, 1 point was scored.

religious movements. For example, Judah has documented the abandonment of drug use among converts to Hare Krishna;[157] Galanter and Buckley have obtained similar results for converts to the Divine Light Mission;[158] Anthony and Robbins have noted the abandonment of drug use among converts to Meher Baba;[159] and Nordquist also found such outcomes for converts to Ananda, a "New Age" community in Sweden.[160]

The low rates of illicit drug use among members of mainstream religions have long been established, as has the abandonment of illicit drug use associated with a change in religious commitment.[161] Both mainstream religions and new religious movements discourage the use of such drugs. However, it appears that prior drug experience varies according to whether one is a member of a mainstream denomination or a new religious movement (whether sect or cult). In denominational religion, norms and beliefs serve to decrease the probability of illicit drug use among participants; among illicit drug users, by contrast, spiritual seeking can result in conversion to new religious movements, which then discourage illicit drug use. Nevertheless, in both cases a change in religiousness is associated with abandonment of illicit drug use. It appears that to become more religiously committed, whether within one's existing faith or in conversion to another faith, is associated with decreased illicit drug use.

Several investigators have described new religious movements as providing an alternative to drug experiences. Some, such as Simmonds, argue that conversion can be a new form of addiction; new religious converts simply substitute one addiction for another.[162] Others, such as Volinn, have focused upon the spiritual experiences of converts to new religious movements as meaningful alternatives to illicit drug "highs."[163]

It would appear that with few exceptions, institutionalized forms of religion—whether denominations, sects, or cults—tend to discourage drug use.[164] Yet many who utilize drugs outside of religion define themselves as spiritual seekers. Roof noted that among his baby boomers, those most exposed to the counterculture of the 1960s were least likely to be conventionally religious but most likely to define themselves as spiritual. Eighty-one percent of those scoring highest on his index of exposure to the 1960s considered themselves as spiritual, whereas 92% of those who scored zero on his index saw themselves as religious.[165] Not surprisingly, 84% of those scoring highest on the index were religious dropouts.[166]

OVERVIEW

Conversion has occupied the interest of social scientists since the beginning of the 20th century. The early research was dominated by psychologists, who focused upon adolescence and sudden emotional conversions. The classic paradigm for conversion was fashioned after Paul's experience. Gradual conversions were recognized to occur, and were linked to an active search for meaning and purpose, but were seldom studied except to be contrasted with sudden conversions.

In the early 1960s, sociologically oriented social psychologists began to study conversion as a phenomenon linked to new religious movements. They have focused upon gradual conversions, postulating models of the conversion process most typically derived from participant observation or interview studies of converts.

Apostasy and deconversion have been studied as phenomena closely linked to conversion. Like conversion, apostasy has been linked to adolescence or young adulthood. Relatively few individuals remain apostates; most return at some point in the life cycle to their religious roots. This typically occurs when one is married, has children, and settles in an established community. However, spiritual seekers may remain outside religion altogether. Deconversion from a new religious movement is likely to be a gradual process of disillusionment, both with the religious group and with its leader.

NOTES

1. James (1902/1985, p. 139).
2. Kundera (1983, p. 308).
3. Poston (1992, p. 158).
4. Rambo (1993, p. 1).
5. Blake (1789/1967, Plate 44).
6. Hall (1904).
7. Coon (1992).
8. Hood (1994).
9. Hall (1917).
10. Gaustad (1966).
11. James (1902/1985, Lectures VI through VIII).
12. Jackson (1908).
13. James (1902/1985, Lectures IX and X).
14. Leuba (1896); Starbuck (1897, 1899).
15. Coe (1916).
16. Pratt (1920).
17. Clark (1958, p. 188).
18. Stephan and Stephan (1985).
19. Beckford and Richardson (1983).
20. Rambo (1982).
21. Capps and Dittes (1990); Capps (1994).
22. Snow and Machalek (1984).
23. Snow and Machalek (1984, p. 168).
24. Cutten (1908); Pratt (1920).
25. Richardson (1985b).
26. Pratt (1920, p. 153).
27. Gorsuch (1988).
28. Gorsuch (1988, p. 202).
29. Travisano (1970, p. 594).
30. Heirich (1977, p. 674).
31. Snow and Machalek (1984, pp. 168–174).
32. Coe (1916, p 54).
33. Brinthaupt and Lipka (1994).
34. Rambo (1993, p. xiii).
35. Snow and Machalek (1984, pp. 170–171).
36. Snow and Machalek (1984, pp. 173–174).
37. Coe (1916, p. 152).
38. James (1902/1985, p. 162).
39. Strickland (1924, p. 123). Emphasis in original.
40. Despite numerous arguments regarding indices of conversion, there are no studies empirically assessing the interrelationship among various operational measures of conversion.
41. There is no consensus in the literature regarding major types of conversion and of related phenomena. "Apostasy" and "deconversion" are generally accepted terms. We have borrowed "intensification" from Rambo (1993, p. 183).
42. Erikson (1968).
43. Berger and Luckmann (1967).
44. Berger (1979).
45. Starbuck (1899, p. 224).
46. Johnson (1959).
47. Roberts (1965).

48. Gillespie (1991).
49. Argyle and Beit-Hallahmi (1975, pp. 58–70).
50. Silverstein (1988).
51. Vernon (1968); Welch (1978).
52. Hadaway (1989).
53. Hadaway (1989, p. 201).
54. Brinkerhoff and Burke (1980).
55. Hadaway and Roof (1988).
56. Hadaway and Roof (1988, pp. 30–31).
57. See Roof and Hadaway (1979); Roof and McKinney (1987).
58. James (1902/1985). If Rambo's distinction between conversion and intensification is used, most of James's examples of conversion are intensification experiences. See Rambo (1993, p. 183).
59. Starbuck (1899).
60. Ames (1910).
61. Coe (1916).
62. Johnson (1959, p. 117).
63. Richardson (1985b, p. 164).
64. See Richardson (1985b, pp. 164–166).
65. Strickland (1924).
66. Clark (1929).
67. Starbuck (1899).
68. Pratt (1920).
69. Watson (1993); Watson, Morris, and Hood (1993).
70. Gordon (1984); Hood (1992c).
71. Hood (1983).
72. Coe (1916).
73. McCallister (1995).
74. Spellman, Baskett, and Byrne (1971).
75. Poston (1992).
76. Woodberry (1992).
77. Downton (1980); Lofland and Stark (1965).
78. Scobie (1973, 1975).
79. Strickland (1924).
80. Richardson (1985b).
81. Lofland and Skonovd (1981).
82. See Spilka, Hood, and Gorsuch 1985, p. 206). All of these contrasts were noted in early research (see Starbuck, 1899).
83. See Richardson (1985b, pp. 166–172).
84. Lofland and Stark (1965); Richardson (1985b, p. 168).
85. Lofland (1977).
86. Barker (1984).
87. Long and Hadden (1983).
88. Rambo (1992).
89. Richardson (1978b).
90. Beckford (1978).
91. Lofland and Skonovd (1981).
92. Lofland and Skonovd (1981, p. 374).
93. Lofland and Skonovd (1981, p. 375).
94. Straus (1976).
95. Lofland and Skonovd (1981, p. 379).
96. Snow and Machalek (1984, p. 173).
97. Beckford (1978); Snow and Machalek (1983); Spilka and McIntosh (1995); Spilka, Shaver, and Kirkpatrick (1985).
98. Balch (1980).
99. Deikman (1966).
100. Wilson (1982).
101. Preston (1981, 1982).
102. Preston (1981, 1982); Wilson (1982); Volinn (1985).
103. Balch (1980).

104. Festinger (1954). Festinger's theory has long been abandoned in psychological social psychology, but sociological social psychology has rediscovered its relevance to conversion. Ironically, Festinger was the first to apply his theory to a new religious movement. See Festinger, Riecken, and Schachter (1956).
105. Gartrell and Shannon (1985).
106. The classic model proposed by sociologists is that of Lofland and Stark (1965). A recent exhaustive model proposed by a psychologist is that of Rambo (1993, pp. 168–169).
107. In this sense, Richardson's use of the concept of "paradigm" to identify classic and contemporary research is illuminating. Paradigms are not capable of either falsification or verification in any straightforward sense. The literature of paradigm and its relevance to the social sciences is as immense as it is controversial. See Kilbourne and Richardson (1989); Richardson (1985b); Kuhn (1962); Masterman (1970).
108. Wallace (1956).
109. Bulliet (1979).
110. Bulliet (1979, pp. 31–32).
111. Rambo (1993).
112. Gerlach and Hine (1970).
113. Heirich (1977).
114. Straus (1979).
115. Seggar and Kunz (1972).
116. Rambo (1993, p. 47).
117. Gerlach and Hine (1970).
118. Heirich (1977).
119. Straus (1976).
120. Staples and Mauss (1987).
121. Seggar and Kunz (1972, pp. 178–184).
122. Ullman (1982).
123. Rambo (1993, pp. 87–123).
124. Snow and Machalek (1984, p. 182).
125. Galanter (1980); Snow, Zurcher, and Ekland-Olson (1980, 1983); Stark and Bainbridge (1980a); Straus (1984).
126. Jacobs (1987, 1989).
127. Pratt (1920, p. 160).
128. Cartwright and Kent (1992).
129. Kirkpatrick and Shaver (1990). Also see Kirkpatrick (1992, 1995).
130. Beckford (1978).
131. Boyer (1994); Morinis (1985).
132. Paloutzian (1981). See also Paloutzian, Jackson, and Crandell (1978).
133. Richardson (1978b).
134. Bird and Remier (1982).
135. Barker and Currie (1985).
136. Wright (1987).
137. Skonovd (1983).
138. Wright (1986).
139. Downton (1980).
140. Galanter, Rabkin, Raskin, and Deutsch (1979).
141. Jacobs (1989).
142. Jacobs (1989, p. 128).
143. Snow and Machalek (1984).
144. Roozen (1980, p. 440).
145. Albrecht, Cornwall, and Cunningham (1983).
146. Albrecht, Cornwall, and Cunningham (1983, p. 65). See also Albrecht and Cornwall (1989).
147. Hoge, McGuire, and Stratman (1981).
148. Roszak (1968).
149. Tipton (1982).
150. Roof (1993, p. 154).
151. Roof (1993, pp. 265–268).
152. Erikson (1968).

153. Keniston (1968, 1971); Roszak (1968).
154. Montgomery (1991).
155. Volinn (1985).
156. Volinn (1985, p. 152).
157. Judah (1974).
158. Galanter and Buckley (1978).
159. Anthony and Robbins (1974).
160. Nordquist (1978).
161. Gorsuch (1976).
162. Simmonds (1977a).
163. Among former drug users converted to new religious movements, the metaphor of a new alternative "high" is quite common. See Volinn (1985).
164. Interesting exceptions include the use of drugs in some religious groups in North America, such as the sacramental use of peyote in some Native American religions. See LaBarre (1969).
165. Roof (1993, p. 123).
166. Roof (1993, p. 57).

Chapter 9

THE SOCIAL PSYCHOLOGY OF RELIGIOUS ORGANIZATIONS

ॐ

> The people of Jonestown could not have had a compelling reason for what they did, for the integrity of our own social existence would thereby be placed in doubt. Giving credence to Jones' account would require concluding the unthinkable: that the people of Jonestown were "justified" in taking the action of terminating the lives of an entire community.[1]

> Between you and God there stands the church.[2]

> The work of the Church ends when knowledge of God begins.[3]

> The novelty which "brainwashing" poses should not prevent legislative or judicial recognition of identifiable and effective methods employed to understand rational thought and critical capacities. The law as an evolving body must adapt to technical developments in psychological theory as well as those of the physical sciences.[4]

> When a society would turn its eyes away from the deepest questions of responsibility, brainwashing becomes an explanation that avoids the responsibility of looking inward.[5]

The process of becoming religious continues to intrigue social scientists and to foster both theoretical and empirical debate. The simple fact that persons are not born religious means they must *become* religious, if they are to be so. The process of becoming religious entails numerous possibilities. Persons may be born into a family with a particular faith commitment and may simply be socialized to adopt that faith as their own. These individuals are those whom William James dubbed "the once-born."[6] On the other hand, persons may be born into one faith tradition and later change to another. Those born outside any faith tradition may later choose to commit to one. Those previously committed may fall away. Or people may have a series of different faith commitments throughout their lives. Some may simply engage in an interminable quest in which spiritual issues absorb their interest but never find a resolution. Much of this flux is the subject matter of religious conversion; converts are James's "twice-born,"[7] as discussed in Chapter 8.

Yet this individual religious change does not take place in a vacuum. The maintenance of faith, as well as conversion, is not an individual affair. Those with faith tend to seek companions in a social context within which their faith may be both shared and practiced. In this flux of individual religious change also lie the rise and fall of churches and the growth and decline of denominations. In addition, the emergence of novel religious forms from within established groups creates the sects, and from without creates the cults. James typifies the psychologist's propensity to emphasize religious experience in individual terms,[8] as we have discussed in Chapter 6. The renowned philosopher Whitehead even went so far as to define religion in terms of what individuals do with their solitude.[9] Yet even solitude is a retreat from the social and takes with it the very language shared by others within which private thoughts are possible.[10] Despite a rich conceptual literature linking spirituality and solitude, religion is inherently social.[11]

Thus, the social characteristics of the groups within which persons are socialized, to which individuals convert, or from which individuals withdraw are of obvious relevance to understanding how persons become religious. Our task in this chapter is to present theory and data on the social psychology of religious organizations. In so doing, we confront issues that have long been of concern to social scientists and that have recently emerged into public debate and controversy. Neither the rise and fall of religious collectivities nor the commitments and disaffections of religious individuals can be discussed for long without controversy.

THE CLASSIFICATION OF RELIGIOUS ORGANIZATIONS

Although it may be true that psychologists are particularly prone to define religious commitments in terms of individuals, it remains abundantly clear that these commitments are shared and under varying degrees of organizational control. Whitehead's focus on the great solitary images of religious imagination[12]—Mohammed brooding in the desert, Buddha resting under the Bodhi tree, and Christ crying out from the cross—is balanced by the fact that such solitary religious figures maintain their importance within great traditions maintained by generations of the faithful, organized into "churches" or "denominations" and "sects." Furthermore, novel forms of religious commitment centered upon newly identified charismatic figures are likely themselves quickly to take an organizational form, however unstructured this may be, if they are to survive. These are the religious "cults." Hence, to be either traditionally or innovatively religious is to be related in some fashion to a religious group. The solitary religious figure is a myth reconstructed and abstracted from the organizational forms that both define this figure and give him or her meaning. The classification of these religious forms has occupied much of the interest of the more sociologically oriented psychologists of religion. Of the various classification schemes proposed, the most influential has been "church–sect theory."

CHURCH–SECT THEORY

Church–sect theory was never intended as a theory of origins, and hence it is a bit surprising that it has so dominated the empirical literature on both established and new religious movements. Furthermore, as Dittes has noted, the careers of church–sect theory and intrinsic–extrinsic theory (discussed in Chapter 1) have numerous parallels.[13] Both theories have dominated their conceptual and empirical literatures; both have numerous critics; and both have, in Dittes's phrasing, "some considerable promise of surviving their obituaries."[14]

A common criticism of both church–sect and intrinsic–extrinsic theories is the confounding of evaluation with description. This often entails implicit claims to "good" and "bad" religion—whether in terms of organizational structure, as in church–sect theory, or in terms of religious motivation, as in intrinsic–extrinsic theory.[15] As we note later in this chapter, religious cults have to a large extent borne the burden of a variety of pejorative connotations. They are typically perceived as "bad" religion. As social psychologists, we must explore the empirical reasons for such connotations. To do so requires an empirical grounding in the relationship between forms of religious organizations and their dominant or host cultures. In this sections, we draw upon the roots of church–sect theory and attempt to show how these have influenced the sociologically oriented social-psychological literature. Only a few would argue against the importance of church–sect theory.[16] We hope that our discussion of the roots of this theory in the work of Troeltsch will demonstrate both its relevance and its usefulness in organizing contemporary empirical studies on the social psychology of religious organizations.

Origins of Church–Sect Theory

The main source of church–sect theory in modern social psychology has been Reinhold Niebuhr's work on the social sources of denominationalism.[17] Denominations are what many persons think of as "churches"—groups commonly accepted as legitimate religious organizations within their host cultures. Most people identify themselves by reporting their denominational membership when asked for their religious identification. Thus, as Wimberley and Christenson have noted, individual religious identity is largely synonymous with group religious membership.[18]

Niebuhr's work is a modification and popularization of church, sect, and mysticism—three types of religious organizations articulated in Troeltsch's classic work, *The Social Teachings of the Christian Churches*.[19] Niebuhr significantly altered Troeltsch's conceptualizations, ignoring his three-part typology (church–sect–mysticism) in favor of a two-part typology (church–sect). Furthermore, Niebuhr added a dynamic tendency to the theory: He suggested that persons who are dissatisfied with the commonness and permissiveness of churches as they successfully appeal to the masses seek more demanding criteria for membership. This exclusiveness creates a sectarian movement. Over time, sects themselves begin to tend toward the characteristics of churches as they too become more successful and accepting of new membership, especially from other than the lower social classes of their host cultures. Eister has referred to this dynamic process as the "paradox of religious organizations": It produces sects from churches, but sects then tend to become like the churches they once criticized.[20]

Niebuhr's modification of Troeltsch's typology is further confounded when it is recognized that Troeltsch's three-part typology was derived from two independent dichotomies elaborated by Max Weber.[21] As Swatos has emphasized,[22] Weber had two typologies: church–sect and mysticism–asceticism. Troeltsch's single typology of church–sect–mysticism was itself a modification, intended both to simplify and to clarify his friend Weber's dual typologies. The extent to which Troeltsch's single typology is compatible with Weber's dual typologies is a matter of dispute among scholars. Steeman argues that Troeltsch's treatment of church–sect–mysticism at least approximates Weber's intent in his dual typology.[23] On the other hand, Garrett argues that a significant disjuncture separates Weber's and Troeltsch's typologies, especially when consideration is given to mysticism.[24]

For our purposes, it is important to emphasize that the Weber and Troeltsch theories share a crucial defining criterion that differentiates churches (denominations) from sects:

Churches are inclusive, whereas sects are exclusive. By focusing upon the single criterion of degree of exclusiveness, church–sect theory can contribute to organizing the empirical literature in value-neutral terms. The criterion of exclusiveness is easily operationalized, and it permits us as social scientists to sidestep issues of evaluating "good" and "bad" religion.

A further clarification of the origins of Troeltsch's theory will aid us greatly in organizing the empirical literature, as well as in suggesting how a focus upon the original intent of Weber's and Troeltsch's typologies makes them less evaluative than subsequent theorists' development of these concepts.[25]

Troeltsch and Church–Sect Theory

Troeltsch's theory has been critiqued or modified by numerous theorists, most of whom ignore Troeltsch's own analytical use of this typology within a limited historical context. Furthermore, Troeltsch's typology was intended only for Christianity. Contemporary theorists apply church–sect theory to a variety of new religious movements, many of which are non-Christian. However, despite these serious limitations, Troeltsch's theory remains viable as it focuses upon two assumptions likely to have universal validity. First, church, sect, and mysticism are logical tendencies within Christianity. Such tendencies are likely to be inherent not only in Christianity, but in any faith tradition centered upon a charismatic figure, regardless of particular histories or contexts.[26] The second assumption is that contingent historical factors often structure the emergence of the types as actual empirical embodiments of these logical tendencies.[27] Troeltsch saw the logical tendencies of church, sect, and mysticism exhausted in their empirical forms as far as Christianity was concerned. He argued that the church form was most purely expressed in medieval Catholicism, the sect form in Calvinism, and the mysticism form in Quakerism. However, mysticism needs little formal organization; instead, it enshrines radical subjectivity and individuality either within or outside faith traditions as forms of spirituality claiming direct access to the transcendent. Hence, mysticism is of little relevance to religious organizations. As Steeman has succinctly noted, the mysticism type is more or less the end of the road in Troeltsch's historical scheme.[28] Thus, we do not discuss mysticism further in this chapter. (It has been separately treated in Chapter 7 of this text.)

The Troeltsch legacy for the modern study of religion is the "free church." Here, new denominations of Christianity emerge, each a free expression of a fellowship of faith. These denominations exhibit dynamic tendencies, competing for universality (an expression of the church type) while also demanding ascetic purity (an expression of the sect type). They are expressions of religious tolerance in a host culture that accepts and demands religious diversity. The historical exhausted realities of Troeltsch's forms of Christianity remain as logical tendencies within denominations, with their propensity for universalization (church) and personal purity (sect). These tendencies are expressed in much of the contemporary empirical literature.

The Empirical Tradition Influenced by Church–Sect Theory

Not surprisingly, contemporary social scientists have divided into two camps regarding church–sect theory. One camp continues the classical tradition of modifying church–sect theory and of debating its validity and value mainly at the conceptual level.[29] Most of the resulting classification systems are qualitatively derived, relying upon appeals to face validity. Few in this camp seek empirical verification of predictive consequences for their typologies. In the rare instances when these classifications have been empirically assessed, they have been found to be less than adequate. As Welch has noted, "Few existing set classification schemes—both unidimensional and multidimensional varieties—are able to offer true discriminatory power when put to the empirical test."[30]

Members of the other camp have opted for more precise operationalization of their typologies, often employing quantitative procedures to construct their typologies,[31] and have sought systematic testing of hypotheses derived from these classifications. One of the most systematic efforts has been made by Stark,[32] whose model has moved the debate beyond mere conceptual criticisms to one of testing of empirical hypotheses based upon operational measures of sects.

Stark owes much to a now-classic paper by Johnson, who first operationalized the essential difference between church and sect that he felt both Weber and Troeltsch set forth with varying degrees of explicitness.[33] Churches are inclusive (e.g., accepting infant baptism) and are widely accommodating to their host cultures, seldom being at significant odds with their major values. On the other hand, sects are exclusive (e.g., often demanding adult baptism) and seek a religious purity that often puts them at odds with their culture. The universalizing tendency of the church type accommodates to the host culture, accepting many persons who meet only minimal criteria for membership. The perfectionist tendency of the sect type sets rigorous criteria for membership; as such, it is less accommodating to the host culture. Johnson operationalized these tendencies as follows: "*A church is a religious group that accepts the social environment in which it exists. A sect is a religious group that rejects the social environment in which it exists.*"[34] Johnson further restricted church and sect to religious groups, stopping by definitional fiat the efforts to extend church–sect typologies to other groups (such as political ones) that some theorists have found useful.[35]

Stark and Bainbridge have refined Johnson's definition by further operationalizing acceptance and rejection according to degree of difference, antagonism, and separation between a religious group and its host culture.[36] In our view, the most fruitful operational indicator is the degree of difference, indicated by belief and behavioral norms, between sects and the dominant host culture. Salient differences are likely to lead to mutual rejection, but whether or not they do is an independent empirical question. Furthermore, antagonism is largely a corollary of different beliefs and behavioral norms. Difference itself can be operationally equated with subcultural deviance when the beliefs produce tension between religious groups and their host culture. Low-tension beliefs are congruent with being part of mainstream culture and are characteristic of denominations (churches).

Given this operationalization of church and sect along a continuum of tension, embedded within a more general theory of religion, numerous novel hypotheses have been generated and empirically tested.[37] Perhaps the most hotly disputed among these is the concept of a general religious economy, in which religious views must compete in an open market. As such, sects become more successful (gain members) by reducing their tension with the host culture. Over time, sects tend to shed their other-worldly and perfectionist tendencies as they accommodate to the culture. They may, but are unlikely to, remain isolated instances of subcultural deviance. Thus, in the Stark and Bainbridge theory, churches reemerge from sects as essentially secularized religious groups—insofar as secularization is recognized to be a process of accommodation to the dominant host culture.

Another novel hypothesis derived from this theory is that in similar religious markets, novel forms of religion can be expected to thrive. As we shall soon see, if cults are defined as novel religious organizations, cults can be expected to thrive precisely where churches or denominations are weak. This follows from the hypothesis that churches have already accommodated to the mainstream culture and that sects are unlikely to maintain for long a novel stance *vis-à-vis* the larger host culture, to which they also must accommodate to be successful. The hypothesis that weak church environments lead to increased probabilities of cult formation has yet to be fully empirically substantiated, but remains as viable a hypothesis as it is controversial.[38] Still, the tendency for sects to lead to churches is inherent in any view arguing that almost by definition, surviving social groups have accommodated to their culture, to at least the degree that their survival is assured. Garrett has referred to this tendency, most evident in Niebuhr, as the "Americanization of the Troeltschian typology."[39]

It is important to emphasize that although accommodation to the host culture can be identified as a secular move, it is inherent in the nature of religious organizations that they devise objective means to permit universality at the expense of ethical perfection. For instance, churches permit membership on the basis of minimal criteria that can be objectively specified. In Troeltsch's terms, the church allows an "institutionalization of grace."[40] Sects can maintain exclusivity by rejecting members who can be objectified as "too worldly." As such, the sect is a religious subculture by definition. Exclusivity both defines and characterizes sects as they emerge from churches. Yet they tend toward universality as they survive. Furthermore, religious subcultures, if sufficiently at odds with their host cultures and not in a process of accommodating to them, are likely to be targets of legal retaliation and control— something that has characterized the history of sects in the Western world.[41] It has also become a major issue with respect to the contemporary analysis of cults, as we note later in this chapter.

With church–sect theory, the useful empirical indicator is not simply the religious group's accommodation to or rejection of the host culture, but the reaction of the host culture in turn to the religious group. What empirically distinguishes churches and sects is the degree to which their host cultures seek to control and minimize the influence of particular religious groups. In many Western cultures, especially North America, the generally favorable attitude toward "religion" suggests that both churches and sects are likely to do fairly well. Churches, or what we might call mainline denominations, are likely to fare better than sects, but both accommodate enough to their host cultures to be acceptable in varying degrees. As Redekop has emphasized, the useful empirical task is to identify the specific aspects of tension with the host culture that creates problems of retaliation.[42] We first focus upon this issue in terms of denominational and sectarian forms of religion. In a later section, we explore it in terms of cults—the area where it has generated the majority of recent empirical research in the face of popular controversies.

Operational Indices on the Church–Sect Continuum

Johnson's operationalization of church–sect theory in terms of degree of tension with the host culture permits Troeltsch's typology to be placed upon a continuum. Religions enforcing norms that are sharply distinct from the more generally accepted norms of the host culture are relatively sectarian; those permitting members to participate freely in all aspects of secular life of the host culture are more church-like.[43] Bainbridge and Stark have provided survey data consistent with Johnson's operationalization.[44] Their data were taken from a sample of church members in four counties of northern California; our focus is upon responses from 2,326 members of different Protestant denominations. Denominations "intuitively"[45] identified as sects included the Church of God, the Church of Christ, the

Church of the Nazarene, Assemblies of God, and Seventh-Day Adventists.[46] Mainstream Protestant denominations were classified into those more compatible (low-tension) and those less compatible (high-tension) with their host culture. Our focus is only upon low-tension denominations contrasted with sectarian groups, which are high-tension by definition. We have selected from the survey data certain behaviors permitted by most of secular society but differentially forbidden by religious groups. It ought to be the case that the more sectarian groups should forbid behaviors permitted by the host culture more frequently than more church-like religious groups (denominations) should do. Table 9.1 compares results from the low-tension mainstream Protestant denominations (grouped together) and the five Protestant sects (separately) on differences in some common cultural behaviors and beliefs.

The fact that more sectarian groups hold beliefs at odds with the dominant culture simply indicates one dimension of tension. To oppose dancing or drinking within the host culture, where they are approved and considered normal, separates sect members by belief and behavior from certain cultural activities. Likewise, to oppose such beliefs as the theory of evolution puts sect members at odds with normative educational forces in the culture. Even the support of more literal religious beliefs, such as the reality of the Devil or Christ's return, may put sect members at odds with members of other, more culturally congruent religions. In the comparisons in Table 9.1, the differences among the sectarian groups are never as large as those between all sectarian groups and mainstream Protestants.[47] This supports the contention that sects are at odds with the dominant culture and with denominations within that culture.

Additional evidence for the usefulness of operationalizing sectarian religions by belief tension with their host culture can be gleaned from Poloma's interesting study of Christian Scientists.[48] Here a single axis of tension, appropriate medical care, is of overriding importance.

It is clearly the case that medical perspectives on physical illness dominate modern cultures; most persons seek medical treatment for illness. However, many persons use religious techniques such as prayer to facilitate healing. Several investigators have emphasized that spiritual healing is not as marginal in modern society as one might expect from the official

TABLE 9.1. Comparison of Mainstream Protestant Denominations and Five Protestant Sects on Selected Behaviors and Beliefs

	Percentage of respondents endorsing behavior/belief					
	Mainstream Protestant ($n = 1,032$)	Church of Christ ($n = 37$)	Church of God ($n = 44$)	Church of the Nazarene ($n = 75$)	Assemblies of God ($n = 44$)	Seventh-Day Adventist ($n = 35$)
	Behaviors					
Disapprove of gambling	62	100	89	92	98	97
Favor censorship	31	57	57	73	82	66
Disapprove of dancing	1	95	77	96	91	100
	Beliefs					
Reject Darwin	11	78	57	80	91	94
Believe Devil exists	14	87	73	91	96	97
Believe Jesus will return	22	78	73	93	100	100

Note. Percentages must be cautiously interpreted, given the variation in sample sizes. Adapted from Bainbridge and Stark (1980b, pp. 111–112). Copyright 1980 by the Religious Research Association. Adapted by permission.

dominance of medical perspectives. For instance, Johnson, Williams, and Bromley found that 14% of their sample of 586 adults claimed to have experienced a healing of a "serious disease or physical condition" as a result of prayer.[49] Likewise, Poloma and Pendleton found that 72% of randomly chosen respondents from a Midwestern population believed that persons sometimes receive physical healing as a result of prayer.[50] Nearly one-third of these (32%) claimed a personal experience of healing, and a third of this subsample (34%) claimed that healing was of an accident or medical problem that was life-threatening. Thus, Poloma rightly concludes that spiritual healing is a widely diffused belief and practice through a broad range of the general population.[51]

Although Poloma is correct in her general assessment, it is important to note that prayer as an adjunct to orthodox medical treatment is not a significant source of tension with the dominant culture. For instance, Trier and Shupe have shown that among participants randomly selected from telephone numbers in the Great Lakes area, prayer was used as an adjunct to traditional, mainstream medical care.[52] They found no evidence that prayer was used in lieu of traditional medical treatments. Furthermore, frequency of prayer was positively correlated with consulting a physician. Thus, prayer is most frequently used in conjunction with and not in opposition to orthodox medical treatment.[53] As such, prayer for recovery is hardly sectarian in nature.

However, the use of prayer as an adjunct to medical treatment is a far cry from the articulation of a religious ideology that argues against both the concept of disease and the relevance of medical treatment to a cure. Christian Science is one religion that argues for healing in opposition to, not in conjunction with, orthodox medical treatment.[54] This is clearly a belief at odds with the dominant host culture, and even with mainstream Christian interpretations of spiritual healings by faith or miraculous intervention.[55] Thus, the sectarian nature of Christian Science can best be revealed when comparisons are made between beliefs of Christian Scientists and mainstream Protestant Christians who claim to have experienced a spiritual healing.

In a follow-up study of the 1985 Akron Area Survey,[56] Poloma contacted 97 of 179 potential participants who had agreed to be interviewed for another study. These were those who reported having "experienced a healing of an illness or disease as a result of prayer."[57] They were interviewed this time on the topic of spiritual healing. The vast majority of participants were "born-again" Christians (82%) and identified themselves as charismatic, Pentecostal, or both (86%). Two were Christian Scientists, who were later used in obtaining an additional sample of 42 members of the Church of Christ, Scientist (Christian Science). Comparisons between the 95 mainstream Protestants and the 44 Christian Scientists on matters on beliefs regarding spiritual healing revealed expected differences, as noted in Table 9.2.

It should be stated that these differences in beliefs of spiritual healing between Christian religious groups were found despite similarities in beliefs on other religious matters. For instance, the majority of both Christian Scientists and mainline Christians in Poloma's sample agreed that Jesus healed in order to show compassion and divinity, as well as to gain followers and to glorify God.[58] Furthermore, in terms of actual reported medical practices, the majority of both mainline Christians and Christian Scientists practiced their beliefs—the former seeking and utilizing orthodox medical care, the latter much less likely to do so. Some of these comparisons are reported in Table 9.3.

As can be seen from Table 9.3, neither the Christian Scientists nor the mainstream Christians acted perfectly in conformity with their stated beliefs: 10% of Christian Scientists reported having visited a doctor within the last year, while an almost equal percentage of

TABLE 9.2. Differences between Mainline Christians and Christian Scientists in Beliefs about Spiritual Healing

Belief	Percentage of respondents endorsing belief	
	Mainline Christians (n = 95)	Christian Scientists (n = 44)
God always heals if faith enough	57	85
God withholds healing for spiritual good	72	10
Healing operates with fixed laws	69	95
God punishes evil with illness	24	0
God usually heals through doctors	73	12
God usually does not use divine healing	47	3

Note. All differences were significant, at least p < .01. Adapted from Poloma (1991, p. 341). Copyright 1991 by the Religious Research Association. Adapted by permission.

mainline Christians had failed to visit one. Still, the Christian Scientists' rejection of orthodox medicine was related to very high rates of nonparticipation in its practices. Clearly, rejecting orthodox medicine is a point of tension that separates Christian Scientists from other Christians and from the mainstream culture as well.

ORGANIZATIONAL DYNAMICS

The operationalization of tension with the host culture along a single continuum is useful, but it can also be misleading. Cultures are not homogeneous entities; they are not defined by a single set of norms. Cultures are heterogeneous, with conflicting and often incompatible norms existing simultaneously. In a word, cultures are pluralist. Some social scientists refer to this state of affairs as "postmodernism."[59] Although little consensus exists on the meaning of this term, the fact that no single perspective dominates postmodern cultures suggests that tension with a culture must be defined in terms of opposition arising in significant power groups within the culture, which have vested interests in the support of particular norms. Deviation from norms whose enforcement is of little concern is less crucial than deviation from norms that arouses reactions from those with significant power within the host culture. More sectarian groups arouse reaction from the powerful, not simply

TABLE 9.3. Differences between Mainline Christians and Christian Scientists in Reasons for Seeking Medical Care and Medical Visits

	Percentage of respondents endorsing item	
	Mainline Christians (n = 95)	Christian Scientists (n = 44)
Likely would seek help for:		
Relief of headache	100	0
Flu-like symptom	35	6
Severe chest pain	76	10
Severe injury	76	5
Visited doctor within last year	88	10

Note. All differences were significant at p < .001. Adapted from Poloma (1991, p. 344). Copyright 1991 by the Religious Research Association. Adapted by permission.

because they harbor different beliefs, but because they harbor different beliefs on a continuum considered salient or important to the powerful within the culture.[60]

To take an obvious example, Christian Science, in its opposition to modern medical science, raises concern among the powerful in a culture dominated by belief in modern medicine. Numerous instances arise when parents from belief traditions such as Christian Science or the Jehovah's Witnesses, which oppose some or all of orthodox medicine, have children in need of medical care. In such cases, the confrontation between the powerfully sanctioned norms of the medical establishment and alternative beliefs within sectarian traditions illustrates a significant tension. Outside of particularly specified religious alternatives, it is simply "common sense" that one treats disease by orthodox medical procedures. Yet common sense is but the culturally shared knowledge of reality defined within a tradition.[61] The criteria for assessing claims to truth are often incommensurate between traditions. The very specifications of the criteria of judgment are themselves contextually bound. Thus, to claim that medical treatment is "obviously" necessary for diseases is not simply to affirm one reality but to reject others such as that articulated within Christian Science. How to treat these issues empirically without imposition of value claims has long plagued the social sciences.

Before we address one possible resolution to this problem, we simply emphasize that the existence of differences in reality claims in which groups within the culture have dominant interests is not simply a source of identity, but one of conflict as well. To identify oneself as a Christian Scientist is both to belong to a group at odds with orthodox medicine and also to be at odds with the educational elite of the culture, who provide the support for and defend the perspective of orthodox medicine. It is almost axiomatic in the social sciences that strong identification of members with divergent groups increases prejudice, as measured by the social distance groups attempt to maintain from one another.[62] Recently, Watson and his colleagues have defined the social distance between groups in terms of their "ideological surround."[63]

Ideological Surround

In a series of empirical studies, Watson and his colleagues have utilized a methodological procedure that permits the identification of different meanings attributed by persons of a given tradition to various phenomena. Consistent with the position that both ideological and methodological pluralism characterizes postmodern culture,[64] Watson utilizes empirical measures corrected for their ideological content. Since all descriptions are theory- and value-laden, it is of little use to attempt arguments across traditions. Furthermore, even within the physical sciences, attempting a neutral, presumably objective context-free description of reality is neither possible nor desirable.[65] It is even less so with the realities dealt with by social psychologists, which are obviously socially constructed. These constructions both define groups and provide identities for their members that can place them at odds with one another. Watson's "ideological surround" method is an empirical procedure that permits identification of different meanings for identical scale items. Empirically, considerations of the ideological surround of any operational measure permit groups to communicate with one another, based upon the differing meanings any measure may have in groups identified with different ideologies.

For instance, the fact that intrinsic religiosity often correlates positively with social desirability measures is not interpreted to mean that the intrinsically religious only wish to appear socially desirable.[66] This interpretation of the empirical data fails to account for the meaning of social desirability items within the ideological surround of the intrinsically religious person. An alternative explanation can readily be derived from simply having individuals rate the various items on social desirability scales for their religious relevance. For instance, among intrinsically religious persons, positive endorsement of social desirability items reflects the ideological surround of their religious tradition, which defines such items as desirable social behaviors.[67] Thus, intrinsic religiosity correlates with social desirability on measures that intrinsically religious persons see as desirable socially. In a similar vein, correcting scales to measure self-actualization for their different ideological surround reveals different meanings of the term for religiously and humanistically committed persons.[68] Thus, whether or not a person describes himself or herself as self-actualized depends upon the relevance or meaning of any measure of self-actualization within a given tradition. Thus, the meaning of any measure is established within a given ideological surround; no measure is an Archimedean point by which all traditions can be judged. Both humanists and religionists can be self-actualized, within criteria acceptable to their beliefs. More importantly, when the ideological surround of any operational measure is understood, communication between groups is established by one's understanding of the different meanings identical operational measures may have for diverse groups.

More sociologically influenced social psychologies, especially those rooted in the work of G. H. Mead,[69] have long held that social phenomena can be predicted best when the meaning of the phenomena from the actors' perspective is taken into account. Most forcefully expressed in symbolic interactionism, this tradition argues that positivistic methods, which assume that an objective measure is equally meaningful across persons, are limited.[70] Persons react to meanings that in terms of religions are defined by their traditions. These meanings are often dismissed as merely subjective, or are assessed by measures assumed to be objective indices of belief, regardless of the particular meaning they may have for a subject. Yet, as Blumer has noted, "To ignore the meaning of things toward which people act is seen as falsifying the behavior under study."[71] Subjective meanings shared among persons define an intersubjectivity that is the normative base of various groups within a culture.

Symbolic interactionists have typically used qualitative methods to study such subjective meanings—a tradition often identified as the "Chicago school."[72] The competing "Iowa school" of symbolic interactionism has tried to establish quantitative indices of meaning, using methods compatible with the use of reliable scales in mainstream social psychology.[73] However, these procedures ignore individual differences in meaning within groups for the same items. Watson's ideological surround permits a measurement and treatment of subjective meanings that combine the quantitative considerations of the Iowa school with the sensitivity to individual subjective meanings of the Chicago school. It does not assume that meanings are identical across groups even when scales have high reliabilities. Instead, subjective meanings are determined for significant clusters of persons within groups, and the scales are differentially scored for the relevance of these meanings.

The ideological surround is directly relevant to the identification of those tensions that differentiate denominations from sects. Again, sects are religious groups that have significant tension with powerfully enforced norms within a host culture, based upon the different meanings they have for sect members and for the enforcers of the dominant culture—each supported by a powerful tradition. To go back to our earlier example, good mothers in religions compatible with the orthodox medical culture seek medical aid for their children's illness; good mothers within the Church of Christ, Scientist do not take ill children to the doctor. Here the obvious tension between sects that reject orthodox medicine and cultures that are committed to orthodox medicine is highlighted. A member of the mainstream culture is likely to wonder, "How could a mother who loves her child reject necessary medical care?" The Christian Scientist has a powerful, if clearly sectarian, response to this question.

Defining Sects versus Denominations in Terms of Change

Applying the notion of ideological surround to religious organizations helps us to grasp the dynamic nature of these groups, which might otherwise be misperceived as having a static quality. All groups are in a continual process of change, denominations no less than sects. Cultures are in a continual process of change as well. However, the issue is whether changes within religious groups are in a direction compatible with the dominant culture (denominations) or not (sects). In most cases, the issue of congruence is a function of the meanings involved. We can identify this dynamic tension as a ratio between "restorative" and "transformative" efforts to maintain a tradition or shared system of meaning. Meanings are seldom if ever merely personal or idiosyncratic; they are almost always shared by some group, and at odds with those shared by other groups.[74] Religious groups undergoing either transformative or restorative changes become sectarian if the dominant culture's commitments remain fairly constant or shift in a direction opposite to the religious group's concerns, respectively.

Restorative Sects

Restorative changes are attempts to maintain or restore beliefs and practices that oppose altered values in the dominant culture. These changes produce tension by supporting a particular system of meaning, with norms and behavioral expectations that the dominant culture now views as archaic. Even though these beliefs and norms may have been dominant at one time, their continuance in the face of cultural change now creates tension. If the changes are defined with a religious system of meaning, we may speak of "restorative sects."

For instance, religious fundamentalism is a modern sectarian movement within North American Protestantism directed at restoring fundamental values and commitments seen as threatened by movements within the dominant culture. It began in the early 20th century when a series of pamphlets, *The Fundamentals: A Testimony to the Truth*, were distributed by Lyon and Milton Stewart, two California businessmen.[75] Essentially, these pamphlets rejected the modernist techniques of textual and scientific criticism that had been applied to Christian scripture; they asserted that historical and literary criticism was not to be utilized to undermine a literal interpretation of scripture. Scripture was declared to be without error and to establish authoritatively and for all time a shared system of meaning. The ideological surround of fundamentalist religion supports the meaningfulness of beliefs in such things as the divinity of Christ, the reality of the Virgin birth, and the factual truth of miracles as literally interpreted from scripture.[76] Thus, fundamentalist groups became sectarian as they refused to participate in religious denominations that accommodated their beliefs to the modernist criticisms, both scientific and literary, supported by mainstream culture.

Almost by definition, few social scientists with religious identities would identify themselves as fundamentalists, since the distance between fundamentalist ideology and that implicit in social science methodologies is great. Not surprisingly, much of the empirical literature on fundamentalism finds it to be characterized by undesirable or deficient traits, such as narrow-mindedness,[77] a lack of cognitive complexity,[78] and a low level of spiritual maturity.[79] However, investigators have often not appropriately noted variations within fundamentalist groups[80] and the consequences of different operational indices used to assess fundamentalism.[81] In terms of an ideological surround, such descriptions suggest the different meanings social scientists give to phenomena that are normative and meaningful within fundamentalism. Fundamentalist groups are by definition socially functional, even when by particular psychological measures individual fundamentalists are found to be psychologically dysfunctional.

Research has demonstrated the lack of sensitivity of many social-scientific measures when applied to fundamentalist traditions. For instance, the original version of the Minnesota Multiphasic Personality Inventory (MMPI), a widely used objective measure of pathological personality assessment, included frequency of prayer and other specific items meaningful within the ideological surround of the Fundamentalist. To cite but one such item, "Christ performed miracles such as changing water into wine." With the exception of an item referring to church attendance, agreement with this and all other religious items was scored to indicate pathology. To make matters even worse, many of these items were part of a subscale used in research to measure ego strength, the lack of which is often perceived as pathological.[82] Obviously, measuring pathology among religious fundamentalists by such items does not give a measure of pathology that is independent of the person's religious belief. Hood demonstrated that correcting for the meaning of such items in terms of ideological surround or removing such items altogether fails to support a relationship between pathology and fundamentalism.[83] Furthermore, as Stark has noted, from a purely sociological perspective ongoing groups are by definition normal, regardless of presumed pathological conditions within their membership.[84]

Within a pluralistic society, fundamentalists maintain their sectarian nature by deliberately utilizing both religious and sectarian means to maintain the boundaries of their beliefs that are functional for their way of life. For instance, several studies have shown that fundamentalists vote as a meaningful bloc only when candidates take significantly different stands on issues crucial to their beliefs. In these instances, fundamentalists vote in a manner congruent with what has been called "boundary maintenance."[85] Thus fundamentalism within Protestantism attempts to maintain a tradition in the face of broader cultural changes that threaten such beliefs, and hence demands the restoration of these beliefs. The restorative sectarian nature of fundamentalism is widely recognized in other traditions, including Islam, despite originating as a North American phenomenon.[86]

Transformative Sects

Although one is often tempted to think of sectarian movements as trying to restore or maintain a tradition in the face of cultural opposition, denominations can become sectarian by attempting to maintain a tradition through transforming aspects of their beliefs or practices. For instance, within many denominations worldwide, there are efforts to alter the traditional roles of women as defined within various religions. These efforts aim to maintain the denominations' traditions through transformative modifications.[87] As women's roles are radically altered within many cultures, pressure for religious groups to change increases.[88] The lessening of tension with the host culture by those who would transform a religious tradition through expanding or changing traditional roles of women within the group may operate to maintain the tradition in the face of a changed culture. Yet adapting beliefs and norms to the dominant culture on a significant axis of tension ironically may increase tension between the host culture, within which roles for women have changed, and the remaining portion of the religious tradition that would maintain the traditional norms for women.

Sectarian change is inevitable, whether it is transformative, restorative, or both. Among mainstream denominations, movements to transform traditional views of women, homosexuals, or abortion are but a few possible sources of tension. Religious groups are continually pressured to accommodate their beliefs and practices to a changing culture. They can maintain their identities by transformative moves compatible with cultural change, or can resist cultural changes in restorative sectarian efforts. In either case, change is a dynamic aspect of any religious group.

Placing Religious Organizations and Cultures on Axes of Change

Both restorative and transformative tendencies exist in all organizations. Within religious organizations, the crucial social dimension is whether the norms that are maintained by either of these processes are sufficiently congruent with the norms that are strongly supported by the host culture. If they are congruent, the religious group has a church (denominational) form, which assures that its members are nonproblematic to the host culture. If they are not congruent, the group has a sectarian nature, which assures that its members are problematic to the host culture. Of course, the issue is complicated by the fact that cultures are changing along with and in opposition to religious groups. The position of the religious group norm relative to the cultural norm on issues of great salience is the key to defining sects and denominations. We can illustrate forms of sectarian and denominational religion along axes of change for both the culture and religious groups within the culture, as we have done in Figure 9.1.

The Position of Sects within the Host Culture

Sects persist, but as Bainbridge and Stark have noted, to be an ongoing, functioning group that is problematic to the host culture is to be a deviant subculture by definition.[89] Thus sects are best viewed as tolerable forms of religious deviance, created when religious groups differ significantly from their host culture on salient values. Sects are problematic to the dominant host culture's interests, but are of the acceptable forms of religious identity characterized by the tolerance for diversity that is common in postmodern cultures.[90]

Occasionally, sectarian practices become targets of legal sanction; however, within a culture that cherishes religious freedom, efforts to constrain sectarian religious practices are likely to meet with serious obstacles. This is particularly likely to be the case where religious freedom is a strong cultural tradition and where religion is a valuable label. As Richardson has noted, being identified as a religion in the United States has numerous benefits, not the least of which is protection from government regulations that would prohibit otherwise problematic behaviors.[91] Benefits include tax exemptions, as well as exemptions from civil rights legislation and many laws that govern business. For instance, religions can refuse to ordain women, even in the United States, where women have achieved additional legal protection from discrimination based upon gender. No Catholic or fundamentalist woman can bring a lawsuit on discrimination because she is refused the right to be a priest or a minister, respectively. Yet religions risk losing their religious identification if they deviate too far from cul-

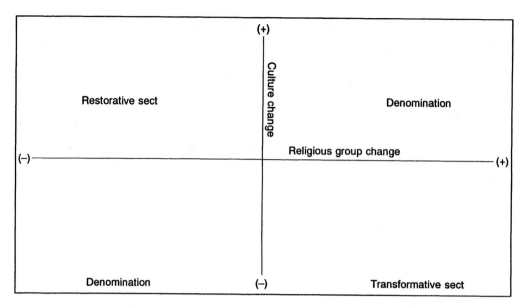

FIGURE 9.1. Sects and denominations relative to patterns of change in the dominant culture and in religious groups. (+) and (−) indicate the presence or absence of change in a salient value for religious groups (horizontal axis) and the host culture (vertical axis). Denominations are in quadrants with equivalent signs; sects are in quadrants with discrepant signs. both religious groups and cultures are in a continual process of change.

tural norms for what constitutes a "religion." As Greil and Robbins have noted, at least in the United States the law does not concern itself with claims to religious heresy; this indicates that within broad limits, religious norms, even those at odds with the dominant culture, are to be protected.[92] However, being protected by the law does not mean that tension with the host culture is minimized. In the United States, the legal acceptance of religious diversity knows few limits. Sectarian groups are allowed to exist and even flourish as pockets of subcultural religious deviance so characteristic of the religious pluralism and dynamism of postmodern culture. Among the more curious of sectarian religious practices is the handling of serpents among the Holiness sects of Appalachia, as we have already noted in Chapter 6, and describe in more detail in Research Box 9.1.

When tensions are extreme and reactions to religious subcultures become more intense, tolerance for diversity is likely to find its limit. In India, fundamentalist Hindus, who continue the practice of *sati* despite its illegality, support a restorative sectarian movement that is unlikely to find sympathy from either men or women influenced by modernity. Yet the practice of *sati* is rooted in the belief that the untimely death of a husband is caused by the failure of his wife to protect him, and hence she must sacrifice herself on his funeral pyre. Recent cases of the reemergence of *sati* and its defense by Hindu fundamentalists have generated much social-scientific commentary and analysis.[93] Here, the tension with most cultural views is extreme, despite the long tradition of *sati* as a minority movement within Hinduism. Legal repercussions in the interest of the dominant culture suggest a retaliation and an appeal to a higher standard unlikely to be heard within the ideological surround of *sati* and its defenders. The resulting conflict has few parallels in the Western world except where cults are concerned.

Research Box 9.1. Serpent-Handling Sects (Hood & Kimbrough, 1995; see also Kimbrough, 1995)

Early in the 20th century in the rural South, George Hensley picked up a serpent in response to Mark 16:17–18: "And these signs shall follow them that believe; In my name shall they cast out devils; they shall speak with new tongues; They shall take up serpents; and if they drink any deadly thing, it shall not hurt them; they shall lay hands on the sick, and they shall recover."[a] Returning to his church, he initiated the practice of serpent handling, unique as a form of religion in the United States. For a while the practice was normative in the Church of God, where Hensley was ordained. Later rejected as a practice by the Church of God, it became normative for Holiness sects in Appalachia. Often identified as "sign-following" sects and long predicted to disappear, these sects continue to outlive their obituaries. Preachers, with their serpent boxes ever present, handle deadly snakes—either when faith alone dictates it or, for some, when they feel they have a special experience of being "anointed." Associated with serpent handling, but less common, is the drinking of poison, often strychnine or lye. About 80 deaths have been documented from serpent bites; Hensley himself was a victim, dying of a snake bite in 1955. Serpent bites are common, and among serpent-handling sects, opinions differ on whether one ought to seek medical aid if bitten. Although many Protestant sects practice some of the signs specified in Mark 16:17–18, only the Holiness sects of Appalachia follow all five signs. For instance, many Pentecostal groups speak in tongues (glossolalia) but reject serpent handling. The tension that serpent handling presents to a modern culture is obvious. Legal sanctions have been directed against the practice in some states, such as Tennessee; in other states, such as West Virginia, the practice carries no sanction.[b] Numerous studies of serpent-handling sects suggest the strong appeal of what to many is a curious religious practice, but to serpent-handling believers is but one of the Biblical signs to be followed. To the outsider, this obedience to the literal Biblical imperative is the major defining characteristic of these sects.

---

[a]Other texts are interpreted by serpent-handling sects to support their practice—for instance, Luke 10:19 ("Behold, I give unto you power to tread on serpents . . .").
[b]For a listing of court cases involving serpent-handling sects, see Burton (1993).

CULTS

If tension with the host culture on salient values best empirically defines a church–sect continuum, what about cults? The term "cult" has such a pejorative quality, especially in the popular media, that some investigators who have profitably utilized the concept in the past are now calling for the elimination of the term altogether.[94] In one sense, it has become the sociological equivalent of psychopathology in the popular mind. Even the sociological literature on cults tends toward the dramatic and extreme, despite wide variations in the nature of cult beliefs and practices.[95] Empirical studies of attitudes toward cults indicate that the majority of respondents have heard of Jonestown and Charlie Manson—names linked to the term "cult" in the popular media.[96] It is as if all sects and cults were identified with the Hindu ritual of *sati*. Yet death and violence are no more essential to cults than to other social groups.

Comparing Cults and Sects

Despite the fact that the cult type was never part of the theoretical development of church–sect theory, it is probably most useful to compare cults and sects. As Stark and Bainbridge have argued, sects tend to rise from within existing religious groups and to move toward a new religious form.[97] Schisms create sects by what we have termed either restorative or transformative movements. Hence, sects are inherently religious protest movements. On the other hand, cults lack prior ties with religious bodies and tend to emerge afresh, often under the direction of a single charismatic leader. Cults are novel forms of religion, which, not surprisingly, are likely to emerge in tension with both established religious groups (such as churches and sects) and the host culture. As such, we can expect that sects and cults share a rejection of their host culture or at least some aspects of their host culture, and are likely to be rejected by their host culture in turn. As with sects, there are belief differences between cults and their host culture. There are also likely to be close patterns of interaction among cult members, as well as retaliatory actions on the part of host cultures toward them—all of which create an even more clearly defined religiously deviant subculture for cults than for sects. This occurs not only because cults are novel and hence lack previous religious legitimation, but also because cult leaders are likely to be solitary, powerful, charismatic figures. Indeed, many characterize cults as lacking a formal organizational structure and as largely controlled in an authoritative manner by their leaders.[98] Cults are often defined and identified by the names of their leaders, at least in the popular media; hence we have the "Manson cult," the "Jim Jones cult," and the "Moonies" (after the Reverend Sun Myung Moon). As Barnes and Becker have noted about charismatic figures in general: "Charismatic domination is established through the extraordinary qualities (real or supposed) of the leader. . . . Law is not the source of authority; on the contrary, he [or she] proclaims new laws on the basis of revelation, oracular utterance, and inspiration."[99]

Given the charismatic nature of cult leadership, combined with the fact that cults (like sects) are in opposition to salient cultural values, there is often some confusion as to whether or not cults are truly "religions." The distinction between religious and secular groups has become blurred in the modern world. As Greil and Rudy have noted, many organizations are best conceived of as parareligious or quasi-religious because they have mixed characteristics, some of which are sacred and some of which are secular.[100] This applies, for example, to Alcoholics Anonymous, astrology, and many healing movements.[101] In congruence with postmodern analyses, we should note that "religion" can be conceived of as a category of discourse, negotiated by groups that would either desire to obtain or wish to refute the label. Although there are often benefits to the label, as noted earlier, there can be liabilities as well. For instance, Transcendental Meditation (TM) was successfully excluded from schools in the United States on the basis of a claim that Maharishi Mahesh Yogi denied—namely, that TM was a religion.[102] Hence, efforts to include TM as a secular activity in schools were rejected, based upon a court ruling that such practices were in fact religious in nature. Thus, the category of religion must be negotiated between groups and a culture; some groups desire the label, whereas others do not want it.[103]

However, as novel forms of religious identity, cults are likely to be severely challenged by mainstream culture. Pfeiffer found that the vast majority of college students in his sample

(82%) described "an average cult member" only in negative terms; not a single student used positive terms.[104] He also randomly divided subjects into three equal groups and had them respond to one of three vignettes describing three groups. None of these three groups was identified as a cult, but each was selected because of popular notions about its alleged authoritarian structures and near-total environmental control of members, who are kept isolated from the wider society. The vignettes were identical except for the groups specified—either "Marines," "Moonies," or "priests." The vignette described a typical recruit, "Bill," at the relevant group facility (with only the identification of the persons surrounding him changed across the three vignettes) as follows:

> While at the facility, Bill is not allowed very much contact with his friends or family and he notices he is seldom left alone. He also notices that he never seems to be able to talk to the other four people who signed up for the program and that he is continually surrounded by (Moonies, Marines, Priests) who make him feel guilty if he questions any of their actions and beliefs.[105]

Among several assessments in this study, participants were asked to select the term that best described the process Bill had undergone in order to reach the facility from among these terms: "initiation," "conversion," "brainwashing," "basic training," "resocialization," or "religious education." The most common term used to describe the process by which Bill was surrounded by Moonies was "brainwashing" (22 of 31, or 71%), whereas this term was used much less frequently to describe joining the Marines (15 of 34, or 44%) or the priesthood (10 of 34, or 29%). Still, as we shall see later in this chapter, "brainwashing" as a term to describe conversion—especially conversion to unpopular groups—has become a major issue, dividing even professional psychologists. Likewise, when participants were asked to characterize cults on the basis of the degree to which they foster "psychological growth," "community programs," "child abuse," or "brainwashing," Pfeiffer found that both negative descriptive terms ("child abuse" and "brainwashing") were seen to characterize cults, whereas neither positive term was seen as characteristic of cults.[106]

In addition, the participants rated Bill on a variety of indices on a bipolar scale, as summarized in Table 9.4. These ratings and statistical analyses of these data[107] indicated that Bill was generally perceived as less happy and responsible if he joined the Moonies, as well as likely to have been coerced into joining them and as powerless to leave. Overall, he was also perceived to have been treated unfairly by the Moonies.

Pfeiffer's study paints a negative picture of the perception of both cults and cult members that is supported by previous research. Zimbardo and Hartley found that the most typical descriptions of cults obtained from students using a semantic differential scale tended to be those with strongly negative connotations, such as "not worthwhile" (64%) and "crazy" (60%).[108] Consistent with the need for cults, as novel forms of religious organization, to negotiate for the validity of their label as "religions," more than one-fifth of these subjects identified cults as "nonreligious."[109]

The problem of novel groups' negotiating to be labeled as "religions" is accentuated when these groups combine charismatic leadership with authoritarian structures that tend toward withdrawal from the dominant culture. For instance, Galanter emphasizes the strong influence on behavior by those group norms supported by the attribution of divine powers to a cult leader.[110] Richardson emphasizes the oppositional nature of cults, which is exacerbated by the fact that they often derive their inspiration and ideology from outside the predominant religious and secular culture.[111] Wallis has emphasized that cults need not

TABLE 9.4. Mean Ratings of "Bill" Based upon Label of Group He Joined

	Marines	Moonies	Priests	
Positive process	4.41	5.22	3.97	Negative process
Happy	3.76	4.90	3.85	Unhappy
Intelligent	3.32	4.16	3.41	Unintelligent
Responsible	3.53	4.33	3.70	Irresponsible
Uncoerced	3.76	4.97	3.68	Coerced
Free to leave	6.03	6.06	5.29	Not free to leave
Treated fairly	3.55	4.71	3.55	Treated unfairly
Power to resist	4.17	5.19	4.29	Powerless to resist

Note. All ratings were made on a 7-point scale (1 = left-hand phrase, 7 = right-hand phrase). Adapted from Pfeiffer (1992, p. 537). Copyright 1992 by V. H. Winston and Son, Inc. Adapted by permission.

always take their ideology from outside the dominant culture.[112] Yet, as novel religious forms, cults clearly have an ideology that is at least distinct from the dominant culture. As Ellwood emphasizes, cults present a distinct alternative to dominant patterns in society, and the tension this creates is exacerbated when the cults are led by charismatic persons who demand high degrees of commitment.[113] Swatos emphasizes that the cult leader may be an imaginary figure, not a real one.[114] Yet to focus religious novelty on a single figure, cultivating fierce commitment from members who are willing to withdraw from significant aspects of both religious and secular culture, is likely to create a powerful deviant subculture.

Thus, models of sects as deviant religious subcultures may actually apply more forcefully to cults than to sects. As innovative deviant subcultures, cults stand in opposition to both culture and sects. Both sects and cults share the fact of tension with the dominant host culture, but cults more frequently emphasize separatist tendencies from a novel base, and hence are more likely to attract intense cultural rejection in turn. As we have seen, sects tend to emerge out of religious organizations. They are likely to find some support for their aims, whether restorative or transformative, from others within the dominant culture. By contrast, cults arise as original movements within the culture and are likely to provoke opposition both from established religions and from the secular host culture.

In a postmodern culture, the acceptance of pluralism may create some added degree of tolerance—a cultic milieu somewhat favorable to both sects and cults.[115] However, tolerance has its limits. This is especially the case in light of two factors. First, as Stark has emphasized, cults tend to appeal for recruits to members of weakened churches or to the unchurched.[116] Thus, in terms of the religious marketplace, denominations are either losing members to cults or failing to attract as members those individuals from the secular culture who join cults. Second, the oppositional nature of cults is directed not only against the churches' claims to appropriate accommodation to the world, but against the sects' claims to renewed efforts to maintain an exclusive religious purity. Not surprisingly, these rejections of both churches and sects as well as the secular culture foster retaliation in turn. Cults are unlikely to have an easy birth or a long life. As we shall see, retaliatory efforts have created recent "anti-cult" movements, especially in the United States.[117] Much of this movement has been aided and abetted by psychologists and psychiatrists who support the claims that cults utilize "brainwashing" to convert members against their will. We confront both of these issues after we first give some consideration to the axis along which tension is likely to occur.

Bainbridge and Stark have properly noted that the nature of the dominant activity of a cult is likely to define its source of tension with the dominant culture.[118] For instance, "client cults" provide personal growth and treatments for their members.[119] Hence, they are likely to be opposed by established groups that claim to provide the only legitimate avenue for these services. To give an analogy, Bergin has noted that psychiatrists and psychologists provide competing services long claimed to be the proper domain of the clergy, including the claim to be authoritative moral agents.[120] Similarly, both London[121] and Gross[122] note that in secularized societies mental health personnel often take roles previously reserved for religious healers. Likewise, Frank[123] and Ellenberger[124] have provided authoritative historical analyses of numerous similarities between religious and psychological systems of healing. Illich has documented the expropriation of health by orthodox medicine.[125] In a similar fashion, competition between client cults providing unorthodox treatments is likely to create significant tension with powerfully established medical and mental health groups, both of which are heavily sanctioned by the dominant culture.

Further exacerbation is readily understandable in light of the research of Kilbourne and Richardson, indicating that both established therapies and new religious movements attract persons seeking to change identities and find new meanings in life.[126] However, cults seek to produce more radical change than orthodox therapies, adding to tension.[127] In terms of an ideological surround, the very success of cults is likely to be seen as pathological by representatives of orthodox therapies. To cite but two extreme cases, who would argue for the validity of the mass suicide indelibly associated with Jonestown, or the violent murders associated with the Charlie Manson family? Yet, even in these cases, serious scholars have raised significant questions beyond the stereotype of madness and cults presented in the mass media. For instance, Zaehner has argued that Manson's crimes are not merely an expression of psychopathology but have a religious significance as well: "Charlie Manson was sane: he had been *there*, where there is neither good nor evil, and he had read and reread the Book of Revelation. These two facts explain his crime."[128] Likewise, Hall notes that Jim Jones, who led the mass suicide in Jonestown, is not simply to be understood in psychopathological terms:

> Ironically, Jones has become far more important for the society at large as a symbolic personification of evil than he has in any way to those who share some of the concerns that animated his movement. It is the opponents of Jim Jones who infused him with a charisma powerful enough to make him play the mythic role of scapegoat that cleanses the world of sin, even if they failed to acknowledge that the sin-offering of Jonestown had wider sources than the evil in Jones.[129]

Thus, we cannot ignore the religious relevance of even the extremist cult leaders. Feuerstein documents the relevance of madness as a category of the holy, especially for cult leaders.[130] It is important to remember that religious extremism is also a normative part of religious history. We must be careful not to identify all religion with cultural accommodations and compatibilities.

Using client cults as an example of an axis of tension identifies a conflict between cults and orthodox healers that is not likely to engage massive cultural concern, except in isolated and highly publicized cases. However, an area of tension that cuts across diverse cultural groups that is perpetually a matter of intense concern is sexuality. A cult's violation of sexual norms is likely to elicit retaliatory responses from the dominant culture. We focus upon the social control of sexuality, since claims to legitimate forms of sexual expression have varied and continue to vary immensely, both within and between cultures; yet few have no opinion about what is appropriate.

Cults and Sexuality

Relating the control of sexuality to varieties of group formation and cohesion has a long history and firm theoretical grounding. Much of the social psychology of classical Freudian theory identifies group formation as being rooted in the control of sexuality and dyadic intimacy. As an inevitable dimension of tension with society, any form of sexuality can become problematic. The social and cultural history of sexuality is largely a religious history.[131] Gardella has shown how Christianity, especially in North America, promoted a view of sexuality that required it to be both innocent and ecstatic.[132] In English-speaking North America, the celibacy of Catholic priests and nuns has been derided as abnormal, as was that of the early Shaker communities in the United States.[133] The polygamy of early Mormons was violently criticized by a monogamous culture that was also equally opposed to what it perceived as the sexual permissiveness of the early Oneida community, which fostered free sexuality between its members.[134]

Although monogamy has been challenged by many religious groups, retaliation is often swift, especially toward groups that put their alternative sexual beliefs into actual practice. Lewis recounts many instances of carefully constructed cultural atrocity tales directed at Catholics and Mormons, who were accused of using a wide variety of techniques of mind control to force persons to be either celibate (in the case of Catholics) or polygamous (in the case of Mormons).[135] As we shall see, these historical instances of retaliation applied to what are now mainstream religions have numerous parallels in contemporary retaliation toward cults. Lewis's discussion of atrocity tales directed at Catholics and Mormons is described in greater detail in Research Box 9.2.

Even mainstream religions have accommodated themselves to the existence of divorce, and hence to a form of serial monogamy, seen by some as a form of polygamy. As Freud noted, there is an antithesis between sexuality and civilization, given that "sexual love is a relationship between two people, in which a third can only be superfluous or disturbing, whereas civilization is founded on relation between large groups of persons."[136] Not surprisingly, theorists influenced by Freud have argued for the crucial importance of sexuality in all types of group formation, not simply religious ones.[137] Thus, religious cults are likely to arouse cultural wrath if they modify established norms of sexuality. Likewise, insofar as conversion to a mainstream religious commitment is one of the best predictors of the delayed loss of virginity (as noted in Chapter 4), modification of sexual norms within cults is likely to incur retaliation from mainstream churches heavily involved in the sexual socialization of adolescents. For instance, the Unification Church has been accused by Horowitz of being a collectivist organization,[138] and chided in particular for supporting arranged marriages in which persons were married who were "in some cases unfamiliar with each other up to minutes prior to the ceremony."[139] Yet not only is there firm theological justification for such marriages within the Unification Church;[140] as Lewis has shown, dyadic intimacy is also a factor in cult defection, insofar as among spouses joining cults, the best predictor is that if one partner leaves the cult the other will leave also.[141] Not surprisingly, then, the Unification Church attempts to exert control over dyadic matching in terms of the larger group's interests, as do other religious groups such as the Hare Krishna.[142] However, in a culture in which both free choice and romanticism are presumed to direct dyadic selection, such novel controls on sexual expression are likely to be serious sources of tension.[143]

When sexuality is controlled in a manner that permits multiple partners (often, several partners are sexually active with a cult leader), the challenge to sexual and religious cultural

ಖ

Research Box 9.2. Catholic and Mormon Atrocity Tales
(Lewis, 1989; see also Gardella, 1985)

Lewis notes that the most popular book written in the United States before *Uncle's Tom's Cabin* was a pseudoautobiography by one "Marie Monk," titled *Awful Disclosures of the Hotel Dieu Nunnery of Montreal*. With more than a quarter of a million copies sold between its publication in 1836 and the Civil War, the book described licentious sex between priests and nuns; it also told of babies born to nuns and quickly baptized after birth, suffocated, and bodily dissolved in lye. Despite being thoroughly discredited, this fraudulent text was part of an anti-Catholic genre fueled by exaggerated tales of genuine ex-nuns and of fallen priests that continues today. For instance, tales of priests forcing ladies to confess sexual sins in order to seduce them were common in English-speaking North America before the 19th century. *The Priest, the Woman, and the Confessional*, a 1984 book by C. Chiniquy, is one example of this genre that is still in print today.

If "unnatural" celibacy fueled atrocity tales against nuns and priests, "unnatural" polygamy fueled atrocity tales against Mormons. Paralleling Marie Monk's book was another fabricated story by Marie Ward entitled *Female Life among the Mormons*. Assuming that no conscientious females would accept polygamy, the text accused Mormon males of using hypnotic techniques to force females to accept a presumably unnatural wedded life. Like ex-nuns, ex-Mormon women told elaborately embellished stories accentuating the misery of women under Mormonism. These helped to enrage the larger culture to retaliation against Mormons, ranging from vigilante justice to government action directed against Mormon leaders and practices.

The insistence by a culture that only wedded monogamy is sanctioned by God provides a context within which other religious sexual practices, whether celibacy or polygamy, must fight to gain legitimacy.

---

norms is obvious. Wangerin has documented how "flirty fishing," or the use of sexual favors to gain adherents, created significant tension for the otherwise fundamentalist Children of God/Family of Love.[144] Further confounding their otherwise fundamentalist beliefs is the confusion they have created within fundamentalist circles by supporting masturbation and a generally masculine point of view regarding sexuality.[145] Jacobs has documented the fact that some male cults foster romantic idealization of the cult leader by female followers.[146] This leads to what some perceive as sexual abuse and exploitation for those who fail to successfully complete their attachment to the cult leader. Then, much as in a more normative love relationship, the socioemotional bonds with both the group and the leader must be broken for defection from the cult to occur (as we have noted in Chapter 8). With a charismatic male leader and a female follower, the process is accentuated, but similar processes operate in male followers as well.

THE ANTI-CULT MOVEMENT

In a partly tongue-in-cheek paper (a rarity in scientific journals), Richardson and Kilbourne described a new mental illness, "cultphobia."[147] Although perhaps not to be taken seriously as a claim to defining a pathology, their effort was directed at "putting the shoe on the other foot."[148] Richardson, a prominent sociologist and lawyer involved in the study of new religious movements, has been a leader in arguing for researchers to abandon the term "cult" altogether.[149] Much of his concern centers upon the well-documented fact that attitudes toward new religious movements are heavily influenced by the mass media, whose presentation of cults has been largely sensationalistic and heavily slanted in a negative direction.[150] Few if any distinctions are made among cults. For instance, Patrick, a prominent activist in the anti-cult movement, has stated: "You name 'em. Hare Krishna, the Divine Light Mission, Guru Maharaj Ji, Brother Julius, Love Israel, the Children of God. Not a brown penny's worth of difference between any one of 'em."[151]

The Empirical Study of Resistance to Cults

Empirically, the identification of resistance from groups within the culture is worthy of study. Thus, we consider the pejorative connotation that cults have acquired within the media to be an important empirical issue—one that is integral to the operationalization of cults as novel forms of subcultural religious deviance. The refusal to differentiate among cults is also worthy of empirical study. As Zimbardo and Hartley noted, similar negative views of cults are held by adolescents, regardless of whether or not they have ever had any contact with recruiters for various cults.[152] Yet, as Wallis has rightly noted, "Not all authoritative groups are the same. Scientology has authoritarian features but most members hold down full time jobs and limit their involvement in terms compatible with their occupation and domestic responsibilities."[153]

Tolerance or hostility toward cults is but an aspect of general tolerance or intolerance for deviance, often associated with political science studies of civil liberties.[154] Perhaps the most consistent finding is that education and tolerance are positively correlated. Although numerous challenges and modifications of this generalization have been made in specific cases, it remains as a "most durable generalization."[155]

The study of tolerance for new religious movements is almost by definition a study for tolerance of cults. Despite a relatively small literature, empirical studies are congruent with the research on support for civil liberties.[156] Within a democratic culture, retaliation against new religious movements can be expressed by attitudes in favor of legal restrictions on cults.[157] Several studies have used this operational indicator in either general or specific cases. For instance, Richardson and van Driel found substantial agreement with the statement that "Legislation should be passed to control the spread of new religions or cults," in a telephone survey of 400 randomly selected voters in Nevada.[158] However, they also noted that some respondents were confused by the phrasing of the question, wanting to control cults but not new religions.[159] This confusion is consistent with the problem already discussed of negotiating a religious identity for a novel group. Cults are often refused such a label, as many do not perceive them as legitimate religions.[160] Thus, although there is generally strong support for the right of freedom of worship for all religions, the support is strongest among educated elites rather than the mass public; it is also tempered when the religions are seen to be too extreme, including cults, which may not be perceived as religious at all.[161]

When questions are more specific, the attitudes toward legal restrictions on cults are more illustrative. For instance, Bromley and Breschel utilized four specific questions to assess favorable attitudes toward cult legislation: a ban on cult recruitment of teenagers; the necessity for Federal Bureau of Investigation (FBI) surveillance of cults; the desirability of restricting solicitation by Hare Krishnas at airports; and whether or not the Reverend Moon should be allowed to publish a newspaper.[162] Overall, they found that a majority of the mass public (66%) and a minority (25%) of the educated elites approved of most items. Furthermore, the more religiously involved respondents were more likely to support legislation to control cults. This is consistent with the tension that cults, as novel religious forms, are likely to have with both secular and sacred groups within mainstream culture.

O'Donnell utilized a similar measure to assess attitudes toward restrictions on new religions; he also added an item indicating opposition to Satan worship.[163] Opposition to Satan worship is an important indicator of media influence on cult perception, since empirical research has failed to establish that there is either a large Satanic movement in America or that Satan worship has any significant following or influence among adolescents.[164] His sample included a mass survey of 1,708 persons and an additional sample of 863 elites, selected from business, government, education, media, and religious leaders. O'Donnell used the five items as a single scale. The overall responses for the various groups are presented in Table 9.5. Not only did the academics within the elites have the greatest tolerance, but among the mass group, education was also the best predictor of tolerance.

Thus, within the study of new religious movements, tolerance has been found to follow the similar pattern of the "most durable generalization" noted for civil liberties in general. Still, we must confront a curious phenomenon proposed by members of some intellectual elites—one that medicalizes religious deviance and also suggests a basis for discounting much of the tolerance expressed by both elites and the educated masses toward religious cults. That phenomenon is coercive persuasion, or, in the inadequate vernacular of the popular media, "brainwashing."

TABLE 9.5. Tolerance for New Religious Movements (Cults)

Group	Overall response (1 = no, 2 = yes)
Mass public (*n* = 1,708)	1.42
Elites (*n* = 863)	
Academics	1.87
Business	1.67
Government	1.74
Media	1.79
Religious leaders	
Ministers	1.58
Priests	1.60
Rabbis	1.68

Note. The survey items were as follows:

1. There should be laws to prevent groups like Hare Krishna from asking people for money at airports.
2. Followers of the Reverend Sun Myung Moon should not be allowed to print a daily newspaper in Washington, D.C.
3. It should be against the law for unusual religious cults to try to convert teenagers.
4. The FBI should keep a close watch on new religious cults.
5. There should be laws against the practice of Satan worship.

Each item was scored on a 2-point scale (1 = no, 2 = yes). The table reports the overall mean response for the five items. Adapted from O'Donnell (1993, p. 361). Copyright 1993 by the Society for the Scientific Study of Religion. Adapted by permission.

The Question of Cults and Coercive Persuasion

The Medicalization of Deviant Religious Groups

The tendency for the educated to be tolerant of new religious movements is confounded by controversies surrounding cults and the "medicalization of deviance." Although varying in precise meaning, this term generally refers to efforts to explain commitment to deviant groups in terms of dysfunctional or pathological processes.[165] Thus, individuals are assumed to be unable to commit freely to a new religious group. Conversion to cult beliefs and adherence to cult norms are interpreted as symptoms of illness or pathology. Not surprisingly, much of the support for this position comes from clinical psychologists and psychiatrists. For instance, in a series of papers, Clark has claimed to clinically identify powerful mental coercion used by cults to create pathological commitments in converts.[166] Likewise, Shapiro has claimed to have clinically identified a syndrome of "destructive cultism" that includes such phenomena as loss of identity, behavioral changes, estrangement from one's family, and mental control by the cult leader.[167] Finally, Singer has gained a considerable reputation for the clinical treatment of former cult members, who, she has argued, are "psychiatric casualties."[168]

In opposition to clinical claims are the claims of most empirical researchers, who have found no evidence that cults utilize unique methods or techniques in order to alter normal psychological processes. Some have seen the empirical response to exaggerated clinical claims as itself overstated. As a result of all this, much of the study of new religious movements has become highly politicized. The process has forced serious debate and disclaimers among investigators as to hidden motives involved in the study of new religious movements.[169] This has led to concerns regarding the academic integrity of research on new religious movements in general,[170] as well as challenges to the integrity of researchers committed to controversial religions such as Wicca, often simply identified as witchcraft.[171] To some, the serious question is "Have the social sciences been converted?"[172] Others note that contemporary perspectives in the philosophy of science make distinctions between the religious and scientific methods of knowing less distinct, blurring the boundaries of what many have tried to separate.[173] The debate is most heated when claims to having identified a process of coercive persuasion unique to cults is linked to the popular but scientifically unwarranted concept of "brainwashing."

A History of the Concept of Brainwashing

The term "brainwashing" has entered the popular language as a summary term for some loosely defined techniques of coercive persuasion that presumably can make persons adopt beliefs and conform to behaviors they would normally reject. Historically, the term was popularized by a U.S. journalist who worked for the Central Intelligence Agency (CIA), Hunter.[174] Hunter claimed to have identified powerful techniques of thought reform utilized by the Chinese Communists, for which he coined the word "brainwashing."[175] Research agencies of several governments—including the Nazi SS and the Gestapo; the U.S. Office of Strategic Services, the forerunner of the CIA; and investigators in Stalinist Russia and in Communist China—had been involved in programs to discover effective procedures for obtaining information from the interrogation of prisoners of war, and to find ways to alter the beliefs of individuals so that they would be cooperative with captive governments.

Despite widely exaggerated popular press accounts of the effects of secret brainwashing techniques, it was quickly recognized that no government had discovered any such techniques that were truly effective. Most efforts to alter beliefs utilized varieties of deception, often combined with the administration of drugs, or with techniques of coercion and force. Although compliance was easily produced by these crude techniques, true belief change was virtually nonexistent. "Compliance" simply means that persons conformed to demands to avoid pain and suffering within a totally controlled environment; however, their true beliefs did not change. Evidence for this is the disappearance of behavioral compliance upon release from the environment. Of 7,000 Korean prisoners of war subjected to harsh treatment techniques by the Chinese Communists, approximately 30% died. Of the remainder, only 21 refused repatriation after secession of hostilities. Of these 21, 10 later changed their minds. Hence, only 11 cases of over 4,500 survivors actually adopted Chinese Communist beliefs and refused ultimate repatriation.[176] Not surprisingly, Hinkle and Wolff, researchers given access to CIA material concerning all claims to brainwashing, noted that no effective techniques existed and that compliance produced by physical coercion, isolation, propaganda, peer pressure, and intense torture—in a context of total control combined with uncertainty about the future—involved no unknown social-psychological principles.[177] Indeed, the desired effects of mind change measured by repatriation indicated the complete failure of the presumed brainwashing. Thus, responsible reviews of the facts indicate that no evidence exists for a technique using advanced psychological knowledge that can alter a person's thoughts against his or her will.

Another phrase closely associated with brainwashing is "thought reform," a more adequate description of the Chinese Communists' intent. The term is closely linked to the research of Lifton, a psychiatrist who studied Korean prisoners of war.[178] Both thought reform and brainwashing are linked to what Schein and colleagues have called "coercive persuasion."[179] Although a scientifically inadequate popular literature extols the unlimited power of coercive techniques, as we shall see, the responsible scientific literature is consistent in agreeing (1) that such techniques can produce only limited attitude change and (2) that such change is highly unstable when controls on the immediate environment are lifted.

Two major varieties of coercive persuasion have been utilized in recent history, the Chinese and the European. Although the two forms overlap, as Somit has noted,[180] their differences are evident in the extreme forms of expression. European-oriented techniques primarily emphasize the obtaining of confessions of guilt from presumably innocent persons, typically singly and in isolation. Chinese-oriented techniques focus upon efforts to change people's total ideological orientation, typically in group situations where many are solicited as volunteers. The Chinese-oriented techniques have much in common with "totalism." Totalism seeks ultimate control of the individual through actual or threatened physical techniques of coercion and torture[181]; it is most often associated with totalitarian states. Totalism assumes the freedom of individuals to resist, and does not postulate a unique technique or method that can make anyone, regardless of predisposing factors or strength of will, change ideological orientation. As such, it is what Anthony and Robbins refer to as a "soft determinism,"[182] quite compatible with theories of modern social science. Cults, like many other groups (both religious and secular), seek to attract persons with identifiable predispositions that can be manipulated in such a manner as to persuade the persons to become converts. Of course, such conversions remain intentional actions. They are not the process of some hard determinant such as brainwashing that abolishes the capacity to choose.

The popularization of a brainwashing model is compatible with neither the European nor the Chinese model of coercive persuasion, each developed independently. Although brainwashing is a thoroughly discredited concept, the broad basis of processes involved in coercive persuasion can be readily identified.

Processes of Coercive Persuasion

Since techniques of coercive persuasion have developed from pragmatic sociopolitical concerns, they have not often been linked to broader theoretical views. Overstated efforts to link a particular technique to a theory, such as Sargent's appeal to Pavlovian theory,[183] are neither adequate to the totality of coercive persuasion nor supported by sufficient empirical evidence to be generally acceptable. Our summary of the components involved in coercive persuasion focuses only upon what is shared across several responsible efforts to reconstruct from historical and personal accounts the processes involved in this kind of influence.[184]

1. *Total control and isolation.* Persons are isolated (individually or in small groups), under the absolute control of authorities.

2. *Physical debilitation and exhaustion.* Persons are physically exhausted and debilitated. Causes can include constant interrogation and/or continual prodding from peers, as well as sleep and food deprivation. In extreme cases, physical torture and starvation may be used.

3. *Confusion and uncertainty.* Personal belief systems and entire ideological orientations are challenged. Persons' uncertainty about their own fate is linked to uncertainty concerning beliefs and values.

4. *Guilt and humiliation.* A sense of guilt and personal humiliation is induced by a variety of techniques. All are directed at making a potential convert feel unworthy if he or she persists in maintaining present commitments.

5. *Release and resolution.* An absolute framework provides only a single "out." Suicide is prohibited. Only by compliance or full conversion can individuals gain release from the isolation, pain, guilt, and confusion induced in them by their persuaders.

It is readily apparent that coercive techniques of persuasion are seldom of an all-or-none nature. It is best to talk about degrees of coercive persuasion, ranging from the extremes of the techniques applied to prisoners of war, to the middle-range examples of draftees into the military, then to the minimal extremes (e.g., a religious summer camp to which parents may send a reluctant child). Although the degree of compliance is rather straightforwardly linked to the degree of control, actual conversion or internalization of beliefs is less clearly empirically understood. What is certain is that conversion is much rarer than compliance under any system of coercive persuasion. However, as Somit has noted, compliance achieved by extreme coercive persuasion has its own limits:

> To be successful it demands a uniquely structured and controlled environmental setting and an inordinate investment in time and manpower. Despite the cost entailed, its effectiveness is limited to individual subjects or, even under the optimum conditions, to a small group of persons.[185]

Coercive Persuasion/Brainwashing and Cults: A Contemporary Appeal to a Discredited Process

It is readily apparent that popular interest in new religious movements and cults cannot be explained by such pseudoscientific concepts as brainwashing. The term has also been thoroughly discredited in the contexts within which it was first applied, since no powerful psychological technique to mandate beliefs or behaviors exists. Techniques of coercive persuasion are readily identifiable and work by methods well established in the social sciences; yet these techniques are variously associated with a variety of groups, and in no sense differentially or uniquely characterize cults.

For some, the popularity of new religious movements to which close friends or relatives convert is troublesome. Yet serious issues of values, differences, and lifestyle are sidestepped by essentially rhetorical schemes directed at delegitimating cults; the Unification Church has been a particular target of such schemes.[186] For others, new religious movements can be discredited if an explanation for conversion can be offered that denies it was voluntary. Pseudoscientific terms such as "snapping"[187] or "mentacide"[188] have been coined. Not only do such terms lack real scientific credibility; claims to a "cult syndrome" have never been substantiated, even in terms of the data provided by the most passionate champions of the claim. For instance, despite the popular appeal of one text—*Snapping: America's Epidemic of Sudden Personality Change*, which claims to document a "cult withdrawal syndrome"[189]— none of the claims have withstood scientific scrutiny.[190] Yet such claims are widely reported in the popular media, paralleling for new religious movements what occurred historically in terms of political ideologies.[191] This medicalization of the conversion process is but part of the larger issue of the medicalization of deviance, which Anthony and Robbins have termed the "medicalization of religion."[192] In a word, however thoroughly discredited the concept of brainwashing may be, the acceptance of brainwashing is the major way in which those who oppose conversion to cults have attempted to circumvent what would otherwise be the rights of choice protected by the First Amendment to the U.S. Constitution.[193]

This contemporary appeal to a discredited process follows the similar fallacious reasoning used previously to discredit political views. Applied to cults as novel (and, hence, to some, threatening) religious views, brainwashing or "snapping" implies that a person's ability to withstand such practices is severely limited. Comments offered to support a person's conversion to cult beliefs and practices are used as evidence of mental aberration, rather than as evidence of a successful search for an alternative religious view by a competent individual. When doctrines are viewed as symptoms of pathology, the process by which the individual was coerced to adopt such views is the target of concern, not the content of the beliefs or the religiously informed lifestyle the beliefs support. The right to choose even unpopular alternatives is denied to converts if the rhetorical strategies of those who would pathologize the process are successful.[194]

Ironically, a largely self-fulfilling prophecy of what the rhetoricians of brainwashing fear most is realized in the anti-cult movement, portions of which support "deprogramming." Deprogrammers utilize many of the techniques of coercive persuasion to undo the presumed effects of brainwashing. The fact that cults appeal disproportionately to the young, and to others who are often in opposition to mainstream culture, fuels the anti-cult movement.[195] Almost by definition, youths are abandoning the faiths of their parents (whether these are secular or religious) to join cults. As discussed in Chapter 3 on socialization, interpersonal factors are important in religious conversion. Not surprisingly, then, parent–youth conflict is both a motivating factor for conversion to cults and often a consequence of such conversion.[196]

Parent–youth conflict plays a major role in the deprogramming controversies, in which parents must often be granted legal rights to forcefully remove their children from cult groups. These legal issues are complex in their own right and are confounded by the courts' need to evaluate scientific claims that are hotly disputed among those who defend or oppose cults as expert witnesses.[197] Paradoxically, this has led to several studies of the process of deprogramming, as there are no identifiable studies on the processes of brainwashing presumably utilized by some of the more controversial cults.[198] Although some have tried to sensationalize deprogramming as a new rite of exorcism[199] and anti-cultists as themselves pathological,[200] such rhetoric among researchers is best taken as empirical evidence for the necessity of paying serious attention to issues of the ideological surround, which inevitably inform social-scientific research. The actual empirical techniques of deprogrammers are no less mysterious than are coercive persuasive techniques. The ability of deprogrammers to isolate their subjects, with extensive control over the environment, permits them to utilize established procedures to reconvert cult members. Kim has summarized this process as involving three steps: (1) motivating the persons to "unfreeze" their commitment to the cult; (2) providing information that requires the reevaluation of the person's cult beliefs in light of the beliefs to which the persons are to be "reconverted"; and (3) obtaining a "refreezing" of the supported perspective to which the persons are now recommitted.[201]

Cults' Actual Ability to Retain and Recruit Members

Ironically, despite controversies surrounding cult practices, the majority of cult members are not likely to stay converted. As we have noted in Chapter 8, most converts to new religious groups are seekers, who explore a variety of beliefs and lifestyles, many associated with new religious movements. Most cults, by their very nature, can be expected to appeal permanently only to a minority of followers. The inability of any group in a pluralist society to maintain complete social isolation, totally regulate its members' lifestyles, channel dyadic intimacy, and articulate and defend one authoritative ideology (to cite but a few examples) assures that cults will have high rates of turnover in membership.[202] Furthermore, most voluntary defectors from cults feel neither angry nor duped over the experience. Most feel wiser for the experience, even though they were unwilling to stay cult members. Table 9.6 indicates the results of a survey of 45 members who voluntarily left cults.

Not only do cults have significant voluntary turnover of members; their ability to recruit members through coercive techniques is also severely limited, especially in a society where civil liberties are protected. For instance, in Galanter's study of Unification Church induction workshops, those who agreed to attend were followed in terms of the success of eight of these workshops to persuade attendees actually to join.[203] Of 104 participants in the workshops, 71 dropped out within 2 days; another 29 dropped out between 2 and 9 days; and an additional 17 dropped out after 9 days. Only 9 workshop participants actually stayed over 21 days to join the Unification Church.[204] Thus, even among persons self-selected to be receptive to recruitment workshops where mild degrees of coercive persuasion were used, the vast majority failed to join. Barker replicated Galanter's findings with a sample of over 1,000 workshop participants in London 1 year later.[205] She noted that after 2 years far fewer than 1% of workshop participants were associated with the Unification Church, despite the fact that workshop participants were likely to be favorably predisposed to the Unification Church

TABLE 9.6. Responses of 45 Voluntary Defectors from Three Cults

Response category	n	%
Felt angry	3	7
Felt duped/"brainwashed"	4	9
Felt wiser for experience	30	67
All other responses	8	18

Note. The three cults were the Children of God/Family of Love, Hare Krishna, and the Unification Church (n = 15 each). Adapted from Wright (1987, p. 87). Copyright 1987 by the Society for the Scientific Study of Religion. Adapted by permission.

and presumably were the targets of powerful coercive techniques.[206] Contrary to media claims, the failure to successfully recruit large numbers of persons who voluntarily stay with deviant religious groups is typical of all cult recruitment and retention efforts.

Discussion and Summary

The research on cult recruitment suggests that the controversy surrounding new religious movements is not simply an issue of the processes such movements employ to attract and convert members. It is more likely one of the significant tensions that mainstream religious and secular groups have with novel religions, which solicit and legitimate diverse interpretations and modes of confrontation with sacred and symbolic realities. Hence, even in the most extreme cases, we must be careful not to naively utilize and uncritically accept delegitimating modes of explanation for perspectives different from our own.[207] The tendency to explain away beliefs and practices distant from our own through labels for the processes presumed to be operating, which need not take into account the content of beliefs, is a pervasive tendency in the social sciences. Yet, as Kroll-Smith has shown, even the most private experiences of members of deviant religious groups are influenced by normal social-psychological processes.[208] Several studies show that conversion to new religious groups helps individuals adapt to social and cultural change, of which these groups by definition are a part.[209] Even converts to deviant religious groups are often socialized by the process of conversion to accept other mainstream cultural values.[210] In addition, deviant religious groups socialize people into subcultures where otherwise maladaptive behaviors are functional.[211] Also, we cannot underestimate the power of such variant religious bodies to reconceptualize commonly accepted social realities, so that they both justify participation in, and legitimate the continuance of, what to mainstream culture are at best puzzling but acceptable instances of subcultural deviance.[212] This is particularly true of many of the practices of cult leaders, whose behaviors to an outsider appear to be no more than trickery, chicanery, or pathology.[213]

The failure of cults to be differentially associated with pathology must be emphasized. It has not yet been confirmed empirically that cults either attract or produce pathology when pathology is judged independently of the cults' own behavioral norms. For instance, Galanter notes that deviant sects shy away from recruiting persons who show obvious pathological characteristics.[214] Likewise, Ungerleider and Welish have documented the absence of obvious pathology in former and current members of a variety of cults.[215] Finally, Taslimi, Hood, and Watson failed to substantiate previous claims to pathology in a follow-up study of former members of a fundamentalist Jesus commune, Shilo.[216] Furthermore, the earlier claims about the maladaptive characteristics of these members while in the Jesus commune failed to account appropriately for the fact that objective indices of maladaptive behavior must be judged within the particular context; behaviors that were otherwise less functional outside the commune may have been adaptive for members while inside the commune.[217]

On the positive side, Robbins and Anthony have critically reviewed the relevant empirical literature and concluded that members of deviant religious groups are socially integrated on many criteria:

1. Likely termination of illicit drug use.
2. Renewed vocational motivation.
3. Mitigation of neurotic distress.
4. Suicide prevention.

5. Decrease in anomie/moral confusion.
6. Increase in social compassion/responsibility.
7. Decrease in psychosomatic symptoms.
8. Improved self-actualization.
9. Clarified sense of identity.
10. Generally positive problem-solving assistance.[218]

Finally, it must be emphasized that judgments of the relative value of identities and lifestyles are inevitably beyond the ability of the social sciences to resolve factually. Efforts to set criteria for authentic spiritual choices must be individually and collectively made, but their existential base is never simply resolved by factual descriptions or explanations of the processes by which such choices are made. Although research clearly demonstrates that identities linked to divergent social groups increase the prejudice of such groups toward one another, the ability of groups to identify superordinate goals, which can only be achieved by the cooperation of all groups, reduces conflict and prejudice.[219] Thus, the seeking of superordinate goals that transcend religious groupings and require the collective effort of all groups to achieve is a worthwhile project, however ambitious it may be, if prejudices and conflicts among religious groups are to be reduced.[220]

SOCIAL-PSYCHOLOGICAL PROCESSES IN RELIGIOUS PARTICIPATION

Are Religion and Mainline Religious Groups Doomed to Extinction?

It has been more than a quarter of a century since two of the major researchers in the sociology of religion raised the issue of whether or not North America was entering a post-Christian era.[221] A major factor in their questioning was survey research documenting a decline in what many perceived as core Christian beliefs—most centrally, the belief in the divinity of Christ. Stark and Glock provided a pessimistic prediction for mainline Christian denominations:

> As matters now stand we can see little long-term future for the church as we know it. A remnant church can be expected to last for a long time if only to provide the psychic comforts which are currently dispensed by orthodoxy. However, eventually substitutes for even this function are likely to emerge leaving churches of the present with no effective rationale for existing.[222]

In a similar vein, the renowned anthropologist Wallace has argued that all supernatural beliefs are doomed to extinction,[223] presumably along with the churches that rely upon such beliefs for the effectiveness of their rituals.

However, associated with predictions of the eventual extinction of churches and supernatural beliefs are two assumptions that can be seriously questioned. One is that religious beliefs and church attendance are heavily correlated, and hence that changes in the one can be used to infer changes in the other. It is assumed that people who change religious beliefs are likely to lower their rate of church attendance, or that persons who lower their rate of church attendance have probably changed beliefs. Yet belief and attendance are far from perfectly correlated, and one can be a very poor predictor of the other.[224] Second, the evidence (largely derived from Gallup Poll data) suggesting declines in church attendance is confounded by variations within denominational groups. For instance, Greeley has documented an increase in church attendance among Catholics, associated with a decrease in commitment to orthodox Catholic beliefs.[225] There is no paradox in these findings when we realize that persons attend churches for a variety of reasons, many of which are only marginally related to belief issues. Furthermore, we have noted earlier that as denominational attendance falters, sectarian and cultic commitments are likely to increase, so that overall levels in religious group participation may remain strong. Yet before we accept evidence for the decline in mainstream denominations, it behooves us to consider denominations that have properties similar to the sects and cults in terms of ideological and behavioral strictness, even though their norms are less in tension with the dominant culture than either the more extreme sects or cults.

The Kelley Thesis: A Strictness Contingency

While many social scientists were predicting doom for traditional Christian denominations, one investigator burst onto the scene with a book that stimulated much controversy and continues to generate empirical research. Kelley argued that an overall decline in church attendance, especially among North American Protestants, masked two contradictory trends: The more liberal and ecumenical denominations were declining in membership, while the more conservative, exclusive, fundamentalist denominations were increasing in membership.[226] Ironically, then, the more a religious group was accommodating itself to mainstream culture, the less effectively it was maintaining its membership.

Kelley's thesis is more relevant to the strictness of religious groups in the enforcement of their beliefs and behavioral norms than to their strictness in the content of the beliefs they profess. However, strict groups are likely to be sectarian in nature, demanding a purity that the more lenient denominations relax as they universalize and welcome a diverse membership, which itself capitulates to the pluralism of mainstream modern or postmodern culture. More sectarian groups demand a seriousness and strictness that are inappropriate to broader universalizing tendencies. Hence, Kelley's thesis is compatible with our earlier discussion of sects as acceptable forms of subcultural deviance, and of cults as more problematic forms of religious deviance eliciting cultural retaliation. However, in Kelley's thesis, it is the stricter denominations, the sects, and the cults that are increasing in membership, at the cost of the more liberal denominations. The simplicity of his thesis can be seen in his ordering of religious groups along a gradient of seriousness or strictness. Denominations that strictly enforce norms taken seriously by their membership tend toward exclusiveness; this differentiates them from mainstream denominations, which cannot (by their very nature of belief and behavioral tolerance) be strong religions, according to Kelley.[227] Another way to identify this gradient is along a continuum from most exclusive (serious/strict) to most ecumenical. It is this continuum that is hypothesized to correlate with church attendance and growth. A listing of religious organizations along Kelley's continuum is presented in Figure 9.2.

Kelley's thesis is strongly stated and needs conceptual refinement, but it does have the merit of identifying the postulated determinants of church growth in terms capable of empirical investigation. Several studies have tested Kelley's basic thesis with respect to particular denominations;[228] some authors have suggested that his thesis applies not to the recruitment of new members, but to the maintenance of adult members and to the retention of children as they mature and stay as adult members of the congregation.[229] Others have argued that not all exclusive groups maintain high membership and attendance rates, and thus that Kelley's thesis is far from a general covering law.[230] Finally, although Kelley uses

```
                                              <Most exclusive
              Jehovah's Witnesses
           Evangelicals and Pentecostals
              Churches of Christ
            Latter-Day Saints (Mormons)
             Seventh-Day Adventists
               Church of God
            Church of Christ, Scientist
             Southern Baptist Convention
            Lutheran Church-Missouri Synod
             American Lutheran Church
              Roman Catholic Church
               Russian Orthodox
                Greek Orthodox
             Lutheran Church in America
            Southern Presbyterian Church
             Reformed Church in America
               Episcopal Church
            American Baptist Convention
             United Presbyterian Church
              United Methodist Church
               United Church of Christ
                Ethical Culture Society
  Most universal>           Unitarian-Universalists
```

FIGURE 9.2. Kelley's exclusive–ecumenical continuum. Adapted from Kelley (1972, p. 89). Copyright 1972 by HarperCollins Publishers. Adapted by permission.

his thesis to contrast the rates of liberal and conservative church growth, the gradient of strictness and seriousness characterizes many sectarian and cult movements, whose rapid growth rates are perceived to be in opposition to mainline (conservative) values. Still, as we have noted in Chapter 3, much religious socialization involves patterns of entering and exiting from mainstream religious groups that have little tension with the culture. Though it is still a matter of empirical investigation, Kelley's thesis forces consideration of the problem that has been a major focus of this chapter: the dynamic processes involved in tensions between religious groups and their cultures.

OVERVIEW

The contemporary debate over forms of religious expression is as old as religion itself. The long tradition of church-sect theory suggests that religious organizations are in a constant process of change—some adapting to cultural changes while others try to resist change. The temptation to postulate unique psychological processes involved in religions distant from one's own is unlikely to be fruitful. Individuals committed to cult and sect forms of religion struggle no less for meaning and significance in their lives than do those committed to more mainstream forms of religious faith. Concepts such as ideological surround are useful in sensitizing the researcher to the fact that measures and assessments are unlikely to be illuminating if they cannot demonstrate a fairness to the believer's own perspective. The claim that unique psychological processes must be involved in the maintenance of deviant religious beliefs is unlikely to be a fruitful avenue for insight into either sectarian or cult forms of faith. Polemical terms such as "brainwashing" are clearly less than useful. At best they distort complex processes in need of careful empirical investigation. Accurate descriptions of phenomena are crucial in science, and perhaps more so in social scientific research on less popular forms of religion. That, in the end, evaluations must be made is but a further plea that before such evaluations researchers make sure that their descriptions of religious groups are accurate and fair.

NOTES

1. Hall (1989, p. xiii).
2. Statement attributed to the bishop presiding at the trial of Joan of Arc; quoted in Stobart (1971, p. 157).
3. Coventry Patmore, quoted in Underhill (1911/1961, p. 164).
4. Rosenzweig (1979, p. 158).
5. Scheflin and Opton (1978, p. 50).
6. James (1902/1985, Lecture VIII).
7. James (1902/1985, Lecture VIII).
8. James (1902/1985).
9. Whitehead (1926).
10. Berger and Luckmann (1967).
11. See Koch (1994); Storr (1988).
12. Whitehead (1926).
13. Dittes (1971c).
14. Dittes (1971c, p. 382).
15. Kirkpatrick and Hood (1990); Dittes (1971c).
16. See Robertson (1975); Snook (1974).
17. Niebuhr (1929).
18. Wimberley and Christenson (1981).
19. Troeltsch (1931).
20. Eister (1973).
21. See Gerth and Mills (1946); Weber (1922/1963).
22. Swatos (1976).
23. Steeman (1975).
24. Garrett (1975).
25. Steeman (1975).
26. Troeltsch (1931, Vol. 2, pp. 993–994).
27. Troeltsch (1931, Vol. 2, pp. 994–1004).
28. Steeman (1975, p. 201).
29. For instance, see Eister (1973); Johnson (1963, 1971); Wilson (1970).
30. Welch (1977, p. 127).
31. See Welch (1979).
32. Stark (1985).
33. Johnson (1963).
34. Johnson (1963, p. 542). Emphasis in original.
35. See Robertson (1975).
36. See Stark and Bainbridge (1979, 1985).
37. Stark and Bainbridge (1980b).
38. See Bibby and Weaver (1985); Wallis (1986).
39. Garrett (1975, p. 211).
40. Troeltsch (1931, Vol. 2, p. 993).
41. Johnson (1963, p. 540).
42. Redekop (1974).
43. Johnson (1963, p. 544).
44. Bainbridge and Stark (1980b).
45. Bainbridge and Stark (1980b, p. 107).
46. Certain groups (Gospel Lighthouse, Foursquare Gospel Church) classified as sects had too few respondents to be included in the statistical tables. We focus upon mainstream denominations only, contrasted with sects, for which the sample size is sufficient. For additional details on the sample, the research instrument, and groups that we have excluded, see Glock and Stark (1966, pp. 86–122).

47. Bainbridge and Stark also present evidence for the separation and encapsulation of sects as part of their deviant subcultural status. These data are less conclusive and are ignored here. However, we do accept the mutual rejection of sects, cults, and their host cultures, as well as the relative encapsulation of sects and cults, as worthwhile operational criteria of tension, along with the more empirically supported belief difference criteria we present in Table 9.1. See our discussion of cults later in this chapter.
48. Poloma (1991).
49. Johnson, Williams, and Bromley (1986).
50. Poloma and Pendleton (1991b).
51. Poloma (1991, p. 337); Johnson, Williams, and Bromley (1986).
52. Trier and Shupe (1991).
53. Trier and Shape (1991, p. 355).
54. Gottschalk (1973).
55. Peel (1987).
56. Poloma and Pendleton (1991b).
57. Poloma (1991, p. 339).
58. Poloma (1991, p. 341).
59. Rosenau (1992).
60. Becker (1963).
61. Berger and Luckmann (1967).
62. See Beit-Hallahmi (1989, pp. 92–106); Tajfel and Turner (1986).
63. Watson (1993).
64. See Rosenau (1992); Roth (1987).
65. Schlagel (1986).
66. Batson, Schoenrade, and Ventis (1993, pp. 331–364).
67. Watson, Morris, Foster, and Hood (1986).
68. See Watson, Morris, and Hood (1987, 1990b).
69. Mead (1934).
70. Blumer (1969).
71. Blumer (1969, p. 3).
72. Blumer (1969).
73. Kuhn and McPartland (1954).
74. Berger and Luckmann (1967).
75. Hood (1983).
76. Hood (1983).
77. See Altemeyer and Hunsberger (1992); Gorsuch and Aleshire (1974); Kirkpatrick (1993).
78. See Kirkpatrick, Hood, and Hartz (1991); Pancer, Jackson, Hunsberger, Pratt, and Lea (1995); Hunsberger, Pratt, and Pancer (1994).
79. See Fowler (1981); Richards and Davison (1992).
80. Ethridge and Feagin (1979).
81. Kellstedt and Smidt (1991).
82. For original MMPI see Hathaway and McKinley (1951). MMPI-2 contains no religious items. See Butcher, Dahlstrom, Graham, Tellegen, and Kaemmer (1989).
83. Hood (1974).
84. Stark (1971).
85. See Hood, Morris, and Watson (1985, 1986).
86. Marty and Appleby (1991). This is the first volume in a projected six-volume series as part of a major effort to study fundamentalism worldwide, The Fundamentalism Project, sponsored by the American Academy of Arts and Sciences.
87. Hawley (1994a).
88. Hawley (1994a).
89. Bainbridge and Stark (1980b).
90. Rosenau (1992).
91. Richardson (1985a).
92. Greil and Robbins (1994).
93. See Hawley (1994b, 1994c).
94. Richardson (1993a).
95. Eister (1979).
96. Pfeiffer (1992, p. 538).
97. Stark and Bainbridge (1979, p. 125).

98. See Ellwood (1986); Wallis (1974).
99. Barnes and Becker (1938, p. 22).
100. Greil and Rudy (1990).
101. See Greil and Robbins (1994); McGuire (1993).
102. Greil and Robbins (1994, p. 13).
103. Greil (1993).
104. Pfeiffer (1992).
105. Pfeiffer (1992, p. 535).
106. Pfeiffer (1992, p. 539).
107. Pfeiffer (1992, pp. 537–538). With the exception of "responsible–irresponsible," all differences among the three means as a set were significant at $p < .05$. Neither post hoc nor a priori comparison between individual means were reported in the original study.
108. Zimbardo and Hartley (1985, p. 114).
109. Zimbardo and Hartley (1985, p. 114).
110. Galanter (1989a, p. 142).
111. Richardson (1978a).
112. Wallis (1974).
113. Ellwood (1986).
114. Swatos (1981).
115. See Kilbourne and Richardson (1984a, pp. 238–239); Rosenau (1992).
116. Stark (1985).
117. See Shupe and Bromley (1985); Shupe, Bromley, and Oliver (1984).
118. Bainbridge and Stark (1980a).
119. Bainbridge and Stark (1980a).
120. Bergin (1980).
121. London (1964).
122. Gross (1978).
123. Frank (1974).
124. Ellenberger (1970).
125. Illich (1976).
126. Kilbourne and Richardson (1984a).
127. See Kilbourne and Richardson (1984a); Schur (1976).
128. Zaehner (1974, p. 18).
129. Hall (1989, p. 311).
130. Feuerstein (1992).
131. See Parrinder (1980); Steinberg (1983); Tennant (1903/1968).
132. Gardella (1985).
133. Foster (1984).
134. Foster (1984).
135. Lewis (1989).
136. Freud (1930/1961, p. 61).
137. See Badcock (1980); Marcuse (1955).
138. Horowitz (1983a).
139. Horowitz (1983a, p. 181).
140. See Barker (1984, pp. 70–93).
141. Lewis (1989).
142. Judah (1974).
143. Gardella (1985).
144. Wangerin (1993).
145. Wangerin (1993, pp. 49–52).
146. See Jacobs (1984, 1987).
147. Kilbourne and Richardson (1986).
148. Kilbourne and Richardson (1986, p. 259).
149. This is true despite earlier works in which Richardson employed the concept of "cult" favorably. Compare Richardson (1978a, 1979) with Richardson (1993a).
150. van Driel and Richardson (1988).
151. Patrick and Dulack (1977, p. 11).
152. Zimbardo and Hartley (1985, p. 115).
153. Wallis (1976).

154. See, for instance, McClosky and Brill (1983); Stouffer (1955); Wilcox et al. (1992).
155. Sullivan, Pierson, and Marcus (1982, p. 29).
156. Bromley and Breschel (1992).
157. See Delgado (1982); Galanter (1989b); Lifton (1985); Stander (1987).
158. Richardson and van Driel (1984, p. 413).
159. Richardson and van Driel (1984, p. 417).
160. Greil (1993, pp. 11–16).
161. McClosky and Brill (1983).
162. Bromley and Breschel (1992).
163. O'Donnell (1993).
164. See Richardson, Best, and Bromley (1991); Swatos (1992).
165. There is a vast literature on this general theme. Among the most relevant works are Conrad and
     Schnelder (1980); Kittrie (1971); Szasz (1970, 1983, 1984).
166. See Clark (1978, 1979); Clark, Langone, Schacter, and Daly (1981).
167. Shapiro (1977).
168. See Singer (1978a, 1978b); Singer and West (1980); Singer and Ofshe (1990).
169. See Barker (1983); Friedrichs (1973); Horowitz (1983a, 1983b); Robbins (1983).
170. Wilson (1983).
171. Scarboro, Campbell, and Stave (1994).
172. Segal (1985).
173. Jones (1994).
174. Anthony and Robbins (1994, pp. 459–460).
175. Hunter (1951).
176. Anthony and Robbins (1994, p. 460).
177. Hinkle and Wolff (1956).
178. Lifton (1961).
179. Schein, Schneier, and Barker (1971).
180. Somit (1968).
181. See Arendt (1979); Friedrich and Brzezinski (1956).
182. Anthony and Robbins (1994).
183. Sargent (1957).
184. Especially useful are Bromley and Richardson (1983); Anthony and Robbins (1994); Robbins and
     Anthony (1980); Lifton (1961); Somit (1968).
185. Somit (1968, p. 142).
186. Robbins (1977).
187. Conway and Siegelman (1978).
188. Shapiro (1977, p. 80).
189. Conway and Siegelman (1978).
190. See Kilbourne (1983); Kirkpatrick (1988); Lewis and Bromley (1987).
191. Verdier (1977).
192. Robbins and Anthony (1982).
193. Anthony and Robbins (1992).
194. Robbins and Anthony (1979).
195. Barker (1986).
196. Pilarzyk (1978).
197. See Beckford (1979); Delgado (1977); Lemoult (1978); Lundé and Segal (1987); Robbins (1985).
198. Kim (1979).
199. Shupe, Spielman, and Stigall (1977).
200. Kilbourne and Richardson (1986).
201. Kim (1979).
202. Wright (1987, p. 87).
203. Galanter (1989a).
204. Galanter (1989a, pp. 140–143).
205. Barker (1984, p. 146).
206. Barker (1984, p. 147).
207. Johnson (1979).
208. Kroll-Smith (1980).
209. See Lebra (1970); Turner (1979); Weigert, D'Antonio, and Rubel (1971).

210. Johnson (1961).
211. Lewellen (1979).
212. See Festinger, Riecken, and Schachter (1956); Weisner (1974).
213. Feuerstein (1992).
214. Galanter (1983, 1989a, p. 142).
215. Ungerleider and Welish (1979).
216. Taslimi, Hood, and Watson (1991).
217. See Richardson, Stewart, and Simmonds (1979); Simmonds (1977b).
218. See Robbins and Anthony (1982, pp. 290–291).
219. Sherif (1953).
220. For an ambitious effort to set such goals, see Anthony, Ecker, and Wilbur (1987).
221. Stark and Glock (1968).
222. Stark and Glock (1968, p. 210).
223. Wallace (1966).
224. Demerath (1965).
225. Greeley (1972b).
226. Kelley (1972). It should be noted that Kelley's ecumenical–exclusive gradient applies only within the Christian tradition, not across traditions. Only Christian groups are ordered; other groups, such as Islam and Judaism, would need their own gradients. See pp. 78–96.
227. Kelley (1972, pp. 56–77).
228. See Bouma (1979); Perry and Hoge (1981).
229. See Bibby (1978); Bibby and Brinkerhoff (1973).
230. Smith (1992).

Chapter 10

RELIGION AND MORALITY

ॐ

[Religion] makes prejudice and it unmakes prejudice. . . . Some people say the only cure for prejudice is more religion; some say the only cure is to abolish religion.[1]

. . . history, down to the present day, is a melancholy record of the horrors which can attend religion: human sacrifice, and in particular the slaughter of children, cannibalism, sensual orgies, abject superstition, hatred as between races, the maintenance of degrading customs, hysteria, bigotry, can all be laid at its charge. Religion is the last refuge of human savagery.[2]

. . . being helpful is a scriptural criterion of true religion (James 1:27), and humans will ultimately be judged on their efforts on behalf of those in need of aid or comfort (Matthew 25:31–46).[3]

At least initially, temperance was part of a new kind of effort to assert the authority of religious ideas in the public sphere, and to regroup religious forces under auspices outside the church.[4]

NO to condom distribution in the schools, NO to taxpayer funding of abortion, NO to sex-education classes in the public schools that promote promiscuity, NO to homosexual adoptions and government-sanctioned gay marriages.[5]

DOES RELIGION DICTATE MORALITY?

Religion has a lot to say about morality. Christians, Jews, Buddhists, Muslims, and Hindus may not agree on the nature of God, or on religious rituals and teachings, but they do tend to agree about moral issues. In fact, when it comes to ethics, major world religions are amazingly consistent in their teachings about right and wrong, especially concerning murder, stealing, and adultery. In Christianity, this distilled essence of morality is captured by the Ten Commandments. And all major world religions seem to teach some version of "Do unto others what you would have them do unto you."

Persons with a proreligious orientation would be inclined to argue that religion has tremendous potential to improve our world by teaching an ethical system that would benefit all of us. In fact, the theologies of such diverse religious bodies as Buddhists, Christians, and Jews have claimed that faith and morality are inseparable.[6] And some groups, such as the conservative "Christian Coalition" in the United States, are apparently "eager to impose what it sees as a Bible-backed morality on the American public at large."[7] On the other hand, some people are not convinced that religion holds the key to morality in the world, and they may argue that it can actually cause problems.

Religion as "Good"

We can all think of examples in which religion apparently served or serves as a source of tolerance, helpfulness, and personal and interpersonal integrity. Mother Teresa spends her life in appalling conditions in order to help the poor, the sick, and the downtrodden, in the cause of Christian charity. Martin Luther King faced considerable danger, and was eventually assassinated, in his religiously based fight for equal rights and self-respect for black Americans. Churches also provide money, housing, and social support for refugees from other lands, and soup kitchens and halfway houses are sponsored by religious organizations. The list could go on and on.

Religion as "Bad"

On the other hand, many examples can be cited in which religion seemed or seems to have no impact at all, or may even have contributed to dishonesty, intolerance, physical violence, and prejudice. Anti-Semitism is preached openly in some North American pulpits. The Christian-based Ku Klux Klan spreads hatred of blacks, Jews, and Catholics. Many wars and other violent conflicts in today's world are religiously based: Catholics battle Protestants in Northern Ireland; fundamentalist Muslims in the Middle East clash with their nonfundamentalist brethren; Muslims and Christians fight in the former Yugoslavia; Sikhs and Hindus die in violent conflicts in India. Some may well wonder whether religion does not directly contribute to violence and injustice.

Considering the Evidence

Clearly, it would be a mistake to oversimplify these issues and to generalize about "religion" contributing to "morality" or "immorality." Faith is complex, and there are many unique religious groups, orientations, and dimensions that may differentially relate to specific aspects of "right and wrong."

Furthermore, we should not assume that religion has an impact on ethics through the process of "moral development" in childhood and adolescence. We have pointed out in Chapter 2 that Kohlberg thought of moral development as quite distinct from its religious counterpart, and he asserted that we should not assume that religion in any way causes or even contributes to the emergence of morality. Reviews of the literature concerning the acquisition of morality typically make little or no mention of religion in this process.[8]

Quite apart from formal moral development in Kohlbergian or other terms, it has been claimed that religiousness is associated with being a "better person" in numerous ways. In addition to broad moral imperatives such as "love thy neighbor," many religions have specific things to say about various personal issues: honesty and cheating, substance use and abuse, sexual behavior, criminal behavior and delinquency, helping others, and prejudice and discrimination. After a brief discussion of moral attitudes and religion, we explore each of these areas in turn, attempting to determine whether or not religion and "morality" are associated. In the case of helping behavior and prejudice, relationships with religion are especially complex and have been of considerable interest in the psychology-of-religion literature, possibly because the associations are not always what we might expect. Thus, our coverage of these latter topics is more detailed.

MORAL ATTITUDES

It is not surprising that religion is related to people's attitudes on a host of morality-related issues. Typically, people who are religious (as measured in many different ways) are "more conservative" in their attitudes. In general, those who are more religious show more opposition to abortion,[9] divorce,[10] pornography,[11] Communism,[12] contraception,[13] homosexuality,[14] feminism,[15] nudity in advertising,[16] suicide,[17] euthanasia,[18] amniocentesis,[19] women going topless on beaches,[20] and so on. The highly religious are also more likely to support marriage,[21] capital punishment,[22] traditional sex roles,[23] conservative political parties,[24] more severe criminal sentences,[25] censorship of sex and violence in the mass media,[26] and the like.

However, it is one thing to oppose premarital sex or alcohol use on the basis of religion, and quite another to act consistently with this attitude when the opportunity presents itself. Furthermore, it is possible that one's personal position on ethical issues may differ from one's "public" stance. For example, it has been found that people who personally oppose abortion on moral or religious grounds may actually *favor* legal abortion.[27] Thus, although associations between faith and moral attitudes are informative, they do not always tell us much about religion and moral *behavior*. So we now turn to a survey of several areas of behavior with strong ethical implications, in order to assess the role of religion in people's actions.

MORAL BEHAVIOR

Honesty and Cheating

In light of the emphasis placed on honesty by most religions, we might expect that their adherents would be less likely to lie, cheat, or otherwise deceive others. Of course, this is a difficult issue to study. One can imagine the problems associated with simply asking people how "religious" and how "honest" they are, to see whether the two variables are correlated. For both practical and ethical reasons, it is also not easy to place people in realistic circumstances that provide an opportunity to lie and cheat in order to observe their reactions. First, it is difficult to construct such situations that are realistic and believable to those being studied. Second, to provide an opportunity for people to lie or cheat could violate ethical standards of research, especially since it might be necessary to conceal the true purpose of such research in order to encourage "real-life" responding.

In spite of these problems, some studies have attempted to investigate these personal morality issues. And although we might expect religion to have some impact in reducing dishonesty and cheating among religious persons, the evidence in general suggests that it has little or no impact in this regard.

Early Research

Hartshorne and May investigated a possible link between religiousness and cheating in their massive studies involving some 11,000 school children in the 1920s.[28] They devised ingenious tests for cheating—for example, by measuring peeking during "eyes-closed" tests, and by checking to see whether students changed their original answers when they were allowed to grade their own exams. In the end, they found essentially no relationship between religion and honesty or cheating. In fact, there was even some tendency for children who attended Sunday school to be less cooperative and helpful. Other early studies, such as that by Hightower, similarly found no relationship between Biblical knowledge on the one hand, and lying and cheating on the other.[29]

More Recent Studies

A 1960 investigation by Goldsen and colleagues even found that 92% of religious college students affirmed that it was morally wrong to cheat, but that 87% of them agreed with the statement "If everyone else cheats, why shouldn't I?"[30] Consistent with this, a 1980s investigation by Spilka and Loffredo reported that 72% of a group of highly religious college students admitted that they had cheated on examinations.[31] And even among Mormons, a group known for its conservative and strict approach to moral issues, 70% of a sample of more than 2,000 adolescents admitted that they had cheated on tests at school.[32]

Other research, involving behavioral measures and diverse samples, has also confirmed that religion does not decrease cheating behavior. Guttman investigated sixth-graders from religious schools in Israel and discovered that religious children indicated some resistance to temptation on a paper-and-pencil test, but were actually more inclined to cheat on a behavioral measure.[33] Smith, Wheeler, and Diener studied undergraduate college students, categorizing them as involved in the "Jesus movement" or as being otherwise religious, nonreligious, or atheistic; no differences emerged among the groups with respect to their tendency to cheat on a class examination when the opportunity was available.[34]

Some studies have found a negative link between religiousness and cheating, but these involved self-reports rather than actual behavioral measures. For example, Grasmick and his colleagues have carried out investigations of the relationship between religion and self-reported admission of the likelihood respondents would cheat on their income taxes (and in one study, commit theft and engage in littering) in the future.[35] There was some tendency for more religious persons to indicate they were less likely to cheat on their taxes (and less likely to litter, but there was no significant relationship for theft). Similarly, in a recent nationwide Dutch survey, ter Voert, Felling, and Peters found that "strong Christian believers" reported holding a stricter moral code with respect to self-interest morality (different forms of cheating).[36] We must be careful in interpreting such findings, however, since they represent self-reports only; as indicated above, what people say they will do is not always consonant with their actual behavior.

Conclusion

In summary, the available research spans a considerable time period (from the 1920s to the present), and has involved many diverse samples and measures. In the end, there is not much evidence from studies of actual behavior to support the position that religious people are somehow more honest, or less likely to lie or cheat, than are their less religious or nonreligious peers. In view of the clear teachings of most faiths on such issues, we are left to ponder why religion does *not* have a significant impact in reducing cheating *behavior*.

Drug and Alcohol Use/Abuse

Religious teachings typically oppose the use and abuse of such substances as alcohol and illicit drugs. One might expect, therefore, that faith would be associated with decreased substance use/abuse. And in fact, the related literature generally does confirm this. Gorsuch and Butler noted this in their survey of studies prior to the mid-1970s,[37] and more recent reviews by Benson and Gorsuch concluded that research since the mid-1970s has quite consistently confirmed the tendency for more religious persons (as defined in many different ways) to be less likely to use and abuse alcohol and drugs.[38]

The range of studies in this area is impressive, focusing variously on alcohol, tobacco, and illicit drugs used for nonmedical purposes (such as cocaine, heroin, amphetamines, barbiturates, and psychedelic substances). Some studies focus on either alcohol *or* "drugs," but many investigate the impact of religion on both. Here we consider the findings of the various studies together, because their results are so similar.

The Negative Relationship between Religion and Substance Use/Abuse

In the early 1980s, Khavari and Harmon analyzed data from almost 5,000 people between the ages of 12 and 85, and concluded that there was a "powerful" negative relationship between religiousness and both alcohol consumption and the use of psychoactive drugs.[39] People who reported that they were "not religious at all" tended to use more tobacco products, marijuana, hashish, and amphetamines, compared with people who considered themselves to be religious. Results such as these seem to suggest that religion somehow contributes to decreased use of a variety of products that have possible negative implications for health.[40]

Similarly, a massive study of over 10,000 youths in Minnesota by Benson and his colleagues found that many indices of religious belief and behavior were negatively related to the use of such drugs as marijuana, LSD, PCP, Quaaludes, and amphetamines.[41] Congruent results were obtained by Perkins in a study of several thousand New York college students between 1982 and 1991.[42]

The Magnitude and Generality of the Relationship. The size of the relationships noted above varies from study to study, but Benson concluded that on average, correlations with alcohol, tobacco, and marijuana use are roughly −.20, and that the corresponding relationships for other illicit drugs are lower.[43] Donahue noted some tendency for the strength of the associations to decline in the 1980s, at least among high school seniors.[44] Although the obtained relationships are fairly weak, they typically remain significant even after the effects of age, gender, race, region, education, income, and other variables are controlled for (see, e.g., studies by Cochran, Beeghley, & Bock[45] and by Benson & Donahue[46]).

Benson has further pointed out that the negative relationship between religion and substance use/abuse has been found in multiple studies of adolescents, college students, and adults, and that it seems to hold for both males and females.[47] With few exceptions, consistent findings have been obtained in diverse parts of the United States,[48] as well as in countries such as Canada,[49] Nigeria,[50] England,[51] Sweden,[52] Israel,[53] Kuwait,[54] and Australia.[55]

New Religions. The negative association between religion and substance use/abuse is not limited to traditional religious groups, as discussed in Chapter 8. Although there is evidence that individuals who become members of cults often have a history of greater drug and alcohol use before joining,[56] research suggests that their subsequent use of these substances often declines, sometimes dramatically (see, e.g., Richardson[57]; Galanter & Buckley[58]). In fact, these sorts of findings led Latkin to suggest that "The study of new religions may provide insights into methods of improving drug treatment programs."[59]

Why Does This Relationship Exist? It is one thing to find an association between variables, and quite another to explain *why* that relationship exists. There are probably many factors involved in the inverse correlation between religion and substance use/abuse, and various theories have been proposed to explain the association.[60] Benson's review of the related empirical literature led him to infer:

> Nearly all of these efforts appeal to the social control function of religion, in which religious institutions and traditions maintain the social order by discouraging deviance, delinquency, and self-destructive behavior. Religion, then, prevents use through a system of norms and values that favor personal restraint.[61]

The impact of reference groups has further been isolated as one means by which religion can influence substance use.[62] It has also been argued that religion has its strongest influence when there is no general social consensus on the acceptability of alcohol and drugs. That is, religious norms may be particularly powerful referents when there is "social dissensus" concerning substance use, since people will then be most likely to look to their religion for guidance.[63]

Benson has argued that in addition to social control mechanisms, religion also decreases alcohol and drug use/abuse indirectly by "promoting environmental and psychological assets that constrain risk-taking."[64] He is referring here to religion's attempts to encourage positive behaviors through family harmony and parental support, by sponsoring prosocial values and social competence. Research is needed to assess the extent to which such indirect mechanisms are effective deterrents to drug and alcohol use/abuse.

There are interesting variations in the relationship between religion and substance use/abuse across faith groups. Cochran, for example, found that for alcohol consumption, this association was strongest for religious bodies that condemn alcohol; faiths that were silent regarding alcohol revealed little influence of religiosity.[65] (See Research Box 10.1 for further details.) In another study, Beeghley, Bock, and Cochran found that when people changed religions, the effects of faith on alcohol consumption were strongest when their new religious group banned the use of alcohol.[66] These findings confirm the importance of religion in the context of reference groups, and also mesh neatly with the important distinction between religiously proscribed and nonproscribed behavior, as conceptualized by Batson, Schoenrade, and Ventis[67] and described in more detail in our discussion of religion and prejudice later in this chapter.

The Role of Religion in Prevention and Treatment of Substance Abuse

The many studies that show religion and substance use/abuse to be negatively related might suggest that religion could be incorporated into treatment programs to combat substance abuse. Of course, the studies illustrating this association are correlational in nature, and we cannot assume a cause-and-effect relationship. It is likely that some prevention, treatment, and support programs could benefit from the aspects of religion that combat substance abuse,

---

Research Box 10.1. Effects of Religiosity and Denomination on Adolescent Self-Reported Alcohol Use (Cochran, 1993)

In this investigation, Cochran sought to assess the possibility that religious proscriptions might vary for different types of alcoholic beverages, and that this might be related to the frequency of use of these beverages. The data base came from an extensive anonymous questionnaire study of 3,065 high school students in three Midwestern states. Personal religiousness was measured by three items that asked how religious respondents were, how important church activities were to them, and what their attitudes were toward alcohol use. They were also asked about the extent to which adults and peers close to them approved or disapproved of alcohol use. Finally, Baptists, Methodists, and Pentecostals were grouped together and contrasted with Catholics, Jews, Episcopalians, Lutherans, Presbyterians, and "nones," under the assumption that the former grouping would be more proscriptive than the latter. Controls were included for age, race, gender, and socioeconomic status.

On the basis of sophisticated regression analyses, Cochran suggested that his findings, combined with those of previous work, led to two important conclusions:

> First, the effects of religiosity vary across faith groups. Where official doctrine proscribes use, the effects are strongest; where doctrine stands mute with regard to use (i.e., the nonproscriptive faith groups), the effects of personal religiosity are attenuated. Second, the effects of religiosity on use vary by beverage type. For alcoholic beverages such as beer and liquor, whose consumption is restricted largely to recreational use, the effects are strongest; for wine, an alcoholic beverage consumed for functional and ceremonial purposes, as well as recreational purposes, the effects of personal religiosity are less evident. (p. 488)

---

though research is needed to clarify what those specific elements are. Gorsuch has suggested that religion may be especially effective for religious people who want their beliefs to be considered in treatment for substance abuse, if it is within a nurturing, supportive faith context.[68] As Benson laments, the potential of religion has not been recognized in the general prevention and treatment literature on alcohol and drug abuse.[69]

This is not to say that prevention and treatment approaches do not include religious elements. Some programs sponsored by churches rely heavily on a religious perspective. Alcoholics Anonymous (AA) is an organization that has had some success in treating alcoholism over the years;[70] although AA is essentially a secular organization, it has incorporated aspects of religious experience and practices in its treatment program, especially a reliance on a higher power (God) as the source of rehabilitation.[71] However, the specific contribution of religion to such programs, as compared to the contribution of their other features, is difficult to assess. Research is needed that attempts to isolate the extent to which religion actually contributes to the success of prevention and treatment programs, and to show how it might better be incorporated into such attempts to better people's lives.

Caveats

One drawback of the many studies on religion and substance use/abuse is that they typically rely on self-reports of the latter. If, as Batson et al. have suggested, religious persons (especially the intrinsically oriented) have an inclination toward socially desirable responses,[72] it is possible that they are reporting a kind of ideal image of themselves, rather than an accurate assessment of their actual substance use and abuse. Apparently, few investigators have considered this possibility.

In addition, most of the studies in this area examined religiousness in a very general sense, relying on measures such as church attendance and affiliation. There is evidence that in some specific contexts, the usual negative relationship between religion and substance use/abuse may disappear, or even be reversed. For example, after an extensive survey of more than 18,000 children and parents, Forliti and Benson concluded that a "restrictive" religious orientation was in fact associated with *increased* alcohol use.[73] Makela has claimed that the liberalization of alcohol policies (both religious and other) would result in increases in *moderate* alcohol consumption, but would decrease *heavy* drinking.[74]

In spite of repeated findings of low negative correlations between religion and substance use/abuse, there are exceptions. Some "failures" to find the expected association may reflect unique cultural or religious situations. For example, studies carried out in Iran,[75] in Colombia,[76] and among Chinese students in Singapore[77] have shown no link between religion and alcohol or drug use.

Finally, we must remember that the "substances" considered in this section sometimes play a part in religious ceremonies or rituals for specific faith groups, and that within this context their use may actually be increased by religious involvement. For example, religious ceremonial use was one justification for drinking alcohol in Nigerian[78] and Mexican and Honduran[79] samples. In the 1960s some new religious groups encouraged the use of LSD, and Clark[80] and Siegel[81] have argued that psychedelic drugs may contribute to religious experiences and behaviors. In a different vein, Westermeyer and Walzer have even suggested that drug use among young people may occur in part because it generates personal and social benefits that would formerly have derived from religious practice.[82]

Summary

The vast majority of studies in this area reveal a negative link between religion and substance use and abuse. The relationship is typically rather weak; there are confounds to consider, and also occasional failures to replicate the effect, but all in all, it is impressive how general and consistent the association is across diverse samples and studies. In light of this, it is somewhat surprising that the overall literature on substance use/abuse makes only token acknowledgment of religion as an important explanatory variable, and then only as one of many possible cultural influences.[83]

Sexual Behavior

Religious institutions have made considerable attempts to control sexual behavior over the years, and one might agree with Shea that these attempts have historically resulted in a great amount of human distress and misery:

> If we consider those people prosecuted and punished for sexual sins or crimes in Christian communities, we might conservatively estimate the number of castrations, whippings, incarcerations, burnings, beheadings, hangings, and other executions attributable directly to Christian teaching to be in the millions.[84]

Shea points out that such treatment has (to some extent) continued to the present time, but suggests that religion's active attempts to control personal sexuality go far beyond such blatant physical punishments. Religion has engendered shame, guilt, fear, and anxiety for a wide variety of sexual "sins."[85] The psychological effects of religiously based conflict over sexuality are considered in Chapter 12. Here, however, we evaluate the evidence that religion does indeed influence the perceived morality of human sexuality, as well as sexual behavior itself.

Traditionally, religion has acknowledged the proper role of sexuality as being for procreative purposes within the marital relationship (see Chapter 4). Consequently, virtually any sort of sexual expression outside of heterosexual marriage was considered to be inappropriate and sinful. These norms have been both strong and stable across the centuries, but recent changes in these standards have occurred, particularly in Europe and North America. The population at large and some religious groups are currently showing an increased tolerance of masturbation, premarital sex, and even some extramarital sexual behavior. As Cochran and Beeghley have pointed out,

> some churches have addressed the problem by adjusting and softening their stand, while others have steadfastly avoided such secularization. As a result, there are significant differences in the official stands taken toward nonmarital, particularly premarital sex, among mainstream religious bodies in America.[86]

Is There a Negative Relationship between Religion and Nonmarital Sex?

In spite of these denominational differences, research has generally found that stronger religious beliefs and involvement are associated with decreased premarital sexual activity in a broad sense. For example, a recent textbook on lifespan development concluded:

> One of the clearest cultural influences on adolescent sexual behavior is religious participation. Adolescents who attend religious services frequently and who value religion as an important aspect of their lives have less permissive attitudes toward premarital sex. This finding applies equally to Catholic, Protestant, and Jewish young people. The relationship is accentuated in adolescents who describe themselves as Fundamentalist Protestant or Baptist.[87]

The reader will recognize that cause and effect are not entirely clear in such correlational relationships. It is tempting to infer that religiousness is influencing sexual beliefs and practices. However, it is also possible that sexual beliefs and practices are affecting religious commitment. Most probably, young people are making their own decisions about both religion and sexuality at approximately the same time. But decisions to have more permissive attitudes concerning sexuality could influence people to be less frequent church attenders, possibly because religious participation is less satisfying to them.[88] Of course, the bulk of the literature assumes that the causal direction is from religion to sexuality; given religious teachings about sexual morality, this is certainly a reasonable position.

Recent work has typically found this negative association between religiousness and nonmarital sexuality, but has also tried to further specify and explain the relationship. For example, Cochran and Beeghley examined cumulative data from the National Opinion Research Center's General Social Surveys conducted in the United States between 1972 and 1989, involving almost 15,000 people.[89] They did find an overall tendency for religious persons to disapprove more strongly of premarital sexuality, extramarital sexuality, and homosexuality than their less religious fellows. However, there were notable variations across different religious groups (see Table 10.1), apparently indicative of the official doctrines of U.S. churches. The more strongly one's (religious) reference group condemns and prohibits various sexual acts, the more likely one is to agree. "That is, as religious proscriptiveness increases, the effect of religiosity on nonmarital sexual permissiveness increases."[90]

Qualifications

It is surprising that there has not been more interest in the relationship between specific religious *orientations* and nonmarital sexual attitudes and behavior. Haerich recently investigated the role of intrinsic and extrinsic religiousness in the sexual attitudes of about 200 undergraduate psychology students.[91] Consistent with other research, Haerich found that lower church attendance and religiousness (by self-report) were weakly but significantly associated with more permissive attitudes toward nonmarital sexuality, as measured by a sexual permissiveness scale. Furthermore, permissive attitudes were inversely linked to intrinsic scores and positively associated with extrinsic scores, usually in the .20 to .30 range. This is consistent with Woodroof's finding that extrinsics were more likely to be nonvirgins and to have had more sexual experience than intrinsics.[92] Haerich interprets these findings as indicating that greater commitment to religious institutions (intrinsic scores) is associated with decreasing permissiveness, whereas people with a religious orientation that focuses on personal comfort and security (extrinsic scores) will, in a similar manner, use sexual intimacy to contribute to their personal comfort and security. However, this interpretation must be considered speculative, pending further research.

The many studies that simply look for relationships between general measures of religiousness and sexual attitudes and behaviors neglect potentially important factors. For example, Reynolds has pointed out that the research investigating premarital sexual experience typically assumes that early sexual activity is consensual, when in many cases it is not, especially for females.[93] Cases of nonconsensual sex should not be included in studies of the

TABLE 10.1. Attitudes toward Nonmarital Sexuality: Percentage Saying Specific Behaviors Are "Almost Always Wrong" or "Always Wrong" among Different Religious Groups

Religious group	Attitude toward		
	Premarital sexuality	Extramarital sexuality	Homosexuality
Nonaffiliated	10	66	49
Jewish	18	75	43
Catholic	36	87	77
Episcopalian	25	85	66
Presbyterian	36	89	76
Lutheran	40	90	81
Methodist	43	91	84
Baptist	49	90	89
Other Protestant	55	93	86
Total sample	40	88	79

Note. Adapted from Cochran and Beeghley (1991, pp. 54–55). Copyright 1991 by the Society for the Scientific Study of Religion. Adapted by permission.

influence of religion on sexuality, she argues, since this could distort the nature and strength of the overall relationship.

Finally, Hammond, Cole, and Beck have noted another complicating factor in the relationship between religion and nonmarital sexuality.[94] Their investigation indicates that at least among white Americans, young people from fundamentalist and sect-like religions are more likely to marry before the age of 20 than are mainline Protestants, even when various other factors are controlled for. They argue that this tendency may result from generally stronger pressures to avoid premarital sexual intercourse. In one sense, this is important because it emphasizes another way in which a person's religious background may influence an aspect of the transition to adulthood—namely, marriage. In another sense, this tendency could also unfairly contribute to the "religion deters premarital sexual activity" finding in many studies, because early marriages in fundamentalist groups will reduce the "opportunity" for premarital sexual interaction between highly religious young people. By definition, one obviously cannot engage in *pre*marital sex *after* marriage.

Summary

There is little dispute about the typically weak but consistent tendency for religion to be negatively related to nonmarital sexual attitudes and behaviors. However, it is also evident that the relationship is not as simple as was once thought. Again, we look to future research to specify these relationships further.

Criminal Behavior and Delinquency

We are all familiar with the statistics on rising crime rates, and recent projections suggest that crime and delinquency will continue to increase, possibly to "epidemic" proportions.[95] As is the case for alcohol and drug use/abuse, and to some extent nonmarital sexuality, churches and synagogues typically take strong stands against criminal or delinquent behavior. One might hope that religion could act as a powerful deterrent to such acts. Of course, the phrase "criminal and delinquent behavior" covers considerable territory. Furthermore, crime statistics themselves may be unreliable: Definitions may vary from one jurisdiction to the next; some governments and police agencies may be more zealous in enforcing laws; and much crime undoubtedly goes unreported. Also, the methodological and statistical challenges in teasing out religion–delinquency relationships are considerable.

The Historical Context

Historically, the theoretical underpinnings of the expectation that low religious involvement may be associated with higher crime rates can be traced to the early years of this century—particularly Durkheim's emphasis on the social roots of religion, and his social integration theory of deviance and religion's place in society.[96] Durkheim felt that religion is integrally tied to the social order, playing an important role in legitimizing and reinforcing society's values and norms. Deviance may then stem from a breakdown in the church's role in this regard. Consistent with what many people would consider "common-sense" reasoning, the Durkheimian tradition links strong religious ties with decreased crime rates. In fact, many of the relevant data available to us today come from sociologists who have carefully scrutinized crime and deviance statistics and their relationship to church attendance, denominational affiliation, religious commitment, and so on. The majority of this work focuses on adolescent delinquency, with fewer investigations of adult crime.

Contradictory Findings

Some early research did indeed show the expected negative religion–delinquency correlations.[97] However, a widely cited paper with the provocative title "Hellfire and Delinquency," published in the late 1960s by Hirschi and Stark, reported that there was little or no association between religiousness and delinquency among several thousand California adolescents.[98] The authors suggested that earlier findings of a negative relationship had been weak and were probably spurious. Possibly because this finding was unexpected, it stimulated numerous subsequent investigations of this topic. Some of this follow-up research seemed to replicate Hirschi and Stark's original finding.[99] However, other investigators have challenged this conclusion by finding that religion was indeed negatively correlated with some kinds of delinquency.[100]

In a notable study, Jensen and Erickson reanalyzed Hirschi and Stark's data, and concluded that the original authors had reached erroneous conclusions because of their methodology.[101] There was actually a negative relationship between religion and delinquency, they claimed, which had remained hidden because of the statistical analyses carried out by Hirschi and Stark. Their own findings, based on several thousand Arizona high school students, confirmed the general inverse religion–delinquency relationship, though specific comparisons were often weak and did not always achieve statistical significance. Furthermore, Jensen and Erickson noted that the importance of religious variables in "explaining" crime statistics was greater for Mormons than it was for Catholics and Protestants. This tendency for correlations to be stronger, relatively speaking, within samples of Mormon adolescents has recently been replicated by Chadwick and Top.[102] That is, denominational variations may affect the results obtained.

The general tendency toward relatively weak and not always consistent findings has continued in more recent research. Some studies find low but significant relationships; others generate few if any statistically reliable results. In an extensive investigation, Bainbridge examined data from 75 U.S. metropolitan areas and, after taking into account some possible intervening variables (e.g., social mobility, poverty), claimed that larceny, burglary, and assault were apparently deterred by religion, but murder, rape, and possibly robbery were not.[103] Pettersson investigated the relationship between religion and a variety of criminal behaviors by analyzing data from almost a thousand Swedes.[104] He noted that relationships varied, depending on the type of crime at issue, but the pattern differed somewhat from that found by Bainbridge in the United States. A negative association was found between church involvement and crimes associated with violence, violations of public order and safety, and alcohol abuse; however, there was no substantial relationship for property, narcotic, or moral offenses. Shaffer and colleagues investigated narcotic addicts and found that a variety of their criminal activity was linked with lack of early religious training, among other things.[105]

To complicate things even more, Cochran and colleagues recently studied more than 1,500 Oklahoma high school students.[106] They observed, similar to Hirschi and Stark 25 years earlier,[107] that for most categories of delinquency the effect of religiosity was reduced to nonsignificant levels when nonreligious control variables were also considered. This led Cochran et al. to assume that in most cases, the religion–delinquency relationship is spurious.

Making Sense of the Contradictions

It is difficult to draw general conclusions from these efforts, given the differences in samples, findings and interpretations of various authors. Recently, Bainbridge offered several important conclusions, based on his review of the relevant research.[108] First, there has been some tendency for studies carried out in areas where organized religion is weak to show no relationship. But work conducted in areas where organized religion is relatively strong usually generate the negative religion–delinquency findings. Thus, consistent with previous inferences by Stark,[109] Bainbridge suggests that the religious community context is critical in explaining the contradictory findings in this area. Religion is more likely to act as a deterrent to delinquency if religious social support exists (e.g., are one's friends also religious?).

Bainbridge also draws an important distinction between "hedonistic" or "antiascetic" acts and other forms of deviance. His own research (as well as that of others) suggests that religion is negatively associated with drug and alcohol use, promiscuous sexuality, and similar "hedonistic" acts, regardless of the religious community context. It is when deviant acts such as theft, assault, and murder are examined that the religious social context apparently becomes important in qualifying the religion–delinquency relationship.

Finally, it is clear that zero-order correlations between gross measures of religion and delinquency can be quite misleading, since the removal of the effects of other social and cultural variables often reduces these associations considerably.

Partner and Child Abuse

Some studies have focused on family violence, such as partner or child abuse. Capps[110] and Greven[111] have suggested that religion may be seen by some people as "justifying" child abuse, in the sense that it may encourage physical punishment of children. These authors point to numerous Biblical passages, as well as books and articles written by Christian authors, that encourage the use of physical force in disciplining children; it is argued that these could serve as a justification for various forms of abuse (e.g., "It is for the child's own good"). Furthermore, Bottoms and colleagues have suggested that religious beliefs can threaten the welfare of children in various ways, including the withholding of medical care and attempts to rid children of evil, as well as direct physical and psychological abuse that adults see as religiously justified.[112]

There is apparently little research to assess religion's possible role in exacerbating or inhibiting abuse of children. Neufeld[113] and Steele and Pollock[114] have suggested that fundamentalist religious parents may be especially prone to punish their children physically, and also possibly to abuse them; Hull and Burke have proposed that members of the "religious right" may be more likely to tolerate family abuse in general.[115] However, these possibilities must be considered conjectural, pending thorough empirical assessment. These issues are further discussed in Chapter 4.

Recently, Elliott investigated childhood sexual abuse among almost 3,000 professional women.[116] She could find no evidence that its prevalence was related to family religious affiliation, but there was a tendency for adult religious practices to mediate the severity of symptoms for those victimized as children. Studies such as this underline the potential of religion to help some adult survivors to cope with their earlier abuse.

There have been suggestions that family abuse, generally speaking, has roots in the strong patriarchal family structure espoused by some religions. This patriarchal system is sometimes interpreted as justifying the subordination of women, particularly in terms of their subjection to powerful male authority,[117] though some women may turn to religion as a source of empowerment in other ways.[118] The problem may be confounded by some clergy, who counsel women to remain with abusive husbands because it is their religious duty and responsibility to stay with and obey their spouses.[119]

Work on courtship and spousal violence has sometimes found links with religion, though few studies have focused on this issue. The findings of Makepeace seem to contradict the line of thinking described above, since religion was found to be negatively associated with courtship violence among college students.[120] Brinkerhoff, Grandin, and Lupri investigated possible religious involvement in spousal violence in a Canadian sample of more than a thousand adults.[121] Their hypothesis that the more fundamentalist, conservative Protestants would be more abusive "because of the stereotypes surrounding their value of patriarchy"[122] received mixed support. Conservative Protestant women (but not men[123]) reported the highest rates of violence (37.8%), compared to mainline Protestants (28.1%), Catholics (23.9%), and the nonaffiliated (30.8%). Furthermore, church attendance was related to spousal violence in a curvilinear manner, with frequent attenders being the least violent. These findings are potentially important, but await corroboration from further research with different samples and measures.

Does Religion Sometimes Contribute to Crime?

Although some studies show that religion and crime are negatively (albeit weakly) associated, we must consider the possibility that religion may also contribute to criminal behavior, at least in some situations. Some religions may emphasize the importance of standing up for one's rights ("an eye for an eye"), or a particular religious group may stress that members of this group are superior to various others; either of these factors could potentially incline individuals to act aggressively in some situations. In a study of regional differences in crimes against persons in the United States, Ellison concluded that there was some evidence that "the public religious culture" of the South played a role in legitimizing this kind of violence.[124] That is, an emphasis on the "an eye for an eye" approach to the world, instead of "turn the other cheek," may have contributed both to greater tolerance of physical force and to personal justification for retaliatory violent acts. There have been few investigations of this issue, however, and research is needed to clarify the specific contexts (if any) in which religion might actually exacerbate such acts.

In recent years, there has been much publicity concerning physical and sexual abuse of children, adolescents, and sometimes adults by members of the clergy. It has been suggested that religion may be a contributing factor to such abuse because of celibacy requirements, rigid rules and expectations concerning sexuality, and so on. This issue is discussed further in Chapter 12.

Summary

The literature on religion and crime or delinquency is somewhat contradictory and ambiguous. Although some studies do show a negative relationship, it tends to be weak and inconsistent. As in some other areas, there has been a tendency to use very general measures of religion (e.g., church attendance, denominational affiliation), and to ignore the important but subtle differences that may be based on religious *orientation*, rather than simple attendance or affiliation. When this deficiency is combined with the unreliability of crime statistics and with other problems, it becomes almost impossible to reach firm conclusions.

Benson, Donahue, and Erickson's survey of the literature on adolescence and religion led them to conclude that the weight of the evidence supports the existence of a weak to moderate negative relationship between religion and delinquency.[125] But, along with others,[126] they point out that much of this association may be attributable to social environment factors other than to religion itself: "After accounting for whether they have friends who engage in deviant behaviors, the adolescents' closeness to their parents, and how important it is for them to do what their parents say, religion contributes little independent constraining effect."[127]

In general, the negative relationship seems most likely to appear for "victimless activities" (e.g., use/abuse of alcohol and drugs, consensual premarital sexual activity), rather than other delinquent behavior.[128] It is important to go beyond simple correlational relationships, as indicated in research carried out by Peek, Curry, and Chalfant.[129] They found evidence that over time, higher delinquency rates appeared among students who declined in religiousness, compared to those who were low in religiousness throughout the same period. Such longitudinal trends may provide the basis for future investigations of adolescent delinquency.

Helping Behavior

"Help those in need." "Love one another." "Treat others as you would have them treat you." These are simple yet powerful imperatives, and similar themes are espoused by all of the world's major religions, as Coward has pointed out.[130] Religion has been identified with humanity and community through terms such as "love," "justice," "compassion," "mercy," "grace," "charity," and so on. The scriptural writings of most religions provide many examples of religious persons being kind to and helping others in need. And even in contemporary society, religious organizations and individuals sometimes stand out in their efforts to assist others, as noted at the beginning of this chapter. Churches become involved in relief efforts to ease the effects of famines, earthquakes, and other disasters. Religious organizations organize and fund soup kitchens in cities large and small; they help refugees to escape from unbelievable horrors and to become established in a new land; they become actively involved as peacemakers in the world's "hot spots." Oliner and Oliner's interviews with hundreds of people who rescued Jews in Nazi Europe revealed some who attributed their behavior to their religious values.[131] The list of religiously sponsored or promoted helping efforts is a long one.

Yet many nonreligious and even antireligious persons assist others as well. Present-day society offers unlimited opportunities to aid others in a secular context, and many people accept this challenge; "religion" apparently has little or nothing to do with their good will. Of course, this is why anecdotes are of little use in clarifying our understanding of the relationship between religion and helping behavior. Examples can be marshaled to show that both religious and nonreligious individuals and organizations assist others, and that both religious and nonreligious persons and organizations can act with callous neglect when other people cry out for assistance. Our challenge is to move beyond rhetoric and anecdotal material—to examine more general links between religion and helping, as revealed in the empirical literature.

Measurement and Definitional Problems

As in many areas of the psychology of religion, psychometric and methodological issues are important in the study of helping behavior. In keeping with many psychological studies of religion, much research in this area relies on questionnaires, asking for self-reports of religiousness and helping behavior. This raises concerns about "self-presentation" issues. For example, it can be argued that religious persons may be concerned about appearing to be good representatives of their faith, and therefore would be inclined to exaggerate the extent to which they help others. Fortunately, there are also some studies in this area that have utilized behavioral measures, as described below, and these serve as an important counterbalance to the many questionnaire studies on helping.

In this section we purposely use the term "helping" rather than "altruism," in order to avoid the thorny issue of whether all helping behavior is egoistically motivated, or whether at least some helping behavior is motivated purely by the ultimate goal of benefiting someone else (i.e., altruistic behavior). The reader interested in this issue might consult Batson's book on altruism, which addresses philosophical, theoretical, and empirical aspects of this distinction.[132]

Early Questionnaire Studies

Early survey studies in this area tended to rely on measures of frequency of church attendance as the primary measure of religiousness, with occasional forays into measures of such factors as belief in God, affiliation, or religious involvement. Assessment of "helping" typically involved self-reports (and occasionally others' reports) of one's inclination to assist others. These studies were fairly "primitive" in the sense that the measures of both religion and helping were quite simple and basic, and investigators merely looked for correlations between such general measures. These studies typically reported low to moderate correlations between religiousness and helping,[133] with some investigations reporting mixed or qualified associations.[134]

Most of these studies failed to take other factors into account. They did not, for example, control for church-related helping as opposed to helping outside of the "church walls." Nelson and Dynes found that when their low but significant associations between religiousness and helping through social service agencies were corrected for some other factors (e.g., helping through one's church, income, age), the correlations essentially disappeared.[135] Similarly, Hunsberger and Platonow found that although religiously orthodox students reported that they were more likely to volunteer to help in religion-related contexts, there was no evidence that they were more helpful in a nonreligious context.[136] Furthermore, when we turn to studies that incorporate actual behavioral measures of helping, there is little evidence that religious people are more helpful than less religious or nonreligious people.

Early Behavioral Studies

Batson, Schoenrade, and Ventis have provided a thorough review of the literature on religion and helping, and point to a considerable difference between "pencil-and-paper" and behavioral studies of helping.[137] The questionnaire investigations often showed at least some positive connection between religion and helping, as indicated above. However, consistent with studies indicating that the positive correlations from questionnaire studies tended to disappear when possible confounding variables were controlled for, Batson et al.'s review of six early studies employing behavioral measures shows that five of the six found no evidence that more religious persons are more helpful.

These early studies were creative in their employment of behavioral measures. For example, Forbes, TeVault, and Gromoll "lost" addressed letters near different churches and examined the extent to which people "helped" by putting these letters into mailboxes.[138] Smith, Wheeler, and Diener gave people the opportunity to volunteer to work with a retarded child.[139] Annis, in two investigations, put people in a situation where they apparently heard a woman in distress after a ladder fell.[140] McKenna measured the extent to which people would call a garage for a stranded woman motorist without any money.[141] Yinon and Sharon examined financial contributions to help a needy family.[142]

Only the last of these studies (the one by Yinon and Sharon) showed any inclination for "more religious" individuals to be more likely to help than their less religious counterparts, and even this finding held only when the request came from a religious person. Batson et al. have concluded that "this evidence strongly suggests that the more religious show no more active concern for others in need than do the less religious. The more religious only present themselves as more concerned."[143]

Dimensions of Religion and Helping

The reader will observe that the studies discussed above did not take into account possible differences in helping tendencies associated with varying religious *orientations*. The distinction between intrinsic and extrinsic orientations, for example, would lead one to expect that intrinsic persons should be more helpful since they tend to "live" their religion, and extrinsic persons should be less helpful because their religion derives from self-interest. Batson, on the other hand, has proposed that intrinsic religiousness relates only to the *appearance* of being more helpful, whereas the "quest" dimension of religion is the best and most direct predictor of helping behavior.[144] Batson has carried out a series of investigations to test these proposals, and we describe this program of research shortly. First, however, we describe several studies that have focused on the extent to which helping may be associated with intrinsic, extrinsic, or related religious orientations.

A number of researchers have relied entirely on self-reports of helping-related values and religious orientation. These have usually resulted in positive correlations between intrinsic scores and self-reports of values associated with aiding others.[145] Batson et al. have argued that this kind of study does not resolve the issue of whether intrinsics are really more helpful, because intrinsic persons are simply trying to "look good" by agreeing with altruistic values.[146] Other studies have found significant correlations between intrinsic–extrinsic orientations and self-reported helping. For example, Benson and colleagues found that "nonspontaneous helping," as measured by self-reports of the kinds of charitable activities that people engaged in to assist others, was positively related to intrinsic scores ($r = .30$).[147] Unfortunately, we do not know the extent to which social desirability might have played a role in this relationship. Also, Benson et al. did not distinguish between church-related helping and secular charitable situations. Hunsberger and Platonow had participants volunteer for *secular* charitable work in their study, and found that there was a weak but significant correlation between such volunteering and intrinsic scores ($r = .17$), as well as a negative association for extrinsic scores ($r = -.27$). Furthermore, a measure of social desirability was *not* related to intrinsic scores ($r = .02$), but it was significantly correlated with extrinsic scores ($r = .22$).[148]

In the end, the evidence suggests that more religious persons, especially intrinsic individuals, tend to help others through their religious organizations in a variety of ways. Also, it would appear that intrinsic religiosity is positively but weakly related to an inclination to say that one helps others, and apparently also to the tendency actually to volunteer in a charitable context. There is some evidence that social desirability does not explain this relationship, though the relevant studies have relied to a large extent on self-reports. The situation is certainly not clear-cut, since the associations that have appeared tend to be weak, and not entirely consistent from one study to the next. Batson has argued that only behavioral studies can resolve the controversy over a possible religion–helping relationship.

Batson's Research Program

C. Daniel Batson is a respected researcher in the general social-psychological literature on helping behavior, who has also investigated the relationship between religion and helping. Much of his religion-related work has focused on the controversy concerning how religious *orientation* is related to assisting others, and he has introduced a number of important behavioral measures of helping which have allowed this area to escape from the problems associated with investigations based solely on self-report.

The Good Samaritan Study. Batson's first study in this area attempted to operationalize the parable of the good Samaritan, and this investigation, highlighted in Research Box 10.2, has served as a model for some subsequent research.[149] In this investigation, there was no tendency for means (similar to extrinsic), end (similar to intrinsic), or quest orientations to be related to helping behavior.

Darley and Batson's conclusion that among those who did offer to help, the more orthodox, intrinsic persons might be helping for their own reasons instead of being sensitive to those needing aid has been challenged.[150] Maybe those higher on quest helped "tentatively" because they really weren't very committed to helping in the first place, and the more assertive assistance of the high intrinsics reflected more genuine caring and concern on their part. Furthermore, we may wonder about the generalizability of findings from the relatively homogeneous and religious sample of seminary students. Another study, by Batson and Gray,[151] extended the original Darley and Batson findings in a very different context.

"Helping Janet." In this follow-up investigation, 60 female introductory psychology students at the University of Kansas, all of whom reported being at least moderately religious, were placed one at a time in an experimental situation involving an exchange of written notes. "Janet," supposedly another participant, was a fictitious person who indicated that she was feeling lonely and needed to work through some problems. Half of the time Janet expressly asked the real participant to meet with her again for further conversation, and the other half of the time Janet indicated quite clearly that she was resolved to work out her problems on her own. How did the participants respond to Janet's clear request for help or no help? Intrinsic scores were positively correlated with participants' previously obtained self-reports of helpfulness and concern for others. But when Batson and Gray examined actual helping responses, intrinsic scores were correlated about .27 with helping, *whether or not* Janet wanted any help. Quest scores, however, were positively associated with helping ($r = .37$) when Janet said she wanted help, and negatively related to helping ($r = -.32$) when Janet indicated she wanted to work things through on her own. This finding supports Darley and Batson's earlier suggestion that high questers are sensitive to the expressed needs of others with respect to help needed, but that people with an intrinsic (end) orientation are rather indiscriminately inclined to help, whether the other person wants help or not.

Research Box 10.2. Situational and Dispositional Variables in Helping Behavior (Darley & Batson, 1973)

In the parable of the good Samaritan, Jesus described a man who is robbed, beaten, and left for dead at the side of the road. Two "religious" individuals, a priest and a Levite, pass by but do not stop to help. However, a Samaritan, a religious outcast, does (at some cost to himself) give the robbery victim the help he needs. Jesus wanted to make the point that people should model their behavior after the Samaritan, not after "religious" people, who may be so caught up in their thoughts that they don't see the needs of people around them.

Would the results differ if this situation were to occur in contemporary society? Darley and Batson attempted to construct a similar "help-needed" situation at Princeton University. Sixty-seven seminary students first completed questionnaires to assess their religious orientation, among other things; then, one at a time, 40 of them showed up for a follow-up experimental session. They were asked to prepare a short talk based on either (1) the parable of the good Samaritan, or (2) jobs that seminary students might pursue. After having a few minutes to prepare for their forthcoming talk, participants were given a map to show them how to get to a room in another building where they would give their talk. Half of the participants were told that they would need to hurry, since they were late for their appointment.

As these students passed down an alley, they met a man in need of help. A confederate of the experimenters was slumped in a doorway, head down, eyes closed, not moving. As each seminarian passed, the victim coughed and groaned; given the geographical setting, it was virtually impossible to miss him. The key dependent measure in this study was whether or not the students stopped to offer any kind of help. In fact, just 16 of the 40 seminarians (40%) offered assistance. And religious orientation (means, end, or quest) did not predict who would stop to offer aid.

However, among those who did stop, an interesting finding emerged. When a seminarian offered help, the victim indicated that he had just taken his medication, he would be fine if he just rested a few minutes, and he would like to be left alone. Some of the "good Samaritans" were quite insistent, however. In spite of the victim's objections, some participants insisted on taking him into a nearby building and pouring some coffee and/or religion into him. Among only those who did stop to help, the intrinsic (end) dimension correlated positively with this "I know what is best for you" helping style ($r = .43$), but the quest orientation was negatively associated with such insistent aid ($r = -.54$). Darley and Batson concluded that the more intrinsic seminarians seemed to be guided by a "preprogrammed" helping response, which was not affected by the expressed needs of the victim. It was almost as if the "super helpers" were satisfying their own internal need to help, rather than meeting the needs of the victim. However, those with a quest orientation had a more "tentative" helping style, sensitive to the person needing help, since they tended to accept the victim's statement that he really just wanted to be left alone and everything would be fine.

Before we leave our consideration of this study, there are some loose ends to tie up. Contrary to expectations, it did not make any difference whether the participant was preparing to give a speech on the parable of the good Samaritan or on jobs for seminary graduates. Apparently, thinking about helping in a Biblical context did not make participants more likely to offer aid in a similar situation. Finally, those participants in the "hurry up, you're late" condition were significantly less likely to stop and offer any kind of help than were those with no "hurry up" instructions. Apparently, the most powerful variable in determining helping behavior overall in this study was a nonreligious one—whether or not a participant was in a hurry.

Additional Research. Three further studies by Batson have attempted to delve into the "altruistic versus egoistic" issue concerning underlying motivation for helping by people with different religious orientations, and these have provided additional valuable data concerning the relationship of intrinsic and quest orientations to helping behavior. Two of these investigations, reported by Batson's group in 1989,[152] are discussed in Research Box 10.3. The findings were generally consistent with the group's interpretation of intrinsic-based helping as motivated by concern for "appearances" and quest-based assistance as stemming from sensitivity to others' needs.

Batson and Flory subsequently attempted to manipulate the extent to which research participants thought they would "look good," by employing a cognitive interference task (involving the Stroop effect) and an appeal involving a family tragedy similar to that in the second Batson et al. study (see Research Box 10.3).[153] As they expected, Batson and Flory found that high intrinsic scores were associated with "looking good," and there was a weak (nonsignificant) tendency for quest scores to be linked with helping stemming from concern for the victim's welfare.

This series of studies has provided substantial but not entirely consistent support for Batson's interpretation of tendencies to help, and motivation for assisting others, depending on religious orientation. These investigations all involved small samples of university students, and the generalizability of the findings may be questioned. Furthermore, the expected correlational relationships did not always achieve significance in specific studies, and the weak psychometric properties of the Quest scale used in these studies is a serious concern. However, the combined impact of these investigations suggests that the tendency for the intrinsically religious to be helpful may stem to some extent from personal need rather than from the needs of others. Moreover, the quest orientation has predicted helping under some circumstances, and the evidence indicates that the resulting assistance is motivated by the needs of others rather than by personal reward or appearance. In this sense, quest-related helping may approach "altruistic" assistance, whereas intrinsic-related helping may have a more "egoistic" basis.[154]

Summary

The study of religion and helping behavior is especially interesting because of the availability of both self-report questionnaires and investigations of actual behavior. Furthermore, few areas have seen such systematic theorizing, accompanied by a systematic research program, as that provided by Batson and his coworkers.

Not all authors are prepared to accept Batson's conclusions that intrinsic religion is related to the *appearance* of helping, and that the assistance provided by such individuals is likely to be a preprogrammed, self-serving type of aid. Nor is there complete acceptance of the finding that the quest orientation is a good predictor of *actual* (behavioral) helping, and that quest-based assistance is motivated by the needs of others.[155] Specific criticisms have been directed at the measures of religion used, as well as the context for helping.[156] However, Batson has provided a systematic program of research, the results of which provide general support for his conclusions. We hope that those who prefer alternate interpretations of the Batson findings will carry out their own multiple-study programs of research to test these interpretations. Until such investigations are forthcoming, we are inclined to cautiously accept Batson's findings and interpretations.

**Research Box 10.3. Religious Prosocial Motivation:
Is It Altruistic or Egoistic? (Batson et al., 1989)**

In the first of two studies, participants were told that they could volunteer to help out a
7-year-old boy with a rare genetic disorder, but that even if they were willing to help, they
would have to pass a sort of physical fitness qualifying task before they could participate
in a walkathon. Some participants were led to believe that the qualifying standard was
relatively easy; others were told that it was "extremely stringent." Batson et al. reasoned
that when the standard was described as difficult, it would be easy to volunteer because
there wasn't much chance that a participant would actually have to follow through with
the volunteer commitment. Consistent with their expectations, the researchers found that
an extrinsic orientation was negatively correlated with volunteering for both the easy and
difficult qualifying standards ($r = -.37$, on average). Intrinsic scores, however, did not
correlate with volunteering when the standard was easy, but they were positively correlated ($r = .50$) when the standard was difficult. Although other interpretations are possible, Batson et al. have suggested that this supports their contention that intrinsically
inclined people want to *look* like helpers, but only if there is actually just a small chance
of their having to carry through with the assistance.

Quest scores did not correlate with helping in either the easy or difficult conditions.
Furthermore, those who volunteered were actually asked to proceed with the qualifying
task (stepping up and down from a block for 30 seconds). There was evidence that
intrinsically inclined individuals tried harder in the difficult condition only if they had
not volunteered to help. Quest scores, on the other hand, were positively related to performance on the qualifying task only for those who *had* volunteered to help. Batson et al.
have interpreted these rather complex findings as being consistent with Batson's earlier
research findings. First, intrinsics' motivation for helping stemmed from a personal need
to appear helpful (without actually having to help), rather than from the needs of others.
Second, questers' motivation for helping was really generated by the needs of others, since
they worked hardest when they thought it would be difficult to qualify to help.

A second investigation reported in the same article focused on a different helping
context— an undergraduate who was coping with family tragedy and needed help from
others to support her siblings. The pattern of correlations suggested that extrinsics were
less likely to volunteer and questers were more likely to volunteer when there was little
pressure to do so, but intrinsic scores were unrelated to offering assistance under either
high- or low-pressure conditions.

Prejudice, Discrimination, and Stereotyping

Few areas in the psychology of religion have generated as much interest, research, and controversy as the relationship between religion and prejudice. Since, as noted above, most world
religions espouse a common theme of "love one another," it might be expected that this
teaching would have a powerful effect in reducing prejudice among the members of these
religions. But research has not been supportive of this generalization. In fact, many studies
have linked various aspects of religiousness with *increased* discriminatory attitudes. Glock
and Stark even built a case that Christianity contributes directly to anti-Semitic prejudice,[157]
and in spite of challenges to this position, it has been confirmed by other researchers—most
recently by Eisinga, Konig, and Scheepers in a Dutch investigation.[158]

Gordon Allport, one of the 20th century's most prominent authorities on prejudice, concluded that the effect of religion on prejudice is paradoxical, since "it makes prejudice and it unmakes prejudice."[159] The reasoning behind this paradox is that different religious orientations may be differentially related to prejudice. First, let us consider the related research in historical perspective. In reviewing the work on religion and prejudice, we do not offer an exhaustive review of the literature that has accumulated in the area (such reviews have been provided in Gorsuch & Aleshire,[160] Batson et al.,[161] and Spilka, Hood, & Gorsuch[162]). Rather, we attempt to summarize different stages in the development of our understanding of the religion–prejudice relationship, and ultimately focus on promising developments that have occurred in the past decade or so, involving religious fundamentalism, quest, and right-wing authoritarianism.

Early Studies

Many studies over the years have found that people's responses to measures of religion and prejudice are related. In light of his review of the literature, Wulff was led to conclude:

> Using a variety of measures of piety—religious affiliation, church attendance, doctrinal orthodoxy, rated importance of religion, and so on—researchers have consistently found positive correlations with ethnocentrism, authoritarianism, dogmatism, social distance, rigidity, intolerance of ambiguity, and specific forms of prejudice, especially against Jews and blacks.[163]

Batson et al.,[164] Dittes,[165] Gorsuch and Aleshire,[166] Meadow and Kahoe,[167] Myers,[168] Paloutzian,[169] and Spilka, Hood, and Gorsuch[170] have similarly concluded that as a broad generalization, the more religious an individual is, the more prejudiced that person is. However, most of these authors are quick to qualify this inference in terms of a possible curvilinear relationship, and also in terms of religious orientation (see below).

Research showing a religion–prejudice link has a long history, dating at least to the 1940s, when Adorno, Frenkel-Brunswik, Levinson, and Sanford's famous studies of the authoritarian personality disclosed a positive association between religion and prejudice.[171] Batson et al. reviewed much work on religion and prejudice, and found that for investigations published in 1960 or earlier, 19 of 23 findings confirmed the positive relationship between religion and prejudice; there was no clear relationship in 3 studies; and just 1 revealed a negative relationship.[172] It is unusual for so many efforts in the social sciences to converge on such a clear conclusion. However, the generalization that religion is positively correlated with prejudice is more complex than it might first appear.

Is the Religion–Prejudice Relationship Curvilinear?

There have been suggestions—for example, by Gorsuch[173] and Wulff[174]—that this relationship is actually curvilinear with respect to church attendance. It has been proposed that nonattenders are relatively unprejudiced, that infrequent to moderately frequent church attenders are the most prejudiced persons, and that "Active church members [are] among the least prejudiced in society."[175] This curvilinear relationship is sometimes idealistically portrayed as a smooth bell-shaped curve.[176] Although the curvilinear relationship has apparently been readily accepted in the relevant literature, there is in fact limited empirical evidence to support it; authors often do not acknowledge the many weaknesses and qualifications associated with the findings, and some researchers have reported data suggesting that the relationship is in fact a reasonably strong linear one.[177]

Figure 10.1 shows where there is general agreement and also some disagreement in the literature. If one includes a broadly representative sample of people, from the nonreligious through to the highly religious, there is little argument concerning the solid line in section B of the graph. That is, moderately religious people are more prejudiced than very weakly religious people. There also seems to be a consensus that *non*religious people are relatively nonprejudiced, though it is not entirely clear whether they are less prejudiced than very weakly religious persons (see section A of Figure 10.1). The greatest controversy, however, is apparent in regard to section C, where contradictory evidence and arguments suggest that the religion–prejudice line either continues to increase (I), levels off (II), drops modestly (III), or declines precipitously (IV). The last of these would be the preferred conclusion in terms of the curvilinear relationship.

Even those studies that seem to have found a curvilinear relationship do not always provide strong evidence of this effect. For example, the tendency for prejudice scores to drop off for the highly religious apparently occurs (when it does appear) for just a tiny portion of the (highly) religious population. In one such study, by Struening, a "drop" in prejudice scores was apparent only for people who attended church more than twice a week (just 2.4% of the sample).[178] Furthermore, as pointed out elsewhere by Hunsberger,[179] there exists little empirical evidence to support the conclusion that very frequent church attenders are any less prejudiced than *non*religious persons,[180] who have been found to be the *least* prejudiced persons by Adorno et al.[181] and by Altemeyer and Hunsberger.[182]

Some of the confusion concerning curvilinear findings may have resulted from the fact that some investigators did not always distinguish between weakly religious and nonreligious persons (e.g., they combined members who attended seldom or never with nonmembers); others did not include nonreligious persons at all, and therefore their research can shed no light on this aspect of the proposed curvilinear relationship (section A of Figure 10.1). Furthermore, there is no agreement in the literature on what constitutes "high," "moderate,"

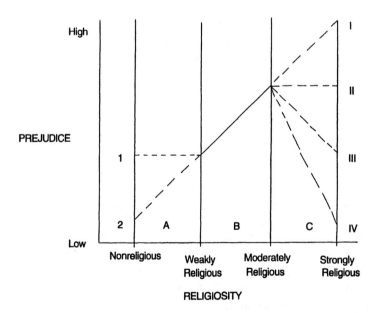

FIGURE 10.1. Possible relationships between religion and prejudice.

and "low" religiosity, and different studies may have used unique reference points in comparing these groups.

For example, the research of both Struening[183] and Friedrichs[184] has been cited as confirmation of the curvilinear effect.[185] As noted above, Struening reported that prejudice scores began to drop off for people who attended church more than twice a month (just 2.4% of the sample). Friedrichs found that those who attended three, four, or five times per month were in fact the *most* prejudiced people in his sample; prejudice scores began to decrease only for those who went to church more than once a week. So, based on frequency of church attendance, Struening's *least* prejudiced people would have been in Friedrich's *most* prejudiced group.

Finally, most authors have failed to mention the numerous qualifications accompanying their curvilinear findings. For example, Struening included five different measures of authoritarianism and prejudice, and only his prejudice measure showed a decrease for frequent church attenders; the other four instruments (authoritarianism, submission, suspicion, and nationalism) all showed increases in this group.[186]

Does Religious Orientation Make a Difference?

Of course, early research on religion did not often take religious *orientation* into account. Indeed, much of this initial work was conducted before the conceptualization and measurement of various religious orientations began in the mid-1960s and later. We might hope that such refinements in our thinking about religion would help to resolve the issue of a possible link between religion and prejudice.

Allport and Ross addressed this issue head-on when they published their famous article outlining the formulation of intrinsic and extrinsic religious orientations, as well as scales developed to measure the concepts, since this was done in the context of their study of prejudice.[187] Ultimately, Allport and Ross concluded that more intrinsic persons were, as expected, less prejudiced than those with an extrinsic religious orientation, who in turn were less prejudiced than those with an "indiscriminately pro" (IP) orientation (i.e., those who scored high on both the intrinsic and extrinsic dimensions). This finding that intrinsics are less prejudiced than extrinsics, who are less prejudiced than IPs, has become firmly embedded in the literature.[188] In fact, in light of these findings, the first edition of the present text concluded over a decade ago that "the problem of religion and prejudice seems to be essentially solved."[189]

However, as Kirkpatrick has eloquently pointed out,[190] there were many problems with the original intrinsic and extrinsic concepts and scales as developed by Allport and Ross. In Research Box 10.4, we describe the original study and its findings; in Research Box 10.5, we critically reevaluate this influential study and its conclusions. The problems in this investigation (and in some subsequent research) make us reluctant simply to accept the Allport and Ross conclusion at face value. Furthermore, Hunsberger has argued that "although the findings of some other studies have paralleled Allport and Ross' results . . . the [intrinsic–extrinsic] conceptualization has not lived up to expectations in identifying or reducing prejudice."[191] Similarly, Donahue's review and meta-analysis of the intrinsic–extrinsic literature led him to conclude that "[the Intrinsic scale] is uncorrelated, rather than negatively correlated, with prejudice across most available measures. [The Extrinsic scale] is positively correlated with prejudice, but not nearly so strongly as Allport's writings might have predicted."[192] The many problems with the Extrinsic scale make its apparent link with prejudice

Research Box 10.4. Personal Religious Orientation and Prejudice (Allport & Ross, 1967)

In light of previous research, which seemed to show a curvilinear relationship between church attendance and prejudice, Allport and Ross used Intrinsic and Extrinsic scales to assess whether people with an extrinsic religious orientation were more prejudiced than people with an intrinsic orientation. This, it was felt, would help to explain why some "religious people" are prejudiced while others are not, and it also fit neatly with Allport's earlier work,[a] in which he had distinguished between "immature" and "mature" religious orientations. It seemed to make sense that intrinsic persons, with a committed, interiorized faith, should live their religion and be less prejudiced, but that extrinsics, with a consensual, exteriorized, utilitarian religious orientation, should be more prejudiced.

Both direct and indirect questionnaire measures of prejudice were included; the former tapped prejudice against blacks, Jews, and other minorities, whereas the latter measured a lack of sympathy with mental patients and a generalized distrust of people. These instruments were administered to 309 Christian churchgoers from six faiths: 94 Roman Catholics from Massachusetts, 55 Lutherans from New York, 44 Nazarenes from South Carolina, 53 Presbyterians from Pennsylvania, 35 Methodists from Tennessee, and 28 Baptists from Massachusetts.

Allport and Ross initially conceptualized the intrinsic and extrinsic orientations as opposite ends of a single dimension, but found a positive correlation between various measures of prejudice and *both* the Extrinsic scale and a "total Extrinsic–Intrinsic scale" (p. 437), whereas they had expected to find a *negative* correlation between prejudice and intrinsic religiosity. In fact, they never reported the correlation between their prejudice measures and the Intrinsic scale alone.

After contemplating these initial results, which did not support their expectations, the authors decided that a "reformulation" was necessary. Instead of simply examining the correlations between intrinsic–extrinsic scores and prejudice, Allport and Ross decided that it might be better to categorize people according to four types determined by median splits on the Intrinsic and Extrinsic scales: consistently intrinsic, consistently extrinsic, "indiscriminately pro" (IP; i.e., high scores on both scales—also referred to as "religious muddle-headedness"), and "indiscriminately anti" (IA; i.e., low scores on both scales). Since they did not include any nonchurchgoers in their sample, they were not able to examine the IA category. Reanalyzing their data for the remaining three religious types (with each of the three types constituting very roughly one-third of the sample), they reported that the extrinsic type was more prejudiced on both direct and indirect measures of prejudice, and also that the IP persons were more prejudiced than either of the two consistent intrinsic and extrinsic types.

Allport and Ross concluded that prejudice is often part of the personality structure, and that this is intertwined with the individual's religious orientation:

> One definable style marks the individual who is bigoted in ethnic matters and extrinsic in his religious orientation. Equally apparent is the style of those who are bigoted and at the same time indiscriminately proreligious. A relatively small number of people show an equally consistent cognitive style in their simultaneous commitment to religion as a dominant, intrinsic value and to ethnic tolerance. (p. 442)

Thus, it seemed that the intrinsic–extrinsic distinction would be a valuable tool in clarifying the links between religion and prejudice. In order of decreasing prejudice came the IPs, then the extrinsics, and finally the intrinsics.

---

[a]Allport (1954, 1956).

difficult to interpret, and Hoge and Carroll even concluded that the only thing they could be sure of was that the extrinsic scale "is *not* tapping extrinsic religious motivation."[193]

Is Social Desirability a Confounding Variable?

There have been attempts to reinterpret the intrinsic–extrinsic findings regarding prejudice. For example, Batson et al. have argued that social desirability may be acting as an intervening variable, confusing the relationship between prejudice and intrinsic–extrinsic religiosity.[194] They have suggested that social desirability and intrinsic religious orientation are positively correlated, making it difficult to assess the real relationship between intrinsicness and prejudice. Intrinsic persons may *seem* to be less prejudiced because they are also concerned with "looking good," and therefore they may respond to questionnaire items on prejudice in a biased manner, making themselves look less prejudiced than they actually are. Batson et al. have suggested that if we could just control for these "social desirability" effects among intrinsics, the negative correlation between intrinsicness and prejudice that sometimes appears may disappear or even be reversed. In fact, Batson and his colleagues carried out two studies that seem to support this interpretation.

Batson, Flink, Schoenrade, Fultz, and Pych[195] and Batson, Naifeh, and Pate[196] both reported that Intrinsic scores were negatively correlated with overt prejudice, but this relationship was not apparent when the effects of social desirability were controlled for in the first study, nor when a covert behavioral measure of prejudice was used in the second study. Extrinsic scores were unrelated to all measures of prejudice. These findings differ from previous research in important ways. As Donahue has pointed out,[197] previous research has typically revealed little or no relationship between Intrinsic and prejudice scores, but does show a weak positive correlation between Extrinsic scores and prejudice. The two Batson studies apparently reveal very different trends—positive associations between Intrinsic and prejudice scores, but no relationship for Extrinsic scores. Also, Batson et al. reported a link in one study between Intrinsic scores and social desirability (.36),[198] whereas other authors, such as Hunsberger and Platonow[199] and Spilka, Kojetin, and McIntosh,[200] have been unable to find a significant relationship in this regard, and Morris, Hood, and Watson found that controlling for social desirability did not change prejudice–religion relationships.[201] Furthermore, it has been argued by Watson and colleagues[202] that weak positive correlations between the intrinsic (or a similar religiousness) dimension and social desirability are unique to the Crowne–Marlowe Social Desirability scale,[203] the measure used by Batson et al.[204] That is, such correlations are not a result of social desirability, but appear because the Social Desirability scale "has a substantial number of items confounded by a religious relevance dimension."[205] More recently, Leak and Fish have challenged Watson et al.'s conclusions in this regard.[206] The reader can understand why these discrepancies make it difficult to come to firm conclusions regarding the role of social desirability in the relationship between intrinsic religiousness and prejudice.

In the end, the assertions of many articles and texts notwithstanding, we suggest that the relationship between prejudice and the intrinsic–extrinsic dichotomy is at best tenuous and difficult to interpret. At times it seems that the intrinsic–extrinsic distinction, which was intended to help us understand Allport's paradoxical assertion that religion both makes (extrinsic religious orientation) and unmakes (intrinsic religious orientation) prejudice, has instead led us into a psychometric and empirical morass of confusion. However, other approaches to religious orientation seem to offer more promise in explaining the religion–prejudice connection.

ॐ

Research Box 10.5. A Critical Reevaluation of
"Personal Religious Orientation and Prejudice" (Allport & Ross, 1967)

A close examination of the Allport and Ross study calls into question its basic conclusions. First, the switch from using one continuous intrinsic–extrinsic scale to examining discrete orientation categories involved some "data analysis gymnastics," resulting in the final "intrinsic < extrinsic < IP" conclusion, which served as the basis for further research and conclusions that appeared regularly in the literature. This is not a minor point; as Donahue has observed,[a] few studies in the literature have actually used the four-way categorization recommended by Allport and Ross. Rather, most studies have simply reported correlations between each of the Intrinsic and Extrinsic scales and other measures—precisely what the original authors decided they should *not* do. In fact, later authors have incorrectly concluded that Allport and Ross reported a positive correlation between intrinsic scores and either humanitarian attitudes[b] or lower prejudice.[c] But all of this aside, if we ignore the reformulations and reanalyses that were necessary to reach the "extrinsics are more prejudiced than intrinsics" conclusion, and instead focus on the research itself, what do we find?

For one thing, although overall comparisons were significant, some considerable inconsistencies appear for the different religious subgroups. For example, just one of Allport and Ross's six religious denominational groups actually showed the intrinsic < extrinsic < IP pattern for the "anti-Negro prejudice" measure. In the other five groups, either the IPs' mean was lower than that for the extrinsics, or the extrinsics' mean was lower than that for the intrinsics.

Questions can also be raised concerning the prejudice measures used, especially their theoretical and psychometric strength, since such properties were typically not reported in this paper. One must wonder about potential biases, which might be stimulated by what Allport and Ross called an "indirect" measure of prejudice. It described the attempts of a black girl to rent a room in an all-white neighborhood, then asked "If you had been Mrs. Williamson, would you have rented to the Negro girl?" We suspect that a proreligious and possibly nondiscriminatory bias might have been aroused in participants by these sorts of measures, especially since apparently all of them knew that they were in this study because they attended a specific church.

We have previously noted the many problems with the Intrinsic scale and especially the Extrinsic scale. In fact, an entire subliterature has evolved, arguing the pros and cons of these two scales. At one extreme, Kirkpatrick and Hood have suggested, as one of several possibilities, that the scales might be abandoned because of their many problems.[d] Relevant to our concerns here, it is worth noting that the psychometric properties of these scales vary from study to study, and in the end are less than convincing. Cronbach's alpha (a measure of internal consistency) tends to be somewhat erratic, and Donahue has concluded that the Extrinsic scale especially suffers from low internal consistency and item–total correlations.[e] It is tempting to speculate that the problems with these scales contributed to Allport and Ross's decision not to report any psychometric information on the scales in their 1967 article. A number of authors have attempted to deal with the scales' problems by rewording, rewriting, reconceptualizing, or restructuring the scales. Most authors who use the Intrinsic and Extrinsic scales today rely on a Likert-type "agree–disagree" response format, although the original scale used different response formats

(*cont.*)

across items. In addition, attempts to consider subdimensions (personal vs. social well-being) of the extrinsic scale have offered some promise.[f]

It might be argued that, regardless of the problems with the scales and the original Allport and Ross report of a link between prejudice and intrinsic–extrinsic religiosity, so many subsequent studies have confirmed their initial conclusions that we should not over-concern ourselves with problems in the initial investigation. That is, the "weight of the evidence" clearly suggests that IP individuals are more prejudiced than are extrinsics, who in turn are more prejudiced than intrinsically oriented people, and that this in turn justifies the intrinsic–extrinsic conceptualization. But others are concerned about the scales' psychometric shortcomings, the lack of conceptual clarity, the inconsistency in Allport and Ross's results and some subsequent findings, and indeed the difficulty in making sense of these findings in light of the problems mentioned above.

---

[a]Donahue (1985a).
[b]Vergote (1993).
[c]Koenig (1992).
[d]Kirkpatrick and Hood (1990).
[e]Donahue (1985a).
[f]Kirkpatrick (1989); Gorsuch and McPherson (1989).

Proscribed versus Nonproscribed Prejudice

It seems logical that for religious people, the stand of their church on issues of prejudice would have some effect on their own attitudes and behavior. However, Batson et al. have noted that the existing research on religion and prejudice rarely considers the potential impact of the formal or informal stance of one's religious group on such issues.[207] If religious communities make serious attempts to eliminate prejudiced attitudes ("proscribed prejudice"), it is argued that highly religious (e.g., intrinsic) individuals will at least give the appearance that they are unprejudiced on overt measures of prejudice such as pencil-and-paper question-naires. They see themselves as religious persons, and their church teaches that a specific prejudice is wrong; therefore, they say that they do not hold that particular prejudice.

Batson et al. go on to suggest that there are situations in which a religious group may not attempt to negate prejudice, and in fact may even formally or informally support specific prejudice ("nonproscribed prejudice"). In such cases, the same religious (e.g., intrinsic) persons will be likely to admit to their prejudice because it is sanctioned by their church. That is, people who try to live their religion will openly include discriminatory attitudes as part of their approach to the world around them. Furthermore, Batson et al. argue that even if prejudice is condemned, religious persons will admit to their discriminatory attitudes if the measure of prejudice is "covert," as in the case of subtle behavioral measures.

Other researchers, such as Griffin, Gorsuch, and Davis[208] and McFarland,[209] have made similar suggestions, though Batson et al. have most clearly articulated the potentially impor-tant distinction between proscribed and nonproscribed prejudice. But how do we decide which prejudices are proscribed and which are not? We might argue that all prejudice is pro-scribed by Christian and some non-Christian religions, which teach that people should be sensitive, caring, and helpful to *all* other people. Of course, specific religious individuals and groups have used religious teachings as justification for many discriminatory attitudes and behaviors. Even within Christianity, interpretations of Biblical passages vary from denomination to denomination, from church to church, and even from individual to individual within a given church. It is not always easy to ascertain whether specific prejudice is proscribed or not, partly because of such variations.

Batson et al. have argued that some prejudice (e.g., racial) is now proscribed by mainline North American Christian churches, but that prejudice against homosexuals and Communists is not. Certainly, the link between religion and negative attitudes toward homosexuality is well established (see Chapter 4).[210] Unfortunately, studies on religion and homosexuality have not attempted to assess the proscribed–nonproscribed distinction. Research is needed to test these proposals—research that attempts to obtain clear estimates of the extent to which different prejudices are proscribed, possibly by analyzing the publications of specific religious groups, public statements by clergy, or even transcripts of sermons or religious services. It is conceivable that some of the previous findings that seemed contradictory could be "explained" by the proscribed versus nonproscribed distinction if we could accurately estimate the extent to which faiths denounce specific prejudices.

Religious Fundamentalism and Quest

Recent evidence suggests that there may be other ways of assessing religious orientation that are more productive in explaining religion's link with prejudice than the traditional intrinsic–extrinsic distinction is. Of particular interest are two concepts: religious fundamentalism and quest. Both of these approaches to religious orientation avoid focusing on the content of beliefs; rather, they emphasize the ways in which beliefs are held, as well as the openness of people to changes in their beliefs.

Defining Fundamentalism. Early in this century, William James anticipated the importance of going beyond the content or orthodoxy of a person's beliefs.[211] He argued that a rigid, dogmatic style of religious belief may be associated with bigotry and prejudice. In fact, over the years, some investigators have used the term "religious fundamentalism" to capture this rigid, dogmatic way of being religious. In this context, some researchers reported a positive relationship between fundamentalism and prejudice. However, definition of the term "fundamentalism" was quite variable, and often did not correspond to religious use of the word. In fact, early researchers often used the term interchangeably with "orthodoxy of belief," "intense interest in religion," or "considerable religious involvement."

More recently, Altemeyer and Hunsberger have offered a definition of religious fundamentalism that is theoretically distinct from these other aspects of religion:

> the belief that there is one set of religious teachings that clearly contains the fundamental, basic, intrinsic, essential, inerrant truth about humanity and deity; that this essential truth is fundamentally opposed by forces of evil which must be vigorously fought; that this truth must be followed today according to the fundamental, unchangeable practices of the past; and that those who believe and follow these fundamental teachings have a special relationship with the deity.[212]

This definition, which is consistent with other recent theoretical work on fundamentalism by Kirkpatrick and colleagues,[213] is potentially applicable to most major world religions, unlike much previous work on fundamentalism. Also, the reader will recognize that we might expect this conceptualization to be negatively related to Batson's quest orientation, which involves a questioning approach to religion, openness and flexibility, and a resistance to clear-cut, pat answers.[214]

Fundamentalism and Quest Scales. Furthermore, scales with good psychometric properties have been generated to measure both of these religious orientations. Altemeyer and Hunsberger (see Research Box 10.6, below) developed a 20-item Religious Fundamentalism scale, balanced against response sets, which generated Cronbach's alphas of .91 to .95 in different studies; they also developed a 16-item balanced Quest scale, which had an alpha of .88.[215] Batson and Schoenrade's revised 12-item Quest scale generated alphas of .81 and .75 in two samples.[216] We must be careful in comparing the two Quest scales, however, since they have little item overlap, and it is not clear to what extent they might tap different conceptualizations of quest.

Relationships with Prejudice. All three of these scales have been found to correlate significantly with measures of prejudice. Batson et al.[217] cited five studies (by Batson et al.,[218] McFarland,[219] and Snook & Gorsuch[220]) that revealed significant negative relationships between Quest scores and prejudice. Two other studies (by Griffin et al.,[221] and Ponton & Gorsuch[222]) did not replicate this negative association. However, all of these studies apparently used the earlier, psychometrically weaker version of Batson's Quest scale.[223]

Altemeyer and Hunsberger reported that their Religious Fundamentalism and Quest scales were strongly negatively correlated (e.g., $r = -.79$ in an adult sample), as expected.[224] They also found that fundamentalism scores were significantly and positively correlated with four measures of prejudice and authoritarian aggression (r's ranged from .23 to .41), and that Quest scores were significantly negatively associated with the same prejudice measures (r's ranged from $-.26$ to $-.39$). The positive relationship between fundamentalism and prejudice has apparently been replicated by Kirkpatrick[225] and McFarland[226] in studies involving somewhat different measures of fundamentalism that had a more Christian focus.

Can Prejudice be Reduced by Decreasing Fundamentalism? Recently, Billiet has argued that among a sample of Flemish Catholics, "sociocultural Christianity" tended to prevent fundamentalism, "a religious orientation that could encourage ethnocentrism."[227] He defines sociocultural Christianity as "the values of solidarity, charity, and social justice, which have been emphasized in the legitimations and the collective identity of the Catholic social organizations [in Belgium] since the late sixties."[228] Thus, Billiet argues that a pattern of specific faith values (sociocultural Christianity), when taught and emphasized by churches, can serve to ameliorate ethnocentrism by counteracting the development of religious fundamentalism. Billiet points out that Flemish "Catholic church leaders and prominent Catholics declared openly that they favored the integration of immigrants, and Catholic organizations promoted the idea."[229] This is certainly consistent with the suggestion that the proscribed–nonproscribed distinction is important in the study of religion and prejudice.

Summary. In the end, these relationships between fundamentalism and quest on the one hand and prejudice on the other emphasize the potential importance and utility of these two approaches to religious orientation in explaining the historical religion–prejudice relationship. However, we need to consider an additional concept, right-wing authoritarianism, in this regard.

The Link with Right-Wing Authoritarianism

Religion, Authoritarianism, and Prejudice.   Nearly 50 years ago, Adorno et al. noted that religiousness was related to authoritarianism, as measured by the California F scale.[230] For example, it was rare for religious people also to score low on authoritarianism. However, this early work on authoritarianism has received considerable criticism on methodological and conceptual grounds,[231] and Adorno et al. used rather unsophisticated operationalizations of religion (e.g., frequency of attendance, importance of religion).

Work by Altemeyer has confirmed that right-wing authoritarianism may help us to understand the relatively high levels of prejudice found among fundamentalist and non-questing religious persons.[232] Altemeyer has done a considerable amount of work on reconceptualizing authoritarianism. He focuses on three attitudinal clusters (authoritarian submission, authoritarian aggression, and conventionalism) instead of Adorno et al.'s proposed nine components of authoritarianism. As Duckitt has noted, Altemeyer's conceptualization of authoritarianism and his development of a reliable and valid Right-Wing Authoritarianism scale to measure this construct "finally seem to have made it possible for the study of authoritarianism to move beyond the unresolved methodological controversies and inconclusive findings that have thus far plagued it."[233]

Adding Fundamentalism and Quest to the Equation.   Altemeyer and Hunsberger conducted a study to assess the links among fundamentalism, quest, prejudice, and right-wing authoritarianism (see Research Box 10.6).[234] They found that people who scored high on the authoritarianism scale were commonly fundamentalist in religious orientation ($r = .68$), and prejudiced in a variety of ways (r's $= .33$ to $.64$). This is not to imply that all highly authoritarian individuals are religious fundamentalists, nor that fundamentalists are necessarily highly authoritarian. However, "off-quadrant" cases (i.e., those high in authoritarianism and low in fundmentalism, or vice versa) were quite rare, and Altemeyer has concluded that religion and authoritarianism do seem to "feed" each other.[235] That is, religious fundamentalism and authoritarianism both encourage obedience to authority, conventionalism, self-righteousness, and feelings of superiority.

Given these relationships, we might wonder whether fundamentalism or authoritarianism (or neither) is the more basic "causative agent" with respect to prejudice. This is not an easy matter to resolve, especially with the available correlational data, but the evidence leans toward authoritarianism as the more basic factor. For example, in Altemeyer and Hunsberger's central study of almost 500 adults, partialing out the effects of authoritarianism from the sizeable fundamentalism–prejudice relationship reduced these correlations to non-significant levels. But removing fundamentalism from the authoritarianism–prejudice associations only slightly reduced them. Although not definitive, this suggests that right-wing authoritarianism is the more basic contributor to prejudice. In other words, fundamentalism correlates with measures of prejudice because fundamentalists tend to be right-wing authoritarians. Thus, as Hunsberger has suggested elsewhere, "fundamentalism might be viewed as a religious manifestation of right-wing authoritarianism."[236] If this is true, one might expect people with right-wing authoritarian personalities to become religious fundamentalists, and religious fundamentalism would be expected to encourage and reinforce this (authoritarian) personality.

What about Non-Christian Religions?   Recently, Hunsberger assessed these relationships in small samples of people from non-Christian religions in Canada.[237] The psychometric

---

**Research Box 10.6. Authoritarianism, Religious Fundamentalism,
Quest, and Prejudice (Altemeyer & Hunsberger, 1992)**

"Are religious persons usually good persons?" Altemeyer and Hunsberger sought to answer this question within the context of their measures of religious fundamentalism, religious quest, prejudice, and right-wing authoritarianism. They proposed a definition of fundamentalism (see text) that allowed the development of a 20-item Religious Fundamentalism scale, including items such as "God has given mankind a complete, unfailing guide to happiness and salvation, which must be totally followed." They developed this measure, as well as a 16-item Quest scale, in several studies of university students in Manitoba and Ontario. Satisfied that their new measures were reliable and that they interrelated as expected among students, the authors then carried out an investigation of 491 Canadian parents of university students.

In addition to the Fundamentalism and Quest scales, these adults completed a 12-item Attitudes Toward Homosexuals scale (e.g., "In many ways, the AIDS disease currently killing homosexuals is just what they deserve"); a 20-item Prejudice scale (e.g., "It is a waste of time to train certain races for good jobs; they simply don't have the drive and determination it takes to learn a complicated skill"); the Right-Wing Authoritarianism scale; and two additional measures of prejudice—a Posse–Radicals survey (in which participants indicated the extent to which they would pursue radicals outlawed by the government), and a Trials measure (in which respondents "passed sentence" in three court cases involving a dope pusher, a pornographer, and someone who spit on a provincial premier). The resulting web of relatively strong and significant correlations led these authors to conclude the following about the answer to their initial question ("Are religious persons usually good persons?"):

> [It] appears to be "no," if one means by "religious" a fundamentalist, nonquesting religious orientation, and by "good" the kind of nonprejudiced, compassionate, accepting attitudes espoused in the Gospels and other writings. But the answer is "yes" if one means by "religious" the nonfundamentalist, questing orientation found most often in persons belonging to no religion. Which irony gives one pause. (pp. 125–126)

The authors have cautioned against overgeneralizing these findings, since there were inevitably exceptions to the rule—people who scored high on the fundamentalism scale and low on the Quest scale who showed nonprejudiced, accepting attitudes, or nonfundamentalist questers who were quite bigoted. But the correlations that emerged were quite strong and clear-cut. Apparently fundamentalists and nonquesters, as defined here, tend to be prejudiced in a variety of ways. The authors speculate that fundamentalist beliefs can be linked to some of the psychological sources of authoritarian aggression (e.g., fear of a dangerous world and self-righteousness), as well as the tendency for authoritarians to reduce guilt over their own misdeeds through their religion.

---

properties of the fundamentalism scale, as well as its relationship to prejudice and right-wing authoritarianism, remained relatively stable in his samples of adult Hindus, Muslims, and Jews (Cronbach's alpha for the fundamentalism scale ranged from .85 to .94; its correlations with attitudes toward homosexuals were .42 to .65; and fundamentalism–authoritarianism correlations ranged from .45 to .74). These results seem to confirm the links among fundamentalism, right-wing authoritarianism and prejudice across various religious groups. However, further research is needed to assess the relationships in larger samples, and also among non-Christian groups outside of North America.

Reactions and Extensions. The findings described above have not gone without comment in the psychology-of-religion literature. Gorsuch has questioned several aspects of the Altemeyer and Hunsberger study,[238] and the original authors have provided additional data and arguments to support their conclusions.[239]

Leak and Randall have suggested that authoritarianism's positive association with religion is limited to measures of "less mature faith development."[240] They found that such "less mature" measures of religion (e.g., measures of Christian Orthodoxy, Fowler's second and third stages of faith development [see Chapter 2], and church attendance) were positively related to authoritarianism scores, but "more mature" measures of religion (e.g., Batson's Quest scale, measures of Fowler's fourth and fifth faith stages, and a Global Faith Development scale) were negatively correlated with authoritarianism. The real issue here may be semantics. Just what *is* "mature faith?" Leak and Randall have chosen to regard a quest sort of orientation as "mature." Their Global Faith Development scale includes items such as "It is very important for me to critically examine my religious beliefs and values,"[241] and in this respect it bears some resemblance to quest scales. It is not surprising that such measures have a negative association with authoritarianism, as previously reported by Altemeyer and Hunsberger. However, it seems a moot point to define, for example, Global Faith Development and Batson's quest orientation as "mature" and religious orthodoxy and fundamentalism as "less mature." Orthodox religious persons and those with a fundamentalist orientation may feel that *their* religion is the mature one and that questing is immature. In the end, we would suggest that Leak and Randall's findings are consistent with earlier findings of fundamentalism–quest–prejudice–authoritarianism relationships.

Finally, it is worth noting that the relationships described here are not unique to the specific measures and North American samples reported above. Recent studies by Eisinga et al.[242] and Billiet[243] in Europe, using very different measures of religiousness, authoritarianism, and prejudice, have found links among these measures which are quite consistent with the findings reported above. Apparently the religion–prejudice–authoritarianism findings cut across differing measures and cultural contexts, at least within Christianity.

Summary

Clearly, the religion–prejudice link is more complicated than the initial suggestion of a linear relationship between church attendance and prejudiced attitudes. However, unlike some other reviewers of the religion–prejudice literature, we have concluded that the intrinsic–extrinsic dichotomy has not been especially helpful in understanding the relationship between religion and prejudice. Furthermore, we now know that it was premature to conclude that Gorsuch and Aleshire's 1974 review of the prejudice–religion literature[244] "marked the end of an era," since "by the early 1970s, mainstream American culture no longer countenanced blatant prejudice. The casual church attender thus stopped admitting to bigoted outlooks, and results became nonreplicable."[245] Developments in the 1990s have shown that we have much to learn about this area. A religious fundamentalist and nonquesting orientation is apparently linked to prejudice and discrimination; there is also some evidence that it is not religious fundamentalism per se that causes prejudice, but rather the tendency for fundamentalists also to be right-wing authoritarians.

In keeping with one of our basic themes, this may be an example of how the meaning, control, and self-esteem that religion offers to people can lead to negative outcomes. In some circumstances, control can contribute to authoritarian submission and aggression, as manifested in prejudice. And meaning and self-esteem can be carried too far, possibly contributing to self-righteousness. However, such unpleasant associations with religion seem to have more to do with the style of holding religious beliefs than with the beliefs themselves.

It is disconcerting to some that those who make the strongest claims to being "true believers" of religious traditions, and who reportedly follow religious teachings most scrupulously, are also those who tend to be the most intolerant of others. That is, prejudice seems relatively unrelated to the content of people's beliefs, but it is associated with the ways in which people hold their religious beliefs, possibly through the influence of right-wing authoritarianism. These conclusions need further investigation, but findings from the past decade suggest considerable promise for this approach to the religion–prejudice relationship.

OVERVIEW

We have taken something of a roller-coaster ride in this chapter. Religion does indeed seem to be related to some aspects of moral attitudes and behaviors. We have seen that in the areas of substance use/abuse, nonmarital sexual behavior, and (to a lesser extent) crime and delinquency, more religious persons generally report that they have stricter moral attitudes and are less likely to engage in behaviors that contravene societal and especially religious norms. However, faith is surprisingly unrelated to some other behaviors, such as cheating/dishonesty and helping behavior. There are indications that religious people *say* they are more honest and helpful, but the data do not bear this out for actual behavior in a secular setting. Within a religious context, the more faithful do indeed help more by giving money, time, and talent to religiously based causes. However, outside such a context, it becomes very difficult to distinguish helpers from nonhelpers on the basis of their religion. Batson and his coresearchers have tried to build a case for the argument that intrinsic religiousness is only related to the *appearance* of helpfulness, not to actual behavior; however, some studies fail to find any association between intrinsicness and self-reported helping. Also, the quest orientation is positively associated with behavioral measures of giving assistance to others. Furthermore, when people do help others, there is some evidence that intrinsic persons may offer a kind of preprogrammed, self-serving aid, whereas individuals scoring high on quest offer a more flexible and victim-focused assistance. Still, there are arguments against this interpretation.

These findings deserve a moment of reflection. Religious persons may derive some consolation from studies showing that personal faith is negatively associated with substance use/abuse, nonmarital sexual behavior, and some criminal and delinquent acts. However, these associations tend to be relatively weak when found. We might wonder why the correlations are not much larger, given the strength and consistency of religious teachings on these moral issues. In addition, there is the failure of religion to relate consistently to honesty versus cheating and to helping behavior. And the tendency for questers to be more apt to help is even more perplexing, in the sense that the quest orientation bears little similarity to what most people think of as religion in a traditional sense. Moreover, high questers tend to score low on measures of religious orthodoxy.[246]

Even more troubling than this, however, is what we find in the area of prejudice. Here, we go beyond the mere absence of a relationship to discover that in some ways, religion is *positively* related to prejudice. This association has been researched and debated over the years, but in the end it seems that it is not religion per se that is linked to prejudice, but rather the ways in which one holds one's faith. Thus, religious fundamentalism is positively, and quest negatively, associated with various measures of prejudice.

One drawback to most of the research discussed in this chapter is that it relies very heavily on self-reports of moral attitudes and behaviors. We have already warned that such self-reports may be inaccurate and unreliable. However, in most cases it is very difficult to measure actual moral behavior, and few studies have attempted to do so, especially in highly sensitive domains such as prejudice. In consequence, we must rely on self-reports as "the next best thing," which in many cases probably gives us a reasonable impression of people's attitudes and behaviors. However, we must recognize the weakness inherent in this approach, and strive wherever possible to supplement these measures with convergent reports (e.g., from parents, friends, teachers) and especially with actual behavioral measures.

In the end, we are left to puzzle over many things. Why do the obtained relationships vary so much for different moral behaviors? Why doesn't religion have a stronger impact in *all* of these areas? How do we explain the "no relationship" findings? Why do some highly religious persons show considerable intolerance of others? We would suggest that styles of being religious (i.e., fundamentalism and quest) must be taken more seriously in research on religion and morality. We must also consider the potential impact of an associated personality variable, right-wing authoritarianism, especially with respect to the religion–prejudice link.

NOTES

1. Allport (1954, p. 444).
2. Whitehead (1926, p. 37).
3. Ritzema (1979, p. 105).
4. Schmidt (1995, p. 111).
5. Excerpt from a fund-raising letter distributed in March 1995 by the Christian Coalition, as quoted in Birnbaum (1995, p. 22).
6. Spilka, Hood, and Gorsuch (1985).
7. Birnbaum (1995, p. 22).
8. See, e.g., Darley and Shultz (1990).
9. Bryan and Freed (1993).
10. Hayes and Hornsby-Smith (1994).
11. Lottes, Weinberg, and Weller (1993).
12. Bibby (1987).
13. Krishnan (1993).
14. Marsiglio (1993).
15. Wilcox and Jelen (1991).
16. Alexander and Judd (1986).
17. Domino and Miller (1992).
18. Shuman, Fournet, Zelhart, Roland, and Estes (1992).
19. Seals, Ekwo, Williamson, and Hanson (1985).
20. Herold, Corbesi, and Collins (1994).
21. Hayes and Hornsby-Smith (1994).
22. Bibby (1987).
23. Larsen and Long (1988).
24. Bibby (1987).
25. Altemeyer and Hunsberger (1992).
26. Fisher, Cook, and Shirkey (1994).

27. Scott (1989).
28. Hartshorne and May (1928, 1929); Hartshorne, May, and Shuttleworth (1930).
29. Hightower (1930).
30. Goldsen, Rosenberg, Williams, and Suchman (1960).
31. Spilka and Loffredo (1982).
32. Chadwick and Top (1993).
33. Guttman (1984).
34. Smith, Wheeler, and Diener (1975).
35. Grasmick, Bursik, and Cochran (1991); Grasmick, Kinsey, and Cochran (1991).
36. ter Voert, Felling, and Peters (1994).
37. Gorsuch and Butler (1976).
38. Benson (1992b); Gorsuch (1995).
39. Khavari and Harmon (1982).
40. Khavari and Harmon (1982).
41. Benson, Wood, Johnson, Eklin, and Mills (1983).
42. Perkins (1994).
43. Benson (1992b).
44. Donahue (1987).
45. Cochran, Beeghley, and Bock (1988).
46. Benson and Donahue (1989).
47. Benson (1992b).
48. Donahue (1987).
49. Adlaf and Smart (1985); Hundleby (1987).
50. Adelekan, Abiodun, Imouokhome-Obayan, Oni, and Ogunremi (1993).
51. Francis and Mullen (1993).
52. Pettersson (1991).
53. Kandel and Sudit (1982).
54. Demerdash, Mizaal, el Farouki, and El Mossalem (1981).
55. Engs (1982); Najman, Williams, Keeping, Morrison, and Anderson (1988).
56. Rochford, Purvis, and NeMar (1989).
57. Richardson (1995).
58. Galanter and Buckley (1978).
59. Latkin (1995, p. 179).
60. See, e.g., Cochran (1992).
61. Benson (1992b, p. 216).
62. See, e.g., Cochran et al. (1988); Cochran, Beeghley, and Bock (1992).
63. See, e.g., Hadaway, Elifson, and Petersen (1984).
64. Benson (1992b, p. 218).
65. Cochran (1993).
66. Beeghley, Bock, and Cochran (1990).
67. Batson, Schoenrade, and Ventis (1993).
68. Gorsuch (1995).
69. Benson (1992b).
70. Some authors have argued that AA's success, especially as portrayed in the mass media, is overrated. See, e.g., Bufe (1991).
71. Maxwell (1984); Morreim (1991).
72. Batson et al. (1993).
73. Forliti and Benson (1986).
74. Makela (1975).
75. Spencer and Agahi (1982).
76. Marin (1976).
77. Isralowitz and Ong (1990).
78. Oshodin (1983).
79. Natera et al. (1983).
80. Clark (1969).
81. Siegel (1977).
82. Westermeyer and Walzer (1975).
83. See, e.g., Gorsuch (1995); Petraitis, Flay, and Miller (1995).

84. Shea (1992, p. 70).
85. See, e.g., Patton (1988).
86. Cochran and Beeghley (1991, p. 46).
87. Newman and Newman (1995, p. 439).
88. Thornton and Camburn (1989).
89. Cochran and Beeghley (1991).
90. Cochran and Beeghley (1991, p. 46).
91. Haerich (1992).
92. Woodroof (1985).
93. Reynolds (1994).
94. Hammond, Cole, and Beck (1993).
95. Walinsky (1995).
96. Durkheim (1915).
97. Jensen and Erickson (1979).
98. Hirschi and Stark (1969).
99. See, e.g., Burkett and White (1974).
100. See, e.g., Elifson, Petersen, and Hadaway (1983); Peek, Curry, and Chalfant (1985).
101. Jensen and Erickson (1979).
102. Chadwick and Top (1993).
103. Bainbridge (1989).
104. Pettersson (1991).
105. Shaffer et al. (1987).
106. Cochran, Wood, and Arneklev (1994).
107. Hirschi and Stark (1969).
108. Bainbridge (1992).
109. Stark (1984).
110. Capps (1992).
111. Greven (1991).
112. Bottoms, Shaver, Goodman, and Qin (1995).
113. Neufeld (1979).
114. Steele and Pollock (1968).
115. Hull and Burke (1991).
116. Elliott (1994).
117. Clarke (1986); Pagelow and Johnson (1988).
118. Ozorak (1996).
119. Alsdurf and Alsdurf (1988).
120. Makepeace (1987).
121. Brinkerhoff, Grandin, and Lupri (1992).
122. Brinkerhoff et al. (1992, p. 28).
123. We must consider the possibility that this male–female difference could represent a self-serving bias on the part of the men.
124. Ellison (1991a).
125. Benson, Donahue, and Erickson (1989).
126. Burkett and Warren (1987); Cochran et al. (1994); Elifson et al. (1983); Welch, Tittle, and Petee (1991).
127. Benson et al. (1989, p. 172).
128. Chadwick and Top (1993).
129. Peek et al. (1985).
130. Coward (1986).
131. Oliner and Oliner (1988).
132. Batson (1991).
133. See, e.g., Langford and Langford (1974); Nelson and Dynes (1976); Rokeach (1969).
134. See, e.g., Friedrichs (1960); Cline and Richards (1965).
135. Nelson and Dynes (1976).
136. Hunsberger and Platonow (1986).
137. Batson et al. (1993).
138. Forbes, TeVault, and Gromoll (1971).
139. Smith et al. (1975).
140. Annis (1975, 1976).

141. McKenna (1976).
142. Yinon and Sharon (1985).
143. Batson et al. (1993, p. 342).
144. Batson (1976, 1990); Batson, Schoenrade, and Pych (1985); Batson et al. (1993).
145. Bernt (1989); Chau, Johnson, Bowers, Darvill, and Danko (1990); Johnson et al. (1989); Tate and Miller (1971); Watson, Hood, Morris, and Hall (1984); Watson, Hood, and Morris (1985).
146. Batson et al. (1993).
147. Benson et al. (1980).
148. Hunsberger and Platonow (1986).
149. Darley and Batson (1973).
150. Gorsuch (1988); Watson et al. (1985).
151. Batson and Gray (1981).
152. Batson et al. (1989).
153. Batson and Flory (1990).
154. Batson et al. (1989).
155. See, e.g., Gorsuch (1988); Watson et al. (1984).
156. Ritzema (1979).
157. Glock and Stark (1966).
158. Eisinga, Konig, and Scheepers (1995).
159. Allport (1954, p. 444).
160. Gorsuch and Aleshire (1974).
161. Batson et al. (1993).
162. Spilka, Hood, and Gorsuch (1985).
163. Wulff (1991, pp. 219–220).
164. Batson et al. (1993).
165. Dittes (1969).
166. Gorsuch and Aleshire (1974).
167. Meadow and Kahoe (1984).
168. Myers (1987).
169. Paloutzian (1996).
170. Spilka, Hood, and Gorsuch (1985).
171. Adorno, Frenkel-Brunswik, Levinson, and Sanford (1950).
172. Batson et al. (1993).
173. Gorsuch (1993); Gorsuch and Aleshire (1974).
174. Wulff (1991).
175. Gorsuch (1988, p. 212).
176. Spilka, Hood, and Gorsuch (1985, p. 271).
177. Altemeyer and Hunsberger (1993).
178. Struening (1963).
179. Hunsberger (1995).
180. See, e.g., Eisinga, Felling, and Peters (1990).
181. Adorno et al. (1950).
182. Altemeyer and Hunsberger (1992).
183. Struening (1963).
184. Friedrichs (1959).
185. Wulff (1991).
186. Struening (1963).
187. Allport and Ross (1967).
188. See, e.g., Gorsuch (1988).
189. Spilka, Hood, and Gorsuch (1985, p. 273).
190. Kirkpatrick (1989); Kirkpatrick and Hood (1990).
191. Hunsberger (1995, p. 117).
192. Donahue (1985b, p. 405).
193. Hoge and Carroll (1973, p. 189). Emphasis added.
194. Batson et al. (1993).
195. Batson, Flink, Schoenrade, Fultz, and Pych (1986).
196. Batson, Naifeh, and Pate (1978).
197. Donahue (1985b).

198. Batson et al. (1978).
199. Hunsberger and Platonow (1986).
200. Spilka, Kojetin, and McIntosh (1985).
201. Morris, Hood, and Watson (1989).
202. Watson, Morris, Foster, and Hood (1986).
203. Crowne and Marlowe (1964).
204. Batson et al. (1978).
205. Watson et al. (1986, p. 230).
206. Leak and Fish (1989).
207. Batson et al. (1993).
208. Griffin, Gorsuch, and Davis (1987).
209. McFarland (1989).
210. See, e.g., Gentry (1987); Herek (1988); Kunkel and Temple (1992); Marsiglio (1993); VanderStoep and Green (1988).
211. James (1902/1985).
212. Altemeyer and Hunsberger (1992, p. 118).
213. Kirkpatrick, Hood, and Hartz (1991).
214. Batson et al. (1993).
215. Altemeyer and Hunsberger (1992).
216. Batson and Schoenrade (1991a, 1991b).
217. Batson et al. (1993).
218. Batson et al. (1978, 1986).
219. McFarland (1989, 1990).
220. Snook and Gorsuch (1985).
221. Griffin et al. (1987).
222. Ponton and Gorsuch (1988).
223. Batson and Ventis (1982).
224. Altemeyer and Hunsberger (1992).
225. Kirkpatrick (1993).
226. McFarland (1989).
227. Billiet (1995, p. 231).
228. Billiet (1995, p. 231).
229. Billiet (1995, p. 232).
230. Adorno et al. (1950).
231. Altemeyer (1981).
232. Altemeyer (1981, 1988).
233. Duckitt (1992, p. 209).
234. Altemeyer and Hunsberger (1992).
235. Altemeyer (1988).
236. Hunsberger (1995, p. 121).
237. Hunsberger (1996).
238. Gorsuch (1993).
239. Altemeyer and Hunsberger (1993).
240. Leak and Randall (1995).
241. Leak and Randall (1995, p. 248).
242. Eisinga et al. (1995).
243. Billiet (1995).
244. Gorsuch and Aleshire (1974).
245. Spilka, Hood, and Gorsuch (1985, p. 274).
246. Altemeyer and Hunsberger (1992); Batson et al. (1993).

Chapter 11

RELIGION, COPING, AND ADJUSTMENT

> They never sought in vain that sought the Lord aright![1]
>
> God loves to help him who strives to help himself.[2]
>
> A mighty fortress is our God,
>   A bulwark never failing;
> Our helper He amid the flood
>   Of mortal ills prevailing.[3]
>
> A little girl repeating the Twenty-Third Psalm said it this way: "The Lord is my shepherd, that's all I want."[4]
>
> Father expected a great deal of God. He didn't actually accuse God of inefficiency, but when he prayed his tone was loud and angry like that of a dissatisfied guest in a carelessly managed hotel.[5]
>
> The prayer does not change God, but it changes the one who offers it.[6]

In North American society, people are usually judged on their ability to cope with what is demanded of them. Life endlessly presents problems, and individuals often turn to their faith for help with these difficulties. As we will see, religion may be an especially important resource people have to deal with those "times that try men's souls"—when crisis strikes and options are limited.

THEORETICAL APPROACHES TO COPING AND RELIGION

The Process of Coping

In recent years, much effort has been directed toward understanding how people handle life's problems. Some researchers have emphasized coping styles or traits—relatively long-lasting, if not permanent, characteristics of individuals. Others have looked to the process of coping and to change in the way difficulties are handled.[7] Though it may be argued that personal religiosity is treated as if it were an attribute of personality, those who have examined the role of religion in coping are mostly concerned with it as a process variable, asking what it does for the person and how it operates when problems arise.

377

The foremost scholar in research on the role of faith in relation to coping behavior is Kenneth Pargament of Bowling Green State University. For a number of years, he has been meticulously defining and assessing the contributions of religion to the various facets of the coping process. He and colleagues have asserted:

> People do not face stressful situations without resources. They rely on a system of beliefs, practices, and relationships which affects how they deal with difficult situations. In the coping process, this orienting system is translated into concrete situation-specific appraisals, activities, and goals. Religion is part of this general orienting system. A person with a strong religious faith who suffers a disabling injury, must find a way to move from the generalities of belief to the specifics of dealing with the injury.[8]

Building upon the work of Lazarus and Folkman, Pargament first looks at the initial step in the coping process—namely, "appraisal."[9] When an event takes place, the person implicitly asks, "What does this mean to me?" In other words, is it irrelevant, positive, or negative? If the answer is that it is negative and stressful, the next question becomes "What can I do about it?" This brings to the fore additional judgments of "harm/loss," "threat," or "challenge." In the case of harm/loss, the individual has already suffered some adverse effects, such as illness or injury. Threat focuses on anticipated difficulties, whereas in challenge the person sees the likelihood of future growth and development. This form of appraisal has also been termed "primary appraisal." Pargament notes the differential role of religion in such appraisal, as a person can view what is happening as an intentional action of God to teach a lesson, or possibly to reward or punish via everyday success or failures.

Dealing with the problem is the second step in the coping process, and this has been labeled "secondary appraisal." A religious person may do a number of things, one of which is praying—a behavior that Holahan and Moos view as an active, cognitive coping strategy.[10] The praying person is doing something, making an appeal to the highest power possible for help in overcoming misfortune and suffering. This may be constructive, as in spurring the person to adopt new means to solve a problem. Prayer, however, may also be dysfunctional if it causes the person to avoid actively seeking to resolve the predicament.

When people attempt to handle various difficulties, they often find that they are confronted with two issues: the problem itself, and the emotions that have been aroused by the threat it poses for them. Chances are that both will be dealt with; however, more attention is commonly directed toward one of these concerns than toward the other, suggesting that the individual's style of coping may be primarily "problem-focused" or "emotion-focused."[11] A person may deal with a problem by using either "approach" or "avoidance" strategies, and the latter can be indicative of poor adjustment to the situation. Though emotion-focused coping may be beneficial and deal with anxiety constructively, the general tendency has often been to look at this concern as largely avoiding the problem.[12] We sometimes see this when life is especially difficult, as among the elderly who are ill.[13] Whether or not religion is distracting under such circumstances, it does seem to stress the reduction of unpleasant emotions first.

Religious activities, especially prayer, are usually regarded as positive coping devices directed toward both the problem and personal growth.[14] This is a controversial position, as some psychologists see religion as simply a means of controlling emotions.[15] Others see it as an effective mechanism of problem-focused coping, in that a person's faith may be the only practical way of dealing with many tragedies, such as the death of a loved one.[16] Apparently, it can perform functions of both problem- and emotion-focused coping.[17]

Evidence suggests that people are likely to use problem-focused cognitions and behaviors when the situation is considered changeable. If circumstances cannot be modified, the tendency is to resort to emotion-focused coping. Those who turn to prayer and religious methods apparently consider the problems toward which these means are directed as changeable. At the same time, particularly among younger people, religion may counter undesirable emotions (disgust and anger) while enhancing pleasure and happiness.[18] In other words, turning to faith in times of difficulty is helpful and constructive in dealing with both problems and emotions.

Religion and Human Survival

The role that religion may play in helping people understand and effectively handle their worlds has been put into a broader context by the sociobiologists. They maintain that religion probably has a biological basis—something we have discussed in Chapter 1. In terms of human evolution, it is claimed that this natural foundation has always been socially expressed. In the long run, such behaviors are said to have aided humanity in its struggle for survival.

The founder of sociobiology, E. O. Wilson, asserts that "if the brain evolved by natural selection . . . religious beliefs must have arisen by the same mechanistic process."[19] He further suggests that "beliefs are really enabling mechanisms for survival."[20] The hypothesized "enabling mechanism" for religion is altruism. Wilson suggests that religion motivates people "to subordinate their immediate self-interest to the interests of the group."[21] Batson supports this thesis by affirming the "possibility of an innate kin-specific altruistic impulse."[22] He also recognizes the potential universalizing of reciprocal altruism through such religious imagery as "we are all the children of God," "the family of God," and so forth. At the same time, Batson calls attention to the fact that many religious groups and people regard themselves as specially favored by the deity, while others are defined as pagans or heathens who should be rejected (if not punished or even killed) for their different views. The troubled history of Christian–Jewish–Muslim relations amply testifies to such behavior.

Though religion is paradoxical in both bringing people together and separating them, sociobiologists emphasize the former behavior, which benefits groups and individuals; hence they infer a biological substrate for both altruism and religion. The work of Waller and colleagues claims such a basis for religion, and similar research indicates that empathy and altruism may also have genetic roots.[23] In like manner, Alister Hardy ties religion to biology and organic evolution, along with a wide variety of behaviors such as submission and altruism.[24] D'Aquili goes a step further and postulates a neurobiological basis for God in actual structures in the nervous system, which he terms "neural operators."[25]

In all of these efforts to anchor religion in biology, the assertion is made that faith is a species-wide coping mechanism that has aided humans to cope successfully with life, and has enhanced their chances for physical survival.

The Coping Functions of Religion

In Chapter 1, the motivational foundations of attribution theory have been given as the needs for meaning, control, and self-esteem. In our view, stress, whether it involves loss, threat, or challenge, reflects a situation in which meaning, control, and self-esteem are in jeopardy. A person has difficulty making sense out of a situation, or is unable to master it, or evaluates the self negatively in relation to the existing circumstances. Religion is one way these needs are met, and the worldwide prevalence of religion testifies in part to the success of faith in attaining these goals.

The Need for Meaning

The search for meaning has been called "the ultimate problem of motivational psychology."[26] This insight is by no means a modern discovery; over 2,000 years ago, Aristotle observed that "all men by nature desire to know."[27] In 1788, the Scottish philosopher Thomas Reid regarded the "desire of knowledge" to be a fundamental "animal principle of action," and hence innate and inherent in human biological nature.[28] Philosophers and psychologists from ancient to modern times have thus, in one form or another, claimed that people possess a primary need to understand what they experience.

In this search for meaning, religion occupies a central place. Michael Argyle maintains that "a major mechanism behind religious beliefs is a purely cognitive desire to understand."[29] Clark's key observation, cited in Chapter 1, bears repeating here: "religion more than any other human function satisfies the need for meaning in life."[30] Baumeister simply and directly tells us that religious meanings help people cope with life's problems.[31] Like Lazarus and Folkman, he views meaningful explanations as helping to solve problems and regulate emotions. Though Baumeister feels that religion is currently less significant than science in realizing this role, he perceives faith as much more important than science when it comes to "regulating one's emotional states, as in coping with misfortune."[32] Finally, Fichter asserts that "religious reality is the only way to make sense out of pain and suffering."[33] That this struggle to understand tragedy may last for a long time is evidenced by one extensive 7-year study.[34] Interviews of flood disaster survivors over this period led the researcher to conclude that "they became theologians by asking how God could have allowed such tragedies to occur to them and their loved ones. They became philosophers by asking the meaning of life when they knew how frail and ephemeral life could be. . . ."[35] Clearly, the need for meaning may never be satisfactorily resolved. In this work, questions still remained unanswered.

Without understanding, without knowledge, without some idea of what is happening—in other words, without meaning—a person is severely handicapped in coping with many of life's problems. Ambiguity, doubt, and uncertainty are the enemies of action. Simply put, being able to comprehend one's world, to make it meaningful, probably constitutes the core of successful coping and adjustment. For many people religion performs this role very well, especially in times of personal crisis.

The Need for Control

Philosophers, theologians, and psychologists have often considered the desire for mastery, power, or control a basic human need, like the search for meaning. From Hesiod and Homer through Aristotle and other Greek thinkers, the notion of active and passive powers and energies was invariably present in their writings.[36] The British philosophers, particularly Hobbes, Locke, and Hume, saw power as inherent in human life.[37] Thomas Reid considered "the desire of power" another of his "animal principles of action."[38] In speaking of Nietzsche's "will to power," Berndtson claims that "the aim of evolving life is not to secure self-preservation through relatively passive adjustment to the environment, but to secure increased power involving mastery and transformation of the environment."[39] In essence, this is the basic view of contemporary psychologists, who see a central role for mastery and control in human motivation.[40] As we will see, religion is considered a source of empowerment for most people.

Faith often conveys the meaning that life's difficulties can be overcome. Whether or not a person can control objective conditions may be of less importance than the belief that even insurmountable obstacles can be mastered. In much of life, the sense of control is really an illusion; yet it is one that can be a powerful force supporting constructive coping behavior. Lefcourt suggests that it "may be the bedrock on which life flourishes."[41]

Locus of Control. Generally, the feeling that a person is in control of his or her own life is associated with successful adjustment, whereas the perception that external forces are in charge suggests unfavorable outlooks and outcomes.[42] This pattern holds, in part, when the external controlling agent is viewed as God. If a "deferring" mode of relationship is adopted (e.g., praying in order to put the problem totally in the hands of God), this does not appear to be as helpful as when a "collaborative" mode of relationship is manifested (e.g., prayer that keeps the individual working on the problem while seeking the support of the deity). A "self-directive" approach is more like collaboration than deference.[43] In self-direction, God is acknowledged, but the problem is regarded as requiring personal rather than godly solution; in both self-direction and collaboration, however, internal control is present. A deferring mode is akin to assigning all control to the external power of God. In collaboration, petitioning for aid from God is best for the individual, who still feels that responsibility for himself or herself cannot be totally surrendered.

Forms of Control. The idea of control is complex. Though it implies "being in charge," or having the ability to change the world (a concept termed "primary control"), very often the change is in oneself, and this is known as "secondary control." The famous writer Nikos Kazantzakis noted this potential when he quoted a mystic's prescription: "Since we cannot change reality, let us change the eyes which see reality."[44] Faith may play an important role in stimulating both primary and secondary forms of control.

People want to be in control of their destinies. Their goal is to have some degree of mastery, especially in dire situations; the greater the anxiety and threat, the more control is sought. Those in hopeless predicaments may be energized by their faith to seek new ways to obtain some measure of primary control. Failure to accomplish this may be countered by the development of beliefs and illusions that something truly substantive and effective has been achieved. The situation per se may not have changed, but people have changed when they come to feel that their faith can move mountains. A kind of "cognitive mediation" has taken place. Religion often provides a number of such possibilities. For instance, in various situations, physicians whose experience tells them that a certain outcome is inevitable may find themselves confounded by spontaneous remissions and unexpected developments that seem to be correlated with the beliefs and religious outlooks of their patients.[45]

We must recognize that primary and secondary forms of control are probably not independent of each other; both are likely to be employed at the same time by most people. Psychologically, the resort to religion falls largely under the realm of secondary control. It can be argued that the various forms of secondary control are a kind of emotion-focused coping. As part of the objective situation, the problem continues to exist, but the person is being altered.

Meaning and Control. In most cases, information gives people the feeling that they can do something about whatever is troubling them. As Sir Francis Bacon put it, "knowledge is power."[46] Baumeister adds that "meaning is used to predict and control the environment,"[47] and religious meaning can help people regulate their emotions. In other words, simply having information may reduce stress.[48] A wonderful anecdotal example of how religion can realize this role was provided by a breast cancer patient, who stated, "I had no idea that God could answer so many of my questions."[49] Though we may call this "informational control," it is intimately tied to three forms of secondary control that have been theorized by Rothbaum, Weisz, and Snyder.[50] These are termed "interpretive control," "predictive control," and "vicarious control," and are especially significant for understanding how religion helps people cope with the problems they confront in both everyday living and in troubled times.

Interpretive Control. When a situation looks grave, it is often natural to feel that there is no way out of the predicament. In seeking to understand such an event and gain some measure of control over what seems hopeless, people often reinterpret what is taking place. They exercise interpretive control and construe a distressing situation in less troubling or even positive terms; for instance, they may claim that "things could be worse" or that "I have it better than a lot of other people." In one study, some young paraplegics facing lifelong paralysis looked to a godly purpose for their plight.[51] In other work, a cancer patient concluded, "I looked upon cancer as a detour in the road, but not a roadblock."[52] People gain control over their emotions through such interpretations, and may be in a better position to handle their difficulties in a constructive way. In other words, emphasizing emotions may actually help a person become increasingly problem-focused.

Predictive Control. The perpetual human dream is to foretell the future. The idea of precognition fascinates people. If they could predict what would happen on future rolls of dice, who would win horse races, what the stock market might do, whether their efforts would result in success or failure, they feel that they would become the beneficiaries of unlimited wealth and happiness. The Bible has said that "the Lord himself shall give you a sign. . . ."[53] The dream holds, and people continue to hope that they will be the favored recipients of cues signifying that the future holds good things for them.

One kind of secondary control is predictive in nature: It assures a person that in the end, things will turn out all right. For example, another cancer patient stated that "Because of my relationship with God, I had faith that this cancer was not going to take my life."[54] There is a poignant example of predictive control in Eliach's *Chassidic Tales of the Holocaust*.[55] Eliach tells the story of a devout Jew who during World War II was brought by the Nazis into the death camp at Auschwitz. The number 145053 was tattooed on his arm. He looked at it and suddenly concluded that he would live. He reached this conclusion by adding the digits together and finding that they totaled 18; 18 is a number that within Judaism means life, and thus he felt assured of survival. Again, it was as if God had offered an omen signifying a secure future. Such predictive control gives a person confidence that tomorrow will be good. We must remember that the critical element here is *perception* of the future; what actually occurs is independent of this aspiration.

Vicarious Control. When people feel that they may not have the strength to cope with their troubles—particularly in cases of serious illness, where death is a possibility—they often turn to their God, and, vicariously, the deity becomes a support or substitute for their own actions. The essence of such vicarious control was stated by one woman cancer patient, who declared, "I could talk to my God and ask for his help in healing."[56] She identified with her God, and derived the strength to face potential death through her perceived divine connection. She thus attained a measure of vicarious control over her circumstances.

The Need for Self-Esteem

It is a simple truism to say that people want to feel good about themselves. Self-regard, if not self-love, has often been considered one of the most basic of human motives. The ancient Greeks regarded the self as the core of identity; early Christianity, by contrast, felt that self-esteem opposed the humility that allowed a person to truly experience God.[57] Thomas Reid, however, included self-esteem among his fundamental animal action principles.[58] Kaplan captures the essence of the current psychological view when he claims, "The self-esteem motive is universally and characteristically a dominant motive."[59] In addition, self-esteem has often been cited as evidence of good adjustment and effective coping. Silver and Wortman concluded that "measures of self-esteem have comprised the central operational definition of coping in several studies."[60]

If there is one pattern of relationships that generally holds, it is that positive views of oneself correlate with favorable judgments about others and the world.[61] Even in difficult times this pattern is likely to be maintained, as high self-esteem moderates the effects of stress and counters feelings of hopelessness. Though it is most evident under conditions of low stress, the effect is still present when stress is high.[62] Clearly, the importance of self-esteem should not be overlooked.

RELIGION AND GENERAL ADJUSTMENT

The realm of coping and adjustment is immense. Most psychology departments give courses in the "psychology of adjustment," and the number of books with this same title or some slight variation of it must be legion. The content of this field varies greatly, from a person's own outlook on life to the way individuals relate to others at home, work, school, and play. Concern is also directed at every possible aspect of daily living, in addition to the most dire and tragic crisis situations that may be encountered. It is a realm bounded by birth and death. There is no sharp dividing line between coping and adjustment on the one hand, and the equally broad field of mental health and illness on the other; however, we will make an arbitrary and expedient distinction here by relegating the relationship of religion and abnormal behavior primarily to the next chapter.

Religion and the Self

A very noteworthy early U.S. psychologist, Mary Whiton Calkins, viewed religion as "the conscious relation of human self to divine self, that is, to a self regarded as greater than this human self."[63] Stressing the conscious relations of selves introduces the view that people make inferences regarding themselves and the nature of their deity. Benson and Spilka showed in one study that a positive outlook toward oneself corresponded to a similar perception of God.[64] Surveying almost 200 studies of relationships among religious orientations and various conceptions of mental health, Batson, Schoenrade, and Ventis were unable to find consistent associations with self-acceptance and self-actualization.[65] When the seven indices these authors used are considered, it is obvious that self-judgments were being offered in a variety of domains, such as "personal competence and control." If all were to be somewhat loosely combined, the dominant tendency would be for positive outlooks on oneself and one's situation to correlate positively with an intrinsic orientation and negatively with an extrinsic perspective. Unhappily, considerable inconsistency would still be evident in these data, whether intrinsic, extrinsic, or quest forms of individual religion were being studied.

In a recent rather sophisticated study in which religious internalization was examined in relation to indices of self-esteem, a deep personal identification with religion was solidly correlated with global self-esteem. This finding also held for an intrinsic religious approach, but not for either an extrinsic or a quest orientation.[66] Foster and Keating conducted a rather ingenious investigation into the relationships between male and female God images for men and women, and observed greater self-esteem when women interacted with a female God, whereas males viewed themselves more favorably when their God was masculine.[67]

Overall, as Jones notes, "extensive studies have found the presence of religious beliefs and attitudes to be the best predictors of life satisfaction and a sense of well-being."[68] As a rule, we may conclude that a solid intrinsic religious commitment and favorable images of God are positively associated with self-esteem and good life adjustment. In general, the opposite is true of an extrinsic religious orientation. A common hypothesis is that a negative self-concept and low self-esteem should be associated with fundamentalist views because of their emphasis on personal sin and guilt; to date, no consistent support has been found for this view.[69]

As important as the above-described findings are, we need to look at the relationship between self-concept and faith in its social context. Rosenberg studied consonance and dissonance between the religious identification of people and the presence of religiously similar or different others in their surroundings.[70] For example, a dissonant context would exist if a person was Jewish but his or her neighborhood was predominantly Christian; consonance would, of course, mean that all shared the same faith. Studying Catholics, Protestants, and Jews, Rosenberg observed that a dissonant religious context meant that a person tended to feel isolated from coreligionists and therefore lacked support from them. Apparently discrimination also often occurred. The long-range effects of such contextual dissonance were likely to be low self-esteem, depressive feelings, and psychosomatic symptoms. A variation on this theme that merits study is dissonance in degree of religious commitment (i.e., a person's residence area is uniform in religious orientation, but the person is either more or less religiously involved than others).

Religion and Explanatory Style

Another factor that contributes to effective coping behavior is the broad perspective a person takes on life and its problems. Primarily viewed as an explanatory style and conceptualized largely in terms of optimism–pessimism, it relates, as we might expect, to self-esteem. Increasingly, this dimension is being treated as a very general trait or outlook that includes a person's overall attitude and approach toward the self and the world.[71] Its significance is well illustrated by a longitudinal study in which a pessimistic explanatory style manifested in early life predicted poor health in middle and old age.[72]

Faith has been shown to be a significant component of optimism. One large-scale study revealed that religious fundamentalists were more optimistic than their more religiously moderate peers, and that the latter demonstrated more optimism than liberal religionists. The researchers claim that a conservative religious perspective engenders hope and long-term optimism.[73] In an earlier study relating religiosity and time perspective, it was found that religious people were more willing to look into the distant future and even to confront their eventual death than were their nonreligious peers.[74] Faith has been shown not only to foster long-range hope, but also to create optimism for the short-term future.[75] This is especially true for senior citizens, for whom religious involvement is a solid correlate of happiness.[76]

The association of religion with personal happiness goes beyond conservative religion to faith in general.[77] Extensive surveys of thousands of people in 14 countries have shown a positive association between being religious and feelings of well-being.[78] Utilizing a variety of religious measures in national samples in the United States, Pollner concluded that "relations with a divine other are a significant correlate of well-being."[79] He did not favor the view that faith works because it supports a relationship with the divine or because it has any special power to cope with problem situations. Among the possible reasons suggested by Pollner for religion's effectiveness are its (1) lending a quality of order and coherence to stressful situations, (2) countering feelings of shame or anger that are aroused by stress, (3) supporting positive feelings about oneself simply because of having a perceived relationship with the deity, and lastly (4) fostering a tendency to see the self and the world in positive terms. Further research to test these possibilities is certainly in order. We ought to add to these considerations the likelihood that religious people often develop a broad network of social support through churches and other religious institutions.

Myers and others feel that faith offers a "sense of meaning and purpose."[80] Krause and Van Tranh provide evidence that religion also helps people to develop and maintain self-esteem and control in stressful situations.[81] Carver and his associates have further shown that optimism and religion go together when the problem is breast cancer.[82]

In short, the evidence would appear to be quite strong that religion, through offering a sense of meaning, control, and self-esteem, does support an optimistic outlook. This in turn helps people deal constructively with life, and seems to have long-range beneficial effects.

RELIGION AND COPING WITH STRESS

It takes no special knowledge or insight to recognize the helpful role religion plays when people confront difficulty and crisis in life. In wartime, the old adage that "there are no atheists in foxholes" is not to be taken lightly. "When misery is the greatest, God is the closest" states this principle well.[83] Bjorck and Cohen point out that "religious coping represents a normative and adaptive coping strategy" for intrinsically religious persons.[84] Culturally, it appears to be normative and adaptive for most people who confront stress as a result of threats and losses.[85]

Surprisingly little research has been done on differences in the way people affiliated with different religious groups may handle stress. Park, Cohen, and Herb point out that various faiths may differentially emphasize the use of prayer, group support, reading of sacred texts, or positive thinking. They conducted a comparison of Catholics and Protestants and found some differences, suggesting that religion may both alleviate and exacerbate stress.[86] Given the over 200 Protestant bodies that exist in the United States, plus the strong ethnic variations found in Catholicism, there is a need for additional work in this area to examine more exactly defined religious bodies and the relative success of their approaches.

Hypothesizing that entering a university constitutes a stressful experience for young people, Hunsberger, Pancer, Pratt, and Alisat attempted to get a very large group of incoming first-year students to take a broad range of psychological tests.[87] These were administered in blocks: prior to coming to the university, early in the first term, and late in the first year. Though a variety of religious measures (including one on fundamentalism) failed to relate to adjustment, indices of religious doubt were consistently and negatively linked to indices of adjustment, including poorer relationships with parents and increased stress. This work suggests that the usual measures of religious belief and behavior may not be enough in studying coping behavior; the issue of religious doubt per se may need to be considered. Rejection of religion and religious doubt may well be different phenomena, and research illustrating their differential significance would make a nice contribution to the literature.

Religion and Coping with Socioeconomic Stress

Stress may be a lifelong event, as in the case of those mired in poverty. Glock has posited economic deprivation as a major source of religious inspiration and activity.[88] One classical sociologist asserted that "the really creative, church-forming, religious movements are the work of the lower strata."[89] The situation is, however, more complex than a simple statement that poverty produces religion would suggest. Illustratively, Wood cites a number of scholars to the effect that "various Holiness churches arise . . . where there are . . . large numbers of dislocated, alienated persons without secure social contacts."[90] This description characterized the members of a Free Will Baptist group that Kaplan studied in Appalachia.[91] Severely economically deprived and socially isolated, these individuals viewed life as basically evil and full of pain and suffering. They looked forward to death as leading to rewards in heaven. Unable to believe that they could cope in this life with the stress of their existence, they retreated into a faith that promised success and happiness only in an afterlife. This is one way religion can be used to adapt to tragic circumstances (albeit arguably not the best way).

Demerath claims that "those of low status and those of high status discrepancy are likely to seek respites from the secular world that judges them."[92] "Status discrepancy" refers to situations in which, for example, a person has attained much education but has low income. The former suggests high status, the latter low status; hence high status discrepancy may exist. Discrepancies among occupations, incomes, and education are often examined in such research, and this has shown that status discrepancy is a major source of stress that can have long-range adverse behavioral and health effects.[93] The one tentative finding reported by Demerath is that a lack of such congruence is positively associated with church attendance, implying that religious activity may counter the stress produced by status discrepancy. Another study that examined the personal significance of church attendance found that it reduced anxiety, which is, of course, a likely correlate of stress.[94] Clearly, more work needs to be done on the role of status discrepancy in relation to religious behavior.

Religion and Coping with Crisis

As already noted and widely shown to be true, people turn to their gods in times of trouble and crisis. Whether this is simply an expression of a utilitarian or extrinsic religion, or just a general human propensity, there can be no doubt of its pervasiveness. Much research has been undertaken on a variety of psychological stressors. Some of these are illness, disability, and other negative life events that can cause both mental and physical distress; the anticipated or actual death of friends and relatives; and dealing with an adverse life situation (e.g., among the elderly).

Coping with Disability, Illness, and Similar Negative Events

One of the earliest studies of this genre dealt with young paraplegics and quadriplegics who were primarily victims of accidents.[95] The 23 men and 6 women studied averaged 22.7 years of age. Though self-blame was related positively to religiosity, it seemed to be an element of successful coping. The most frequent explanation for the event and the disability involved reference to the deity. The general idea was that God caused the event to teach the person a lesson—not just punitively, but to orient him or her toward a different life direction. These attributions were interpreted by the authors as efforts to make this situation meaningful in as broad a sense as possible, and to allow self-esteem to be maintained. For both of these needs, religion was an effective coping aid.

Pargament and his colleagues have shown that when religion is used to deal with life's problems, it may be used in a number of ways:

Spiritually based coping	A generalized form emphasizing God and Christ as sources of strength and knowledge
Doing good deeds	Changing one's behavior by engaging in more positive social and religious activities
Religious discontent	Questioning and doubting God and church
Religious support	Getting support from clergy and church members
Religious pleading	Petitioning God for information and help
Religious avoidance	Trying to avoid the problem by turning it over to God; thinking about or engaging in other diverting religious activities[96]

These researchers looked at the contribution of forms of religious coping such as these to three possible outcomes of the coping process: effect on mental health status, the general outcome of the event, and its influence on the religious views of the person (see Research Box 11.1). In keeping with earlier work, these researchers observed that viewing God in a positive and benevolent light can buttress an individual's sense of meaning, self-esteem, and peronal control in life. They further noted the constructive role of religious ritual and prayer in enhancing feelings of mastery and predictability under stress.[97] The positive effects of spiritual coping on mental health status noted here were also found in another study, but the results were present only for females, not males.[98]

In a large-scale community investigation, these results were further supported, but it was noted that religion was of particular benefit when people were dealing with chronic illness or the death of loved ones.[99] In another study, resorting to one's faith was found to be the most useful coping device for dealing with various losses.[100] Bjorck and Cohen claim that different types of stress are differentially related to religious coping. Further threats, defined as the anticipation of damage, elicit greater use of religion than losses, which require acceptance. Since events that challenge people call upon personal effort and resources, they are seen as most controllable; resort to faith as a coping aid is *least* often employed in these situations.[101]

**Research Box 11.1. Coping Efforts and Significant Negative Life Events
(Pargament et al., 1990)**

In this landmark research, a very basic question was addressed: "What kinds of religious coping are helpful, harmful, or irrelevant to people dealing with significant negative events?" (p. 798). The authors also attempted to find out whether measures of religious coping predicted outcomes of coping better than measures of nonreligious coping techniques.

A sample of 586 Christian church members responded to questionnaires assessing religious and nonreligious coping activities and outcomes in regard to negative events that they had experienced during the preceding year. Six kinds of religious coping and four kinds of nonreligious coping were identified. Three outcome measures were assessed: mental health status, general outcome of the negative event, and its religious outcome. The religious variables did, to varying degrees, predict all three of the outcomes. This was most evident for spiritually based activities plus faith and trust in God. Religious discontent and concern with punishment from God hindered coping and adjustment. Positive effects were specifically predictable from perceptions of a just, loving, and supportive deity; involvement in religious rituals, such as attendance at services; prayer; Bible reading; focusing on the afterlife; living a good life; and getting support from clergy and church members. It was also observed that an extrinsic, utilitarian faith was also helpful. The authors concluded that at least among church members, religious coping is an important and beneficial part of the overall process of coping with stress.

Hayden researched the potential utility of religion in coping with pain, and noted tendencies for a conservative religiosity and meaning in life to counter pain perceptions.[102] Other researchers have found that this works best with individuals who are not very depressed to begin with, and who believe that their faith can address their pain effectively, such as some arthritis patients.[103] That there is a significant psychological component in the perception of pain goes without saying. Physical and psychological pain often go together, and a strong faith combined with being religiously active seems to counter distress, depression, and anxiety.[104]

The stress-buffering role of faith seems to have very broad applications. Maton has shown that it relates positively to college adjustment among new students who have experienced high stress during the preceding 6 months.[105] Newman and Pargament observed that religion provides emotional support among college students and helps them redefine their problems.[106] The need for new and positive meanings may be met this way. This redefining or "reframing" is a coping strategy that should not be looked on negatively. Research on caregivers of dementia patients—whose role is an extremely trying one—indicates that they utilize their faith to make their situation more acceptable and manageable.[107]

When serious, potentially fatal illness strikes, religion is often invoked rapidly and with telling effect. This is especially true when the problem is cancer. There is apparently a pervasive tendency to avoid blaming God for the bad things that happen to people, and to credit God for positive possibilities and outcomes.[108] To the degree that God is viewed by cancer patients as being in control of things, the sense of threat to one's life decreases, and self-esteem improves.[109] An intrinsic religious orientation also counteracts feelings of anger, hostility, and social isolation.[110] In fact, intrinsic individuals may well receive much social support from their coreligionists.

When people feel that they can be active (e.g., do something constructive) in coping with their disease, they appear to benefit. Prayer, as we have already noted, is an active, cognitive coping strategy,[111] and cancer patients who pray feel that it is helpful both in combating their pain and in aiding them to deal with their disease.[112] The objective evidence supports such a position.

Coping with Death

As indicated in Chapter 5, religious perspectives on death are multidimensional in character. The data indicate clearly that a strong religious commitment and an intrinsic faith are positively correlated with the acceptance of death; it is perceived in such cases as a test of life and courage. Such an approach counters interpretations of mortality as failure, pain, and the desertion of loved ones.[113] Most often, studies in this area are conducted on people who are young and for whom death is a distant, if not unreal, likelihood for some time to come. Unhappily, there are many situations in which death is a reality with immediate repercussions. Among these are cases in which parents are anticipating the death of a child, or coping with such a tragedy after it has occurred.

McIntosh and his colleagues have examined the role of faith in coping with the death of an infant from sudden infant death syndrome (SIDS) (see Research Box 11.2). They found that coping was positively related to faith in several ways. Religious participation facilitated social support and the enhancement of meaning for the bereaved parents. The importance of religion per se to the parents also contributed to making the SIDS loss more meaningful, while, at the same time, it helped the parents to cognitively process and come to grips with the death of their child.[114] This study revealed that religion may not directly affect postdeath adjustment and distress; rather, it may work indirectly by bolstering the perception of social support, aiding cognitive processing, and increasing the meaningfulness of the death, probably by putting it in the context of a positive religious framework. Research such as this, by clarifying some of the mechanisms that are operative when a person's faith is tested by crisis and tragedy, indicates the complexity of the role of religion in the coping process.

Research Box 11.2. Religion's Role in Adjustment to a Negative Life Event (McIntosh, Silver, & Wortman, 1993)

This significant study examined how religion helped parents who lost an infant to sudden infant death syndrome (SIDS) adjust to this tragedy. A sample of 124 parents was interviewed within 15 to 30 days after a child's death from SIDS, and reinterviewed 18 months later. Adjustment and coping were related to four factors: religion, social support, cognitive processing, and meaning. The researchers hypothesized that religious participation would promote perceptions of social support and adjustment. They also expected that when religion per se was important to the parents, it would help them find meaning in the loss and aid them in their cognitive processing of the event, and would enhance adjustment through these avenues. All these hypotheses were supported. In addition, religious participation helped the parents derive meaning from their loss.

These studies suggest the possibility that religion as a coping device may be especially important when death or other devastating, uncontrollable events occur. For most people, naturalistic explanations of death are unsatisfactory, for they imply no future, no hope—simply termination. In contrast, religious interpretations offer the potential of future life, reward, and other-worldly gratification for the deceased, and this-worldly answers that offer a measure of contentment for survivors. Whereas McIntosh and his coworkers have found this to be true for parents who lose an infant to SIDS, this has also been demonstrated for those who anticipate the death of a child from illness.[115] Similar findings hold when parents have to deal with the deaths of premature and newborn infants.[116]

Maton offers evidence that spiritual support is particularly effective in countering depression and bolstering the self-esteem of parents who have recently lost a child, as opposed to those whose offspring died more than 2 years previously.[117] Another study found that church attendance was associated with a reduction in death anxiety for both fathers and mothers who had lost a child, particularly for mothers, for whom it seemed to lessen grief "related to feelings of anger, guilt, loss of control, rumination, depersonalization, and optimism/despair."[118] In addition, there were indications that religious beliefs were strengthened by such a tragedy when the parents already had a religious commitment.

Three different theodicies have been observed among bereaved parents: "1) reunion with the deceased in an afterlife; 2) death as a purposive event; and 3) death as punishment for wrong-doing on the part of survivors."[119] These are regarded as attempts to make the death meaningful, and even to experience guilt feelings. Attributions to a purposeful God are also invoked when a friend dies, but intrinsic religionists may undergo much cognitive restructuring in order to understand what has occurred, possibly because of their positive image of the deity. There is also the possibility that it is cognitively easier to deal with one's own death than with that of another valued person.[120]

Religion, Stress, and the Elderly

The famous psychoanalyst Erik Erikson may have been the first modern thinker to develop a lifespan developmental psychology. Looking at the final period in life, he pictured it as a struggle between ego integrity and despair. The individual must confront the issue of loss— the loss of physical and often mental skills; the loss of personal significance through work as retirement takes place; the loss of friends through death; and finally the knowledge that one's own life will shortly conclude.[121] As a 90-year-old Papago woman said over 60 years ago to an anthropologist, "It is not good to be old. Not beautiful. When you come again, I will not be here."[122] In other words, to be elderly is itself stressful.

In reviewing his or her life, the elderly person is called upon to decide whether this life has been basically meaningful or meaningless. An ever-present awareness of and probable fear of death can be mitigated by emotional integration, which will in all probability involve religion. This is especially true for the oldest segment of the population, who, when they were young, were more strongly exposed to religious teachings than succeeding generations have been.[123]

Research on the elderly has consistently revealed that religious coping mechanisms are the ones this group most frequently employs when dealing with health-related stress. Prayer and turning to the deity for support are also often the most effective strategies available to seniors; this holds true for persons of different ethnic groups, socioeconomic statuses, and widely varying levels of education.[124] Among those over 65, when the problem is physical, social, economic, or medical, prayer is the most commonly employed means of coping.[125] In like manner, the rural elderly employ religion in general for coping more than any other referent.[126] Whether the specific religious variable is attendance at services, beliefs, prayer, or church social support, many studies indicate that all of these possibilities are positively correlated with combating depression and loneliness among the elderly.[127]

Examining the use of faith in regard to loss, threat, and challenge situations, McRae observed that of 28 coping possibilities, religion was the first to be employed when loss occurred; it came in third when threat was present; and it ranked 15th in challenge situations.[128] One's own impending demise is obviously a threat, and thinking about personal death is positively related to the religious activities in which the elderly participate. Research on the latter suggests that spiritual involvement may reduce seniors' fears about physical pain and suffering during the dying process, concerns about what will happen to their possessions following death, and uncertainty about what they will experience after they die. These entail thoughts about rejection by God, the role of the devil, afterlife punishment, reincarnation, and the like.[129] Such findings may suggest that the motivation to utilize religion is wholly negative, but this is not so. Turning to one's faith increases with the number of positive life events a person has experienced, and among the benefits of such religious involvement is the great amount of social support that coreligionists often provide.[130] In addition, the salience of an individual's religion to self-image also increases with age.[131]

To sum up, the data show clearly that religion is a powerful buffer against stress among the elderly. As Myers puts it, "the happiest of senior citizens are those who are actively religious . . ."[132] The powerful effects of religious faith among the elderly go far beyond just feeling good. A study by Idler and Kasl speaks to the potential influence of faith on health and mortality (see Research Box 11.3).

Research Box 11.3. Religion, Disability, Depression, and the Timing of Death (Idler & Kasl, 1992)

In this interesting study, the authors examined the effects of public and private religiosity on health, the ways in which these varied for Christians and Jews, and mortality rates around religious holidays. Starting with a sample of 2,812 people over 65 in 1982, Idler and Kasl reinterviewed the members of this group in 1983, 1984, and 1985.

By means of sophisticated data analyses, public religious participation in 1982 was found to be related to low functional disability in the following 3 years. Things were more complex with private religiousness: This was associated with greater disability in 1984, but an examination of those who died and those who lived revealed that those engaging in private religiosity seemed to be protected against mortality.

Studying who lived and who died in the 30 days preceding and following religious holidays showed very strong effects relative to Easter for the Christian groups; the death rate was significantly lower prior to the holiday than after it. This did not occur for Jews relative to the Christian holiday, but was found for the Jewish holidays of Passover, Rosh Hashanah, and Yom Kippur. The pattern of reduced deaths prior to a Jewish holiday held for Jewish males but not for females; this variation was seen as a function of the greater role and investment of Jewish males than females in these holidays. This work shows a considerable potential for religious influence on both the health and mortality of the elderly.

RELIGION AND HEALTH

Over the past two decades, psychologists, physiologists, and physicians have increasingly recognized that personality and attitudes may play significant roles in health and illness. It was therefore just a matter of time before psychologists would probe possible relationships between faith and physical health. In sum, this literature indicates that optimistic explanatory styles and effective coping behavior go along with good health.[133]

Levin and Schiller reviewed over 200 studies that related faith and health, and concluded that the two tend to go together. They raised the interesting question whether "perhaps the nervous system represents the locus of a mechanism by which religious faith or religious beliefs . . . promote well-being."[134] The mechanism may well be the sense of control that is often associated with religion.[135] Perceptions that one is personally in control of life situations, along with similar views that God is in control, relate to good health.[136] Another possibility has been advanced by Benson—namely, that certain religious rituals, prayer, meditation, and so forth may stimulate a "relaxation response" that is broadly healthful.[137]

A different approach was taken by Hannay, who studied Indian and Irish immigrants to Scotland. Among these immigrants, again, better health was associated with greater religious activity. The suggestion was made that religion may act as a "stabilizing factor" for minorities who have left their home cultural base.[138] Such stabilization may reduce tension and, in Benson's terms, stimulate relaxation. In our framework, this would be tantamount to an increased sense of personal control.

One may argue that the final test of the relationship between religion and health may be found in longevity. Do religious people live longer than their less religious counterparts? At least one study claims that this is true for elderly people who are in poor health.[139] Idler and Kasl extended this to Christians and Jews, in general, for 1 month prior to significant religious holidays (see Research Box 11.3, above).[140] Obviously, findings like these merit much more research.

These relationships are not simple, for even though direct connections have been found between physical well-being and religion, the latter often seems to work indirectly by fostering good health habits. Among these, faith (particularly an intrinsic religious orientation) counters smoking, drinking, and the use of illicit drugs, and supports the use of seat belts, among other possibilities. Beliefs about prevention may also relate to religious commitment. A comparison of highly religious mothers with their less committed counterparts revealed that the former were significantly more likely to engage in active illness prevention behaviors than the latter group; still, the more religious mothers felt that they had less control over illness.[141] Since a major prevention category in this study was to "go to the doctor," there might be an inclination here for religion to sponsor a deference both to God and to medical authorities. This possibility merits further assessment. Finally, churches often actively sponsor a wide variety of healthful practices (e.g., dietary restrictions, prohibitions against alcohol and tobacco), and such ideas are often adopted by believers.[142]

Even though religious groups differ in vulnerability to many illnesses because of dietary and other cultural factors, faith is associated with a low incidence of a number of cardiovascular conditions, hypertension, stroke, and different forms of cancer.[143] Another possibility is that since religiosity is positively correlated with optimism, life satisfaction, and a sense of purpose in life, the more religious people are, the less inclined they may be to report symptoms of illness (and therefore the more likely they may be to downplay their possible significance).[144] This, of course, would work to their detriment, and does not appear to be generally true.

Despite much research in these areas, there remain many unanswered questions. The mechanisms through which faith may operate in maintaining health have yet to be identified. There is a definite need for more studies that control for religious affiliation, cultural differences, and health-promoting or health-damaging behaviors.[145] In addition, issues of response bias remain unaddressed. Clearly, here is a fertile topic for further study.

HOW RELIGION WORKS IN COPING

The Role of Belief

A central theme in this chapter, if not this book, is that religion is extremely significant in life because it offers people meaning, control, and self-esteem. We have also suggested that these factors work through religious beliefs, experiences, and practices. The question then must be posed as to how these aspects of religion function to aid a person to cope with the trials, stresses, and vicissitudes of everyday life.

Subjectively, the distance between belief and the feeling that one "knows," and therefore possesses valid knowledge, is in many instances rather small. This is often true where religious beliefs are concerned. These constitute a system of meanings that appear applicable to virtually every situation a person may encounter. Often premised upon scripture and/or a popular or civil religion, God images have the potential to explain both world and personal events.[146] The deity is simultaneously forgiving, loving, merciful, blessed, wrathful, involved in all human affairs, and simultaneously uninvolved since people have been "given free will."[147] The many concepts of God that are held can be called upon as needed to explain occurrences that seem to defy naturalistic interpretations. For example, people are loath to rely on chance; hence the winner in a lottery often credits God for success. Fate, luck, and chance are poor referents for understanding, but the deity in all its possible manifestations can fill the void of meaninglessness admirably.

God is usually conceived of in terms of love and power. Thus, as Pargament and his coworkers have observed, some people may defer to the deity, asking for aid when they see no personal potential for action; others may feel they must collaborate, working along with the divine in realizing some master plan. Finally, there are those who delineate a role for humanity in which God is not directly involved.[148] In all of these relationships, there is a place for one's God—simply watching, guiding, supporting, or actively solving a problem. The image of an omnipresent, omniscient, and omnipotent deity endows stressful situations with meaning, and this form of informational control may have beneficial results in the effort to cope with life.

As noted above, to hold a belief is to "know" something. As Herbert Benson has claimed, "the faith factor" is a powerful force in coping. He also feels that "the placebo effect reflects the power of belief."[149] The internal mechanisms by which such beliefs work have not been determined, but no one can doubt that they can have profound effects.

The Role of Ritual

Ritual has fascinated scholars in fields ranging from anthropology and linguistics to psychoanalysis.[150] Such scholars are unanimous in concluding that an innate need for ritual is always present, and serves the deepest, even unconscious needs of people. Reik suggested that "ritual [is] at the centre of an analytical investigation of religious questions."[151] Pruyser has pointed out that "religious belief is embedded in religious practices."[152] Whereas psychoanalysts have usually associated ritual with psychopathology, or have described religion as the "universal obsessional neurosis," other observations indicate that ritual and ceremony perform many roles and functions that have nothing to do with mental disorder, immaturity, or personal inadequacy.[153]

Erikson perceived ritual as fulfilling a variety of central roles throughout life, among which are the development of trust, identity, conviction, commitment, and authority.[154] If a person's encounter with social rules and regulations stifles the constructive use of ritual, a short-circuiting of maturity is theorized, in which practice becomes mechanical and the real meaning of ritual is lost. In essence, ritual connects generations and individuals with one another in sharing relationships.

These positive functions find expression in the fact that ritual orders and organizes life; it counters chaos, distress, ambiguity, and randomness. In this sense, it is invariably measured, precise, stereotyped, and often repetitive. These characteristics led Pruyser to view ritual as structuring, shaping, and limiting emotion and feeling, especially in regard to intensity.[155] Ceremony is thus an agency of control that works against doubt, fear, guilt, and anxiety. It imparts a feeling of rigor and comfort under conditions of tension and instability.

Ritual also conveys a sense of predictability and mastery. When religion is involved, these accomplishments result from the fact that ritual may be regarded as the structured call of the religious community to its deity, in order to solemnize, legitimate, and make significant the joint desires of the group and the individuals within it. Ritual offers both God's and the community's sanction for major life events—birth of a child, marriage, death, war, the planting and harvesting of crops, and so on. In other words, ritual connects people to the divine. It symbolizes godly actions or the actions the deity desires of humanity; it brings people closer to God, and surrounds them with the perception and security of godly protection and power. Constructive, basic meanings are thus provided, particularly when people are under stress. Viewed from another perspective, ritual is organized action: In ritual, people are not passive, but are doing something that implies capability, mastery, and control. Our hypothesized fundamental needs for meaning and control are thus met, and one major outcome is the enhancement of self-esteem.

Empirical data support these views. Fullerton and her associates found that ritual moderated stress among firefighters.[156] Religious ritual has also been shown to be a relatively powerful mediator for negative life events.[157]

The Role of Prayer

Probably the most intensely personal type of religious ritual is prayer. It is also extremely widely employed. In one Gallup poll, approximately 90% of the U.S. population reported praying, and 76% regarded it as very important in everyday life.[158]

Forms of Prayer

The idea and practice of prayer cover many possibilities. From a spiritual perspective, one scholar identified 21 different forms of prayer.[159] A recent research effort resulted in the classification of eight distinct types of prayer: "petitionary," "ritualistic," "meditational," "confessional," "thanksgiving," "intercessory," "self-improvement," and "habitual." All have been confirmed and measured by separate, reliable scales.[160] A U.S. national study has variously spoken of "contemplative," "conversational," "colloquial," "ritual," "petitionary," and "meditative" prayers.[161] Obviously, there is considerable overlap among these schemes, and future research will have to sort out the issue of what the different forms of prayer actually are.

Though empirical work in this realm is relatively scarce, writing by professionals and laypersons alike on prayer is prodigious. It is clearly of immense popular and personal interest. If any general conclusion may be drawn from the data on prayer, it would appear to be that the more people pray, the more forms of prayer they utilize.[162] In addition, frequency of prayer goes with praying for more things—health, interpersonal concerns, and financial matters.[163] Finally, we may well agree with Trier and Shupe that "prayer [is] the most often practiced form of religiosity."[164]

Usage and Efficacy of Different Forms of Prayer

There is evidence that people are selective in their praying, and that different forms of prayer may be employed in different circumstances. For example, breast cancer patients who have survived more than 5 years since their diagnosis are likely to stress prayers of thanksgiving.[165] Petitionary prayers, which are said to be the oldest and most common prayer form, are employed to counter frustration and threat, whereas contemplative prayer (an attempt to relate deeply to one's God) seems to aid internal self-integration.[166] Meditational prayer (concern with one's relationship to God) seems to reduce anger, anxiety, and aid relaxation.[167] Contemplative prayer has also been shown to aid psychotherapy by lessening distress and specific kinds of complaints.[168]

The Issue of Intercessory Prayer

The issue of intercessory prayer is a controversial one. The idea that prayers in behalf of another can influence the health of that other person has a long history. It has been subjected to research generally leaves much to be desired.

In a mid-1960s study, Joyce and Weldon matched patients with chronic or progressively deteriorating rheumatic or psychological illness on sex, age, and clinical diagnosis.[169] Two groups of 19 patients each were created. The "treatment" group participants were prayed for by members of a prayer group; the "nontreatment" group served as a control. Each patient in the "treatment" group was the recipient of a total of 15 hours of prayer over a 6-month period. This was a double-blind study, in which neither the patients nor their physicians knew of the prayer "treatment." After 6 months of intercessory prayer, no differences between the two groups could be demonstrated.

Within a few years, another intercessory prayer study was reported by Colipp.[170] This involved 18 leukemic children, 10 of whom were randomly chosen to be the objects of prayer by the author's friends and church members. After 15 months of prayer, the "treatment" group seemed to have a slight advantage over the control group in survival ($p < .10$).

A third study utilizing 393 coronary patients was undertaken by Byrd.[171] Patients, doctors, and the author were all kept "blind" in this work. The results seemed to support the power of intercessory prayer, as the "treatment" group appeared to do better than the controls. Though this work looks impressive on the surface, many serious questions may be posed regarding its design, data analysis, and interpretation. In fact, strong challenges to the validity of all these studies can be advanced, based on the nature (and often the size) of the samples, the evaluation procedures, the methodology, and the statistical analyses. If scientific doubts are not enough, many theologians should be able to mount their own criticisms of this kind of work. We must conclude that at this stage of research on intercessory prayer, its power and significance have yet to be demonstrated.

Prayer as a Means of Coping with Serious Illness and Other Problems

We have already seen that prayer is the religious coping device most commonly employed among the sick and well elderly. Park, Cohen, and Herb further claim that it is the most widely used means of coping found among Catholics and Protestants who deal with stressful situations.[172] Unhappily, in most research no distinction is made regarding how an individual prays or what types of prayer are utilized, so all we know is that prayer is used, and that it often appears to be rather effective. The major question here is what "effective" means. If, for example, we mean that prayer is objectively effective (meaning that it can change events in the world), this is scientifically very open to question. Still, about one-third of the U.S. population believes that it does have such influence.[173]

If we conceive of prayer as changing oneself, then the evidence is much stronger. Holahan and Moos's conception of prayer as an active, cognitive coping strategy has gained much support.[174] It has been shown to alleviate the depression that is stimulated by stress.[175] Considering prayer as picturing a link with God, Bickel found that a collaborative relationship with the deity, in which the person and God worked together, was more effective in combating stress than was a self-directive effort by the person without resorting to God; he also found that a deferring relationship, leaving all to God, was unrelated to the reduction of stress.[176] Poloma and colleagues have found that engaging in prayer is positively correlated with well-being and life satisfaction.[177] In a somewhat related investigation, Richards found that the intensity of prayer was associated positively with a sense of purpose in life and internal control.[178]

When serious illness strikes, prayer becomes of the utmost importance. Among the coping methods that a sample of hemodialysis patients used, prayer came in second only to efforts to maintain control over the situation and hope that things would get better (the latter two efforts tied for first place).[179] Prayer, however, came in first as a coping pattern among renal transplant patients.[180]

Ninety percent of a sample of breast cancer patients revealed that they prayed for help in dealing with their cancer; only 9% stated that they prayed "a few times."[181] Much the same appears to be true of those dealing with the stress of cardiac surgery. Of 100 patients, 70 gave prayer the highest possible helpfulness rating on a 15-point scale; 93 assigned it a helpfulness rating of 10 or above.[182] Other research suggests that the more serious a symptom is judged to be by an ill person, the more that individual will both pray about it and, concurrently, seek medical aid for the problem.[183] This is a sensible example of the old adage that "God helps those that help themselves."

Prayer is also considered useful by arthritics who employ it. One study of black and Hispanic arthritis patients found that both groups utilized prayer and felt it was effective.[184] Hispanics were also more likely to use self-administered heat for their arthritis. Heat and prayer were combined with traditional medical therapies, and were sanctioned because of cultural support and the fact that they were practical and inexpensive. Lest we lose sight of the fact that prayer serves other functions, we must recognize that the frequency of prayer and the belief that it is effective do result in measurable tension reduction.[185]

Further examination of the functions that prayer may serve in coping comes from a study of the Spiritual Baptist Church, a black Christian group in the Caribbean and the United States.[186] The members of one Spiritual Baptist congregation pointed to seven benefits resulting from their practice of prayer, which they termed "mourning." This involves an extended period of fasting, prayer, and isolation designed to emulate bodily death, from which one's spirit rises. The claimed results (as perceived by the participants) were (1) alleviation of depression; (2) increased ability to predict and avoid danger; (3) the enhancement of decision-making ability; (4) greater felt ease of communication with God, and increased capacity to meditate; (5) amplified pride and appreciation of ethnic origins; (6) strengthened commitment to their church and its officials; and (7) recovery from physical ills.

According to Brown, engaging in petitionary prayer is a function of whether it is appropriate and/or effective; when it is appropriate, one may not believe it is effective, and vice versa.[187] Clearly, motives for the use of such prayer are more complex than may be evident.

The Purposes of Prayer

Much evidence has been presented that prayer is effective in many frustrating and threatening situations and circumstances. One study gets to the heart of the matter by noting that the more pain people have, the greater the risk to their self-esteem, and the more they are uncertain about life after death, the more they pray.[188]

Obviously people pray for many reasons; however, we have stressed the function of prayer relative to stress and coping. Examination of the motives for prayer in such circumstances returns us to our original suggestion that issues of meaning, control, and self-esteem may be paramount in this picture. The verbalizations of those who pray for aid bring such considerations to the fore. What we must keep in mind is that "prayer is a cognitive activity";[189] as such, it performs cognitive functions. Not the least of these is the enhancement of meaning. It is also action with profound emotional consequences.

Prayer is reflective of both a need to make sense out of a situation and a further need to change what is taking place. To return to the notions of primary and secondary control, though the person would like to alter reality, he or she must often be satisfied with changing the self—the way the world is seen and interpreted. Interpretive control suggests that real knowledge lies in the mind of the deity, and by engaging in prayer, the individual seeks new meanings that portend hope.[190] The purpose is to change the pray-er—to modify the way things are perceived. Kierkegaard is quoted by Phillips as saying, "The prayer does not change God, but it changes the one who offers it."[191] Phillips thus contends that the hope the person seeks and obtains is fundamentally a set of meanings that sponsor "living with oneself."[192] This comes about because prayer is talking to God, and "talking to God is a meaningful activity."[193] In any event, the core of this process is premised upon the idea that "people believe that their prayers may make a difference to what transpires."[194] New meaning comes about because prayer is largely a new interpretation or reinterpretation of what is already known.

One major psychological mechanism through which prayer works returns us to our earlier consideration of attribution processes. We have theorized that these are called into play when something out of the ordinary occurs—when meaning, control, and self-esteem are threatened. In such a case, a person's goal is to understand the whys and wherefores of what has taken place. Prayer is first and foremost an interpretive activity. It is premised upon learned and experienced religious frameworks—images of God and how faith may "work wonders." A person who prays sees the "hand of God" in both worldly and personal events. It has a role in what the person does; nothing is left to chance. Such a point of view is founded upon the belief in a "just world," which functions according to a divine master plan; hence all people are God's tools, as are all aspects of the universe.[195] An excellent example of the influence of belief in a "just world" is offered by Pargament and Hahn,[196] and is described in Research Box 11.4. In other words, people are especially likely to make attributions to God when naturalistic explanations are unsatisfactory—as they often are in dire circumstances, and not infrequently when great or unexpected success occurs.

Research Box 11.4. Causal and Coping Attributions to God in Health Situations (Pargament & Hahn, 1986)

Claiming that "people have a need to feel a sense of meaning, justice, and control in their lives" (p. 193), Pargament and Hahn focused on the attributions made in health-related situations. They noted that these may reflect personally responsible behavior (e.g., exercising) or personal irresponsibility (e.g., smoking). In addition, these actions may result in positive or negative outcomes. The expectation is that responsible behavior ought to eventuate in positive outcomes, whereas irresponsible conduct ought to produce negative outcomes. Stated differently, outcomes are supposed to be contingent on behaviors. In one sense this idea of contingency is illusory, for bad things do happen to good people, and vice versa. This association of action and result leads to four possibilities that are pertinent to health relationships: (1) Behaving wrongly should be followed by negative outcomes; (2) doing the right thing ought to result in positive consequences; (3) behaving responsibly may have negative repercussions; and (4) irresponsible actions are possibly succeeded by good outcomes. These two pairs of alternatives (1–2 and 3–4) result in what may be defined as "contingent/just" and "noncontingent/unjust" situations, respectively.

The researchers had a sample of 124 undergraduates react to 16 event scenarios. These pictured responsible and irresponsible behaviors with positive and negative outcomes. In checking for explanations, the researchers assessed attributions to oneself, chance, God's will, God's love, and God's anger. When situations were contingent/just, they elicited more attributions to oneself than when they were noncontingent/unjust. Respondents wanted to believe they would get what was merited when good actions and good outcomes went together, and the same was true for negative behavior and results. Noncontingent/unjust situations eventuated in attributions to chance and God's will. God's will and love tended to be invoked when irresponsible actions were followed by positive outcomes. When responsible behavior had negative outcomes, God was included along with oneself in the interpretations. God's will and God's love were both treated as benevolent expressions of the divine. God's anger was viewed as present in negative outcome situations. A person might be "punished" for irresponsibility.

Negative outcomes apparently stimulated "a functional view of a God who acts as a source of support or strength . . . in times of stress" (p. 202). This was true for negative outcomes of both responsible and irresponsible behavior, and was viewed by the researchers in terms of a need to perceive the world as just and controllable. The results of this work are more complex than this summary indicates, and suggest further research into the motivation to perceive a "just world" that involves a benevolent deity.

This last point about the need to believe that the world is "just," and that what happens is based on a justice principle, seems to be a strong factor when people evaluate behavior. The strength of one's God belief, self-rated religiosity, and church attendance are positively correlated with trust that the world is indeed a just place.[197]

Regardless of the form of prayer employed (petitionary, thanksgiving, meditational, confessional, etc.), prayer conveys and internally reinforces various meanings. In addition, since the act of praying assumes that there is an ultimately powerful listener, strength is gained through the belief that the omnipotent hearer has a likelihood of responding in a supportive way. A person is thus afforded power by contacting its most fundamental source—God. Finally, through such inferences and connections, the prayer is put "right" with the deity; the praying individual feels personally fortified, sustained, and encouraged, which redounds to his or her sense of self-esteem and worth. On a more popular level, isn't this the message of the title of the book *Positive Prayers for Power-Filled Living*?[198] In a similar mode, Buttrick has written of *The Power of Prayer Today*, and Allen has declared that *All Things Are Possible through Prayer.*[199] The message is clear: Prayer makes life meaningful, endows people with strength, and makes them feel good.

The Role of Religious Experience and Conversion

Personal problems can be made worse or improved by the way one views them. Secondary control emphasizes this understanding. The effects of the objectively unchangeable can be greatly mollified when adaptation "change[s] the eyes which see reality."[200] This has a high probability of occurring when one has a religious experience or undergoes conversion. The world *appears* to have changed. Though conversion and religious experience need not go together, they are often associated, and their effects are frequently similar; hence they are treated here together.

For almost a century, the religionists and psychologists who study religious experience and conversion have commented on their precursors. Chief among these are conflict, turmoil, anxiety, personal problems, distress, and the like. Paul Johnson claimed that "a genuine religious conversion is the outcome of a crisis . . . a crisis of ultimate concern . . . a sense of desperate conflict."[201] Surveying five studies conducted between 1899 and 1929 on over 15,000 people, Johnson noted that the average age of conversion was 15.2 years. Starbuck attributed this to the "storm and stress" of adolescence, which he described as a time of "ferment of feeling, distress, despondency and anxiety."[202] De Sanctis claimed that "all the converted speak of their crises, of their efforts, and of their conflicts which they have endured."[203] The outcome, according to William James, is as follows:

> To be converted, to be regenerated, to receive grace, to experience religion, to gain an assurance . . . [these phrases] denote the process, gradual or sudden, by which a self hitherto divided, and consciously wrong inferior and unhappy, becomes unified and consciously right superior and happy, in consequence of its firmer hold upon religious realities. This is what conversion signifies in general terms. . . . [204]

Whether such an experience is identified as mysticism, religious experience, or conversion, many factors contribute to its occurrence. Clark has noted that mystical experience "is conditioned by temperament, tradition, suggestion, sexual urges in some cases, and the desire for security or escape in others."[205] We are mostly concerned with the last consideration, and agree with contemporary psychologists and sociologists that religious experience and conversion come to those who are actively seeking such security or escape, usually out of personal need.[206]

The motivation for religious experience or conversion is often seen in its effects, chief among which is the feeling that one has gained new knowledge and enlightenment. Greeley refers to experiential ecstasy as "a way of knowing."[207] In other words, the initial result is the gaining of a new set of meanings and new ways of seeing things. This stress on knowledge and meaning has been repeatedly demonstrated in empirical work.[208] The attainment of meaning is probably also the first step in gaining control of crisis situations

Virtually by definition, as we have indicated earlier, a crisis is a set of circumstances in which one lacks control. Rambo cites research to the effect that conversion enables "people to gain new ego control and strength."[209] Many converts' accounts speak to these elements, as those who describe their experiences and the effects of these repeatedly affirm a sense of heightened mastery over their lives and problems. This is widely discussed in the literature on Alcoholics Anonymous and drug addiction.[210]

In like manner, religious experiences and conversion are overwhelmingly associated with self-descriptive outcomes that cite joy, happiness, "up feelings," peace, calm, bliss, and satisfaction, among other similar terms and concepts.[211] Stated differently, these effects reflect improved self-esteem. To summarize, we may infer that religious experience and conversion, in the main, change people for the better and help them to resolve problems. They are often very effective means of coping with severe and/or long-standing difficulties. Though the issue is left to the next chapter, these encounters are not frequently symptomatic of mental disturbance.[212] Research Box 11.5 shows both sides of this issue.

Research Box 11.5. The Structure of Mystical Experience in Relation to Lifestyle (Spilka, Brown, & Cassidy, 1993)

In this study, 192 persons who reported having had religious mystical experiences responded to questions regarding their pre- and postexperience lives and the nature of their experiences. By means of utilizing factor analysis, six preexperience scales were constructed: general satisfaction, religious background, negativity toward mystical experience, self-satisfaction, health concerns, and religiosity. Eight reliable experience composites assessed unity/completeness, sacredness/holiness, presence of God, emotional and physical reactions, enlightenment/new knowledge, joy and bliss, extreme sensory stimulation, and hallucinations. Postexperience factors were a sense of spiritual oneness, positive change, and general mysticism.

Relationships among these three domains revealed a number of patterns. The strongest were as follows. First, older persons with health concerns and low self-esteem who were also likely to have had psychological counseling experienced a sense of unity/completeness, enlightenment/new knowledge, the presence of God, and much sensory stimulation. Second, those who reported these kinds of experiences now manifested enhanced feelings of spiritual oneness, positive change, and mystical inclinations. Though some configurations among the variables suggested maladjustment, the overall effects of the mystical experience were positive.

OVERVIEW

There can be little doubt that religion is an important resource in the coping and adjustment of many people. This is especially true when severe health difficulties or other life-threatening problems are present. Faith may help individuals marshal their personal capabilities and strengths, so that they can confront their troubles and handle them properly. When there are no effective means of changing a situation, religion may actually change a person: New interpretations are introduced that make the problem less distressing.

Religion probably helps because it provides individuals with personally useful meanings for upsetting circumstances. Concurrently, it offers, through a variety of avenues, opportunities for an enhanced sense of power and control over what is taking place. The result of both of these tendencies and of faith itself is a buttressing of self-esteem. Things no longer seem as bad as they once were, and since the individuals now believe they are doing the best that is possible, they can feel good about themselves. For the overwhelming majority of North Americans, the message of the 46th Psalm thus holds: "God is our refuge and strength, a very present help in trouble."[213]

NOTES

1. Robert Burns, quoted in Davidoff (1952, p. 291).
2. Aeschylus, quoted in Bartlett (1955, p. 13).
3. Martin Luther, quoted in Bartlett (1955, p. 86).
4. Quoted in Mead (1965, p. 166).
5. Clarence Day, quoted in Davidoff (1952, pp. 114–115).
6. Søren Kierkegaard, quoted in Phillips (1981, p. 56).
7. Lazarus and Folkman (1984).
8. Silverman and Pargament (1990, p. 2).
9. Lazarus and Folkman (1984, pp. 31–54).
10. Holahan and Moos (1987).
11. Lazarus and Folkman (1984).
12. Holahan and Moos (1987).
13. Conway (1985–1986).
14. Folkman, Lazarus, Dunkel-Schetter, De Longis, and Gruen (1986).
15. Koenig, George, and Siegler (1988).
16. Bjorck and Cohen (1993); Rollins-Bohannon (1991).
17. Carver, Scheier, and Weintraub (1989).
18. Folkman and Lazarus (1988).
19. E. O. Wilson (1978, p. 2).
20. E. O. Wilson (1978, p. 3).
21. E. O. Wilson (1978, p. 176).
22. Batson (1983, p. 1385).
23. Waller, Kojetin, Bouchard, Lykken, and Tellegen (1990); Matthews, Batson, Horn, and Rosenman (1981).
24. Hardy (1975).
25. D'Aquili (1978).
26. Maddi (1970, p. 137).
27. McKeon (1941, p. 689).
28. Reid (1788/1969, p. 128).
29. Argyle (1959, p. 147).
30. Clark (1958, p. 419).
31. Baumeister (1991).
32. Baumeister (1991, p. 183).
33. Fichter (1981, p. 20).

34. Echterling (1993).
35. Echterling (1993, p. 5).
36. Brett (1912).
37. Russell (1945).
38. Reid (1788/1969, p. 128).
39. Berndtson (1950, p. 379).
40. Langer (1983); Phares (1976); Seligman (1975).
41. Lefcourt (1973, p. 425).
42. Lefcourt and Davidson-Katz (1991).
43. McIntosh and Spilka (1990); Pargament et al. (1988).
44. Kazantzakis (1961, p. 45).
45. Adler (1991); Cousins (1979); Sklar and Anisman (1981).
46. Quoted in Bartlett (1955, p. 118).
47. Baumeister (1991, p. 183).
48. Andrew (1970).
49. Quoted in Johnson and Spilka (1988, p. 12).
50. Rothbaum, Weisz, and Snyder (1982).
51. Bulman and Wortman (1977).
52. Quoted in Johnson and Spilka (1988, p. 13).
53. Isaiah 7:14 (*The Holy Bible*, Authorized King James Version).
54. Quoted in Johnson and Spilka (1988, p. 12).
55. Eliach (1982).
56. Quoted in Johnson and Spilka (1988, p. 12).
57. Gergen (1971).
58. Reid (1788/1969).
59. Kaplan (1982, p. 139).
60. Silver and Wortman (1980, p. 329).
61. Wylie (1979).
62. Whisman and Kwon (1993).
63. Calkins (1910, pp. 262–263).
64. Benson and Spilka (1973).
65. Batson, Schoenrade, and Ventis (1993).
66. Ryan, Rigby, and King (1993).
67. Foster and Keating (1990).
68. Jones (1993, p. 2).
69. Hood (1992c).
70. Rosenberg (1962).
71. Myers (1992); Seligman (1991).
72. Peterson, Seligman, and Vaillant (1988).
73. Sethi and Seligman (1993).
74. Hooper and Spilka (1970).
75. Myers (1992, p. 201).
76. Myers (1992, p. 75).
77. Ellison (1991b).
78. Myers (1992, p. 183).
79. Pollner (1989, p. 100).
80. Myers (1992, p. 189).
81. Krause and Van Tranh (1989).
82. Carver et al. (1993).
83. Gross (1982, p. 242).
84. Bjorck and Cohen (1993, p. 67).
85. Ross (1990).
86. Park, Cohen, and Herb (1990).
87. Hunsberger, Pancer, Pratt, and Alisat (in press).
88. Glock (1964).
89. Niebuhr (1929, p. 29).
90. Wood (1965, p. 109).
91. Kaplan (1965).

92. Demerath (1965, p. 203).
93. Sampson (1969).
94. Peterson and Roy (1985).
95. Bulman and Wortman (1977).
96. Pargament et al. (1990).
97. Pargament et al. (1990).
98. Crawford, Handal, and Wiener (1989).
99. Mattlin, Wethington, and Kessler (1990).
100. McRae and Costa (1986).
101. Bjorck and Cohen (1993).
102. Hayden (1991).
103. Greenberg and Revenson (1993).
104. Ross (1990).
105. Maton (1989).
106. Newman and Pargament (1990).
107. Wright, Pratt, and Schmall (1985).
108. Johnson and Spilka (1991); Spilka and Schmidt (1983).
109. Jenkins and Pargament (1988).
110. Acklin, Brown, and Mauger (1983); Johnson and Spilka (1991).
111. Holahan and Moos (1987, p. 949).
112. Meyer, Altmaier, and Burns (1992); Yates, Chalmer, St. James, Follansbee, and McKegney (1981).
113. Minton and Spilka (1976); Spilka, Stout, Minton, and Sizemore (1977).
114. McIntosh, Silver, and Wortman (1993).
115. Friedman, Chodoff, Mason, and Hamburg (1963).
116. Palmer and Noble (1986).
117. Maton (1989).
118. Rollins-Bohannon (1991).
119. Cook and Wimberly (1983, p. 237).
120. Park and Cohen (1993); Schoenrade, Ludwig, Atkinson, and Shane (1990).
121. Erikson (1963).
122. Underhill (1936, p. 64).
123. Benson and Eklin (1990).
124. Koenig, George, and Siegler (1988); Krause and Van Tranh (1989).
125. Koenig, George, and Siegler (1988); Conway (1985–1986); Manfredi and Pickett (1987).
126. Rosen (1982).
127. Johnson and Mullins (1989); Koenig, Kvale, and Ferrel (1988); Pressman, Lyons, Larson, and Strain (1990).
128. McRae (1984).
129. Fry (1990).
130. Albrecht and Cornwall (1989).
131. Moberg (1965).
132. Myers (1992, p. 75).
133. Levin and Schiller (1987).
134. Levin and Schiller (1987, p. 24).
135. McIntosh, Kojetin, and Spilka (1985); McIntosh and Spilka (1990); Strickland and Shaffer (1971).
136. Loewenthal and Cornwall (1993); McIntosh and Spilka (1990); Sarafino (1990).
137. Benson, cited in Goleman (1984, p. 51).
138. Hannay (1980).
139. Zuckerman, Kasl, and Ostfeld (1984).
140. Idler and Kasl (1992).
141. Ameika, Eck, Ivers, Clifford, and Malcarne (1994).
142. Sarafino (1990); King (1990); Levin and Schiller (1987); Oleckno and Blacconiere (1991).
143. Levin and Schiller (1987).
144. Kass, Friedman, Leserman, Zuttermeister, and Benson (1991).
145. King (1990); Levin and Schiller (1987).
146. Spilka, Shaver, and Kirkpatrick (1985).
147. Gorsuch (1968); Spilka, Armatas, and Nussbaum (1964).
148. Pargament et al. (1988).

149. Benson, quoted in Goleman (1984, p. 52).
150. Lawson and McCauley (1990); Reik (1946).
151. Reik (1946, p. 17).
152. Pruyser (1974, p. 205).
153. Pruyser (1974, pp. 208–209).
154. Wright (1982, p. 57).
155. Pruyser (1968, pp. 143, 168).
156. Fullerton, McCarroll, Ursano, and Wright (1992).
157. Pargament et al. (1990).
158. Poloma and Gallup (1991).
159. Foster (1992).
160. David, Ladd, and Spilka (1992).
161. Poloma and Gallup (1991).
162. David et al. (1992).
163. Trier and Shupe (1991).
164. Trier and Shupe (1991, p. 354).
165. Ladd, Milmoe, and Spilka (1994).
166. Janssen, de Hart, and den Draak (1989); Poloma and Gallup (1991, pp. 8–10).
167. Carlson, Bacaseta, and Simanton (1988).
168. Finney and Malony (1985a).
169. Joyce and Weldon (1965).
170. Colipp (1969).
171. Byrd (1988).
172. Park et al. (1990).
173. Trier and Shupe (1991).
174. Holahan and Moos (1987).
175. Parker and Brown (1982); Veroff, Douvan, and Kulka (1981).
176. Bickel (1993).
177. Poloma and Gallup (1990); Poloma and Pendleton (1991a).
178. D. G. Richards (1991).
179. Baldree, Murphy, and Powers (1982).
180. Sutton and Murphy (1989).
181. Spilka, Ladd, and David (1993).
182. Saudia, Kinney, Brown, and Young-Ward (1991).
183. Bearon and Koenig (1990).
184. Bill-Harvey, Rippey, Abeles, and Pfeiffer (1989).
185. Elkins (1977).
186. Griffiths and Mahy (1984).
187. Brown (1966, 1968).
188. Fry (1990).
189. Watts and Williams (1988, p. 109).
190. Weisz, Rothbaum, and Blackburn (1984).
191. Phillips (1981, p. 56).
192. Phillips (1981, p. 67).
193. Phillips (1981, p. 72).
194. Watts and Williams (1988, p. 114).
195. Lerner (1980).
196. Pargament and Hahn (1986).
197. Rubin and Peplau (1973).
198. Schuller (1976).
199. Buttrick (1970); Allen (1958).
200. Kazantzakis (1961, p. 45).
201. Johnson (1959, p. 117).
202. Starbuck (1899, p. 213).
203. De Sanctis (1927, p. 67).
204. James (1902/1985, p. 157).
205. Clark (1958, p. 290).
206. Malony (1973); Rambo (1992).

207. Greeley (1974).
208. Laski (1961); Spilka, Brown, and Cassidy (1993).
209. Rambo (1992, p. 177).
210. Clark (1971).
211. Greeley (1974, p. 21); Spilka, Brown, and Cassidy (1993).
212. Spilka, Brown, and Cassidy (1993).
213. Psalms 46:1 (*The Holy Bible*, Authorized King James Version).

Chapter 12

RELIGION AND MENTAL DISORDER

Religion as we know it today serves as an institutionalized defense against anxiety.[1]

God should be brought forth to meet Satan and then Satan could go and teach the people the right. . . . It was my job to start it and get the spirit working. . . . I am the true spirit of God. . . . When I was in the rage, there was something telling me that I was the true spirit of Christ.[2]

She wore a crown of thorns. She scarred her face with pepper so no man would find her attractive. Someone had the bad taste to praise her hands, so she dipped them in lye.[3]

Once in direst distress, no way out, Jesus sat beside me in my car and said "Do not look at me. All will be well."[4]

I was carried outside my body. . . . I saw God, and it seemed his holiness scared me and about four hours later I came back to earth.[5]

PAST AND PRESENT: CONFUSION IN VALUES AND PRACTICES

The association of religion and mental disorder goes well back into antiquity. Biblical citation is antedated by primitive and Asian references, and the Greeks and Romans usually invoked supernatural explanations when psychological aberration was manifested.[6] At no time in history have religious institutions ignored expressions of mental and emotional disturbances.

Not too long ago, mental deviation was defined and controlled by religious authorities operating on the Biblical principle that "the Lord shall smite thee with madness" for not obeying God's commandments (and religious leaders' pronouncements).[7] In reacting to mental disturbance during its first 1,500 years, the Christian tradition combined kindness and compassion with cruelty and punishment. At first, the early church associated tolerance and sympathy with prayer and supportive religious practices.[8] Threats to ecclesiastical authority from competing political and economic forces paralleled a growing concern with sin, confession, repentance, and punishment. Renaissance, Reformation, and Enlightenment ideas brought new challenges to religious institutions, which accordingly often hardened their position even further. One late expression of this conflict may be found in a readiness to make the accusation of witchcraft. Literally thousands of mentally disturbed persons suffered and met their deaths because of such responses from religious communities.[9]

Even though ecclesiastical power in this realm slowly gave way to medicine, psychiatry, and psychology, the notion of sin and wrongdoing as causative of mental problems still has a grip on the popular mind, and such themes even persist among the helping professions.[10] Though the cruder versions of these ideas seem to be fading, some may be found today in certain religiously conservative quarters, particularly in relatively isolated groups.

Intimations of abnormality and psychopathology have plagued the relationship between religion and psychology in the contemporary world.[11] Largely emanating from classical psychoanalysis, this tradition offered the triad of "becoming weak-minded, religious, and credulous."[12] Freud supplemented this judgment with even more pejorative suggestions that "religion is comparable to a childhood neurosis."[13] He and his followers soon argued for an analogy between acts of faith and "obsessional neurosis."[14] The long-range outcome turned out to be a latent (and often not so latent) feeling on the part of many psychologists that to be religious signified at least intellectual and emotional immaturity, and possibly a need for therapy. This view was kept alive by the widespread use of illustrations of religion in mental illness in psychological texts, and even in the third edition of the American Psychiatric Association's *Diagnostic and Statistical Manual of Mental Disorders* (DSM-III).[15] With respect to DSM-III, Kilbourne and Richardson claimed that it had "an implicit and sometimes explicit tendency to devalue experiences common to many religions and to cast them into the pale of psychopathology."[16]

The situation, however, seems to be changing, as the latest edition of the DSM (DSM-IV) recognizes "religious and spiritual difficulties as a distinct mental disorder deserving treatment."[17] As part of this new awareness, religion and spirituality can be considered psychotherapeutic tools. Antireligious statements, such as Ellis's view that "the less religious they [patients] are, the more emotionally healthy they will tend to be,"[18] are apparently becoming passé.

For at least three decades, psychologists and religionists have been replacing previous doubts and antagonisms with a new spirit of mutual concern and cooperation. The rapidly growing pastoral psychology movement has united both lay and religious clinicians in the common endeavor of enhancing human potential. This and similar aspirations are finding considerable support in a thriving research literature on coping and adjustment (see Chapter 11). Among other groups, the Psychology of Religion division of the American Psychological Association plays a central part in furthering these developments. Stern and Marino, in speaking of what they term "psychotheology," claim that "religion and psychology have come to the point of seeing each other as polar ends of a workable compromise."[19] Toward such a goal, Sanborn has written a book entitled *Mental–Spiritual Health Models*, showing ways in which pastoral psychology and theology relate to mental and spiritual health and illness.[20] In a similar manner, many psychoanalytically oriented practitioners currently work toward harmonizing their approach with patients' faith. In this spirit, Linn and Schwarz have written on "ways in which religion and the social sciences, especially psychiatry, may join forces."[21] Contradicting Freud, they present clinical data to the effect "that emotional growth by way of psychoanalysis can result in an upsurge of religious feeling."[22] In sum, the integration of contemporary religion and psychology supports Hiltner's position of "psychology as a theological discipline internal to theology itself."[23] Simply put, we have come full circle to the realization that cooperation between religion and the behavioral sciences is essential to human betterment.

DIRECTIONS, CONCERNS, AND CAUTIONS

The relationship of religion to psychopathology has a long and complex history, which is worthy of study in its own right. Insofar as we are products of our collective past, a full appreciation of this heritage is essential; however, it goes far beyond what we can offer here. The purpose of this chapter is to show the many ways in which faith and psychological problems are interrelated. Among these possibilities are the following:

1. Religion may be an expression of mental disorder.
2. Institutionalized faith can be a socializing and suppressing force, helping (or forcing) people to cope with their difficulties and therefore to function as contributing members of society.
3. Religion can serve as a haven, a protective agency for some disturbed people.
4. Spiritual commitment and involvement may perform therapeutic roles in alleviating mental distress.
5. Religion can be a stressor, a source of problems; in a sense, it can be "hazardous to one's mental health."[24]

In addition to these possible relational patterns, much research has been conducted on connections between personal faith and the following: a variety of behavioral disturbances, such as substance abuse, crime, and delinquency (see Chapter 10 for our treatment of these problems); mild to severe forms of psychopathology; and special areas of concern that have only recently been recognized, such as mental disorder among women, the elderly, and persons who affiliate with what are pejoratively termed "cults." Issues such as sexual abuse among the clergy have received considerable attention in the mass media and are also worthy of examination. There are few matters in the psychology of religion more complex and controversial than the relationship of religion to sexual abuse and other behaviors that are most accurately termed "psychosocial disorders"; this is an area that has been greatly studied, and yet it continues to merit much more investigation. At the outset, however, let us say that the overwhelming mass of research evidence suggests far more beneficial associations between religion and mental well-being than adverse effects of religion on mental health.

Problems of Definition

Although scientists always hope to achieve truly definitive and final answers, they generally consider these unobtainable luxuries. If anything is constant in the scientific community, it is change, and as far as the diagnosis of mental disorder is concerned, measured and orderly change has been an ideal for over 40 years. As already noted, DSM-IV has recently appeared to supplant its predecessor, DSM-III-R. Since research on religion and abnormality spans many decades, the language employed in earlier work may not be in use any more. Translating older terminology into the terms acceptable today may actually not be possible. For example, the more or less generic rubrics "neurosis" and "psychosis" have been out of favor for about 15 years. In addition, within psychology and psychiatry, those who have worked with one classification system for psychopathology are frequently reluctant to adopt new frameworks, and may mix the concepts and ideas with which they are familiar with the latest categories. In other words, the application of diagnostic labels is likely to be considerably less precise than is desirable from either a research or an applied perspective.[25] Much inconsistency may be present when clinical identifications are offered. Caution must therefore be the rule in reading about any psychological/psychiatric grouping. For example, over the years the syndrome of schizophrenia has undergone many changes, so that a rough correspondence to what was meant a short time ago obscures new understandings and classifications.

The situation is no better when we review the religious facets of work in this area. Not uncommon are studies that simply designate their respondents as Catholic, Protestant, Jewish, and "other."[26] Once these labels are applied, little or no explanation is provided for variations among these broad groups. Confounding factors such as socioeconomic status or ethnic group are ignored, and both of these factors are very significant correlates of mental disorder. In addition, issues such as degree of religious commitment and church or synagogue participation are not considered. It must also be noted that these classifications are simplifications. Are the Jews Orthodox, Conservative, or Reform? Being an Italian Catholic is sometimes very different from being an Irish Catholic in religious expression. And just what does it mean to be Protestant? The *Yearbook of American and Canadian Churches* lists about 260 religious bodies, of which about 220 are said to be Protestant.[27] The futility of conducting research when the religious variable is poorly defined is obvious. Furthermore, the habit has developed of providing demographic information without a theory that makes such classification meaningful.

In Chapter 1, we have discussed the complexity of the religious domain, and we have suggested that categories such as "intrinsic" and "extrinsic" or "committed" and "consensual" faith forms, among other possibilities, might be useful. Unhappily, virtually no study dealing with mental disorder goes beyond some vague breakdown of religiosity based on frequency of church attendance or a designation of individuals as Protestant, Catholic, Jewish, and "other." An interesting variation is to classify persons as orthodox, fundamentalist, evangelical, or Pentecostal. Simplistic indicators of religion often mask a poor understanding of this highly complex realm by researchers. Still, consistency over multiple studies suggests reliable findings, and even when respondents have been poorly classified, such work can offer clues to more sophisticated workers and thus stimulate better research. Unfortunately, this is a costly and time- and energy-consuming path to follow, and a much more efficient approach is possible. This entails the development of adequate theory to guide such studies; more exacting definitions on both sides of the issue of religion and mental disturbance are an essential prerequisite in such work.

A Possible Theoretical Direction

In Chapter 11, coping and adjustment have been related to the assumption that humans have at least three basic needs. Though others can similarly be hypothesized, we have emphasized the elemental desires for meaning, control, and self-esteem. Earlier in this volume, and in its predecessor, discussion has been directed at the cognitive social-psychological idea of attributions. Also in Chapter 11, we have attempted to show that the attributions people make are efforts to maximize meaning, control, and self-esteem. In many instances, religious attributions perform these roles.

Let us now apply these ideas to the realm of religion and mental disorder. The origins of mental disorders are complex, often involving biological factors; however, the translation of their influences into the domain of social conduct is our main concern. As effects, these frequently entail deviant attributions to the world and to the self. They imply that in order to achieve meaning and maintain a sense of control and self-esteem, a person is psychologically forced, usually by the stresses of life, to seek explanations outside of the normal range. Such is the stuff of delusions and reality distortions, and of their expression in the categories of the DSM. This is a rather bare theoretical statement that needs much further specification, but it should suffice as a guide.

Religion may be described in a number of ways that have already been cited: as an expression of mental disorder; as a suppressing or socializing device; as a haven; as therapy; and as a hazard to mental health. These possibilities are not necessarily independent of one another. Suppression/socialization and therapy may at times overlap, and may take place in a haven-like atmosphere. The suppression/socialization functions of faith may act both constructively, keeping a person in the community, and stressfully, creating for the individual an internal struggle; the long-range result of all this may be either positive or negative. Similarly, the haven function of institutionalized religion, with its own rules and regulations that often limit member options, may eventually create severe stress that culminates in serious breakdown. Recognizing such complexity is essential. However, to start our analysis, we must begin on a simpler note, and examine the roles of faith in relation to the way people cope with what Thomas Szasz terms "problems of living."[28]

RELIGION AS AN EXPRESSION OF MENTAL DISORDER

Mystical Experience[29]

The often extremely unusual and graphic nature of religious or mystical experiences can readily lead an observer to conclude that these are signs of mental disturbance. Indeed they may be, but let us first accept a well-established research finding described Chapter 7 on mysticism—namely, that considerable proportions of the U.S. and British populations report such encounters. Depending on the way the question eliciting this information is phrased, up to 50% of those sampled indicate having had such experiences.[30] If religiously active people are selected, the incidence is even higher. In fact, certain religious bodies (usually quite conservative ones) expect their members to have these episodes and to disclose them publicly. In these groups, such experiences help integrate people into the church and therefore support their adjustment. In addition, in both Western and other cultures, reports of such occurrences frequently contribute to the reputations of spiritual figures such as saints.[31] In other words, having a religious experience seems to be quite normal, may aid adjustment, and may be regarded quite positively.

Even though it has been acknowledged that "some mystics are badly disoriented personalities,"[32] a committee of the Group for the Advancement of Psychiatry indicated that it was unable "to make a firm distinction between a mystical state and a psychopathological state."[33] The committee did feel that mysticism "serves certain psychic needs, or that it constitutes an attempt to resolve certain ubiquitous problems."[34] Even though this committee offered some comments on the possibly favorable outcomes of mystical experiences, it was still too strongly attached to classic psychoanalytic and psychiatric views to make a full and truly balanced break with its negative historical tradition. It thus identified mystical behaviors as "intermediate between normality and frank psychosis; a form of ego regression."[35] Other psychiatrists have suggested, however, that mystical experience can be a constructive rejection of aggression or even a suicide preventative.[36] Research has also been conducted that distinguishes between mystical states and schizophrenic thinking and behavior.[37]

The association of religious and mystical episodes with the use of drugs has been widely noted.[38] Insofar as drug use may be activated by abnormality, psychedelic experiences with a religious flavor can be regarded as expressive of deviance in personality.

Almost three-quarters of a century ago, Leuba looked at the role of epilepsy in mystical expression, implying aberrant nervous system function as underlying such experiences in many people. He thus spoke of "the presence in our great mystics of nervous disorders, perhaps of hysteria."[39] Leuba also felt that mental problems such as "neurasthenia" and depression predisposed people to have mystical experiences.

In a highly significant theoretical and research paper, Rodney Stark has offered a breakdown of religious/mystical experiences that range from the normal to the possibly pathological.[40] For example, his "salvational" type is said to be motivated by a sense of "sin and guilt."[41] Of a more extreme nature, with much potential for illustrating a mentally disturbed condition, is what Stark terms the "revelational" experience. It is clearly the rarest and most deviant form he discusses, and finds expression in visual and auditory hallucinations that the individual regards as true messages from the deity, angels, or Satan. It has received some confirmation from work showing that personality and adjustment problems may be associated with religious experiences involving extreme physical and emotional reactions and/or hallucinations.[42] Similar connections have been offered by other scholars.[43]

Summarizing the research literature, Lukoff and his associates point out that "studies have found that people reporting mystical experiences scored lower on psychopathology scales and higher on measures of psychological well-being than controls."[44] There is no doubt that religious and mystical encounters may reflect mental disturbance; however, the weight of the evidence suggests that such experiences are often normal, and even have beneficial effects.[45] This is discussed further in Chapters 6 and 7.

Glossolalia

The phenomenon of glossolalia, or "speaking in tongues," can be quite impressive and awe-inspiring in its effects. Commonly associated with religious experience and found frequently among Pentecostal, revivalist, and charismatic sects, it easily led to interpretations of psychopathology, especially in the past. In some instances, when it is observed outside of its approved religious setting, recommendations for psychiatric involvement are likely to occur.[46] There is reason to believe that the presence of glossolalia may be increasing in more mainline Christian groups. One recent estimate suggests that there are at least 2 million glossolalics in the United States.[47]

The question "Is glossolalia a normal or abnormal behavior?" has been with us for some time. Clinical psychological and psychiatric professionals are inclined toward explanations that stress deviance. Researchers lean toward seeing minor personality differences, or, more commonly, find no distinctions between glossolalics and nonglossolalics. Kildahl has described glossolalics as suggestible, passive, submissive, and dependent.[48] In contrast, Teshome found glossolalics to be more independent and to rely on others less than nonglossolalics.[49] He found few differences between his groups on personality measures.

Taking the deviance perspective, Pattison claims that glossolalic individuals demonstrate "overt psychopathology of a sociopathic, hysterical, or hypochondriacal nature."[50] This certainly indicates serious disorder. Kelsey notes an implied correlation with schizophrenia, but rejects such an identification.[51] He is more willing to accept glossolalia as a lesser neurotic symptom, but also expresses doubt about applying such a label to these people. There is evidence that speaking in tongues usually follows a period of crisis, and works to resolve the resulting anxiety.[52] Similarly, Preus sees glossolalia as a "release from tension and an answer to personal stress and trauma . . . and [it] can be accomplished by almost any person who really wants to. . . ."[53] These last views moderate the extreme position of Pattison, but still maintain some potentially aberrant motivation (i.e., stress and anxiety). Goodman uses the phrase "hyperarousal dissociation," which verbally implies abnormality, but really speaks more to an altered state of consciousness. She further asserts that "beyond the threshold of the conscious there is not disorder but structure."[54]

The confusion about the normality or abnormality of glossolalic behavior is slowly being resolved in the direction of normality. There is currently little doubt that it is learned behavior, which is reinforced in certain group settings into which the person is socialized.[55] Undoubtedly, there are instances of individuals whose glossolalia may be symptomatic of personal problems, but these seem to be the exception rather than the rule. A representative example of research in this area is provided in Research Box 12.1.

Conversion[56]

Like religious experience and glossolalia, which are sometimes associated with conversion, conversion itself has been the object of clinical and psychiatric concern. (In recent years, this has been especially true when a person affiliates with a group pejoratively described as a "cult." This, however, is a topic worthy of consideration in its own right, and it is more extensively discussed in Chapters 8 and 9.) As will be evident, we are concerned here with only one part of the multifaceted phenomenon termed "conversion."

Research Box 12.1. The Psychology of Speaking in Tongues
(Kildahl, 1972)

In this study, two groups—one of 20 glossolalics, the other of 20 nonglossolalics—were interviewed in depth about their lives and tongue-speaking experiences. The groups were equated for religiosity, which was evidently high. Three projective tests (the Rorschach ink blot, the Thematic Apperception Test, and the Draw-a-Person) and one objective test (the Minnesota Multiphasic Personality Inventory) were administered to the participants.

It was observed that the nonglossolalics tended to be more independent and autonomous, but also more depressed, than their glossolalic peers. Tongue speaking appeared to be associated with strong trust in a religious group leader. Though no real differences existed between the two groups on mental well-being, the glossolalics were characterized as being more dependent on the guidance of a trusted religious authority. They appeared inclined to relinquish personal independence and control to this leader, and became indifferent to glossolalia or ceased being glossolalic when they lost faith in their spiritual guide.

In his book, Kildahl cited another researcher who asserted that "more than 85 percent of tongue-speakers had experienced a clearly defined anxiety crisis preceding their speaking in tongues" (p. 57). The glossolalia seemed to be constructive and anxiety-reducing in these cases.

Without question, most conversions are not symptomatic of mental disturbance. Some, indeed, do mirror personal problems, but they may also reflect constructive solutions to those difficulties. Even early researchers pointed to both possibilities. Though negative perceptions prevailed in their writings, room was still left for favorable interpretations of the causes and outcomes of conversion. Probably the earliest such study was conducted by E. D. Starbuck in the late 1890s, and it illustrates these considerations well. High among the motives he found to motivate conversion were "fear of Death or Hell," and "Remorse, Conviction for Sin, etc."[57] The most common emotional states he found to be associated with conversion were "depression, sadness, pensiveness," with "restlessness, anxiety, uncertainty" following closely.[58]

In another classic study of over 2,000 people, E. T. Clark reported three kinds of "religious awakening."[59] Two of these, the "definite crisis awakening" and the "emotional stimulus awakening," were judged to have the highest potential of expressing psychological problems. Most often they were accompanied by sin, guilt, and depression, frequently affiliated with sexual problems. Clark's "gradual awakening" type pictured a positive form of conversion.

More recent work that illustrates the influence of underlying disturbance reveals that persons suffering from affective disorders show an increased likelihood of having conversion and salvational experiences when either ill or well. This has been explained by noting the heightened emotional responsiveness of such individuals. The outcomes of these religious manifestations span the entire range from pain and depression to great personal benefit.[60]

The research of Starbuck and Clark brought to the fore the question of sudden versus gradual conversion. The literature has tended to indict the former as an expression of underlying pathology, while approving of the latter as suggestive of mental health and well-being. The general position has been that, on average, those who convert suddenly tend to be emotionally unstable and are likely to relapse. In many instances, their transformation has been considered superficial, since they may engage in repeated conversions, particularly in revival-type situations.[61] A follow-up of persons who made such "decisions" during a Billy Graham crusade in Great Britain revealed that about half had lapsed during the subsequent year.[62] Another investigation reported that 87% of these converts had reverted within 6 months to their former religious behavior.[63] Apparently, some of these people had converted up to six times. Psychiatrist Leon Salzman termed these sudden and superficial conversions "regressive-pathological."[64]

Other work on the sudden–gradual distinction has fairly consistently shown that the sudden form is associated with higher anxiety and poorer chronic adjustment than is true of those who acquire their faith and commitment over a longer period of time.[65] Severe depression and the potential for suicide have also been components in these sudden conversions.[66] However, as popular as the image of the sudden conversion seems to be in the popular mind, the evidence suggests that it is relatively uncommon, usually affecting about 7% of converts.[67]

Family concerns have often been emphasized by psychologists and psychiatrists in their work on conversion. Christensen reported parent–child difficulties prior to conversion, particularly among persons with early fundamentalist training.[68] Ullman's work on converts to Catholicism, Judaism, Baha'i, and Hare Krishna also resulted in a focus on early family life and pointed at disturbed relationships on the part of the converts with their fathers, plus other signs of a distressed childhood.[69] Salzman had earlier identified his "regressive-pathological" conversions with authority conflicts, notably with one's father.[70] The same theme pervades the work of Allison, whose study of converts also stressed the role of alcoholic, absent, or weak fathers.[71] Though claims such as these are made by knowledgeable clinicians, it is sometimes difficult for readers to reach the same conclusions from the data as those reporting such work. Still, this kind of thinking is popular in certain psychological/psychiatric quarters. Especially illustrative is an extensive and informative case history in which Levin and Zegans viewed the conversion of a young man as a "replacement for his deficient, weak father."[72] This theme of conversion reflecting paternal problems is commonly found among psychoanalytically oriented scholars, but needs confirmation by more exacting research. This is part of a broader negative view of conversion as "generally a regressive, disintegrative, pathological phenomenon."[73] This position has, however, failed to gain any substantial support in almost a century of research.

We may say that conversion, though often graphically impressive, is infrequently a manifestation of underlying psychological disturbance. Most large-scale studies demonstrate that conversions are positive and constructive events.[74] The rapid acquisition of a new religious faith is apparently more likely than its gradual counterpart to reflect problems in coping with impulses and relating to others and the world.

Scrupulosity

A rather clear example of mental pathology being manifested in religious thinking and behavior has been termed "scrupulosity."[75] Simply put, it has been called "the religious manifestation of Obsessive–Compulsive Disorder, and is regarded in DSM-IV as one of the Anxiety Disorders."[76] Specifically, it is considered "a condition involving continuous worry about religious issues or compulsions to perform religious rituals."[77] Askin and her colleagues have been able to develop a relatively short objective measure of scrupulosity that correlates very strongly with indices of obsessive–compulsiveness.[78] Similar findings have been reported for a group of disturbed Catholic children.[79]

Primary among the expressions associated with scrupulosity are a fear of sin and compulsive doubt.[80] Those suffering from this condition are continually seeking assurance from religious authorities. In addition, they engage in rigid ritualistic observances and practices in order to gain some sense of purification—a sense that they can never attain. This is because of their views of the self as bad and sinful, and of the deity as unforgiving and tolerating no deviation from the most extreme religious strictures that can be imagined.

The Religion of Mentally Disordered Persons

Psychopathology can affect religious expression in many ways. Many illustrations can be found in textbooks on abnormal psychology and psychiatry.[81] Furthermore, we have noted that DSM-III focused unduly on case study religious illustrations for a wide variety of disorders, probably as a partial reflection of antireligious bias. This prejudice is a function of the highly questionable psychoanalytic inference of "similarities between mental illness and religion."[82]

Since religious identification, beliefs, and practices are very normal (though highly variable) in every known culture, if they mirror abnormal mental states, distinctions between such conditions and customary religious expressions may be evident. This has been shown to be true. There is little doubt that mental deviance has its parallels in spiritual aberrance. Argyle has pointed out that religious mental patients often manifest their faith in troubled and bizarre ways.[83] Oates found that psychotics who believed religion was involved in their problems had distorted memories of religion in their early years.[84] Reifsnyder and Campbell claimed that the religion of psychiatric patients was often inconsistent, shallow, and confused.[85] Apparently, many disturbed people commonly perceive their deity as controlling, vindictive, and unforgiving, ready to punish those who violate godly prescriptions. A consonant perception is that these individuals are themselves sinners and transgressors, and deserving of divine punishment.[86]

That the situation is more complex than these findings imply is illustrated by Lowe and Braaten's research,[87] which is presented in Research Box 12.2. We may, however, conclude that the faith of mentally disturbed persons has a high probability of also being deviant. We must also agree with Beit-Hallahmi, who wisely observes that "the specific content of psychiatric symptoms seems to be determined by social background factors. Individual psychodynamics determine the appearance of symptoms, but their particular form will be the result of these background factors, one of which is religion."[88]

RELIGION AS A SOCIALIZING AND SUPPRESSING AGENT

The Control Functions of the Religious Community

As a sociocultural institution, religion may function to actively socialize, suppress, and inhibit what the community defines as deviant and unacceptable behavior. Both sociologists and psychologists affirm that churchgoers overwhelmingly represent the more conservative and conforming members of the North American social order.[89] Stark and Glock refer to "churches as moral communities"; as such, mental deviance is often redefined as a moral problem, since it threatens social cohesion.[90] Whether a religious institution is socially regarded as liberal or conservative, it attempts to suppress conflict among its own adherents even if this increases dissension in the larger community.[91] This can extend into all aspects of an individual's life, not the least of which are child-rearing practices that attempt to con-

---

෫

**Research Box 12.2. Differences in Religious Attitudes
in Mental Illness (Lowe & Braaten, 1966)**

Inferring that "religious concern and conflict characterize patients in psychiatric hospitals" (p. 435), these researchers attempted to determine objectively the religious attitudes of 508 hospitalized mental patients. A 27-item religion questionnaire was developed, 18 items of which dealt with religion in relation to the patient's pathology.

No differences were found in the religious attitudes of patients with different diagnoses. A major influence was the time a patient had spent in the hospital; this related positively to self-concern and negatively to religious influence. When those who had been patients for more than 7 years were compared with their peers who had been hospitalized for less than this time, the former expressed more doubts about the existence of God, were less certain that God loved them, and felt that their faith was less comforting and less likely to provide a sense of purpose. They were, however, more apt to feel that it was an aid for self-improvement. The researchers felt that the longer people were in the hospital, the greater their withdrawal from the world. Viewing religion as a form of social interest, they concluded that religious involvement and ideas suffered during hospitalization, along with other social commitments.

trol displeasing and socially inappropriate behavior (e.g., aggression).[92] Studying maladaptive behavior among mainline Protestants, MacDonald and Luckett suggested that failures to adapt in this core group may result from early exposure at home to overly strong and repressive controls. Such experiences, rather than aiding adjustment to reality, may foster rigid identifications with ideals that simply may not be realizable in modern life.[93]

Social disapproval and ostracism are strong weapons for shaping thought and action. Little is more distressing than the loss of friendships and affectional support. When an individual departs from group norms, pressure is exerted to bring the person into line with social standards. If that fails, contact with the offender is reduced until the person is isolated.[94] By such means, the religious community creates a learning environment that can direct abnormal thinking and activity into approved channels. This is mediated both through the social values and responses of the church members and through religious doctrines. Socializing an individual by these means apparently strengthens impulse controls and counters deviant tendencies.[95] This is evidently true for Hare Krishna members, whose adjustment improves with the length of time that they are affiliated with this group. The social controls exercised by this organization clearly constitute a learning environment for its adherents.[96]

A considerable research literature also shows that the social environment of a religious group can suppress undesirable delinquent behavior and the use of drugs and alcohol (see also Chapter 10).[97] Among Jews, as one goes from Reform to Orthodox groups, intoxication decreases.[98] The traditional Orthodox Jewish home tightly circumscribes the use of alcohol, primarily permitting it to be used in religious rituals. In contrast, among more liberal Reform Jews, the strong identification that is made with general North American values permits considerable social drinking, with a greater likelihood of alcohol abuse.[99]

The Control Functions of Religious Ideas and Institutions

In the preceding section, we have been concerned with the internalization of the control functions of religion. As Pruyser has noted, religion is "a perennial form of wish-fulfillment and need gratification . . . it condones [infantile wishes] by symbolic satisfactions."[100] The implication is that mental disturbance may be socially shaped, focused, and controlled by religious ideas and their embodiment in the form of churches and their representatives.

Institutionalized faith lives by both formal and informal rules and referents—the Ten Commandments, the Golden Rule, the Bible, papal statements, interpretations and decisions of denominational conclaves, and so forth. The ecclesiastical climate also sponsors notions of how a "good Jew" or a "good Christian" thinks and acts. These are supported by images of God's love, mercy, or vengeance—which are not taken lightly by the faithful, whether they be normal or disordered individuals. When adopted as guides for personal action, they may be very effective forces for the suppression and socialization of abnormal impulses.

Even if psychopathology comes to the surface, the argument has often been made that the use of religion may prevent worse things from happening. One paper suggests that "occasionally religiosity in paranoid schizophrenia might itself be a mechanism to control underlying hostility and aggressive behavior."[101] In a case study, two psychiatrists claimed that a patient's "religious conversion enabled him to find a new and potentially viable self-definition."[102] It apparently functioned as a substitute for the "overwhelming panic of his acute psychosis."[103] In a similar manner, Allison refers to intense religious experiences and conversion as "adaptive regression" that may "help reorganize a weakened ego."[104]

The power of religious doctrine is nowhere more evident than in the association of faith and suicide. There is no need to document the very negative attitude of Western religious institutions toward suicide. Dublin has emphasized that "suicide . . . is infrequent where the guidance and authority of religion are accepted without question, where the church forms the background of communal life, where duties are rigidly prescribed."[105] This relationship is most evident in such bodies as Roman Catholicism, Greek Orthodoxy, and Orthodox Judaism. Countries in which these faiths predominate report the lowest suicide rates. The greater emphasis of Protestantism on individualism and personal freedom may work to set the troubled person adrift in an anomic world; hence suicide rates for Protestants are two to three times higher than for Jews and Catholics.[106] There is, of course, the confounding factor that a religious setting that condemns suicide is not likely to produce medical and civil authorities who are willing to define a death as suicide, except when the evidence is irrefutable and/or has become public knowledge.[107]

There are both historical and contemporary examples of the extremes to which religious leaders may go when exercising control over their followers. Most of us may look in admiring awe at the self-sacrifice carried out at Masada in 73 A.D., when a group of Jewish Zealots, in their quest for freedom, left only their corpses to greet the Roman conquerors. Quite different was the mass suicide of those in Jim Jones's People's Temple movement, where socioreligious control appears to have resulted partly from the megalomania of its leader.[108] The more recent example of David Koresh and the mass death of his Branch Davidians may be another tragic example of this same abuse of power.

The socializing function of religious doctrine has been well summarized by Feifel: "Religion . . . tries to school us in those wise restraints—self-discipline, the capacity for sacrifice and service to others—that make the repressive control of impulses unnecessary."[109] This is an ideal that many disturbed people attempt to realize.

Religious Role Models

Children and adults often learn how to behave by modeling themselves after those whom they admire or who represent ideas and ideals that speak to success in attaining desired goals. In other words, they learn by observing others who serve as models. These others may be people with whom children and adults interact or about whom they read, hear, or are informed. Social learning theory suggests that "the power of a moral model . . . can be an important component in the development of self-control."[110] In other words, one can learn to be "normal" or "abnormal" by emulating others.

Ministers, priests, rabbis, Biblical heroes, Jesus and his apostles, saints, and so forth, stand as sanctified models to be imitated. Explicitly and implicitly, these figures enact roles that may significantly influence the behavior and thinking of religious people along approved lines. In one study of over 3,000 children and adolescents, clergy were rated as more supportive than parents, suggesting the potential of priests and ministers as positive role models.[111] In all likelihood, these images may serve as significant referents for some mentally disturbed individuals. As Bandura affirms, "modeling influences can strengthen or weaken inhibitions over behavior."[112]

This role model approach to controlling behavior has recently been formalized in the study of religious experience by the Swedish scholar Hjalmar Sunden. His role theory (which has also been discussed in Chapter 6) appears applicable to religious behavior in general as it stresses perception, motivation, and learning. Holm points out that "these roles need not necessarily always be socially given models but can equally well be literary or mythical narratives."[113] He adds that "when an individual in a certain religious tradition absorbs descriptions from sacred history, he learns models for his attitudes toward the supernatural."[114] We are told that "this description will function as a structuring role pattern."[115] Here is a theoretical framework that usefully connects religious role models with the socialized control of thinking and behavior on the part of the mentally distressed person.

Religion and Control: When Does It Work?

It has been well established that religious activity is negatively associated with deviance in both cognition and action. Stark has shown that mentally disturbed persons who continue to live in a community outside of an institution assign less personal importance to religion and are less active than more normal citizens.[116] He theorizes that "psychopathology seems to *impede* the manifestation of conventional religious beliefs and activities."[117] This confirms the findings of a number of researchers who have reported that the faith of mentally disordered individuals is itself disturbed and deviant.[118] Other work indicates that the more severe the psychopathology, the less the involvement of the individual in both personal and organized religious activity.[119]

In a number of areas in which the line between mental disorder and morality is not always easily drawn—particularly crime, drug and alcohol usage, and sexual promiscuity—the findings reveal some confusion (see also Chapter 10). Sometimes these behaviors correlate negatively with religiosity; at other times they appear to be independent of religion. Bainbridge explains some of these results by referring to what he calls "the Stark effect." Stark observed that crime and delinquency rates were low in communities where organized religion was strong, but not where it was weak. In cases where few people in the community were religious, neither individual nor community religiousness had the power to inhibit deviance, even among religious youths.[120]

Bainbridge's own research has suggested an even more complicated explanation. Examining a variety of data, he indicates that individual religiousness suppresses deviance when the person is part of a religious community, even if the overall community is religiously weak.[121] In all probability, community effects will hold not only for immoral responses, but for a wide variety of mental aberrations that mark the individual's behavior as psychologically disordered.

Another approach to this problem of controlling abnormality relates to the way people view themselves. It is not unexpected that deviant behavior may both result from and contribute to the social ostracism of disturbed persons, and, furthermore, that such people possess negative views of themselves. We also know that unfavorable self-attributions parallel similar attributions for the deity and religion.[122] In some instances, this pattern may prevent these individuals from benefiting either from their personal faith or from association with similar others in religious institutions. Jensen and Erickson suggest that strict religious group attitudes, along with the positive role models provided by clergy and coreligionists, may act both to socialize and to restrain expressions of abnormality.[123]

It is evident that religious systems and their supporters can suppress abnormal thinking and behavior, and thus can help mentally disordered people to become part of the larger community. Such social and ideological sustenance may also contribute to ego strength and integration. Stated differently, adherence to a faith that is in line with cultural norms can reduce abnormality and psychopathology. Stark's work, which is presented in Research Box 12.3, illustrates this principle.

❧

Research Box 12.3. Psychopathology and Religious Commitment
(Stark, 1971)

Theorizing that conventional religious involvement would be incompatible with deviant thinking and behavior, Rodney Stark hypothesized a negative relationship between these two variables. In his study, 100 mentally disturbed persons were carefully matched with 100 normals and compared on a variety of religious items. The basic findings were as follows:

Percentage claiming	Mentally ill	Normals
No religious affiliation	16	3
Religion not important at all	16	4
Not belonging to any church	54	40
Never attending church	21	5

Note. Adapted from Stark (1971). Copyright 1971 by the Religious Research Association. Adapted by permission.

The hypothesis was clearly confirmed, as the mentally disturbed persons demonstrated less conventional religious involvement than the normal sample. In another part of this study, a national sample of Protestants and Catholics who scored low on indices of psychic difficulties were more likely to be religiously orthodox and to attend church frequently than those revealing such problems. Again, the hypothesis was supported.

RELIGION AS A HAVEN

Religion has been known to offer mentally distressed individuals a refuge from the stresses of daily life—a safe harbor from the turmoil and turbulence of living. This can take place in three ways: (1) Everyday existence may be circumscribed and controlled by rules that leave little doubt about how to behave; (2) being part of a religious organization may alleviate fears of social isolation and rejection; and (3) strong identification with a religious body can provide the mentally disordered with the perceived security of divine protection. It can also do this within three different types of religious organizations: (1) groups or movements that are out of the religious mainstream (so-called "sects" or "cults"); (2) encapsulated religious communities, such as the Amish and the Hutterites; and (3) separate communities within mainline religions, such as sisterhoods of nuns.

Groups or Movements That Are Out of the Mainstream

"Deviant" religious movements can attract mentally disturbed individuals (see Chapter 9). We have noted above that if such persons are not socialized by mainline churches, they may become estranged from traditional religion. This is a two-way street: The average churchgoer is probably sympathetic to the plight of the mentally disordered, but may still prefer not to be associated with such people. The inability of the mentally disturbed to fit in may cause them to respond in a reciprocal manner and to reject conventional beliefs and believers. They may, however, find a home in religious or spiritual subcultures that are out of the mainstream—the so-called "sects" or "cults." Since members of these groups often feel that they are ostracized by society (and in many instances they actually are), they may find common cause with others who are rejected for reasons of individual mental deviance. If the latter are seeking divine guidance and support, so much the better, from the viewpoint of those with missionary zeal.

It is very important at this point to recognize that the majority of members of what are socially regarded as deviant religious groups are quite normal and mentally healthy.[124] Most of those who join such bodies do not suffer from psychological problems. Some individuals may, of course, find a haven that functions as a source of meaning and a framework of needed control in these religious groups, but this is probably the exception and not the rule.[125]

Alienated individuals can be attracted by a wide variety of religious and ecclesiastical elements. Unquestioning attachment to a spiritual leader may reflect emotional immaturity and extreme dependency needs. The charismatic quality of some of the founders of these groups can entice persons whose reality contacts are weak. One study of the Unification Church (pejoratively called the "Moonies") revealed that about 40% admitted having mental difficulties prior to joining the church, a third had sought professional help, and 6% had been hospitalized.[126] As Research Box 12.4 (below) notes, the outcome of affiliation with the Unification Church was psychologically beneficial.

Snelling and Whitley studied four of what they termed "problem-solving groups," including a Hare Krishna temple. They suggested that, instead of obvious abnormality predominating, there seemed to be "a noticeable strain or predisposition toward reductionism in the sense of cutting down or narrowing the 'size' of the world in order to make it more manageable."[127] Though such a reaction may indicate some coping difficulties, it may be a rather wise choice on the part of some devotees; also, since the great majority of these individuals return to society, their experience in such "manageable" environments may permit them needed time to develop better ways to adjust to the world.

Another example of the way in which sects or cults may serve a temporary haven function is implied by work showing that some young people who affiliate with these bodies come from troubled homes and families.[128] Such a religious group may serve as a substitute family, offering needed social and psychological backing until the person is able to cope with a North American milieu that highly values personal autonomy.

The haven role not only offers a defense against a possibly unappreciative and potentially threatening society outside of the chosen religious group, but also usually provides much positive acceptance and support. We see this in Kildahl's description of the fellowship of glossolalics. He cited them as exhibiting "a tremendous openness, concern, and care for one another . . . they bore each other's burdens . . . were with each other in spirit and in physical presence."[129]

A variation on this theme may exist among Jehovah's Witnesses, a religiously conservative and strongly proselytizing group. Said to have an incidence of schizophrenia three to four times higher than that found in the general population (a finding that needs further confirmation), it may appeal to some distressed people who feel they need a spiritual foundation that incorporates a very strict moral code.[130] This may protect such individuals from life stresses and temptations, while helping them to internalize necessary controls that permit a modicum of adjustment. The research of Galanter and his associates, which illustrates such a tendency in the Unification Church, is presented in Research Box 12.4.

Finding a spiritual haven is not easy. Especially among the cults and sects, troubled people frequently move rather easily from one such group to another. The unstable membership of these bodies is well documented.[131] There are, however, some data suggesting that these shifts of commitment increase with the severity of mental problems.[132] Still, such mov-

---

Research Box 12.4. The Moonies: A Study of Conversion and Membership (Galanter, Rabkin, Rabkin, & Deutsch, 1979)

With the cooperation of the Unification Church, an extensive questionnaire dealing with mental health issues was administered to 237 church members. A pattern of disruption and emotional difficulties preceded their joining the church in many instances; about one-third had sought professional help for these problems, and 6% had been hospitalized. Psychological distress scores for the time prior to church affiliation were 48% higher than at the time the testing took place. In addition, church members still showed more personal disturbance than was found in the general population. Though there were indications that adjustment initially declined when conversion to the church took place, as religious and communal ties to the group increased, so did psychological well-being. The greater a person's religious involvement and commitment, the less distress was evidenced.

---

ing about may also benefit seekers in their search for meaning, control, and self-esteem. Sometimes satisfactory answers are elusive.

Encapsulated Religious Communities: The Amish and the Hutterites

Though they are usually considered sects, their long history of relative isolation, combined with a reasonable degree of acceptance by the general society, makes groups like the Amish and Hutterites of special interest to mental health researchers. The nature of their separation allows social scientists to regard them as "laboratory-like" sociocultural cases, worthy of much study. Neither group has attempted to bring in new members by proselytizing. People are born into these groups; rarely do they seek to join from the outside. Because of these bodies' isolation and the formal and informal controls they exercise over their adherents, they manifest the haven functions of religion well. They also provide information on some of the causes of various kinds of mental disorder.

Among the Amish, the doctrine of separation is evident in the proscription against marrying outsiders or even entering business partnerships with non-Amish persons. Basically, this view holds for any deep or long-lasting social involvement or contact with any outsiders.[133] Such self-segregation, when combined with very strict internal controls on behavior, creates great stress for many Amish. The expectations these rules engender have been cited as a cause of anxiety, and may in part account for an incidence of suicidal tendencies above the national average among Amish hospitalized for mental problems.[134] Unfortunately, there is not enough information available to indicate whether the incidence of neurotic or psychotic disorders is unusual. The community acts as a haven, preferring to care for its own whenever possible.

The Hutterites are a different matter; good observational data have been collected from them. Eaton and Weil carried out a highly regarded study on religion and mental disorder with this group more than 40 years ago.[135] Like the Amish, the Hutterites are a separationist Anabaptist sect; they live in relatively isolated communities in southern Canada and along the northwest tier of the United States from the Dakotas westward. Because the group is a close-knit and highly supportive communal organization, the authors expected low rates of mental disturbance. Where such disturbance does occur, as with the Amish, a loving community with its own apparently constructive therapeutic views is present to aid the distressed individual.

Eaton and Weil found that the frequency of the less severe neurotic states tended to be low, particularly those in which aggressive or antisocial expressions were primary. In lieu of these symptoms, guilt and depression were commonly found; these seemed to be a product of both the highly controlling social milieu and failure to live up to the strict expectations of the community. Moreover, the low rates of neurotic disorders were countered by a high incidence of severe psychotic disorders. Four centuries of relative isolation may have concentrated the genetic and constitutional potential for such illnesses; these propensities could also be activated by the often inflexible demands of daily life. Furthermore, Eaton and Weil had reason to believe that the Hutterite communities they studied might operate much better as refuges for the less disturbed group members than for their more seriously affected counterparts.

Separate Communities within Mainline Religious Groups

Some mentally disturbed persons may believe that they are "called" to a religious vocation, and subsequently may find a haven in a religious community that separates them from the world. This view has been confirmed by Kelley, who studied Catholic nuns. Finding a variety of disordered states among the sisters, she concluded that these were a function of pre-existing difficulties rather than of the chosen religious life.[136] Reference has also been made to a high frequency of hypochondriacal complaints.[137] Similar findings have been reported in other studies of nuns.[138] Research Box 12.5 describes Kelley's significant study.

Additional work on disturbed sisters attributes their motivation to enter orders to a desire for security because of emotional starvation and/or a view of the world as dangerous. These needs are frustrated by organizational pressures and restraints, which are thought to exacerbate the nuns' tenuous grip on reality.[139] Kurth has claimed that two factors should be recognized as contributing to this situation. First, "many mentally ill individuals seek to

---

Research Box 12.5. Hospitalized Mental Illness among Religious Sisters
(Kelley, 1958)

Kelley, a nun herself, gathered data from 357 U.S. private and public mental hospitals regarding 783 Catholic sisters who were hospitalized for mental disorders in 1956. High rates for depression and schizophrenia were observed; yet, prior to being committed, the sisters had spent an average of 17 to 20 years in their order.

The incidence of severe disorders among sisters who performed domestic functions was over seven times higher than the rate for those involved in teaching. The rates for cloistered nuns were also higher than for those in noncloistered orders. Among the hospitalized nuns, 80% suffered from psychotic states, 65% of which were schizophrenic. Depressive symptomatology was also quite common. Kelley theorized that the highly structured life in these religious communities often led to feelings of failure and ensuing breakdown on the part of those unable to cope with the stringent demands of such an existence.

enter religious life. Such neurotic and pre-psychotic individuals are especially attracted to cloistered life, which by its very nature caters to the needs of schizoid individuals."[140] Second, according to Kurth, "too many Superiors of convents in the United States think that all their candidates are psychologically sound and enjoy good mental health."[141]

In some instances, the requirement of chastity and celibacy is too much of a psychological burden for priests and nuns to bear, and abnormal expressions of anxiety and other behaviors may result.[142] Toward the end of this chapter, we take up this theme again when we look specifically at the mental health of the clergy.

RELIGION AS THERAPY

We have seen that the suppression/socialization functions of religion may work to inhibit deviant mental expression, if not to improve abnormal mental states. The constructive role of religion, however, continues beyond this limited possibility and can actually be therapeutic. Specifically, therapeutic roles may be played by such activities as ritual, prayer, religious experience, glossolalia, and conversion.

Ritual

The early psychoanalytic approach to religion identified ritual with abnormality. Ritual was viewed as an expression of religion as "obsessional neurosis," designed to alleviate unconscious guilt.[143] This view has been strongly rejected by later psychologists of religion, some of whom have viewed religious ritual as performing healing and beneficial roles.[144] Its compulsive cathartic nature, the implication of appeasement, and the exercise of control are seen as reducing fear and anxiety; repressed motives are said to be worked through, expressed, and dispelled.[145] Kiev points out that such ritual explicitly promotes "therapeutic emotional reactions" via the opportunity to "express in socially approved ways ordinarily inhibited impulses and desires."[146]

Central to these therapeutic possibilities is the relation of ritual to emotion. Pruyser suggests that ritual is adaptive when it creates a "structure for emotional expression" or performs "dynamically as a defense against the intensity of any emotion or the unpleasantness of some."[147] Scheff sees the critical function of ritual as "distancing" a person from emotion, particularly affect that is universal (e.g., that which may be aroused by death concerns).[148] Such emotions are actually confronted in group rituals; however, the setting is both secure and social, permitting individuals to deal safely with their feelings.

Jacobs stresses the social aspect of ritual, in that it strengthens one's connections to significant and powerful figures in the community.[149] She emphasizes the cathartic role of ritual as countering shame and guilt and as supporting self-esteem. Attention is also directed at the control of, and distancing from, emotion in healing and mourning rituals.

A study committee of the Group for the Advancement of Psychiatry has compared ritual to psychoanalytic therapy, in that both have the "intention of facilitating growth.... Ritual not only stimulates regression, but controls and guides it."[150] Erik Erikson spoke of ritualization as "creative formalization" that controls both impulsiveness and compulsive restrictiveness, such as in constructive play.[151] Because of such channeling, parallels have been drawn between pastoral care and counseling and ritualistic expression.[152]

The rather ubiquitous nature of religious ritual is well demonstrated by Moberg, who covers the range from the individual level through family, churches, and synagogues to literally nationwide forms that utilize the mass media.[153] Given such possibilities, the healing and therapeutic possibilities inherent in rites and ceremonies must be regarded as very impressive.

There can be little doubt about the theoretical importance of ritual. The observations of astute anthropologists and clinicians concerning its theoretical effects are quite striking; however, it must be noted that objective empirical work in this realm is lacking. It is a topic worthy of considerable study by rigorous research psychologists.

Prayer

In Chapter 11, we have described the essentially supportive and therapeutic place of prayer in one's personal armamentarium. Because of this, only a few major points need to be made here. Publicly and privately, prayer is probably the most commonly employed religious rite, with approximately 90% of the U.S. population engaging in this activity.[154] We accept the view of Holahan and Moos that prayer is an active, cognitive coping strategy.[155] In other words, it is most often an attempt to deal with distress—a kind of self-therapy. Much research has been conducted on the beneficial uses of prayer by the elderly, the seriously ill, and average persons in a wide variety of circumstances (again, see Chapter 11).

Psychiatrist Kenneth Appel claims that prayer plays a personality-integrative role in life.[156] Kidorf views the *shiva*, a collective Jewish mourning ceremony, as a form of group therapy.[157] Generally, in death-related situations, the incidence of prayer increases and helps the bereaved cope with loss.[158]

The therapeutic role of prayer needs little further explication, but readers should recognize that this is only one of its major functions. Its complexity in this and other domains is well detailed in the fine scholarly works of Brown and Buttrick.[159] Research Box 12.6 presents Parker and Brown's study on coping with depression; the role of prayer in this work is significant.

Religious Experience

We have also described in Chapter 11 the constructively therapeutic role of religious experience. In recent work, it was shown that the vast majority of distressed people who reported

---

Research Box 12.6. Coping Behaviors that Mediate between Life Events and Depression (Parker & Brown, 1982)

In an initial study, 176 general medical patients responded to items indicating factors that made them feel depressed, plus behaviors that seemed effective in reducing these stresses. After the initial measures were refined, a new sample of 103 patients was obtained. Using factor analysis, the authors found that the inclination to pray contributed strongly to a problem-solving dimension. A subsample of 20 clinically depressed patients was then compared with a control group; this revealed that the problem-solving behaviors were more likely to be used by the control group. Prayer therefore related positively to the percentage of those reporting prayer as increasing behavioral change and as effective in the process. The implication is that prayer can be a significant element in coping with depression.

such incidents benefited greatly from them.[160] This has been known for some time. In 1936 Anton Boisen viewed psychotic behavior as an effort at problem-solving that is "closely related to certain types of religious experience."[161] He then documented many cases testifying to the curative and restorative possibilities inherent in religious experience. Research by Bergin confirms Boisen's examples.[162] Bergin observed that participants in his study who were not coping well "appeared to have their adjustment level boosted considerably by intense religious experiences that were like Maslow's peak experiences."[163] Maslow himself compared his "peak experiences" to religious and mystical encounters, taking a positive view of their outcomes, and explicitly interpreting these events as therapeutic.[164] Unhappily, this is not always true, as many distressing and terrifying religious experiences have also been reported.[165]

Specific therapeutic outcomes for religious experience have included reductions in guilt feelings, a heightened sense of security and belonging, improved control of aggression and hostility, and suicide prevention.[166] Drug-induced religious experience has also been cited positively with regard to its influence on alcoholics, narcotic addicts, neurotics, and terminal cancer patients.[167] Clark feels that these positive effects are enhanced when the experiencer explicitly denotes these events as religious.[168] Mystical encounters have further been likened to creative experiences as "attempts at integration or reintegration by people who have not achieved satisfying results in identity formation."[169]

Prince puts religious experience back into its social context by noting that it may be defined as pathological or therapeutic, depending on culture and group values. In situations where they are approved manifestations, he claims that some "may be channeled into socially valuable roles."[170] This seems to be true among Pentecostal sects that encourage mystical encounters. Hine suggests that these aid adjustment and integrate people into their groups, which also provide quite supportive environments.[171]

Glossolalia

Glossolalia, like mystical experience and conversion, is not only a possible expression of mental disorder, but may operate therapeutically as well. For example, many open-minded observers subscribe to what Brown calls "a benign form of the 'abnormal theory,'"[172]— namely, that speaking in tongues is adaptive. In addition to its social function of integrating a glossolalic individual into a religious group that places such behavior in a positive light, it has been associated with increased well-being, social sensitivity, religious maturity, the resolution of neurotic conflicts, and the reduction of anxiety and tension.[173] It would appear, therefore, to be therapeutic. Although this possibility must not be dismissed, some research has failed to support any of these findings.[174] Much good work has already been undertaken in this area, but there is still a need to resolve the pathology–therapy issue.

Conversion

The beneficial and therapeutic effects of conversion have been celebrated for millenia. We hear about being "born again," "twice born," "finding God," "coming home," and so forth. Almost a century ago, Starbuck claimed that for converts "the joy, the relief, and the acceptance are qualities of feeling, perhaps, which give the truest picture of what is going on in conversion—the free exercise of new powers, and escape from something, and the birth into Larger Life. . . ."[175] Though clinicians might employ different language, these are unquestioningly therapeutic goals.

Invariably, the psychological bias has been toward viewing conversion as the outgrowth and resolution of personal crisis.[176] Jones and Cesarman offer illustrations of the alleviation of sexual and other conflicts, which are then replaced by an "inner calm."[177] Though there may be both positive and negative outcomes to conversion (as discussed earlier in this chapter), on the positive side there are indications of increased openness, improved contacts with the world and others, greater emotional responsivity, a heightened sense of personal satisfaction and happiness, conflict resolution, and productive identity formation.[178] On another level, conversion among Mexican-Americans from Catholicism to Protestantism relates positively to a success/achievement orientation that is valued in mainstream U.S. society.[179]

It must be noted that these beneficial effects of conversion are not restricted to the well-accepted and established churches in the North American social order, but also extend to cults, such as the Unification Church and Hare Krishna.[180] Richardson summarizes this work simply: "The personality assessments of these groups reveals that life in the new religions is often therapeutic instead of harmful."[181]

In more than a few instances, conversion may be explicitly associated with or play a role in psychotherapy.[182] Both can also be regarded as forms of cognitive restructuring.[183] Though there may be many reasons for conversion, clinicians are becoming increasingly sensitive to both the potential benefits and the adverse effects of conversion experiences.[184]

RELIGION AS A HAZARD TO MENTAL HEALTH

As we have already commented, in the history of psychology, the dominant view of faith has been to associate it with psychopathology. Thus far, the opposite has been demonstrated. However, religious institutions and doctrines are not always beneficial; they can create stress and cause psychological problems. Indeed, there is truth in the title of one book, *Religion Can Be Hazardous to Your Health*.[185] In a similar vein, Pruyser has referred in an article title to "The Seamy Side of Current Religious Beliefs."[186] The message is simply that religion contains elements that can adversely affect the mental well-being of its adherents.

Religion as a Source of Abnormal Mental Content

The doctrines and sources of institutional faith sometimes contain the seeds of psychopathology. Though most individuals who accept religious mandates live happy and fruitful lives, there are those who misinterpret and misapply the core elements of their faith. Others are, in a sense, victimized by parents, clergy, or influential others who misuse religion to gain power and personal gratification. This can happen when people deal with religious precepts in a rigid and inflexible manner.[187] One study dealing with some mental disorder correlates of "rigid religiosity" is described in Research Box 12.7. Simply put, clinicians perceive strict religious upbringing as an element in the development of emotional disorders, depression, suicidal potential, and a generally fearful response to life.[188]

The inability to interpret church tenets and scripture for modern life is an accusation that has usually been directed at fundamentalist groups and conservative religious bodies, often in an unbalanced manner. In fact, such research, particularly on fundamentalism, suffers from a wide variety of biases. At the same time, some individuals are attracted to these bodies because of what Ostow calls an "illusory defense against reality."[189]

The great reliance of orthodox groups on scripture may be one of those defenses. For

━━━━━━━━━━━━━━━━━ ❧ ━━━━━━━━━━━━━━━

Research Box 12.7. Rigid Religiosity and Mental Health
(Stifoss-Hanssen, 1994)

Religious bodies possess rules and regulations that people can often interpret in ways ranging from an easy flexibility to a rigid absolutism. The latter has been defined in one major study as a "law-orientation."[a] In the present study, a scale of rigid–flexible religiosity
was developed and administered to 56 volunteer hospitalized neurotic patients and a
control group of 70 nonpatients. The first group scored significantly higher than the controls on the scale, demonstrating that a rigid religiosity is a correlate of, at least, severely
neurotic thinking and behavior. The author is inclined to suggest a positive relationship
between mental disturbance and an extrinsic religious orientation.

―――――――――

[a]Strommen, Brekke, Underwager, and Johnson (1972).

example, it has been used to justify the abuse of women and children, and some officials in
these churches have also supported such behavior.[190] Partner and child abuse in these groups
has been associated with much conflict about sexual issues and with the blaming of victims.
These tendencies have been invoked to explain the claim of high rates of multiple personality disorder in families with fundamentalist religious backgrounds.[191]

Fundamentalist religion is often quite authoritarian in its structure, endowing its leaders with the image of having a special relationship with the deity. Control and the suppression of dissent are seen as the natural prerogatives of those holding high church positions.
These factors have been used to explain the anxiety, "guilt, low self-esteem, sexual inhibitions, and vivid fears of divine punishment" noted among individuals who leave these
churches.[192] The argument is made that the absolutist structure and dictates of these churches
produce a "fundamentalist mindset" that creates adjustment problems for their members.[193]
This has been further described as involving extreme dogmatism and a need for simplistic
"quick fixes for problems involving marriage, children, sexuality, or society."[194]

Despite all of these unpleasant inferences, research supporting such ideas is rather sparse,
and these claims have yet to be convincingly demonstrated. In fact, in Chapter 11, we have
noted work suggesting the association of fundamentalism with an optimistic outlook on
life.[195] Similarly, recent research has failed to provide any evidence of any adverse effects on
the ego development or adaptive capacity of fundamentalists.[196] When such contradictions
exist, the only answer is to call for more research; however, we must keep in mind that this
is a very controversial area, and objectivity is imperative.

Religious doctrines are rich sources of ideas for use by mentally disturbed persons.
Southard has shown how identification with higher powers may help such individuals to deny
reality and counter therapy; he described one patient who used hymn singing to frustrate
psychotherapy.[197] The presentation of miracles and other unusual occurrences found in religious writings can stimulate magical thinking that is suggestive of psychopathology.

Commonly, religious groups and doctrines offer their members meanings that make
life bearable, but at a cost—namely, a "sacrifice of intellect."[198] Complex matters are often
simplified into a dichotomy of good versus evil. Difficult and intricate issues are denied attempts at understanding by reference to such clichés as "God works in mysterious ways."

At times, however, objective need and cognitive dissonance may cause individuals to challenge polarized beliefs and "stop thinking" phrases. The outcome in such instances may be a serious crisis of faith, extreme personal stress, depression, and the potential for suicide.

Religion as a Source of Abnormal Mental Motives

Religious systems affect the motives and behaviors of their followers. Just as they can strengthen moral commitments, they may stimulate disordered thinking and action.[199] We see this in religion's concern with sin. A book chapter by O'Connell asks, "Is Mental Illness a Result of Sin?", and the well-known psychologist O. H. Mowrer attempted to bring the sin concept into psychotherapy.[200] It was thus examined positively and negatively—as a constructive control on behavior, and as an activator of guilt, depression, and distress. Obsession with sin and guilt seems to be a correlate of religious frameworks that stress moral perfection.[201] An emphasis on perfection often incites feelings of low self-esteem and worthlessness, which can contribute to mental disorders.[202] We also find the presence of sin and associated guilt in the motivation for mysticism, conversion, prayer, scrupulosity, confession, bizarre rituals, self-denial, and self-mutilation.[203]

The need to expunge sin and reduce guilt is a powerful motive, and one that may eventuate in serious mental pathology. McGinley's fascinating presentation of the behavior of saints abounds in examples of grotesque, brutal, and painful masochistic behavior, which today we would regard as indicative of profound psychopathology.[204]

Religious institutions and leaders that demand absolute subservience and unquestioning obedience from followers frequently use punitive threats and devices to eliminate individuality. Pruyser points out that those subject to such control must suspend any semblance of critical reasoning and substitute "unbridled and untutored fantasy."[205] Blind faith of this sort requires an immature, if not extremely childish, denial of reality for its maintenance. The pathetic extremes to which such belief may drive people have been evidenced many times in recent years. We need only consider such tragedies as the mass suicides and deaths of those in the People's Temple in Guyana, the Branch Davidians in Texas, and the Solar Temple group in Europe and Canada.

TOPICS OF SPECIAL CONCERN

Even with all its shortcomings, one of the hallmarks of present-day Western society has been an increasing openness and receptivity about matters to which previous generations closed their eyes. Platitudes such as "That's life," "That's the way things are," or some variation on "It's the natural scheme of things" have given way to a new awareness of what was either ignored, denied, taken for granted, or blindly not even recognized. Among these concerns are the mental health of clergy, and the plight of women and the elderly. Religion plays significant roles for all three groups.

The Mental Health of the Clergy

The mental state of those who have formally and professionally committed their lives to their faith merits special attention. Because members of the clergy are often among the most admired and respected members of their community, their parishioners and others frequently regard them as somehow above the daily struggle and not subject to the strains and pressures of everyday life. A closer look rapidly shatters this idyllic picture, however. One small bibliography on religion and mental health that only covered a 4-year period listed 42 research and discussion books and papers dealing with abnormality among the clergy.[206] If we can conclude anything regarding this topic, it is (1) that being a minister, priest, rabbi, or nun is stressful, and (2) that emotional conflicts among the clergy are increasing.[207]

Personality and Psychological Problems

In terms of personality and psychological difficulties, the problem was initially studied in theological students. Claims of deviant findings have dominated this literature; for instance, one researcher asserted that Catholic seminarians are poorly integrated and show depressive tendencies, in addition to possessing a variety of interpersonal and identity problems.[208] Finch has emphasized that circumstances can lead mentally disordered individuals to feel that they should become clergy.[209] Also noted are early parental conflicts, ambivalent attitudes of parents toward their children, possible rejection of the children, and maternal dominance and control.[210] Other studies of seminary students have indicated that they score higher on indices of neuroticism, are in poorer mental health than nonseminarians, and tend to be either somewhat aggressive or quite submissive and dependent.[211] In other words, anything that implies some psychological difficulty has been inferred at one time or another. Increasingly, seminaries are using mental tests in order to eliminate applicants with emotional problems. Apparently, many if not most troubled individuals withdraw themselves from clerical training programs.[212]

There is also an extensive literature on the mental status of active clergy; as in the work on seminary students, the entire range of possible findings on personality and psychological problems has been offered. In a sample of disturbed ministers, similar early life influences were supplemented by a late adolescence choice of a clerical future after the arousal of considerable guilt over a sexual encounter.[213] As noted earlier, work on nuns suggests high rates of schizophrenia, with the incidence being greater for cloistered than for active orders. The suggestion has been made that a life that values meditation and withdrawal from the community may appeal to schizophrenic women.[214] Signs of depression have also been reported in such groups.[215]

Where psychological and emotional problems have been identified among the clergy, it is not clear whether such difficulties motivate persons to become clerics, or result from the considerable stress that has been observed in this profession.[216] Recent writing, for example, has pointed to the issue of "burnout" potential among pastors.[217]

Sexual Abuse by Clergy

As troubling as these indications are, a much more distressing situation has come to the fore in recent years—namely, the issue of sexual abuse by members of the clergy. This is a problem caught between morality and mental disturbance; though we treat it in greater detail here, it has repercussions for the area of religion and morality, and is thus briefly mentioned in Chapter 10. We are, however, not simply speaking about socially irresponsible and illegal behavior, but what lies behind it. Much that is counter to the law is properly excused when mental aberration that can be defined by the courts as insanity is present. In most instances, this does not appear to be true here.

The potential for sexual abuse may have been initially detected in research over 30 years ago that used the very widely employed psychological test, the Minnesota Multiphasic Personality Inventory (MMPI). At that time, note was made in two studies of elevated clerical MMPI Psychopathic Deviate scores.[218] This language gave way to the term "character disorder," which Stewart observes appears to be increasing in the clergy as various neurotic expressions decrease.[219] Persons so affected are not regarded as mentally disturbed, in that they know right from wrong and possess adequate control over their impulses. They may, however, be described as egocentric, immature, and narcissistic individuals who want gratification of their desires as rapidly as possible, without concern for the needs and feelings of others. As is known, the rates of such individuals in prisons tend to be high. It may therefore be argued that this condition, though it is indeed deviant, is not usually considered a form of mental disorder. Unfortunately, more time and energy have been spent on documenting the prevalence of clergy sexual abuse than on formally conducting research and gathering data on those who have engaged in abusive behavior. One effort is described in Research Box 12.8.

The situation is, however, more complicated than simple reference to a pattern of personality traits can explain. For example, it has been pointed out that the clerical profession exposes clergy to sexual temptation—women or men who "fall in love" with their pastors, or parishioners who bare their most intimate problems to ministers, rabbis, or priests. Such actions make both the clergy and those who seek their help vulnerable to exploitation. Given

---

Research Box 12.8. Clergy Sexual Involvement with Young People: Distinctive Characteristics (Camargo & Loftus, 1993)

This sophisticated statistical study of clerics (primarily Catholic priests) who sexually abused young people attempted to determine demographic, personality, and intellectual factors that would distinguish among five different groups: (1) a "youth-sexual" group (male clergy sexually involved with youths—also designated the "age-inappropriate" group) ($n = 117$); (2) adult heterosexuals exclusively involved with adults ($n = 133$); (3) adult homosexuals exclusively involved with adult homosexuals ($n = 121$); (4) bisexuals ($n = 38$); and (5) controls (no sexual activity or nonspecified sexual activity) ($n = 140$).

Relative to the other groups, the youth-sexual clergy tended to be lowest in socioeconomic status; were mostly Catholic diocesan priests; and scored high on a passivity pattern versus low on an angry cluster of traits, or vice versa. On the Minnesota Multiphasic Personality Inventory (MMPI) and some associated measures, the youth-sexual group were lowest in hypochondriasis, depression, masculinity, obsessive–compulsivity, social introversion, and anxiety. They scored highest in ego strength. Comparisons among the groups implied the possibility of distinguishing potential youth abusers from the other groups of abusers and from the control group.

This is a very brief summary of a highly complex piece of research, and it suggests (to us, at least) the possibility of character disorder even if the Psychopathic Deviate scale of the MMPI failed to demonstrate statistical significance. This could be a function of the nature of the groups that were compared. Comparative data on a "real" control group of successful nonabusing clergy currently working in parish settings might have been more helpful. Still, this is an impressive piece of research.

such encounters, it may not come as a surprise that one study of 1,500 Catholic priests over a 25-year period indicated that about half had violated their celibacy vows.[220] Other work reports that between 47% and 77% of female clergy claim that they have been sexually harassed or abused.[221] Though some estimates suggest that up to one-third of North American ministers admit to having engaged in sexual misconduct, most work indicates that about 25% of pastors have had some kind of sexual involvement with a parishioner. Actual intercourse rates between 10% and 15% are usually found.[222] In the 1983–1993 decade, one concerned organization documented over 1,150 such incidents.[223]

Despite these numbers, efforts at psychological characterization of clergy abusers have met with limited success, in part because of the variety of such abuse. These episodes involve both heterosexual and homosexual behavior, and the mistreatment of both children and adults. Among other possibilities, one scheme identifies what might be termed "passive/neurotic" abusers and "angry/impulsive" abusers.[224] Another framework distinguishes six different types, but we still do not know how to recognize any of these clerics before they do damage.[225] The application of psychological and psychiatric labels has not proven useful, for although such behavior is unacceptable, individual cases often reveal many unique (if not tragic) circumstances that also influence average people.[226] This is a problem that seems to be increasing, and clearly demands continuing study and action.

In any profession, perfection is an unrealizable ideal. This fact is especially distressing where religion is concerned. The population frequently looks to the clergy as ideal role models, forgetting that clerics are subject to the same stresses, problems, motives, and shortcomings that parishioners and congregants themselves possess. Better procedures are needed to select those who enter the religious professions; however, screening processes will undoubtedly contain a fair amount of error for some time to come. Psychological and character disorders will therefore persist in religious institutions. Little, however, can be done about such difficulties until they become evident; the tragedy is that when they do come to light, there will be victims—clerics and laity alike.

Religion and the Mental Health of Women

The women's movement of the past 30 years has highlighted the many forms of economic, political, social, and familial injustice and discrimination that have plagued women throughout the world for millenia. In essence, these are fundamental to basic sociocultural institutions, and therefore involve religion at its most elemental levels. The inevitable consequence of these inequities has been the subjection of women to extreme stress, the outcome of which can be mental disorder.

We have seen a few of the more blatant roles of religion in female victimization and abuse when men justify their actions and power over women by reference to scripture and church tenets.[227] Theological considerations are buttressed by more subtle social and psychological ones. For example, DSM-III and DSM III-R have been shown to contain gender biases that disadvantage women.[228]

The association of religion with female mental health begins with early childhood socialization. As McGuire observes, "religious symbols and images . . . shape the individual's gender role concept."[229] Future women are thus taught their socially approved identity, and variation from accepted role expectations may result in guilt, poor self-evaluations, and the self-attribution of abnormality.[230] Rothblum further asserts that "women are socialized to be unassertive, passive, or helpless, all of which behaviors lead to depression rather than action under stress."[231]

Both the socialization practices described above and traditional gender roles relate positively to religious commitment.[232] In extreme situations, such as those often existing in fundamentalist families, great frustration, anger, and depression have been reported among wives who have to deal with the severe religious norms of their group.[233] This "homebound behavior" has been indicted in the development of agoraphobia (the pathological fear of open spaces).[234] The best evidence suggests that the combination of traditional sex roles and a strict religious framework is a notable risk factor for depression.[235]

An interesting side issue concerns the fact that the dominant God image in North American society is masculine. Foster and Keating claim that identification with such a deity is easier for males and accords them high esteem; the opposite is said to be true for females.[236] Other research suggests that such a disadvantage can be mitigated by women's viewing a male God as a supportive rather than a punitive figure.[237] Research Box 12.9 offers some insight into the way this issue may be studied.

There is little doubt that in sponsoring traditional sex roles, religion can be an impediment to female aspirations, empowerment, and mental health. Concurrently, as Chapter 11 indicates, faith may be an aid in coping with adversity. Obviously, this is a complex issue, both sides of which have been extensively discussed.[238]

Religion and the Mental Health of the Elderly

Old age carries with it many mental and physical health perils, not the least of which is that no one gets out of this world alive. People of all ages think of aging and death as going together, and faith constitutes one of the strongest defenses against the fear of death.

Religious involvement (e.g., church attendance, worship, prayer, Bible reading, etc.) apparently counter suicide, depression, death anxiety, poor adjustment to bereavement, and aggression and hostility among the elderly.[239] Work among the old who are medically ill similarly reveals that religious coping protects such individuals against mild to severe depressive conditions.[240] Public expressions of religiosity, however, seem best for older women, whereas

---

Research Box 12.9. The Male God Concept and Self-Esteem (Foster & Keating, 1990)

A total of 89 males and females were asked to write a story about meeting and having a conversation with either a male or a female God. Under the assumption that this would activate a schema of God as male or female, the respondents were then asked to fill out a number of questionnaires that dealt with self-esteem, masculinity, and femininity.

A significant interaction was found between participant gender and God gender. After relating to a female God, the women scored higher on a femininity scale, whereas the men scored lower. In this God condition, the tendency to respond stereotypically was reduced for both males and females, though much more for the latter. Lastly, for the male God condition, women scored higher on masculinity; when the God was female, as noted above, they scored higher on femininity. The implication is that even though direct measures of self-esteem were not affected by the gender of the God schema, participants' personal orientations toward their sexual identification were influenced by the "encounter" with a male or female deity.

their male peers benefit more from private religiousness.[241] In addition, the more religious coping behavior is used, the more effective faith appears to be in combating depression and anxiety.[242]

It has been theorized that one of the advantages of religion for the elderly is that it offers them hope.[243] Empirically, hope per se relates negatively to depression and positively to self-esteem and optimism.[244]

In addition, religious doctrines function as a bulwark against life's adversities, and institutional involvement brings in social support and personal help, often from individuals in similar life circumstances. The effects of these influences are discussed in Chapter 11. The entire topic is, however, well summarized by Koenig, Smiley, and Gonzales, who conclude that "religious activity, particularly group-related, is inversely associated with mental illness such as depression and its consequences."[245] This is indirectly evidenced in the study described in Research Box 12.10.

RELIGION, PERSONALITY, AND MENTAL DISORDER: ISSUES AND CONCERNS

Personality and the Religious Context: The Jewish Example

Biases in psychology regarding the role of religion in mental health initially directed researchers to search for negative religious influences. Early studies suggested such adverse effects, but the more refined studies of recent decades have increasingly observed the opposite. Contemporary work has also attempted to understand personality and abnormality in relation to the social context. A good illustration of this kind of research was undertaken by Rosenberg, who noted that stress may be a function of the relationship of one's group to the broader social setting.[246] Since different groups possess different values and expectations for people, a collective may find itself at variance with others if it resides in an area in which it is a minority. Rosenberg termed this "contextual dissonance." He observed that children reared in such an environment (one in which their faith differs from that of their more numerous neighbors) are likely to evidence low self-esteem, anxiety, and emotional distress.

ε&

Research Box 12.10. The Use of Religion and Other Emotion-Regulating Coping Strategies (Koenig, George, & Siegler, 1988)

In this large-sample study, over 800 people ranging in age from 55 to 94 completed a number of questionnaires. These dealt with formal, organizational ritual activity and nonorganizational, personal religiosity. Other measures dealt with coping success and morale. The latter contained three subscales designed to assess agitation, attitude toward one's aging, and loneliness/dissatisfaction.

All of the religiosity variables correlated positively and significantly with the morale measure. These relationships held for both those under and over the age of 75, but they tended to be stronger for women than for men. Noting the association between morale and depression, the authors see their findings as supporting the view that religion is likely to counter depression among the elderly.

In virtually all nations, Israel excepted, this is the situation in which Jews find themselves. Moreover, they have been victims of prejudice, discrimination, and persecution for over two millenia. If ever a group lived in a state of contextual dissonance, it has been the Jewish minority. In terms of Rosenberg's hypothesis, we might therefore expect higher rates of mental disturbance among Jews than among their Christian peers; there are data that support this proposition, but it must be qualified. These statistics show that higher rates of mental disturbance may be found among Jews for mild to moderate conditions, but not for the more severe forms of psychopathology.[247]

Various explanations may be offered for this observation. For example, we may ask whether Jews are more likely than other religionists to seek aid and therapy early in the breakdown process, reducing the likelihood of more serious difficulties. Is it also possible that Jews may not show up in the public hospital statistics because they seek help from private agencies and practitioners? These remain unresolved questions. Srole and his colleagues have suggested that Jewish religious and familial supports may protect individuals from developing more profound forms of disorder.[248] Yet another thesis intimates that a long history of dealing with prejudice and discrimination may somehow act as an immunizing force against severe disorder.[249] The possible influence of socioeconomic differences can also be posited; this is discussed below.

The Rosenberg dissonance hypothesis may gain support from the long history of anti-Semitism. Images of a high incidence of mental and physical illnesses have been part of this past, and these may have been internalized by many Jews. They may have also subtly become a stimulus for Jews to enter medicine and psychiatry.[250] This background of victimization can prepare the way for a negative view of oneself and one's heritage and group; such has been evidenced in the well-known phenomenon of Jewish self-hatred. It has also been proposed as a factor contributing to the development of mental disorder among Jews.[251]

As this example has demonstrated, when we are looking at religion in relation to mental disorder, we cannot take the social context lightly. It is clearly significant on many levels—the level of the immediate group; that of its place in society and valuation in the culture at large; and finally that of its place in history.

Confounding Factors: Gender, Socioeconomic Status, and Ethnicity

Just as religion per se may influence personality and the development of mental disorder, so within cultures, the interaction of faith with other broad sociocultural factors can affect both abnormality and religion.

Gender

We have already discussed the bias that considerations of gender bring to the evaluation of abnormality. McGuire points out that "women's versions of a certain religion are probably very different from men's versions."[252] Comparing gender to a caste system, particularly within a religious framework, McGuire further makes us aware that male–female status differences and concomitant exploitation are endemic in religious systems. The accompanying gender-associated learning and stress involve long-term adjustments that have a high likelihood of resulting in disturbed thinking and behavior. Psychiatric and psychological biases compound the problem and can define the observed actions as normal or abnormal, depending on their potential disrupting effects on the social system rather than the individual. Challenges to the existing power structure, often legitimated by religion, are not usually accepted easily. We are, however, living in a time when women's movements and feminist theology are bringing such issues to the fore; these developments may, in the not too distant future, benefit the coping behavior and adjustment of women. In the interim, when religion is related to mental disorder in men and women, it may be important to look more closely at sex roles as disposing factors in psychopathology.

Socioeconomic Status

For some time, sociologists have demonstrated that religious groups and expressions are affiliated with class distinctions. We know that Episcopalians, Presbyterians, and Jews tend to be high in socioeconomic status, whereas Catholics, Pentecostal sects, and Baptist bodies are much lower on the class ladder.[253] The same holds true for educational attainment.

The association of these same distinctions with mental disorder has also been repeatedly shown. That is, the religious groups higher in socioeconomic status and educational attainment have lower rates of disorder, and vice versa.[254] We do, however, need research that is also more sophisticated in understanding even the demographics of religion. For example, in one study, first admissions for mental disorders are classified by religion as Protestants, Catholics, Jews, and "other." The last category is totally undefined,[255] permitting us to speculate that we may be less informed with this information than without it.

The plot thickens further when we note that the rates of serious disorder decline for groups higher up the class ladder.[256] Unhappily, this work is probably marred by diagnostic biases, as clinicians appear to assign more severe diagnoses to clients who are unlike themselves in ethnic group and class level. Those coming from poorer backgrounds are therefore more often regarded as suffering from serious abnormality than their upper-class peers.[257] In addition, the latter may fail to show up in the statistics, because they go to private practitioners and undergo outpatient therapy more often.

Another supportive influence may merit attention here. Roberts summarizes a number of observations indicating that lower-class churches stress sin and guilt—tendencies that may produce stress and activate latent psychopathology. In contrast, higher-class religious institutions more often support one's sense of personal dignity, self-worth, and self-esteem.[258] Could such be involved in the suppression functions of religion discussed earlier?

Significant questions must be raised when psychological tests are used to diagnose abnormality. The appearance of objectivity may be only skin-deep. Many, if not most, of these instruments have been standardized on middle- and upper-middle-class persons, and penalize deviance from these referent groups. Since many tests are also susceptible to social desirability response biases, particularly in terms of what the middle class considers approved thinking and behavior, those from lower-class settings may never have learned the "right" answers.[259]

Ethnicity

The influence of ethnic group on mental disorder has often been studied, but rarely in relation to religion. This realm is very often confounded with socioeconomic status and questions about the degree to which an ethnic group is acculturated into general North American society. For example, studies of Hispanic groups in the United States definitely suggest the influence of culture. Depression and psychosomatic disorders among Mexican-American women reveal a complex pattern of associations with abuse and acculturation. Theoretically, religion may support the continued existence of abusive marriage and home situations, but objective data on such possibilities have yet to be obtained.[260] The fact that Hispanics are overwhelmingly Catholic implies a role for Catholicism in understanding mental disorder in this group. However, we must ask whether this faith is differently understood by the various Hispanic peoples in the United States, and, if so, how such differences might influence adjustment and coping behavior. Unfortunately, data on these issues are also lacking.

Similar questions may be raised about religion in African-American groups. The importance of faith and religious activities such as prayer has been shown in Chapter 11 to be of great importance in the coping efforts of older, poor blacks.[261] Though most African-Americans embrace Protestantism, many indigenous ethnic expressions are found in these churches; again, however, we do not know of research relating these religious styles to mental disorder. Obviously, acculturation and poverty must be considered when such work is conducted. This is clearly an area worthy of investigation.

RELIGION AND PSYCHOTHERAPY

No treatment of the domain of religion and mental disorder would be complete without some mention of the increasing role of religious ideas and practitioners in treating psychological problems. The widespread use of pastoral care and pastoral counseling has for a long time been supplemented by such concepts as Biblical and spiritual therapies. Some of these ideas go back more than 50 years.[262] We have also noted that religious problems are now included in DSM-IV, bringing a new perspective to mainstream clinical psychology and psychiatry regarding the place of religion in personal life. Bergin poignantly observes the need for clinical psychology to broaden its perspectives on religion, as the religious outlooks of clients and therapists are often markedly discrepant.[263] Research Box 12.11 summarizes a recent survey of a private mental health facility's staff and patients in regard to such matters. This study reveals a growing recognition of the need to consider religious and spiritual issues.[264]

As a final consideration, attention needs to be directed to the fine research of Propst on the place and uses of religion in the therapeutic process.[265] Propst has also been able to offer guidance to clinicians and clergy on how a cognitive-behavioral type of psychotherapy can utilize patients' faith to beneficial and constructive ends.[266]

OVERVIEW

The realm of religion and mental disorder is obviously vast and growing rapidly. Students of this area still have to examine faith in its many expressions, though some work along these lines has already been reported.[267] To date, however, research has not been organized along productive theoretical lines. Those who employ coping approaches and see mental disorders as fundamentally "problems of living" seem to be establishing some potentially fruitful avenues for future exploration.[268] Such directions are described in Chapter 11.

Serious defects exist in many of the earlier studies—defects that often stemmed from antireligious perspectives. The more modern view is that religion functions largely as a means of countering abnormal thinking and behavior. Personal religious expressions may still reflect underlying mental disturbance, and for some, institutional faith remains a danger to their mental health. In most instances, however, faith buttresses people's sense of control and

꒰ꍏ꒱

Research Box 12.11. Religion and Psychotherapy
(Bethesda PsycHealth, 1994)

A survey dealing with religious/spiritual issues was administered to 60 professional staff members (physicians, etc.), 50 line staff members (aides, etc.), and 51 patients of a private mental health facility. Some representative questions and responses are as follows.

1. "How important to you is the inclusion of a spiritual focus as a part of the psychotherapy process?" Percentages responding "somewhat to very important": professional staff, 73%; line staff, 55%; patients, 72%.
2. "Is there a need to increase medical/professional staff's awareness of the use of a spiritual focus in psychotherapy?" Percentages responding "some to much need": professional staff, 66%; line staff, 80%.
3. "What percentage of your patients would benefit from a spiritual focus as part of the psychotherapy process?" Percentages mentioned: professional staff, 34%; line staff, 54%. (When patients were asked whether their spiritual beliefs helped in their recovery, 45% said "yes.")
4. "How important do you consider spiritual values to be?" Percentages responding "moderately to very important": professional staff, 78%; line staff, 90%.

Note that even though 73% of the medical and professional staff considered a spiritual approach important, they still felt that only 34% of their patients would benefit from this approach. This discrepancy might be worthy of further investigation.

This is only a small sampling of the questions asked. In addition, detailed open-ended responses were also obtained. For the samples obtained here, the importance of a religious/spiritual approach in therapy is apparent.

self-esteem, offers meanings that oppose anxiety, provides hope, sanctions socially facilitating behavior, enhances personal well-being, and promotes social integration. All of these possibilities work to the benefit of distressed persons; ideally, they will be increasingly employed by mental health professionals, to the advantage of those who seek their aid.

NOTES

1. Symonds (1946, p. 187).
2. Interviewee quoted in Boisen (1936, pp. 168–169).
3. McGinley (1969, p. 129).
4. Respondent quoted in Beardsworth (1977, p. 71).
5. Interviewee quoted in Clark (1929, p. 131).
6. McNeill (1951); Zilboorg and Henry (1941).
7. Deuteronomy 28:28 (*The Holy Bible*, Authorized King James Version).
8. McNeill (1951); Zilboorg and Henry (1941).
9. Bromberg (1937); Deutsch (1946).
10. Kirk and Kutchins (1992); Mowrer (1961); Ramsey and Seipp (1948); Rotenberg (1978).
11. Freud (1907/1924).
12. Freud (1933/1953, p. 107).
13. Freud (1927/1961, p. 53).

14. Freud (1907/1924); Reik (1946).
15. Coleman, Butcher, and Carson (1984); American Psychiatric Association (1980); Richardson (1993b).
16. Kilbourne and Richardson (1984b, p. 2).
17. Sleek (1994, p. 8). See American Psychiatric Association (1994).
18. Ellis (1980, p. 637).
19. Stern and Marino (1970, p. 1).
20. Sanborn (1979).
21. Linn and Schwarz (1958, p. vii).
22. Linn and Schwartz (1958, p. 20).
23. Hiltner (1961, p. 251).
24. With the exception of the last role for religion, we are deeply indebted to Dr. James E. Dittes for this scheme, which was first used in Spilka and Werme (1971).
25. Kirk and Kutchins (1992).
26. Hollingshead and Redlich (1958); Rose (1955); Srole, Langner, Michael, Opler, and Rennie (1962).
27. Bedell (1994).
28. Szasz (1960).
29. Some pertinent discussion of material that bears on the relationship of mystical experience and psychopathology may be found in Chapter 7, "Mysticism," and readers may want to coordinate that information with what is mentioned here.
30. Greeley (1974); Hardy (1979); Hay and Morisy (1978); Thomas and Cooper (1978).
31. Prince (1992).
32. Greeley (1974, p. 81).
33. Group for the Advancement of Psychiatry (1976, p. 815).
34. Group for the Advancement of Psychiatry (1976, p. 715).
35. Group for the Advancement of Psychiatry (1976, p. 731).
36. Horton (1973); *Roche Report: Frontiers of Psychiatry* (1972).
37. Siglag (1987).
38. Batson, Schoenrade, and Ventis (1993); Bridges (1970).
39. Leuba (1925, p. 191).
40. Stark (1965).
41. Stark (1965, p. 102).
42. Jackson and Spilka (1980).
43. Boisen (1936); Spilka, Brown, and Cassidy (1993); Prince (1992).
44. Lukoff, Lu, and Turner (1992).
45. Beit-Hallahmi and Argyle (1977).
46. Prince (1992, pp. 286–287).
47. Greenberg and Witztum (1992).
48. Kildahl (1972).
49. Teshome (1992).
50. Pattison (1968, p. 76).
51. Kelsey (1964).
52. Kildahl (1972, p. 57).
53. Preus (1982, p. 290).
54. Goodman (1972, p. 152).
55. Goodman (1972); Preus (1982); Samarin (1959).
56. Readers are referred to Chapter 8, "Conversion." Some of the present ideas are developed in greater detail there. In addition, the complexity of conversion must be appreciated; this complexity is well beyond our ability to describe in the present chapter.
57. Starbuck (1899, p. 52).
58. Starbuck (1899, p. 63).
59. Clark (1929).
60. Gallemore, Wilson, and Rhoads (1969).
61. Lutoslawski (1923).
62. Argyle (1959).
63. Argyle (1959).
64. Salzman (1953).
65. Kildahl (1965); Roberts (1965); Spellman, Baskett, and Byrne (1971).
66. Cavenar and Spaulding (1977).
67. Clark (1929); Starbuck (1899).

68. Christensen (1963).
69. Ullman (1982).
70. Salzman (1953).
71. Allison (1969).
72. Levin and Zegans (1974).
73. Rambo (1982, p. 155).
74. Srole et al. (1962, see especially pp. 314–315).
75. Mora (1969).
76. Askin, Paultre, White, and Van Ornum (1993, p. 3).
77. Askin et al. (1993, pp. 3–4).
78. Askin et al. (1993); Askin, Paultre, Van Ornum, and White (1992).
79. Weisner and Riffel (1960).
80. Overholser (1963).
81. Beit-Hallahmi and Argyle (1977, p. 26).
82. Group for the Advancement of Psychiatry (1968, p. 654).
83. Argyle (1959).
84. Oates (1955).
85. Reifsnyder and Campbell (1960).
86. Hardt (1963).
87. Lowe and Braaten (1966).
88. Beit-Hallahmi (1977, p. 29).
89. Adorno, Frenkel-Brunswik, Levinson, and Sanford (1950); Glock and Stark (1965); Herberg (1960); McGuire (1992); Stark and Glock (1968).
90. Stark and Glock (1968, pp. 163–173).
91. McGuire (1992, pp. 175–211).
92. Bateman and Jensen (1958); Nunn (1964).
93. MacDonald and Luckett (1983).
94. Schachter (1951).
95. Rohrbaugh and Jessor (1975).
96. Ross (1983).
97. Bainbridge (1992); Benson (1992b).
98. Snyder (1962).
99. Snyder (1962).
100. Pruyser (1971, p. 79).
101. MacDonald and Luckett (1983, p. 33).
102. Levin and Zegans (1974, p. 80).
103. Levin and Zegans (1974, p. 79).
104. Allison (1968, p. 459).
105. Dublin (1963, p. 74).
106. Argyle (1959).
107. Gibbs (1966).
108. Levi (1982).
109. Feifel, quoted in Mowrer (1958, p. 579).
110. Casey and Burton (1986, p. 82).
111. Nelsen, Potvin, and Shields (1976).
112. Bandura (1977, p. 49).
113. Holm (1987, p. 41).
114. Holm (1987, p. 41).
115. Holm (1987, p. 41).
116. Stark (1971).
117. Stark (1971, p. 175). Emphasis in original.
118. Hardt (1963); Lowe (1955); Lowe and Braaten (1966); Reifsnyder and Campbell (1960).
119. MacDonald and Luckett (1983, p. 15).
120. Bainbridge (1992).
121. Bainbridge (1992, p. 203).
122. Benson and Spilka (1973).
123. Jensen and Erickson (1979).
124. Richardson (1995); Rovner (1983).
125. Ross (1983).

126. Galanter, Rabkin, Rabkin, and Deutsch (1979).
127. Snelling and Whitley (1974).
128. Schwartz and Kaslow (1979).
129. Kildahl (1972, p. 299).
130. Spencer (1975).
131. McLoughlin (1978); Sasaki (1979); Wood (1965).
132. Galanter et al. (1979).
133. Hostetler (1968).
134. Hostetler (1968, pp. 293–300).
135. Eaton and Weil (1955).
136. Kelley (1958).
137. Sister Margaret Louise (1961).
138. Jahreiss (1942); Kurth (1961).
139. De Maria, Giulani, Annese, Corfiati (1971).
140. Kurth (1961, p. 20).
141. Kurth (1961, p. 23).
142. Gratton (1959), cited in Menges and Dittes (1965); Sipe (1990); Slawson (1973).
143. Freud (1907/1924); Reik (1946).
144. Argyle (1959); Scobie (1975).
145. Heelas (1985).
146. Kiev (1966, p. 170).
147. Pruyser (1968, p. 143).
148. Scheff (1977).
149. Jacobs (1992).
150. Group for the Advancement of Psychiatry (1968, p. 704).
151. Erikson, quoted in Couture (1990, p. 1089).
152. Couture (1990, p. 1090).
153. Moberg (1971).
154. Poloma and Gallup (1991).
155. Holahan and Moos (1987).
156. Appel (1959).
157. Kidorf (1966).
158. Loveland (1968).
159. Brown (1994); Buttrick (1942).
160. Spilka, Brown and Cassidy (1993).
161. Boisen (1936, p. 53).
162. Bergin (1994).
163. Bergin (1994, p. 88).
164. Maslow (1964).
165. Greeley (1974); Leuba (1925); Spilka, Brown, and Cassidy (1993); Stark (1965).
166. Hartocollis (1976); Horton (1973); Trew (1971).
167. Clark (1968); Pahnke (1969).
168. Clark (1968).
169. Group for the Advancement of Psychiatry (1976, p. 819).
170. Prince (1992, p. 289).
171. Hine (1969).
172. Brown (1987, p. 158).
173. Hutch (1980); Kelsey (1964); Kildahl (1972); Pattison (1968).
174. Lovekin and Malony (1977).
175. Starbuck (1899, p. 122).
176. Rambo (1992).
177. Jones (1937, p. 171); Cesarman (1957).
178. Bragan (1977); Gallemore et al. (1969); Gordon (1964).
179. Bronson (1966); Bronson and Meadow (1968).
180. Kilbourne and Richardson (1984a); Richardson (1992); Ross (1983); Snelling and Whitley (1974).
181. Richardson (1992, p. 233).
182. Bergman (1953); Levin and Zegans (1974); Propst (1988).
183. Batson et al. (1993); Propst (1988).
184. Bergman (1953); Levin and Zegans (1974).

185. Chesen (1972).
186. Pruyser (1977).
187. Stifoss-Hanssen (1994).
188. Culver (1988).
189. Ostow (1990, p. 122).
190. Alsdurf and Alsdurf (1988); Pagelow and Johnson (1988).
191. Higdon (1986).
192. Hartz and Everett (1989, p. 209).
193. Kirkpatrick, Hood, and Hartz (1991).
194. Hartz and Everett (1989, p. 208).
195. Sethi and Seligman (1993).
196. Weaver, Berry, and Pittel (1994).
197. Southard (1956).
198. Pruyser (1977, p. 332).
199. Andreason (1972); Bock and Warren (1972).
200. O'Connell (1961); Mowrer (1961).
201. Miller (1973).
202. Andrews (1987).
203. E. T. Clark (1929); W. H. Clark (1958); Cutten (1908); James (1902/1985).
204. McGinley (1969).
205. Pruyser (1977, pp. 333–334).
206. National Clearinghouse for Mental Health Information (1967).
207. Anderson (1963); Kelley (1961); Rayburn, Richmond, and Rogers (1983, 1986).
208. Rabinowitz (1969).
209. Finch (1965).
210. Christensen (1960).
211. Ranck (1961); Roe (1956); Strunk (1959); Webster (1967).
212. Aloyse (1961); Booth (n.d.); Menges and Dittes (1965, pp. 168–179); Wauck (1957).
213. Christensen (1963).
214. Jahreiss (1942); Kelley (1958).
215. Kelley (1961).
216. Moracco and Richardson (1985); Sammon, Reznikoff, and Geisinger (1985).
217. Daniel and Rogers (1981).
218. Aloyse (1961); Wauck (1957).
219. Stewart (1974, p. 45).
220. Schaffer (1990).
221. Fortune and Poling (1994).
222. Culver (1994); Lebacqz and Barton (1991, p. 69).
223. Fortune and Poling (1994, p. 21).
224. Camargo and Loftus (1993).
225. Hands (1992).
226. Lebacqz and Barton (1991).
227. Hawley (1994a); Horton and Williamson (1988).
228. Kaplan (1983); Landrine (1989).
229. McGuire (1992, p. 112).
230. Miller (1986).
231. Rothblum (1983, p. 88).
232. Holter (1970).
233. Ammerman (1987).
234. Brehony (1983).
235. Bridges and Spilka (1992).
236. Foster and Keating (1990).
237. Nelsen, Cheek, and Au (1985).
238. Bridges and Spilka (1992).
239. Koenig (1992).
240. Koenig (1992, p. 185).
241. Idler (1987).
242. Atkinson and Malony (1994).
243. Pruyser (1986).

244. Dalfiume (1993).
245. Koenig, Smiley, and Gonzales (1988, p. 75).
246. Rosenberg (1962).
247. Argyle (1959); Silberman (1985); Srole et al. (1962).
248. Srole et al. (1962).
249. Becker (1971).
250. Gilman (1984).
251. Gilman (1986).
252. McGuire (1992, p. 112).
253. Roberts (1984).
254. Chalfant, Beckley, and Palmer (1981); Hollingshead and Redlich (1958); Rose and Stub (1955).
255. Malzberg (1973).
256. Dohrenwend and Dohrenwend (1969); Hollingshead and Redlich (1958).
257. Hollingshead and Redlich (1958).
258. Roberts (1984).
259. Auld (1952); Berg (1967); Edwards (1957).
260. Duran (1995).
261. Krause and Van Tranh (1989).
262. Stolz (1940, 1943); Young and Meiburg (1960).
263. Bergin (1980).
264. Bethesda PsycHealth (1994).
265. Propst (1980, 1982, 1992).
266. Propst (1988).
267. Pargament, Steele, and Tyler (1979); VanderPlate (1973).
268. Szasz (1960).

Chapter 13

EPILOGUE

At the end of our review of the psychology of religion, it is fitting to take stock of the field—both as it is and as it is likely to develop in the immediate future. There is a heavy dose of evaluation in the former effort, and a bit of prophecy in the latter. To paraphrase the subtitle of one of Malony's texts,[1] the problems and possibilities of the psychology of religion are intimately a function of the notable personalities involved in the field. Even among ourselves, the authors of this text, there are differences in emphasis and orientation that reflect some of the diversity characterizing contemporary psychology in general and the contemporary psychology of religion in particular.

RESEARCH IN THE PSYCHOLOGY OF RELIGION

Our immediate focus in this text has been upon the empirical psychology of religion, because the empirical approach most adequately characterizes the academic study of religion in North American psychology departments. As we have seen, the empirical psychology of religion is as old as scientific psychology itself. Yet from its inception, scientific psychology has often been more of an ideal than a fact. The term "empirical" has undergone a curious change over time, so that entire orientations historically identified as empirical are not granted that description today by mainstream psychologists.[2] For many, classical psychoanalytic, object relations, Jungian, and phenomenological psychology are not empirical. "Empirical" has come to mean reliance upon the triad of observation, experimentation, and measurement. This is the paradigm that Gorsuch argues identifies our domain and places it firmly within a natural-scientific framework.[3] Historically, this has not always been the case.

A Historical Reminder

The Two Stances of Wilhelm Wundt

Authorities such as Robinson remind us that psychology as a natural science emerged in the 19th century, and that its success was largely a North American phenomenon associated with professionalization.[4] However, its origins were in philosophical developments utilizing natural-scientific assumptions to describe phenomena in the light of principles based upon observation, measurement, and experimentation. Textbooks commonly cite Willhelm Wundt and his psychological laboratory at Leipzig as the beginning of scientific psychology. The establishment of this laboratory in 1879 meant that psychology was moving from speculative philosophy to natural science. The bridge was experimentation, which involved measurement, manipulation, and observation. Yet Wundt actually fostered two psychologies—limiting the applicability of natural-scientific assumptions to some phenomena, but applying different assumptions and methods to other, more social phenomena ("folk psychology").[5]

From the beginning, psychology and social psychology never quite met in terms of natural-scientific assumptions. Even less could psychology maintain its grasp on the entire range and scope of religion with natural-scientific hands—aspects of religion, maybe, but not religion itself. The reduction of religion to categories of science, a persistent goal of early Enlightenment social scientists, can fairly be judged to have failed.[6] The split between psychology as a natural science and social psychology is today as firmly debated as in Wundt's time.[7] From the efforts to reconstruct social psychology proposed by Armstead,[8] to the efforts to deconstruct social psychology proposed by Parker and Shotter,[9] the identity of social psychology as a natural science has always been and remains perpetually problematic. This is important, insofar as the major sources of the contemporary measurement-based psychology of religion are social psychologists.

The Two Stances of William James

William James, a contemporary of Wundt and the founder of North American psychology, also failed to apply laboratory- and measurement-based methodologies to the study of religion. Twice president of the American Psychological Association, James also helped establish the American Society of Psychical Research. The two organizations made strange bedfellows. Coon reminds us that psychology gained its professional standing in North America within a population that equated psychology ("psychical") with things spiritual.[10] The study of things psychical was a bridging concept that allowed psychologists to gain popular support for their science, while aiming to use natural-scientific methods to debunk the claims of spiritualists.

James, as in so many instances, was an exception. His most consistently psychological work, *The Principles of Psychology*, took a rigorous stance that psychology was to be a natural science.[11] However, as Hood[12] has emphasized, James took this stance provisionally, seeking to expose its limits. These limits were both revealed and transcended in James's confrontation with religion. Religious experience was the subject matter of his Gifford lectures and the basis for James's other undisputed classic text in the psychology of religion.

James's *The Varieties of Religious Experience* explored the range and depth of religious experience, using personal documents placed within the context of their development so that their fruits could be assessed.[13] The stress upon measurement and the use of questionnaires, already established by such notables as Pratt and Starbuck, were ignored by James in favor of the existential thrust of experience, defined and interpreted within a more historical, narrative context. In modern terms, James's research was qualitative, not quantitative. His psychological treatment of religion specifically expanded the boundaries of a natural-science-based psychology articulated in *The Principles*.[14] *The Varieties* still remains the single most frequently assigned text in the psychology of religion.[15] This should not, however, convey the idea that the contemporary empirical psychology of religion is heavily influenced by James.

Despite the fact that empirical psychologists of religion tend to be primarily social psychologists, they come from the *psychological* tradition of social psychology, not the *sociological* tradition. Ironically, as Schellenberg has noted, the latter has been influenced more by James than the former.[16] The natural-scientific assumptions of psychology remain firm for most of the psychologically oriented social psychologists who do empirical research. Those who confine themselves to natural-scientific assumptions tend to produce what Beit-Hallahmi identifies as a psychology of religion rather than a religious psychology per se.[17] A psychology of religion places psychological categories at the forefront, and would have psychology explain religion only insofar as its phenomena of religion can be captured within natural-scientific constructs from mainstream psychology. On the other hand, religious psychology gives supremacy to religious constructs, and finds psychology to follow from and to be constrained within the conceptual limits of a natural science whose explanatory power is superseded by religion. There is an uneasy tension between psychologists of religion and religious psychologists, which promises to persist in the foreseeable future.

As we have noted in this text, not simply measurement, but the ontological status assigned to what is measured, is crucial in developing theory within the psychology of religion. William James remains the most significant figure in identifying the tensions between a psychology of religion and the tendency to move toward a religious psychology. Measurement has often been the fence that separates these two.

The Measurement Paradigm in the Psychology of Religion

Hood has argued for a compromise position—neither a psychology of religion nor a religious psychology, but rather psychology *and* religion.[18] This stance admits the validity of concepts from both disciplines and encourages their interaction. At odds is to what extent a genuine interaction can occur, given the limited empirical characteristics of many religious constructs. Still, psychology has its nonempirical assumptions, as well as a rigorous perspective as to what constitutes both measurement and empiricism. The psychology of religion is both broadened and challenged by newer orientations such as transpersonal psychology and the human sciences—both of which accept a broader definition of "empiricalism," much of it compatible with religious and spiritual traditions. *The Journal of Transpersonal Psychology* has established itself as a major journal representing spiritual phenomena studied by means of admittedly sympathetic psychological methods. Such studies and methods contrast with those of more objective measurement-based journals, such as the *Journal for the Scientific Study of Religion* whose focus has been on mainstream social-scientific methods applied to religious (and, to a lesser extent, spiritual) phenomena. The *Review of Religious Research* focuses upon theory and empirical research with some relevance or application to religious institutions. The boundaries between these journals promise to become more permeable as social scientists sympathetic to both religious and spiritual phenomena begin to develop scientific theories compatible with concepts central to religion. Likewise, as proponents of more traditionally measurement-based psychology broaden their theoretical horizons, new measurement techniques are likely to arise to permit a more adequate assessment of variables or religious and spiritual relevance.

The classical non-measurement-based theories of religion, many derived from psychoanalysis or its analytical and object relations offshoots, continue to spawn an immense literature.[19] Largely interpretative of religion, as in the case of psychoanalysis, or interpretative of spirituality, in the case of analytical (Jungian) or object relations theory, this literature promises to influence measurement psychology in two ways. First, it provides hypotheses that can be subject to measurement-based tests; many of these tests are controversial, but legitimately empirical nonetheless. Second, as competing qualitative methodologies, approaches such as these gain credibility as other narrative and interpretive psychologies emerge and influence mainstream social psychology. In addition, the long tradition of qualitative sociological social psychology, such as symbolic interactionism, is beginning to influence the more measurement-based psychological social psychology. Measurement is on the defensive as an all-inclusive methodological claim. As Roth has noted, methodological pluralism is the emerging norm in the social sciences.[20] The psychology of religion promises to benefit from interchange between theories and methods that were previously perceived as mutually exclusive.

Measurement-based psychology is likely to rise to the challenge by articulating more meaningful and inclusive theory that nevertheless is susceptible to empirical test. Works such as that of Spilka and McIntosh,[21] which respond to the critical demand for theoretical advancement in the empirical psychology of religion, are welcome harbingers. One major challenge to a measurement-based psychology of religion is simply put—interest. It is not clear whether the massive literature spawned in psychology in general has yielded fruits relative to the effort. When one considers the explosion of literature in mainstream psychology, it is obvious that no psychologist can master even a small portion of it. Hearnshaw reminds us that writing in psychology since 1950 exceeds the total output of works on the subject produced since the time of the Greeks.[22] Yet this massive literature has spawned no agreed-upon theoretical integration. There is no such theory in general psychology, much less in the psychology of religion. Despite the vast amount of research produced in the North American resurgence of interest in the psychology of religion since 1950, much of it is, in Dittes's term, promiscuous empiricism.[23] The rigors of measurement and the cleverness of experimental design fail if the ultimate result is, as is so often the case, trivial or uninformative. The psychology of religion is likely to become more like a quilt, in which measurement will at best sew together patches derived from diverse theoretical perspectives.

THE NEED FOR THEORY IN THE PSYCHOLOGY OF RELIGION

Within the psychology of religion, the cry for good theory has reached the level of cacophony. Our guess is that the older generation of researchers will want to make their theoretical contributions in light of the plea for such guidance across the disciplines concerned with the study of religion. Likewise, a younger generation of researchers will be trained to demand good theory as a prerequisite to the collection of meaningful empirical data. The field should profit from the emerging consensus that theory congruent with the passion and interest elicited by religion is needed. Theory and measurement need not be incompatible endeavors, but the latter alone will not rise to the level of adequate theory.

General Changes and Developments

Consistent with theory development in the psychology of religion is similar growth in general psychology as it is forced to confront religious issues. Religion is no longer a marginal concern of psychology; whether in the challenges of therapy or in the collective confrontation with cults, it occupies much of the center stage of general culture. Mainstream psychology will begin to confront religion in terms of its theories, if for no other reason than to show the meaningful relevance of psychology to the interests of a culture that supports and in the process seeks guidance from this science, natural or otherwise. In many cases, the vacuum left by some religions will be filled by psychology. Vitz has made the case that for some, psychology has become a religion.[24] Some areas, such as transpersonal psychology, blur the boundaries between psychology as a science and as a spiritual discipline. In the future, religionists will probably need to be more psychologically skilled, and psychologists more religiously sophisticated, if there are to remain identifiable boundaries between psychology on the one hand and spirituality/religion on the other.

In a similar vein, journals devoted to a faith commitment—either by constraining their psychology within the more narrow confines of a particular faith (e.g., the *Journal of Psychology and Christianity*, the *Journal of Psychology and Judaism*), or by interrelating or integrating psychology and religion (e.g., the *Journal of Psychology and Theology*)—will assure that psychology is itself appropriately reflective on its own limits. Religion and psychology may confront similar questions, but how they are asked defines what constitutes an appropriate answer. Precisely what it is within religion that admits of an empirical answer must be more clearly theoretically determined. So, too, the limits of empiricism must be acknowledged theoretically. The *Journal of the Psychology of Religion* is among the most recent of the new publications committed to broadening the methodological basis of the psychology of religion.

The continual debate between nomothetic and idiographic methodologies within mainstream psychology has long parallels in the history of religion. General covering laws have long been psychology's goal, but are no longer thought to exclude the individual case. Idiographic studies are of immense value, both as unique narratives in their own right, and as instances of a general law concretely particularized. Tageson's "objective phenomenology" is not an oxymoron.[25] The radically subjective can enter a rigorous psychology of religion. The discussion of mysticism in this text also indicates the interface between phenomenological and measurement psychology, in which the results of phenomenological analysis can be operationalized and can fulfill the requirements of a measurement paradigm. Once again, the issue is not only that multiple methods can be of value in the psychology of religion, but that measurement can be based upon a variety of theoretical and even alternative methodological perspectives. It is long past the time when the psychological illumination of religious issues can be assumed to deny the validity of the religious nature of what is illuminated psychologically. Boundaries must be identified theoretically even if they are to be crossed.

If there is a change in the psychology of religion, it is likely to be most evident in the North American dominance of the field. The success of psychology in the United States and Canada has always been associated with its development as a profession. The recent split in allegiances between the American Psychological Association, long the dominant organization for psychologists (whether teachers, researchers, or practitioners), and the recently formed American Psychological Society (which focuses more upon research and teaching than upon practice) suggests that even within North American psychology, tensions between research and practice, knowledge and application are considerable. The tension is reflected in religion as a specialty in the American Psychological Society and religion as a division within the American Psychological Association. Practitioners are more likely to foster a religious psychology than are researchers. It is unlikely that this emphasis will gain as strong an academic foothold in North American universities as the research-based empirical psychology of religion.

With the emergence of the *International Journal for the Psychology of Religion*, the global dimensions of psychology and religion have been highlighted. The psychology of religion in European cultures has been substantial, even though it has a relatively short history. For these cultures, there has been no reemergence of the study of religion, but rather only a gradual emergence of its study since World War II.[26] Compared to North American psychologists of religion, Europeans are less measurement-oriented and more receptive to phenomenological and dynamic studies. These cultures are also less overtly committed to institutional religion. Thus the European psychology of religion promises to challenge North American supremacy in this area, both because of European psychology's greater breadth and scope, and because of North American psychology's tendency to take apologetic religious-psychological stances. In addition, Asian studies in the psychology of religion are emerging—with much less distinct lines between psychology, religion, and science. To date, mainly transpersonal psychologists have examined these traditions, but their influence will undoubtedly affect measurement psychology. Again, the challenge to a psychology of religion premised upon measurement and experimentation is for theoretical meaningfulness as well as greater breadth and scope. It is unlikely that another *Annual Review of Psychology* will include a review of psychology of religion in which the data base consists exclusively of convenience samples of Protestant Christians selected primarily from North American universities.[27]

What seems most clearly on the horizon that will assure the vigor, relevance, and compatibility of the psychology of religion with mainstream psychology is theory. The complaint that the psychology of religion has largely been atheoretical, piecemeal, and lacking in sustained development is unlikely to characterize the future. Mainstream psychology has proposed a variety of theories that integrate and guide meaningful empirical research, and many of them are beginning to influence the study of religion. Likewise, more restricted theories are being developed within our field that can sustain significant research. In any case, whether new theories are broad or narrow, the demand for theory will guide the future psychology of religion. Promising illustrations of emerging theory from the more narrow confines of the psychology of religion as a specialty, from mainstream psychology, and from the practical concerns of psychology as a profession are readily available and worth noting.

Theories from within the Specialty of the Psychology of Religion

Bodies of empirical research are emerging that are theory-driven with respect to particular topics more common in the psychology of religion than in other specialties. In some cases, concepts central to religion have become the foci of theoretical development within the area.

Fundamentalism has emerged as a major construct of concern to both sociologists and psychologists. The massive Fundamentalism Project is a major theoretical effort, largely sociologically oriented.[28] Yet psychologists have also begun a rather systematic study of fundamentalism. What is important is that a term integral to religious traditions is the basis of systematic empirical clarification by psychologists. Hood's warning that the earlier empirical literature on fundamentalism read more like a caricature than like scientific findings[29] no longer applies. As we have seen in many places in this text, fundamentalism is being illuminated as both an enduring form of religious life and, as Hunsberger and his colleagues have been demonstrating,[30] a religious commitment that is meaningfully related to complexity of both thought and attitudes toward others. Likewise, Kirkpatrick, Hood, and Hartz have proposed a theoretical model of fundamentalism conceptualized in terms of Rokeach's dogmatism theory, a mainstream measurement-based social-psychological perspective.[31] Although much research remains to be done, the psychological illumination of fundamentalism is an empirical challenge that future psychology of religion is quite capable of meeting—in terms neither apologetic nor demeaning, but theoretically pertinent and empirically substantiated.

Within the North American psychology of religion, we have more than a quarter of a century of measurement-based research on intrinsic faith. Yet, as Gorsuch has recently noted, doubts and concerns regarding intrinsic religion persist.[32] We could count on one hand the notable psychologists of religion who have failed to utilize some aspect of an intrinsic orientation in their measurement studies. Most have used the variable as independent, exploring its relationship to a variety of phenomena, perhaps most typically prejudice and helping behavior. Yet since then there have been pleas for a more sophisticated theoretical treatment of this construct. Most recently, Kirkpatrick and Hood have often been misinterpreted as suggesting that the concept must be abandoned.[33] In fact, this is but one of the options suggested. Others include a return to Allport's own theorizing and a more sophisticated research program that is explicitly theory-driven. Gorsuch has taken a similar approach, but argues that theory must come not from Allport's original intent, but from within religious commitment as an evolving research program.[34] Gorsuch's suggestion for motivational theories of religious commitment may revitalize intrinsic–extrinsic research by linking it to theories of motivation within general psychology. In Dittes's apt phrasing over a quarter of a century ago, despite continual criticism, intrinsic–extrinsic theory continues to survive its obituaries.[35] It is likely to do so again.

Batson's research program can be understood in a similar vein.[36] The quest orientation was initially an effort to operationalize aspects of intrinsic religiosity ignored in Allport's own operationalization of the intrinsic concept. Batson and his colleagues are the most consistent representatives of a measurement-premised, quasi-experimental approach to the psychology of religion. They continue to pave the way for others to develop internally consistent research programs, so that constructs and theories can be appropriately developed, revised, and ultimately evaluated in terms of their empirical fruitfulness and adequacy.

Theories from Mainstream Psychology

Social psychology continues to drive the empirical psychology of religion. Most of the notable measurement-oriented researchers have their doctorates in social psychology. Systematic efforts to apply major social-psychological theories, such as attribution theory (championed by Spilka),[37] are not surprisingly stressed by these social psychologists of religion. Despite the controversies surrounding social psychology noted above, this specialty is likely to continue to be a major source of empirical work in our field, at least in North America. Related to this is the "cognitive revolution" that has influenced both general psychology and social psychology. McIntosh has proposed that religion be viewed as schema, and in the process has proposed another inducement for the psychology of religion to seek haven within theories from mainstream social psychology.[38] His appeal to cognitive theory parallels McCallister's enthusiasm for a psychology of religion that can emerge out of cognitive psychology.[39]

Developmental psychology has come to play a more dominant role in the psychology of religion. There are significant new developmental research findings in the psychology of religion, such as Tamminen's study of patterns of faith development in childhood and adolescence.[40] As Hyde's massive survey reveals, developmental psychology remains heavily influential in terms of theoretical possibilities for the future of the psychology of religion.[41] Attachment theory, bridging mainstream developmental and social psychology, has also been the focus of systematic research (primarily by Kirkpatrick) in terms of its relevance to the psychology of religion.[42] Attachment theory is rigorous in formulation, measurement-based, and firmly rooted within the tradition of psychology as a natural science. Its place in the future development of an empirical psychology of religion seems secure.

The natural-scientific basis for attachment theory is ultimately rooted in evolutionary theory. Evolution is the overarching theoretical umbrella for a variety of orientations that would keep the psychology of religion firmly within natural-scientific boundaries.[43] Clearly an evolutionary psychology is on the horizon, and this promises great significance for the psychology of religion.

Virtually every major theoretical orientation has its evolutionary basis. Classic psychoanalysis, strongly based on Freud's use of evolution, is reemerging as a formidable force. Freud's discredited reliance upon Lamarckian ideas (and the unlikely inheritance of acquired characteristics) is giving way to a modern version compatible with Darwinian theory. Badcock's work is particularly impressive in this respect, linking psychoanalytic psychology not only to mainstream science, but to topics of interest in the psychology of religion (e.g., altruism).[44]

Bowlby, the theoretical architect of attachment theory, relied upon evolutionary theory to explain the mechanisms for the emergence of basic attachment types.[45] Although attachment theory is not yet fully developed within the psychology of religion, it is, as noted above, a prime example of an empirical theory that is firmly rooted in a natural-scientific perspective. Attachment theorists will be forced to confront more psychoanalytically oriented theorists as they utilize evolutionary theory to provide a thoroughly natural-science-based theoretical interpretation of religion. The experimental attachment tradition is likely to confront the considerable scope of the more clinically and anthropologically based psychoanalytic interpretations of religion. Both theoretical camps mine the rich fields of evolutionary theory as the paradigmatic base for their theories of religion.

Religious experience in general, as well as mystical experience in particular, will probably be drawn into this debate. Theories of mysticism have long had an evolutionary basis, as have many conceptual perspectives on religious experience. The correlation of experience with neurophysiological states assures a future interest in religious experience, if for no other reason than such experiences can be identified in terms of neurophysiological structures known to have an evolutionary history. This natural-science-based approach, which is compatible with a psychology of religion, is likely to be challenged by evolutionary theories with a more spiritual, "religious" psychology orientation. Wilber's recent theoretical effort is subtitled *The Spirit of Evolution*,[46] reflecting the fact that even within paradigms based on evolutionary science, boundaries between science and spirituality—like those between religion and science—can become blurred. Nevertheless, the long-sought paradigm that would incorporate divergent views in a forced dialogue may be on the horizon as psychological theory becomes more explicitly informed by evolutionary views. Only evolutionary theory seems to be a foundational focus for so many diverse theories. Here varieties of data can be meaningfully understood from a methodologically pluralistic perspective.

Theories from Psychology as a Profession

Among clinically oriented investigators, issues of religion and mental health have moved away from earlier naive views of religion as necessarily pathological. Fowler's conceptualization of stages of faith development,[47] though lacking a firm empirical base, has provided a theoretical framework within which questions such as "Is religion healthy?" are no longer meaningful. The issue is what type of religion can be expected to foster what view of health. It is unlikely that discussions of religion in general are likely to be theoretically useful. Fowler has gone on to explicate a specific view of Christian faith development.[48] However, in the process, the notion of what constitutes appropriate faith development even within a given tradition has produced interminable debate as to which methodologies can empirically identify differences in value and meaning. The systematic development of the notion of "ideological surround" by Watson and his colleagues is a strong contender for a meaningful empirical way to identify differences in value and meaning inherent in any discussion of religion and mental health.[49]

Closely related to the issue of ideological surround will be the demand for a more sophisticated theological literacy among researchers in the psychology of religion.[50] For instance, Gorsuch has emphasized that if intrinsic religion is treated as a motivational construct, then its independent assessment from belief content is essential.[51] Low correlations among measures of general intrinsic religiousness and other variables may be attributable to the fact that only when specific beliefs are taken into account can more powerful predictions be made. Thus, whether or not one is intrinsically motivated is less powerful a predictor than one's intrinsic motivation within a particular belief context. In a similar vein, Hood has argued that psychological processes, empirically identified, are of little use in making predictions unless the content of specific faith traditions is taken into account.[52] The psychology of religion, even when not a religious psychology, will nevertheless need to be religiously informed in order to make meaningful empirical predictions.

The move from a concern with religion and mental health to an interest in religion and coping is one of the more striking changes in the present text from the first edition. This can be attributed in large part to the systematic empirical and theoretical work of Kenneth Pargament.[53] His treatment of both coping and religion presages a likely future trend noted above. His work is neither a pure psychology of religion nor a religious psychology; rather, his is a psychology of religion *and* coping. It is apparent that investigators who are most intimately familiar with the interaction of religion and psychology produce the more meaningful empirically based theories, which are neither purely psychological nor religious.

Finally, training in the practice of psychology needs to become more sensitive to cultural, gender, and religious differences. This need makes the psychology of religion a legitimate—indeed, essential—subject for psychologists seeking to be practitioners. Jones has made a case for the inclusion of religious values and perspectives within modern clinical psychology.[54] At a minimum, sensitivity to clients' values, often religious ones, is an ethical imperative for clinicians and other social service providers. In many cases, psychotherapy may be best conductded within a religious framework.[55] At this writing, the American Psychological Association is about to publish Shafranske's major edited text on religion and the practice of clinical psychology.[56] In the extreme, awareness of religious motivations and schemas is necessary for effective intervention when law enforcement confronts religiously based deviance, as in recent confrontations with religious sects and cults. It has long been established that whether or not they are true in some ultimate sense, things believed and acted upon as true have real consequences. An understanding of religious perspectives, however different from researchers' own beliefs they may be, is another tool in interacting effectively with those whose religiously based views provide meaning, security, and mastery—if not for the researchers, then at least for those who believe. Theory, empirically supported, will properly dominate the future of the psychology of religion; ideally, it will illuminate religious and spiritual phenomena that otherwise may only be seen "through a glass darkly."

NOTES

1. Malony (1991).
2. See Hamlyn (1967); Hearnshaw (1987).
3. Gorsuch (1984).
4. Robinson (1981).
5. See Wundt (1901, 1916).
6. Preus (1987).
7. See Parker (1989).
8. Armstead (1974).
9. Parker and Shotter (1987).
10. Coon (1992).
11. James (1890/1950).
12. Hood (1995c).
13. James (1902/1985).
14. Hood (1992a).
15. Vande Kemp (1976).
16. Schellenberg (1990).
17. Beit-Hallahmi (1991).
18. Hood (1994).
19. See Hood (l995a).
20. Roth (1987).
21. Spilka and McIntosh (in press).
22. Hearnshaw (1987, p. 246).
23. Dittes (1971a).
24. Vitz (1977).
25. Tageson (1982).
26. Belzen (1994).
27. Gorsuch (1988).
28. See Marty and Appleby (1991).
29. Hood (1983).
30. Hunsberger, Pratt, and Pancer (1994).
31. Kirkpatrick, Hood, and Hartz (1991).
32. Gorsuch (1994).
33. Kirkpatrick and Hood (1990).
34. Gorsuch (1994, p. 316).
35. Dittes (1971c).
36. Batson, Schoenrade, and Ventis (1993).
37. Spilka and McIntosh (1995).
38. McIntosh (1995).
39. McCallister (1995).
40. Tamminen (1991).
41. Hyde (1990).
42. Kirkpatrick (1995).
43. Wright (1994).
44. See Badcock (1980, 1986, 1991).
45. See Bowlby (1969, 1973, 1980).
46. Wilber (1995).

47. Fowler (1981).
48. Fowler (1984).
49. See Watson (1993).
50. Hunter (1989).
51. Gorsuch (1994).
52. Hood (1992c).
53. See Pargament (in press).
54. Jones (1994).
55. Propst (1988).
56. Shafranske (1996).

REFERENCES

Aarson, B., & Osmond, H. (1970). *Psychedelics: The use and implications of psychedelic drugs.* Garden City, NY: Doubleday.

Abraham, K. G. (1981). The influence of cognitive conflict on religious thinking in fifth and sixth grade children. *Journal of Early Adolescence, 1,* 147–154.

Acklin, M. W., Brown, E. C., & Mauger, P.A. (1983). The role of religious values in coping with cancer. *Journal of Religion and Health, 22,* 322–333.

Acock, A. C., & Bengtson, V. L. (1978). On the relative influence of mothers and fathers: A covariance analysis of political and religious socialization. *Journal of Marriage and the Family, 40,* 519–530.

Acock, A. C., & Bengtson, V. L. (1980). Socialization and attribution processes: Actual versus perceived similarity among parents and youth. *Journal of Marriage and the Family, 42,* 501–515.

Adelekan, M. L., Abiodun, O. A., Imouokhome-Obayan, A. O., Oni, G. A., & Ogunremi, O. O. (1993). Psychosocial correlates of alcohol, tobacco and cannabis use: Findings from a Nigerian university. *Drug and Alcohol Dependence, 33,* 247–256.

Adlaf, E. M., & Smart, R. G. (1985). Drug use and religious affiliation, feelings and behaviour. *British Journal of Addiction, 80,* 163–171.

Adler, A. (1931). *What life should mean to you.* New York: Grosset & Dunlap.

Adler, A. (1935). Introduction: The fundamental views of individual psychology. *International Journal of Individual Psychology, 1*(1), 5–8.

Adler, T. (1991, February). Cancer patients helped by therapy, study finds. *APA Monitor,* p. 9.

Adorno, T. W., Frenkel-Brunswik, E., Levinson, D. J., & Sanford, R. N. (1950). *The authoritarian personality.* New York: Harper & Row.

Ahern, G. (1990). *Spiritual/religious experience in modern society.* Oxford: Alister Hardy Research Centre, Westminister College.

Albert, A. A., & Porter, J. R. (1986). Children's gender role stereotypes: A comparison of the United States and South Africa. *Journal of Cross-Cultural Psychology, 17,* 45–65.

Albrecht, S. L., & Cornwall, M. (1989). Life events and religious change. *Review of Religious Research, 31,* 23–38.

Albrecht, S. L., Cornwall, M., & Cunningham, P. H. (1988). Religious leave-taking: Disengagement and disaffiliation among Mormons. In D. G. Bromley (Ed.), *Falling from the faith: Causes and consequences of religious apostasy* (pp. 62–80). Newbury Park, CA: Sage.

Alexander, M. W., & Judd, B. B. (1986). Differences in attitudes toward nudity in advertising. *Psychology: A Quarterly Journal of Behavior, 23,* 26–29.

Al-Issa, I. (1977). Social and cultural aspects of hallucinations. *Psychological Reports, 84,* 570–587.

Allegro, J. M. (1971). *The sacred mushroom and the cross.* New York: Bantam.

Allen, C. L. (1958). *All things are possible through prayer.* New York: Revell.

Allen, R. O., & Spilka, B. (1967). Committed and consensual religion: A specification of religion–prejudice relationships. *Journal for the Scientific Study of Religion, 6,* 191–206.

Allison, J. (1961). Recent empirical studies of conversion experiences. *Pastoral Psychology, 17,* 21–33.

Allison, J. (1968). Adaptive regression and intense religious experiences. *Journal of Nervous and Mental Disease, 145,* 452–463.

Allison, J. (1969). Religious conversion: Regression and progression in an adolescent experience. *Journal for the Scientific Study of Religion, 8,* 23–38.

Allport, G. W. (1950). *The individual and his religion.* New York: Macmillan.

Allport, G. W. (1954). *The nature of prejudice.* Cambridge, MA: Addison-Wesley.

Allport, G. W. (1959). Religion and prejudice. *The Crane Review, 1,* 1–10.

Allport, G. W. (1966). The religious context of prejudice. *Journal for the Scientific Study of Religion, 5,* 447–457.

Allport, G. W., Gillespie, J. M., & Young, J. (1948). The religion of the post-war college student. *Journal of Psychology, 25,* 3–33.

Allport, G. W., & Ross, J. M. (1967). Personal religious orientation and prejudice. *Journal of Personality and Social Psychology, 5,* 432–443.

Aloyse, Sister M. (1961). Evaluation of candidates for the religious life. *Guild of Catholic Psychiatrists Bulletin, 8,* 199–204.

Alsdurf, P., & Alsdurf, J. M. (1988). Wife abuse and scripture. In A. L. Horton & J. A. Williamson (Eds.), *Abuse and religion: When praying isn't enough* (pp. 221–227). Lexington, MA: Lexington Books.

Altemeyer, B. (1981). *Right-wing authoritarianism.* Winnipeg: University of Manitoba Press.

Altemeyer, B. (1988). *Enemies of freedom: Understanding right-wing authoritarianism.* San Francisco: Jossey-Bass.

Altemeyer, B., & Hunsberger, B. (1992). Authoritarianism, religious fundamentalism, quest, and prejudice. *International Journal for the Psychology of Religion, 2,* 113–133.

Altemeyer, B., & Hunsberger, B. (1993). Response to Gorsuch. *International Journal for the Psychology of Religion, 3,* 33–37.

Ambert, A.-M. (1992). *The effects of children on parents.* New York: Haworth Press.

Ameika, C., Eck, N. H., Ivers, B. J., Clifford, J. M., & Malcarne, V. (1994, April). *Religiosity and illness prevention.* Paper presented at the annual meeting of the Rocky Mountain Psychological Association, Las Vegas, NV.

American Psychiatric Association. (1980). *Diagnostic and statistical manual of mental disorders* (3rd ed.). Washington, DC: Author.

American Psychiatric Association. (1994). *Diagnostic and statistical manual of mental disorders* (4th ed.). Washington, DC: Author.

Ames, E. S. (1910). *The psychology of religious experience.* Boston: Houghton Mifflin.

Ammerman, N. T. (1987). *Bible believers: Fundamentalists in the modern world.* New Brunswick, NJ: Rutgers University Press.

Anand, B. K., Chhina, G. S., & Singh, B. (1961). Some aspects of electroencephalographic studies on yogis. *Electroencephalography and Clinical Neurophysiology, 13,* 452–456.

Anderson, G. C. (1963). Who is ministering to ministers? *Christianity Today, 7,* 362–363.

Andreason, N. J. C. (1972). The role of religion in depression. *Journal of Religion and Health, 11,* 153–166.

Andrew, J. M. (1970). Recovery from surgery, with and without preparatory instructions for three coping styles. *Journal of Personality and Social Psychology, 15,* 223–226.

Andrews, L. M. (1987). *To thine own self be true.* Garden City, NY: Doubleday/Anchor.

Annis, L. V. (1975). Study of values as a predictor of helping behavior. *Psychological Reports, 37,* 717–718.

Annis, L. V. (1976). Emergency helping and religious behavior. *Psychological Reports, 39,* 151–158.

Anthony, D., Ecker, B., & Wilbur, K. (Eds.). (1987). *Spiritual choices.* New York: Paragon House.

Anthony, D., & Robbins, T. (1974). The Meher Baba movement: Its effect on post-adolescent social alienation. In I. I. Zaretsky & M. P. Leone (Eds.), *Religious movements in contemporary America* (pp. 228–243). Princeton, NJ: Princeton University Press.

Anthony, D., & Robbins, T. (1992). Law, social science and the "brainwashing" exception to the First Amendment. *Behavioral Sciences and the Law, 10*, 5–29.

Anthony, D., & Robbins, T. (1994). Brainwashing and totalitarian influence. In U. S. Ramachdran (Ed.), *Encyclopaedia of human behavior* (Vol. 1, pp. 457–471). New York: Academic Press.

Appel, K. E. (1959). Religion. In S. Arieti (Ed.), *American handbook of psychiatry* (Vol. 2, pp. 1777–1810.) New York: Basic Books.

Archer, S. L. (1989). Gender differences in identity development: Issues of process, domain and timing. *Journal of Adolescence, 12*, 117–138.

Arendt, H. (1979). *The origins of totalitarianism.* San Diego: Harcourt Brace Jovanovich.

Argyle, M. (1959). *Religious behavior.* Glencoe, IL: Free Press.

Argyle, M., & Beit-Hallahmi, B. (1975). *The social psychology of religion.* London: Routledge & Kegan Paul.

Arinze, F. C. (1986). Globalization of theological education. *Theological Education, 23*, 7–31.

Armstead, N. (Ed.). (1974). *Reconstructing social psychology.* Harmondsworth, England: Penguin.

Askin, H., Paultre, Y., Van Ornum, W., & White, R. (1992, August). *Family dysfunction and scrupulosity and obsessive compulsive disorder.* Paper presented at the annual meeting of the American Psychological Association, Washington, DC.

Askin, H., Paultre, Y., White, R., & Van Ornum, W. (1993, August). *The quantitative and qualitative aspects of scrupulosity.* Paper presented at the annual meeting of the American Psychological Association, Toronto.

Atkinson, B. E., & Malony, H. N. (1994). Religious maturity and psychological distress among older Christian women. *International Journal for the Psychology of Religion, 4*, 165–179.

Auld, F., Jr. (1952). Influence of social class on personality test responses. *Psychological Bulletin, 49*, 318–332.

Austin, W. H. (1980). Are religious beliefs "enabling mechanisms for survival"? *Zygon, 15*, 193–201.

Babchuk, N., & Whitt, H. P. (1990). R-order and religious switching. *Journal for the Scientific Study of Religion, 29*, 246–254.

Bach, G. R., & Wyden, P. (1969). *The intimate enemy.* New York: William Morrow.

Back, K., & Bourque, L. (1970). Can feelings be enumerated? *Behavioral Science, 15*, 487–496.

Badcock, C. R. (1980). *Psychoanalysis of culture.* Oxford: Basil Blackwell.

Badcock, C. R. (1986). *The problem of altruism: Freudian–Darwinian solutions.* Oxford: Basil Blackwell.

Badcock, C. R. (1991). *Evolution and individual behavior: An introduction to human sociobiology.* Oxford: Basil Blackwell.

Badham, P. (1976). *Christian beliefs about life after death.* London: Macmillan.

Bagchi, B. K., & Wenger, M. A. (1957). Electro-physiological correlates of some yogi exercises. *Electroencephalography and Clinical Neurophysiology, 2*(Suppl. 7), 132–139.

Bahr, H. M., & Albrecht, S. L. (1989). Strangers once more: Patterns of disaffiliation from Mormonism. *Journal for the Scientific Study of Religion, 28*, 180–200.

Bahr, H. M., & Harvey, C. D. (1980). Correlates of morale among the newly widowed. *Journal of Social Psychology, 110*, 219–233.

Bainbridge, W. S. (1989). The religious ecology of deviance. *American Sociological Review, 54*, 288–295.

Bainbridge, W. S. (1992). Crime, delinquency, and religion. In J. F. Schumaker (Ed.), *Religion and mental health* (pp. 199–210). New York: Oxford University Press.

Bainbridge, W. S., & Stark, R. (1980a). Client and audience cults in America. *Sociological Analysis, 41*, 199–214.

Bainbridge, W. S., & Stark, R. (1980b). Sectarian tension. *Review of Religious Research, 22*, 105–124.

Bains, G. (1983). Explanations and the need for control. In M. Hewstone (Ed.), *Attribution theory: Social and functional extensions* (pp. 117–143). Oxford: Basil Blackwell.

Bakalar, J., & Grinspoon, L. (1989). Testing psychotherapies and drug therapies: The case of psychedelic drugs. In S. Peroutka (Ed.), *Ecstasy: The clinical, pharmacological, and neurotoxicological effects of the drug MDMAS.* Norwell, MA: Kluver Academic.

Baker-Brown, G., Ballard, E. J., Bluck, S., de Vries, B., Suedfeld, P., & Tetlock, P. E. (1992). The conceptual integrative complexity scoring manual. In C. P. Smith (Ed.), *Motivation and personality:*

Handbook of thematic content analysis (pp. 401–418). Cambridge, England: Cambridge University Press.

Balch, R. W. (1980). Looking behind the scenes in a religious cult: Implications for the study of conversion. *Sociological Analysis, 45,* 301–314.

Baldree, K. S., Murphy, S. P., & Powers, M. J. (1982). Stress identification and coping patterns in patients on hemodialysis. *Nursing Research, 31,* 107–112.

Bales, R. F. (1962). Attitudes toward drinking in the Irish culture. In D. J. Pittman & C. R. Snyder (Eds.), *Society, culture, and drinking patterns* (pp. 157–187). New York: Wiley.

Balk, D. E. (1995). *Adolescent development: Early through late adolescence.* Pacific Grove, CA: Brooks/Cole.

Ballard, S. N., & Fleck, J. R. (1975). The teaching of religious concepts: A three stage model. *Journal of Psychology and Theology, 3,* 164–171.

Baltzell, E. D. (1966). *The Protestant establishment.* New York: Random House/Vintage.

Bandura, A. (1977). *Social learning theory.* Englewood Cliffs, NJ: Prentice-Hall.

Barber, T. X. (1970). *LSD, marijuana, yoga, and hypnosis.* Chicago: Aldine.

Barker, E. (1983). Supping with the devil: How long a spoon does the sociologist need? *Sociological Analysis, 44,* 197–206.

Barker, E. (1984). *The making of a Moonie.* Oxford: Basil Blackwell.

Barker, E. (1986). Religious movements: Cult and anticult since Jonestown. *Annual Review of Sociology, 12,* 329–346.

Barker, I. R., & Currie, R. F. (1985). Do converts always make the most committed Christians? *Journal for the Scientific Study of Religion, 24,* 305–313.

Barnes, H. R., & Becker, H. (1938). *Social thought from lore to science* (Vol. 1). Boston: D. C. Heath.

Barnes, M., & Doyles, D. (1989). The formation of a Fowler scale: An empirical assessment among Catholics. *Review of Religious Research, 30,* 412–420.

Barr, H. L., Langs, R. J., Holt, R. R., Goldberger, L., & Klein, C. S. (1972). *LSD, personality and experience.* New York: Wiley.

Barron, F. (1953). An ego-strength scale which predicts response to psychotherapy. *Journal of Consulting Psychology, 17,* 327–333.

Bartlett, J. (Ed.). (1955). *Familiar quotations by John Bartlett* (13th and centennial ed.). Boston: Little, Brown.

Bassett, R. L., Miller, S., Anstey, K., Crafts, K., Harmon, J., Lee, Y., Parks, J., Robinson, M., Smid, H., Sterner, W., Stevens, C., Wheeler, B., & Stevenson, D. H. (1990). Picturing God: A nonverbal measure of God concept for conservative Protestants. *Journal of Psychology and Christianity, 9,* 73–81.

Bateman, M. M., & Jensen, J. S. (1958). The effect of religious background on modes of handling anger. *Journal of Social Psychology, 47,* 133–141.

Batson, C. D. (1976). Religion as prosocial: Agent or double agent? *Journal for the Scientific Study of Religion, 15,* 29–45.

Batson, C. D. (1983). Sociobiology and the role of religion in promoting prosocial behavior: An alternative view. *Journal of Personality and Social Psychology, 45,* 1380–1385.

Batson, C. D. (1990). Good Samaritans—or priests and Levites? Using William James as a guide in the study of religious prosocial motivation. *Personality and Social Psychology Bulletin, 16,* 758–768.

Batson, C. D. (1991). *The altruism question: Toward a social-psychological answer.* Hillsdale, NJ: Erlbaum.

Batson, C. D., Flink, C. H., Schoenrade, P. A., Fultz, J., & Pych, V. (1986). Religious orientation and overt versus covert racial prejudice. *Journal of Personality and Social Psychology, 50,* 175–181.

Batson, C. D., & Flory, J. D. (1990). Goal-relevant cognitions associated with helping by individuals high on intrinsic, end religion. *Journal for the Scientific Study of Religion, 29,* 346–360.

Batson, C. D., & Gray, R. A. (1981). Religious orientation and helping behavior: Responding to one's own or to the victim's needs? *Journal of Personality and Social Psychology, 40,* 511–520.

Batson, C. D., Naifeh, S. J., & Pate, S. (1978). Social desirability, religious orientation, and racial prejudice. *Journal for the Scientific Study of Religion, 17,* 31–41.

Batson, C. D., Oleson, K. C., Weeks, J. L., Healy, S. P., Reeves, P. J., Jennings, P., & Brown, T. (1989). Religious prosocial motivation: Is it altruistic or egoistic? *Journal of Personality and Social Psychology, 57*, 873–884.

Batson, C., D., & Raynor-Prince, L. (1983). Religious orientation and complexity of thought about existential concerns. *Journal for the Scientific Study of Religion, 22*, 38–50.

Batson, C. D., & Schoenrade, P. A. (1991a). Measuring religion as quest: 1. Validity concerns. *Journal for the Scientific Study of Religion, 30*, 416–429.

Batson, C. D., & Schoenrade, P. A. (1991b). Measuring religion as quest: 2. Reliability concerns. *Journal for the Scientific Study of Religion, 30*, 430–447.

Batson, C. D., Schoenrade, P. A., & Pych, V. (1985). Brotherly love or self-concern? Behavioural consequences of religion. In L. B. Brown (Ed.), *Advances in the psychology of religion* (pp. 185–208). New York: Oxford University Press.

Batson, C. D., Schoenrade, P., & Ventis, W. L. (1993). *Religion and the individual: A social-psychological perspective.* New York: Oxford University Press.

Batson, C. D., & Ventis, W. L. (1982). *The religious experience: A social-psychological perspective.* New York: Oxford University Press.

Baumeister, R. F. (1991). *Meanings of life.* New York: Guilford Press.

Baumrind, D. (1967). Child care practices anteceding three patterns of preschool behavior. *Genetic Psychology Monographs, 75*, 43–88.

Baumrind, D. (1991). Parenting styles and adolescent development. In R. M. Lerner, A. C. Petersen, & J. Brooks-Gunn (Eds.), *The encyclopedia of adolescence* (Vol. 2, pp. 746–458). New York: Garland Press.

Beardsworth, T. (1977). *A sense of presence.* Oxford: Manchester College Religious Experience Research Unit.

Bearon, L. B., & Koenig, H. G. (1990). Religious cognitions and use of prayer in health and illness. *The Gerontologist, 30*, 249–253.

Beck, J. R., Spilka, B., & Mason, R. (1991, August). *Prayer, globalization attitudes, and faith orientation in an evangelical seminary sample.* Paper presented at the annual meeting of the American Psychological Association, San Francisco.

Becker, E. (1973). *The denial of death.* New York: Free Press.

Becker, H. S. (1963). *Outsiders.* New York: Free Press.

Becker, J. (1986, December 19–21). We believe—and we believe. *USA Weekend,* pp. 4–5.

Becker, R. J. (1971). Religion and psychological health. In M. B. Strommen (Ed.), *Research on religious development: A comprehensive handbook* (pp. 391–421). New York: Hawthorn Books.

Beckford, J. A. (1978). Accounting for conversion. *British Journal of Sociology, 29*, 249–262.

Beckford, J. A. (1979). Politics and the anti-cult movement. *Annual Review of the Social Sciences of Religion, 3*, 169–190.

Beckford, J. A., & Richardson, J. T. (1983). A bibliography of social scientific studies of new religious movements. *Social Compass, 30*, 111–135.

Bedell, K. B. (Ed.). (1994). *Yearbook of American and Canadian churches 1994.* Nashville, TN: Abingdon Press.

Beeghley, L., Bock, E. W., & Cochran, J. K. (1990). Religious change and alcohol use: An application of reference group and socialization theory. *Sociological Forum, 5*, 261–278.

Beit-Hallahmi, B. (1989). *Prolegomena to the psychological study of religion.* Lewisburgh, PA: Bucknell University Press.

Beit-Hallahmi, B. (1991). Goring the sacred ox: Towards a psychology of religion. In H. N. Malony (Ed.), *Psychology of religion: Personalities, problems, possibilities* (pp. 189–194). Grand Rapids, MI: Baker.

Beit-Hallahmi, B. (1995). Object relations theory and religious experience. In R. W. Hood, Jr. (Ed.), *Handbook of religious experience* (pp. 254–268). Birmingham, AL: Religious Education Press.

Beit-Hallahmi, B., & Argyle, M. (1977). Religious ideas and psychiatric disorders. *International Journal of Social Psychiatry, 23*, 26–30.

Bellah, R. N. (1967). Civil religion in America. *Daedalus, 96*, 1–21.

Bellah, R. N. (1970). *Beyond belief.* New York: Harper & Row.

Bellah, R. N., & Hammond, P. E. (1980). *Varieties of civil religion.* New York: Harper & Row.

Belzen, J. A. (1994). Between feast and famine: A sketch of the develoment of the psychology of religion in the Netherlands. *International Journal for the Psychology of Religion, 4,* 181–197.

Bendiksen, R., Hewitt, M., & Vinge, D. (1979, October). *Cancer residence for clergy: A preliminary evaluation of an institutional response to clergy involvement in cancer management.* Paper presented at the annual meeting of the Society for the Scientific Study of Religion, San Antonio, TX.

Bengtson, V. L., & Troll, L. (1978). Youth and their parents: Feedback and intergenerational influence in socialization. In R. M. Lerner & G. B. Spanier (Eds.), *Child influences on marital and family interaction: A life-span perspective* (pp. 215–240). New York: Academic Press.

Benham, W. G. (Ed.), (1927). *Putnam's complete book of quotations.* New York: Putnam.

Benson, P. L. (1981, December). God is alive in the U.S. Congress, but not always voting against civil liberties and for military spending. *Psychology Today,* pp. 47–57.

Benson, P. L. (1988, October). *The religious development of adults.* Paper presented at the annual meeting of the Religious Research Association, Chicago.

Benson, P. L. (1992a). Patterns of religious development in adolescence and adulthood. *Psychologists Interested in Religious Issues Newsletter, 17,* 2–9.

Benson, P. L. (1992b). Religion and substance use. In J. F. Schumaker (Ed.), *Religion and mental health* (pp. 211–220). New York: Oxford University Press.

Benson, P. L., Dehority, J., Garman, L., Hanson, E., Hochschwender, M., Lebold, C., Rohr, R., & Sullivan, J. (1980). Intrapersonal correlates of nonspontaneous helping behavior. *Journal of Social Psychology, 110,* 87–95.

Benson, P. L., & Donahue, M. J. (1989). Ten year trends in at-risk behavior: A national study of black adolescents. *Journal of Adolescent Research, 4,* 125–139.

Benson, P. L., Donahue, M. J., & Erickson, J. A. (1989). Adolescence and religion: A review of the literature from 1970 to 1986. *Research in the Social Scientific Study of Religion, 1,* 153–181.

Benson, P. L., & Eklin, C. H. (1990). *Effective Christian education: A national study of Protestant congregations.* Minneapolis: Search Institute.

Benson, P. L., & Spilka, B. (1973). God image as a function of self-esteem and locus of control. *Journal for the Scientific Study of Religion, 13,* 297–310.

Benson, P. L., & Williams, D. L. (1982). *Religion on Capitol Hill: Myths and realities.* New York: Harper & Row.

Benson, P. L., Williams, D. L., & Johnson, A. L. (1987). *The quicksilver years: The hopes and fears of young adolescents.* San Francisco: Harper & Row.

Benson, P. L., Wood, P. K., Johnson, A. L., Eklin, C. H., & Mills, J. E. (1983). *Report on 1983 Minnesota survey on drug use and drug-related activities.* Minneapolis: Search Institute.

Benson, P. L., Yeager, P. K., Wood, M. J., Guerra, M. J., & Manno, B. V. (1986). *Catholic high schools: Their impact on low-income students.* Washington, DC: National Catholic Educational Association.

Berg, I. A. (1967). *Response set in personality adjustment.* Chicago: Aldine.

Berger, P. (1979). *The heretical imperative: Contemporary possibilities of religious affirmation.* Garden City, NY: Doubleday/Anchor.

Berger, P., & Luckmann, T. (1967). *The social construction of reality: A treatise in the sociology of knowledge.* Garden City, NY: Doubleday.

Bergin, A. E. (1964). Psychology as a science of inner experience. *Journal of Humanistic Psychology, 4,* 95–103.

Bergin, A. E. (1980). Psychotherapy and religious values. *Journal of Consulting and Clinical Psychology, 48,* 95–105.

Bergin, A. E. (1994). Religious life styles and mental health. In L. B. Brown (Ed.), *Religion, personality, and mental health* (pp. 69–93). New York: Springer-Verlag.

Bergling, K. (1981). *Moral development: The validity of Kohlberg's theory.* Stockholm: Almqvist & Wiksell.

Bergman, P. (1953). A religious conversion in the course of psychotherapy. *American Journal of Psychotherapy, 7,* 41–58.

Bergman, R. L. (1971). Navajo peyote use: Its apparent safety. *American Journal of Psychiatry, 128,* 695–699.

Berke, R. L. (1995, May 18). Coalition poses social agenda. *The Denver Post,* p. 2A.

Berlyne, D. E. (1960). *Conflict, arousal, and curiosity.* New York: McGraw-Hill.

Berman, A. L. (1974). Belief in afterlife, religion, religiosity, and life threatening experiences. *Omega, 5,* 127–135.

Bernard, L. L. (1924). *Instinct.* New York: Henry Holt.

Berndtson, A. (1950). Vitalism. In V. Ferm (Ed.), *A history of philosophical systems* (pp. 375–386). New York: Philosophical Library.

Bernt, F. M. (1989). Being religious and being altruistic: A study of college service volunteers. *Personality and Individual Differences, 10,* 663–669.

Bertocci, P. A. (1958). *Religion as creative insecurity.* New York: Association Press.

Bethesda PsycHealth. (1994). *Results of the Bethesda professional staff chaplain support services advisory committee survey of professional staff, line staff, and patients.* Denver, CO: Author.

Bettelheim, B. (1976). *The uses of enchantment.* New York: Knopf.

Bibby, R. W. (1978). Why conservative churches are growing: Kelley revisited. *Journal for the Scientific Study of Religion, 17,* 129–137.

Bibby, R. W. (1987). *Fragmented gods: The poverty and potential of religion in Canada.* Toronto: Irwin.

Bibby, R. W. (1993). *Unknown gods: The ongoing story of religion in Canada.* Toronto: Stoddart.

Bibby, R. W., & Brinkerhoff, M. B. (1973). The circulation of the saints: A study of people who join conservative churches. *Journal for the Scientific Study of Religion, 12,* 273–283.

Bibby, R. W., & Weaver, H. R. (1985). Cult consumption in Canada: A further criticism of Stark and Bainbridge. *Sociological Analysis, 46,* 445–460.

Bickel, C. O. (1993). *Perceived stress, religious coping styles, and depressive affect.* Unpublished doctoral dissertation, Loyola College, Baltimore, MD.

Bierce, A. (1967). *The enlarged devil's dictionary.* Garden City, NY: Doubleday. (Original work published 1911)

Bill-Harvey, D., Rippey, R. M., Abeles, M., & Pfeiffer, C. A. (1989). Methods used by urban, low-income minorities to care for their arthritis. *Arthritis Care and Research, 2,* 60–64.

Billiet, J. B. (1995). Church involvement, individuals, and ethnic prejudice among Flemish Roman Catholics: New evidence of a moderating effect. *Journal for the Scientific Study of Religion, 34,* 224–233.

Bird, F., & Remier, B. (1982). Participation rates in new religious movements and para-religious movements. *Journal for the Scientific Study of Religion, 21,* 1–14.

Birnbaum, J. H. (1995, May 15). The gospel according to Ralph. *Time,* pp. 18–27.

Bivens, A. J., Neimeyer, R. A., Kirchberg, T. M., & Moore, M. K. (1994–1995). Death concern and religious beliefs among gays and bisexuals of variable proximity to AIDS. *Omega, 30,* 105–120.

Bjorck, J. P., & Cohen, L. H. (1993). Coping with threats, losses, and challenges. *Journal of Social and Clinical Psychology, 12,* 56–72.

Blake, W. (1967). The garden of love. In *Songs of innocence and experience* (Plate 44). New York: Orion Press. (Original work published 1789)

Blazer, D., & Palmore, E. (1976). Religion and aging in a longitudinal panel. *The Gerontologist, 16,* 82–85.

Blofeld, J. (1970). *The Tantric mysticism of Tibet.* New York: E. P. Dutton.

Blumer, H. (1969). *Symbolic interactionism: Perspective and method.* Englewood Cliffs, NJ: Prentice-Hall.

Bock, D. C., & Warren, N. C. (1972). Religious belief as a factor in obedience to destructive demands. *Review of Religious Research, 13,* 185–191.

Bohannon, J. R. (1991). Religiosity related to grief levels of bereaved mothers and fathers. *Omega, 23,* 153–159.

Boisen, A. T. (1936). *Exploration of the inner world.* Chicago: Willet, Clark.

Boisen, A. T. (1960). *Out of the depths: An autobiographical study of mental disorder and religious experience.* New York: Harper.

Bolt, M., Pyne, C., & Shoemaker, A. (1984, August). *Religious orientation, responsibility denial, and nonspontaneous helping.* Paper presented at the annual meeting of the American Psychological Association, Toronto.

Bolt, M., & Vermeulen, D. (1986, August). *Religious orientation and social compassion.* Paper presented at the annual meeting of the American Psychological Association, Washington, DC.

Booth, C. (n.d.). *The psychological examination of candidates for the ministry.* New York: Academy of Religion and Mental Health.

Boswell, J. (n.d.). *The life of Samuel Johnson, LL.D.* New York: Modern Library. (Original work published 1791)

Bottomley, F. (1979). *Attitudes toward the body in Western Christendom.* London: Lupus.

Bottoms, B. L., Shaver, P. R., Goodman, G. S., & Qin, J. (1995). In the name of God: A profile of religion-related child abuse. *Journal of Social Issues, 51,* 85–111.

Bouchard, R. J., Jr., Lykken, D. T., McGue, M., Segal, N. L., & Tellegen, A. (1990). Sources of human psychological differences: The Minnesota study of twins reared apart. *Science, 250,* 223–250.

Bouhmama, D. (1984). Assessment of Kohlberg's stages of moral development in two cultures. *Journal of Moral Education, 13,* 124–132.

Bouma, G. D. (1979). The real reason one conservative church grew. *Review of Religious Research, 20,* 127–137.

Bourque, L. B. (1969). Social correlates of transcendental experience. *Sociological Analysis, 30,* 151–163.

Bourque, L. B., & Back, K. W. (1971). Language, society, and subjective experience. *Sociometry, 34,* 1–21.

Bowker, J. (1973). *The sense of God: Sociological, anthropological, and psychological approaches to the origin of the sense of God.* Oxford: Clarendon Press.

Bowlby, J. (1969). *Attachment and loss: Vol. 1. Attachment.* New York: Basic Books.

Bowlby, J. (1973). *Attachment and loss: Vol. 2. Separation: Anxiety and anger.* New York: Basic Books.

Bowlby, J. (1980). *Attachment and loss: Vol. 3. Loss: Sadness and depression.* New York: Basic Books.

Boyer, P. (1994). *The naturalness of religious ideas.* Berkeley: University of California Press.

Brabant, S., Forsyth, C., & McFarlain, G. (1995). Life after the death of a child: Initial and long term support from others. *Omega, 31,* 67–85.

Bragan, K. (1977). The psychological gains and losses of religious conversion. *Journal of Medical Psychology, 50,* 177–180.

Brehony, K. A. (1983). Women and agoraphobia: A case for the etiological significance of the feminine sex-role stereotype. In V. Franks & E. D. Rothblum (Eds.), *The stereotyping of women: Its effects on mental health* (pp. 112–128). New York: Springer.

Brereton, V. L., & Klein, C. R. (1979). American women in ministry: A history of Protestant beginning points. In R. Ruether & E. McLaughlin (Eds.), *Women of spirit* (pp. 301–332). New York: Simon & Schuster.

Brett, G. S. (1912). *A history of psychology* (Vol. 1). London: Allen & Unwin.

Bridges, H. (1970). *American mysticism from William James to Zen.* New York: Harper & Row.

Bridges, R. A., & Spilka, B. (1992). Religion and the mental health of women. In J. F. Schumaker (Ed.), *Religion and mental health* (pp. 43–53). New York: Oxford University Press.

Brinkerhoff, M. B., & Burke, K. L. (1980). Disaffiliation: Some notes on "falling from the faith." *Sociological Analysis, 41,* 41–54.

Brinkerhoff, M. B., Grandin, E., & Lupri, E. (1992). Religious involvement and spousal violence: The Canadian case. *Journal for the Scientific Study of Religion, 31,* 15–31.

Brinkerhoff, M. B., & Mackie, M. M. (1993). Casting off the bonds of organized religion: A religious-careers approach to the study of apostasy. *Review of Religious Research, 34,* 235–257.

Brinthaupt, T. M., & Lipka, R. P. (Eds.). (1994). *Changing the self.* Albany: State University of New York Press.

Bromberg, W. (1937). *The mind of man.* New York: Harper.

Bromley, D. G. (1988). Religious disaffiliation: A neglected social process. In D. G. Bromley (Ed.), *Falling from the faith: Causes and consequences of religious apostasy* (pp. 9–25). Newbury Park, CA: Sage.

Bromley, D. G., & Breschel, E. F. (1992). General population and institutional support for social control of new religious movements: Evidence from national survey data. *Behavioral Sciences and the Law, 10,* 39–52.

Bromley, D. G., & Richardson, J. T. (Eds.). (1983). *The brainwashing/deprogramming controversy: Sociological, psychological, legal and historical perspectives.* Lewiston, NY: Edwin Mellon.

Bronson, L. (1966). *Changes in personality needs and values after conversion to Protestantism in a traditionally Roman Catholic group.* Unpublished doctoral dissertation, University of Arizona.

Bronson, L., & Meadow, A. (1968). The need achievement orientation of Catholic and Protestant Mexican-Americans. *Revista Interamericana de Psicologia, 2,* 159–168.

Brown, F. C. (1972). *Hallucinogenic drugs.* Springfield, IL: Charles C Thomas.

Brown, L. B. (1962). A study of religious belief. *British Journal of Psychology, 53,* 259–272.

Brown, L. B. (1966). Egocentric thought in petitionary prayer: A cross-cultural study. *Journal of Social Psychology, 68,* 197–210.

Brown, L. B. (1968). Some attitudes underlying petitionary prayer. In A. Godin (Ed.), *From cry to word: Contributions toward a psychology of prayer* (pp. 65–84). Brussels, Belgium: Lumen Vitae Press.

Brown, L. B. (1987). *The psychology of religious belief.* London: Academic Press.

Brown, L. B. (1994). *The human side of prayer: The psychology of praying.* Birmingham, AL: Religious Education Press.

Browning, D. S. (1975). *Generative man: Psychoanalytic perspectives.* New York: Dell.

Browning, D. S. (1986). Globalization and the task of theological education. *Theological Education, 23,* 43–59.

Browning, R. (1895). Pippa passes. In H. E. Scudder (Ed.), *The complete practical works of Browning* (pp. 128–145). Cambridge, MA: Riverside Press. (Original work published 1841)

Bryan, J. W., & Freed, F. W. (1993). Abortion research: Attitudes, sexual behavior, and problems in a community college population. *Journal of Youth andAdolescence, 22,* 1–22.

Bryer, K. B. (1979). The Amish way of death: A study of family support systems. *American Psychologist, 34,* 255–261.

Buber, M. (1965). *Between man and man.* New York: Macmillan.

Bucher, A. A. (1991). Understanding parables: A developmental analysis. In F. K. Oser & W. G. Scarlett (Eds.), *Religious development in childhood and adolescence* (New Directions for Child Development, No. 52, pp. 101–105). San Francisco: Jossey-Bass.

Bucke, R. M. (1961). *Cosmic consciousness: A study of the evolution of the human mind.* Hyde Park, NY: University Books. (Original work published 1901)

Bufe, C. (1991). *Alcoholics Anonymous: Cult or cure?* San Francisco: Sharp Press.

Bulka, R. P. (1979). *The quest for ultimate meaning.* New York: Philosophical Library.

Bulliet, R. W. (1979). *Conversion to Islam in the medieval period: An essay in quantitative history.* Cambridge, MA: Harvard University Press.

Bulman, R. J., & Wortman, C. B. (1977). Attributions of blame and coping in the "real world": Severe accident victims react to their lot. *Journal of Personality and Social Psychology, 35,* 351–363.

Burhoe, R. W. (1979). Religion's role in human evolution: The missing link between ape-man's selfish genes and civilized altruism. *Zygon, 14,* 135–162.

Buri, J. R., Louiselle, P. A., Misukanis, T. M., & Mueller, R., A. (1988). Effects of parental authoritarianism and authoritativeness on self-esteem. *Personality and Social Psychology Bulletin, 14,* 271–282.

Burkett, S. R., & Warren, B. O. (1987). Religiosity, peer associations, and adolescent marijuana use: A panel study of underlying causal structures. *Criminology, 25,* 109–131.

Burkett, S. R., & White, M. (1974). Hellfire and delinquency: Another look. *Journal for the Scientific Study of Religion, 13,* 455–462.

Burris, C. T. (1994). Curvilinearity and religious types: A second look at intrinsic, extrinsic, and quest relations. *International Journal for the Psychology of Religion, 4,* 245–260.

Burris, C. T., Batson, C. D., Altstaedten, M., & Stephens, K. (1994). "What a friend . . .": Loneliness as a motivator of intrinsic religion. *Journal for the Scientific Study of Religion, 33*, 326–334.

Burton, T. (1993). *Serpent-handling believers*. Knoxville: University of Tennessee Press.

Butcher, J. N., Dahlstrom, W. G., Graham, J. R., Tellegen, A. M., & Kaemmer, B. (1989). *MMPI-2: Manual for administration and scoring*. Minneapolis: University of Minnesota Press.

Buttrick, G. A. (1942). *Prayer*. New York: Abingdon-Cokesbury Press.

Buttrick, G. A. (1970). *The power of prayer today*. New York: World.

Byrd, R. C. (1988). Positive therapeutic effects of intercessory prayer in a coronary care unit population. *Southern Medical Journal, 81*, 826–829.

Caird, D. (1988). The structure of Hood's Mysticism Scale: A factor analytic study. *Journal for the Scientific Study of Religion, 27*, 122–127.

Calkins, M. W. (1910). *A first book in psychology* (2nd rev. ed.). New York: Macmillan.

Camargo, R. J., & Loftus, J. A. (1993, August). *Clergy sexual involvement with young people: Distinctive characteristics*. Paper presented at the annual meeting of the American Psychological Association, Toronto.

Campbell, A. (1981). *The sense of well-being in America*. New York: McGraw-Hill.

Campbell, D. T. (1975). On the conflicts between biological and social evolution and between psychology and moral tradition. *American Psychologist, 30*, 1103–1126.

Campbell, E. Q. (1969). Adolescent socialization. In D. A. Goslin (Ed.), *Handbook of socialization theory and research* (pp. 821–859). Chicago: Rand McNally.

Campbell, R. A., & Curtis, J. E. (1994). Religious involvement across societies: Analyses for alternative measures in national surveys. *Journal for the Scientific Study of Religion, 33*, 217–229.

Cannon, L. (1984, February 14). Reagan's recruitment of God in his campaign. *The Denver Post*, p. 21A.

Caplovitz, D., & Sherrow, F. (1977). *The religious drop-outs: Apostasy among college graduates*. Beverly Hills, CA: Sage.

Capps, D. (1992). Religion and child abuse: Perfect together. *Journal for the Scientific Study of Religion, 31*, 1–14.

Capps, D. (1994). An Allportian analysis of Augustine. *International Journal for the Psychology of Religion, 4*, 205–228.

Capps, D., & Dittes, J. E. (Eds.). (1990). *The hunger of the heart: The confessions of Augustine*. West Lafayette, IN: Society for the Scientific Study of Religion.

Carey, R. G. (1971). Influence of peers in shaping religious behavior. *Journal for the Scientific Study of Religion, 10*, 157–159.

Carey, R. G. (1979–1980). Weathering widowhood: Problems and adjustment of the widowed during the first year. *Omega, 10*, 163–174.

Carey, R. G., & Posavec, E. J. (1978–1979). Attitudes of physicians on disclosing information to and maintaining life for terminal patients. *Omega, 10*, 163–174.

Carlson, C. R., Bacaseta, P. E., & Simanton, D. A. (1988). A controlled evaluation of devotional meditation and progressive relaxation. *Journal of Psychology and Theology, 16*, 362–368.

Carroll, J. B. (Ed.). (1956). *Language, thought, and reality: Selected writings of Benjamin Lee Whorf*. New York: Wiley.

Carroll, M. P. (1983). Vision of the Virgin Mary: The effects of family structures on Marian apparitions. *Journal for the Scientific Study of Religion, 22*, 205–221.

Carroll, M. P. (1986). *The cult of the Virgin Mary: Psychological origins*. Princeton, NJ: Princeton University Press.

Carter, S. L. (1993). *The culture of disbelief: How American law and politics trivilize religious devotion*. New York: Basic Books.

Cartwright, R. H., & Kent, S. A. (1992). Social control in alternative religions: A familial perspective. *Sociological Analysis, 53*, 345–361.

Carver, C. S., Pozo, C., Harris, S. D., Noriega, V., Scheier, M. F., Robinson, D. S., Ketcham, A. S., Moffat, F. L., Jr., & Clark, K. C. (1993). How coping mediates the effect of optimism on distress: A study of women with early stage breast cancer. *Journal of Personality and Social Psychology, 65*, 375–390.

Carver, C. S., Scheier, M. F., & Weintraub, J. K. (1989). Assessing coping strategies: A theoretically based approach. *Journal of Personality and Social Psychology, 56,* 267–283.

Casey, W. M., & Burton, R. V. (1986). The social-learning theory approach. In G. L. Sapp (Ed.), *Handbook of moral development* (pp. 74–91). Birmingham, AL: Religious Education Press.

The Catholic Worker. (1991, May). The aims and means of the Catholic Worker movement. p. 5.

Cavenar, J. O., & Spaulding, J. G. (1977). Depressive disorders and religious conversions. *Journal of Nervous and Mental Disease, 165,* 200–212.

Cecil, Lord D. (1966). *Melbourne.* Indianapolis, IN: Bobbs-Merrill.

Cerny, L. J., II, & Carter, J. D. (1977). *Death perspectives and religious orientation as a function of Christian faith.* Paper presented at the annual meeting of the Society for the Scientific Study of Religion, Chicago.

Cesarman, F. C. (1957). Religious conversion of sex offenders. *Journal of Pastoral Care, 11,* 25–35.

Chadwick, B. A., & Garrett, H. D. (1995). Women's religiosity and employment: The LDS experience. *Review of Religious Research, 36,* 277–293.

Chadwick, B. A., & Top, B. L. (1993). Religiosity and delinquency among LDS adolescents. *Journal for the Scientific Study of Religion, 32,* 51–67.

Chalfant, P. H., Beckley, R. E., & Palmer, C. E. (1981). *Religion in contemporary society.* Sherman Oaks, CA: Alfred.

Chamberlain, K., & Zika, S. (1992). Religiosity, meaning in life, and psychological well-being. In J. F. Schumaker (Ed.), *Religion and mental health* (pp. 138–148). New York: Oxford University Press.

Chau, L. L., Johnson, R. C., Bowers, J. K., Darvill, T. J., & Danko, G. P. (1990). Intrinsic and extrinsic religiosity as related to conscience, adjustment, and altruism. *Personality and Individual Differences, 11,* 397–400.

Chave, E. J. (1939). *Measure religion: Fifty-two experimental forms.* Chicago: University of Chicago Press.

Chaves, M. (1989). Secularization and religious revival: Evidence for U.S. church attendance rates, 1972–1986. *Journal for the Scientific Study of Religion, 28,* 464–477.

Chaves, M. (1990). Holding the cohort: Reply to Hout and Greeley. *Journal for the Scientific Study of Religion, 29,* 525–530.

Chaves, M. (1991). Family structure and Protestant church attendance: The sociological basis of cohort and age-effects. *Journal for the Scientific Study of Religion, 30,* 501–514.

Chaves, M., & Cavendish, J. C. (1994). More evidence on U.S. Catholic church attendance. *Journal for the Scientific Study of Religion, 33,* 376–381.

Chesen, E. S. (1972). *Religion may be hazardous to your health.* New York: Macmillan.

Christensen, C. W. (1960). The occurrence of mental illness in the ministry: Family origins. *Journal of Pastoral Care, 14,* 13–20.

Christensen, C. W. (1963). Religious conversion. *Archives of General Psychiatry, 9,* 207–216.

Clark, E. T. (1929). *The psychology of religious awakening.* New York: Macmillan.

Clark, J. (1978). Problems in the referral of cult members. *Journal of the National Association of Private Psychiatric Hospitals, 9,* 19–21.

Clark, J. (1979). Cults. *Journal of the American Medical Association, 242,* 279–281.

Clark, J., Langone, M. D., Schacter, R., & Daly, R. C. G. (1981). *Destructive cult conversion: Theory, research and practice.* Weston, MA: American Family Foundation.

Clark, J. H. (1983). *A map of mental states.* London: Routledge & Kegan Paul.

Clark, J. M., Brown, J. C., & Hochstein, L. M. (1989). Institutional religion and gay/lesbian oppression. *Marriage and Family Review, 14,* 265–284.

Clark, R. W. (1984). The evidential value of religious experiences. *International Journal of Philosophy of Religion, 16,* 189–201.

Clark, S. L., & Carter, J. D. (1978, June). *Death perspectives: Fear of death, guilt and hope as functions of Christian faith.* Paper presented at the meeting of the Western Association of Christians for Psychological Studies, Malibu, CA.

Clark, W. H. (1958). *The psychology of religion.* New York: Macmillan.

Clark, W. H. (1968). The relation between drugs and religious experience. *Catholic Psychological Record, 6*, 146–155.

Clark, W. H. (1969). *Chemical ecstasy: Psychedelic drugs and religion.* New York: Sheed & Ward.

Clark, W. H. (1971). Intense religious experience. In M. B. Strommen (Ed.), *Research on religious development: A comprehensive handbook* (pp. 521–550). New York: Hawthorn Books.

Clarke, R.-L. (1986). *Pastoral care of battered women.* Philadelphia: Westminster Press.

Clemens, N. A. (1976). An intensive course for clergy on death, dying, and loss. *Journal of Religion and Health, 15*, 223–229.

Cline, V. B., & Richards, J. M. (1965). A factor-analytic study of religious belief and behavior. *Journal of Personality and Social Psychology, 1*, 569–578.

Clouse, B. (1986). Church conflict and moral stages: A Kohlbergian interpretation. *Journal of Psychology and Christianity, 5*, 14–19.

Clouse, B. (1991). Religious experience, religious belief and moral development of students at a state university. *Journal of Psychology and Christianity, 10*, 337–349.

Cobb, N. J. (1992). *Adolescence.* Mountain View, CA: Mayfield.

Cobb, N. J. (1995). *Adolescence: Continuity, change, and diversity* (2nd ed.). Mountain View, CA: Mayfield.

Cochran, J. K. (1992). The effects of religiosity on adolescent self-reported frequency of drug and alcohol use. *Journal of Drug Issues, 22*, 91–104.

Cochran, J. K. (1993). The variable effects of religiosity and denomination on adolescent self-reported alcohol use by beverage type. *Journal of Drug Issues, 23*, 479–491.

Cochran, J. K., & Beeghley, L. (1991). The influence of religion on attitudes toward nonmarital sexuality: A preliminary assessment of reference group theory. *Journal for the Scientific Study of Religion, 30*, 45–62.

Cochran, J. K., Beeghley, L., & Bock, E. W. (1988). Religiosity and alcohol behavior: An exploration of reference group theory. *Sociological Forum, 3*, 256–276.

Cochran, J. K., Beeghley, L., & Bock, E. W. (1992). The influence of religious stability and homogamy on the relationship between religiosity and alcohol use among Protestants. *Journal for the Scientific Study of Religion, 31*, 441–456.

Cochran, J. K., Wood, P. B., & Arneklev, B. J. (1994). Is the religiosity–delinquency relationship spurious? Social control theories. *Journal of Research in Crime and Delinquency, 31*, 92–123.

Coe, G. A. (1900). *The spiritual life: Studies in the science of religion.* New York: Eaton & Mains.

Coe, G. A. (1916). *The psychology of religion.* Chicago: University of Chicago Press.

Cohn, W. (1962). Is religion universal? Problems of definition. *Journal for the Scientific Study of Religion, 2*, 25–33.

Coleman, J. C., Butcher, J. N., & Carson, R. C. (1984). *Abnormal psychology and modern life* (7th ed.). Glenview, IL: Scott, Foresman.

Colipp, P. J. (1969). The efficacy of prayer: A triple-blind study. *Medical Times, 97*, 201–204.

Colombo, F. (1984). *God in America: Religion and politics in the United States.* New York: Columbia University Press.

Condran, J. G., & Tamney, J. B. (1985). Religious "nones": 1957–1982. *Sociological Analysis, 46*, 415–423.

Conrad, P., & Schnelder, J. W. (1980). *Deviance and medicalization: From badness to sickness.* St. Louis, MO: C. V. Mosby.

Conway, K. (1985–1986). Coping with the stress of medical problems among black and white elderly. *International Journal of Aging and Human Development, 21*, 39–48.

Conway, F., & Siegelman, J. (1978). *Snapping: America's epidemic of sudden personality change.* Philadelphia: J. B. Lippincott.

Cook, A. S., & Oltjenbruns, K. A. (1989). *Dying and grieving.* New York: Holt, Rinehart & Winston.

Cook, T., & Wimberly, D. (1983). If I should die before I wake: Religious commitment and adjustment to the death of a child. *Journal for the Scientific Study of Religion, 22*, 222–238.

Coon, D. J. (1992). Testing the limits of sense and science: American experimental psychologists combat spiritualism, 1880–1920. *American Psychologist, 47*, 143–151.

Coopersmith, S., Regan, M., & Dick, L. (1975). *The myth of the generation gap.* San Francisco: Albion.

Cornwall, M. (1987). The social bases of religion: A study of factors influencing religious belief and commitment. *Review of Religious Research, 29,* 44–56.

Cornwall, M. (1988). The influence of three agents of religious socialization: Family, church, and peers. In D. L. Thomas (Ed.), *The religion and family connection* (pp. 207–231). Provo, UT: Religious Studies Center, Brigham Young University.

Cornwall, M. (1989). The determinants of religious behavior: A theoretical model and empirical test. *Social Forces, 68,* 572–592.

Cornwall, M., & Thomas, D. L. (1990). Family, religion, and personal communities: Examples from Mormonism. *Marriage and Family Review, 15,* 229–252.

Corssan, J. D. (1975). *The dark interval.* Niles, IL: Argus Communication.

Council of Evangelical Churches of Nicaragua. (n.d.). *Brochure describing the Council's activities.* Managua: Author.

Cousins, N. (1979). *Anatomy of an illness.* New York: Norton.

Couture, P. (1990). Ritual and pastoral care. In R. J. Hunter (Ed.), *Dictionary of pastoral care and counseling* (pp. 1088–1090). Nashville, TN: Abingdon Press.

Coward, H. (1986). Intolerance in the world's religions. *Studies in Religion, 15,* 419–431.

Crawford, M. E., Handal, P. J., & Wiener, R. I. (1989). The relationship between religion and mental health/distress. *Review of Religious Research, 31,* 16–22.

Crooks, E. B. (1913). Professor James and the psychology of religion. *Monist, 23,* 122–130.

Crowne, D. P., & Marlowe, D. (1964). *The approval motive: Studies in evaluative dependence.* New York: Wiley.

Culver, V. (1988, April 17). Emotional upset linked to strictness in religion. *The Denver Post,* pp. 1B–2B.

Culver, V. (1994, May 11). Clergy sex misconduct prevalent. *The Denver Post,* pp. 1B, 8B.

Curb, R., & Manahan, N. (1985). *Lesbian nuns: Breaking silence.* Tallahassee, FL: Naiad Press.

Cutten, G. B. (1908). *The psychological phenomena of Christianity.* New York: Scribner.

Dalfiume, L. (1993, April). *Hope as a life structuring variable for the transition to midlife.* Paper presented at the joint meeting of the Rocky Mountain and Western Psychological Associations, Phoenix, AZ.

Daniel, S. P., & Rogers, M. L. (1981). Burnout and the pastorate: A critical review with implications for pastors. *Journal of Psychology and Theology, 9,* 232–249.

D'Antonio, W. V., Newman, W. M., & Wright, S. A. (1982). Religion and family life: How social scientists view the relationship. *Journal for the Scientific Study of Religion, 21,* 218–225.

D'Aquili, E. G. (1978). The neurobiological bases of myth and concepts of deity. *Zygon, 13,* 257–275.

Darley, J. M., & Batson, C. D. (1973). "From Jersualem to Jericho": A study of situational and dispositional variables in helping behavior. *Journal of Personality and Social Psychology, 27,* 100–108.

Darley, J. M., & Shultz, T. R. (1990). Moral rules: Their content and acquisition. *Annual Review of Psychology, 41,* 525–556.

Darling, N., & Steinberg, L. (1993). Parenting style as context: An integrative model. *Psychological Bulletin, 113,* 487–496.

Datta, L. E. (1967). Family religious background and early scientific creativity. *American Sociological Review, 32,* 626–635.

David, J., Ladd, K., & Spilka, B. (1992, August). *The multidimensionality of prayer and its role as a source of secondary control.* Paper presented at the annual meeting of the American Psychological Association, Washington, DC.

Davidoff, H. (Ed.). (1952). *The pocket book of quotations.* New York: Pocket Books.

Davids, A. (1955). Alienation, social apperception, and ego structure. *Journal of Consulting Psychology, 19,* 21–27.

Davidson, J. D. (1972). Patterns of belief at the denominational and congregational levels. *Review of Religious Research, 13,* 197–205.

Davidson, J. D. (1975). Glock's model of religious commitment: Assessing some different approaches and results. *Review of Religious Research, 16,* 83–93.

Davidson, J. D., & Pyle, R. E. (1994). Passing the plate in affluent churches: Why some members give more than others. *Review of Religious Research, 36,* 181–196.

Davidson, J. D., Pyle, R. E., & Reyes, D. V. (1995). Persistence and change in the Protestant establishment. *Social Forces, 74,* 157–175.

Davis, C. F. (1989). *The evidential force of religious experience.* Oxford: Clarendon Press.

Davis, J. A., & Smith, T. W. (1994). *General Social Surveys, 1972–1994* [Machine-readable data file]. Chicago: National Opinion Research Center [Producer]; Storrs: Roper Center for Public Opinion Research, University of Connecticut [Distributor].

Day, J. M. (1994). Moral development, belief, and unbelief: Young adult accounts of religion in the process of moral growth. In J. Corveleyn & D. Hutsebaut (Eds.), *Belief and unbelief: Psychological perspectives* (pp. 155–173). Atlanta: Rodopi.

Dean, D. G. (1961). Alienation: Its meaning and measurement. *American Sociological Review, 26,* 753–758.

Deconchy, J.-P. (1965). The idea of God: Its emergence between 7 and 16 years. In A. Godin (Ed.), *From religious experience to a religious attitude* (pp. 97–108). Chicago: Loyola University Press.

De Frain, J. D., Jakub, D. K., & Mendoza, B. L. (1991–1992). The psychological effects of sudden infant death on grandmothers and grandfathers. *Omega, 24,* 165–182.

Degelman, D., Mullen, P., & Mullen, N. (1984). Development of abstract religious thinking: A comparison of Roman Catholic and Nazarene youth. *Journal of Psychology and Christianity, 3,* 44–49.

Deikman, A. (1966). Implications of experimentally produced contemplative meditation. *Journal of Nervous and Mental Disease, 142,* 101–116.

Delgado, R. (1977). Religious totalism. *University of Southern California Law Review, 15,* 1–99.

Delgado, R. (1982). Cult and conversions: The case for informed consent. *Georgia Law Review, 16,* 533–574.

Deluty, R. H. (1988–1989). Factors affecting the acceptability of suicide. *Omega, 19,* 315–326.

De Maria, F., Giulani, B., Annese, A., & Corfiati, I. (1971). A picture of psychopathological conditions in members of religious communities. *Acta Neurologica, 26,* 79–86.

de Mello, A. (1984). *Sadhana: A way to God.* New York: Image Books.

Demerath, N. J. (1965). *Social class and American Protestantism.* Chicago: Rand McNally.

Demerdash, A. M., Mizaal, H., el Farouki, S., & el Mossalem, H. (1981). Some behavioural and psychosocial aspects of alcohol and drug dependence in Kuwait Psychiatric Hospital. *Acta Psychiatrica Scandinavica, 63,* 173–185.

The Denver Post. (1988, June 17). Fewer Americans attending church, but most remain religious, Gallup says. p. 3A.

The Denver Post. (1993, January 21). Fax now available for messages to God. p. 17A.

De Sahagun, B. (1974). The Aztec funerary ritual. In M. Eliade (Ed.), *Death, afterlife, and eschatology* (pp. 26–34). New York: Harper & Row.

De Sanctis, S. (1927). *Religious conversion: A bio-psychological study.* New York: Harcourt, Brace.

Deutsch, A. (1946). *The mentally ill in America.* New York: Columbia University Press.

de Vaus, D. A. (1983). The relative importance of parents and peers for adolescent religious orientation: An Australian study. *Adolescence, 18,* 147–158.

de Vaus, D. A., & McAllister, I. (1987). Gender differences in religion: A test of the structural location theory. *American Sociological Review, 52,* 472–481.

De Vellis, B. M., De Vellis, R. F., & Spilsbury, J. C. (1988). Parental actions when children are sick: The role of belief in divine influence. *Basic and Applied Social Psychology, 9,* 185–196.

Dewey, J. (1929). *The quest for certainty.* New York: Minton, Balch.

DiBlasio, F. A., & Benda, B. B. (1990). Adolescent sexual behavior: Multivariate analysis of a social learning model. *Journal of Adolescent Research, 5,* 449–466.

Dienstbier, R. A. (1979). Emotion-attribution theory: Establishing roots and exploring future perspectives. In R. A. Dienstbier (Ed.), *Nebraska Symposium on Motivation* (Vol. 26, pp. 237–306). Lincoln: University of Nebraska Press.

Dittes, J. E. (1969). Psychology of religion. In G. Lindzey & E. Aronson (Eds.), *Handbook of social psychology* (Vol. 5, 2nd ed., pp. 602–659). Reading, MA: Addison-Wesley.

Dittes, J. E. (1971a). Conceptual derivation and statistical rigor. *Journal for the Scientific Study of Religion, 10*, 392–395.

Dittes, J. E. (1971b). Psychological characteristics of religious professionals. In M. P. Strommen (Ed.), *Research on religious development: A comprehensive handbook* (pp. 422–460). New York: Hawthorn Books.

Dittes, J.E. (1971c). Typing the typologies: Some parallels in the career of church–sect and extrinsic–intrinsic religion. *Journal for the Scientific Study of Religion, 10*, 375–383.

Dixon, R. D., & Kinlaw, B. J. R. (1982–1983). Belief in the existence and nature of life after death: A research note. *Omega, 13*, 287–292.

Dobkin de Rios, M. (1984). *Hallucinogens: Cross-cultural perspectives.* Albuquerque: University of New Mexico Press.

Doblin, R. (1991). Pahnke's "Good Friday" experiment: A long-term follow-up and methodological critique. *Journal of Transpersonal Psychology, 23*, 1–28.

Dohrenwend, B. P., & Dohrenwend, B. S. (1969). *Social status and psychological disorder.* New York: Wiley.

Domino, G., & Miller, K. (1992). Religiosity and attitudes toward suicide. *Omega, 25*, 271–282.

Donahue, M. J. (1985a). Intrinsic and extrinsic religiousness: The empirical research. *Journal for the Scientific Study of Religion, 24*, 418–423.

Donahue, M. J. (1985b). Intrinsic and extrinsic religiousness: Review and meta-analysis. *Journal of Personality and Social Psychology, 48*, 400–419.

Donahue, M. J. (1987). *Religiousness and drug use: 1976–1985.* Paper presented at the annual meeting of the Society for the Scientific Study of Religion, Louisville, Kentucky.

Donahue, M. J. (1994). Correlates of religious giving in six Protestant denominations. *Review of Religious Research, 36*, 149–157.

Donovan, D. C., & De Jong, J. A. (1986). *Age, experience of God, religious practices, and the concerns and satisfactions of priests.* Paper presented at the annual meeting of the American Psychological Association, Washington, DC.

Douglass, J. D. (1974). Women and the continental reformation. In R. R. Ruether, (Ed.), *Religion and sexism: Images of women in the Jewish and Christian traditions* (pp. 292–318). New York: Simon & Schuster.

Downton, J. V., Jr. (1980). An evolutionary theory of spiritual conversion and commitment: The case of the Divine Light Mission. *Journal for the Scientific Study of Religion, 19*, 381–396.

Dresser, H. W. (1929). *Outlines of the psychology of religion.* New York: Thomas Y. Crowell.

Dublin, L. I. (1963). *Suicide.* New York: Ronald Press.

Duckitt, J. (1992). *The social psychology of prejudice.* New York: Praeger.

Dudley, R. L. (1978). Alienation from religion in adolescents from fundamentalist religious homes. *Journal for the Scientific Study of Religion, 17*, 389–398.

Dudley, R. L. (1993). Indicators of commitment to the church: A longitudinal study of church affiliated youth. *Adolescence, 28*, 21–28.

Dudley, R. L., & Dudley, M. G. (1986). Transmission of religious values from parents to adolescents. *Review of Religious Research, 28*, 3–15.

Dunlap, K. (1925). *Social psychology.* Baltimore: Williams & Wilkins.

Duran, D. G. (1995, June). *Impact of psychosocial factors, depression and the patient–provider relationship on somatic complaints of the distressed Latina.* Unpublished doctoral dissertation, University of Denver.

Durkheim, E. (1915). *The elementary forms of the religious life: A study in religious sociology* (J. W. Swain, Trans.). London: Allen & Unwin.

Durr, R. A. (1970). *Poetic vision and the psychedelic experience.* New York: Dell.

Eaton, J. W., & Weil, R. J. (1955). *Culture and mental disorders.* Glencoe, IL: Free Press.

Echterling, L. G. (1993, August). *Making do and making sense: Long-term coping of disaster survivors.* Paper presented at the annual meeting of the American Psychological Association, Toronto.

Edsall, T. B. (1995, May 15). Christian right presses agenda. *The Denver Post*, p. 2A.

Edwards, A. L. (1957). *The social desirability variable in personality assessment and research.* New York: Dryden Press.

Edwards, K. J., & Wessels, S. J. (1980). *Relationship of psychosocial maturity to intrapersonal, interpersonal, and spiritual functioning.* Paper presented at the annual meeting of the American Psychological Association, Montreal.

Edwards, T. (1955). *The new dictionary of thoughts* (rev. & enlarged ed.). New York: Standard.

Einstein, A. (1931). Religion and science. In A. M. Drummond & R. H. Wagner (Eds.), *Problems and opinions* (pp. 355–358). New York: Century.

Eisenberg-Berg, N., & Roth, K. (1980). Development of young children's prosocial moral judgment: A longitudinal follow-up. *Developmental Psychology, 16,* 375–376.

Eisenstein, V. W. (Ed.). (1956). *Neurotic interaction in marriage.* New York: Basic Books.

Eisinga, R., Felling, A., & Peters, J. (1990). Religious belief, church involvement, and ethnocentrism in the Netherlands. *Journal for the Scientific Study of Religion, 29,* 54–75.

Eisinga, R., Konig, R., & Scheepers, P. (1995). Orthodox religious beliefs and anti-Semitism: A replication of Glock and Stark in the Netherlands. *Journal for the Scientific Study of Religion, 34,* 214–223.

Eister, A. W. (1973). H. Reinhold Niebuhr and the paradox of religious organizations: A radical critique. In C. Y. Glock & P. E. Hammond (Eds.), *Beyond the classics? Essays in the scientific study of religion* (pp. 355–408). New York: Harper & Row.

Eister, A. W. (1979). An outline of a structural theory of cults. *Journal for the Scientific Study of Religion, 11,* 319–330.

Eliach, Y. (1982). *Hassidic tales of the Holocaust.* New York: Avon.

Elifson, K. W., Petersen, D. M., & Hadaway, C. K. (1983). Religion and delinquency: A contextual analysis. *Criminology, 21,* 505–527.

Elkind, D. (1961). The child's concept of his religious denomination: I. The Jewish child. *Journal of Genetic Psychology, 99,* 209–225.

Elkind, D. (1962). The child's concept of his religious denomination: II. The Catholic child. *Journal of Genetic Psychology, 101,* 185–193.

Elkind, D. (1963). The child's concept of his religious denomination: III. The Protestant child. *Journal of Genetic Psychology, 103,* 291–304.

Elkind, D. (1964). Piaget's semi-clinical interview and the study of spontaneous religion. *Journal for the Scientific Study of Religion, 4,* 40–46.

Elkind, D. (1970). The origins of religion in the child. *Review of Religious Research, 12,* 35–42.

Elkind, D. (1971). The development of religious understanding in children and adolescents. In M. P. Strommen (Ed.), *Research on religious development: A comprehensive handbook* (pp. 655–685). New York: Hawthorn Books.

Elkind, D., & Elkind, S. (1970). Varieties of religious experience in young adolescents. *Journal for the Scientific Study of Religion, 2,* 102–112.

Elkins, J. D. (1977). *The effect of prayer on tension reduction.* Unpublished doctoral dissertation, George Peabody College for Teachers.

Ellenberger, H. F. (1970). *The discovery of the unconscious: The history and evolution of dynamic psychiatry.* New York: Basic Books.

Elliott, D. M. (1994). The impact of Christian faith on the prevalence and sequelae of sexual abuse. *Journal of Interpersonal Violence, 9,* 95–108.

Ellis, A. (1980). Psychotherapy and atheistic values: A response to A. E. Bergin's "Psychotherapy and religious issues." *Journal of Consulting and Clinical Psychology, 48,* 635–639.

Ellison, C. G. (1991a). An eye for an eye? A note on the Southern subculture of violence thesis. *Social Forces, 69,* 1223–1239.

Ellison, C. G. (1991b). Religious involvement and subjective well-being. *Journal of Health and Social Behavior, 32,* 80–89.

Ellison, C. G., & Sherkat, D. E. (1993). Obedience and autonomy: Religion and parental values reconsidered. *Journal for the Scientific Study of Religion, 32,* 313–329.

Ellman, I. (1971). Jewish intermarriage in the United States of America. In B. Schlesinger (Ed.), *The Jewish family* (pp. 25–62). Toronto: University of Toronto Press.

Ellwood, C. A. (1922). *The reconstruction of religion.* New York: Macmillan.

Ellwood, R. (1986). The several meanings of cult. *Thought, 61,* 212–224.

Elmore, T. M. (1962). *The development of a scale to measure psychological anomie.* Unpublished doctoral dissertation, Ohio State University.

Embree, R. A. (1968, May). *Special leading and natural leading: An interpretive investigation of motivation for the Christian ministry.* Paper presented at the annual meeting of the Rocky Mountain Psychological Association, Denver, CO.

Engs, R. C. (1982). Drinking patterns and attitudes toward alcoholism of Australian human-service students. *Journal of Studies on Alcohol, 43,* 517–531.

Epstein, S., & O'Brien, E. J. (1985). The person–situation debate in historical and current perspective. *Psychological Bulletin, 98,* 513–537.

Erickson, D. A. (1964). Religious consequences of public and sectarian schooling. *School Review, 72,* 21–33.

Erickson, J. A. (1992). Adolescent development and commitment: A structural equation model of the role of family, peer group, and educational influences. *Journal for the Scientific Study of Religion, 31,* 131–152.

Erikson, E. H. (1958). *Young man Luther: A study in psychoanalysis and history.* London: Faber & Faber.

Erikson, E. H. (1963). *Childhood and society* (2nd ed.). New York: Norton.

Erikson, E. H. (1968). *Identity: Youth and crisis.* New York: Norton.

Erikson, E. H. (1969). Identity and the life cycle [Special issue]. *Psychological Issues, 1.*

Erikson, E. H., Erikson, J. M., & Kivinick, H. Q. (1986). *Vital involvement in old age.* New York: Norton.

Ernsberger, D. J., & Manaster, G. J. (1981). Moral development, intrinsic/extrinsic religious orientation and denominational teachings. *GeneticPsychology Monographs, 104,* 23–41.

Ethridge, F. M., & Feagin, J. R. (1979). Varieties of "fundamentalism": A conceptual and empirical analysis of two Protestant denominations. *Sociological Quarterly, 20,* 37–48.

Etxebarria, I. (1992). Sentimientos de culpa y abandono de los valores paternos [Guilt feelings and abandoning parental values]. *Infancia y Aprendizaje, 57,* 67–88.

Eysenck, H. J. (1981). *A model for personality.* New York: Springer.

Fabry, J. B. (1968). *The pursuit of meaning: Logotherapy applied to life.* Boston: Beacon.

Fahs, S. L. (1950). The beginnings of mysticism in children's growth. *Religious Education, 45,* 139–147.

Fairchild, R. W. (1971). Delayed gratification: A psychological and religious analysis. In M. P. Strommen (Ed.), *Research on religious development: A comprehensive handbook* (pp. 155–210). New York: Hawthorn Books.

Feifel, H. (1974). Religious conviction and fear of death among the healthy and the terminally ill. *Journal for the Scientific Study of Religion, 13,* 353–360.

Feifel, H., & Tong Nagy, V. (1981). Another look at fear of death. *Journal of Consulting and Clinical Psychology, 49,* 278–286.

Feldman, K. A. (1969). Change and stability of religious orientations during college: Part I. Freshman–senior comparisions. *Review of Religious Research, 11,* 40–60.

Feldman, K. A., & Newcomb, T. M. (1969). *The impact of college on students.* San Francisco: Jossey-Bass.

Fernhout, H., & Boyd, D. (1985). Faith in autonomy: Development in Kohlberg's perspectives in religion and morality. *Religious Education, 80,* 287–307.

Festinger, L. (1954). *A theory of cognitive dissonance.* Stanford, CA: Stanford University Press.

Festinger, L., Riecken, H. W., & Schachter, S. (1956). *When prophecy fails.* Minneapolis: University of Minnesota Press.

Feuerbach, L. (1967). *Lectures on the essence of religion.* New York: Harper & Row.

Feuerstein, G. (1992). *Holy madness.* New York: Arcana.

Fichter, J. H. (1961). *Religion as an occupation.* Notre Dame, IN: University of Notre Dame Press.

Fichter, J. H. (1965). *Priest and people.* New York: Sheed & Ward.

Fichter, J. H. (1968). *America's forgotten priests: What are they saying?* New York: Harper & Row.

Fichter, J. H. (1981). *Religion and pain.* New York: Crossroads.

Field, P. B. (1965). An inventory scale of hypnotic depth. *International Journal of Clinical and Experimental Hypnosis, 13,* 238–249.

Finch, J. C. (1965). Motivations for the ministry. *Insight, 4,* 26–31.

Finke, R., & Stark, R. (1992). *The churching of America, 1776–1990: Winners and losers in our religious economy.* New Brunswick, NJ: Rutgers University Press.

Finney, J. R., & Malony, H. N. (1985a). An empirical study of contemplative prayer as an adjunct to psychotherapy. *Journal of Psychology and Theology, 13,* 284–290.

Finney, J. R., & Malony, H. N. (1985b). Contemplative prayer and its use in psychotherapy: A theoretical model. *Journal of Psychology and Theology, 13,* 172–181.

Finney, J. R., & Malony, H. N. (1985c). Empirical studies of Christian prayer: A review of the literature. *Journal of Psychology and Theology, 13,* 104–115.

Fiorenza, E. S. (1979). Word, spirit, and power: Women in early Christian communities. In R. Ruether & E. McLaughlin (Eds.), *Women of spirit* (pp. 29–70). New York: Simon & Schuster.

Firebaugh, G., & Harley, B. (1991). Trends in U.S. church attendance: Secularization and revival, or merely life cycle effects? *Journal for the Scientific Study of Religion, 30,* 487–500.

Fischer, R. (1969). The perception–hallucination continuum (a re-examination). *Diseases of the Nervous System, 30,* 161–171.

Fischer, R. (1971). A cartography of ecstatic and meditative states. *Science, 174,* 897–904.

Fischer, R. (1978). Cartography of conscious states: Integration of East and West. In A. A. Sugerman & R. E. Tarter (Eds.), *Expanding dimensions of consciousness* (pp. 24–57). New York: Springer.

Fisher, R. D., Cook, I. J., & Shirkey, E. C. (1994). Correlates of support for censorship of sexual, sexually violent, and violent media. *Journal of Sex Research, 31,* 229–240.

Fiske, S. T., & Taylor, S. E. (1991). *Social cognition* (2nd ed.). New York: McGraw-Hill.

Fitzgibbons, J. (1987). Developmental approaches to the psychology of religion. *Psychoanalytic Review, 74,* 125–134.

Flatt, B. (1987). Some stages of grief. *Journal of Religion and Health, 26,* 143–148.

Flavell, J. (1963). *The developmental psychology of Jean Piaget.* Princeton, NJ: Van Nostrand.

Fleck, J. R. (1981). Dimensions of personal religion: A trichotomous view. In J. R. Fleck & J. D. Carter (Eds.), *Psychology and Christianity* (pp. 66–80). New York: Abingdon Press.

Florian, V., & Kravetz, S. (1983). Fear of personal death: Attribution, structure, and relation to religious belief. *Journal of Personality and Social Psychology, 44,* 600–607.

Florian, V., & Kravetz, S. (1985). Children's concepts of death: A cross-cultural comparison among Muslims, Druze, Christians, and Jews in Israel. *Journal of Cross-Cultural Psychology, 16,* 174–189.

Florian, V., & Mikulincer, M. (1992–1993). The impact of death-risk experiences and religiosity on the fear of personal death: The case of Israeli soldiers in Lebanon. *Omega, 26,* 101–111.

Folkman, S., & Lazarus, R. S. (1988). Coping as a mediator of emotion. *Journal of Personality and Social Psychology, 54,* 466–475.

Folkman, S., Lazarus, R. S., Dunkel-Schetter, C., De Longis, A., & Gruen, R. J. (1986). Dynamics of a stressful encounter: Cognitive appraisal, coping, and encounter outcomes. *Journal of Personality and Social Psychology, 50,* 992–1003.

Forbes, G. B., TeVault, R. K., & Gromoll, H. F. (1971). Willingness to help strangers as a function of liberal, conservative, or Catholic church membership: A field study with the lost-letter technique. *Psychological Reports, 28,* 947–949.

Forliti, J. E., & Benson, P. L. (1986). Young adolescents: A national study. *Religious Education, 81,* 199–224.

Forman, R. K. (1990). Mysticism, constructivism, and forgetting. In R. K. Forman (Ed.), *The problem of pure consciousness* (pp. 3–49). New York: Oxford University Press.

Forster, B., & Tabachnik, J. (1993). Jews-by-choice: Conversion factors and outcomes. In M. L. Lynn & D. O. Moberg (Eds.), *Research in the social scientific study of religion* (Vol. 5, pp. 123–155). Greenwich, CT: JAI Press.

Fortune, M. M., & Poling, J. N. (1994). *Sexual abuse by clergy: A crisis for the church* (JPCP Monograph No. 6). Decatur, GA: *Journal of Pastoral Care.*

Foster, L. (1984). *Religion and sexuality: The Shakers, the Mormons, and the Oneida community.* Urbana: University of Illinois Press.

Foster, R. A., & Keating, J. P. (1990, November). *The male God-concept and self-esteem: A theoretical framework*. Paper presented at the annual meeting of the Society for the Scientific Study of Religion, Virginia Beach, VA.

Foster, R. A., & Keating, J. P. (1992). Measuring androcentrism in the western God-concept. *Journal for the Scientific Study of Religion, 31*, 366–375.

Foster, R. J. (1992). *Prayer: Finding the heart's true home*. San Francisco: Harper & Row.

Fowler, J. W. (1981). *Stages of faith: The psychology of human development and the quest for meaning*. San Francisco: Harper & Row.

Fowler, J. W. (1984). *Becoming adult; becoming Christian*. San Francisco: Harper & Row.

Fowler, J. W. (1991a). Stages in faith consciousness. In F. K. Oser & W. G. Scarlett (Eds.), *Religious development in childhood and adolescence* (New Directions for Child Development, No. 52, pp. 27–45). San Francisco: Jossey-Bass.

Fowler, J. W. (1991b). *Weaving the new creation: Stages of faith and the public church*. San Francisco: Harper & Row.

Fowler, J. W. (1993). Response to Helmut Reich: Overview or apologetic? *International Journal for the Psychology of Religion, 3*, 173–179.

Fox, J. W. (1992). The structure, stability, and social antecedents of reported paranormal experiences. *Sociological Analysis, 53*, 417–431.

Francis, L. J. (1979). The priest as test administrator in attitude research. *Journal for the Scientific Study of Religion, 18*, 78–81.

Francis, L. J. (1980). Paths of holiness? Attitudes towards religion among 9–11 year old children in England. *Character Potential: A Record of Research, 9*, 129–138.

Francis, L. J. (1982). *Youth in transit: A profile of 16–25 year olds*. Aldershot, England: Gower.

Francis, L. J. (1986). Denominational schools and pupil attitude toward Christianity. *British Educational Research Journal, 12*, 145–152.

Francis, L. J. (1989a). Measuring attitude towards Christianity during childhood and adolescence. *Personality and Individual Differences, 10*, 695–698.

Francis, L. J. (1989b). Monitoring changing attitudes towards Christianity among secondary school pupils between 1974 and 1986. *British Journal of Educational Psychology, 59*, 86–91.

Francis, L. J. (1994). Personality and religious development during childhood and adolescence. In L. B. Brown (Ed.), *Religion, personality, and mental health* (pp. 94–118). New York: Springer-Verlag.

Francis, L. J., & Brown, L. B. (1990). The predisposition to pray: A study of the social influence on the predisposition to pray among eleven-year-old children in England. *Journal of Empirical Theology, 3*, 23–34.

Francis, L. J., & Brown, L. B. (1991). The influence of home, church and school on prayer among sixteen-year-old adolescents in England. *Review of Religious Research, 33*, 112–122.

Francis, L. J., & Gibson, H. M. (1993). Parental influence and adolescent religiosity: A study of church attendance and attitude toward Christianity among adolescents 11 to 12 and 15 to 16 years old. *International Journal for the Psychology of Religion, 3*, 241–253.

Francis, L. J., & Mullen, K. (1993). Religiosity and attitudes towards drug use among 13–15 year olds in England. *Addiction, 88*, 665–672.

Francis, L. J., Pearson, P. R., & Kay, W. K. (1982). Eysenck's personality quadrants and religiosity. *British Journal of Social Psychology, 21*, 262–264.

Francis, L. J., Pearson, P. R., & Kay, W. K. (1983). Are introverts still more religious? *Personality and Individual Differences, 4*, 211–212.

Francis, L. J., Pearson, P. R., & Kay, W. K. (1988). Religiosity and lie scores: A question of interpretation. *Social Behavior and Personality, 16*, 91–95.

Frank, J. (1974). *Persuasion and healing: A comparative study of psychotherapy* (rev. ed.). New York: Schocken Books.

Frankl, V. (1955). *The doctor and the soul*. New York: Knopf.

Frankl, V. (1963). *Man's search for meaning*. New York: Washington Square Press.

Frankl, V. (1969). *The will to meaning*. New York: New American Library.

Franks, K., Templer, D. I., Cappelletty, G. G., & Kauffman, I. (1990–1991). Exploration of death anxiety as a function of religious variables in gay men with and without AIDS. *Omega, 22*, 43–50.

Freud, S. (1919). *Totem and taboo* (A. A. Brill, Trans.). London: Routledge. (Original work published 1913)

Freud, S. (1924). Obsessive acts and religious practices (R. C. McWalters, Trans.). In E. Jones (Ed.), *Sigmund Freud: Collected papers* (Vol. 2, pp. 25–35). London: Hogarth Press. (Original work published 1907)

Freud, S. (1953). Dreams and the occult (W. H. Sprott, Trans.). In G. Devereux (Ed.), *Psychoanalysis and the occult* (pp. 91–127). New York: International Universities Press. (Original work published 1933)

Freud, S. (1961). *The future of an illusion* (J. Strachey, Trans.). New York: Norton. (Original work published 1927)

Freud, S. (1961). *Civilization and its discontents* (J. Strachey, Trans.). New York: Norton. (Original work published 1930)

Friedenberg, E. (1969). Current patterns of a generation conflict. *Journal of Social Issues, 25,* 21–38.

Friedman, E. H. (1985). *Generation to generation: Family process in church and synagogue.* New York: Guilford Press.

Friedman, S. B., Chodoff, P., Mason, J. W., & Hamburg, D. A. (1963). Behavioral observations on parents anticipating the death of a child. *Pediatrics, 32,* 610–625.

Friedrich, C., & Brzezinski, Z. (1956). *Totalitarian dictatorship and autocracy.* New York: Praeger.

Friedrichs, R. W. (1959). Christians and residential exclusion: An empirical study of a Northern dilemma. *Journal of Social Issues, 15,* 14–23.

Friedrichs, R. W. (1960). Alter versus ego: An exploratory assessment of altruism. *American Sociological Review, 25,* 496–508.

Friedrichs, R. W. (1973). Social research and theology: End of the detente? *Review of Religious Research, 15,* 113–137.

Fromm, E. (1950). *Psychoanalysis and religion.* New Haven, CT: Yale University Press.

Fry, P. S. (1990). A factor analytic investigation of home-bound elderly individuals' concerns about death and dying, and their coping responses. *Journal of Clinical Psychology, 46,* 737–748.

Fugate, J. R. (1980). *What the Bible says about . . . child training.* Tempe, AZ: Alpha Omega.

Fukuyama, Y. (1961). The major dimensions of church membership. *Review of Religious Research, 2,* 154–161.

Fullerton, C. S., McCarroll, J. E., Ursano, R. J., & Wright, K. M. (1992). Psychological responses of rescue workers: Fire fighters and trauma. *American Journal of Orthopsychiatry, 62,* 371–377.

Fullerton, J. T., & Hunsberger, B. E. (1982). A unidimensional measure of Christian orthodoxy. *Journal for the Scientific Study of Religion, 21,* 317–326.

Fulton, A. S. & Gorsuch, R. (1990). *Intrinsic and quest religious orientation, anti-homosexual sentiment, fundamentalism and identity status: In search of mature religion.* Unpublished manuscript.

Furnham, A. F. (1982). Locus of control and theological beliefs. *Journal of Psychology and Theology, 10,* 130–136.

Galanter, M. (1980). Psychological induction into the large group: Findings from a large modern religious sect. *American Journal of Psychiatry, 137,* 1574–1579.

Galanter, M. (1983). Group induction techniques in a charismatic sect. In D. G. Bromley & J. T. Richardson (Eds.), *The brainwashing/deprogramming controversy: Sociological, psychological, legal and historical perspectives* (pp.182–193). Lewiston, NY: Edwin Mellon.

Galanter, M. (1989a). *Cults: Faith, healing, and coercion.* New York: Oxford University Press.

Galanter, M. (Ed.). (1989b). *Cults and new religious movements.* Washington, DC: American Psychological Association.

Galanter, M., & Buckley, P. (1978). Evangelical religion and meditation: Psychotherapeutic effects. *Journal of Nervous and Mental Disease, 166,* 685–691.

Galanter, M., Rabkin, R., Rabkin, J., & Deutsch, A. (1979). The "Moonies": A psychological study of conversion and membership in a contemporary religious sect. *American Journal of Psychiatry, 136,* 165–170.

Gallemore, J. L., Jr., Wilson, W. P., & Rhoads, J. M. (1969). The religious life of patients with affective disorders. *Diseases of the Nervous System, 30,* 483–487.

Gallup, G., Jr. (1978). *The Gallup poll: Public opinion 1972–1977.* Washington, DC: Scholarly Resources.

Gallup, G., Jr. (1992). *The Gallup poll: Public opinion 1991.* Wilmington, DE: Scholarly Resources.

Gallup, G., Jr., & Casteli, J. (1990, June 27). Poll results reported in Los Angeles Times Syndicate.

Gallup, G., Jr., & Newport, F. (1990, September 7). Poll results reported in Los Angeles Times Syndicate.

Gallup, G., Jr., & Proctor, W. (1982). *Adventures in immortality.* New York: McGraw-Hill.

The Gallup Poll Monthly. (1992, December). No. 327, pp. 32–39.

The Gallup Poll Monthly. (1993, December). No. 339, pp. 43–58.

The Gallup Poll Monthly. (1994, July). No. 346, pp. 32–53.

Galton, F. (1869). *Hereditary genius: An inquiry into its laws and consequences* (2nd ed.) London: Macmillan.

Gardella, P. (1985). *Innocent ecstasy.* New York: Oxford University Press.

Gardner, H. (1978). What we know (and don't know) about the two halves of the brain. *Harvard Magazine, 80,* 24–27.

Gardner, J. W. (1978). *Morale.* New York: Norton.

Garrett, W. R. (1974). Troublesome transcendence: The supernatural in the scientific study of religion. *Sociological Analysis, 35,* 167–180.

Garrett, W. R. (1975). Maligned mysticism: The maledicted career of Troeltsch's third type. *Sociological Analysis, 36,* 205–223.

Gartner, J., Larson, D. B., & Allen, G. D. (1991). Religious commitment and mental health: A review of the empirical literature. *Journal of Psychology and Theology, 19,* 6–25.

Gartrell, C. D., & Shannon, Z. K. (1985). Contacts, cognitions, and conversions: A rational choice approach. *Review of Religious Research, 27,* 32–48.

Gaustad, E. S. (1966). *A religious history of America* (rev. ed.). San Francisco: Harper & Row.

Gentry, C. S. (1987). Social distance regarding male and female homosexuals. *Journal of Social Psychology, 127,* 199–208.

Gergen, K. J. (1971). *The concept of self.* New York: Holt, Rinehart & Winston.

Gerlach, L. P., & Hine, V. H. (1970). *People, power, change: Movements of social transformation.* Indianapolis, IN: Bobbs-Merrill.

Gerson, G. S. (1977). The psychology of grief and mourning in Judaism. *Journal of Religion and Health, 16,* 260–274.

Gerth, H. H., & Mills, C. W. (Eds. and Trans.). (1946). *From Max Weber: Essays in sociology.* New York: Oxford University Press.

Getz, I. R. (1984). Moral judgment and religion: A review of the literature. *Counseling and Values, 28,* 94–116.

Geyer, A. F. (1963). *Piety and politics.* Richmond, VA: John Knox Press.

Gibbons, D. E., & Jarnette, J. (1972). Hypnotic susceptibility and religious experience. *Journal for the Scientific Study of Religion, 11,* 152–156.

Gibbs, J. C. (1988). Three perspectives on tragedy and suffering: The relevance of near-death experience research. *Journal of Psychology and Theology, 16,* 21–33.

Gibbs, J. P. (1966). Suicide. In R. K. Merton & R. A. Nisbet (Eds.), *Contemporary social problems* (pp. 281–321). New York: Harcourt, Brace & World.

Gibran, K. (1923). *The prophet.* New York: Knopf.

Gilbert, K. (1992). Religion as a resource for bereaved parents. *Journal of Religion and Health, 31,* 19–30.

Gillespie, D. P. (1983). *An analysis of the relationship between denominational affiliation and religious orientation and death perspectives of the clergy.* Unpublished doctoral dissertation, Western Michigan University.

Gilligan, C. (1977). In a different voice: Women's conceptions of self and morality. *Harvard Educational Review, 47,* 481–517.

Gilligan, C. (1982). *In a different voice: Psychological theory and women's development.* Cambridge, MA: Harvard University Press.

Gilman, S. L. (1984). Jews and mental illness: Medical metaphors, anti-Semitism, and the Jewish response. *Journal of the History of the Behavioral Sciences, 20,* 150–159.

Gilman, S. L. (1986). *Jewish self-hatred*. Baltimore: Johns Hopkins University Press.

Glass, J., Bengtson, V. L., & Dunham, C. C. (1986). Attitude similarity in three-generation families: Socialization, status inheritance or reciprocal influence? *American Sociological Review, 51*, 685–698.

Glick, I. O., Weiss, R. A., & Parkes, C. M. (1974). *The first year of bereavement*. New York: Wiley.

Glock, C. Y. (1962). On the study of religious commitment. *Religious Education, 57*(Research Suppl.), S98–S110.

Glock, C. Y. (1964). The role of deprivation in the origin and evolution of religious groups. In R. Lee & M. E. Marty (Eds.), *Religion and social conflict* (pp. 24–36). New York: Oxford University Press.

Glock, C. Y., & Stark, R. (1965). *Religion and society in tension*. Chicago: Rand McNally.

Glock, C. Y., & Stark, R. (1966). *Christian beliefs and anti-semitism*. New York: Harper & Row.

Gochman, E. R. G., & Fantasia, S. C. (1979). *The concept of immortality as related to planning one's life*. Paper presented at the annual meeting of the American Psychological Association, New York.

Godin, A. (Ed.). (1968). *From cry to word: Contributions toward a psychology of prayer*. Brussels: Lumen Vitae Press.

Godin, A. (1968). Genetic development of the symbolic function: Meaning and limits of the work of R. Goldman. *Religious Education, 63*, 439–445.

Godin, A. (1985). *The psychodynamics of religious experience*. Birmingham, AL: Religious Education Press.

Godin, A., & Hallez, M. (1964). Parental images and divine paternity. *Lumen Vitae, 19*, 253–284.

Goldman, R. (1964). *Religious thinking from childhood to adolescence*. New York: Seabury Press.

Goldsen, R. K., Rosenberg, M., Williams, R. M., Jr., & Suchman, E. A. (1960). *What college students think*. Princeton, NJ: Van Nostrand.

Goldstein, K. (1939). *The organism*. New York: American.

Goldstein, S., & Goldscheider, G. (1968). *Jewish-Americans*. Englewood Cliffs, NJ: Prentice-Hall.

Goleman, D. (1977). *The varieties of meditative experience*. New York: E. P. Dutton.

Goleman, D. (1984, May). The faith factor. *American Health*, pp. 48–53.

Goleman, D. (1988). *The meditative mind: The varieties of meditative experience*. Los Angeles: Jeremy Tarcher/Perigee Books.

Goode, E. (1968). Class styles of religious sociation. *British Journal of Sociology, 19*, 1–16.

Goodman, F. D. (1969). Phonetic analysis of glossolalia in four cultural settings. *Journal for the Scientific Study of Religion, 8*, 227–239.

Goodman, F. D. (1972). *Speaking in tongues: A cross-cultural study of glossolalia*. Chicago: University of Chicago Press.

Goodman, F. D. (1988). *Ecstasy, religious ritual, and alternate reality*. Bloomington: University of Indiana Press.

Goodman, F. D. (1990). *Where the spirits ride the wind: Trance journeys and other ecstatic experiences*. Bloomington: University of Indiana Press.

Gordon, A. I. (1967). *The nature of conversion*. Boston: Beacon Press.

Gordon, D. F. (1984). Dying to self: Self-control through self-abandonment. *Sociological Analysis, 5*, 41–56.

Gordon, S. (1964). Personality and attitude correlates of religious conversion. *Journal for the Scientific Study of Religion, 4*, 60–63.

Gorsuch, R. L. (1968). The conceptualization of God as seen in adjective ratings. *Journal for the Scientific Study of Religion, 7*, 56–64.

Gorsuch, R. L. (1976). Religion as a significant predictor of important human behavior. In W. J. Donaldson, Jr. (Ed.), *Research in mental health and religious behavior* (pp. 206–221). Atlanta, GA: Psychological Studies Institute.

Gorsuch, R. L. (1984). Measurement: The boon and bane of investigating religion. *American Psychologist, 39*, 228–236.

Gorsuch, R. L. (1988). Psychology of religion. *Annual Review of Psychology, 39*, 201–221.

Gorsuch, R. L. (1993). Religion and prejudice: Lessons not learned from the past. *International Journal for the Psychology of Religion, 3*, 29–31.

Gorsuch, R. L. (1994). Toward motivational theories of intrinsic religious commitment. *Journal for the Scientific Study of Religion, 33,* 315–325.

Gorsuch, R. L. (1995). Religious aspects of substance abuse and recovery. *Journal of Social Issues, 51,* 65–83.

Gorsuch, R. L., & Aleshire, D. (1974). Christian faith and ethnic prejudice: A review and interpretation of research. *Journal for the Scientific Study of Religion, 13,* 281–307.

Gorsuch, R. L., & Butler, M. C. (1976). Initial drug abuse: A review of predisposing social psychological factors. *Psychological Bulletin, 83,* 120–137.

Gorsuch, R. L., & McFarland, S. (1972). Single vs. multiple-item scales for measuring religious values. *Journal for the Scientific Study of Religion, 11,* 53–64.

Gorsuch, R. L., & McPherson, S. E. (1989). Intrinsic/extrinsic measurement: I/E-revised and single-item scales. *Journal for the Scientific Study of Religion, 28,* 348–354.

Gorsuch, R. L., & Smith, C. S. (1983). Attributions of responsibility to God: An interaction of religious beliefs and outcomes. *Journal for the Scientific Study of Religion, 22,* 340–352.

Gorsuch, R. L., & Wakeman, E. P. (1991). A test and expansion of the Fishbein model on religious attitudes and behavior in Thailand. *International Journal for the Psychology of Religion, 1,* 33–40.

Gottschalk, S. (1973). *The emergence of Christian Science in American religious life.* Berkeley: University of California Press.

Graebner, O. E. (1964). Child concepts of God. *Religious Education, 59,* 234–241.

Grasmick, H. G., Bursik, R. J., & Cochran, J. K. (1991). "Render unto Casear what is Caesar's": Religiosity and taxpayers' inclinations to cheat. *Sociological Quarterly, 32,* 251–266.

Grasmick, H. G., Kinsey, K., & Cochran, J. K. (1991). Denomination, religiosity and compliance with the law: A study of adults. *Journal for the Scientific Study of Religion, 30,* 99–107.

Grasmick, H. G., Morgan, C. S., & Kennedy, M. B. (1992). Support for corporal punishment in the schools: A comparison of the effects of socioeconomic status and religion. *Social Science Quarterly, 73,* 177–187.

Greeley, A. M. (1963). Influence of the "religious factor" on career graduates plans and occupational values of college. *American Journal of Sociology, 68,* 658–671.

Greeley, A. M. (1967). *The changing Catholic college.* Chicago: Aldine.

Greeley, A. M. (1972a). *The Catholic priest in the United States: Sociological investigations.* Washington, DC: United States Catholic Conference.

Greeley, A. M. (1972b). *The denominational society.* Glenview, IL: Scott, Foresman.

Greeley, A. M. (1974). *Ecstasy: A way of knowing.* Englewood Cliffs, NJ: Prentice-Hall.

Greeley, A. M. (1975). *Sociology of the paranormal: A reconnaissance* (Sage Research Papers in the Social Sciences, Vol. 3, No. 90–023). Beverly Hills, CA: Sage.

Greeley, A. M. (1981). Religious musical chairs. In T. Robbins & D. Anthony (Eds.), *In gods we trust: New patterns of religious pluralism in America* (pp. 101–126). New Brunswick, NJ: Transaction.

Greeley, A. M., & Gockel, G. L. (1971). The religious effects of parochial education. In M. P. Strommen (Ed.), *Research on religious development: A comprehensive handbook* (pp. 264–301). New York: Hawthorne Books.

Greeley, A. M., & Rossi, P. H. (1966). *The education of Catholic Americans.* Chicago: Aldine.

Greenberg, D., & Witztum, E. (1992). Content and prevalence of psychopathology in world religions. In J. F. Schumaker (Ed.), *Religion and mental health* (pp. 300–314). New York: Oxford University Press.

Greenberg, M. A., & Revenson, T. A. (1993, August). *Coping with chronic illness: A closer look at coping efficacy.* Paper presented at the annual meeting of the American Psychological Association, Toronto.

Greenberg, S. (1960). Jewish educational institutions. In L. Finkelstein (Ed.), *The Jews: Their history, culture, and religion* (3rd ed., Vol. 2, pp. 1254–1287). New York: Jewish Publication Society of America.

Greenwood, S. F. (1995). Transpersonal theory and religious experience. In R. W. Hood, Jr. (Ed.), *Handbook of religious experience* (pp. 495–519). Birmingham, AL: Religious Education Press.

Greer, J. E. (1983). A critical study of "Thinking about the Bible." *British Journal of Religious Education, 5,* 113–125.

Greil, A. L. (1993). Explorations along the sacred frontier: Notes on para-religions, quasi-religions, and other boundary phenomena. In D. G. Bromley & J. K. Hadden (Eds.), *Handbook of cults and sects in America: Assessing two decades of research and theory development* (pp. 153–172). Greenwich, CT: JAI Press.

Greil, A. L., & Robbins, T. (1994). Introduction: Exploring the boundaries of the sacred. In A. L. Greil & T. Robbins (Eds.), *Between sacred and secular: Research and theory on quasi-religion* (pp. 1–23). Greenwich, CT: JAI Press.

Greil, A. L., & Rudy, D. R. (1990). On the margins of the sacred. In T. Robbins & D. Anthony (Eds.), *In gods we trust: New patterns of religious pluralism in America* (pp. 219–232). New Brunswick, NJ: Transaction.

Greven, P. (1991). *Spare the child: The religious roots of punishment and the psychological impact of physical abuse.* New York: Knopf.

Griffin, G. A. E., Gorsuch, R., & Davis, A.-L. (1987). A cross-cultural investigation of religious orientation, social norms, and prejudice. *Journal for the Scientific Study of Religion, 26,* 358–365.

Griffiths, E. E. H., & Mahy, G. E. (1984). Psychological benefits of Spiritual Baptist "mourning." *American Journal of Psychiatry, 141,* 769–773.

Grof, S. (1980). *LSD psychotherapy.* Pomona, CA: Hunter House.

Gross, L. (1982). *The last Jews in Berlin.* New York: Simon & Schuster.

Gross, M. L. (1978). *The psychological society.* New York: Random House.

Grossman, J. D. (1975). *The dark interval.* Nile, IL: Argus Communications.

Groth-Marnat, G. (1992). Buddhism and mental health: A comparative analysis. In J. F. Schumaker (Ed.), *Religion and mental health* (pp. 270–280). New York: Oxford University Press.

Group for the Advancement of Psychiatry. (1968). *The psychic function of religion in mental illness and health* (Report No. 67, formulated by the Committee on Psychiatry and Religion). New York: Author.

Group for the Advancement of Psychiatry. (1976). *Mysticism: Spiritual quest or psychic disorder?* New York: Author.

Guttman, J. (1984). Cognitive morality and cheating behavior in religious and secular school children. *Journal of Educational Research, 77,* 249–254.

Hadaway, C. K. (1980). Denominational switching and religiosity. *Review of Religious Research, 21,* 451–461.

Hadaway, C. K. (1989). Identifying American apostates: A cluster analysis. *Journal for the Scientific Study of Religion, 28,* 201–215.

Hadaway, C. K., Elifson, K. W., & Petersen, D. M. (1984). Religious involvement and drug use among urban adolescents. *Journal for the Scientific Study of Religion, 23,* 109–128.

Hadaway, C. K., & Marler, P. L. (1993). All in the family: Religious mobility in America. *Review of Religious Research, 35,* 97–116.

Hadaway, C. K., Marler, P. L., & Chaves, M. (1993). What the polls don't show: A closer look at U.S. church attendance. *American Sociological Review, 58,* 741–752.

Hadaway, C. K., & Roof, W. C. (1988). Apostasy in American churches: Evidence from national survey data. In D. G. Bromley (Ed.), *Falling from the faith: Causes and consequences of religious apostasy* (pp. 29–46). Newbury Park, CA: Sage.

Hadden, J. K. (1969). *The gathering storm in the churches.* Garden City, NY: Doubleday.

Hadden, J. K., & Swain, C. E. (1981). *Prime time preachers.* Reading, MA: Addison-Wesley.

Haerich, P. (1992). Premarital sexual permissiveness and religious orientation: A preliminary investigation. *Journal for the Scientific Study of Religion, 31,* 361–365.

Hall, C. S., & Lindsay, G. (1978). *Theories of personality* (3rd ed.). New York: Wiley.

Hall, G. S. (1904). *Adolescence: Its psychology and relations to physiology, anthropology, sociology, sex, crime, religion and education* (2 vols.). New York: Appleton.

Hall, G. S. (1917). *Jesus, the Christ, in light of psychology* (2 vols.). Garden City, NY: Doubleday.

Hall, J. R. (1989). *Gone from the promised land: Jonestown in American cultural history.* New Brunswick, NJ: Transaction.

Halligan, F. R. (1995). Jungian theory and religious experience. In R. W. Hood, Jr. (Ed.), *Handbook of religious experience* (pp. 231–253). Birmingham, AL: Religious Education Press.

Hamberg, E. M. (1991). Stability and change in religious beliefs, practice, and attitudes: A Swedish panel study. *Journal for the Scientific Study of Religion, 30,* 63–80.

Hamlyn, D. W. (1967). Empiricism. In P. Edwards (Ed.), *The encyclopaedia of philosophy* (Vol. 2, pp. 499–504). New York: Crowell, Collier & Macmillan.

Hammond, J. A., Cole, B. S., & Beck, S. H. (1993). Religious heritage and teenage marriage. *Review of Religious Research, 35,* 117–133.

Hands, D. (1992, Fall). Clergy sexual abuse. *Saint Barnabas Community Chronicle,* pp. 1–3.

Hanford, J. T. (1991). The relationship between faith development of James Fowler and moral development of Lawrence Kohlberg: A theoretical review. *Journal of Psychology and Christianity, 10,* 306–310.

Hannay, D. R. (1980). Religion and health. *Social Science and Medicine, 14A,* 683–685.

Hansen, K. J. (1981). *Mormonism and the American experience.* Chicago: University of Chicago Press.

Hanson, R. A. (1991). The development of moral reasoning: Some observations about Christian fundamentalism. *Journal of Psychology and Theology, 19,* 249–256.

Hardt, H. D. (1963). *Mental health status and religious attitudes of hospitalized veterans.* Unpublished doctoral dissertation, University of Texas.

Hardy, A. (1965). *The living stream.* London: Collins

Hardy, A. (1966). *The divine flame.* London: Collins.

Hardy, A. (1975). *The biology of God.* New York: Taplinger.

Hardy, A. (1979). *The spiritual nature of man: A study of contemporary religious experience.* Oxford: Clarendon Press.

Hardy, T. J. (1913). *The religious instinct.* London: Longmans, Green.

Harley, B., & Firebaugh, G. (1993). Americans' belief in an afterlife: Trends over the past two decades. *Journal for the Scientific Study of Religion, 32,* 269–278.

Harms, E. (1944). The development of religious experience in children. *American Journal of Sociology, 50,* 112–122.

Hartley, L. H. (1973). *Clergy occupational satisfaction.* Paper presented at the annual meeting of the Society for the Scientific Study of Religion, San Francisco.

Hartocollis, P. (1976). Aggression and mysticism. *Contemporary Psychoanalysis, 12,* 214–226.

Hartshorne, H., & May, M. A. (1928). *Studies in the nature of character: Vol. 1. Studies in deceit.* New York: Macmillan.

Hartshorne, H., & May, M. A. (1929). *Studies in the nature of character: Vol. 2. Studies in service and self-control.* New York: Macmillan.

Hartshorne, H., May, M. A., & Shuttleworth, F. K. (1930). *Studies in the nature of character: Vol. 3. Studies in the organization of character.* New York: Macmillan.

Hartz, G. W., & Everett, H. C. (1989). Fundamentalist religion and its effect on mental health. *Journal of Religion and Health, 28,* 207–217.

Hastings, P. K., & Hoge, D. R. (1976). Changes in religion among college students, 1948 to 1974. *Journal for the Scientific Study of Religion, 15,* 237–249.

Hathaway, S. R., & McKinley, J. C. (1951). *The Minnesota Multiphastic Personality Inventory manual.* New York: Psychological Corporation.

Haun, D. L. (1977). Perceptions of the bereaved, clergy, and funeral directors concerning bereavement. *Dissertation Abstracts International, 37,* 6791A.

Havens, J. (1963). The changing climate of research on the college student and his religion. *Journal for the Scientific Study of Religion, 3,* 52–69.

Havighurst, R. J., & Keating, B. (1971). The religion of youth. In M. P. Strommen (Ed.), *Research on religious development: A comprehensive handbook* (pp. 686–723). New York: Hawthorne Books.

Hawley, J. S. (Ed.). (1994a). *Fundamentalism and gender.* New York: Oxford University Press.

Hawley, J. S. (1994b). Hinduism: *Sati* and its defenders. In J. S. Hawley (Ed.), *Fundamentalism and gender* (pp. 79–110). New York: Oxford University Press.

Hawley, J. S. (Ed.). (1994c). Sati, *the blessing and the curse*. New York: Oxford University Press.

Hay, D. (1979). Religious experience amongst a group of postgraduate students: A qualitative study. *Journal for the Scientific Study of Religion, 18*, 164–182.

Hay, D. (1987). *Exploring inner space: Scientists and religious experience* (2nd ed.). London: Mowbray.

Hay, D. (1994). "The biology of God": What is the current status of Hardy's hypothesis? *International Journal for the Psychology of Religion, 4*, 1–23.

Hay, D., & Heald, G. (1987). Religion is good for you. *New Society, 80*, 20–22.

Hay, D., & Morisy, A. (1978). Reports of ecstatic, paranormal, or religious experience in Great Britain and the United States: A comparison of trends. *Journal for the Scientific Study of Religion, 17*, 255–268.

Hay, D., & Morisy, A. (1985). Secular society, religious meanings: A contemporary paradox. *Review of Religious Research, 26*, 213–227.

Hayden, J. J. (1991, August). *Rheumatic disease and chronic pain: Religious and affective variables*. Paper presented at the annual meeting of the American Psychological Association, San Francisco.

Hayes, B. C., & Hornsby-Smith, M. P. (1994). Religious identification and family attitudes: An international comparison. In M. L. Lynn & D. O. Moberg (Eds.), *Research in the social scientific study of religion* (Vol. 6, pp. 167–186). Greenwich, CT: JAI Press.

Hearnshaw, C. S. (1987). *The shaping of modern psychology*. New York: Routledge.

Heelas, P. (1985). Social anthropology and the psychology of religion. In L. B. Brown (Ed.), *Advances in the psychology of religion* (pp. 34–51). Elmsford, NY: Pergamon Press.

Heider, F. (1958). *The psychology of interpersonal relations*. New York: Wiley.

Heiler, F. (1932). *Prayer: A study in the history and psychology of religion*. New York: Oxford University Press.

Heimbrock, H. G. (1991). Psychoanalytic understanding of religion. *International Journal for the Psychology of Religion, 1*, 71–89.

Heirich, M. (1977). Change of heart: A test of some widely held theories of religious conversion. *American Sociological Review, 83*, 653–680.

Helfaer, P. (1972). *The psychology of religious doubt*. Boston: Beacon Press.

Herberg, W. (1960). *Protestant, Catholic, Jew*. Garden City, NY: Doubleday.

Herbert, F. (1965). *Dune*. New York: Berkeley.

Herek, G. M. (1988). Heterosexuals' attitudes toward lesbians and gay men: Correlates and gender differences. *Journal of Sex Research, 25*, 451–477.

Herold, E., Corbesi, B., & Collins, J. (1994). Psychosocial aspects of female topless behavior on Australian beaches. *Journal of Sex Research, 31*, 133–142.

Herzbrun, M. B. (1993). Father–adolescent religious consensus in the Jewish community: A preliminary report. *Journal for the Scientific Study of Religion, 32*, 163–168.

Hewstone, M. (Ed.). (1983a). *Attribution theory: Social and functional extensions*. Oxford: Basil Blackwell.

Hewstone, M. (1983b). Attribution theory and common-sense explanations: an introductory overview. In M. Hewstone (Ed.), *Attribution theory: Social and functional extensions* (pp. 1–27). Oxford: Basil Blackwell.

Hick, J. (1989). *An interpretation of religion*. New Haven, CT: Yale University Press.

Hickman, F. S. (1926). *Introduction to the psychology of religion*. New York: Abingdon Press.

Higdon, J. F. (1986, September). *Association of fundamentalism with MPD*. Paper presented at the Third International Conference on Multiple Personality Disorder, Chicago.

Higgins, E. T. (1989). Continuities and discontinuities in self-regulatory and self-evaluative processes: A developmental theory relating self and affect. *Journal of Personality, 57*, 407–444.

Hightower, P. R. (1930). Biblical information in relation to character and conduct. *University of Iowa Studies in Character, 3*(2).

Hilgard, E. R. (1973). A neodissociation interpretation of pain reduction in hypnosis. *Psychological Review, 80*, 396–411.

Hilgard, E. R. (1986). *Divided consciousness: Multiple controls in human thought and action* (expanded ed.). New York: Wiley.

Hill, P. C. (1994). Toward an attitude process model of religious experience. *Journal for the Scientific Study of Religion, 33,* 303–314.

Hill, P. C. (1995). Affective theory and religious experience. In R. W. Hood, Jr. (Ed.), *Handbook of religious experience* (pp. 353–377). Birmingham, AL: Religious Education Press.

Hill, P. C., & Bassett, R. L. (1992). Getting to the heart of the matter: What the social-psychological study of attitudes has to offer psychology of religion. In M. L. Lynn & D. O. Moberg (Eds.), *Research in the social scientific study of religion* (Vol. 4, pp. 159–162). Greenwich, CT: JAI Press.

Hill, S. S., & Owen, D. E. (1982). *The new religious right in America.* Nashville, TN: Abingdon Press.

Hiltner, S. (1962). Conclusion: The dialogue on man's nature. In S. Doniger(Ed.), *The nature of man in theological and psychological perspective* (pp. 237–261). New York: Harper.

Himmelfarb, H. S. (1979). Agents of religious socialization among American Jews. *Sociological Quarterly, 20,* 477–494.

Hine, V. H. (1969). Pentecostal glossolalia: Toward a functional interpretation. *Journal for the Scientific Study of Religion, 8,* 211–226.

Hinkle, L. E., Jr., & Wolff, H. E. (1956). Communist interrogation and the indoctrination of "enemies of the states." *Archives of Neurology and Psychiatry, 76,* 117.

Hirschi, T., & Stark, R. (1969). Hellfire and delinquency. *Social Problems, 17,* 202–213.

Hochstein, L. M. (1986). Pastoral counselors: Their attitudes toward gay and lesbian clients. *Journal of Pastoral Care, 40,* 158–165.

Hodges, D. L. (1974). Breaking a scientific taboo: Putting assumptions about the supernatural into scientific theories of religion. *Journal for the Scientific Study of Religion, 13,* 393–408.

Hoelter, J. W. (1979). Religiosity, fear of death, and suicide acceptability. *Suicide and Life-Threatening Behavior, 9,* 163–172.

Hoelter, J. W., & Epley, R. J. (1979). Religious correlates of the fear of death. *Journal for the Scientific Study of Religion, 9,* 163–172.

Hoffman, M. S. (Ed.). (1992). *The world almanac and book of facts.* New York: Pharos Books.

Hoffman, S. J. (1992, November). *Prayers, piety and pigskins: Religion in modern sports.* Paper presented at the annual meeting of the Society for the Scientific Study of Religion, Washington, DC.

Hoge, D. R. (1988). Why Catholics drop out. In D. G. Bromley (Ed.), *Falling from the faith: Causes and consequences of religious apostasy* (pp. 81–99). Newbury Park, CA: Sage.

Hoge, D. R. (1994). Introduction: The problem of understanding church giving. *Review of Religious Research, 36,* 101–110.

Hoge, D. R., & Carroll, J. W. (1973). Religiosity and prejudice in Northern and Southern churches. *Journal for the Scientific Study of Religion, 12,* 181–197.

Hoge, D. R., Heffernan, E., Hemrick, E. F., Nelsen, H. M., O'Connor, J. P., Philibert, P. J., & Thompson, A. D. (1982). Desired outcomes of religious education and youth ministry in six denominations. *Review of Religious Research, 23,* 230–254.

Hoge, D. R., Johnson, B., & Luidens, D. A. (1993). Determinants of church involvement of young adults who grew up in Presbyterian churches. *Journal for the Scientific Study of Religion, 32,* 242–255.

Hoge, D. R., & Keeter, L. G. (1976). Determinants of college teachers' religious beliefs and participation. *Journal for the Scientific Study of Religion, 15,* 221–235.

Hoge, D. R., with McGuire, K., & Stratman, B. F. (1981). *Converts, dropouts, returnees: A study of religious change among Catholics.* New York: Pilgrim Press.

Hoge, D. R., & Petrillo, G. H. (1978a). Determinants of church participation among high school youth. *Journal for the Scientific Study of Religion, 17,* 359–379.

Hoge, D. R., & Petrillo, G. H. (1978b). Development of religious thinking in adolescence: A test of Goldman's theories. *Journal for the Scientific Study of Religion, 17,* 139–154.

Hoge, D. R., Petrillo, G. H., & Smith, E. I. (1982). Transmission of religious and social values from parents to teenage children. *Journal of Marriage and the Family, 44,* 569–580.

Hoge, D. R., & Thompson, A. D. (1982). Different conceptualizations of goals of religious education and youth ministry in six denominations. *Review of Religious Research, 23,* 297–304.

Hoge, D. R., & Yang, F. (1994). Determinants of religious giving in religious denominations: Data from two nationwide surveys. *Review of Religious Research, 36,* 123–148.

Hoggatt, L., & Spilka, B. (1978). The nurse and the terminally ill patient. *Omega, 9,* 255–256.

Holahan, C. J., & Moos, R. H. (1987). Personal and contextual determinants of coping strategies. *Journal of Personality and Social Psychology, 52,* 946–955.

Holden, G. W., & Edwards, L. A. (1989). Parental attitudes toward child rearing: Instruments, issues, and implications. *Psychological Bulletin, 106,* 29–58.

Holley, R. T. (1991). Assessing potential bias: The effects of adding religious content to the Defining Issues Test. *Journal of Psychology and Christianity, 10,* 323–336.

Hollingshead, A. B., & Redlich, F. C. (1958). *Social class and mental illness.* New York: Wiley.

Holm, N. G. (1982). Mysticism and intense experiences. *Journal for the Scientific Study of Religion, 21,* 268–276.

Holm, N. G. (1987a). *Scandinavian psychology of religion.* Åbo, Finland: Åbo Akademi.

Holm, N. G. (1987b). Sunden's role theory and glossolalia. *Journal for the Scientific Study of Religion, 26,* 383–389.

Holm, N. G. (1991). Pentecostalism: Conversion and charismata. *International Journal for the Psychology of Religion, 1,* 135–151.

Holm, N. G. (1995). Role theory and religious experience. In R. W. Hood, Jr. (Ed.), *Handbook of religious experience* (pp. 397–420). Birmingham, AL: Religious Education Press.

Holm, N. G., & Belzen, J. A. (Eds.). (1995). *Sundén's role theory: An impetus to contemporary psychology of religion.* Åbo, Finland: Åbo Akademi.

Holmes, U. T. (1980). *A history of Christian spirituality.* New York: Seabury Press.

Holt, R. R. (1964). Imagery: The return of the ostracized. *American Psychologist, 19,* 254–264.

Holter, H. (1970). *Sex roles and social structure.* Oslo: Universitetsforlaget.

Hong, G.-Y. (1995). Buddhism and religious experience. In R. W. Hood, Jr. (Ed.), *Handbook of religious experience* (pp. 87–121). Birmingham, AL: Religious Education Press.

Honigmann, J. J. (1959). *The world of man.* New York: Harper & Row.

Hood, R. W., Jr. (1970). Religious orientation and the report of religious experience. *Journal for the Scientific Study of Religion, 9,* 285–291.

Hood, R. W., Jr. (1972). Normative and motivational determinants of religious experience in two Baptist samples. *Review of Religious Research, 13,* 192–196.

Hood, R. W., Jr. (1973a). Hypnotic susceptibility and reported religious experience. *Psychological Reports, 33,* 549–550.

Hood, R. W., Jr. (1973b). Religious orientation and the experience of transcendence. *Journal for the Scientific Study of Religion, 12,* 441–448.

Hood, R. W., Jr. (1974). Psychological strength and the report of intense religious experience. *Journal for the Scientific Study of Religion, 13,* 65–71.

Hood, R. W., Jr. (1975). The construction and preliminary validation of a measure of reported mystical experience. *Journal for the Scientific Study of Religion, 14,* 29–41.

Hood, R. W., Jr. (1976a). Conceptual criticisms of regressive explanations of mysticism. *Review of Religious Research, 7,* 179–188.

Hood, R. W., Jr. (1976b). Mystical experience as related to present and anticipated future church participation. *Psychological Reports, 39,* 1127–1136.

Hood, R. W., Jr. (1977a). Differential triggering of mystical experience as a function of self-actualization. *Review of Religious Research, 18,* 264–270.

Hood, R. W., Jr. (1977b). Eliciting mystical states of consciousness with semistructured nature experiences. *Journal for the Scientific Study of Religion, 16,* 155–163.

Hood, R. W., Jr. (1978a). Anticipatory set and setting: Stress incongruity as elicitors of mystical experience in solitary nature situations. *Journal for the Scientific Study of Religion, 17,* 278–287.

Hood, R. W., Jr. (1978b). The usefulness of the indiscriminatively pro and anti categories of religious orientation. *Journal for the Scientific Study of Religion, 17,* 419–431.

Hood, R. W., Jr. (1980). Social legitimacy, dogmatism, and the evaluation of intense experiences. *Review of Religious Research, 21,* 184–194.

Hood, R. W., Jr. (1983). Social psychology and religious fundamentalism. In A. W. Childs & G. B. Melton (Eds.), *Rural psychology* (pp. 169–198). New York: Plenum Press.

Hood, R. W., Jr. (1985). Mysticism. In P. Hammond (Ed.), *The sacred in a secular age* (pp. 285–297). Berkeley: University of California Press.

Hood, R. W., Jr. (1989). Mysticism, the unity thesis, and the paranormal. In G. K. Zollschan, J. F. Schumaker, & G. F. Walsh (Eds). *Exploring the paranormal: Perspectives on belief and experience* (pp. 117–130). New York: Avery.

Hood, R. W., Jr. (1991). Holm's use of role theory: Empirical and hermeneutical considerations of sacred text as a source of role adoption. *International Journal for the Psychology of Religion, 1*, 153–159.

Hood, R. W., Jr. (1992a). A Jamesean look at self and self loss in mysticism. *Journal of the Psychology of Religion, 1*, 1–14.

Hood, R. W., Jr. (1992b). Mysticism, reality, illusion and the Freudian critique of religion. *International Journal for the Psychology of Religion, 2*, 141–159.

Hood, R. W., Jr. (1992c). Sin and guilt in faith traditions: Issues for self-esteem. In J. F. Schumaker (Ed.), *Religion and mental health* (pp. 110–121). New York: Oxford Univerity Press.

Hood, R. W., Jr. (1994). Psychology and religion. In U. S. Ramachdran (Ed.), *Encyclopaedia of human behavior* (Vol. 3, pp. 619–629). New York: Academic Press.

Hood, R. W., Jr. (Ed.). (1995a). *Handbook of religious experience*. Birmingham, AL: Religious Education Press.

Hood, R. W., Jr. (1995b). The facilitation of religious experience. In R. W. Hood, Jr. (Ed.), *Handbook of religious experience* (pp. 569–597). Birmingham, AL: Religious Education Press.

Hood, R. W., Jr. (1995c). The soulful self of William James. In D. Capps & J. L. Jacobs (Eds.), *The struggle for life: A companion to William James's* The varieties of religious experience (Society for the Scientific Study of Religion Monograph Series, Whole No. 9, pp. 209–219). West Lafayette, IN: Society for the Scientific Study of Religion.

Hood, R. W., Jr., & Hall, J. R. (1977). Comparison of reported religious experience in Caucasian, American Indian, and two Mexican American samples. *Psychological Reports, 41*, 657–658.

Hood, R. W., Jr., & Hall, J. R. (1980). Gender differences in the description of erotic and mystical experience. *Review of Religious Research, 21*, 195–207.

Hood, R. W., Jr., Hall, J. R., Watson, P. J., & Biderman, M. (1979). Personality correlates of the report of mystical experience. *Psychological reports, 44*, 804–806.

Hood, R. W., Jr., & Kimbrough, D. (1995). Serpent-handling Holiness sects: Theoretical considerations. *Journal for the Scientific Study of Religion, 34*, 311–322.

Hood, R. W., Jr., & Morris, R. J. (1981a). Knowledge and experience criteria in the report of mystical experience. *Review of Religious Research, 23*, 76–84.

Hood, R. W., Jr., & Morris, R. J. (1981b). Sensory isolation and the differential elicitation of religious imagery in intrinsic and extrinsic persons. *Journal for the Scientific Study of Religion, 20*, 261–273.

Hood, R. W., Jr., & Morris, R. J. (1983). Toward a theory of death transcendence. *Journal for the Scientific Study of Religion, 22*, 353–365.

Hood, R. W., Jr., Morris, R. J., & Harvey, D. K. (1993, October). *Religiosity, prayer and their relationship to mystical experience.* Paper presented at the annual meeting of the Religious Research Association, Raleigh, NC.

Hood, R. W., Jr., Morris, R. J., & Watson, P. J. (1985). Boundary maintenance, socio-political views, and presidential preference. *Review of Religious Research, 27*, 134–145.

Hood, R. W., Jr., Morris, R. J., & Watson, P. J. (1986). Maintenance of religious fundamentalism. *Psychological Reports, 9*, 547–559.

Hood, R. W., Jr., Morris, R. J., & Watson, P. J. (1987). Religious orientation and prayer experience. *Psychological Reports, 60*, 1201–1202.

Hood, R. W., Jr., Morris, R. J., & Watson, P. J. (1989). Prayer experience and religious orientation. *Review of Religious Research, 31*, 39–45.

Hood, R. W., Jr., Morris, R. J., & Watson, P. J. (1990). Quasi-experimental elicitation of the differential report of mystical experience among intrinsic indiscriminatively pro-religious types. *Journal for the Scientific Study of Religion, 29*, 164–172.

Hood, R. W., Jr., Morris, R. J., & Watson, P. J. (1991). Male commitment to the cult of the Virgin Mary and the passion of Christ as a function of early maternal bonding. *International Journal for the Psychology of Religion, 1,* 221–231.

Hood, R. W., Jr., Morris, R. J., & Watson, P. J. (1993). Further factor analysis of Hood's Mysticism Scale. *Psychological Reports, 3,* 1176–1178.

Hooper, T. (1962). *Some meanings and correlates of future time and death among college students.* Unpublished doctoral dissertation, University of Denver.

Hooper, T., & Spilka, B. (1970). Some meanings and correlates of future time and death perspectives among college students. *Omega, 1,* 49–56.

Horowitz, I. L. (1983a). Symposium on scholarship and sponsorship: Universal standards, not universal beliefs. Further reflections on scientific method and religious sponsors. *Sociological Analysis, 44,* 179–182.

Horowitz, I. L. (1983b). A reply to critics and crusaders. *Sociological Analysis, 44,* 221–225.

Horton, A. L., & Williamson, J. A. (Eds.). (1988). *Abuse and religion.* Lexington, MA: Lexington Books.

Horton, P. C. (1973). The mystical experience as a suicide preventative. *American Journal of Psychiatry, 130,* 294–296.

Hostetler, J. A. (1968). *Amish society* (rev. ed.). Baltimore: Johns Hopkins University Press.

Hout, M., & Greeley, A. M. (1990). The cohort doesn't hold: Comment on Chaves (1989). *Journal for the Scientific Study of Religion, 29,* 519–524.

Howkins, K. G. (1966). *Religious thinking and religious education.* London: Tyndale Press.

Hsu, F. L. K. (1952). *Religion, science, and human crises.* London: Routledge & Kegan Paul.

Hudson, W. H. (1939). *Far away and long ago.* London: Dent.

Hughey, M. W. (1983). *Civil religion and moral order.* Westport, CT: Greenwood Press.

Hull, D. B., & Burke, J. (1991). The religious right, attitudes toward women, and tolerance for sexual abuse. *Journal of Offender Rehabilitation, 17,* 1–12.

Hundleby, J. D. (1987). Adolescent drug use in a behavioral matrix: A confirmation and comparison of the sexes. *Addictive Behaviors, 12,* 103–112.

Hunsberger, B. (1976). Background religious denomination, parental emphasis, and the religious orientation of university students. *Journal for the Scientific Study of Religion, 15,* 251–255.

Hunsberger, B. (1977). A reconsideration of parochial schools: The case of Mennonites and Roman Catholics. *Mennonite Quarterly Review, 51,* 140–151.

Hunsberger, B. (1978). The religiosity of college students: Stability and change over years at university. *Journal for the Scientific Study of Religion, 17,* 159–164.

Hunsberger, B. (1980). A reexamination of the antecedents of apostasy. *Review of Religious Research, 21,* 158–170.

Hunsberger, B. (1983a). Apostasy: A social learning perspective. *Review of Religious Research, 25,* 21–38.

Hunsberger, B. (1983b). *Current religious position and self-reports of religious socialization influences.* Paper presented at the annual meeting of the Society for the Scientific Study of Religion, Knoxville, TN.

Hunsberger, B. (1983c). *Religion and attribution theory: A test of the actor–observer bias.* Paper presented at the annual meeting of the Society for the Scientific Study of Religion, Knoxville, TN.

Hunsberger, B. (1985a). Parent–university student agreement on religious and nonreligious issues. *Journal for the Scientific Study of Religion, 24,* 314–320.

Hunsberger, B. (1985b). Religion, age, life satisfaction, and perceived sources of religiousness: A study of older persons. *Journal of Gerontology, 40,* 615–620

Hunsberger, B. (1995). Religion and prejudice: The role of religious fundamentalism, quest, and right-wing authoritarianism. *Journal of Social Issues, 51,* 113–129.

Hunsberger, B. (1996). Religious fundamentalism, right-wing authoritarianism and hostility toward homosexuals in non-Christian religious groups. *International Journal for the Psychology of Religion, 6,* 39–49.

Hunsberger, B., Alisat, S., Pancer, S. M., & Pratt, M. (1996). Religious fundamentalism and religious doubts: Content, connections and complexity of thinking. *International Journal for the Psychology of Religion, 6,* 201–220.

Hunsberger, B., & Altemeyer, B. (1995, June). *Apostates from highly religious homes: Socialization anomalies.* Paper presented at the annual meeting of the Canadian Psychological Association, Charlottetown, Prince Edward Island.

Hunsberger, B., & Brown, L. B. (1984). Religious socialization, apostasy, and the impact of family background. *Journal for the Scientific Study of Religion, 23,* 239–251.

Hunsberger, B., & Ennis, J. (1982). Experimenter effects in studies of religious attitudes. *Journal for the Scientific Study of Religion, 21,* 131–137.

Hunsberger, B., Lea, J., Pancer, S. M., Pratt, M., & McKenzie, B. (1992). Making life complicated: Prompting the use of integratively complex thinking. *Journal of Personality, 60,* 95–114.

Hunsberger, B., McKenzie, B., Pratt, M., & Pancer, S. M. (1993). Religious doubt: A social psychological analysis. In M. L. Lynn & D. O. Moberg (Eds.), *Research in the social scientific study of religion* (Vol. 5, pp. 27–51). Greenwich, CT: JAI Press.

Hunsberger, B., Pancer, S. M., Pratt, M., & Alisat, S. (1996). The transition to university: Is religion related to adjustment? In J. M. Greer & D. O. Moberg (Eds.), *Research in the social scientific study of religion* (Vol. 7, pp. 181–199). Greenwich, CT: JAI Press.

Hunsberger, B., & Platonow, E. (1986). Religion and helping charitable causes. *Journal of Psychology, 120,* 517–528.

Hunsberger, B., Pratt, M., & Pancer, S. M. (1994). Religious fundamentalism and integrative complexity of thought: A relationship for existential content only? *Journal for the Scientific Study of Religion, 33,* 335–346.

Hunsberger, B., & Watson, B. (1986, November). *The devil made me do it: Attributions of responsibility to God and Satan.* Paper presented at the annual meeting of the Society for the Scientific Study of Religion, Washington, DC.

Hunt, R. A. (1972). Mythological–symbolic religious commitment: The LAM scales. *Journal for the Scientific Study of Religion, 11,* 42–52.

Hunt, R. A., & King, M. M. (1971). The intrinsic–extrinsic concept: A review and evaluation. *Journal for the Scientific Study of Religion, 10,* 339–356.

Hunt, R. A., & King, M. B. (1978). Religiosity and marriage. *Journal for the Scientific Study of Religion, 17,* 399–406.

Hunter, E. (1951). *Brainwashing in Red China.* New York: Vanguard.

Hunter, W. F. (1989). Theme issue: The case for theological literacy in the psychology of religion. *Journal of Psychology and Theology, 17,* 327–422.

Hutch, R. A. (1980). The personal ritual of glossolalia. *Journal for the Scientific Study of Religion, 19,* 255–266.

Hutsebaut, D., & Verhoeven, D. (1995). Studying dimensions of God representation: Choosing closed or open-ended research questions. *International Journal for the Psychology of Religion, 5,* 49–60.

Hyde, K. E. (1990). *Religion in childhood and adolescence: A comprehensive review of the research.* Brimingham, AL: Religious Education Press.

Ice, M. L. (1987). *Clergy women and their worldviews.* New York: Praeger.

Idler, E. L. (1987). Religious involvement and the health of the elderly: Some hypotheses and an initial test. *Social Forces, 66,* 226–238.

Idler, E. L., & Kasl, S. V. (1992). Religion, disability, depression and the timing of death. *American Journal of Sociology, 97,* 1052–1079.

Illich, I. (1976). *Medical nemesis: The expropriation of health.* New York: Pantheon Books.

Inge, D. (1899). *Christian mysticism.* London: Methuen.

Institute for Ecology, Justice and Faith. (1995, March). *Program for "Aspects and models of the green theological community: An intensive cross-disciplinary seminar for faculty and graduate students and leaders of religious and environmental organizations."* Chicago: Author.

Isralowitz, R. E., & Ong, T. (1990). Religious values and beliefs and place of residence as predictors of alcohol use among Chinese college students in Singapore. *International Journal of the Addictions, 25,* 515–529.

Jackson, C. W., Jr., & Kelly, E. L. (1962). Influence of suggestion and subject's prior knowledge in research on sensory deprivation. *Science, 132,* 211–212.

Jackson, D. N. (1976). *Jackson Personality Inventory manual.* Goshen, NY: Research Psychology Press.

Jackson, D. N. (1978). Interpreter's guide to the Jackson Personality Inventory. In P. McReynolds (Ed.), *Advances in psychological assessment* (Vol. 4, pp. 56–102). San Francisco: Jossey-Bass.

Jackson, G. (1908). *The fact of conversion: The Cole lectures for 1908.* New York: Revell.

Jackson, N. J., & Spilka, B. (1980, April). *Correlates of religious mystical experience: A selective study.* Paper presented at the annual meeting of the Rocky Mountain Psychological Association, Tucson, AZ.

Jacobs, J. L. (1984). The economy of love in religious commitment: The deconversion of women from nontraditional religious movements. *Journal for the Scientific Study of Religion, 23,* 155–171.

Jacobs, J. L. (1987). Deconversion from religious movements: An analysis of charismatic bonding and spiritual commitment. *Journal for the Scientific Study of Religion, 26,* 294–308.

Jacobs, J. L. (1989). *Divine disenchantment.* Bloomington: Indiana University Press.

Jacobs, J. L. (1992). Religious ritual and mental health. In J. F. Schumaker (Ed.), *Religion and mental health* (pp. 291–299). New York: Oxford University Press.

Jacquet, C. H., Jr. (1983). *Yearbook of American and Canadian churches 1983.* Nashville, TN: Abingdon Press.

Jahreiss, W. O. (1942). Some influences of Catholic education and creed upon psychotic reactions. *Diseases of the Nervous System, 3,* 377–381.

James, W. (1950). *The principles of psychology* (2 vols.). New York: Dover. (Original work published 1890)

James, W. (1967). The final impressions of a psychical researcher. In J. McDermott (Ed.), *The Writings of William James* (pp. 787–799). New York: Random House. (Original work published 1909)

James, W. (1985). *The varieties of religious experience.* Cambridge, MA: Harvard University Press. (Original work published 1902)

Janssen, J., de Hart, J., & den Draak, C. (1989). Praying practices. *Journal of Empirical Theology, 2,* 28–38.

Janssen, J., de Hart, J., & den Draak, C. (1990). A content analysis of the praying practices of Dutch youth. *Journal for the Scientific Study of Religion, 29,* 99–107.

Janssen, J., de Hart, J., & Gerardts, M. (1994). Images of God in adolescence. *International Journal for the Psychology of Religion, 4,* 105–121.

Janus, S. S., & Janus, C. L. (1993). *The Janus report on sexual behavior.* New York: Wiley.

Jaynes, J. (1976). *The origin of consciousness in the breakdown of the bicameral mind.* Boston: Houghton Mifflin.

Jenkins, R. A., & Pargament, K. I. (1988). The relationship between cognitive appraisals and psychological adjustment in cancer patients. *Social Science and Medicine, 26,* 625–633.

Jensen, G. F., & Erickson, M. L. (1979). The religious factor and delinquency: Another look at the hellfire hypotheses. In R. Wuthnow (Ed.), *The religious dimension: New directions in quantitative research* (pp. 157–177). New York: Academic Press.

Jernigan, H. L. (1976). Bringing together psychology and theology: Reflections on ministry to the bereaved. *Journal of Pastoral Care, 30,* 88–102.

Johnson, A. L., Brekke, M. L., Strommen, M. B., & Underwager, R. C. (1974). Age differences and dimensions of religious behavior. *Journal of Social Issues, 30,* 43–67.

Johnson, B. (1961). Do Holiness sects socialize in dominant values? *Social Forces, 39,* 309–317.

Johnson, B. (1963). On church and sect. *American Sociological Review, 28,* 539–549.

Johnson, B. (1971). Church and sect revisited. *Journal for the Scientific Study of Religion, 10,* 124–137.

Johnson, B. L., Eberly, S., Duke, J. T., & Sartain, D. H. (1988). Wives' employment status and marital happiness of religious couples. *Review of Religious Research, 29,* 259–270.

Johnson, D. M., Williams, J. S., & Bromley, D. G. (1986). Religion, health and healing: Findings from a Southern city. *Sociological Analysis, 47,* 66–73.

Johnson, D. P. (1979). Dilemmas of charismatic leadership: The case of the People's Temple. *Sociological Analysis, 40,* 315–323.

Johnson, D. P., & Mullins, L. C. (1989). Subjective and social dimensions of religiosity and loneliness among the well elderly. *Review of Religious Research, 31,* 3–15.

Johnson, M. A. (1973). Family life and religious commitment. *Review of Religious Research, 14,* 144–150.

Johnson, P. E. (1959). *Psychology of religion* (rev. ed.). New York: Abingdon Press.

Johnson, R. C., Danko, G. P., Darvill, R. J., Bochner, S., Bowers, J. K., Huang, Y.-H., Park, J. Y., Pecjak, V., Rahim, A. R. A., & Pennington, D. (1989). Cross-cultural assessment of altruism and its correlates. *Personality and Individual Differences, 10*, 855–868.

Johnson, S., & Spilka, B. (1988, October). *Coping with breast cancer: The role of religion.* Paper presented at the annual meeting of the Society for the Scientific Study of Religion, Chicago.

Johnson, S., & Spilka, B. (1991). Religion and the breast cancer patient: The roles of clergy and faith. *Journal of Religion and Health, 30*, 21–33.

Johnson, W. (1974). *The search for transcendence.* New York: Harper & Row.

Johnston, W. (1974). *Silent music.* New York: Harper.

Johnstone, R. L. (1966). *The effectiveness of Lutheran elementary and secondary schools as agencies of Christian education.* St. Louis, MO: Concordia Seminary Research Center.

Johnstone, R. L. (1988). *Religion in society: A sociology of religion* (3rd ed.). Englewood Cliffs, NJ: Prentice-Hall.

Jones, E. (1955a). *The life and work of Sigmund Freud* (Vol. 1). New York: Basic Books.

Jones, E. (1955b). *The life and work of Sigmund Freud* (Vol. 2). New York: Basic Books.

Jones, J. W. (1993). Living on the boundary between psychology and religion. *Religion Newsletter, 18*(4), 1–7.

Jones, R. H. (1986). *Science and mysticism.* London: Associated Universities Press.

Jones, S. L. (1994). A constructive relationship for religion with the science and profession of psychology: Perhaps the boldest model yet. *American Psychologist, 49*, 184–199.

Jones, W. L. (1937). *A psychological study of conversion.* London: Epworth.

Joyce, C. R. B., & Weldon, R. M. C. (1965). The objective efficacy of prayer: A double-blind clinical trial. *Journal of Chronic Diseases, 18*, 367–377.

Judah, J. S. (1974). *Hare Krishna and the counterculture.* New York: Wiley.

Jung, C. G. (1933). *Modern man in search of a soul* (W. S. Dell & C. F. Baynes, Trans.). New York: Harcourt, Brace.

Jung, C. G. (1938). *Psychology and religion.* New Haven, CT: Yale University Press.

Jung, C. G. (1968). Archetypes of the collective unconscious. In H. Read, M. Fordham, & G. Adler (Eds.) and R. F. C. Hull (Trans.), *The collected works of C. G. Jung* (2nd ed., Vol. 9, Part I, pp. 3–41). Princeton, NJ: Princeton University Press. (Original work published 1954)

Jung, C. G. (1969). A psychological approach to the dogma of the Trinity. In H. Read, M. Fordham, & G. Adler (Eds.) and R. F. C. Hull (Trans.), *The collected works of C. G. Jung* (2nd ed., Vol. 11, pp. 107–200). Princeton, NJ: Princeton University Press. (Original work published 1948)

Kahoe, R. D., & Dunn, R. F. (1975). The fear of death and religious attitudes and behavior. *Journal for the Scientific Study of Religion, 14*, 379–382.

Kalish, R. A., & Dunn, L. (1976). Death and dying: A survey of credit offerings in theological schools and some possible implications. *Review of Religious Research, 17*, 134–140.

Kalish, R. A., & Reynolds, D. K. (1976). *Death and ethnicity: A psychocultural study.* Los Angeles: University of Southern California Press.

Kandel, D. B., & Sudit, M. (1982). Drinking practices among urban adults in Israel: A cross-cultural comparison. *Journal of Studies on Alcohol, 43*, 1–16.

Kantrowitz, B., King, P., Rosenberg, D., Springen, K., Wingert, P., Namuth, T., & Gegax, T. X. (1994, November 28). In search of the sacred. *Newsweek,* pp. 52–62.

Kaplan, B. H. (1965). The structure of adaptive sentiments in a lower class religious group in Appalachia. *Journal of Social Issues, 21*, 126–141.

Kaplan, H. B. (1982). Prevalence of the self-esteem motive. In M. Rosenberg & H. B. Kaplan (Eds.), *Social psychology of the self-concept* (pp. 139–151). Arlington Heights, IL: Harlan Davidson.

Kaplan, M. (1983). A woman's view of DSM-III. *American Psychologist, 38*, 786–803.

Kasamatsu, M., & Hirai, T. (1969). An electroencephalographic study on the Zen meditation (*zazen*). In C. Tart (Ed.), *Altered states of consciousness* (pp. 489–501). New York: Wiley.

Kass, J. D., Friedman, R., Leserman, J., Zuttermeister, P. C., & Benson, H. (1991). Health outcomes and a new index of spiritual experience. *Journal for the Scientific Study of Religion, 30*, 203–211.

Kastenbaum, R. J. (1981). *Death, society, and human experience.* St. Louis, MO: C. V. Mosby.

Kastenbaum, R. J., & Aisenberg, R. (1972). *The psychology of death.* New York: Springer.

Katz, J. (1961). *Exclusiveness and tolerance.* Oxford: Oxford University Press.

Katz, S. T. (1977). *Mysticism and philosophical analysis.* New York: Oxford University Press.

Katz, S. T. (1983). *Mysticism and religious traditions.* New York: Oxford University Press.

Katz, S. T. (1992). *Mysticism and language.* New York: Oxford University Press.

Kaufman, W. (1958). *Critique of religion and philosophy.* New York: Harper.

Kazantzakis, N. (1961). *Report to Greco.* New York: Simon & Schuster.

Kearl, M. (1989). *Endings: A sociology of death and dying.* New York: Oxford University Press.

Kedem, P., & Cohen, D. W. (1987). The effects of religious education on moral judgment. *Journal of Psychology and Judaism, 11,* 4–14.

Kelley, D. M. (1972). *Why conservative churches are growing.* New York: Harper & Row.

Kelley, H. H. (1967). Attribution theory in social psychology. In D. Levine (Ed.), *Nebraska Symposium on Motivation* (Vol. 15, pp. 192–238). Lincoln: University of Nebraska Press.

Kelley, M. L., Power, T. G., & Wimbush, D. D. (1992). Determinants of disciplinary practices in low-income black mothers. *Child Development, 63,* 573–582.

Kelley, Sister M. W. (1958). The incidence of hospitalized mental illness among religious sisters in the United States. *American Journal of Psychiatry, 115,* 72–75.

Kelley, Sister M. W. (1961). Depression in the psychoses of members of religious communities of women. *American Journal of Psychiatry, 118,* 423–425.

Kellstedt, L., & Smidt, C. (1991). Measuring fundamentalism: An analysis of different operational strategies. *Journal for the Scientific Study of Religion, 30,* 259–278.

Kelly, G. A. (1983). Faith, freedom, and disenchantment: Politics and the American religious establishment. In M. Douglas & S. Tipton (Eds.), *Religion and America* (pp. 207–228). Boston: Beacon Press.

Kelsey, M. T. (1964). *Tongue speaking: An experiment in spiritual experience.* Garden City, NY: Doubleday.

Kemper, T. D. (1978). *A social interaction theory of emotions.* New York: Wiley.

Keniston, K. (1968). *Young radicals.* New York: Harcourt, Brace & World.

Keniston, K. (1971). *Youth and dissent.* New York: Harcourt Brace Jovanovich.

Kennedy, E. C., & Heckler, V. J. (1972). *The Catholic priest in the United States: Psychological investigations.* Washington, DC: United States Catholic Conference.

Keysar, A., & Kosmin, B. A. (1995). The impact of religious identification on differences in educational attainment among American women in 1990. *Journal for the Scientific Study of Religion, 34,* 49–62.

Khavari, K. A., & Harmon, T. M. (1982). The relationship between the degree of professed religious belief and use of drugs. *International Journal of the Addictions, 17,* 847–857.

Kidorf, I. W. (1966). The *shiva*: A form of group psychotherapy. *Journal of Religion and Health, 5,* 43–46.

Kieren, D. K., & Munro, B. (1987). Following the leaders: Parents' influence on adolescent religious activity. *Journal for the Scientific Study of Religion, 26,* 249–255.

Kierniesky, N., & Groelinger, L. (1977). General anxiety and death imagery in Catholic seminarians and college students. *Journal of Psychology, 97,* 199–203.

Kiev, A. (1966). Prescientific psychiatry. In S. Arieti (Ed.), *American handbook of psychiatry* (Vol. 3, pp. 166–179). New York: Basic Books.

Kilbourne, B. K. (1983). The Conway and Siegelman claim against religious cults: An assessment of their data. *Journal for the Scientific Study of Religion, 22,* 380–385.

Kilbourne, B. K., & Richardson, J. T. (1984a). Psychotherapy and new religions in a pluralistic society. *American Psychologist, 39,* 237–251.

Kilbourne, B. K., & Richardson, J. T. (1984b). *The DSM-III and its relation to psychotherapy for cult-converts.* Unpublished manuscript.

Kilbourne, B. K., & Richardson, J. T. (1986). Cultphobia. *Thought, 61,* 258–266.

Kilbourne, B. K., & Richardson, J. T. (1989). Paradigm conflict, types of conversion, and conversion theories. *Sociological Analysis, 50,* 1–21.

Kildahl, J. P. (1965). The personalities of sudden religious converts. *Pastoral Psychology, 16,* 37–44.

Kildahl, J. P. (1972). *The psychology of speaking in tongues.* New York: Harper & Row.

Kim, B. (1979). Religious deprogramming and subjective reality. *Sociological Analysis, 40,* 197–207.

Kimbrough, D. L. (1995). *Taking up serpents: Snake handling in eastern Kentucky.* Chapel Hill: University of North Carolina Press.

King, D. G. (1990). Religion and health relationships: A review. *Journal of Religion and Health, 29,* 101–112.

Kinsey, A. C., Pomeroy, W. B., & Martin, C. E. (1948). *Sexual behavior in the human male.* Philadelphia: W. B. Saunders.

Kinsey, A. C., Pomeroy, W. B., Martin, C. E., & Gebhard, P. H. (1953). *Sexual behavior in the human female.* Philadelphia: W. B. Saunders.

Kirk, S. A., & Kutchins, H. (1992). *The selling of DSM: The rhetoric of science in psychiatry.* New York: Aldine/de Gruyter.

Kirkpatrick, C. (1949). Religion and humanitarianism: A study of institutional implications. *Psychological Monographs, 63*(No. 9).

Kirkpatrick, L. A. (1986). *Empirical research on images of God: A methodological and conceptual critique.* Paper presented at the annual meeting of the Society for the Scientific Study of Religion, Savannah, GA.

Kirkpatrick, L. A. (1988). The Conway–Siegelman data on religious cults: Kilbourne's analysis reassessed (again). *Journal for the Scientific Study of Religion, 27,* 117–121.

Kirkpatrick, L. A. (1989). A psychometric analysis of the Allport–Ross and Feagin measures of intrinsic-extrinsic religious orientation. In M. L. Lynn & D. O. Moberg (Eds.), *Research in the social scientific study of religion* (Vol. 1, pp. 1–31). Greenwich, CT.: JAI Press.

Kirkpatrick, L. A. (1992). An attachment-theory approach to the psychology of religion. *International Journal for the Psychology of Religion, 2,* 3–28.

Kirkpatrick, L. A. (1993). Fundamentalism, Christian orthodoxy, and intrinsic religious orientation as predictors of discriminatory attitudes. *Journal for the Scientific Study of Religion, 32,* 256–268.

Kirkpatrick, L. A. (1995). Attachment theory and religious experience. In R. W. Hood, Jr. (Ed.), *Handbook of religious experience* (pp. 446–475). Birmingham, AL: Religious Education Press.

Kirkpatrick, L. A., & Hood, R. W., Jr. (1990). Intrinsic–extrinsic religious orientation: The boon or bane of contemporary psychology of religion? *Journal for the Scientific Study of Religion, 29,* 442–462.

Kirkpatrick, L. A., Hood, R. W., Jr., & Hartz, G. W. (1991). Fundamentalist religion conceptualized in terms of Rokeach's theory of the open and closed mind: New perspectives on some old ideas. In M. Lynn & D. Moberg (Eds.), *Research in the social scientific study of religion* (Vol. 3, pp. 157–179). Greenwich, CT: JAI Press.

Kirkpatrick, L. A., & Shaver, P. R. (1990). Attachment theory and religion: Childhood attachments, religious beliefs, and conversion. *Journal for the Scientific Study of Religion, 29,* 315–334.

Kirkpatrick, L. A., & Shaver, P. R. (1992). An attachment-theoretical approach to romantic love and religious belief. *Personality and Social Psychology Bulletin, 18,* 266–275.

Kittrie, N. (1971). *The right to be different.* Baltimore: John Hopkins University Press.

Kling, F. R. (1958). A study of testing related to the ministry. *Religious Education, 53,* 243–248.

Kling, F. R. (1959). *The motivation of ministerial candidates* (Research Bulletin No. 59–2). Princeton, NJ: Educational Testing Service.

Kling, F. R., Pierson, E., & Dittes, J. E. (1964). *Relation of TSI scores and selected items of biographical information* (Theological School Inventory Research Bulletin No. 1). Dayton, OH: Ministry Studies Board.

Klingberg, G. (1959). A study of religious experience in children from nine to thirteen years of age. *Religious Education, 54,* 211–216.

Klinger, E. (1971). *Structure and functions of fantasy.* New York: Wiley.

Klopfer, F. J., & Price, W. F. (1979). Euthanasia acceptance as related to afterlife belief and other attitudes. *Omega, 9,* 245–253.

Kluegel, J. R. (1980). Denominational mobility: Current patterns and recent trends. *Journal for the Scientific Study of Religion, 19,* 26–39.

Kobasa, S. C. O. (1986). *The choice of priesthood at mid-life.* Paper presented at the annual meeting of the American Psychological Association, Washington, DC.

Koch, P. (1994). *Solitude: A philosophical encounter.* Chicago: Open Court.

Koenig, H. G. (1992). Religion and mental health in later life. In J. F. Schumaker (Ed.), *Religion and mental health* (pp. 177–188). New York: Oxford University Press.

Koenig, H. G. (1994a). *Aging and God: Spiritual pathways to mental health in midlife and later years.* New York: Haworth Press.

Koenig, H. G. (1994b). *Self-destructive behaviors related to death in physically ill elderly men: Pilot data.* Unpublished manuscript, Duke University Medical Center.

Koenig, H. G. (1995). Use of acute hospital services and mortality among religious and non-religious copers with medical illness. *Journal of Religious Gerontology, 9,* 1–22.

Koenig, H. G., George, L. K., & Siegler, I. C. (1988). The use of religion and other emotion-regulating coping strategies among older adults. *The Gerontologist, 28,* 303–310.

Koenig, H. G., Kvale, J. N., & Ferrel, C. (1988). Religion and well-being in later life. *The Gerontologist, 28,* 18–28.

Koenig, H. G., Smiley, M., & Gonzales, J. A. P. (1988). *Religion, health, and aging.* New York: Greenwood Press.

Kohlberg, L. (1964). Development of moral character and moral ideology. In M. L. Hoffman & L. W. Hoffman (Eds.), *Review of child development research* (pp. 383–431). New York: Russell Sage Foundation.

Kohlberg, L. (1969). Stage and sequence: The cognitive-developmental approach to socialization. In D. A. Goslin (Ed.), *Handbook of socialization theory and research* (pp. 347–480). Chicago: Rand McNally.

Kohlberg, L. (1980). Stages of moral development as a basis for moral education. In B. Munsey (Ed.), *Moral development, moral education, and Kohlberg* (pp. 15–98). Birmingham, AL: Religious Education Press.

Kohlberg, L. (1981). *Essays in moral development: Vol. 1. The philosophy of moral development: Moral stages and the idea of justice.* San Francisco: Harper & Row.

Kohlberg, L. (1984). *Essays on moral development: Vol. 2. The psychology of moral development: The nature and validity of moral stages.* San Francisco: Harper & Row.

Kolakowski, L. (1985). *Bergson.* New York: Oxford University Press.

Kolb, B., & Whishaw, I. Q. (1990). *Fundamentals of human neuropsychology* (3rd ed.). New York: W. H. Freeman.

Koltko, M. E. (1993, August). *Religion and vocational development: The neglected relationship.* Paper presented at the annual meeting of the American Psychological Association, Toronto.

Kopplin, D. (1976). *Religious orientations of college students and related personality characteristics.* Paper presented at the annual meeting of the American Psychological Association, Washington, DC.

Kosmin, B. A., & Lachman, S. P. (1993). *One nation under God.* New York: Harmony Books.

Kotre, J. N. (1971). *The view from the border.* Chicago: Aldine/Atherton.

Kramrisch, S., Otto, J., Ruck, C., & Wasson, R. (1986). *Persephone's quest: Etheogens and the origin of religion.* New Haven, CT: Yale University Press.

Krause, N. (1986). Social support, stress, and well-being among older adults. *Journal of Gerontology, 41,* 512–519.

Krause, N., & Van Tranh, T. (1989). Stress and religious involvement among older blacks. *Journal of Gerontology: Social Sciences, 44,* S4–S13.

Kraybill, D. B. (1977). *Ethnic education: The impact of Mennonite schooling.* San Francisco: R & E Research Associates.

Krishnan, V. (1993). Gender of children and contraceptive use. *Journal of Biosocial Science, 25,* 213–221.

Kroll-Smith, J. S. (1980). The testimony as performance: The relationship of an expressive event to the belief system of a Holiness sect. *Journal for the Scientific Study of Religion, 19,* 16–25.

Kruglanski, A. W., Hasmel, I. Z., Maides, S. A., & Schwartz, J. M. (1978). Attribution theory as a special case of lay epistemology. In J. H. Harvey, W. Ickes, & R. F. Kidd (Eds.), *New directions in attribution research* (Vol. 2, pp. 299–333). Hillsdale, NJ: Erlbaum.

Kuhn, M. H., & McPartland, T. S. (1954). An empirical investigation of self-attitudes. *American Sociological Review, 19*, 68–76.

Kuhn, T. (1962). *The structure of scientific revolutions.* Chicago: University of Chicago Press.

Kundera, M. (1983). *The unbearable lightness of being.* London: Faber & Faber.

Küng, H. (1979). *Freud and the problem of God.* New Haven, CT: Yale University Press.

Kunkel, L. E., & Temple, L. L. (1992). Attitudes towards AIDS and homosexuals: Gender, marital status, and religion. *Journal of Applied Social Psychology, 22*, 1030–1040.

Kurth, C. J. (1961). Psychiatric and psychological selection of candidates for the sisterhood. *Guild of Catholic Psychiatrists Bulletin, 8*, 19–25.

Kushner, H. (1981). *When bad things happen to good people.* New York: Schocken Books.

LaBarre, W. (1969). *The peyote cult* (enlarged ed.) New York: Schocken Books.

LaBarre, W. (1972a). Hallucinations and the shamanantic origins of religion. In P. T. Furst (Ed.), *The flesh of the gods* (pp. 261–278). New York: Praeger.

LaBarre, W. (1972b). *The ghost dance: The origins of religion* (rev. ed.). New York: Delta.

Ladd, K. L., McIntosh, D. N., & Spilka, B. (1994, November). *The development of God schemata: The influence of denomination, age, and gender.* Paper presented at the annual meeting of the Society for the Scientific Study of Religion, Albuquerque, NM.

Ladd, K. L., Milmoe, S., & Spilka, B. (1994, April). *Religious schemata: Coping with breast cancer.* Paper presented at the annual meeting of the Rocky Mountain Psychological Association, Las Vegas, NV.

Lafal, J., Monahan, J., & Richman, P. (1974). Communication of meaning in glossolalia. *Journal of Social Psychology, 92*, 277–291.

Landrine, H. (1989). The politics of personality disorder. *Psychology of Women Quarterly, 13*, 325–339.

Lane, R. E. (1969). *Political thinking and consciousness.* Chicago: Markham.

Langer, E. J. (1983). *The psychology of control.* Beverly Hills, CA: Sage.

Langford, B. J., & Langford, C. C. (1974). Review of the polls. *Journal for the Scientific Study of Religion, 13*, 221–222.

Larsen, K. S., & Long, E. (1988). Attitudes toward sex roles: Traditional or egalitarian? *Sex Roles, 19*, 1–12.

Larsen, S. (1976). *The shaman's doorway.* New York: Harper & Row.

Laski, M. (1961). *Ecstasy: A study of some secular and religious experiences.* Bloomington: University of Indiana Press.

Latkin, C. A. (1995). New directions in applying psychological theory to the study of new religions. *International Journal for the Psychology of Religion, 5*, 177–180.

Lawless, E. J. (1988). *Handmaidens of the Lord.* Philadelphia: University of Pennsylvania Press.

Lawrence, B. B. (1989). *Defenders of God.* New York: I. B. Tauris.

Lawson, E. T., & McCauley, R. N. (1990). *Rethinking religion: Connecting cognition and culture.* Cambridge, England: Cambridge University Press.

Lazarus, R. S. (1990). Constructs of the mind in adaptation. In N. L. Stein, B. Leventhal, & T. Trabasso (Eds.), *Psychological and biological approaches to emotion* (pp. 3–20). Hillsdale, NJ: Erlbaum.

Lazarus, R. S., & Folkman, S. (1984). *Stress, appraisal, and coping.* New York: Springer.

Leak, G. K., & Fish, S. (1989). Religious orientation, impression management, and self-deception: Toward a clarification of the link between religiosity and social desirability. *Journal for the Scientific Study of Religion, 28*, 355–359.

Leak, G. K., & Randall, B. A. (1995). Clarification of the link between right-wing authoritarianism and religiousness: The role of religious maturity. *Journal for the Scientific Study of Religion, 34*, 245–252.

Leary, T. (1964). Religious experience: Its production and interpretation. *Psychedelic Review, 1*, 324–346.

Lebacqz, K., & Barton, R. G. (1991). *Sex in the parish.* Louisville, KY: Westminster/John Knox.

Le Bon, G. (1903). *The crowd.* London: T. Fisher Unwin.

Lebra, T. S. (1970). Religious conversion as a breakthrough for transculturation: A Japanese sect in Hawaii. *Journal for the Scientific Study of Religion, 9*, 181–186.

Lee, J. M. (1980). Christian religious education and moral development. In B. Munsey (Ed.), *Moral development, moral education, and Kohlberg* (pp. 326–355). Birmingham, AL: Religious Education Press.

Leech, K. (1985). *Experiencing God: Theology as spirituality.* New York: Harper & Row.

Lefcourt, H. M. (1973). The function of the illusions of control and freedom. *American Psychologist, 28,* 417–425.

Lefcourt, H. M., & Davidson-Katz, K. (1991). Locus of control and health. In C. R. Snyder & D. R. Forsyth (Eds.), *Handbook of social and clinical psychology* (pp. 246–266). Elmsford, NY: Pergamon Press.

Lehman, E. C., Jr. (1985). *Women clergy: Breaking through gender barriers.* New Brunswick, NJ: Transaction.

Lehman, E. C., Jr. (1994). *Women in ministry.* Melbourne, Australia: Joint Board of Christian Education.

Lehrer, E. L., & Chiswick, C. U. (1993). Religion as a determinant of marital stability. *Demography, 30,* 385–403.

Leming, M. R. (1979, October). *The effects of personal and institutionalized religion upon death attitudes.* Paper presented at the annual meeting of the Society for the Scientific Study of Religion, San Antonio, TX.

Leming, M. R. (1980). Religion and death: A test of Homan's thesis. *Omega, 10,* 347–364

Lemoult, J. (1978). Deprogramming members of religious sects. *Fordham Law Review, 46,* 599–640.

Lenski, G. E. (1961). *The religious factor: A sociological study of religious impact on politics, economics and family life.* Garden City, NY: Doubleday.

Lerner, M. (1957). *America as a civilization.* New York: Simon & Schuster.

Lerner, M. J. (1980). *The belief in a just world.* New York: Plenum Press.

Lerner, R. M., & Spanier, G. B. (1980). *Adolescent development: A life-span perspective.* New York: McGraw-Hill.

Lester, D. (1967). Experimental and correlational studies of the fear of death. *Psychological Bulletin, 67,* 27–36.

Lester, D. (1972). Religious behaviors and attitudes toward death. In A. Godin (Ed.), *Death and presence* (pp. 107–124). Brussels: Lumen Vitae Press.

Leuba, J. H. (1896). A study in the psychology of religious phenomena. *American Journal of Psychology, 7,* 309–385.

Leuba, J. H. (1921). *The psychological origin and the nature of religion.* London: Constable.

Leuba, J. H. (1925). *The psychology of religious mysticism.* New York: Hacourt, Brace.

Levenson, H. (1973). Multidimensional locus of control in psychiatric patients. *Journal of Consulting and Clinical Psychology, 41,* 397–404.

Levi, K. (1982). *Violence and religious commitment: Implications of the Jim Jones People's Temple movement.* University Park: Pennsylvania State University Press.

Levin, J. S., & Schiller, P. L. (1987). Is there a religious factor in health? *Journal of Religion and Health, 26,* 9–36.

Levin, T. M., & Zegans, L. S. (1974). Adolescent identity and religious conversion: Implications for psychotherapy. *British Journal of Medical Psychology, 47,* 73–82.

Levinson, D. J., Darrow, C. N., Klein, E. B., Levinson, M. H., & McKee, B. (1978). *The seasons of a man's life.* New York: Knopf.

Levitan, T. (1960). *The laureates: Jewish winners of the Nobel Prize.* New York: Twayne.

Levy, L. H., Martinkowski, K. S., & Derby, J. F. (1994). Differences in patterns of adaptation in conjugal bereavement: Their sources and potential significance. *Omega, 29,* 71–87.

Lewellen, T. C. (1979). Deviant religion and cultural evolution: The Aymara Case. *Journal for the Scientific Study of Religion, 81,* 243–251.

Lewis, C. S. (1956). *Surprised by joy: The shape of my early life.* New York: Harcourt Brace.

Lewis, I. M. (1971). *Ecstatic religion: An anthropological study of spirit possession and Shamanism.* Baltimore: Penguin Books.

Lewis, J. R. (1989). Apostates and the legitimation of repression: Some historical and empirical perspectives on the cult controversy. *Sociological Analysis, 49,* 386–396.

Lewis, J. R., & Bromley, D. G. (1987). The cult withdrawal syndrome: A case of misattribution of cause. *Journal for the Scientific Study of Religion, 26,* 508–522.

Lifton, R. J. (1961). *Thought reform and the psychology of totalism.* NewYork: Norton.

Lifton, R. J. (1973). The sense of immortality: On death and the continuity of life. *American Journal of Psychoanalysis, 33,* 3–15.

Lifton, R. J. (1985). Cult processes, religious liberty and religious totalism. In T. Robbins, W. Shepherd, & J. McBride (Eds.), *Cults, culture, and law* (pp. 59–70). Chico, CA: Scholars Press.

Lilly, J. C. (1956). Mental effects on reduction of ordinary levels of physical stimuli on intact healthy persons. *Psychiatric Research Reports, 5,* 1–19.

Lilly, J. C. (1977). *The deep self.* New York: Warner Books.

Lilly, J. C., & Lilly, A. (1976). *The dyadic cyclone.* New York: Simon & Schuster.

Linn, L., & Schwarz, L. W. (1958). *Psychiatry and religious experience.* New York: Random House.

Lippy, C. H. (1994). *Being religious, American style.* Westport, CT: Praeger.

Lipset, S. M. (1964). Religion and politics in the American past and present. In R. E. Lee & M. E. Marty (Eds.), *Religion and social conflict* (pp. 69–126). New York: Oxford University Press.

Litke, J. (1983, August 5). Ideas of afterlife a heavenly mix, survey indicates. *The Denver Post,* p. 15D.

Loehr, F. (1959). *The power of prayer on plants.* Garden City, NY: Doubleday.

Loewenthal, K. M., & Cornwall, N. (1993). Religiosity and perceived control of life events. *International Journal for the Psychology of Religion, 3,* 39–45.

Lofland, J. (1977). *Doomsday cult* (Rev. ed.) New York: Irvington Press.

Lofland, J., & Skonovd, N. (1981). Conversion motifs. *Journal for the Scientific Study of Religion, 20,* 373–385.

Lofland, J., & Stark, R. (1965). Becoming a world saver: A theory of conversion to a deviant perspective. *American Sociological Review, 30,* 862–874.

London, P. (1964). *The modes and morals of psychotherapy.* New York: Holt, Rinehart & Winston.

Long, D., Elkind, D., & Spilka, B. (1967). The child's conception of prayer. *Journal for the Scientific Study of Religion, 6,* 101–109.

Long, T. E., & Hadden, J. K. (1983). Religious conversion and the concept of socialization: Integrating the brainwashing and drift models. *Journal for the Scientific Study of Religion, 22,* 1–14.

Lo Presto, C. T., Sherman, M. F., & Dicarlo, M. A. (1994–1995). Factors affecting the unacceptability of suicide and the effects of evaluator depression and religiosity. *Omega, 30,* 205–221.

Lottes, I., Weinberg, M., & Weller, I. (1993). Reactions to pornography on a college campus: For or against? *Sex Roles, 29,* 69–89.

Lovekin, A., & Malony, H. N. (1977). Religious glossolalia: A longitudinal study of personality changes. *Journal for the Scientific Study of Religion, 16,* 383–393.

Loveland, G. G. (1968). The effects of bereavement on certain religious attitudes. *Sociological Symposium, 1,* 17–27.

Lowe, C. M. (1955). Religious beliefs and religious delusions. *American Journal of Psychotherapy, 9,* 54–61.

Lowe, C. M., & Braaten, R. O. (1966). Differences in religious attitudes in mental illness. *Journal for the Scientific Study of Religion, 5,* 435–445.

Ludwig, D. J., Weber, T., & Iben, D. (1974). Letters to God: A study of children's religious concepts. *Journal of Psychology and Theology, 2,* 31–35.

Luft, G. A., & Sorell, G. T. (1987). Parenting style and parent–adolescent religious value consensus. *Journal of Adolescent Research, 2,* 53–68.

Lukoff, D., & Lu, F. G. (1988). Transpersonal psychology research review topic: Mystical experience. *Journal of Transpersonal Psychology, 20,* 161–184.

Lukoff, D., Lu, F., & Turner, R. (1992). Toward a more culturally sensitive DSM-IV: Psychoreligious and psychospiritual problems. *Journal of Nervous and Mental Disease. 180,* 673–682.

Lukoff, D., Zanger, R., & Lu, F. (1990). Transpersonal psychology research review: Psychoactive substances and transpersonal states. *Journal of Transpersonal Psychology, 22,* 107–148.

Lundberg, F. (1968). *The rich and the super-rich.* New York: Lyle Stuart.

Lundé, D., & Segal, H. (1987). Psychiatric testimony in "cult" litigation. *Bulletin of the American Academy of Psychiatry and the Law, 15,* 205–210.

Lupfer, M. B., Brock, K. F., & DePaola, S. J. (1992). The use of secular and religious attributions to explain everyday behavior. *Journal for the Scientific Study of Religion, 31,* 486–503.

Lupfer, M. B., DePaola, S., Brock, K. F., & Clement, L. (1994). Making secular and religious attributions: The availability hypothesis revisited. *Journal for the Scientific Study of Religion, 33,* 162–171.

Lutoslawski, W. (1923). The conversion of a psychologist. *Hibbert Journal, 21,* 697–710.

MacDonald, C. B., & Luckett, J. B. (1983). Religious affiliation and psychiatric diagnoses. *Journal for the Scientific Study of Religion, 22,* 15–37.

MacDonald, W. L. (1992). Idionecrophanies: The social construction of perceived contact with the dead. *Journal for the Scientific Study of Religion, 31,* 215–223.

Maddi, S. (1970). The search for meaning. In W. J. Arnold & M. M. Page (Eds.), *Nebraska symposium on motivation* (Vol. 18, pp. 137–186). Lincoln: University of Nebraska Press.

Madsen, G. E., & Vernon, G. M. (1983). Maintaining the faith during college: A study of campus religious group participation. *Review of Religious Research, 25,* 127–141.

Magni, K. G. (1972). The fear of death: Studies of its character and concomitants. In A. Godin (Ed.), *Death and presence* (pp. 129–142). Brussels: Lumn Vitae Press.

Magnusson, D. (Ed.). (1981). *Toward a psychology of situations.* Hillsdale, NJ: Erlbaum.

Makela, K. (1975). Consumption level and cultural drinking patterns as determinants of alcohol problems. *Journal of Drug Issues, 5,* 433–357.

Makepeace, J. M. (1987). Social and victim–offender differences in courtship violence. *Family Relations Journal of Applied Family and Child Studies, 36,* 87–91.

Malinowski, B. (1965). The role of magic and religion. In W. A. Lessa & E. Z. Vogt (Eds.), *A reader in contemporary religion* (pp. 63–72). New York: Harper & Row.

Maller, J. B. (1960). The role of education in Jewish history. In L. Finkelstein (Ed.), *The Jews: Their history, culture, and religion* (3rd ed., Vol. 2, pp. 1234–1253). New York: Jewish Publication Society of America.

Malony, H. N. (1973). Religious experience: Inclusive and exclusive. In W. H. Clark, H. N. Malony, J. Daane, & A. R. Tippett (Eds.), *Religious experience: Its nature and function in the human psyche* (pp. 77–91). Springfield, IL: Charles C Thomas.

Malony, H. N. (1978, June). Pastoring about death to dying persons. *Theology: News and Notes,* pp. 16–18.

Malony, H. N. (Ed.). (1991). *Psychology of religion: Personalities, problems, possibilities.* Grand Rapids, MI: Baker.

Malony, H. N., & Lovekin, A. A. (1985). *Glossolalia: Behavioral science perspectives on speaking in tongues.* New York: Oxford University Press.

Malzberg, B. (1973). The distribution of mental disease according to religious affiliation in New York State 1949–1951. In A. Shiloh & C. Cohen (Eds.), *Ethnic groups of America: Their morbidity, mortality, and behavior disorders: Vol. 1. The Jews* (pp. 284–295). Springfield, IL: Charles C Thomas.

Manfredi, C., & Pickett, M. (1987). Perceived stressful situations and coping strategies utilized by the elderly. *Journal of Community Mental Health Nursing, 4,* 99–110.

Maranell, G. M. (1974). *Responses to religion.* Lawrence: University of Kansas Press.

Margaret Louise, Sister. (1961). Psychological problems to vocation candidates. *National Catholic Education Association Bulletin, 58,* 450–454.

Margolis, R. D., & Elifson, K. W. (1979). Typology of religious experience. *Journal for the Scientific Study of Religion, 18,* 61–67.

Marin, G. (1976). Social-psychological correlates of drug use among Colombian university students. *International Journal of the Addictions, 11,* 199–207.

Marlasch, C. (1979). The emotional consequences of arousal without reason. In C. E. Izard (Ed.), *Emotions in personality and psychophysiology* (pp. 565–590). New York: Plenum Press.

Marshall, J. L. (1994a, November). *Lesbian relationships and pastoral care: Covenants and holy unions in the context of church and synagogue.* Paper presented at the annual meeting of the Society for the Scientific Study of Religion, Albuquerque, NM.

Marshall, J. L. (1994b). *Sexual identity and pastoral concerns: Caring with women who are developing lesbian identities.* Unpublished manuscript.

Marsiglio, W. (1993). Attitudes toward homosexual activity and gays as friends: A national survey of heterosexual 15- to 19-year-old males. *Journal of Sex Research, 30,* 12–17.

Martin, D., & Wrightsman, L. S., Jr. (1964). Religion and fears about death: A critical review. *Religious Education, 59,* 174–176.

Martin, W. T. (1984). Religiosity and United States suicide rates, 1972–1978. *Journal of Clinical Psychology, 40,* 1166–1169.

Marty, M. E. (1959). *The new shape of American religion.* New York: Harper & Row.

Marty, M. E., & Appleby, R. S. (Eds.). (1991). *Fundamentalisms observed.* Chicago: University of Chicago Press.

Marty, M. E., Rosenberg, S. E., & Greeley, A. M. (1968). *What do we believe?* New York: Meredith.

Maslow, A. H. (1954). *Motivation and personality.* New York: Harper.

Maslow, A. H. (1964). *Religions, values, and peak-experiences.* Columbus: Ohio State University Press.

Masterman, M. (1970). The nature of paradigm. In I. Lakotos & A. Musgraves (Eds.), *Criticism and the growth of knowledge* (pp. 59–89). Cambridge, England: Cambridge University Press.

Masters, K. S., & Bergin, A. E. (1992). Religious orientation and mental health. In J. F. Schumaker (Ed.), *Religion and mental health* (pp. 221–232). New York: Oxford University Press.

Masters, R. E. L., & Houston, J. (1966). *The varieties of psychedelic experience.* New York: Delta.

Masters, R. E. L., & Houston, J. (1973). Subjective realities. In B. Schwartz (Ed.), *Human connection and the new media* (pp. 88–106). Englewood Cliffs, NJ: Prentice-Hall.

Mathes, E. W. (1982). Mystical experience, romantic love, and hypnotic susceptibility. *Psychological Reports, 50,* 701–702.

Mathes, E. W., Zevon, M., Roter, P., & Joerger, S. (1982). Peak experience tendencies: Scale development and theory testing. *Journal of Humanistic Psychology, 22,* 92–108.

Mathews, S., & Smith, G. B. (Eds.). (1923). *A dictionary of religion and ethics.* New York: Macmillan.

Maton, K. I. (1989). The stress-buffering role of spiritual support: Cross-sectional and prospective investigations. *Journal for the Scientific Study of Religion, 28,* 310–323.

Matthews, A. P. (1994, November). *The sexuality of submissive wives.* Paper presented at the annual meeting of the Society for the Scientific Study of Religion, Albuquerque, NM.

Matthews, K. A., Batson, C. D., Horn, J., & Rosenman, R. H. (1981). "Principles in his nature which interest him in the fortune of others . . .": The heritability of empathic concern for others. *Journal of Personality, 49,* 237–247.

Mattlin, J. A., Wethington, E., & Kessler, R. C. (1990). Situational determinants of coping and coping effectiveness. *Journal of Health and Social Behavior, 31,* 103–122.

Maupin, E. W. (1965). Individual differences in response to a Zen meditation exercise. *Consulting Psychology, 29,* 139–143.

Maxwell, M., & Tschudin, V. (Eds.). (1990). *Seeing the invisible: Modern religious and other transcendent experiences.* London: Penguin Books.

Maxwell, M. A. (1984). *The Alcoholics Anonymous experience: A close-up view for professionals.* New York: McGraw-Hill.

May, C. L. (1956). A survey of glossolalia and related phenomena in non-Christian religions. *American Anthropologist, 58,* 75–96.

Mazlish, B. (1975). *James and John Stuart Mill.* New York: Basic Books.

McCallister, B. J. (1995). Cognitive psychology and religious experience. In R. W. Hood, Jr. (Ed.), *Handbook of religious experience* (pp. 312–352). Birmingham, AL: Religious Education Press.

McCartin, R., & Freehill, M. (1986). Values of early adolescents compared by type of school. *Journal of Early Adolescence, 6,* 369–380.

McClelland, D. C. (1955). Some social consequences of achievement motivation. In M. R. Jones (Ed.), *Nebraska Symposium on Motivation* (Vol. 3, pp. 41–65). Lincoln: University of Nebraska Press.

McClelland, D. C., Atkinson, J. W., Clark, R. A., & Lowell, E. L. (1953). *The achievement motive.* New York: Appleton-Century-Crofts.

McClelland, D. C., Rindlisbacher, A., & DeCharms, R. (1955). Religious and other sources of parental attitudes toward independence training. In D. C. McClelland (Ed.), *Studies in motivation* (pp. 389–397). New York: Appleton-Century-Crofts.

McClenon, J. (1984). *Deviant science.* Philadelphia: University of Pennsylvania Press.

McClenon, J. (1990). Chinese and American anomalous experiences. *Sociological Analysis, 51,* 53–67.

McClosky, H., & Brill, A. (1983). *Dimensions of tolerance: What Americans believe about civil liberties.* New York: Russell Sage Foundation.

McConahay, J. B., & Hough, J. C., Jr. (1973). Love and guilt-oriented dimensions of Christian belief. *Journal for the Scientific Study of Religion, 12,* 53–64.

McCutcheon, A. L. (1988). Denominations and religious intermarriage: Trends among white Americans in the twentieth century. *Review of Religious Research, 29,* 213–227.

McDargh, J. (1983). *Object-relations theory and the psychology of religion.* Lanham, MD: University Press of America.

McDougall, W. (1909). *An introduction to social psychology* (2nd ed.). Boston: J. W. Luce.

McFarland, S. G. (1989). Religious orientations and the targets of discrimination. *Journal for the Scientific Study of Religion, 28,* 324–336.

McFarland, S. G. (1990). *Religiously oriented prejudice in communism and Christianity: The role of quest.* Paper presented at the annual meeting of the Southeastern Psychological Association, Atlanta.

McGinley, P. (1969). *Saint-watching.* New York: Viking.

McGinn, B. (1991). Appendix: Theoretical foundations: The modern study of mysticism. In B. McGinn (Ed.), *The foundations of mysticism* (pp. 265–343). New York: Crossroads.

McGuire, M. B. (1990). Religion and the body: Rematerializing the human body in the social sciences of religion. *Journal for the Scientific Study of Religion, 29,* 283–296.

McGuire, M. B. (1992). *Religion: The social context* (3rd ed.). Belmont, CA: Wadsworth.

McGuire, M. B. (1993). Health and healing in new religious movements. *Annals of the American Academy of Political and Social Science, 527,* 144–154.

McIntosh, D. N. (1995). Religion as schema, with implications for the relation between religion and coping. *International Journal for the Psychology of Religion, 5,* 1–16.

McIntosh, D. N., Kojetin, B. A., & Spilka, B. (1985). *Form of personal faith and general and specific locus of control.* Paper presented at the annual meeting of the Rocky Mountain Psychological Association, Tucson, AZ.

McIntosh, D. N., Silver, R. C., & Wortman, C. B. (1989, October). *Parental religious change in response to their child's death.* Paper presented at the annual meeting of the Society for the Scientific Study of Religion, Salt Lake City, UT.

McIntosh, D. N., Silver, R. C., & Wortman, C. B. (1993). Religion's role in adjustment to a negative life event: Coping with the loss of a child. *Journal of Personality and Social Psychology, 65,* 812–821.

McIntosh, D. N., & Spilka, B. (1990). Religion and physical health: The role of personal faith and control beliefs. In M. L. Lynn & D. O. Moberg (Eds.), *Research in the social scientific study of religion* (Vol. 2, pp. 167–194). Greenwich, CT: JAI Press.

McKenna, R. H. (1976). Good Samaritanism in rural and urban settings: A nonreactive comparison of helping behavior of clergy and control subjects. *Representative Research in Social Psychology, 7,* 58–65.

McKeon, R. (Ed.). (1941). *The basic works of Aristotle.* New York: Random House.

McLoughlin, W. F. (1978). *Revivals, awakenings, and reform.* Chicago: University of Chicago Press.

McNeill, J. T. (1951). *A history of the cure of souls.* New York: Harper.

McRae, R. R. (1984). Situational determinants of coping responses: Loss, threat, and challenge. *Journal of Personality and Social Psychology, 46,* 919–928.

McRae, R. R., & Costa, P. T. (1986). Personality, coping, and coping effectiveness in an adult sample. *Journal of Personality, 54,* 385–405.

Mead, F. S. (Ed.). (1965). *The encyclopedia of quotations.* Westwood, NJ: Fleming H. Revell.

Mead, G. H. (1934). *Mind, self, and society.* Chicago: University of Chicago Press.

Meadow, M. J., & Kahoe, R. D. (1984). *Psychology of religion: Religion in individual lives.* New York: Harper & Row.

Meier, P. D. (1977). *Christian child-rearing and personality development.* Grand Rapids, MI: Baker.

Menges, R. J., & Dittes, J. E. (1965). *Psychological studies of clergymen: Abstracts of research.* New York: Nelson.

Meyer, M. S., Altmaier, E. M., & Burns, C. P. (1992). Religious orientation and coping with cancer. *Journal of Religion and Health, 31,* 273–279.

Miller, A. S., & Hoffman, J. P. (1995). Risk and religion: An explanation of gender differences in religiosity. *Journal for the Scientific Study of Religion, 34,* 63–75.

Miller, J. B. (1986). *Toward a new psychology of women* (2nd ed.). Boston: Beacon Press.

Miller, W. (1973). *Why do Christians break down?* Minneapolis: Augsburg.

Mills, C. W. (1959). *The sociological imagination.* New York: OxfordUniversity Press.

Minton, B., & Spilka, B. (1976). Perspectives on death in relation to powerlessness and form of personal religion. *Omega, 7,* 261–267.

Mitchell, C. E. (1988). Paralleling cognitive and moral development with spiritual development and denominational choice. *Psychology: A Quarterly Journal of Human Behavior, 25,* 1–9.

Moberg, D. O. (1965). The integration of older members in the church congregation. In A. M. Rose & W. A. Peterson (Eds.), *Older people and their social worlds* (pp. 125–140). Philadelphia: F. A. Davis.

Moberg, D. O. (1971). Religious practices. In M. P. Strommen (Ed.), *Research on religious development: A comprehensive handbook* (pp. 551–598). New York: Hawthorn Books.

Moberg, D. O., & Hoge, D. R. (1986). Catholic college students' religious and moral attitudes, 1961 to 1982: Effects of the sixties and seventies. *Review of Religious Research, 28,* 104–117.

Moen, M. C. (1990). Ronald Reagan and the social issues: Rhetorical support for the Christian right. *Social Science Journal, 27,* 199–207.

Monaghan, R. R. (1967). Three faces of the true believer: Motivations for attending a fundamentalist church. *Journal for the Scientific Study of Religion, 6,* 236–245.

Montgomery, R. L. (1991). The spread of religions and macrosocial relations. *Sociological Analysis, 52,* 14–22.

Moody, R. (1976). *Life after life.* New York: Bantam.

Mora, G. (1969). The scrupulosity syndrome. In E. M. Pattison (Ed.), *Clinical psychiatry and religion* (pp. 163–174). Boston: Little, Brown.

Moracco, J. C., & Richardson, G. (1985). *Stress in the clergy: The relationship of demographic and personal variables on perceptions.* Paper presented at the annual meeting of the American Psychological Association, Los Angeles.

Morinis, A. (1985). The religious experience: Pain and the transformation of consciousness in ordeals of initiation. *Ethos, 13,* 150–174.

Morreim, D. C. (1991). *Changed lives: The story of Alcoholics Anonymous.* Minneapolis: Augsburg.

Morris, R. J., & Hood, R. W., Jr. (1980). Religious and unity criteria of Baptists and nones in the report of mystical experience. *Psychological Reports, 46,* 728–730.

Morris, R. J., Hood, R. W., Jr., & Watson, P. J. (1989). A second look at religious orientation, social desirability and prejudice. *Bulletin of the Psychonomic Society, 27,* 81–84.

Mowrer, O. H. (1958). Discussion: Symposium on relationships between religion and mental health. *American Psychologist, 13,* 576–579.

Mowrer, O. H. (1961). *The crisis in psychiatry and religion.* Princeton, NJ: Van Nostrand.

Mueller, D. J. (1967). Effects and effectiveness of parochial elementary schools: An empirical study. *Review of Religious Research, 9,* 48–51.

Muller, M. (1889). *Natural religion.* New York: Longmans, Green.

Munnichs, J. M. A. (1980). *Old age and finitude.* New York: Arno Press.

Myers, D. (1987). *Social psychology* (2nd ed.). New York: McGraw-Hill.

Myers, D. G. (1992). *The pursuit of happiness.* New York: William Morrow.

Myers, F. W. H. (1961). *Human personality and its survival of bodily death.* New Hyde Park, NY: University Books. (Original work published 1903)

Nagi, M. H., Pugh, M. D., & Lazerine, N. G. (1977–1978). Attitudes of Catholic and Protestant clergy toward euthanasia. *Omega, 8*, 153–164.

Naisbitt, J., & Aburdene, P. (1990). *Megatrends 2000*. New York: William Morrow.

Najman, J. M., Williams, G. M., Keeping, J. D., Morrison, J., & Anderson, M. L. (1988). Religious values, practices and pregnancy outcomes: A comparison of the impact of sect and mainstream Christian affiliation. *Social Science and Medicine, 26*, 401–407.

Naranjo, C., & Ornstein, R. E. (1971). *On the psychology of meditation*. New York: Viking.

Natera, G., et al. (1983). Patterns of alcohol consumption in two semirural areas between Honduras and Mexico. *Acta Psiquiatrica y Psicologica de America Latina, 29*, 116–127.

National Clearinghouse for Mental Health Information. (1967). *Bibliography on religion and mental health 1960–1964*. Washington, DC: U.S. Department of Health, Education and Welfare.

Nelsen, H. M. (1980). Religious transmission versus religious formation: Preadolescent–parent interaction. *Sociological Quarterly, 21*, 207–218.

Nelsen, H. M. (1981a). Gender differences in the effects of parental discord on preadolescent religiousness. *Journal for the Scientific Study of Religion, 20*, 351–360.

Nelsen, H. M. (1981b). Life without afterlife: Toward congruency of belief across generations. *Journal for the Scientific Study of Religion, 20*, 109–118.

Nelsen, H. M. (1981c). Religious conformity in an age of disbelief: Contextual effects of time, denomination, and family processes upon church decline and apostasy. *American Sociological Review, 46*, 632–640.

Nelsen, H. M. (1982). The influence of social and theological factors upon the goals of religious education. *Review of Religious Research, 23*, 255–263.

Nelsen, H. M., Cheek, N. H., Jr., & Au, P. (1985). Gender differences in images of God. *Journal for the Scientific Study of Religion, 24*, 396–402.

Nelsen, H. M., & Kroliczak, A. (1984). Parental use of the threat "God will punish": Replication and extension. *Journal for the Scientific Study of Religion, 23*, 267–277.

Nelsen, H. M., & Potvin, R. H. (1981). Gender and regional differences in the religiosity of Protestant adolescents. *Review of Religious Research, 22*, 268–285.

Nelsen, H. M., Potvin, R. H., & Shields, J. (1976). *The religion of children*. Unpublished manuscript, Catholic University of America.

Nelson, F. I. (1977). Religiosity and self-destructive crises in the institutionalized elderly. *Suicide and Life-threatening Behavior, 7*, 67–74.

Nelson, L. D., & Cantrell, C. H. (1980). Religiosity and death anxiety: A multidimensional analysis. *Review of Religious Research, 21*, 148–157.

Nelson, L. D., & Dynes, R. R. (1976). The impact of devotionalism and attendance on ordinary and emergency helping behavior. *Journal for the Scientific Study of Religion, 15*, 47–59.

Nelson, L. D., & Nelson, C. C. (1975). A factor-analytic investigation of the multidimensionality of death anxiety. *Omega, 6*, 171–178.

Nelson, M. O. (1971). The concept of God and feelings toward parents. *Journal of Individual Psychology, 27*, 46–49.

Nesbitt, P. D. (1990). *Feminization of American clergy: Occupational life in the ordained ministry*. Unpublished doctoral dissertation, Harvard University.

Nesbitt, P. D. (1993a). Dual ordination tracks: Differential benefits and costs for men and women clergy. *Sociology of Religion, 54*, 13–30.

Nesbitt, P. D. (1993b, August). *The democracy of experience in the ministry*. Paper presented at the meeting of the Association for the Sociology of Religion, Miami, FL.

Nesbitt, P. D. (1994, April). *Plausible but how progressive? A century of Unitarian and Universalist women in ministry*. Paper presented at the meeting of the American Academy of Religion, Rocky Mountain/Great Plains Region, Boulder, CO.

Neufeld, K. (1979). Child-rearing, religion and abusive parents. *Religious Education, 74*, 234–244.

Newcomb, T. M. (1962). Student peer-group influence. In N. Sanford (Ed.), *The American college: A psychological and social interpretation of the higher learning* (pp. 469–488). New York: Wiley.

Newman, B. M., & Newman, P. R. (1995). *Development through life: A psychosocial approach.* Pacific Grove, CA: Brooks/Cole.

Newman, J. S., & Pargament, K. I. (1990). The role of religion in the problem-solving process. *Review of Religious Research, 31,* 390–403.

Niebuhr, H. R. (1929). *The social sources of denominationalism.* New York: Holt, Rinehart & Winston.

Nipkow, K. E., & Schweitzer, F. (1991). Adolescents' justifications for faith or doubt in God: A study of fulfilled and unfulfilled expectations. In F. K. Oser & W. G. Scarlett (Eds.), *Religious development in childhood and adolescence* (New Directions for Child Development, No. 52, pp. 91–100). San Francisco: Jossey-Bass.

Nordquist, T. A. (1978). *Ananda cooperative village: A study in the beliefs, values and attitudes of a new age religious community.* Uppsala, Sweden: Borgstroms Tryckeri.

Nottingham, E. K. (1954). *Religion and society.* New York: Random House.

Nucci, L., & Turiel, E. (1993). God's word, religious rules, and their relation to Christian and Jewish children's concepts of morality. *Child Development, 64,* 1475–1491.

Nunn, C. Z. (1964). Child-control through a "coalition with God." *Child Development, 35,* 417–432.

Nuttin, J. (1962). *Psychoanalysis and personality.* New York: New American Library.

Nye, W. C., & Carlson, J. S. (1984). The development of the concept of God in children. *Journal of Genetic Psychology, 145,* 137–142.

Oates, W. (1955). *Religious factors in mental illness.* New York: Association Press.

O'Brien, C. R. (1979). Pastoral dimensions in death education research. *Journal of Religion and Health, 18,* 74–77.

O'Brien, E. (Ed.). (1965). *The varieties of mystical experience.* Garden City, NY: Doubleday/Anchor.

O'Brien, M. E. (1982). Religious faith and adjustment to long-term hemodialysis. *Journal of Religion and Health, 21,* 68–80.

O'Connell, D. C. (1961). Is mental illness a result of sin? In A. Godin (Ed.), *Child and adult before God* (pp. 55–64). Brussels: Lumen Vitae Press.

O'Dea, T. F. (1961). Five dilemmas in the institutionalization of religion. *Journal for the Scientific Study of Religion, 1,* 30–39.

O'Donnell, J. P. (1993). Predicting tolerance for new religious movements: A multivariate analysis. *Journal for the Scientific Study of Religion, 32,* 356–365.

O'Faolain, J., & Martinez, L. (Eds.). (1973). *Not in God's image.* New York: Harper & Row.

Oken, D. (1973). Alienation and identity: Some comments on adolescence, the counter-culture, and contemporary adaptations. In F. Johnson (Ed.), *Alienation: Concept, term, and meanings* (pp. 83–110). New York: Seminar Press.

Oleckno, W. A., & Blacconiere, M.J. (1991). Relationship of religiosity to wellness and other health-related behaviors and outcomes. *Psychological Reports, 68,* 819–826.

Oliner, S. P., & Oliner, P. M. (1988). *The altruistic personality: Rescuers of Jews in Nazi Europe.* New York: Free Press.

Olson, D. V. A. (1989). Church friendships: Boon or barrier to church growth? *Journal for the Scientific Study of Religion, 28,* 432–447.

Ornstein, R. O. (1986). *The psychology of human consciousness* (3rd. ed.). New York: Viking Press.

Osarchuk, M., & Tatz, S. J. (1973). Effect of induced fear of death on belief in an afterlife. *Journal of Personality and Social Psychology, 27,* 256–260.

Oser, F. K. (1991). The development of religious judgment. In F. K. Oser & W. G. Scarlett (Eds.), *Religious development in childhood and adolescence* (New Directions for Child Development, No. 52, pp. 5–25). San Francisco: Jossey-Bass.

Oser, F. K., & Gmunder, P. (1991). *Religious judgement: A developmental approach* (H. F. Hahn, Trans.). Birmingham, AL: Religious Education Press. (Original work published 1984)

Oser, F., & Reich, K. H. (1990a). Moral judgment, religious judgment, worldview, and logical thought: A review of their relationship—Part one. *British Journal of Religious Education, 12,* 94–101.

Oser, F., & Reich, H. (1990b). Moral judgment, religious judgment, world view and logical thought: A review of their relationship—Part two. *British Journal of Religious Education, 12,* 172–180.

Oser, F. K., Reich, K. H., & Bucher, A. A. (1994). Development of belief and unbelief in childhood and adolescence. In J. Corveleyn & D. Hutsebaut (Eds.), *Belief and unbelief: Psychological perspectives* (pp. 39–62). Atlanta: Rodopi.

Oser, F. K., & Scarlett, W. G. (Eds.). (1991). *Religious development in childhood and adolesence* (New Directions for Child Development, No. 52.) San Francisco: Jossey-Bass.

Oshodin, O. G. (1983). Alcohol abuse: A case study of secondary school students in a rural area of Benin district, Nigeria. *Journal of Alcohol and Drug Education, 29,* 40–47.

Ostow, M. (1990). The fundamentalist phenomenon: A psychological perspective. In N. J. Cohen (Ed.), *The fundamentalist phenomenon* (pp. 99–125). Grand Rapids, MI: William B. Eerdmans.

Ostow, M., & Scharfstein, B. A. (1954). *The need to believe.* New York: International Universities Press.

Otto, R. (1932). *Mysticism East and West* (B. L. Bracey & R. C. Payne, Trans.). New York: Macmillan.

Otto, R. (1958). *The idea of the holy* (J. W. Harvey, Trans.). London: Oxford University Press. (Original work published 1917)

Overholser, W. (1963). Psychopathology in religious experience. In *Research in religion and mental health: Proceedings of the Fifth Academy Symposium, 1961, of the Academy of Religion and Mental Health* (pp. 100–116). New York: Fordham University Press.

Owens, C. M. (1972). The mystical experience: Facts and values. In J. White (Ed.), *The highest state of consciousness* (pp. 135–152). Garden City, NY: Doubleday/Anchor.

Oxman, T. E., Rosenberg, S. D., Schnurr, P. P., Tucker, G. J., & Gala, G. G. (1988). The language of altered states. *Journal of Nervous and Mental Disease, 176,* 401–408.

Ozorak, E. W. (1989). Social and cognitive influences on the development of religious beliefs and commitment in adolescence. *Journal for the Scientific Study of Religion, 28,* 448–463.

Ozorak, E. W. (1996). The power, but not the glory: How women empower themselves through religion. *Journal for the Scientific Study of Religion, 35,* 17–29.

Pafford, M. (1973). *Inglorious Wordsworths: A study of some transcendental experiences in childhood and adolescence.* London: Hodder & Stoughton.

Pagelow, M. D., & Johnson, P. (1988). Abuse in the American family: The role of religion. In A. L. Horton & J. A. Williamson (Eds.), *Abuse and religion: When praying isn't enough* (pp. 1–12). Lexington, MA: Lexington Books.

Pahnke, W. N. (1966). Drugs and mysticism. *International Journal of Parapsychology, 8,* 295–320.

Pahnke, W. N. (1969). Psychedelic drugs and mystical experience. In E. M. Pattison (Ed.), *Clinical psychiatry and religion* (pp. 149–162). Boston: Little, Brown.

Paine, T. (1897). *The political works of Thomas Paine.* Chicago: Donahue.

Palmer, C. E., & Noble, D. N. (1986). Premature death: Dilemmas of infant mortality. *Social Casework, 67,* 332–339.

Paloutzian, R. F. (1981). Purpose-in-life and value changes following religious conversion. *Journal of Personality and Social Psychology, 41,* 1153–1168.

Paloutzian, R. F. (1996). *Invitation to the psychology of religion* (2nd ed.). Boston: Allyn & Bacon.

Paloutzian, R. F., Jackson, S. L., & Crandell, J. E. (1978). Conversion experience, belief system, and personal and ethical attitudes. *Journal of Psychology and Theology, 6,* 266–275.

Pancer, S. M., Jackson, L. M., Hunsberger, B., Pratt, M., & Lea, J. (1995). Religious orthodoxy and the complexity of thought about religious and non-religious issues. *Journal of Personality, 63,* 213–232.

Pargament, K. I. (1992). Of means and ends: Religion and the search for significance. *International Journal for the Psychology of Religion, 2,* 201–229.

Pargament, K. (in press). *God help me: The psychology of religion and coping.* New York: Guilford Press.

Pargament, K. I., Brannick, M. T., Adamakos, D. S., Ensing, M., Keleman, M. L., Warren, R. K., Falgout, K., Cook, P., & Myers, J. (1987). Indiscriminate proreligiousness: Conceptualization and measurement. *Journal for the Scientific Study of Religion, 26,* 182–200.

Pargament, K. I., Ensing, D. S., Falgout, K., Olsen, H., Reilly, B., Van Haitsma, K., & Warren, R. (1990). God help me: I. Coping efforts as predictors of the outcomes to significant negative life events. *American Journal of Community Psychology, 18,* 793–824.

Pargament, K. I., & Hahn, J. (1986). God and the just world: Causal and coping attributions to God in health situations. *Journal for the Scientific Study of Religion, 25,* 193–207.

Pargament, K. I., Kennell, J., Hathaway, W., Grevengoed, N., Newman, J., & Jones, W. (1988). Religion and the problem-solving process: Three styles of coping. *Journal for the Scientific Study of Religion, 27,* 90–104.

Pargament, K. I., Steele, R. E., & Tyler, F. B. (1979). Religious participation, religious motivation, and individual psychosocial competence. *Journal for the Scientific Study of Religion, 18,* 412–419.

Park, C., & Cohen, L. H. (1993). Religious and nonreligious coping with the death of a friend. *Cognitive Therapy and Research, 17,* 561–577.

Park, C., Cohen, L. H., & Herb, L. (1990). Intrinsic religiousness and religious coping as life stress moderators for Catholics versus Protestants. *Journal of Personality and Social Psychology, 59,* 562–574.

Parker, C. A. (1971). Changes in religious beliefs of college students. In M. P. Strommen (Ed.), *Research on religious development: A comprehensive handbook* (pp. 724–776). New York: Hawthorn Books.

Parker, G. (1983). *Parental overprotection.* New York: Grune & Stratton.

Parker, G., Tupling, H., & Brown, L. B. (1979). A parental bonding instrument. *British Journal of Medical Psychology, 52,* 1–10.

Parker, G., & Brown, L. B. (1982). Coping behaviors that mediate between life events and depression. *Archives of General Psychiatry, 39,* 1386–1391.

Parker, I. (1989). *The crisis in social psychology and how to end it.* New York: Routledge.

Parker, I., & Shotter, J. (Eds.). (1987). *Deconstructing social psychology.* New York: Routledge.

Parker, M., & Gaier, E. L. (1980). Religion, religious beliefs, and religious practices among Conservative Jewish adolescents. *Adolescence, 15,* 361–374.

Parkes, C. M. (1972). *Bereavement: Studies of grief in later life.* New York: International Universities Press.

Parrinder, G. (1980). *Sex in the world's religions.* New York: Oxford University Press.

Patrick, T., & Dulack, T. (1977). *Let our children go!* New York: Ballantine Books.

Pattison, M. (1968). Behavioral science research on the nature of glossolalia. *Journal of the American Scientific Affiliation, 20,* 73–86.

Patton, M. S. (1988). Suffering and damage in Catholic sexuality. *Journal of Religion and Health, 27,* 129–142.

Peatling, J. H. (1974). Cognitive development in pupils in grades four through twelve: The incidence of concrete and religious thinking. *Character Potential, 7,* 52–61.

Peatling, J. H. (1977). Cognitive development: Religious thinking in children, youth and adults. *Character Potential, 8,* 100–115.

Peatling, J. H., & Laabs, C. W. (1975). Cognitive development in pupils in grades four through twelve: The incidence of concrete and abstract religious thinking. *Character Potential, 7,* 107–115.

Peek, C. W., Curry, E. W., & Chalfant, H. P. (1985). Religiosity and delinquency over time: Deviance, deterrence and deviance amplification. *Social Science Quarterly, 66,* 120–131.

Peel, R. (1987). *Spiritual healing in a scientific age.* San Francisco: Harper & Row.

Pelletier, K. R., & Garfield, C. (1976). *Consciousness: East and West.* New York: Harper & Row.

Perkins, H. W. (1994). The contextual effect of secular norms on religiosity as moderator of student alcohol and other drug use. In M. L. Lynn & D. O Moberg (Eds.), *Research in the social scientific study of religion* (Vol. 6, pp. 187–208). Greenwich, CT: JAI Press.

Perry, E. L., Davis, J. H., Doyle, R. T., & Dyble, J. E. (1980). Toward a typology of unchurched Protestants. *Review of Religious Research, 21,* 388–404.

Perry, E. L., & Hoge, D. R. (1981). Faith priorities of pastor and laity as a factor in the growth and decline of Presbyterian congregations. *Review of Religious Research, 22,* 221–241.

Perry, N., & Echeverría, L. (1988). *Under the heal of Mary.* London: Routledge & Kegan Paul.

Perry, R. B. (1935). *The thought and character of William James* (2 vols.). Boston: Little, Brown.

Persinger, M. A. (1987). *Neurophysiological basis of God beliefs.* New York: Praeger.

Persinger, M. A., & Makarec, K. (1987). Temporal lobe epileptic signs and correlative behaviors displayed in normal populations. *Journal of General Psychology, 114,* 1790–1795.

Peter, L. (Ed.). (1977). *Peter's quotations.* New York: Bantam.

Peters, J. F. (1985). Adolescents as socialization agents to parents. *Adolescence, 20,* 921–933.

Petersen, A. C. (1988). Adolescent development. *Annual Review of Psychology, 39*, 583–607.

Peterson, C., Seligman, M. E. P., & Vaillant, G. E. (1988). Pessimistic explanatory style is a risk factor for physical illness: A thirty-five year longitudinal study. *Journal of Personality and Social Psychology, 55*, 23–27.

Peterson, L. R., & Roy, A. (1985). Religiosity, and meaning and purpose: Religion's consequences for psychological well-being. *Review of Religious Research, 27*, 49–63.

Petraitis, J., Flay, B. R., & Miller, T. Q. (1995). Reviewing theories of adolescent substance use: Organizing pieces in the puzzle. *Psychological Bulletin, 117*, 67–86.

Pettersson, T. (1991). Religion and criminality: Structural relationships between church involvement and crime rates in contemporary Sweden. *Journal for the Scientific Study of Religion, 30*, 279–291.

Pevey, C. (1994, November). *Submission and power among Southern Baptist Ladies.* Paper presented at the annual meeting of the Society for the Scientific Study of Religion, Albuquerque, NM.

Pfeiffer, J. E. (1992). The psychological framing of cults: Schematic representations and cult evaluations. *Journal of Applied Social Psychology, 22*, 531–544.

Phares, E. J. (1976). *Locus of control in personality.* Morristown, NJ: General Learning Press.

Philibert, P. J., & Hoge, D. R. (1982). Teachers, pedagogy and the process of religious education. *Review of Religious Research, 23*, 264–285.

Phillips, D. Z. (1981). *The concept of prayer.* New York: Seabury Press.

Piaget, J. (1948). *The moral judgment of the child* (M. Gabain, Trans.). Glencoe, IL: Free Press. (Original work published 1932)

Piaget, J. (1952). *The origins of intelligence in children* (M. Cook, Trans.). New York: International Universities Press. (Original work published 1936)

Piaget, J. (1954). *The construction of reality in the child* (M. Cook, Trans.). New York: Basic Books. (Original work published 1937)

Pilarzyk, K. T. (1978). The origin, development and decline of a youth culture movement: An application of sectarianization theory. *Review of Religious Research, 20*, 23–43.

Pilkington, G. W., Poppleton, P. K., Gould, J. B., & McCourt, M. M. (1976). Changes in religious beliefs, practices and attitudes among university students over an eleven-year period in relation to sex differences, denominational differences and differences between faculties and years of study. *British Journal of Social and Clinical Psychology, 15*, 1–9.

Plaskow, J., & Romero, J. A. (Eds.). (1974). *Women and religion* (rev. ed.). Missoula, MT: Scholars Press.

Ploch, D. R., & Hastings, D. W. (1994). Graphic presentations of church attendance using General Social Survey data. *Journal for the Scientific Study of Religion, 33*, 16–33.

Plutchik, R., & Ax, F. A. (1967). A critique of "Determinants of emotional state" by Schachter and Singer. *Psychophysiology, 4*, 79–82.

Polanyi, M., & Prosch, H. (1975). *Meaning.* Chicago: University of Chicago Press.

Pollner, M. (1989). Divine relations, social relations, and well-being. *Journal of Health and Social Behavior, 30*, 92–104.

Poloma, M. M. (1991). A comparison of Christian Science and mainline Christian healing ideologies and practices. *Review of Religious Research, 32*, 337–350.

Poloma, M. M., & Gallup, G. H., Jr. (1990, November). *Religiosity, forgiveness and life satisfaction: An exploratory study.* Paper presented at the annual meeting of the Society for the Scientific Study of Religion, Virginia Beach, VA.

Poloma, M. M., & Gallup, G. H., Jr. (1991). *Varieties of prayer: A survey report.* Philadelphia: Trinity Press International.

Poloma, M. M., & Pendleton, B. F. (1989). Exploring types of prayer and quality of life research: A research note. *Review of Religious Research, 31*, 46–53.

Poloma, M. M., & Pendleton, B. (1991a). The effects of prayer and prayer experiences on measures of general well-being. *Journal of Psychology and Theology, 19*, 71–83.

Poloma, M. M., & Pendleton, B. F. (1991b). *Exploring neglected dimensions of quality of life research.* Lewiston, NY: Edwin Mellen.

Ponton, M. O., & Gorsuch, R. L. (1988). Prejudice and religion revisited: A cross-cultural investigation with a Venezuelan sample. *Journal for the Scientific Study of Religion, 27*, 260–271.

Poston, L. (1992). *Islamic* da wah *in the West.* Oxford: Oxford University Press.

Potvin, R. H. (1977). Adolescent God images. *Review of Religious Research, 19,* 43–53.

Potvin, R. H., Hoge, D. R., & Nelsen, H. M. (1976). *Religion and American youth: With emphasis on Catholic adolescents and young adults.* Washington, DC: United States Catholic Conference.

Potvin, R. H., & Sloane, D. M. (1985). Parental control, age, and religious practice. *Review of Religious Research, 27,* 3–14.

Pratt, J. B. (1920). *The religious consciousness: A psychological study.* New York: Macmillan.

Pratt, M. W., Hunsberger, B., Pancer, S. M., & Roth, D. (1992). Reflections on religion: Aging, belief orthodoxy, and interpersonal conflict in adult thinking about religious issues. *Journal for the Scientific Study of Religion, 31,* 514–522.

Pressman, P., Lyons, J. S., Larson, D. B., & Gartner, J. (1992). Religion, anxiety, and fear of death. In J. F. Schumaker (Ed.), *Religion and mental health* (pp. 98–109). New York: Oxford University Press.

Pressman, P., Lyons, J. S., Larson, D. B., & Strain, J. J. (1990). Religious belief, depression, and ambulation status in elderly women with broken hips. *American Journal of Psychiatry, 147,* 758–760.

Preston, D. L. (1981). Becoming a Zen practitioner. *Sociological Analysis, 42,* 47–55.

Preston, D. L. (1982). Meditative–ritual practice and spiritual conversion–commitment: Theoretical implications based upon the case of Zen. *Sociological Analysis, 43,* 257–270.

Preston, D. L. (1988). *The social organization of Zen practice.* Cambridge, England: Cambridge University Press.

Preus, J. S. (1987). *Explaining religion.* New Haven, CT: Yale University Press.

Preus, K. (1982). Tongues: An evaluation from a scientific perspective. *Concordia Theological Quarterly, 46,* 277–293.

Prince, R. H. (1992). Religious experience and psychopathology. In J. F. Schumaker (Ed.), *Religion and mental health* (pp. 281–290). New York: Oxford University Press.

Prince, R., & Savage, C. (1972). Mystical states and the concept of regression. In J. White (Ed.), *The highest state of consciousness* (pp. 114–134). Garden City, NY: Doubleday/Anchor.

Princeton Research Center. (1978). *The unchurched American.* Princeton, NJ: American Institute of Public Opinion.

Propst, L. R. (1980). The comparative efficacy of religious and nonreligious imagery for the treatment of mild depression in religious individuals. *Cognitive Therapy and Research, 4,* 167–178.

Propst, L. R. (1982). A model for counseling religious women: Depression and rape cases. *Counseling and Values, 26,* 141–149.

Propst, L. R. (1988). *Psychotherapy in a religious framework.* New York: Human Sciences Press.

Propst, L. R. (1992). Comparative efficacy of religious and nonreligious cognitive-behavioral therapy for the treatment of clinical depression in religious individuals. *Journal of Consulting and Clinical Psychology, 60,* 94–103.

Proudfoot, W. (1985). *Religious experience.* Berkeley: University of California Press.

Proudfoot, W., & Shaver, P. (1975). Attribution theory and the psychology of religion. *Journal for the Scientific Study of Religion, 14,* 317–330.

Pruyser, P. W. (1968). *A dynamic psychology of religion.* New York: Harper & Row.

Pruyser, P. W. (1971). A psychological view of religion in the 1970s. *Bulletin of the Menninger Clinic, 35,* 77–97.

Pruyser, P. W. (1974). *Between belief and unbelief.* New York: Harper & Row.

Pruyser, P. W. (1977). The seamy side of current religious beliefs. *Bulletin of the Menninger Clinic, 41,* 329–348.

Pruyser, P. W. (1986). Maintaining hope in adversity. *Pastoral Psychology, 35,* 120–131.

Putney, S., & Middleton, R. (1961). Rebellion, conformity, and parental religious ideologies. *Sociometry, 24,* 125–135.

Pylyshyn, Z. W. (1973). What a mind's eye tells the mind's brain. *Psychological Bulletin, 80,* 1–24.

Quebedeaux, R. A. (1989). Conservative Protestants in modern American society: Who's influencing whom? In W. R. Garrett (Ed.), *Social consequences of religious belief* (pp. 128–142). New York: Paragon House.

Quinley, H. E. (1974). *The prophetic clergy: Social activism among Protestant ministers.* New York: Wiley.

Rabinowitz, S. (1969). Developmental problems in Catholic seminarians. *Psychiatry, 32,* 107–117.

Rambo, L. R. (1982). Bibliography: Current research on religious conversion. *Religious Studies Review, 8,* 146–159.

Rambo, L. R. (1992). The psychology of conversion. In H. N. Malony & S. Southard (Eds.), *Handbook of religious conversion* (pp. 159–177). Birmingham, AL: Religious Education Press.

Rambo, L. R. (1993). *Understanding religious conversion.* New Haven, CT: Yale University Press.

Ramsey, G. V., & Seipp, M. (1948). Public opinion and information concerning mental health. *Journal of Clinical Psychology, 4,* 397–406.

Ranck, J. G. (1961). Religious conservatism–liberalism and mental health. *Pastoral Psychology, 12,* 34–40.

Randall, T. M., & Desrosiers, M. (1980). Measurement of supernatural belief: Sex differences and locus of control. *Journal of Personality Assessment, 44,* 493–498.

Rätsch, C. (Ed.). (1990). *Gateway to inner space: Sacred plants, mysticism and psychotherapy.* Dorset, England: Prism Press.

Rayburn, C. A., Richmond, L. J., & Rogers, L. (1983). Stress among religious leaders. *Thought, 58,* 329–344.

Rayburn, C. A., Richmond, L. J., & Rogers, L. (1986). Men, women, and religion: Stress within leadership roles. *Journal of Clinical Psychology, 42,* 540–546.

Rea, M. P., Greenspoon, S., & Spilka, B. (1975). Physicians and the terminal patient: Some selected attitudes and behavior. *Omega, 6,* 291–302.

Redekop, C. A. (1974). A new look at sect development. *Journal for the Scientific Study of Religion, 13,* 345–352.

Reed, G. (1974). *The psychology of anomalous experience.* Boston: Houghton Mifflin.

Reeves, N. C., & Boersma, F. J. (1989–1990). The therapeutic use of ritual in maladaptive grieving. *Omega, 20,* 281–291.

Reich, K. H. (1989). Between religion and science: Complementarity in the religious thinking of young people. *British Journal of Religious Education, 11,* 62–69.

Reich, K. H. (1991). The role of complementarity reasoning in religious development. In F. K. Oser & W. G. Scarlett (Eds.), *Religious development in childhood and adolescence* (New Directions for Child Development, No. 52, pp. 77–89). San Francisco: Jossey-Bass.

Reich, K. H. (1992). Religious development across the lifespan: Conventional and cognitive developmental approaches. In D. L. Featherman, R. M. Lerner, & M. Perlmutter (Eds.), *Life-span development and behavior* (Vol. 11, pp. 145–188). Hillsdale, NJ: Erlbaum.

Reich, K. H. (1993a). Cognitive-developmental approaches to religiousness: Which version for which purpose? *International Journal for the Psychology of Religion, 3,* 145–171.

Reich, K. H. (1993b). Integrating differing theories: The case of religious development. *Journal of Empirical Theology, 6,* 39–49.

Reich, K. H. (1994). Can one rationally understand Christian doctrines? An empirical study. *British Journal of Religious Education, 16,* 114–126.

Reich, K. H. (in press). Do we need a theory for the religious development of women? *International Journal for the Psychology of Religion.*

Reid, T. (1969). *The active powers of the human mind.* Cambridge, MA: MIT Press. (Original work published 1788)

Reifsnyder, W. E., & Campbell, E. I. (1960). Religious attitudes of male neuropsychiatric patients: I. Most frequently expressed attitudes. *Journal of Pastoral Care, 14,* 92–97.

Reik, T. (1946). *Ritual: Psychoanalytic studies.* New York: Farrar, Straus.

Reinert, D. F., & Stifler, K. R. (1993). Hood's Mysticism Scale revisited: A factor-analytic replication. *Journal for the Scientific Study of Religion, 32,* 383–388.

Rest, J. R. (1979). *Development in judging moral issues.* Minneappolis: University of Minnesota Press.

Rest, J. R. (1983). Morality. In J. H. Flavell & E. M. Markham (Vol. Eds.), *Handbook of child psychology* (4th ed.): *Vol. 3. Cognitive development* (pp. 556–629). New York: Wiley.

Rest, J., Cooper, D., Coder, R., Masanz, J., & Anderson, D. (1974). Judging the important issues in moral dilemmas: An objective measure of development. *Developmental Psychology, 10,* 491–501.

Reynolds, D. I. (1994). Religious influence and premarital sexual experience: Critical observations on the validity of a relationship. *Journal for the Scientific Study of Religion, 33,* 382–387.

Reynolds, D. K., & Nelson, F. L. (1981). Personality, life situation, and life expectancy. *Suicide and Life-Threatening Behavior, 11,* 99–110.

Reynolds, F. E., & Waugh, E. H. (1977). *Religious encounters with death.* University Park: Pennsylvania State University Press.

Reynolds, V., & Tanner, R. (1995). *The social ecology of religion.* New York: Oxford University Press.

Richards, D. G. (1991). The phenomenology and psychological correlates of verbal prayer. *Journal of Psychology and Theology, 19,* 354–363.

Richards, P. S. (1991). The relation between conservative religious ideology and principled moral reasoning: A review. *Review of Religious Research, 32,* 359–368.

Richards, P. S., & Davison, M. L. (1992). Religious bias in moral development research: A psychometric investigation. *Journal for the Scientific Study of Religion, 31,* 467–485.

Richardson, A. H. (1973). Social and medical correlates of survival among octogenarians: United Automobile Worker retirees and Spanish American War veterans. *Journal of Gerontology, 28,* 207–215.

Richardson, J. G., & Weatherby, G. A. (1983). Belief in an afterlife as symbolic sanction. *Review of Religious Research, 25,* 162–169.

Richardson, J. T. (1973). Psychological interpretation of glossolalia: A reexamination of research. *Journal for the Scientific Study of Religion, 12,* 199–207.

Richardson, J. T. (1978a). An oppositional and general conceptualization of cult. *Social Research, 41,* 299–327.

Richardson, J. T. (Ed.). (1978b). *Conversion careers: In and out of the new religions.* Beverly Hills, CA: Sage.

Richardson, J. T. (1979). From cult to sect: Creative eclecticism in new religious movements. *Pacific Sociological Review, 22,* 139–166.

Richardson, J. T. (1985a, October). *Legal and practical reasons for claiming to be a religion.* Paper presented at the annual meeting of the Society for the Scientific Study of Religion, Savannah, GA.

Richardson, J. T. (1985b). The active vs. passive convert: Paradigm conflict in conversion/recruitment research. *Journal for the Scientific Study of Religion, 24,* 163–179.

Richardson, J. T. (1992). Mental health of cult consumers. In J. F. Schumaker (Ed.), *Religion and mental health* (pp. 233–244). New York: Oxford University Press.

Richardson, J. T. (1993a). Definitions of cult: From sociological–technical to popular–negative. *Review of Religious Research, 34,* 348–356.

Richardson, J. T. (1993b). Religiosity as deviance: Negative religious bias in and misuse of the DSM-III. *Deviant Behaviors, 14,* 1–21.

Richardson, J. T. (1995). Clinical and personality assessment of participants in new religions. *International Journal for the Psychology of Religion, 5,* 145–170.

Richardson, J. T., Best, J., & Bromley, D. G. (Eds.). (1991). *The Satanism scare.* Hawthorne, NY: Aldine/de Gruyter.

Richardson, J. T., Stewart, T. M., & Simmonds, R. (1979). *Organized miracles: A study of a communal youth fundamentalist group.* New Brunswick, NJ: Transaction.

Richardson, J. T., & van Driel, B. (1984). Public support for anti-cult legislation. *Journal for the Scientific Study of Religion, 23,* 412–418.

Ring, K. (1984). *Heading toward omega: In search of the meaning of the near death experience.* New York: William Morrow.

Ritzema, R. J. (1979). Religiosity and altruism: Faith without works? *Journal of Psychology and Theology, 7,* 105–113.

Rizzuto, A.-M. (1979). *The birth of the living God: A psychoanalytic study.* Chicago: University of Chicago Press.

Rizzuto, A.-M. (1991). Religious development: A psychoanalytic point of view. In F. K. Oser & W. G. Scarlett (Eds.), *Religions development in childhood and adolescence* (New Directions for Child Development, No. 52, pp. 47–60). San Francisco: Jossey-Bass.

Robbins, A. (1985). New religious movements, brainwashing and deprogramming: The view from the law journals. *Religious Studies Review, 11*, 361–370.

Robbins, T. (1977, February 26). Even a Moonie has civil rights. *The Nation*, pp. 233–242.

Robbins, T. (1983). The beach is washing away: Controversial religion and the sociology of religion. *Sociological Analysis, 7*, 197–206.

Robbins, T., & Anthony, D. (1979). Cults, brainwashing, and countersubversion. *Annals of the American Academy of Political and Social Science, 446*, 78–90.

Robbins, T., & Anthony, D. (1980). The limits of "coercive persuasion" as an explanation for conversion to authoritarian sects. *Political Psychology, 3*, 22–37.

Robbins, T., & Anthony, D. (1982). Deprogramming, brainwashing and the medicalization of deviant religious groups. *Social Problems, 29*, 284–296.

Roberts, C. W. (1989). Imagining God: Who is created in whose image? *Review of Religious Research, 30*, 375–386.

Roberts, F. J. (1965). Some psychological factors in religious conversion. *British Journal of Social and Religious Psychology, 4*, 185–187.

Roberts, K. A. (1984). *Religion in sociological perspective.* Homewood, IL: Dorsey Press.

Robertson, R. (1975). On the analysis of mysticism: Pre-Weberian, Weberian, and post-Weberian perspectives. *Sociological Analysis, 36*, 241–266.

Robinson, D. N. (1981). *An intellectual history of psychology* (rev. ed.). New York: Macmillan.

Robinson, E. (1983). *The original vision.* New York: Seabury Press.

Roche Report: Frontiers of Psychiatry. (1972, April 15). Search for mysticism held rejection of aggression. p. 1.

Rochford, E. B., Jr., Purvis, S., & NeMar, E. (1989). New religions, mental health, and social control. In M. L. Lynn & D. O. Moberg (Eds.), *Research in the social scientific study of religion* (Vol. 1, pp. 57–82). Greenwich, CT: JAI Press.

Roe, A. (1956). *The psychology of occupations.* New York: Wiley.

Rogers, M. (Ed.). (1983). *Contradictory quotations.* England: Longman.

Rohner, R. P. (1994). Patterns of parenting: The warmth dimension in worldwide perspective. In W. J. Lonner & R. Malpass (Eds.), *Psychology and culture.* Boston: Allyn & Bacon.

Rohrbaugh, J., & Jessor, R. (1975). Religiosity in youth: A personal control against deviant behavior. *Journal of Personality, 43*, 136–155.

Rokeach, M. (1969). Value systems and religion. *Review of Religious Research, 11*, 24–38.

Rollins-Bohannon, J. (1991). Religiosity, related to grief levels of bereaved mothers and fathers. *Omega, 23*, 153–159.

Roof, W. C. (1989). Multiple religious switching: A research note. *Journal for the Scientific Study of Religion, 28*, 530–535.

Roof, W. C. (1993). *A generation of seekers: The spiritual journeys of the boom generation.* San Francisco: Harper.

Roof, W. C., & Hadaway, C. K. (1979). Denominational switching in the seventies: Going beyond Stark and Glock. *Journal for the Scientific Study of Religion, 18*, 363–379.

Roof, W. C., & McKinney, W. (1987). *American mainline religion: Its changing shape and future.* New Brunswick, NJ: Rutgers University Press.

Roof, W. C., & Perkins, R. B. (1975). On conceptualizing salience in religious commitment. *Journal for the Scientific Study of Religion, 14*, 111–128.

Roozen, D. A. (1980). Church dropouts: Changing patterns of disengagement and re-entry. *Review of Religious Research, 21*, 427–450.

Rose, A. M. (Ed.). (1955). *Mental health and mental disorder.* New York: Norton.

Rose, A. M., & Stub, H. R. (1955). Summary of studies on the incidence of mental disorders. In A. M. Rose (Ed.), *Mental health and mental disorder* (pp. 87–116). New York: Norton.

Rosegrant, J. (1976). The impact of set and setting on religious experience in nature. *Journal for the Scientific Study of Religion, 15,* 301–310.

Rosen, C. E. (1982). Ethnic difference among impoverished rural elderly in use of religion as a coping mechanism. *Journal of Rural Community Psychology, 3,* 27–34.

Rosenau, P. M. (1992). *Postmodernism and the social sciences: Insights, inroads, and intrusions.* Princeton, NJ: University of Princeton Press.

Rosenberg, M. (1962). The dissonant religious context and emotional disturbance. *American Journal of Sociology, 68,* 1–10.

Rosenheim, E., & Muchnik, B. (1984–1985). Death concerns in differential levels of consciousness as functions of defense strategy and religious belief. *Omega, 15,* 15–23.

Rosenzweig, C. (1979). High-demand sects: Disclosure legislation and the free exercise clause. *New England Law Review, 15,* 128–159.

Ross, C. E. (1990). Religion and psychological distress. *Journal for the Scientific Study of Religion, 29,* 236–245.

Ross, L., & Nisbett, R. E. (1991). *The person and the situation: Perspectives of social psychology.* New York: McGraw-Hill.

Ross, M. W. (1983). Clinical profiles of Hare Krishna devotees. *American Journal of Psychiatry, 140,* 416–420.

Rossi, A. M., Sturrock, J. B., & Solomon, P. (1963). Suggestion effects on reported imagery in sensory deprivation. *Perceptual and Motor Skills, 16,* 39–45.

Rosten, L. (1975). *Religions of America.* New York: Simon & Schuster.

Roszak, T. (1968). *The making of a counterculture.* Garden City, NY: Doubleday.

Roszak, T. (1975). *The unfinished animal.* New York: Harper & Row.

Rotenberg, M. (1978). *Damnation and deviance: The Protestant ethic and the spirit of failure.* New York: Free Press.

Roth, P. A. (1987). *Meaning and method in the social sciences: The case for methodological pluralism.* Ithaca, NY: Cornell University Press.

Rothbaum, F., Weisz, J. R., & Snyder, S. S. (1982). Changing the world and changing the self: A two process model of perceived control. *Journal of Personality and Social Psychology, 42,* 5–37.

Rothblum, E. D. (1983). Sex-role stereotypes and depression in women. In V. Franks & E. D. Rothblum (Eds.), *The stereotyping of women* (pp. 83–111). New York: Springer.

Rovner, S. (1983, May 1). Study shows cult members may be mentally healthy. *The Denver Post,* p. 54.

Rowe, D. C. (1987). Resolving the person–situation debate: Invitation to an interdisciplinary dialogue. *American Psychologist, 42,* 218–227.

Royce, J. (1912). *The sources of religious insight.* New York: Scribner.

Rubin, Z. (1970). Measurement of romantic love. *Journal of Personality and Social Psychology, 16,* 265–273.

Rubin, Z., & Peplau, A. (1973). Belief in a just world and reactions to another's lot: A study of participants in the national draft lottery. *Journal of Social Issues, 29,* 73–93.

Ruether, R. R. (1972, September). *St. Augustine's penis: Sources of misogynism in Christian theology and prospects for liberation today.* Paper presented at the meeting of the International Congress of Learned Societies in the Field of Religion, Los Angeles.

Ruether, R. R. (Ed.). (1974). *Religion and sexism: Images of women in the Jewish and Christian traditions.* New York: Simon & Schuster.

Russell, B. (1945). *A history of Western philosophy.* New York: Simon & Schuster.

Ryan, R. M., Rigby, S., & King, K. (1993). Two types of religious internalization and their relations to religious orientations and mental health. *Journal of Personality and Social Psychology, 65,* 586–596.

Saigh, P. A. (1979). The effect of perceived examiner religion on the Digit Span performance of Lebanese elementary schoolchildren. *Journal of Social Psychology, 109,* 167–173.

Saigh, P. A., O'Keefe, T., & Antoun, F. (1984). Religious symbols and the WISC-R performance of Roman Catholic parochial school students. *Journal of Genetic Psychology, 145,* 159–166.

Salzman, L. (1953). The psychology of religious and ideological conversion. *Psychiatry, 16,* 177–187.

Samarin, W. J. (1959). Glossolalia as learned behavior. *Canadian Journal of Theology, 19,* 60–64.

Samarin, W. J. (1972). *Tongues of men and angels.* New York: Macmillan.

Sammon, S. D., Reznikoff, M., & Geisinger, K. F. (1985). Psychosocial development and stressful life events among religious professionals. *Journal of Personality and Social Psychology, 48,* 676–687.

Sampson, E. E. (1969). Studies of status congruence. In L. Berkowitz (Ed.), *Advances in experimental social psychology* (Vol. 4, pp. 225–270). New York: Academic.

Sanborn, H. W. (1979). *Mental–spiritual health models.* Lanham, MD: University Press of America.

Sanders, C. M. (1979–1980). A comparison of adult bereavement in the death of a spouse, child, and parent. *Omega, 10,* 303–322.

Sandomirsky, S., & Wilson, J. (1990). Process of disaffiliation: Religious mobility among men and women. *Social Forces, 68,* 1211–1299.

Sapp, G. L. (1986). Moral judgment and religious orientation. In G. L. Sapp (Ed.), *Handbook of moral development* (pp. 271–286). Birmingham, AL: Religious Education Press.

Sarafino, E. P. (1990). *Health psychology.* New York: Wiley.

Sargent, W. (1957). *Battle for the mind.* London: Heinemann.

Saroyan, W. (1937). *My name is Aram.* New York: Harcourt, Brace.

Sasaki, M. A. (1979). Status inconsistency and religious commitment. In R. Wuthnow (Ed.), *The religious dimension: New directions in quantitative research* (pp. 135–156). New York: Academic Press.

Saudia, T. L., Kinney, M. R., Brown, K. C., & Young-Ward, L. (1991). Health locus of control and helpfulness of prayer. *Heart and Lung, 20,* 60–65.

Scarboro, A., Campbell, N., & Stave, S. (1994). *Living witchcraft: An American coven.* Westport, CT: Praeger.

Scarlett, W. G. (1994). Cognitive-developmental and psychoanalytic comments on Tamminen's essay. *International Journal for the Psychology of Religion, 4,* 87–90.

Scarlett, W. G., & Perriello, L. (1991). The development of prayer in adolescence. In F. K. Oser & W. G. Scarlett (Eds.), *Religious development in childhood and adolescence* (New Directions for Child Development, No. 52, pp. 63–76). San Francisco: Jossey-Bass.

Schachter, S. (1951). Deviation, rejection, and communication. *Journal of Abnormal and Social Psychology, 46,* 190–207.

Schachter, S. (1964). The interaction of cognitive and physiological determinants of emotional states. In L. Berkowitz (Ed.), *Advances in experimental social psychology* (Vol. 1, pp. 49–80). New York: Academic Press.

Schachter, S. (1971). *Emotion, obesity, and crime.* New York: Academic Press.

Schachter, S., & Singer, J. E. (1962). Cognitive, social, and physiological determinants of emotional states. *Psychological Review, 69,* 379–399.

Schaefer, C. A., & Gorsuch, R. L. (1991). Psychological adjustment and religiousness: The multivariate belief–motivation theory of religiousness. *Journal for the Scientific Study of Religion, 30,* 448–461.

Schaffer, M. D. (1990, August 15). Sex a special challenge for many clergy members. *The Denver Post,* p. 6B.

Scharfstein, B.-A. (1973). *Mystical experience.* Indianapolis, IN: Bobbs-Merrill.

Scharfstein, B.-A. (1993). *Ineffability.* Albany: State University of New York Press.

Scheff, T. J. (1977). The distancing of emotion in ritual. *Current Anthropology, 18,* 483–505.

Scheffel, D. (1991). *In the shadow of the antichrist: The Old Believers of Alberta.* Lewiston, NY: Broadview Press.

Scheflin, A., & Opton, E. (1978). *The mind manipulators.* New York: Paddington.

Schein, E., Schneier, I., & Barker, C. H. (1971). *Coercive persuasion.* New York: Norton.

Schellenberg, J. A. (1990). William James and symbolic interactionism. *Personality and Social Psychology Bulletin, 16,* 769–773.

Schlagel, R. H. (1986). *Contextual realism: A metaphysical framework for modern science.* New York: Paragon House.

Schmidt, L. A. (1995). "A battle not man's but God's": Origins of the American temperance crusade in the struggle for religious authority. *Journal of Studies on Alcohol, 56,* 110–121.

Schoenrade, P., Ludwig, C., Atkinson, T., & Shane, R. (1990, November). *Whose loss? Intrinsic religion and the consideration of one's own or another's death.* Paper presented at the annual meeting of the Society for the Scientific Study of Religion, Virginia Beach, VA.

Scholem, G. G. (1969). *On the Kabbalah and its symbolism* (R. Manheim, Trans.). New York: Schocken Books.

Schuller, D. S. (1986). Globalization in theological education: Summary and analysis of survey data. *Theological Education, 22,* 19–56.

Schuller, D. S., Strommen, M. P., & Brekke, M. L. (Eds.). (1980). *Ministry in America.* San Francisco: Harper & Row.

Schuller, R. H. (1976). *Positive prayers for power-filled living.* Houston, TX: J. Countryman.

Schuon, F. (1975). *The transcendent unity of religion* (Rev. ed., P. Townsend, Trans.). New York: Harper & Row.

Schur, E. (1976). *The awareness trap: Self absorption instead of social change.* Chicago: Quadrangle.

Schwartz, L. L., & Kaslow, F. W. (1979). Religious cults, the individual and the family. *Journal of Marital and Family Therapy, 5,* 15–26.

Scobie, G. E. W. (1973). Types of religious conversion. *Journal of Behavioral Science, 1,* 265–271.

Scobie, G. E. W. (1975). *Psychology of religion.* New York: Wiley.

Scott, J. (1989). Conflicting beliefs about abortion: Legal approval and moral doubts. *Social Psychology Quarterly, 52,* 319–326.

Seals, B. F., Ekwo, E. E., Williamson, R. A., & Hanson, J. W. (1985). Moral and religious influences on the amniocentesis decision. *Social Biology, 32,* 13–30.

Seeman, M. (1959). The meaning of alienation. *American Sociological Review, 24,* 783–790.

Segal, R. A. (1985). Have the social sciences been converted? *Journal for the Scientific Study of Religion, 24,* 321–324.

Segalowitz, S. J. (1983). *Two sides of the brain: Brain lateralization explained.* Englewood Cliffs, NJ: Prentice-Hall.

Seggar, J., & Kunz, P. (1972). Conversion: Analysis of a step-like process for problem solving. *Review of Religious Research, 13,* 178–184.

Selig, S., & Teller, G. (1975). The moral development of children in three different school settings. *Religious Education, 70,* 406–415.

Seligman, M. E. P. (1975). *Helplessness: On depression, development, and death.* San Francisco: W. H. Freeman.

Seligman, M. E. P. (1991). *Learned optimism.* New York: Knopf.

Sensky, T. (1983). Religiosity, mystical experience and epilepsy. In F. C. Rose (Ed.), *Research in epilepsy* (pp. 214–220). New York: Pitman.

Sethi, S., & Seligman, M. E. P. (1993). Optimism and fundamentalism. *Psychological Science, 4,* 256–259.

Shaffer, J. W., Nurco, D. N., Ball, J. C., Kinlock, T. W., Duszynsk, K. R., & Langrod, J. (1987). The relationship of preaddiction characteristics to the types and amounts of crime committed by narcotic addicts. *International Journal of the Addictions, 22,* 153–165.

Shafranske, E. (1995). Freudian theory and religious experience. In R. W. Hood, Jr. (Ed.), *Handbook of religious experience* (pp. 200–232). Birmingham, AL: Religious Education Press.

Shafranske, E. P. (Ed.). (1996). *Religion and the clinical practice of psychology.* New York: Human Sciences Press.

Shand, J. D. (1990). A forty-year followup of the religious beliefs and attitudes of a sample of Amherst College grads. In M. L. Lynn & D. O. Moberg (Eds.), *Research in the social Scientific study of religion* (Vol. 2, pp. 117–136) Greenwich, CT: JAI Press.

Shapiro, E. (1977). Destructive cultism. *American Family Physician, 15,* 80–83.

Shaver, P. (1986). Consciousness without the body. *Contemporary Psychology, 31,* 645–647.

Shea, J. (1992). Religion and sexual adjustment. In J. F. Schumaker (Ed.), *Religion and mental health* (pp. 70–84). New York: Oxford University Press.

Shephard, R. N. (1978). The mental image. *American Psychologist, 33,* 125–137.

Sherif, M. (1953). *Groups in harmony and tension.* New York: Harper & Row.

Shneidman, E. (1982). *Voices of death*. New York: Bantam.

Shor, R. E., & Orne, E. C. (1962). *Harvard Group Scale of Hypnotic Susceptibility*. Palo Alto, CA: Consulting Psychologists Press.

Shostrom, E. L. (1964). A test for the ensurement of self-actualization. *Educational and Psychological Measurement, 24*, 207–218.

Shrauger, J. S., & Silverman, R. E. (1971). The relationship of religious background and participation to locus of control. *Journal for the Scientific Study of Religion, 10*, 11–16.

Shuman, C. R., Fournet, G. P., Zelhart, P. F., Roland, B. C., & Estes, R. E. (1992). Attitudes of registered nurses toward euthanasia. *Death Studies, 16*, 1–15.

Shupe, A. D., Jr., & Bromley, D. (1985). Social response to cults. In P. Hammond (Ed.), *The sacred in a secular age* (pp. 58–69). Berkeley: University of California Press.

Shupe, A. D., Jr., Bromley, D. G., & Oliver, D. L. (1984). *The anti-cult movement in America*. New York: Garland Press.

Shupe, A. D., Jr., Spielman, R., & Stigall, S. (1977). Deprogramming. *American Behavioral Scientist, 20*, 941–956.

Siegel, R. K. (1977). Religious behavior in animals and man: Drug-induced effects. *Journal of Drug Issues, 7*, 219–236.

Siglag, M. A. (1987, August). *Schizophrenic and mystical experiences*. Paper presented at the annual meeting of the American Psychological Association, New York.

Silberman, C. E. (1985). *A certain people*. New York: Summit.

Silver, R. L., & Wortman, C. B. (1980). Coping with undesirable life events. In J. Garber & M. E. P. Seligman (Eds.), *Human helplessness: Theory and applications* (pp. 279–343). New York: Academic Press.

Silverman, M. K., & Pargament, K. I. (1990). *God help me: III. Longitudinal and prospective studies on effects of religious coping efforts on the outcomes of significant negative life events*. Paper presented at the annual meeting of the American Psychological Association, San Francisco.

Silverstein, S. A. (1988). A study of religious conversion in North America. *Genetic, Social, and General Psychological Monographs, 114*, 261–305.

Silvestri, P. J. (1979). Locus of control and God dependence. *Psychological Reports, 45*, 89–90.

Simmonds, R. B. (1977a). Conversion or addiction? *American Behavioral Scientist, 20*, 909–924.

Simmonds, R. B. (1977b). *The people of the Jesus movement: A personality assessment of members of a fundamentalist religious community*. Unpublished doctoral dissertation, University of Nevada at Reno.

Singer, J. L. (1966). *Daydreaming: An introduction to the experimental study of inner experience*. New York: Random House.

Singer, M. T. (1978a, January). Coming out of the cults. *Psychology Today*, pp. 72–82.

Singer, M. T. (1978b). Therapy with ex-cult members. *Journal of the National Association of Private Psychiatric Hospitals, 9*, 14–18.

Singer, M. T., & Ofshe, R. (1990). Thought reform programs and the production of psychiatric casualties. *Psychiatric Annals, 20*, 188–193.

Singer, M. T., & West, L. J. (1980). Cults, quacks, and non-professional therapies. In H. I. Kaplan & J. B. Sadock (Eds.) *Comprehensive textbook of psychiatry* (Vol. 3, pp. 3245–3258). Baltimore: Williams & Wilkins.

Sipe, A. W. R. (1990). *A secret world: Sexuality and the search for celibacy*. New York: Brunner/Mazel.

Skidmore, D. (1993, October). 8000 from world religions look for unity. *Episcopal Life*, p. 15.

Skinner, B. F. (1953). *Science and human behavior*. New York: Macmillan.

Sklar, L. S., & Anisman, H. (1981). Stress and cancer. *Psychological Bulletin, 89*, 369–406.

Skonovd, L. N. (1983). Leaving the cultic religious milieu. In D. Bromley & J. Richardson (Eds.), *The brainwashing/deprogramming controversy: Sociological, psychological, legal and historical perspectives* (pp. 91–105). Lewiston, NY: Edward Mellon.

Slaughter-Defoe, D. T. (1995). Revisiting the concept of socialization: Caregiving and teaching in the 90s—a personal perspective. *American Psychologist, 50*, 276–286.

Slawson, P. F. (1973). Treatment of a clergyman: Anxiety neurosis in a celibate. *American Journal of Psychotherapy, 27*, 52–60.

Sleek, S. (1994, June). Spiritual problems included in DSM-IV. *APA Monitor*, p. 8.

Sloane, D. M., & Potvin, R. H. (1983). Age differences in adolescent religiousness. *Review of Religious Research, 25*, 142–154.

Smart, N. (Ed.). (1964). *Philosophers and religious truth.* New York: Macmillan.

Smart, N. (1978). Understanding religious experience. In S. Katz (Ed.), *Mysticism and philosophical analysis* (pp. 10–21). New York: Oxford University Press.

Smith, E. R., & Mackie, D. M. (1995). *Social psychology.* NewYork: Worth.

Smith, M. (1978). *The way of the mystics.* New York: Oxford University Press.

Smith, P. C., Range, L. M., & Ulmer, A. (1991–1992). Belief in afterlife as a buffer in suicidal and other bereavement. *Omega, 24*, 217–225.

Smith, R. E., Wheeler, G., & Diener, E. (1975). Faith without works: Jesus people, resistance to temptation, and altruism. *Journal of Applied Social Psychology, 5*, 320–330.

Smith, T. W. (1992). Are conservative churches growing? *Review of Religious Research, 33*, 305–329.

Snarey, J. R. (1985). Cross-cultural universality of social–moral development: A critical review of Kohlbergian research. *Psychological Bulletin, 97*, 202–233.

Snelling, C. H., & Whitley, O. R. (1974). Problem-solving behavior in religious and para-religious groups: An initial report. In A. W. Eister (Ed.), *Changing perspectives in the scientific study of religion* (pp. 315–334). New York: Wiley.

Snook, J. B. (1974). An alternative to church–sect. *Journal for the Scientific Study of Religion, 13*, 191–204.

Snook, S. C., & Gorsuch, R. L. (1985, August). *Religion and racial prejudice in South Africa.* Paper presented at the annual meeting of the American Psychological Association, Los Angeles.

Snow, D. A., & Machalek, R. (1983). The convert as a social type. In R. Collins (Ed.), *Sociological theory* (pp. 259–289). San Francisco: Jossey-Bass.

Snow, D. A., & Machalek, R. (1984). The sociology of conversion. *Annual Review of Sociology, 10*, 167–190.

Snow, D. A., Zurcher, L. A., Jr., & Ekland-Olson, S. (1980). Social networks and social movements: A microstructural approach to differential recruitment. *American Sociological Review, 45*, 797–801.

Snow, D. A., Zurcher, L. A., Jr., & Ekland-Olson, S. (1983). Further thoughts on social networks and movement recruitment. *Sociology, 17*, 112–120.

Snyder, C. R. (1962). Culture and Jewish sobriety: The ingroup–outgroup factor. In D. J. Pittman & C. R. Snyder (Eds.), *Society, culture, and drinking patterns* (pp. 188–225). New York: Wiley.

Somit, A. (1968). Brainwashing. In D. Solls (Ed.), *International encyclopaedia of the social sciences* (Vol. 2, pp. 138–143). New York: Macmillan.

Southard, S. (1956). Religious concern in the psychoses. *Journal of Pastoral Care, 10*, 226–233.

Spanos, N. P., & Moretti, P. (1988). Correlates of mystical and diabolical experiences in a sample of female university students. *Journal for the Scientific Study of Religion, 27*, 105–116.

Spanos, N. P., Radtke, H. L., Hodgins, D. C., Stam, H. J., & Bertrand, L. D. (1983). The Carleton University Responsiveness to Suggestion Scale: Normative data and psychometric properties. *Psychological Reports, 53*, 523–535.

Spellman, C. M., Baskett, G. D., & Byrne, D. (1971). Manifest anxiety as a contributing factor in religious conversion. *Journal of Consulting and Clinical Psychology, 36*, 245–247.

Spencer, C., & Agahi, C. (1982). Social background, personal relationships, and self-descriptions as predictors of drug-user status: A study of adolescents in post-revolutionary Iran. *Drug and Alcohol Dependence, 10*, 77–84.

Spencer, J. (1975). The mental health of Jehovah's Witnesses. *British Journal of Psychiatry, 126*, 556–559.

Spilka, B. (1970). Images of man and dimensions of personal religion: Values for an empirical psychology of religion. *Review of Religious Research, 11*, 171–182.

Spilka, B. (1976). The compleat person: Some theoretical views and research findings for a theological-psychology of religion. *Journal of Psychology and Theology, 4*, 15–24.

Spilka, B. (1977). Utilitarianism and personal faith. *Journal of Psychology and Theology, 5*, 226–233.

Spilka, B. (1993, August). *Spirituality: Problems and directions in operationalizing a fuzzy concept.* Paper presented at the annual meeting of the American Psychological Association, Toronto.

Spilka, B., Addison, J., & Rosensohn, M. (1975). Parents, self and God: A test of competing theories of individual–religion relationships. *Review of Religious Research, 16*, 154–165.

Spilka, B., Armatas, F., & Nussbaum, J. (1964). The concept of God: A factor analytic approach. *Review of Religious Research, 6*, 28–36.

Spilka, B., Brown, G. A., & Cassidy, S. A. (1993). The structure of religious mystical experience in relation to pre- and post-lifestyles. *International Journal for the Psychology of Religion. 2*, 241–257.

Spilka, B., Hood, R. W., Jr., & Gorsuch, R. L. (1985). *The psychology of religion: An empirical approach.* Englewood Cliffs, NJ: Prentice-Hall.

Spilka, B., Kojetin, B., & McIntosh, D. (1985). Forms and measures of personal faith: Questions, correlates and distinctions. *Journal for the Scientific Study of Religion, 24*, 437–442.

Spilka, B., Ladd, K., & David, J. (1993). *Religion and coping with breast cancer: Possible roles for prayer and form of personal faith.* Unpublished manuscript.

Spilka, B., & Loffredo, L. (1982). *Classroom cheating among religious students: Some factors affecting perspectives, actions and justifications.* Paper presented at the meeting of the Rocky Mountain Psychological Association, Albuquerque, NM.

Spilka, B., & McIntosh, D. (1995). Attribution theory and religious experience. In R. W. Hood, Jr. (Ed.), *Handbook of religious experience* (pp. 421–445). Birmingham, AL: Religious Education Press.

Spilka, B., & McIntosh, D. N. (Eds.). (in press). *The psychology of religion: Theoretical approaches.* Boulder, CO: Westview Press.

Spilka, B., & Mullin, M. (1977). Personal religion and psychosocial schemata: A research approach to a theological-psychology of religion. *Character Potential, 8*, 57–66.

Spilka, B., & Schmidt, G. (1983). General attribution theory for the psychology of religion: The influence of event-character on attributions to God. *Journal for the Scientific Study of Religion, 22*, 326–339.

Spilka, B., Shaver, P., & Kirkpatrick, L. A. (1985). A general attribution theory for the psychology of religion. *Journal for the Scientific Study of Religion, 24*, 1–20.

Spilka, B., & Spangler, J. D. (1979, October). *Spiritual support in life-threatening illness.* Paper presented at the annual meeting of the Society for the Scientific Study of Religion, San Antonio, TX.

Spilka, B., Spangler, J. D., & Nelson, C. B. (1983). Spiritual support in life-threatening illness. *Journal of Religion and Health, 22*, 98–104.

Spilka, B., Spangler, J. D., & Rea, M. P. (1981). The role of theology in pastoral care for the dying. *Theology Today, 38*, 16–29.

Spilka, B., Spangler, J. D., Rea, M. P., & Nelson, C. B. (1981). Religion and death: The clerical perspective. *Journal of Religion and Health, 20*, 299–306.

Spilka, B., Stout, L., Minton, B., & Sizemore, D. (1977). Death and personal faith: A psychometric investigation. *Journal for the Scientific Study of Religion, 16*, 169–178.

Spilka, B., & Werme, P. (1971). Religion and mental disorder: A scritical review and theoretical perspective. In M. Strommen (Ed.), *Research on religious development: A comprehensive handbook* (pp. 461–484). New York: Hawthorn Books.

Springer, S. P., & Deutsch, G. (1981). *Left brain, right brain.* San Francisco: W. H. Freeman.

Sprinthall, N. A., & Collins, W. A. (1995). *Adolescent psychology: A developmental view* (3rd ed.) New York: McGraw-Hill.

Srole, L., Langner, T. S., Michael, S. T., Opler, M. K., & Rennie, T. A. C. (1962). *Mental health in the metropolis.* New York: McGraw-Hill.

Stace, W. T. (1960). *Mysticism and philosophy.* Philadelphia: J. B. Lippincott.

Stack, S. (1983). The effect of religious commitment on suicide: A cross-national analysis. *Journal of Health and Social Behavior, 24*, 362–374.

Stack, S., & Wasserman, I. (1992). The effect of religion on suicide ideology: An analysis of the networks perspective. *Journal for the Scientific Study of Religion, 31*, 457–466.

Stambrook, M., & Parker, K. C. H. (1987). The development of the concept of death in childhood: A review of the literature. *Merrill–Palmer Quarterly, 33*, 133–157.

Stander, F. (1987). Some rigors of our time: The First Amendment and real life and death. *Cultic Studies Journal, 4*, 1–17.

Stanley, S. M. (1986). *Commitment and the maintenance and enhancement of relationships.* Unpublished doctoral dissertation, University of Denver.

Stanley, S. M., & Markman, H. J. (1992). Assessing commitment in personal relationships. *Journal of Marriage and the Family, 54,* 595–608.

Staples, C. L., & Mauss, A. L. (1987). Conversion or commitment? A reassessment of the Snow and Machalek approach to the study of conversion. *Journal for the Scientific Study of Religion, 26,* 133–147.

Starbuck, E. D. (1897). A study of conversion. *American Journal of Psychology, 8,* 268–308.

Starbuck, E. D. (1899). *The psychology of religion.* New York: Scribner.

Starbuck, E. D. (1904). The varieties of religious experience. *The Biblical World, 24*(N.S.), 100–111.

Stark, R. (1965). A taxonomy of religious experience. *Journal for the Scientific Study of Religion, 5,* 97–116.

Stark, R. (1971). Psychopathology and religious commitment. *Review of Religious Research, 12,* 165–176.

Stark, R. (1972). The economics of piety: Religious commitment and social class. In G. W. Thielbar & S. D. Feldman (Eds.), *Issues in social inequality* (pp. 483–503). Boston: Little, Brown.

Stark, R. (1984). Religion and conformity: Reaffirming a *sociology* of religion. *Sociological Analysis, 45,* 273–282.

Stark, R. (1985). Church and sect. In P. E. Hammond (Ed.), *The sacred in a secular age* (pp. 139–149). Berkeley: University of California Press.

Stark, R., & Bainbridge, W. S. (1979). Of churches, sects and cults: Preliminary concepts for a theory of religious movements. *Journal for the Scientific Study of Religion, 18,* 117–133.

Stark, R., & Bainbridge, W. S. (1980a). Networks of faith: Interpersonal bonds and recruitment to cults and sects. *American Journal of Sociology, 85,* 1376–1395.

Stark, R., & Bainbridge, W. S. (1980b). Towards a theory of religion. *Journal for the Scientific Study of Religion, 19,* 114–128.

Stark, R., & Bainbridge, W. S. (1985). *The future of religion.* Berkeley, CA: University of California Press.

Stark, R., Foster, B. D., Glock, C. Y., & Quinley, H. (1970, April). Sounds of silence. *Psychology Today,* pp. 38–41, 60–61.

Stark, R., & Glock, C. Y. (1968). *American piety: The nature of religious commitment.* Berkeley: University of California Press.

Starr, M., Buckley, L., & Elan, R. (1989, March 27). Heaven: This is the season to search for new meaning in old familiar places. *Newsweek,* p. 53.

Steele, B. F., & Pollock, C. B. (1968). A psychiatric study of parents who abuse infants and small children. In R. E. Helfer & C. H. Kempe (Eds.), *The battered child* (pp. 103–147). Chicago: University of Chicago Press.

Steeman, T. M. (1975). Church, sect, mysticism, denomination: Periodological aspects of Troeltsch's types. *Sociological Analysis, 26,* 181–204.

Steinberg, L. (1983). *The sexuality of Christ in Renaissance art and in modern oblivion.* New York: Pantheon.

Steinberg, L., Lamborn, S. D., Dornbusch, S. M., & Darling, N. (1992). Impact of parenting practices on adolescent achievement: Authoritative parenting, school involvement, and encouragement to succeed. *Child Development, 63,* 1266–1281.

Steinfels, P. (1992, October 18). Debating intermarriage and Jewish survival. *The New York Times,* pp. 1, 40.

Stephan, C. W., & Stephan, W. G. (1985). *Two social psychologies.* Homewood, IL: Dorsey Press.

Stern, E. M., & Marino, B. G. (1970). *Psychotheology.* New York: Newman.

Stevens, J. (1987). *Storming heaven: LSD and the American dream.* New York: Harper & Row.

Stewart, C. W. (1974). *Person and profession: Career development in the ministry.* Nashville, TN: Abingdon Press.

Stifler, K., Greer, J., Sneck, W., & Dovenmuehle, R. (1993). An empirical investigation of the discriminability of reported mystical experiences among religious contemplatives, psychotic inpatients, and normal adults. *Journal for the Scientific Study of Religion, 32,* 366–372.

Stifoss-Hanssen, H. (1994). Rigid religiosity and mental health: An empirical study. In L. B. Brown (Ed.), *Religion, personality, and mental health* (pp. 138–143). New York: Springer-Verlag.

Stobart, St. C. (1971). *Torchbearers of spiritualism*. New York: Kennikat.

Stolz, K. R. (1940). *Pastoral psychology* (rev. ed.). New York: Abingdon Press.

Stolz, K. R. (1943). *The church and psychotherapy*. New York: Abingdon–Cokesbury Press.

Stolzenberg, R. M., Blair-Loy, M., & Waite, L. J. (1995). Religious participation in early adulthood: Age and family life cycle effects on church membership. *American Sociological Review, 60*, 84–103.

Stone, P. J., Dunphy, D. C., Smith, M. S., & Ogilvie, D. M. (1966). *The general inquirer: A computer approach to content analysis*. Cambridge, MA: MIT Press.

Storr, A. (1988). *Solitude: A return to the self*. New York: Ballantine Books.

Stouffer, S. (1955). *Communism, conformity, and civil liberty*. Garden City, NY: Doubleday.

Straus, R. A. (1976). Changing oneself: Seekers and the creative transformation of experience. In J. Lofland (Ed.), *Doing social life* (pp. 252–272). New York: Wiley.

Straus, R. A. (1979). Religious conversion as a personal and collective accomplishment. *Sociological Analysis, 40*, 158–165.

Strickland, B. R., & Shaffer, S. (1971). I-E, I-E, & F. *Journal for the Scientific Study of Religion, 10*, 366–369.

Strickland, M. P. (1924). *Psychology of religious experience*. New York: Abingdon Press.

Strommen, M. P. (Ed.). (1971). *Research on religious development: A comprehensive handbook*. New York: Hawthorn Books.

Strommen, M. P., Brekke, M. L., Underwager, R. C., & Johnson, A. L. (1972). *A study of generations*. Minneapolis: Augsburg.

Struening, E. L. (1963). Anti-democratic attitudes in Midwest univerity. In H. H. Remmers (Ed.), *Anti-democratic attitudes in American schools* (pp. 210–258). Evanston, IL: Northwestern University Press.

Strunk, O., Jr. (1959). Interests and personality patterns of pre-ministerial students. *Psychological Reports, 5*, 740.

Suedfeld, P. (1975). The benefits of boredom: Sensory deprivation reconsidered. *American Scientist, 63*, 60–69.

Suedfeld, P., & Vernon, J. (1964). Visual hallucination in sensory deprivation: A problem of criteria. *Science, 145*, 412–413.

Sullivan, J. L., Pierson, J. E., & Marcus, G. E. (1982). *Political tolerance in American democracy*. Chicago: University of Chicago Press.

Sutherland, P. (1988). A longitudinal study of religious and moral values in late adolescence. *British Educational Research Journal, 14*, 73–78.

Sutton, T. D., & Murphy, S. P. (1989). Stressors and patterns of coping in renal transplant patients. *Nursing Research, 38*, 46–49.

Swatos, W. H. (1976). Weber or Troeltsch?: Methodology, syndrome, and the development of church--sect theory. *Journal for the Scientific Study of Religion, 15*, 129–144.

Swatos, W. H. (1981). Church, sect and cult: Bringing mysticism back in. *Sociological Analysis, 42*, 17–26.

Swatos, W. H., Jr. (1992). Adolescent Satanism: A research note on exploratory survey data. *Review of Religious Research, 34*, 161–169.

Swinburne, R. (1981). The evidential value of religious experience. In A. R. Peacoke (Ed.), *The sciences and theology in the twentieth century* (pp. 182–196). Notre Dame, IN: University of Notre Dame Press.

Symonds, P. M. (1946). *Dynamics of human adjustment*. New York: Appleton-Century.

Szasz, T. (1960). The myth of mental illness. *American Psychologist, 15*, 113–118.

Szasz, T. (1970). *Ideology and insanity: Essays on the psychiatric dehumanization of man*. Garden City, NY: Doubleday.

Szasz, T. (1983). *The manufacture of madness*. New York: Harper & Row.

Szasz, T. (1984). *The therapeutic states: Psychiatry in the mirror of current events*. Buffalo, NY: Prometheus Books.

Taft, R. (1970). The measurement of the dimensions of ego permissiveness. *Personality: An International Journal, 1*, 163–184.

Tageson, C. W. (1982). *Humanistic psychology: A synthesis.* Homewood, IL: Dorsey Press.

Tajfel, H., & Turner, J. C. (1986). The social identity theory of intergroup behavior. In S. Worchel & W. G. Austin (Eds.), *Psychology of intergroup relationships* (pp. 7–24). Chicago: Nelson-Hall.

Tamminen, K. (1976). Research concerning the development of religious thinking in Finnish students: A report of results. *Character Potential, 7*, 206–219.

Tamminen, K. (1991). *Religious development in childhood and adolescence: An empirical study.* Helsinki: Suomalainen Tiedeakatemia.

Tamminen, K. (1994). Religious experiences in childhood and adolescence: A viewpoint of religious development between the ages of 7 and 20. *International Journal for the Psychology of Religion, 4*, 61–85.

Tamminen, K., Vianello, R., Jaspard, J.-M., & Ratcliff, D. (1988). The religious concepts of preschoolers. In D. Ratcliff (Ed.), *Handbook of preschool religious education* (pp. 97–108). Birmingham, AL: Religious Education Press.

Tart, C. (Ed.). (1969). *Altered states of consciousness.* New York: Wiley.

Tart, C. (1975a). Science, state of consciousness, and spiritual experiences: The need for state-specific sciences. In C. Tart (Ed.), *Transpersonal psychologies* (pp. 9–58). New York: Harper & Row.

Tart, C. (Ed.). (1975b). *Transpersonal psychologies.* New York: Harper & Row.

Taslimi, C. R., Hood, R. W., Jr., & Watson, P. J. (1991). Assessment of former members of Shiloh: The adjective check list 17 years later. *Journal for the Scientific Study of Religion. 30*, 306–311.

Tate, E. D., & Miller, G. R. (1971). Differences in value systems of persons with varying religious orientations. *Journal for the Scientific Study of Religion, 10*, 357–365.

Tavris, C., & Sadd, S. (1977). *The Redbook report on female sexuality.* New York: Dell.

Tellegen, A., & Atkinson, G. (1974). Openness to absorbing and self-altering experiences ("absorption"), a trait related to hypnotic susceptibility. *Journal of Abnormal Psychology, 83*, 268–277.

Tellegen, A., Gerrard, N. L., & Butcher, J. N. (1969). Personality characteristics of members of a serpent-handling religious cult. In J. N. Butcher (Ed.), *MMPI: Research developments and clinical applications* (pp. 221–242). New York: McGraw-Hill.

Tennant, F. (1968). *The sources of the doctrine of the fall and original sin.* New York: Schocken Books. (Original work published 1903)

ter Voert, M., Felling, A., & Peters, J. (1994). The effect of religion on self-interest morality. *Review of Religious Research, 35*, 302–323.

Teshome, M. J. (1992, August). *Separation–individuation among glossolalics and nonglossolalics.* Paper presented at the annual meeting of the American Psychological Association, Washington, DC.

Thomas, D. L., & Weigert, A. J. (1971). Socialization and adolescent conformity to significant others: A cross-national analysis. *American Sociological Review, 36*, 835–847.

Thomas, L. E. (1974). Generational discontinuity in beliefs: An exploration of the generation gap. *Journal of Social Issues, 30*, 1–22.

Thomas, L. E., & Cooper, P. E. (1978). Measurement and incidence of mystical experiences: An exploratory study. *Journal for the Scientific Study of Religion, 17*, 433–437.

Thomas, L. E., & Cooper, P. E. (1980). Incidence and psychological correlates of intense spiritual experiences. *Journal of Transpersonal Psychology, 12*, 75–85.

Thorner, I. (1966). Prophetic and mystic experiences: Comparisons and consequences. *Journal for the Scientific Study of Religion, 5*, 2–96.

Thornton, A., & Camburn, D. (1989). Religious participation and adolescent sexual behavior. *Journal of Marriage and the Family, 51*, 641–654.

Tillich, P. (1952). *The courage to be.* New Haven, CT: Yale University Press.

Tillich, P. (1957). *Dynamics of faith.* New York: Harper & Row.

Tipton, R. M., Harrison, B. M., & Mahoney, J. (1980). Faith and locus of control. *Psychological Reports, 46*, 1151–1154.

Tipton, S. M. (1982). *Getting saved from the sixties: Moral meaning in conversion and cultural change.* Berkeley: University of California Press.

Tobin, S. S., Fullmer, E. M., & Smith, G. C. (1994). Religiosity and fear of death in non-normative aging. In L. E. Thomas & S. A. Eisenhandler (Eds.), *Aging and the religious dimension* (pp. 183–202). Westport, CT: Auburn House.

Travisano, R. (1970). Alternation and conversion as qualitatively different transformations. In G. P. Stone & H. A. Faberman (Eds.), *Social psychology through symbolic interaction* (pp. 594–606). Waltham, MA: Ginn-Blaisdell.

Trew, A. (1971). The religious factor in mental illness. *Pastoral Psychology, 22,* 21–28.

Trier, K. K., & Shupe, A. (1991). Prayer, religiosity and healing in the heartland, USA: A research note. *Review of Religious Research, 32,* 351–358.

Troeltsch, E. (1931). *The social teachings of the Christian churches* (O.Wyon, Trans.). New York: Macmillan.

Trotter, W. (1919). *Instincts of the herd in peace and war.* New York: Macmillan.

Turner, P. R. (1979). Religious conversion and community development. *Journal for the Scientific Study of Religion, 18,* 252–269.

Ulanov, B. (1959). *Death: A book of preparation and consolation.* New York: Sheed & Ward.

Ullman, C. (1982). Cognitive and emotional antecedents of religious conversion. *Journal of Personality and Social Psychology, 43,* 183–192.

Ullman, C. (1989). *The transformed self.* New York: Plenum Press.

Unamuno, M. de. (1954). *The tragic sense of life* (J. E. Crawford Fitch, Trans.). New York: Dover. (Original work published 1921)

Underhill, E. (1961). *Mysticism.* New York: Dutton. (Original work published 1911)

Underhill, R. M. (1936). *The autobiography of a Papago woman* (Memoirs of the American Anthropological Association, No. 46). Menasha, WI: American Anthropological Association.

Ungerleider, J. T., & Welish, D. K. (1979). Coercive persuasion (brainwashing), religious cults, and deprogramming. *American Journal of Psychiatry, 136,* 279–282.

Ungersma, A. J. (1961). *The search for meaning.* London: Allen & Unwin.

U.S. Bureau of the Census. (1992). *Statistical abstract of the United States: 1992.* Washington, DC: U.S. Government Printing Office.

U.S. Bureau of the Census. (1994). *Statistical abstract of the United States: 1994.* Washington, DC: U.S. Government Printing Office.

Valins, S., & Nisbett, R. E. (1971). *Attribution processes in the development and treatment of emotional disorders.* Morristown, NJ: General Learning Press.

Vande Kemp, H. (1976). Teaching psychology/religion in the seventies: Monopoly or cooperation? *Teaching of Psychology, 3,* 15–18.

van der Lans, J. (1985). Frame of reference as a prerequisite for the induction of religious experience through meditation: An experimental study. In L. B. Brown (Ed.), *Advances in the psychology of religion* (pp. 127–134). Oxford: Pergamon Press.

van der Lans, J. (1987). The value of Sunden's role-theory demonstrated and tested with respect to religious experiences in meditation. *Journal for the Scientific Study of Religion, 26,* 401–412.

van der Lans, J. M. (1991). Interpretation of religious language and cognitive style: A pilot study with the LAM scale. *International Journal for the Psychology of Religion, 1,* 107–123.

VanderPlate, C. (1973). Religious orientation in psychiatric patients and normals. In *Proceedings of the 20th Annual Convention of the Christian Association for Psychological Studies* (pp. 93–104). Grand Rapids, MI.

VanderStoep, S. W., & Green, C. W. (1988). Religiosity and homonegativism: A path-analytic study. *Basic and Applied Social Psychology, 9,* 135–147.

van Driel, B., & Richardson, J. T. (1988). Categorization of new religions in American print media. *Sociological Analysis, 49,* 171–183.

Venable, G. D. (1984). *Intrinsic and extrinsic religiosity in developmental perspective.* Unpublished doctoral dissertation, Fuller Theological Seminary.

Verbit, M. F. (1970). The components and dimensions of religious behavior: Toward a reconceptualization of religiosity. In P. E. Hammond & B. Johnson (Eds.), *American mosaic* (pp. 24–39). New York: Random House.

Verdier, P. (1977). *Brainwashing and the cults.* Redondo Beach, CA: Institute of Behavioral Conditioning.

Vergote, A. (1993). What the psychology of religion is and what it is not. *International Journal for the Psychology of Religion, 3,* 73–86.

Vergote, A., & Tamayo, A. (Eds.). (1981). *The parental figures and the representation of God: A psychological and cross-cultural study.* The Hague: Mouton.

Vernon, G. M. (1968). The religious "nones": A neglected category. *Journal for the Scientific Study of Religion, 7,* 219–229.

Vernon, G. M., & Waddell, C. E. (1974). Dying as social behavior. *Omega, 5,* 199–206.

Veroff, J., Douvan, E., & Kulka, R. A. (1981). *The inner American: A self-portrait.* New York: Basic Books.

Vitz, P. C. (1977). *Psychology as religion.* Grand Rapids, MI: Eerdmans.

Volinn, E. (1985). Eastern meditative groups: Why join? *Sociological Analysis, 46,* 147–156.

Volken, L. (1961). *Vision, revelations, and the church.* New York: J. P. Kennedy.

Walinsky, A. (1995, July). The crisis of public order. *Atlantic Monthly,* pp. 39–54.

Wallace, A. F. C. (1956). Revitalization movements. *American Anthropologist, 58,* 264–281.

Wallace, C. W. (1966). *Religion: An anthropological view.* New York: Random House.

Waller, N., Kojetin, B., Bouchard, T., Jr., Lykken, D., & Tellegen, A. (1990). Genetic and environmental influences on religious interests, attitudes, and values: A study of twins reared apart and together. *Psychological Science, 1,* 138–142.

Wallin, T., & Clark, A. (1964). Religiosity, sexual gratification, and marital satisfaction. *Social Forces, 42,* 303–309.

Wallis, R. (1974). Ideology, authority, and the development of cultic movements. *Social Research, 41,* 299–327.

Wallis, R. (1976). *The road to total freedom: A sociological analysis of Scientology.* New York: Columbia University Press.

Wallis, R. (1986). Figuring out cult receptivity. *Journal for the Scientific Study of Religion, 25,* 494–503.

Wallwork, E. (1980). Morality, religion, and Kohlberg's theory. In B. Munsey (Ed.), *Moral development, moral education, and Kohlberg* (pp. 269–297). Birmingham, AL: Religious Education Press.

Walsh, R. (1982). Psychedelics and psychological well-being. *Journal of Humanistic Psychology, 22,* 22–32.

Walsh, W. J. (1906). *The apparitions of the shrines of heaven's bright queen* (4 vols.). New York: Cary-Stafford.

Walters, A., & Bradley, R. (1971). Motivation and religious behavior. In M. Strommen (Ed.), *Research on religious development: A comprehensive handbook* (pp. 599–651). New York: Hawthorn Books.

Wangerin, R. (1993). *The children of God.* Westport, CT: Bergin & Garvey.

Warner, M. (1976). *Alone of all her sex: The myth and the cult of the Virgin Mary.* New York: Knopf.

Warren, B. L. (1970). Socioeconomic achievement and religion: The American case. *Sociological Inquiry, 40,* 130–155.

Wasserman, I., & Stack, S. (1993). The effect of religion on suicide: An analysis of cultural context. *Omega, 27,* 295–305.

Wasson, R. G. (1969). *Soma: Divine mushroom of immortality.* New York: Harcourt Brace Jovanovich.

Wasson, R. G., Hofmann, A., & Ruck, C. (1978). *The road to Eleusis: Unveiling the secret of mysteries.* New York: Harcourt Brace Jovanovich.

Watkins, M. M. (1976). *Waking dreams.* New York: Harper & Row.

Watson, P. J. (1993). Apologetics and ethnocentrism: Psychology and religion within an ideological surround. *International Journal for the Psychology of Religion, 3,* 1–20.

Watson, P. J., Hood, R. W., Jr., & Morris, R. J. (1985). Dimensions of religiosity and empathy. *Journal of Psychology and Christianity, 4,* 73–85.

Watson, P. J., Hood, R. W., Jr., Morris, R. J., & Hall, J. R. (1984). Empathy, religious orientation, and social desirability. *Journal of Psychology, 117,* 211–216.

Watson, P. J., Howard, R., Hood, R. W., Jr., & Morris, R. J. (1988). Age and religious orientation. *Review of Religious Research, 29,* 271–280.

Watson, P. J., Morris, R. J., Foster, J. E., & Hood, R. W., Jr. (1986). Religiosity and social desirability. *Journal for the Scientific Study of Religion, 25*, 215–232.

Watson, P. J., Morris, R. J., & Hood, R. W., Jr. (1987). Antireligious humanistic values, guilt, and self esteem. *Journal for the Scientific Study of Religion, 26*, 535–546.

Watson, P. J., Morris, R. J., & Hood, R. W., Jr. (1988). Sin and self-functioning: Part I. Grace, guilt, and self-consciousness. *Journal of Psychology and Theology, 16*, 254–269.

Watson, P. J., Morris, R. J., & Hood, R. W., Jr. (1990a). Attributional complexity, religious orientation, and indiscriminate proreligiousness. *Review of Religious Research, 32*, 110–121.

Watson, P. J., Morris, R. J., & Hood, R. W., Jr. (1990b). Intrinsicness, self-actualization and the ideological surround. *Journal of Psychology and Theology, 18*, 40–53.

Watson, P. J., Morris, R. J., & Hood, R. W., Jr. (1993). Mental health, religion and the ideology of irrationality. In M. L. Lynn & D. O. Moberg (Eds.), *Research in the social scientific study of religion* (Vol. 5, pp. 53–88). Greenwich, CT: JAI Press.

Watts, F., & Williams, M. (1988). *The psychology of religious knowing.* Cambridge, England: Cambridge University Press.

Wauck, L. (1957). *An investigation into the use of psychological tests as an aid in the selection of candidates for the diocesan priesthood.* Unpublished doctoral dissertation, Loyola University, Chicago.

Weaver, A. J., Berry, J. W., & Pittel, S. M. (1994). Ego development in fundamentalist and nonfundamentalist Protestants. *Journal of Psychology and Theology, 22*, 215–225.

Webb, S. C., & Hultgren, D. D. (1973). Differentiation of clergy subgroups on the basis of vocational interests. *Journal for the Scientific Study of Religion, 12*, 311–324.

Weber, M. (1930). *The Protestant ethic and the spirit of capitalism* (T. Parsons, Trans.). New York: Scribner. (Original work published 1904)

Weber, M. (1963). *The sociology of religion* (E. Frischoff, Trans.). Boston: Beacon Press. (Original work published 1922)

Webster, A. C. (1967). Patterns and relations of dogmatism, mental health, and psychological health in selected religious groups. *Dissertation Abstracts, 27*, 4142A.

Webster, H., Freedman, M., & Heist, P. (1962). Personality changes in college students. In N. Sanford (Ed.), *The American college: A psychological and social interpretation of the higher learning* (pp. 811–846). New York: Wiley.

Weigert, A. J., D'Antonio, W. V., & Rubel, A. J. (1971). Protestantism and assimilation among Mexican Americans: An exploratory study of minister's reports. *Journal for the Scientific Study of Religion, 10*, 219–232.

Weil, A. (1986). *The natural mind* (rev. ed.). Boston: Houghton Mifflin.

Weisman, A. D. (1972). *On dying and denying.* New York: Behavioral.

Weisner, N. (1974). The effect of prophetic disconfirmation of the committee. *Review of Religious Research, 16*, 19–30.

Weisner, W. M., & Riffel, P. A. (1960). Scrupulosity: Religion and obsessive compulsive behavior in children. *American Journal of Psychiatry, 117*, 314–318.

Weisz, J. R., Rothbaum, F. M., & Blackburn, T. C. (1984). Standing out and standing in: The psychology of control in America and Japan. *American Psychologist, 39*, 955–969.

Weitzenhoffer, A. M., & Hilgard, E. R. (1962). *Stanford Hypnotic Susceptibility Scale, Form C.* Palo Alto, CA: Consulting Psychologists Press.

Welch, M. R. (1977). Empirical examination of Wilson's sect typology. *Journal for the Scientific Study of Religion, 16*, 125–139.

Welch, M. R. (1978). Religious non-affiliation and worldly success. *Journal for the Scientific Study of Religion, 17*, 59–61.

Welch, M. R. (1979). Quantitative approaches to sect classification and the study of sect development. In R. Wuthnow (Ed.), *The religious dimension: New directions in quantitative research* (pp. 93–109). New York: Academic Press.

Welch, M. R., Tittle, C. R., & Petee, T. (1991). Religion and deviance among adult Catholics: A test of the "moral communities" hypothesis. *Journal for the Scientific Study of Religion, 30*, 159–172.

Wells, T., & Triplett, W. (1992). *Drug wars: An oral history from the trenches.* New York: William Morrow.

Wenegrat, B. (1990). *The divine archetype: The sociobiology and psychology of religion.* Lexington, MA: Lexington Books.

Westermeyer, J., & Walzer, V. (1975). Drug usage: An alternative to religion? *Diseases of the Nervous System, 36,* 492–495.

Whisman, M. A., & Kwon, P. (1993). Life stress and dysphoria: The role of self-esteem and hopelessness. *Journal of Personality and Social Psychology, 65,* 1054–1060.

Whitehead, A. N. (1926). *Religion in the making.* New York: Macmillan.

Wiehe, V. R. (1990). Religious influence on parental attitudes toward the use of corporal punishment. *Journal of Family Violence, 5,* 173–186.

Wieman, H. H., & Westcott-Wieman, R. (1935). *Normative psychology of religion.* New York: Crowell.

Wikstrom, O. (1987). Attribution, roles and religion: A theoretical analysis of Sunden's role theory of religion and the attributional approach to religious experience. *Journal for the Scientific Study of Religion, 26,* 390–400.

Wilber, K. (1995). *Sex, ecology, spirituality: The spirit of evolution.* Boston: Shambhala.

Wilcox, C., Ferrara, J., O'Donnell, J., Bendyna, M., Gehan, S., & Taylor, R. (1992). Public attitudes toward church–state issues: Elite–masses differences. *Journal of Church and State, 34,* 259–277.

Wilcox, C., & Jelen, T. G. (1991). The effects of employment and religion on women's feminist attitudes. *International Journal for the Psychology of Religion, 1,* 161–171.

Wilde, O. (1965). *The importance of being earnest.* New York: Avon. (Original work published 1895)

Williams, J. P. (1962). The nature of religion. *Journal for the Scientific Study of Religion, 2,* 3–14.

Williams, R. (1971). A theory of God-concept readiness: From Piagetian theories of child artificialism and the origin of religious feeling in children. *Religious Education, 66,* 62–66.

Williamson, P. (1995). *An attributional basis of the Church of God's rejection of serpent handling.* Paper presented at the annual meeting of the Southeastern Psychological Association, Savannah, GA.

Willits, F. K., & Crider, D. M. (1989). Church attendance and traditional religious beliefs in adolescence and young adulthood: A panel study. *Review of Religious Research, 31,* 68–81.

Wills, G. (1990). *Under God: Religion and American politics.* New York: Simon & Schuster.

Wilson, B. R. (1970). *Religious sects.* New York: McGraw Hill.

Wilson, B. R. (1983). Sympathetic detachment and disinterested involvement: A note on academic integrity. *Sociological Analysis, 44,* 183–188.

Wilson, E. O. (1978). *On human nature.* Cambridge, MA: Harvard University Press.

Wilson, J. (1978). *Religion in American society: The effective presence.* Englewood Cliffs, NJ: Prentice-Hall.

Wilson, J., & Sherkat, D. E. (1994). Returning to the fold. *Journal for the Scientific Study of Religion, 33,* 148–161.

Wilson, S. R. (1982). In pursuit of spiritual energy: Spiritual growth in a yoga ashram. *Journal of Humanistic Psychology, 22,* 43–55.

Wimberley, R. C., & Christenson, J. A. (1981). Civil religion and other religious identities. *Sociological Analysis, 42,* 91–100.

Wittgenstein, L. (1953). *Philosophical investigations* (G. E. M. Anscombe, Trans.). New York: Routledge & Kegan Paul. (Original work published 1945–1949)

Wolf, J. G. (Ed.). (1989). *Gay priests.* New York: Harper & Row.

Wong, P. T. P. (1979). Frustration, exploration, and learning. *Canadian Psychological Review, 20,* 133–144.

Wong, P. T. P., & Weiner, B. (1981). When people ask "why" questions, and the heuristics of attributional search. *Journal of Personality and Social Psychology, 40,* 650–663.

Wood, J. (1976). The structure of concern: Ministry in death-related situations. In L. H. Lofland (Ed.), *Toward a sociology of death and dying* (pp. 135–150). Beverly Hills, CA: Sage.

Wood, W. W. (1965). *Culture and personality aspects of the pentecostal holiness religion.* The Hague: Mouton.

Woodberry, J. D. (1992). Conversion in Islam. In H. N. Malony & S. Southard (Eds.), *Handbook of religious conversion* (pp. 22–40). Birmingham, AL: Religious Education Press.

Woodroof, J. T. (1985). Premarital sexual behavior and religious adolescents. *Journal for the Scientific Study of Religion, 24,* 343–366.

Woodruff, M. L. (1993). Report: Electroencephalograph taken from Pastor Liston Pack, 4:00 p.m., 7 Nov. 1985. In T. Burton, *Serpent-handling believers* (pp. 142–144). Knoxville: University of Tennessee Press.

Woodward, K. L. (1970, April 6). How America lives with death. *Time*, pp. 81–88.

Woodward, K. L., Gordon, J., de la Pena, N., King, P., Peyser, M., Mason, M., Joseph, N., Rosenberg, D., & Hammill, R. (1990, December 17). A time to seek. *Newsweek*, pp. 50–56.

Worten, S. A., & Dollinger, S. J. (1986). Mothers' intrinsic religious motivation, disciplinary preferences, and children's conceptions of prayer. *Psychological Reports, 58*, 218.

Wortman, C. B. (1976). Causal attributions and personal control. In J. H. Harvey, W. J. Ickes, & R. F. Kidd (Eds.), *New directions in attribution research* (Vol. 1, pp. 23–52). Hillsdale, NJ: Erlbaum.

Wright, J. E., Jr. (1982). *Erikson: Identity and religion*. New York: Seabury Press.

Wright, R. (1994). *The moral animal*. New York: Pantheon.

Wright, S. A. (1986). Dyadic intimacy and social control in three cult movements. *Sociological Analysis, 47*, 137–150.

Wright, S. A. (1987). *Leaving cults: The dynamics of defection* (Monograph No. 7). Washington, DC: Society for the Scientific Study of Religion.

Wright, S. D., Pratt, C. C., & Schmall, V. L. (1985). Spiritual support for caregivers of dementia patients. *Journal of Religion and Health, 24*, 31–38.

Wulff, D. M. (1991). *Psychology of religion: Classic and contemporary views*. New York: Wiley.

Wulff, D. M. (1993). On the origins and goals of religious development. *International Journal for the Psychology of Religion, 3*, 181–186.

Wulff, D. M. (1995). Phenomenological psychology. In R. W. Hood, Jr. (Ed.), *Handbook of religious experience* (pp. 183–199). Birmingham, AL: Religious Education Press.

Wundt, W. (1901). *Lectures on human and animal psychology* (J. E. Creighton & E. B. Titchner, Trans.). New York: Macmillan.

Wundt, W. (1916). *Elements of folk psychology*. London: Allen & Unwin.

Wuthnow, R. (1978). *Experimentation in American religion*. Berkeley: University of California Press.

Wuthnow, R. (1994). *God and mammon in America*. New York: Free Press.

Wuthnow, R., & Glock, C. Y. (1973). Religious loyalty, defection, and experimentation among college youth. *Journal for the Scientific Study of Religion, 12*, 157–180.

Wuthnow, R., & Mellinger, G. (1978). Religious loyalty, defection, and experimentation: A longitudinal analysis of university men. *Review of Religious Research, 19*, 231–245.

Wylie, R. C. (1979). *The self concept* (2nd ed., 2 vols.). Lincoln: University of Nebraska Press.

Wyllie, I. G. (1966). *The self-made man in America*. New York: Free Press.

Yalom, I. D. (1980). *Existential psychotherapy*. New York: Basic Books.

Yamane, D., & Polzer, M. (1994). Ways of seeing ecstasy in modern society: Experimental–expressive and cultural–linguistic views. *Sociology of Religion, 55*, 1–25.

Yates, J. W., Chalmer, B. J., St. James, P., Follansbee, M., & McKegney, F. P. (1981). Religion in patients with advanced cancer. *Medical and Pediatric Oncology, 9*, 121–128.

Yensen, R. (1990). LSD and psychotherapy. *Journal of Psychoactive Drugs, 17*, 267–277.

Yinger, J. M. (1967). Pluralism, religion, and secularism. *Journal for the Scientific Study of Religion, 6*, 17–28.

Yinger, J. M. (1968a). A research note on interfaith marriage. *Journal for the Scientific Study of Religion, 7*, 97–103.

Yinger, J. M. (1968b). On the definition of interfaith marriage. *Journal for the Scientific Study of Religion, 7*, 104–107.

Yinger, J. M. (1970). *The scientific study of religion*. New York: Macmillan.

Yinon, Y., & Sharon, I. (1985). Similarity in religiousness of the solicitor, the potential helper, and the recipient as determinants of donating behavior. *Journal of Applied Social Psychology, 15*, 726–734.

Young, R. K., & Meiburg, A. L. (1960). *Spiritual therapy*. New York: Harper.

Youth Indicators. (1993). *Trends in the well-being of American youth*. Washington, DC: U.S. Government Printing Office.

Yudell, C. (1978, November). Are clergy afraid to die too? *U.S. Catholic*, pp. 33–39.

Zachry, W. H. (1990). Correlation of abstract religious thought and formal operations in high school and college students. *Review of Religious Research, 31,* 405–412.

Zaehner, R. C. (1957). *Mysticism, sacred and profane: An inquiry into some varieties of praenatural experience.* London: Oxford University Press.

Zaehner, R. C. (1972). *Zen, drugs and mysticism.* New York: Pantheon.

Zaehner, R. C. (1974). *Our savage God.* New York: Sheed & Ward.

Zaleski, C. (1987). *Otherworld journeys: Accounts of near-death experience in medieval and modern times.* New York: Oxford University Press.

Zern, D. S. (1984). Religiousness related to cultural complexity and pressures to obey cultural norms. *Genetic Psychology Monographs, 110,* 207–227.

Zern, D. S. (1987). Positive links among obedience pressure, religiosity, and measures of cognitive accomplishment: Evidence for the secular value of being religious. *Journal of Psychology and Theology, 15,* 31–39.

Zilboorg, G., & Henry, G. W. (1941). *A history of medical psychology.* New York: Norton.

Zimbardo, P. G., & Hartley, C.F. (1985). Cults go to high school: A theoretical and empirical analysis of the initial stage in the recruitment process. *Cultic Studies Journal, 2,* 91–147.

Zinberg, N. (Ed.). (1977). *Alternate states of consciousness.* New York: Free Press.

Zollschan, G. K., Schumaker, J. F., & Walsh, G. F. (Eds.). (1995). *Exploring the paranormal.* Great Britain: Prism Press.

Zubeck, J. P. (Ed.). (1969). *Sensory deprivation: Fifty years of research.* New York: Appleton-Century-Crofts.

Zuckerman, D. M., Kasl, S. V., & Ostfeld, A. M. (1984). Psychosocial predictors of mortality among the elderly poor. *American Journal of Epidemiology, 119,* 410–423.

Zusne, L., & Jones, W. H. (1989). *Anomalistic psychology: A study of magical thinking* (2nd ed.). Hillsdale, NJ: Erlbaum.

AUTHOR INDEX

SUBJECT INDEX